AMERICAN GOVERNMENT:

The Clash of Issues

THIRD EDITION

AMERICAN GOVERNMENT:

The Clash of Issues

Edited by

JAMES A. BURKHART

Stephens College

SAMUEL KRISLOV

University of Minnesota

RAYMOND L. LEE

Indiana University of Pennsylvania

PRENTICE-HALL, Inc., *Englewood Cliffs, New Jersey*

Library of Congress Catalog Card Number: 68-19969

PRINTED IN THE UNITED STATES OF AMERICA

Current printing (last digit):

10   9   8   7   6   5   4   3   2   1

Prentice-Hall International, Inc. *(London)*
Prentice-Hall of Australia, Pty. Ltd. *(Sydney)*
Prentice-Hall of Canada, Ltd. *(Toronto)*
Prentice-Hall of India Private Ltd. *(New Delhi)*
Prentice-Hall of Japan, Inc. *(Tokyo)*

Preface

When the first edition of this book was being planned, the authors agreed that it should emphasize questions which were significant, controversial, and relevant. Now, ten years later, the authors are even more convinced of the validity of their original intention. Unless the study of American government comes to grips with the issues of the day, it does not, in our opinion, maximize the time and effort expended in preparing a study. In this regard, we are in accord with the late Professor Eugene Burdick who asserted, "The *romantic* heart of politics is partisan rather than neutral and deals with issues rather than statistics." We have tried to maintain this heart, while including more technical material relevant to the approach, in accordance with developments in the field of political science.

In previous editions we spelled out our convictions that students must become involved in the political dialogue of our time. We would like to repeat and to reemphasize these objectives:

1. A recognition that controversy and disagreement are natural parts of the democratic process and that their absence rather than their presence should cause alarm.
2. A realization that even though acceptance of political conditions as fixed or "given" can frequently be bad, the opposite—polarized, irreconcilable standing on principle—is equally dangerous.
3. An idea of how emotionally loaded a major issue is, what makes such an issue, and what courses lead to compromise or stalemate.
4. A personal involvement in many of the issues—if not on an action basis, at least an intellectual identification.
5. An awareness that political practices, rights, and liberties are a function of groups of persons and entail a great deal more than the mere passing of a law.

It is impossible to fully express the indebtedness which we owe to our former colleague, Henry G. Bush. Professor Bush was one of the original authors; however, his commitments to the United States Agency for International Development in Southeast Asia during the past seven years made it impossible for him to work on this edition. We regard his absence as another academic casualty to the continuing problems in that area of the world.

Our debt to the many teachers and students who have used earlier editions of this book is very great. Particularly valuable has been the constructive criticism we have received on a day-to-day basis from our colleagues: Patrick A. Carone, Richard F. Heiges, Bruce Jenkins, David Keene, Robert L. Morris, Dorothy A. Palmer, Edward Platt, James L. Reiley, Bert A. Smith, and John W. Smith. We also wish to acknowledge comments and suggestions which have been given to us through the years by various members of the Departments of Political Science at the University of Missouri, the University of Minnesota, and Michigan State University. Needless to say, the authors alone are responsible for all errors and shortcomings of this edition.

JAMES A. BURKHART
SAMUEL KRISLOV
RAYMOND L. LEE

Contents

CHAPTER ONE

THE STATE OF AMERICA: WHERE DO WE STAND?   1

THE POLITICAL SCENE:
CHALLENGE AND RESPONSE

1. *The Abdication of Political Will and Political Leadership*   3
   Hans J. Morgenthau

2. *The Action-Intellectuals*   5
   Theodore H. White

3. *Needed: A Clear-Eyed American*   9
   Milton Eisenhower

SOCIAL STIRRINGS:
THE GENERATIONAL REVOLUTION!

4. *Tell It Like It Really Is— The Opted-Out World*   12
   David Andrew Seeley

5. *Don't Trust Anyone over Thirty*   15
   Morton M. Hunt

6. *Youth in the Context of American Society*   21
Talcott Parsons

CHAPTER TWO
DEMOCRACY OR DIRECTION:
THEORY AND PRACTICE   25

IS THE COMMON MAN TOO COMMON?

1. *Dissection of the Mass Man*   29
Jose Ortega y Gasset

2. *The Elite and the Electorate*   33
Viscount Hailsham

WHAT SYSTEM OF GOVERNMENT
BEST SATISFIES MAN'S NEEDS?

3. *The Case for Control and Direction*   35
Mao Tse-Tung

4. *The Corruption of Absolute Power: The*
Testimony of Hermann Friedrich Graebe   37

5. *Comparative Politics—*
A Developmental Approach?   40
Gabriel A. Almond and
G. Bingham Powell, Jr.

IS THE UNITED STATES REALLY DEMOCRATIC?

6. *Pluralist Democracy in the United States*   43
Robert A. Dahl

7. *The Decline of Liberal Democracy*   46
Harvey Wheeler

ARE SYSTEMS OF GOVERNMENT CONVERGING?

8. *Are Russia and the United States Converging?*   50
Zbigniew Brzezinski and
Samuel P. Huntington

CHAPTER THREE

THE CONSTITUTION: FRAME OR FRAMEWORK?   56

THE CONSTITUTION: FLEXIBLE SYMBOL
OR EMBODIMENT OF AN IDEOLOGY?

1. *American Society*   57
   Robin M. Williams, Jr.

2. *This Is a Republic, Not a Democracy*   59
   The John Birch Society

3. *Reading the Constitution Anew*   61
   Richard Hofstadter

THE CONSTITUTION AS INSTRUMENT:
WHO BENEFITS?

4. *Yesterday's Constitution or Today's?*   63
   Charles P. Curtis

5. *Constitutions: The Politics of Power*   66
   Harold Norris

6. *Unwritten Rules of American Politics*   68
   John Fischer

CHAPTER FOUR

THE FEDERAL SYSTEM: INSTRUMENT OF LIBERTY OR INEFFICIENCY?   70

STATES' RIGHTS: PRINCIPLE OR PRETEXT?

1. *Freedom and Federalism*   72
   Nelson Rockefeller

2. *Federalism and Freedom: A Critique*   74
   Franz L. Neumann

3. *How to Keep Our Liberty*   77
   Raymond Moley

4. *There Is No State Point of View*   79
   Edward W. Weidner

FEDERAL AID TO THE STATES:
HELP OR HINDRANCE?

5. *Federalism and Political Culture:*
   A View from the States   82
   Daniel J. Elazar

6. *Creative Federalism*   84
   Max Ways

7. *Whistlin' Dixie:*
   Creative Federalism in Action   88
   Jessie Hill Ford

NATION, STATE, CITIES: PARTNERS OR RIVALS?

8. *Why Cities Are Turning to*
   Washington for Cash   90
   Mayor Jerome Cavanagh

9. *Minority Views on S. 1633*   93

10. *The Politics of Tax-Sharing*   95
    William V. Shannon

11. *Mayors Oppose U.S. Tax-Sharing*
    with the States   97
    John Herbers

12. *The Political Side of Urban*
    Development: Fragmentation   98
    Scott Greer and David W. Minar

13. *The Federal System:*
    Overcoming Fragmentation   101
    Morton Grodzins

CHAPTER FIVE

CIVIL LIBERTIES:
THE BILL OF RIGHTS   109

HOW FREE CAN WE BE WITHOUT CHAOS?

1. *Free Speech and Free Government*   112
   Alexander Meiklejohn

2. *Heresy, Yes: Conspiracy, No*   114
   Sidney Hook

THE RIGHT TO BE LET ALONE VERSUS THE
NEED TO ORGANIZE SOCIETY

3. *The President's Crime Commission
   Meets the Press*   116
   Meet the Press

4. *The First Amendment Has Served Us Well*   123
   Robert F. Drinan, S. J.

5. *"Absolute Is in the Dark"*   126
   Erwin N. Griswold

6. *The Supreme Court Enunciates a
   Constitutional Right of Privacy*   129
   U.S. Supreme Court

NEGROES AND WHITES: THE CHALLENGE OF
EQUAL PROTECTION OF THE LAWS

7. *Letter from Birmingham City Jail*   132
   Martin Luther King, Jr.

8. *Civil Rights Must Not Destroy Liberty*   136
   William F. Buckley, Jr.

9. *Which Way for the Negro?*   139
   The Editors of *Newsweek*

CHAPTER SIX
*PUBLIC OPINION AND INTEREST GROUPS:
WHO SPEAKS FOR ME?*   144

THE VOICE OF THE PEOPLE OR THE
ECHO OF THE MAKERS OF OPINION?

1. *The New Underworld*   146
   Eugene Burdick

2. *The Nature of Public Opinion*   148
   Herbert Blumer

3. *A Case Study in Change in Public Opinion*   150
Angus Campbell, Philip E. Converse,
Warren Miller and Donald E. Stokes

LOBBYING: PRESSURE POLITICS OR COMMUNICATION
AND THE RIGHT OF PETITION

4. *A Washington Correspondent
Looks at Lobbying*   159
James Deakin

5. *A Political Scientist Looks at Lobbying*   164
Lester W. Milbrath

6. *Pressure Politics: A Case Study*   167
James Deakin

CHAPTER SEVEN
*POLITICAL PARTIES AND POLITICAL
PHILOSOPHIES: THE WILL AND THE WAY*   169

DO AMERICAN POLITICAL PARTIES
MEAN ANYTHING?

1. *How to Tell a Democrat from a Republican*   171
Will Stanton

2. *Democrats or Republicans:
What Difference Does It Make?*   175
Clinton Rossiter

3. *American Political Parties*   183
Stephen K. Bailey

WHICH WAY AMERICA—
LEFT, RIGHT, NEITHER?

4. *The Conscience of a Conservative*   188
Barry Goldwater

5. *The Conscience of a Liberal*   190
Eugene J. McCarthy

6. *Our Radical Right—The Dispossessed*   194
   Daniel Bell

7. *"The New Left—What Is It?"*   201

CHAPTER EIGHT

NOMINATIONS AND ELECTIONS:
CAN GREAT MEN GET ELECTED?   206

THE IDEAL CANDIDATE: AVAILABILITY
VS. THE MAN OF STATURE?

1. *The Ideal Candidate*   208
   Art Buchwald

2. *Is There a Presidential Type?*   210
   Paul T. David, Ralph M. Goldman, and
   Richard C. Bain

THE NATIONAL NOMINATING CONVENTION:
PREFABRICATED PAGEANTRY OR
UNDERRATED POLITICAL INSTITUTION?

3. *Our National Nominating Conventions
   Are a Disgrace*   215
   Dwight D. Eisenhower

4. *The Hiring of Presidents*   219
   Clinton Rossiter

DO CAMPAIGNS CHANGE VOTES?

5. *The Almost Perfect Campaign*   221
   James M. Perry

ELECTIONS: WHAT DOES AN ELECTION MEAN?

6. *Voting*   229
   Bernard R. Berelson, Paul F. Lazarsfeld
   and William N. McPhee

7. *Voters Are Not Fools*   232
   Arthur Maass

CHAPTER NINE

THE PRESIDENCY:
THE HARDEST JOB IN THE WORLD?   237

THE PRESIDENCY: TRANSITION OR
MAJOR TRANSFORMATION?

1. *John F. Kennedy Looks at the Presidency*   239
   John F. Kennedy

2. *The Two Presidencies*   241
   Aaron Wildavsky

3. *The Presidency at the Crossroads*   253
   James MacGregor Burns

4. *Leave Your Presidency Alone*   258
   Clinton Rossiter

THE DILEMMA OF POWER: A DEBATE—
THE PRESIDENCY VS. CONGRESS

5. *The Case for Today's Presidency*   260
   Arthur M. Schlesinger, Jr.

6. *The Case for Congress*   264
   Alfred de Grazia

CHAPTER TEN

CONGRESS:
THE NEW, OLD, OR LAST FRONTIER?   269

CONGRESS: ALTERATION OR ADAPTATION?

1. *Congressional Responses to the
   Twentieth Century*   271
   Samuel P. Huntington

2. *To Move Congress Out of Its Ruts*   276
   Hubert H. Humphrey

3. *The Prospects for Change*   279
   David B. Truman

POWER IN CONGRESS:
THREE VIEWS OF THE "HILL"

4. The Congressional Establishment   284
   Senator Joseph S. Clark

5. Who Belongs to the Senate's Inner Club   287
   Clayton Fritchey

6. Power in the House   293
   Clem Miller

CHAPTER ELEVEN

THE SUPREME COURT:
SUPREME IN WHAT?   296

WHAT MANNER OF INSTITUTION?

1. How the Supreme Court Reaches Decisions   300
   Anthony Lewis

2. Powerful, Irresponsible, and Human   303
   Fred Rodell

WHERE DO THE JUDGES AND THE LAW
COME FROM?

3. Are Judges Politicians?   305
   Charles A. Beard

4. A Political Approach to the Courts   308
   Martin Shapiro

5. Elect Supreme Court Justices?   311
   David Lawrence

6. We Must Go Back in Order to Go Forward   313
   John T. Flynn

WHAT CAN THE COURT DO?

7. A Tenant at Sufferance   315
   Charles P. Curtis

8. *The High Court's Role in Policy*   317

9. *Is the Supreme Court Attempting Too Much?*   318
   Robert G. McCloskey

10. *Can the Supreme Court Defend
    Civil Liberties?*   321
    Edmond Cahn

CHAPTER TWELVE

UNITED STATES FOREIGN POLICY   325

WHICH APPROACH TO WORLD AFFAIRS:
REALISTIC, LEGALISTIC, HUMANISTIC,
OR MILITARISTIC?

1. *In Search of a Realistic Foreign Policy*   327
   Senator J. W. Fulbright

2. *Our Foreign Policy Is Based on
   International Law*   330
   Dean Rusk

3. *The Anglo-American Traditional Policy
   Is Humanistic*   334
   Sir Patrick Dean

4. *Military Power Is the Foundation of
   Foreign Policy*   338
   Barry Goldwater

THE UNITED STATES AND THE
COMMUNIST BLOC: PERMANENT HOSTILITY
OR DECREASING TENSIONS?

5. *The United States Must Not Negotiate
   with the Soviet Union*   341
   Slobodan M. Draskovich

6. *A Fresh Look at the Communist Bloc*   345
   Senator J. W. Fulbright

THE UNITED STATES AND WESTERN
EUROPE: AN ATLANTIC COMMUNITY
OR TWO SEPARATE ENTITIES?

7. *Creating an Atlantic Community*   349
   John F. Kennedy

8. *The Crisis in the Western Alliance*   353
   Hans J. Morgenthau

CHAPTER THIRTEEN

GOVERNMENT AND THE ECONOMY: DIRECTION WITHOUT DOMINATION?   356

OVERALL DIRECTION: CAN GOVERNMENT
CURB THE BUSINESS CYCLE?

1. *The "New Economists" Take Over*   359
   Neil W. Chamberlain

2. *The Other Side of the "New Economics"*   363
   Maurice H. Stans

3. *Applying the New Economics*   368
   Paul A. Samuelson

BIG BUSINESS AND GOVERNMENT:
LOGICAL PARTNERS OR NATURAL ENEMIES?

4. *The Power of Big Business*   370
   Robert L. Heilbroner

5. *Big Business, Militarism, and Democracy*   375
   Dwight D. Eisenhower

AMERICA FACES AUTOMATION:
BOON OR BLIGHT?

6. *Caught on the Horn of Plenty*   378
   W. H. Ferry

7. *Labor Unions Wrestle with Automation*   383
   Neil W. Chamberlain

CHAPTER FOURTEEN

THE POLITICS OF POVERTY: ALLEVIATION OR ELIMINATION?   389

AMERICAN POVERTY: WHO AND WHY?

1. *Penury amid Affluence*   391
   John K. Galbraith

2. *Our Invisible Poor*   393
   Dwight Macdonald

3. *Poverty on the Land*   399
   John Stanley

WHAT ROLE FOR GOVERNMENT: ALLEVIATION OR ELIMINATION?

4. *Government Can't Cure Poverty* 402
   Barry Goldwater

5. *The War on Poverty*   405
   Lyndon B. Johnson

CHAPTER FIFTEEN

THE CRISIS IN URBAN GOVERNMENT: WILL CITIES REMAIN HABITABLE?   411

DOES A CRISIS EXIST?

1. *The American City in Travail*   413
   Peter F. Drucker

2. *A Second Look at the Urban Crisis* 415
   Irving Kristol

WHAT ARE THE MAJOR PROBLEMS?

3. *The Commuting Motorist: Urban Enemy Number One* 418
   C. W. Griffin, Jr.

4. *America, the Dirty*   422
   Clare Boothe Luce

5. *Towards a Super-Ghetto*   424
   Joseph Alsop

WHAT IS THE CITY'S FUTURE?

6. *Urban America in the Year 2000*   426
   Mitchell Gordon

CHAPTER SIXTEEN
AMERCAN CIVILIZATION:
GOVERNMENT'S QUEST FOR A GREAT SOCIETY   432

A GREAT SOCIETY: CAN POLITICAL
LEADERS POINT THE WAY?

1. *Towards a Sane Society*   434
   Eric Fromm

2. *Towards a Great Society*   439
   Lyndon B. Johnson

BEYOND ECONOMICS:
WHAT GOALS FOR AMERICANS?

3. *American Civilization: Beyond Economics*   441
   Peter F. Drucker

4. *Leisure Time: The Age of Fulfillment*   448
   Ralph Lazarus

5. *Technology and Education*   454
   Lewis Paul Todd

AMERICAN GOVERNMENT:

The Clash of Issues

CHAPTER ONE

•

The State of America:
Where Do We Stand?

It is a mistake to try to study a nation's government and political system in isolation. Only in the context of economic, social, intellectual, and historical forces can politics and government be put in proper perspective. However, the job of synthesizing is virtually impossible. Anyone who attempts to encompass American life within the narrow confines of a chapter, book, or even a series of books, faces an insuperable task. The constantly changing, complex, and richly varied character of American life precludes summary observations and automatic responses.

In the following chapter we will not attempt to describe the total scene, but we will try to identify a few current positions, possible trends, and future directions. In the process of doing this, the focus will be on major issues. Like a searchlight in the night, visibility will be restricted to a few well-defined landmarks.

In the following essays the spotlight of attention flashes upon two significant segments of American society—"The Political Scene: Challenge and Response," and "Social Stirrings: The Generational Revolution." In each of these sections we will cite problems and potential problems, and the manner in which American society is responding to these issues.

THE POLITICAL SCENE: CHALLENGE AND RESPONSE

It is difficult to strike a balance in assessing the challenges to American government. Democracy is an open society, and hence its ills and shortcomings are very apparent. In addition, critics and dissenters are, as they should be, very articulate. Yet after making allowances for the natural role of dissent and criticism, there does seem to be more concern expressed in recent years over destructive dissent, political disinterest, and the lack of political will. The following section discusses these challenges to the American political system and then looks at some of the responses.

Professor Hans J. Morgenthau begins with a commentary on political will and political leadership. This is followed by Theodore H. White's account of "The Action Intellectuals," which suggests a changing attitude among some intellectuals. The final note by Milton Eisenhower presents some of the problems facing every citizen but also offers some hopeful suggestions on how these problems can be met.

SOCIAL STIRRINGS: THE GENERATIONAL REVOLUTION!

Much attention today centers on young people, and for a very good reason. They are rapidly becoming a new majority. The United States, along with virtually every country in Western Europe, is experiencing a "youngering" problem as well as an "aging" problem. The swing to youth, however, is something unprecedented, unexpected and, among some adults, perhaps unwelcomed. But welcomed or not, it is upon us. In 1960, when John F. Kennedy ran for President, the average age in America was 33. By 1965 this age level had dropped to 25, and Peter Drucker estimates that by 1970 the United States will be the youngest nation in the free world.

To assume that there would be no consequences of this generational change would be ignoring reality. On the other hand, an attitude that "anything goes" as long as individuals under 30 are involved would also be unrealistic. In the problem, "Social Stirrings: The Generational Revolution!" David Andrew Seeley writes sympathetically on what the far-out youth world is like. Morton M. Hunt reviews the national picture on youth today. Talcott Parsons concludes the section with his article which places the problem of youth culture in the context of American society.

1

The Abdication of Political Will and Political Leadership*

HANS J. MORGENTHAU

Why does Professor Morgenthau contend that creative tensions have gone out of politics? Would you agree that it was easier a century ago to have clear-cut issues than it is today? What is Morgenthau's answer to the increasing complexity and novelty of contemporary issues?

Throughout history, political life has drawn its vitality from the creative contrast between the political world in which men found themselves and the political world which men thought to be ethically, rationally, or pragmatically necessary. Political philosophy performed the political function of demonstrating either that the actual political world and the necessary one were identical or that another one, imagined once to have existed in the past or susceptible of creation *de novo*, had to replace it. That creative intellectual tension between conservation and innovation has been the lifeblood of politics. With that creative tension having gone out of politics, all seemingly antagonistic political movements—and this is as true of Germany, France, and Great Britain as it is of the United States—express in different ways a stagnant mood, a hedonism of the status quo that equates what exists

with what ought to exist, if not with the ultimate purposes of the universe. Thus we are approaching a moribund state of political life which Karl Mannheim analyzed with prophetic insight in these words thirty-five years ago: "It is possible, therefore, that in the future, in a world in which there is never anything new, in which all is finished and each moment is a repetition of the past, there can exist a condition in which thoughts will be utterly devoid of all ideological and utopian elements. But the complete elimination of reality-transcending elements from our world would lead us to 'matter-of-factness' which ultimately would mean the decay of the human will . . . human nature and human development would take on a totally new character. The disappearance of utopia brings about a static state of affairs in which man himself becomes no more than a thing. We would be faced then with the greatest paradox imaginable, namely, that man, who has achieved the highest degree of rational mastery of existence, left without any ideals, becomes a mere creature of impulses. Thus, after a long, tortuous, but heroic

* Hans J. Morgenthau, "Introduction: The Great Issues," in *The Crossroad Papers*, ed. Hans J. Morgenthau (New York: W. W. Norton and Company, Inc., 1965), pp. 12-15. Reprinted by permission of the publisher.

development, just at the highest stage of awareness, when history is ceasing to be blind fate, and is becoming more and more man's creation, with the relinquishment of utopias, man would lose his will to shape history and therewith his ability to understand it."

What, then, accounts for the contrast between the apathy and complacency of the popular mood and the existence and even urgency of the issues before us? Some of these issues transcend in importance, not only for society as a whole but for each individual citizen, most of the issues that in the past have commanded the passionate commitment of the people. Is the nuclear-armaments race, for instance, not more important than a tax on tea or the expansion of slavery to new territories? Objectively, there can of course be no doubt that it is, but it has not aroused the political passions of the American people one way or the other to make it a political issue. Why is this so? Two interrelated answers suggest themselves.

The great unresolved issues, while intellectually recognized by at least a minority, are not experienced by the mass of the people as being of direct concern to, or manageable by, them. A century ago, the legal issue of slavery could be settled by a presidential proclamation emancipating the slaves; yet it takes more than a decision of the Supreme Court to stop the treatment of their descendants as though they were still slaves. It was easier to free the slaves than it is to ensure that their descendants will be dealt with as equals. And a century ago the issue of slavery presented itself in so clearcut a fashion that a civil war could be fought about it. On the other hand, the contemporary issue of equality in all its practical ramifications is too complex to allow at least thoughtful

and responsible people to take so simple a position pro or con.

Admitted that the nuclear-armaments race threatens all of us with destruction, that our public education is inadequate, that our economic system is wasteful and potentially destructive. "I personally," says the man in the street, "have nothing to complain about, I am satisfied. And if I were not, what could I do about it?" The vital link between the intellectual awareness of unresolved issues and the resolution not to leave them unresolved is missing. The man in the street is no longer convinced that public issues will, or even ought to, yield to concerted popular action. They have become remote, unintelligible, and intractable; they are the province of technical experts. And if the experts cannot cope with them, how can he?

This abdication of political will on the part of the electorate is duplicated by the abdication of political leadership. The potential political leaders justify that abdication by citing the political apathy of the electorate. There is no political mileage, they say, for instance, in stopping the nuclear-arms race, in a radical reform of the economic and educational systems. The failure of isolated attempts, such as Adlai Stevenson's in the campaign of 1956, to identify the electorate with the solution of these issues seems to bear out their reluctance. So does the success of Barry Goldwater, who either denies the existence of the great issues of the age or proposes simple and painless solutions for them.

How can the gap be bridged between these great issues and our modes of thought and action? Both the nature of the issues and the American tradition indicate the answer to that question. The novelty and complexity of the issues preclude one comprehensive, systematic solution in the grand manner. What is possible and necessary is what American society has always done when it had to come to terms with a new and vital problem: to carry it toward at least a provisional solution, suggested by some general philosophic principle, through a series of piecemeal pragmatic attacks. . . .

2

*The Action-Intellectuals**

THEODORE H. WHITE

The previous selection tended to stress destructive dissent and disinterest on the part of a number of groups in our society. The following account asserts that at least a certain segment of the intellectuals are not disinterested and apathetic. Are there any pitfalls in recruiting intellectuals for government service? Do you see any dangers to democracy in the increase in action-intellectuals? What is the relevancy of the statement, "to act is to sin and you have to sin a little"?

This is the story of a new power-system in American life—and the new priesthood, unique to this country and this time, of American action-intellectuals.

In the past decade this brotherhood of scholars has become the most provocative and propelling influence on all American government and politics. Their ideas are the drivewheels of the Great Society: shaping our defenses, guiding our foreign policy, redesigning our cities, reorganizing our schools, deciding what our dollar is worth.

Change has called this new power-system into being—raw, dislocating change rushing over us in such torrents that the problems left in its wake overpower our understanding.

As the world outruns its comprehension of itself, inherited knowledge and tradition no longer grip onto reality. "Folk-wisdom," said the late Robert Oppenheimer, "can cry out in pain. But it can't provide solutions."

Yet governments must have solutions. They cannot let change simply happen; their duty is to place a discipline on events. Thus, with almost primitive faith, American government has turned to the priesthood of action-intellectuals—the men who believe they understand what change is doing, and who suggest that they can chart the future. For such intellectuals now is a Golden Age, and America is the place. Never have ideas been sought more hungrily or tested against reality more quickly. From White House to city hall, scholars stalk the corridors of American power:

Last year one half the Cabinet of

* Theodore H. White, "The Action Intellectuals," *Life*, June 9, 1967. © 1967, Time Inc.

the U.S. was drawn, not from politicians, but from the brotherhood of learning: Secretaries Gardner, Katzenbach, Weaver, Wirtz, McNamara, Rusk—all were, at one time or another, college professors or teachers. One catches best the temper of the time as HEW Secretary John Gardner begins a sentence with a slip of the tongue: "When the faculty gets together—I mean, when the *Cabinet* gets together . . ."

For decades, the largest office in the West Wing of the White House, facing out on the Executive Office Building, has usually been the lair of the President's most important assistant. During the last seven years, however, it has been chiefly occupied by Theodore Sorensen, Bill Moyers, Joseph Califano—the successive chiefs of the task forces that ceaselessly scout the campuses and foundations of the nation in search of brains and ideas; and, from basement to third floor of the White House, professors and scholars have sifted what the scouts have brought back. The Presidency, in fact, has become almost a transmission belt, packaging and processing scholars' ideas to be sold to Congress as a program.

No political reporter travels the campaign trail today without realizing that backroom bosses are steadily being pushed out by backroom professors who define the issues, draw up position papers, draft the speeches the candidates will voice. "We are a new establishment without initiation rites," says one of them. "You never know when you're in, but you certainly know when you're out."

By now, beachheads of scholarship are being set up even in the city halls. In his first year in office, Mayor John Lindsay of New York City appointed no fewer than 17 college deans, professors and lecturers to his staff. "If you got together all the books they'd

written," says an old city hall hand, "They'd fill every shelf in this room."

No one can describe to any intellectual's satisfaction what the word "intellectual" means—let alone define the elite new category of action-intellectuals who generate such waves of impact on the American government. Yet, broadly speaking, intellectuals are men for whom ideas provide more than the thought patterns that weave connections among facts—as ideas do for most thoughtful men. For the true intellectual, ideas have an electric vitality of their own which is sensed only by other artists-of-the-mind; ideas engaged his passion more than reality or humanity itself.

*   *   *

Says Richard N. Goodwin, one of the youngest and most creative of the new breed, former adviser to Presidents Kennedy and Johnson, now at Wesleyan University: "The ultimate commitment to ideas is to act on them; action can involve a commitment to an idea that the most brilliant thinking never approaches. It's easy to be pure when you're detached. But Goethe said to act is to sin, and so you have to be willing to sin a little. It's only when the necessity for compromise or accommodation begins to drown the ultimate conviction that led you to act in the first place that you have to withdraw—and that's a matter of individual conscience and judgment."

If the action-intellectuals recognize that peril is hidden in their new roles, so, too, does government. For the flood of new learning flows in no patterns tested by the past; it flows in separate streams, bubbling wildly from separate sources of restless curiosity.

By now, to be sure, the authority of those scholars who explore the stream of science and technology has been fully established in Washington. More recently, with greater difficulty, the government has learned to absorb the wisdom of economists whose way of thinking in symbolic aggregates colors all Washington decisions from defense to urban housing. Today, with utmost difficulty, government is groping to find guidance from a third category of scholars—social scientists, the men nominated by history to explain how communities shall master the changes provoked by the physical scientists and economists. And it is just here that controversy blisters. Do social scientists yet know enough to guide us to the very different world we must live in tomorrow? Do they offer wisdom as well as knowledge?

Says Professor Edward C. Banfield of Harvard: "The premium of scholarship for a professor is all too often originality—not correctness. A politician or businessman must pay a price for being wrong; the academic never does. The college professor has no knowledge of what people want now, or what they are going to want; he deals in generalities, and there is no way of applying a general theory to a unique event. I think it's a national tragedy that people in decision-making roles turn over to intellectuals or computers the right to make their decisions. And it's bad for scholarship, too. No one should tell a professor what to think about. A good professor is a bastard perverse enough to think about what *he* thinks is important, not what government thinks is important."

❀   ❀   ❀

. . . A quick glance at Harvard's files one morning turned up a random and incomplete list of 50 names, but their range of penetration covered everything from national strategy (Professor Thomas Schelling, who urged on the government the hot line between Moscow and the White House) to steel-pricing (Professor Otto Eckstein, whose research braced John F. Kennedy for his crackdown on Big Steel). And beyond these were the Harvard laboratory men whose quiet, unpublicized work, generally benign, has been able nonetheless to deliver to the world such masterpieces of fright as napalm (Professor Louis Fieser) and LSD (first explored by the Harvard Medical School in 1952, then prostituted by Lecturer Timothy Leary, who was fired by Harvard before becoming high priest of psychedelics).

Now broaden the focus to include Harvard's chief partner in public adventures, M.I.T., and examine the substance of their joint contributions to American policy.

Most major universities casually credit themselves with acts of Congress or of their state which their professors have written into law. The University of Chicago proudly asserts that in the halls of its Law School, its scientists and law professors drafted the first version of the McMahon Act which placed control of atomic energy in the hands of civilians rather than the military. Berkeley can boast of atomic legislation and of enforcing federal land laws. But Harvard and M.I.T together are responsible for an almost unbelievable range of statutes.

As early as 1954, for example, a group of Harvard and M.I.T. professors began to get together privately on Friday afternoons. Their knowledge told them the world was at the rim of nuclear destruction, and they felt it was their duty to peer beyond the rim and think about arms control. By 1956 the original group had grown to a formal seminar in which defense scientists, political scientists and historians joined as a working group. By 1960 they were hammering their ideas into the speeches of John F. Kennedy's presidential campaign. By 1961 four of the members of their seminar (Jerome Wiesner, McGeorge Bundy, Arthur Schlesinger Jr., Carl Kaysen) held White House posts. By 1963 they had seen their ideas written into international law as the test ban treaty. In response to pleas from presidents, senators, congressmen, the Harvard-M.I.T. professors have by now written a dozen major laws, from investment-tax credits to labor legislation, from civil rights to education and model cities and metropolitan development.

The outburst of public activity, as we have seen, disturbs other scholars, even at Harvard and M.I.T., who interpret it as a subtle betrayal of the real purpose of scholarship, the pursuit of truth for its own sake.

In Washington and at other political centers, however, it disturbs other men for different reasons—not so much for the power that Harvard and M.I.T. wield in national thinking (or the right and wrong of their contributions) as for the way this great center links together with the other centers at Ford, in California, in the Ivy League belt, in Washington itself. "If I had my way," burst out one of the highest executives of the Johnson Administration, "there wouldn't be another federal dollar going to those schools or laboratories in Boston and California. They're draining the rest of the country of its brains."

Those who see a brain cartel inexorably taking over the nation's thinking can trace, like all amateurs of cartel theory, neat and precise interlockings and directorates: Harvard Dean McGeorge Bundy leaves Cambridge to go to the White House as presidential security assistant, then emerges as president of the Ford Foundation to be central banker for all American ideas. Carl Kaysen teaches at Harvard, is simultaneously a consultant at RAND, then leaves for the White House as a Kennedy assistant, then emerges to become head of the Institute for Advanced Study in Princeton. Dean Rusk, professor of government at Mills College in California, enters government during World War II, leaves it 12 years later to become head of the Rockefeller Foundation in New York, then returns to become Secretary of State. Kermit Gordon leaves Williams, becomes a member of the Council of Economic Advisers, then Director of the Bureau of the Budget, then emerges to become head of the Brookings Institution. Charles Hitch goes from Oxford to RAND to Yale and to RAND again, achieves distinction as a RAND economist, becomes comptroller of the Department of Defense at the Pentagon, then emerges at Berkeley as a vice president of the University of California.

John F. Kennedy sets up a task force in the election of 1960 to screen names for candidates to run his Department of State. Of the first 82 names on the list handed him, 63 are members of the Council on Foreign Relations in New York. Johnson succeeds Kennedy and creates a new Department of Housing and Urban Development. Its No. 1 man, Secretary Robert Weaver, is an exprofessor at Columbia; its No. 2 man, Under Secretary Robert C. Wood, is a professor on leave from M.I.T.; its No. 3 man, Assistant Secretary Charles M. Haar, is a professor on leave from Harvard.

Those who like to draw lines between boxes with names in them ask: Is this truly a community of scholars? Or a new kind of political machine?

Nothing annoys the senior action-intellectuals more than this kind of cartel diagram. They see themselves as a community, with recognizable community centers across the nation. But a community is different from a cartel. A cartel sets out to exclude; a community reaches out to include.

And their community, they insist, is the most open in the U.S. Credentials for entry are, simply, brains—plus the ability, the cunning, or know-how to get their ideas listened to in high places. . . .

3

Needed: A Clear-Eyed American *

MILTON EISENHOWER

What specific recommendations does Milton Eisenhower have for creating "clear-eyed Americans"? Is there any evidence that this type of citizen is emerging? What are some of the forces which make it difficult for a citizen to think critically and discerningly?

A single life span is a mere wink in historic time. Yet more awesome changes have taken place in my 67 years than in any previous period, and, I sometimes feel, in all of man's earlier time on earth. When I look backward from this bewildering era, I occasionally indulge in the luxury of nostalgia. Then I see in the sleepy town of Abilene a cozy white house, surrounded by colorful hollyhocks, a flourishing orchard, and a generous vegetable garden. My brothers and I sit on the front porch in rocking chairs observing the drift of the seasons and the passing of the small segment of the world we know. There is no war, no domestic turmoil, no protest marches, on or off campuses, no complex problems to bother us. We, like others of our town, are isolated. Our community is self-contained economically, physically, socially. We have not heard of world interdependence. All is peaceful and we are quite content. But the essence of nostalgia is an awareness that what has been will never be again. In Abilene, we had rude awakenings as we came to understand the nature and consequences of modern change. We had supposed that our economic welfare depended solely upon weather conducive to crop growth and upon hard work, but suddenly, despite perfect weather and efficient work, we found our farmers going broke because Italy raised its tariff on wheat and later because Britain devalued the pound. Soon, and not unrelated to our difficulty, the United States suffered its worst depression. Abilene's economic self-containment—and that of the nation too—was shattered.

Our physical isolation disappeared. I was a freshman in high school before I ventured so far away as Kansas City, Mo. But in a few years thereafter I was traveling to most nations of the world, with greater physical comfort, less fear of the unknown, and in not much more time

---

* Milton Eisenhower, "Needed: A Clear-Eyed American," *Alma Mater*, January, 1967. Reprinted by permission of the publisher.

than I experienced on that first trip away from Abilene.

And our social self-containment was viciously destroyed, for we of Abilene found ourselves in one world war caused, not seemingly by anything we of my town had done, but by an explosion in the Balkans; in a few more years we were in another conflict, due to an infamy at Pearl Harbor, and the insane ambitions of a corporal in Germany.

So we were forced to recognize that the streams of events were toward the unification of our world, a unification which, to succeed, required genuine intercultural understanding, juridical equality of nations, mutuality in human relations, and a global willingness to forego lesser and more selfish purposes in order to concentrate successfully on the transcendent goal of positive peace and raising levels of well-being for all, wherever they lived, whatever their color, nationality, or basic philosophy.

Unhappily, our social concepts were not ready for this imperative.

* * *

Our unpreparedness is contaminated with apathy and sometimes with despair. For there is evidence that in all this the individual citizen tends to feel that he can do little of consequence to help control the streams of history. Not long ago I said: "There is a dangerous myth abroad in this land that an ordinary citizen can do nothing to influence the destiny of his country and the world. I have not decided whether this is a rationalization or an epitaph."

To suggest what a citizen can do may sound pollyannaish. But surely each of us—all of us—must *study*. We must understand all the facts, forces, and circumstances surrounding each of the parts of the fateful

decisions we must make. That problems such as Viet Nam, the disarray of the Atlantic Alliance, imbalances in international payments, the East-West conflict, Cuba, and so on are complex, often requiring expert knowledge, does not exempt a democratic citizen from the obligation of *decision*. The basic social power in our country, and hence the responsibility for its actions, are in the hands of *all* the people.

As I seek to shape my own views, I honestly at moments would welcome a return to the isolation, contentment, and lesser affluence of my youth in Abilene. Of course I know the futility of such passing thoughts. So I try to consider things as they now are and without implying any criticism of any action now under way or policy now in effect, I must in candor say I am persuaded that the time is here when we should reappraise our posture and our methods in the world.

* * *

Where do we begin? Highest priority, in any reappraisal of our posture and methods, must in my judgment begin with power: Peace, wherever it exists—in Philadelphia, in the United States, or in the larger world around us—is partly the product of power to enforce peace, nor would its exercise by a single power, even if possessed in abundance, be acceptable to others. So we must, I suggest, moderate preconceptions about absolute sovereignty and address ourselves to the methods by which nations, all believing in human dignity, mutuality in human relations, and the free choice of peoples, may pool their power, or create new power, to enforce global peace. This has been achieved to a limited extent by the United Nations and by NATO. The need now is to expand the NATO concept, which is transnational rather than multinational, to all free nations and, eventually, to every country of the world.

This *negative* approach must yield us the time, very much time, so desperately needed by men everywhere to foster education and genuine mutual understanding; to improve health and increase productivity; to develop more enlightened trade, aid, and credit relationships; to do all the multitude of things which must be done to build the *positive* peace that will give peoples everywhere the assurance of a better life with dignity, justice, and equality.

This is, as one statesman has said, the century of the common man. The valid aspirations of the oceans of common peoples of all nationalities, colors, religions, and circumstances, can be achieved only in a world at peace. The common peoples of East and West, of the advanced and underdeveloped nations, instinctively want to live in a world free of conflict; but governments, influencing the thinking of citizens, stubbornly cling to the outmoded strategy of competitive power, thus dangerously postponing acceptance of the modern imperative.

All of this is, of course, relevant to us in higher education. Change is the currency we deal in; indeed, our colleges and universities are more and more architects of the world we inhabit. We surely should be the last to condemn revolutionary changes because of the dangers and complex problems that arise from them.

But as the instigator of change, higher education has a special responsibility to create the conditions in which it will be the most constructive and productive. We are obliged to develop men and women who can humanize the scientific revolution, who can harness the power and the potential of technology for the good of all men, who can promote intercultural understanding and action so essential to positive peace, who can give content to the form and direction to the means. This is no task for small minds.

*   *   *

I fear that too few of the millions of young people who pass through our institutions of higher learning meet these qualifications. I rather think that in too many of them we fail to light the light. No individual is wise enough to say precisely why we fail or what we must do to succeed. But I can point to some guide-posts:

We must view learning as a vital and continuing human process with emphasis on genuine understanding rather than mere knowledge.

We must practice what we preach about character building and love of freedom. John Sloan Dickey has said that "to create power of competence without creating a corresponding sense of moral direction to guide the use of power is bad education." Higher education must abandon the comfortable haven of objectivity, the sterile pinnacle of moral neutrality. In our perilous world, we cannot avoid moral judgments; this is a privilege only of the uninvolved.

We must educate more generalists, more leaders who understand the totality of human existence, who are as skillful at devising a total program of peace and progress as specialists are in constructing the engines of destruction. This does not mean a lessening of specialization. Indeed, I boggle at the semantic absurdity of the term "overspecialization" as though a physician, or a chemist, or a mathematician could know too much about his specialty. It does mean that we should educate our students both as men of broad comprehension and as specialists.

We must make the humanities more vital in education. It may be heresy, but I believe that there is no *inherent* value in the humanities. That is, they are meaningful only if they humanize a man, if they enable him to understand the human situation and his own place in it, if they equip a man to live creatively in his own times and contribute to them. Unfortunately, the humanities often become just an academic specialty like physics or biology. It does not necessarily follow that a scholar in the humanities is also a humanist—but it should. For what does it avail a man to be the greatest expert on John Donne if he cannot hear the bell tolling?

We must teach people to communicate with logic and clarity, for this is the prerequisite to understanding. We cannot call a man educated who does not know how to use the language, including the language of science and mathematics. But our specialized men today all too often speak in strangely fractionated jargons and do not understand even the words—let alone the rationale—of other eminent specialists. To make communication more meaningful, to make possible wiser judgments on modern complex problems, the ivory tower of Babel must come down.

In sum, our unalterable purpose must be to help all students learn to think objectively, critically, and creatively with a moral framework, and to employ their talents insistently to the solution of all the key problems presented in a rapidly changing environment.

4

Tell It Like It Really Is — The Opted-Out World *

DAVID ANDREW SEELEY

How does David Seeley's account of nonconventional youth groups differ from the public image of these groups? Do you think his account is too uncritical? What does the author mean by the quotation that "their politics is nonviolent and so is their life-style"?

Let me tell it like it *really* is. Let me tell you who it is we speak of. There are perhaps a score of recognizable and distinct groups, all of which would be classed together by the too-

* David Andrew Seeley, "Tell It Like It Really Is . . . ," *Center Diary: 18*, (Santa Barbara: The Fund for the Republic, Inc., 1967), pp. 60-61. Reprinted by permission of the publisher.

casual observer, and nearly all of these would—and justifiably—resent it. They "all look alike" to the superficial observer, but they wear very obvious marks, easily distinguishable by themselves. They are all thought to behave alike, and "everybody knows" how that is. Actually, group activities vary from beer parties to poetry readings, from pot-smoking to modern dance—

and often those who indulge in one wouldn't touch the other. They are all believed to think and feel alike, yet they range from anarchists to Communists to those politically indifferent, from violent revolutionaries to those who reject violence altogether, both as a political weapon and as a personal way of life. All of them do have one thing very much in common—a great tolerance, both for personal hang-ups and for philosophical differences. In large part because of this tolerance, there is considerable overlap of groups; that is, there are many people who reflect characteristics of two or more of these distinct groups.

Let me take five groups, all of which would be classed together, as "beatniks," by the uncritical observer. There are the teeny-bopper "beatniks" (the name is supposed to be self-explanatory), there are the "beat" surfers, there are the folk "beatniks," the Movement-New Left "beatniks," and the "hippies." In spite of the free flow and movement between groups, the distinct groups and the core members are still easily recognized by a person inside any one of them. And the groups, and their life-styles, are maintained because the groups have, and live, different philosophies.

Let me tell you what they look like. The common badges that the public looks for are beards, long hair, sandals, boots, bare feet, tight pants, and "shabby" clothes. Many of these *are* common badges, but there are often obvious and significant variations of these badges. When they are worn and how they are worn signify things, beyond "rebellion" or "non-conformity." Beards, for example, generally correlate with social concern. The teeny-boppers have no beards, nor do the surfers. The folk and Movement and hippy "beatniks" often have beards, and these are the groups with the social concerns and consciences.

Many, of all the groups, have long hair, but there are significant differences of style, length, and cleanness. Most teeny-boppers wear theirs in the Beatles-Prince Charles style, usually very neat and soft and clean. The surfers often have theirs with a long forelock and short sides and back. The folk and Movement and hippy styles vary from Beatle to a cut like that shown in conventional pictures of Jesus, to a normal haircut with long sideburns, to simply a normal haircut, and not as clean and pampered as the teeny-boppers'. Sandals are unpopular among the teeny-boppers—they wear Beatle-boots more—while the other groups wear sandals or boots or bare feet or regular shoes almost indiscriminately. Sandals are most popular among the folk set, and among the girls especially. The common image of the tightness of pants is way off. The teeny-boppers wear the tightest pants. Surfer types wear theirs about as tight as do "normal" people. As you get farther from the "rock" scene, the pants grow looser and looser, and the folk and Movement and hippy pants are often rather baggier than the average student's. "Shabby" clothes are almost never worn by teeny-boppers, seldom by surfers, but often by the others, and usually for one reason—they are poor. They are often living in voluntary poverty; and besides, they believe, "one has better and more important things to do than heed fashion."

But I said that the groups would resent being classed together. They want to maintain a visible group identity because each group is different in life styles, philosophies, and actions. The teeny-boppers aren't concerned with social reform, nor particularly with sharing, even among themselves. The surfers aren't socially concerned either, but their life-style is less intense than that of the teeny-boppers.

The Movement, folk, and hippy philosophies of social reform, which each of them cares about, differ rather importantly. The Movement people believe more in direct action; the folk people have less faith that one can work within the structure to change the structure without being corrupted by it; the hippies have still less faith in that, and believe generally that the only way really to create a love-ful world is by living the kind of life *now* that they want the world to have later. These are important differences. However, in most other respects these three socially concerned groups are not dissimilar.

Let me tell you what they do, both for leisure and for serious work. For leisure they listen to music, draw, paint, sculpt, write, read, and turn on. Most of the music in their record collections is, contrary to public opinion, classical; and this is followed in popularity by folk, rock, and jazz. They read, mostly poetry and serious nonfiction, from Plato to Sartre to Marx to Freud to Camus to Berne to Lenny Bruce. Most write, draw, paint, or sculpt for themselves; a few, for publication or sale. They turn on, mostly to marijuana, less to LSD, virtually not at all to addictive drugs. They do many and various things in their serious life-work. They don't consider the accumulation of money or possessions to be very important, in spite of, or perhaps because of, the fact that they are mostly children of upper-middle-class suburbia. They are poor, generally for one of two reasons. One is that they are forced to live in poverty by the work they choose as important to do, such as earning $25 a week (with luck) working for SNCC. The other is that they are forced to live in poverty by the work they choose *not* to do, the work they opt out of because they feel it is improper or immoral. Many are students, and they are the

best and brightest students. (Ask any university president, or see the Byrne Report on Berkeley.) Many work as teachers (such as "teaching assistants"), and they are the best and most creative teachers. (Ask any department head, or, better yet, ask the students.) Many others work in the Movement, from the Peace Corps to Students for a Democratic Society. Most have at least been in the Movement, in the South or in community projects, or in anti-war activities. This, the reform of the society and of the world, is what they consider to be more important and more worthwhile than taking over Daddy's business. The hippies want to reform it by becoming a community, and living the kind of life that they would want to have "filter up."

Now, let me tell you where they're really at, what they feel, what they love, what they care about. They care about love, truth, and beauty. True, there is probably no one who would deny that he cares about love, truth, and beauty. But there's a difference. The "beatniks" care about love over life and limb. They care about truth over personal security and liberty. They care about beauty over "bread." For love, they rejected violence when provoked or attacked, in Mississippi, at Berkeley, and in countless other places. For truth, many are going to jail because they refused to register for the draft, rather than cooperate—even to get their student deferment—with an immoral system. For beauty, they will often rather spend grocery money on more paint or more film.

Many of them live the life everyone claims we would or should. They are honest and open, both with insiders and outsiders. They share whatever food or shelter they have, again with insiders and any outsiders who venture to ask. They have one characteristic that makes them difficult to study—

their tolerance. They accept anyone, and they accept people with widely various backgrounds and hang-ups. They are the gentlest and tenderest group of people, especially young people, that we see today. Their dress is gentle and soft. Their long hair is soft. Their music is gentle (the Beatles, for example). Their faces are gentle. Their speech is quiet. Their politics is non-violent, and so is their life-style: no status-consciousness, no one-upmanship, no put-downs. Even in an area of relatively little importance (compared to social reform and anti-war concerns), that of politeness, their gentleness is shown. They are even polite to the cops who dragged them down Sproul Hall's steps on their heads— more polite than the cops are to them. One of their leaders, a president of Students for a Democratic Society, said, "We want to create a world in which love is more possible." They intend to do that, by tearing down the old one, socially and politically reforming it, and by beginning to live the loving life now.

One of their heroes, Bob Dylan, wrote in one of his songs, ". . . something is happening here, but you don't know what it is. Do you, Mr. Jones?" I've told here some of what's happening and what it is and what it means. I've seen it from the inside. If any one of you wants to find out for himself, just go there—to Haight-Ashbury in San Francisco, to Telegraph Avenue in Berkeley, to the Village in New York—just go there, tell them you'd like to know them and to watch them, and they'll take you in, even if you're an F.B.I. man. As long as you come on straight, and say so.

5

Don't Trust Anyone Over Thirty *

MORTON M. HUNT

What is the significance of the title, "Don't Trust Anyone Over Thirty"? In what ways is this "not just a new generation but a new kind of generation"? Are the current generational "styles" a fad or are they indicative of long-range trends and general movements?

❋   ❋   ❋

I talked with hippies and drug users, dropouts and cop-outs; and with Peace Corps volunteers, housewives, salesmen, teachers, medical stu-

dents and countless other young people who were neat, polite, brisk and ambitious.

I wanted to know how much of what had been printed was true about this "new, different generation" on the threshold of adult life.

Time, for example, has said: "This is not just a new generation, but a new kind of generation."

* Morton M. Hunt, "Don't Trust Anyone Over Thirty." From the June 1967 issue of *Redbook* magazine, copyright © by McCall Corporation, 1967.

Author Gene Marine wrote in *Ramparts:*

You who go around judging them [the young adults] are alienated from reality. . . . To you, marijuana is still the road to heroin, LSD is still an infantile escape (from what you still think is reality), obscenity is still what you wouldn't have wanted your children to read because your mother wouldn't have approved of it. To you, Bob Dylan is just this generation's Frank Sinatra. Poor you.

Said a young Californian quoted in the book *It's Happening,* by J. L. Simmons and Barry Winograd:

Look at you [the middle-aged generation], needing a couple of stiff drinks before you have the guts to talk with another human being. Look at you, makit with your neighbor's wife just to prove that you're really alive. Look at you, screwing up the land and the water and the air for profit, and calling this nowhere scene the Great Society! And you're gonna tell us how to live! You've got to be kidding!

Berkeley student protest leader Mario Savio has attempted to close off all lines of communication with the middle-aged enemy by advising, "Never trust anybody over thirty." And Bob Dylan summed up his contempt for everyone on the other side of this time barrier: "Something's happening and you don't know what it is, do you, Mr. Jones?"

All these statements suggest that something new *is* going on in the world; but as a result of my inquiries I now doubt that Bob Dylan really knows what is happening any more than Mr. Jones does.

In matters of politics, religion, sex, intoxicants, moral commitments and even dress and haircuts, there are indeed young people who distress the middle-aged by behaving in ways vastly different from theirs. But during my travels I kept coming across evidence that the behavior and opinions of these far-out young people are also vastly different from the behavior and opinions of the large majority of their middle-class contemporaries.

Yet even if the young extremists are only a minority, it is they who are alarming the older people and exciting the younger ones, who are pioneering in fashions and ideas, who are sounding the call to battle. They are not all of a piece: some are runaways from a world they reject or cannot deal with; some are primarily enthusiastic faddists of new styles and new sensations; and some are impassioned critics and reformers. To what extent they represent their generation and how much of what they do or say today will affect tomorrow's society may be debatable, but few of their activities are truly incomprehensible, even if they often seem so.

Perhaps the hardest to understand of today's young men and women are the cop-outs—the runaways who find their native culture sordid, corrupt and controlled by a power elite too strong to struggle against. Disgusted by contemporary society but feeling incapable of changing it, the cop-outs withdraw and live apart from society and all its values in enclaves of bohemianism and relative poverty. They work just enough to support themselves, and take pride in the simplicity of their way of life and in their freedom from possessions ("Things own *you;* you don't own them," they explain). They spend their leisure time in various ways—reading, talking, painting, experimenting with drugs, and in general seeking a euphoric state of mind in which they say they feel perfectly free from conflicts, perfectly loving. "I love everybody," says one young man who looks deceptively like a cutthroat. "Sometimes I love so much it makes me dizzy."

The Haight-Ashbury section of San Francisco—a run-down, formerly middle-class neighborhood—is headquarters and home for some of the farthest-out young hippies in America today. A bearded, bespectacled young man with the face of a religious ascetic explains his moral philosophy:

I think any behavior is appropriate that makes you happy and doesn't interfere with the happiness of others. People should just leave one another alone.

A long-haired girl in a poor boy sweater tells about seeking comfort through sex and drugs:

Sex is much groovier when there is love, but there is nothing wrong with just sex for sex. As for LSD, I think it's really a drag that you can be put in jail for just feeling good.

A weary young man with shoulder-length hair speaks with great effort:

What I would really like to do is be in the country by myself, and just groove in on what I want to do, whatever I happen to do.

Some hippies are so withdrawn from the society around them, so "tuned out" from its demands, that they can't even borrow books from the library because, as one of them explains: "Man, it's just too much of a drag, filling out those forms to get a card."

The San Francisco cop-outs have their counterparts elsewhere. In a handful of major cities and on a number of campuses there are coffee-houses where one can always find a cluster of self-consciously rebellious-looking—but passive—social drop-outs. Around them are an assortment of marginal types, half-hearted hippies who make the far-out scene as much as they dare to or have time for (by day they may have jobs or go to school; at night or on weekends they play at being cop-outs). Bizarre clothing, rampaging hair and beards, public displays of physical affection, the open assertion of sexual freedom, are some of their ways of dissenting from society. But lately their most important way of dissenting has been through the use of drugs; and advocates of LSD, such as Timothy Leary and novelist Ken Kesey, have attained almost the stature of folk heroes among them.

No one knows how many young adults are now using marijuana and the stronger, more dangerous drugs such as LSD, amphetamines and others, and estimates vary so widely as to make all of them lack credibility. But for what it may be worth, most estimates seem to indicate that from 10 to 30 per cent of American college students have used drugs of one sort or another at some time, although only a very small number uses them regularly. Most young adults who are in on the "drug scene" consider the pot-head (the heavy user of marijuana) or acid-head (the regular user of LSD) a "sickie," and the user of heroin a lost soul. But they also feel strongly that it is their own business whether they do or don't try drugs. Says a 29-year-old high school teacher in Los Angeles,

I fear LSD for its psychological dangers, but I don't like society's forbidding me to try it. I feel sophisticated enough to make my own decision about it. Besides, it's *my* mind—what right has society to tell me how to treat part of myself?

Even though the use of drugs as a symptom of youthful rebelliousness has pre-empted the attention of the nation, some young people—as always —continue to make sex their way of defying "the Establishment." One finds, for example, in *IN New York* (a magazine for "singles"):

The scene today is sexual freedom. No guilt. No phony taboos. No blinds. No questioning why. You make love if, when and how you want to. It's spontaneous, natural, rational.

The New Left—in some ways the most meaningful choice of today's young people in revolt—is an unorganized aggregation of many left-of-center viewpoints. It is not altogether a student movement, but on certain campuses—notably Berkeley, Wisconsin and Michigan—it has made the most news. Its demonstrations, strikes and teach-ins, protesting U.S. involvement in Vietnam or furthering civil rights causes or objecting to university regulations, have been taken to indicate a nationwide spirit of dissent and rebellion among college students in general. This is a misinterpretation. On occasion the great mass of students sympathize with and rally behind some cause championed by members of the New Left, but in general it is a tiny, though very vocal, minority. The most generous estimate of its size has been made by sociologist Amitai Etzioni, of Columbia University, who says about 4 per cent of American college students are involved in New Left activism.

Nonetheless, both on campus and off, a somewhat larger minority of the new generation agrees with some of the New Left positions. These young people make up the bulk of the volunteers who work for civil rights, peace and allied causes. They are not necessarily radical in their social philosophy or even in their dress and behavior; most of them are hard-working, earnest and basically serious people. As a wholesome-looking, blue-eyed girl of 24 explained to me in a Washington coffee shop, she and her friends are not "way out," as her parents think, but are "people with social consciousness."

"We see around us a world filled with grave inequities, great wrongs perpetrated by the older generation—poverty, segregation, war," she said. "Just reading the paper every morning is a profoundly emotional experience for us. Young people like us are willing to risk our lives down South, or our careers by protesting against the war in Vietnam. We're not politically doctrinaire, but we *care* about things."

A few of the New Left attitudes seep downward from the activists to a fairly large but politically inactive part of the young adult population. Bob Dylan's huge audience of admirers apparently accepts or agrees with the singer's feelings about American society and the older generation, which pop-music critic Ralph Gleason sums up as follows:

He sneers at the groves of academe ("the old folks' home in the college"), at religion ("The phantom of the opera in the perfect image of a priest"), at Madison Avenue ("gray-flannel dwarfs"), at the war machine, at hard work. What he is saying is getting an unbelievably intense reaction from a generation thirsting for answers other than those in the college textbooks.

Implicit in much of this is the feeling of at least some of today's young adults that their entire generation is morally superior to older ones—for they see themselves as honest, candid, loving, uncorrupted by ambition. In contrast, they see the older generation as venal "sell-outs," hypocrites and despoilers. Paul Goodman, Allen Ginsberg and other writers who assure the young that they are the good but exploited people get a wildly enthusiastic reception from the young New Left intellectuals and those who have absorbed their key attitudes toward contemporary American society.

But a great number of the alleged moral and political differences between Americans under and over 30 disappear when subjected to the light of impartial research. Gallup polls, for instance, have repeatedly shown that there is very little difference between what people in their 20s and people over 30 expect of the future, or feel the Federal government should concentrate on, or think about capitalism and communism.

Student protest leaders to the contrary, research conducted by the Wisconsin Survey Research Laboratory showed that it is not the young who reject the U.S. role in the Vietnam war so much as older people.

And although the attitudes of most college students toward premarital sexual intercourse have apparently become much more permissive in the last decade or so, sociologist John Gagnon of the Institute for Sex Research, reviewing reports and studies on student sexuality, finds that there is little change in the numbers actually having such sexual relations.

The fact is that the great majority of young adults are not in any revolt at all; they look, think and behave very much like merely younger versions of the older people all around them. All over this country, millions of young men and women rise early, dress carefully, take the train or subway or car to work, try to do their best, hope for promotion, fall in love, marry, have babies and take out insurance.

On the campuses of the great universities the hippies are only stray leaves floating on the smooth river of conventionality. Sociologist Seymour Lipset, of Harvard, says that while radicalism, drugs and dropping out are three ways that students can react to the extreme pressures on them to succeed, the greatest majority by far react in a fourth way—by conforming and studying harder.

And conforming includes accepting without question the basic goals and actions of the Establishment. Even on those campuses where there have been the most vociferous student protests against the war in Vietnam, for instance, most students are politically middle-of-the-road or uninterested.

It is true, however, that both in their student years and afterward most young adults do have certain new and distinctive traits that make them different from the older generation. The great majority, for one thing, are optimistic and unconcerned about the future of the American economy in a way their parents never could be. Young adults have heard about the depression of the 1930s, but to them it is all one with the War of the Roses and the Black Plague. "My folks used to tell me about those days," says a young real-estate man in Atlanta, "but I can't really feel what they felt. And I can't imagine anything like that ever happening again. I never give it a thought."

Being basically confident, today's young adult is unconcerned about saving money. "Our folks are always after us to save something," said a young bride in Detroit, "and we know that they can't help feeling nervous for us. But *we* don't feel nervous, and that's what counts."

*   *   *

In the course of traveling thousands of miles and talking to hundreds of people, I struggled to see the shape of things; and at last homeward bound, I felt that I began to see the real outlines.

There *is* a generational gap, and it seems far wider than at any time in recent history. But it yawns very wide only for a small minority of young adults—a minority that is publicized and talked about out of all proportion to its size.

The majority of young adults are really conventional, which may be reassuring to many of their conservative-minded elders. But I cannot help feeling that this is unfortunate for the young adults themselves; they never go through periods of creative ferment and re-evaluation. Both left-wing and right-wing intellectuals attest to, and deplore, this fact. A left-liberal professor who is studying attitudes at a large state university told me:

For all the folderol about campus radicalism, most students are virtually unconscious concerning social and political matters. They're willing to live life as it is granted them, in a sort of cocoon. They're hell-bent on career and family, and have no time to ponder or disagree with the way things are.

Much the same sentiments were echoed by a college president who heads an ultraconservative political organization in California.

The great majority of young adults don't care about political issues. They haven't any thoughts about tomorrow except whether they're going to have a good job and a nice house and drive a nice car. People in their twenties today are basically old people.

Says a brilliant young sociologist at a Midwestern university:

I feel rather *deprived* because I always got along with my parents. There was no generational gap. Had I been more at odds with my parents, I might have been a better person—less sophisticated and smooth, but harder-working and more probing.

The actual impact on society of the young people who do feel at odds with their parents is far smaller than the conservatives fear or than the radicals hope. For one thing, they swing from one enthusiasm to another so rapidly that few of their innovations take thorough hold. Among college students, for instance, the focus of revolt has shifted from peace to civil rights to drugs with little apparent logic or continuity.

Already the revolt of the Radical Right on campus is forgotten and erased, though only a handful of years ago it seemed to foretell major changes. The New Left of today also may have only a short period of importance. Not only is it torn by factional disputes between the moderates and the all-out radicals, but also it is lacking in a constructive ideology. Unlike the Marxist campus radicals of the 1930s, those of today have no blueprint for social reconstruction. They are *against* war, segregation and poverty, but they seem to have no specific cures in mind, no new social programs, no real ideology.

* * *

It is perhaps the inevitable conclusion of almost all youthful rebellion, and true for all time, that whatever way in which the young differ or dissent—whether by civil disobedience or outlandish clothing, whether through drugs or sex, whether through strange forms of art and music or merely through the use of dirty words—most of them moderate and temper their behavior, and some of them their thinking as well, as they approach the threshold of adult life. The closer they come to the beginnings of a career or of marriage, or both, the narrower the generational gap becomes. For previously they were nobody special, and needed to establish their identity. Opposition, rebellion, newness, offered them a way. Now they are about to become somebody special—careerists, husbands and wives, parents—and they can lay the other identity aside. Whether this is "growing up" or "selling out" all depends on where you view it from—all too often it is a matter of really giving up a dream or daring or originality for comfort and possessions and ease.

And so, to a greater or lesser degree, they begin to enter the ruling order they have scorned—some gladly, some reluctantly, some with dismay. And some without even realizing what is happening to them.

6

Youth in the Context of American Society *

TALCOTT PARSONS

In what important ways is the current youth culture different from that of previous generations? Why does there seem to be a serious concern among young people about meaningfulness? Would you agree that among the American youth there is "not a basic alienation, but an eagerness to learn, to accept higher orders of responsibility and to 'fit' . . ."?

❊   ❊   ❊

Perhaps the most significant fact about current youth culture is its concern with meaningfulness. This preoccupation definitely lies on the serious and progressive side of the division I have outlined. Furthermore, it represents a rise in the level of concern from the earlier preoccupation with social justice—even though the problem of race relations is understandably a prominent one. Another prominent example is the much discussed concern with problems of "identity." This is wholly natural and to be expected in the light of *anomie*. In a society that is changing as rapidly as ours and in which

there is so much mobility of status, it is only natural that the older generation cannot provide direct guidance and role models that would present the young person with a neatly structured definition of the situation. Rather, he must find his own way, because he is pushed out of the nest and expected to fly. Even the nature of the medium in which he is to fly is continually changing, so that, when he enters college, there are many uncertainties about the nature of opportunities in his chosen field on completing graduate school. His elders simply do not have the knowledge to guide him in detail.

It is highly significant that the primary concern has been shifting since early in the century from the field of social justice to that of meaningfulness, as exemplified by the problem of identity—except for the status of special groups such as the Negro. In terms of the social structure, this enhances the problem of integration, and

* Talcott Parsons, "Youth in the Context of American Society," in *Youth: Change and Challenge*, ed. Erik H. Erikson (New York: Basic Books, Inc., Publishers, 1963). © 1961 by the American Academy of Arts and Sciences; © 1963 by Basic Books, Inc., Publishers. Reprinted by permission of the publishers.

focuses concern more on problems of meaning than on those of situation and opportunity in the simpler sense. It is a consequence of the process of social change we have outlined.

It is also understandable and significant that the components of anxiety that inevitably characterize this type of strained situation should find appropriate fields of displacement in the very serious, real dangers of the modern world, particularly those of war. It may also be suggested that the elite youth's resonance to the diagnosis of the current social situation in terms of conformity and mass culture should be expected.[1] Essentially, this diagnosis is an easy disparagement of the society, which youth can consider to be the source of difficulty and (so it seems to them) partially unmanageable problems.

*   *   *

The above analysis suggests in the main that contemporary American society is of a type in which one would expect the situation of youth to involve (certainly, by the standards of the society from which it is emerging) rather special conditions of strain. As part of the more general process of differentiation to which we have alluded, youth groups themselves are coming to occupy an increasingly differentiated position, most conspicuously, in the field of formal education. Though an expanding educational system is vital in preparing for future function, it has the effect of segregating (more sharply and extensively than ever before) an increasing proportion of the younger age groups. The extension of education to increasingly older age levels is a striking example.

The other main focus of strain is the impact on youth of the pace and nature of the general process of social change. This is especially observable in the problem of *anomie.* In view of this change, youth's expectations cannot be defined either very early or very precisely, and this results in considerable insecurity. Indeed, the situation is such that a marked degree of legitimate grievance is inevitable. Every young person is entitled in some respects to complain that he has been brought into "a world I never made."

To assess the situation of American youth within the present frame of reference presents an especially difficult problem of balance. This is an era that lays great stress, both internally and externally, on the urgencies of the times, precisely in the more sensitive and responsible quarters. Such a temper highlights what is felt to be wrong and emphasizes the need for change through active intervention. With reference to the actual state of society, therefore, the tendency is to lean toward a negative evaluation of the status quo, because both the concrete deficiencies and the obstacles to improvement are so great.

That this tendency should be particularly prominent in the younger age groups is natural. It is both to be expected and to be welcomed. The main feature of the youth situation is perhaps the combination of current dependence with the expectation of an early assumption of responsibility. I think that evidence has been presented above that this conflict is accentuated under present conditions. The current youthful indictments of the present state of our society may be interpreted as a kind of campaign position, which prepares the way for the definition of their role when they take over the primary responsibilities, as they inevitably will.

[1] For an analysis of this complex in society, see Winston R. White, *Beyond Conformity* (New York: Free Press of Glencoe, Inc., 1966).

It seems highly probable that the more immediate situation is strongly influenced by the present phase of the society with respect to a certain cyclical pattern that is especially conspicuous in the political sphere. This is the cycle between periods of "activism" in developing and implementing a sense of the urgency of collective goals, and of "consolidation" in the sense of withdrawing from too active commitments and on the whole giving security and "soundness" the primary emphasis. There is little doubt that in this meaning, the most recent phase (the "Eisenhower era") has been one of consolidation, and that we are now involved in the transition to a more activistic phase.

Broadly speaking, youth in a developing society of the American type, in its deepest values and commitments, is likely to be favorable to the activistic side. It is inculcated with the major values of the society, and strongly impressed with the importance of its future responsibilities. At the same time, however, it is frustrated by being deprived of power and influence in the current situation, though it recognizes that such a deprivation is in certain respects essential, if its segregation for purposes of training is to be effective—a segregation which increases with each step in the process of differentiation. A certain impatience, however, is to be expected, and with it a certain discontent with the present situation. Since it is relatively difficult to challenge the basic structure of the youth situation in such respects (e.g., as that one should not be permitted to start the full practice of medicine before graduating from college), this impatience tends to be displaced on the total society as a system, rather than on the younger generation in its specific situation. From this point of view, a generous measure of youthful dissatisfac-

tion with the state of American society may be a sign of the healthy commitment of youth to the activist component of the value system. However good the current society may be from various points of view, *it is not good enough to meet their standards.* It goes almost without saying that a fallibility of empirical judgment in detail is to be expected.

The task of the social scientist, as a scientific observer of society, is to develop the closest possible approach to an objective account of the character and processes of the society. To him, therefore, this problem must appear in a slightly different light: he must try to see it in as broad a historical and comparative perspective as he can, and he must test his judgments as far as possible in terms of available empirical facts and logically precise and coherent theoretical analyses.

Viewed in this way (subject, of course, to the inevitable fallibilities of all cognitive undertakings), American society in a sense appears to be running a scheduled course. We find no cogent evidence of a major change in the essential pattern of its governing values. Nor do we find that—considering the expected strains and complications of such processes as rapid industrialization, the assimilation of many millions of immigrants, and a new order of change in the power structure, the social characteristics, and the the balances of its relation to the outside world—American society is not doing reasonably well (as distinguished from outstandingly) in implementing these values. Our society on the whole seems to remain committed to its essential mandate.

The broad features of the situation of American youth seem to accord with this pattern. There are many elements of strain, but on the whole they may be considered normal for this type of society. Furthermore, the patterns of reaction on the part of American youth also seem well within normal limits. Given the American value system we have outlined, it seems fair to conclude that youth cannot help giving a *relative* sanction to the general outline of society as it has come to be institutionalized. On the other hand, it is impossible for youth to be satisfied with the status quo, which must be treated only as a point of departure for the far higher attainments that are not only desirable but also obligatory.

Clearly, American youth is in a ferment. On the whole, this ferment seems to accord relatively well with the sociologist's expectations. It ex-presses many dissatisfactions with the current state of society, some of which are fully justified, others are of a more dubious validity. Yet the general orientation appears to be, not a basic alienation, but an eagerness to learn, to accept higher orders of responsibility, and to "fit," not in the sense of passive conformity, but in the sense of their readiness to work within the system, rather than in basic opposition to it. The future of American society and the future place of that society in the larger world appear to present in the main a *challenge* to American youth. To cope with that challenge, an intensive psychological preparation is now taking place.

CHAPTER TWO

Democracy or Direction:
Theory and Practice

The competition between democracy and its rivals takes two forms. On one level it is a contest of ideas, an intellectual disagreement. On the other level it is a confrontation of societies of political and social systems carrying out day-to-day activities, presumably in accordance with the prescriptions of the ideology.

The paradox is that on both of these levels democracy today seems more successful and more vital than a decade ago, certainly than three decades ago; yet the confident mood of democratic thought is gone. Questioning and deprecation are more common than hope and easy affirmation.

The success of democracy as an ideology, the almost universal appeal of its assertions, can be proven by its use as a propaganda device, even by its enemies. Even those who deny majoritarian control try to justify their actions in the name of some purer form of democracy. We get very peculiar arguments about "democratic centralism" and "guided democracy" to name only two of the more prominent variants. No doubt they represent something quite different from what has traditionally been claimed for the democratic philosophy; the important point, though, is that the mantle of democracy is wrapped around their shoulders, even by its detractors.

The success of democracy as a system is, perhaps, more open to doubt, yet there are strong indications of its endurance in any race for superiority with other systems. Democracy has proven more capable of change without convulsion than have the structures of Eastern Europe and Communist China. It is more permeable to day-to-day demands as well, as witnessed by the stagnation of personnel and policies that characterizes most of the Eastern European countries.

Why, then, has there been a defensive note in democratic thought of recent years? A small amount of the answer can perhaps be found in the ethos of democracy itself. A system devoted to extolling criticism and deprecating absolutes is likely to be self-critical and self-deprecating.

But there are more substantial reasons. By studying American government in a more precise way through real research and conceptual thought, we have found that the system just doesn't work the way Fourth-of-July orators say it should. Facing up to the consequences of the less than perfect division of power in our society and the less than godlike behavior of our citizens, raises problems for democratic theory. The new efforts to salvage democratic theory have not yet satisfied most thinking observers of politics.

The second reason is also a consequence of greater experience and candor. At the turn of the twentieth century and well into it, Americans and other Westerners believed in the manifest destiny of our form of government as the hope of mankind. Experience has shown that peoples don't automatically leap up and introduce our type of legal order into their society, and when they do accept it, often experience grave difficulties in making it work. That even France, a country rich both materially and in the democratic tradition, has found it difficult to solve its real problems by anything even remotely resembling the democratic process is, to say the least, disquieting.

To some extent the pessimism that was the reaction to the failures of democracy after World War I persists; to some extent it is mitigated. We see the mote in our eye, but take perhaps perverse pleasure in the beam in the eye of others. As Winston Churchill pointed out, democracy is, indeed, a very bad form of government, but thus far it seems able to vindicate its superiority over Brand X. The conviction persists that it is a governmental arrangement profoundly rooted in the needs of the human personality. Even so skeptical a thinker as Paul Goodman—the spiritual father of the New Left movement—has recently written: "The question is whether or not our beautiful libertarian, pluralist and populist experiment is viable in modern conditions. If it's not, I don't know any other acceptable politics, and I am a man without a country."

Is the Common Man Too Common?

The traditional objection to democracy is an aristocratic one; the average citizen is incapable of self-control and self-direction. The traditional answer is as old as the objection. As Aristotle said, the guest can judge at the banquet better than the chef, though he might not be able to cook the meal. Or, as has been suggested as a variant, not even scientific machinery can really determine whether the shoe pinches. But the modern form of this argument against the average man goes further. Not only is he, as valid scientific studies indicate, often irrational in politics, but he doesn't even know where the shoe pinches. The modern common man is even worse than his predecessor. In the past society institutionalized and rewarded excellence. Today the common man is jealous and self-confident. In short, it is argued that democratic theory has destroyed the basis for leadership and thoughtful decision making. This argument is represented in our readings by the classic statement of Ortega y Gasset, but it has been argued, for example, on the conduct of foreign policy by Walter Lippman. It raises the question, too, of whether in day-to-day life the demands of equality may not extinguish individuality and distinctive excellence in every field. In a sense the claims of current youthful "rebellions" such as the Berkeley effort and Haight-Ashbury living, have been in the name of individuality. But observers note that, at least in part, it is based upon a desire to egalitize all living. The tension between the amateur and the specialist, the leader and the led, then, permeates democratic theory, and the issue is as live in current faddish thinking as it was at the time of Plato.

WHAT SYSTEM OF GOVERNMENT BEST SATISFIES MAN'S NEEDS?

From the standpoint of "a decent respect for the opinions of mankind," democratic values clearly win the contest. The civilized tone of discussion in even the less well-established democracies must be contrasted to the pronouncements of non-democratic governments that their critics are worms, jackals, and sometimes less flattering creatures. The humaneness of rotation in office and the congratulatory exchange of telegrams after an election is evident in contrast to the firing squad, the concentration camp, and the mysterious disappearance.

But non-democratic systems often can generate more excitement, involvement with a charismatic leader, a sense of doing things and going places. It is not even clear—probably the bulk of the evidence suggests the opposite—that people really want to make decisions for themselves, as much as they resent it when decisions they dislike are made.

But the most important argument and deterrent to the spread of democracy has been the claim that tighter systems of control are necessary in economically less advanced countries. The example of the Soviet Union in developing heavy industry has been the model for countries that claim that greater responsiveness to the public will lead to consumer orientation and waste.

Then, too, it has been suggested that democracy is a fragile system not easily exported. It requires, it would appear, unique social and economic underpinnings not usually present in most countries of the world. Where a society is fragmented on religious, ethnic, or even tribal grounds, the charismatic leader can be the only integrating force in a society. Pluralistic expression of views, it is argued, will only lead to disintegration and secession.

In studying developing countries, students of comparative government seem to have found confirmation for some of the claims of advantage of tightly knit decision systems in coping with particular stages of development and particular types of decisions. But they have also found that there are times when autocracy is a very bad system, even for economic development. Indeed, the growing emphasis has been not upon one system or the other as being more desirable, but upon a statement of under what conditions democracy and direction are most useful.

Is the United States Really Democratic?

In recent years the political scientists have developed more precise information on the nature of our political system. Instead of broad assertions and discussions about "the boss system," or vague claims about "sinister interests," we have studies of the exact relative influence of differing groups, and the ways in which different institutions favor specific interests. There have been studies of the decision-making process in various cities to discover just who prevails under what conditions. The scientific posture of these studies is somewhat tainted; most such observors have found in the communities they studied the type of power structure they had expected to find before the study began. Nonetheless, we know considerably more about community power structures, as well as national decision making, than we did a decade ago. Hand in hand with this information have gone more sophisticated ways of thinking about the processes of power and decision. (Indeed some of the rhetoric of the civil rights movement—power structure, for example—has been borrowed from such conceptualization.)

The picture that emerges is of a pluralistic organization of power groups, with decisions negotiated largely within the leadership strata. This is not truly a "one man, one vote" operation, and, indeed, in some aspects it makes the American system appear more like some of the systems normally described as oligarchical.

Does this then mean that our democracy is only a pretext? Has there been a change to this system from something pure, more democratic? Have the new institutional arrangements of mass society eroded individual power? Have mass communications reversed the pattern of messages so that the leadership can manipulate people at their will? Or has the opposite happened? Has power now found a new pattern of distribution in which even the formerly powerless have gained a share of control through the weapon of group structure? "If the meek are to inherit the earth, they first have to get organized." Do mass communication and universal education disperse information that allows greater participation? Unfortunately the evidence here is murky, although the answers to these questions seem rather urgent.

Are Systems of Government Converging?

Such writers as Isaac Deutscher have suggested that industrial societies require governmental systems that are roughly equivalent to each other. A minimal amount of decentralization of decisions and freedom of criticism must be allowed to make the system work. A scientist, it is argued, has to be allowed his freedom or he cannot function. The same is true, although it is temporarily disguised, of a plant manager, or other head of a business enterprise. In short, the argument is that the Soviet Union is not merely experiencing an "accidental thaw," a loosening up of restrictions because of the particular leadership it presently has, but rather one that was historically inevitable. China, too, would presumably go through a period of "modernizing autocracy," in which dictatorship would impose industrialization, but that very process of industrialization would result in a political system approaching our own.

At the same time, it is pointed out that the United States is moving from discrete, individual enterprises to social enterprises like the corporation, the foundation, and the pension fund. The development of an industrial bureaucracy, largely independent of stockholder control, makes our system a little bit more like that of the non-capitalist world. (It must be recognized that this is not a really new thesis. James Burnham enunciated such notions prior to World War II in *The Managerial Revolution*.)

But it is not clear that "convergence" is a very useful or precise concept. Systems can be alike on one level of thinking, and yet be vastly different on any meaningful plane. Some scholars, indeed, are most skeptical about the concept of "historical inevitability," and even suggest that the notion of "convergence" is a profound example of wishful thinking.

1

Dissection of the Mass Man *

JOSE ORTEGA Y GASSET

The arguments of Jose Ortega y Gasset are that the rise of the common man in politics has everywhere meant a decline in standards. The common man is a creature of appetites, no more. He is convinced he is perfect. He listens to almost no one. He is like a spoiled child. He is using politics and mass democracy for his own advantages, particularly for his own economic advantages, but he contributes nothing to the further growth and development of democratic politics and government. He recognizes no standards other than his own whims and desires. The more he comes into political power and is wooed and solicited for his biases and whims (called public opinion), the more civilization weakens.

There is one fact which, whether for good or ill, is of utmost importance

<hr style="opacity:0" />

* Jose Ortega y Gasset, *The Revolt of the Masses* (New York: W. W. Norton & Company, Inc., 1932). Pp. 11-15, 17-18, 55, 60-65. Copyright renewed 1960. Reprinted by permission of the publisher.

in the public life of Europe at the present moment. This fact is the accession of the masses to complete social power. . . .

Perhaps the best line of approach to this historical phenomenon may be found in turning our attention to a visual experience, stressing one aspect of our epoch which is plain to our very eyes. This fact is quite simple to enunciate, though not so to analyze. I shall call it the fact of agglomeration, of "plentitude." Towns are full of people, houses full of tenants, hotels full of guests, trains full of travelers, cafés full of customers, parks full of promenaders, consulting-rooms of famous doctors full of patients, theatres full of spectators, and beaches full of bathers. What previously was, in general, no problem, now begins to be an everyday one, namely, to find room. . . .

What about it? Is this not the ideal state of things? . . .

The concept of the multitude is quantitative and visual. Without changing its nature, let us translate it into terms of sociology. We then meet with the notion of the "social mass." Society is always a dynamic unity of two component factors: minorities and masses. The minorities are individuals or groups of individuals which are specially qualified. The mass is the assemblage of persons not especially qualified. By masses, then, is not to be understood, solely or mainly, "the working masses." The mass is the average man. In this way what was mere quantity—the multitude—is converted into a qualitative determination: it becomes the common social quality, man as undifferentiated from other men, but as repeating in himself a generic type.

The mass is all that which sets no value on itself—good or ill—based on specific grounds, but which feels itself "just like everybody," and nevertheless is not concerned about it; in fact, quite happy to feel itself as one with everybody else. . . .

For there is no doubt that the most radical division that it is possible to make of humanity is that which splits it into two classes of creatures: those who make great demands on themselves, piling up difficulties and duties; and those who demand nothing special of themselves, but for whom to live is to be every moment what they already are, without imposing on themselves any effort towards perfection; mere buoys that float on the waves. . . .

The old democracy was tempered by a generous dose of liberalism and of enthusiasm for law. . . . Today we are witnessing the triumphs of a hyperdemocracy in which the mass acts directly, outside the law, imposing its aspirations and its desires by means of material pressure. It is a false interpretation of the new situation to say that the mass has grown tired of politics and handed over the exercise of it to specialized persons. . . . Now, on the other hand, the mass believes that it has the right to impose and to give force of law to notions born in the café. I doubt whether there have been other periods of history in which the multitude has come to govern more directly than in our own. That is why I speak of hyperdemocracy. . . .

The characteristic of the hour is that the commonplace mind, knowing itself to be commonplace, has the assurance to proclaim the rights of the commonplace and to impose them where it will. . . .

Public authority is in the hands of a representative of the masses. These are so powerful that they have wiped out all opposition. They are in possession of power in such an unassailable manner that it would be difficult to find in history examples of a Government so all-powerful as these. And yet public authority—the Government—exists from hand to mouth, it does not offer itself as a frank solution for the future, it represents no clear announcement of the future, it does not stand out as the beginning of something whose development or evolution is conceivable. In short, it lives without

any vital program, any plan of existence. It does not know where it is
going, because, strictly speaking, it
has no fixed road, no predetermined
trajectory before it. When such a public authority attempts to justify itself
it makes no reference at all to the future. On the contrary, it shuts itself
up in the present, and says with perfect sincerity: "I am an abnormal
form of Government imposed by circumstances." Hence its activities are
reduced to dodging the difficulties of
the hour; not solving them, but escaping from them for the time being,
employing any methods whatsoever,
even at the cost of accumulating
thereby still greater difficulties for the
hour which follows. Such has public
power always been when exercised directly by the masses: omnipotent and
ephemeral. The mass-man is he whose
life lacks any purpose, and who simply goes drifting along. Consequently,
though his possibilities and his powers
be enormous, he constructs nothing.
And it is this type of man who decides
in our time. . . .

In the schools, which were such a
source of pride to the last century, it
has been impossible to do more than
instruct the masses in the technique of
modern life; it has been found impossible to educate them. They have been
given tools for an intenser form of
existence, but no feeling for their great
historic duties; they have been hur-
riedly inoculated with the pride and
power of modern instruments, but not
with their spirit. Hence they will have
nothing to do with their spirit, and the
new generations are getting ready to
take over command of the world as if
the world were a paradise without
trace of former footsteps, without traditional and highly complex problems. . . .

What appearance did life present to
that multitudinous man who in ever-
increasing abundance the nineteenth

century kept producing? To start
with, an appearance of universal material ease. Never had the average
man been able to solve his economic
problem with greater facility. . . .

To this ease and security of economic conditions are to be added the
physical ones, comfort and public
order. Life runs on smooth rails, and
there is no likelihood of anything violent or dangerous breaking in on it.
. . . That is to say, in all its primary
and decisive aspects, life presented
itself to the new man as exempt from
restrictions. . . .

But still more evident is the contrast
of situations, if we pass from the material to the civil and moral. The average man, from the second half of the
nineteenth century on, finds no social
barriers raised against him. . . . There
are no civil privileges. The ordinary
man learns that all men are equal before the law. . . .

Three principles have made possible
this new world: liberal democracy, scientific experiment, and industrialism.
. . . The world which surrounds the
new man from his birth does not compel him to limit himself in any fashion,
it sets up no veto in opposition to him;
on the contrary, it incites his appetite,
which in principle can increase indefinitely. . . . Even today, in spite of
some signs which are making a tiny
breach in that sturdy faith, even today, there are few men who doubt
that motorcars will in five years' time
be more comfortable and cheaper than
today. They believe in this as they believe that the sun will rise in the morning. The metaphor is an exact one.
For, in fact, the common man, finding
himself in a world so excellent, technically and socially, believes that it
has been produced by nature, and
never thinks of the personal efforts of
highly endowed individuals which the
creation of this new world presup-
posed. Still less will he admit the

notion that all these facilities still require the support of certain difficult human virtues, the least failure of which would cause the rapid disappearance of the whole magnificent edifice. . . .

This leads us to note down in our psychological chart of the mass-man of today two fundamental traits: the free expansion of his vital desires, and therefore, of his personality; and his radical ingratitude towards all that has made possible the ease of his existence. These traits together make up the well-known psychology of the spoilt child. And in fact it would entail no error to use this psychology as a "sight" through which to observe the soul of the masses of today. Heir to an ample and generous past—generous both in ideals and in activities—the new commonalty has been spoiled by the world around it. To spoil means to put no limit on caprice, to give one the impression that everything is permitted to him and that he has no obligations. The young child exposed to this regime has no experience of its own limits. By reason of the removal of all external restraint, all clashing with other things, he comes actually to believe that he is the only one that exists and gets used to not considering others, especially not considering them as superior to himself. This feeling of another's superiority could only be instilled into him by someone who, being stronger than he is, should force him to give up some desire, to restrict himself, to restrain himself. He would then have learned this fundamental discipline: "Here I end and here begins another more powerful than I am. In the world, apparently, there are two people: I myself and another superior to me." The ordinary man of past times was daily taught this elemental wisdom by the world about him, because it was a world so rudely organized, that catastrophes were frequent, and there was nothing in it certain, abundant, stable. But the new masses find themselves in the presence of a prospect full of possibilities, and furthermore, quite secure, with everything ready to their hands, independent of any previous efforts on their part, just as we find the sun in the heavens without hoisting it up on our shoulders. No human being thanks another for the air he breathes, for no one has produced the air for him; it belongs to the sum total of what "is there," of which we say "it is natural," because it never fails. And these spoiled masses are unintelligent enough to believe that the material and social organization, placed at their disposition like the air, is of the same origin, since apparently it never fails them, and is almost as perfect as the natural scheme of things.

My thesis, therefore, is this: the very perfection with which the nineteenth century gave an organization to certain orders of existence has caused the masses benefited thereby to consider it, not as an organized, but as a natural system. Thus is explained and defined the absurd state of mind revealed by these masses; they are only concerned with their own well-being, and at the same time they remain alien to the cause of that well-being. As they do not see, beyond the benefits of civilization, marvels of invention and construction which can only be maintained by great effort and foresight, they imagine that their role is limited to demanding these benefits peremptorily, as if they were natural rights. . . .

2

The Elite and the Electorate *

VISCOUNT HAILSHAM

Ortega y Gasset's comments suggest that democracy means the end of excellence in leadership and in public affairs, as well as in other aspects of life. If true, this would be a grievous weakness, for modern society entails a greater role for government. Both political leadership and bureaucratic administration become crucial aspects of democratic political systems. When government was a casual thing, amateur leadership by a small aristocracy could handle matters on a dilettante basis. Can modern democracy do more? A favorable answer comes from Viscount Hailsham, an answer that is perhaps more impressive because he is not only a member of the nobility, but also a leader of the British Conservative Party.

* * *

The traditional objection to democracy both in theory and in practice, ever since Plato and Thucydides began to notice its defects in the fifth century B.C., has been exactly the contrast between the elite and the electorate, the classes and the masses, as they used to be called. The contradiction has been that the complexities of administration and the maintenance of adequate civilized and cultural standards demand the existence of a class of men enjoying amenities and leisure and education up to age twenty-four or above, whereas the facts of life have been that the means of production are adequate to support such a class only on a limited scale, and thus in a state of privilege over

the majority. The mere existence of such a class therefore presupposes a contrast between rich and poor, between elite and electorate, between those who actually carry the responsibility of government and administration of all sorts and those who are governed, a contrast that it is said a democracy will never continue to tolerate for long.

I have not the leisure to demonstrate how far the various criticisms of the democratic thesis, the fear of mob rule, or the experience of the more sordid side of electioneering are really all variations upon this single theme. My case is that both the requirements of the technological society and the potentialities of modern production virtually drive society forward toward a fully educated society in which the contrast between electorate and elite has virtually disappeared—not because men will necessarily have moved any closer to equality of achievement or of reward, but because quantitative production has provided the means, and the require-

* Viscount Hailsham, "The Elite and the Electorate," in *Challenges to Democracy,* ed. Edward Reed; published by Frederick A. Praeger, Inc., Publishers, New York, 1964, for the Center for the Study of Democratic Institutions. Copyright 1963 by The Fund for the Republic, Inc. Reprinted by permission of the publisher.

ments of technology the necessity, to train or educate human beings without regard to wealth, birth, color, religion, or race to their limit, and to reward the remainder for their services, if they are prepared to work, to the limit of *their* capacity.

I am not describing a society in which everyone is equal, and I am certainly not describing a utopia. I do not claim to have discovered an antidote to original sin, which seems to me the only doctrine of the church for which there is ample empirical evidence *a posteriori*. I do not claim that such a society will be particularly agreeable, particularly moral, or even pleasantly secure. All I have said is that this is the logic of modern technology, that it is a development of democracy and not of Communism, and that it is something that the democrats of today would do well to further and to bring about precisely because it eliminates the inner contradiction of elite and electorate that has been the destruction of so many democratic regimes in the past.

The essence of my thesis is that it is Communism and not democracy that will be destroyed by its inner contradictions, contradictions, I may say, that become more and more apparent every day. Yet even this destruction could happen by evolutionary means. No nation, not even Russia and far less China, has willingly embraced Communism, and only fear, force, or fraud holds nations within the Communist embrace. As education and wealth and modern industrial techniques progress there, the logic of the technological revolution may be expected also to produce comparable results.

❖   ❖   ❖

As it exists today, democracy is not so much a system of government as a principal power and a means of changing political and economic systems without war. The differences between democracies are as important as their resemblances. . . . When democracy is first installed, it generally inherits from aristocracy a fine tradition of amateurism. It is the Caesars who produce the professional governors, the Chinese and the Roman Emperors, the Indian Civil Service, Napoleon's *carrière ouverte aux talents,* Pharaoh's appointment of Joseph as his Grand Vizier.

Yet, of course, it is clear enough that without a degree of professionalism no modern regime can exist. In the middle of the nineteenth century, Britain discovered that her Indian possessions had copied the mandarinate from the Chinese Empire and, by a second act of plagiarism, imported into the homeland a career civil service recruited by examination, administratively competent, incorrupt, and politically neutral, whose size and importance in Britain today possibly makes for a more fundamental difference between American and British democracy than the absence in the United States of a titular monarch and a hereditary peerage.

Does America need a mandarinate? I suspect that it is acquiring one with great speed. Yet even now it is strange to an Englishman to observe the number and the relatively low level of the appointments that require to be changed in Washington with the coming and going of consecutive administrations of different political color. But neither in America nor in Britain does the professionalism of the mandarinate extend to the real occupants of power—the President or the recipients of his confidence in the United States, the Prime Minister or the members of the British Cabinet in Britain.

❖   ❖   ❖

. . . A modern society requires that it be governed by professionals; in fact, it entrusts its confidence to semi-amateurs, whose know-how is at best empirical and who must rely for the more technical business of administration on a career civil service to do their bidding. Nor is there the smallest reason to suppose that the business of government could in fact be carried on by political neutrals. An element of sheer amateurism is an essential characteristic of democracy if democracy is to be given effective choices of policy; the politician who forgets his grass roots in order to become a professional administrator will both lose his seat and deserve to do so.

*　　*　　*

The essence of democracy is, of course, one man, one vote, and it is the perpetual terror of its critics that this principle will swamp the educated, pull down standards, set aside morality, devalue civilization. As a mere matter of history, this has seldom happened at the ballot box. The real instances of mob rule have been the result of violence or usurpation, not manhood suffrage. The weakness of democracy in the past has lain more in the capacity of the electorate for self-deception than in their violence. But this is no more than to say that the real logic of democracy is universal education, and this means something different in character nowadays from the minimum schooling of the past.

3

The Case for Control and Direction *

MAO TSE-TUNG

But there is another kind of nondemocratic government in the world. There are a lot of examples—40 or 50 at any moment in time. These (which we call dictatorships), are ruled by one party led by a strong personality, a charismatic leader. We find them in many countries recently emerged from the timeless, changeless past which economists and sociologists call "traditional society." Revolution leaves a society in turmoil. It is a break, a shattering break, with the institutions of the past. The Asian and African nations in which it has recently occurred are not industrialized. Without exception they are backward technologically and politically. The argument by their authoritarian leaders is that only by direct action and a good deal of compulsion can the backward nation they govern be driven and pushed toward modernization and a complete break with its backward, timeless, mindless past. In this respect, they may feel an affinity for the Chinese above all others. In the statement of the problem, Mao's views may typify those of many noncommunist leaders of such countries.

"You are dictatorial." My dear sirs, what you say is correct. That is just

* From Mao Tse-Tung, "On the Present Situation and Our Tasks," report to the Central Committee of the Chinese Com-

what we are. All the experiences of the Chinese people, accumulated in the course of many successive decades, tell us to carry out a people's democratic dictatorship. . . .

"You are not benevolent." Exactly. We definitely have no benevolent policies toward the reactionaries or the reactionary deeds of such classes. Our benevolent policy does not apply to such deeds or to such persons, who are outside the ranks of the people; it applies only to the people. . . .

The job of reforming the reactionary classes can be handled only by a state having a people's . . . dictatorship. . . .

Our party is entirely different from the political parties of the bourgeoisie. They are afraid to speak of the elimination of classes, state power, and parties. We, however, openly declare that we are energetically striving to set up conditions just for the sake of eliminating these things. The Communist Party and the state power of the people's dictatorship constitute such conditions.

. . . Communists everywhere are more competent than the bourgeoisie. They understand the laws governing the existence and development of things. They understand dialectics and can see further ahead. . . .

In this our land of China, the People's Liberation Army has already reversed the counterrevolutionary course. . . . This is a turning point in history. . . . This is a great event. . . .

The victory of China's New Democratic revolution is impossible with-

out the broadest united front. . . . But this is not all. This united front must also be firmly led by the Chinese Communist Party. Without the firm leadership of the Chinese Communist Party, no revolutionary united front can be victorious. . . .

As long as their reactionary tendencies can still influence the masses, we must expose them among the masses who are open to their influence, and strike at their political influence in order to liberate the masses from it. But political blows are one thing and economic extermination is another. . . . The existence and development of small and middle capitalist elements is not at all dangerous. The same thing applies to the new-rich peasant economy, which, after agrarian revolution, will inevitably come into existence. . . .

Many of China's conditions are identical with or similar to those of Russia before the October Revolution. Both had the same sort of feudal oppression. Economically and culturally they were similarly backward, though China was the more so. . . .

We must take our destinies into our own hands. We must rid our ranks of all flabby and incompetent thinking. . . . We are well aware of the fact that there will still be all kinds of obstacles and difficulties in the path of our advance. . . . We must be up and doing! . . .

. . . they [the business men] have monopolized the economic life of the entire country. . . . This monopoly capitalism, closely combined with foreign imperialism and the native landlord class and old type of rich peasants, becomes comprador-feudal state-monopoly capitalism. . . . This . . . not only oppresses the workers and peasants but also oppresses the petty bourgeoisie and harms the middle bourgeoisie. . . .

. . . the Party must do its utmost to

munist Party, December 25, 1947; from Report of the Second Plenary Session of the Central Committee of the Seventh Party Congress, Communist Party of China, released in Peking March 23, 1949; and from Mao Tse-Tung, "On People's Democratic Dictatorship," July 1, 1949. The English versions used are from Part IV, "Documents," in *New China: Three Views*, by Otto B. van der Sprenkel, Robert Guillain, and Michael Lindsay (New York: The John Day Company, Inc., 1951) pp. 154, 156, 165-67, 171, 174-75, 177-78, 180-81, 185-86, 190-92, 197. Reprinted by permission of the publisher.

learn how to lead the urban people . . . and how to administer and build up the cities. . . . The Plenary Session called on all Party comrades to devote all their energies to learning the technique and management of industrial production; and to learning commercial banking and other work closely related to production. . . . if the Party is ignorant in production work . . . the Party . . . will fail. . . .

We must overcome all difficulties and must learn the things we do not understand. We must learn to do economic work from all who know . . . (no matter who they are). We must respect them as teachers, learning from them attentively and earnestly. We must not pretend that we know when we do not know. We must not put on bureaucratic airs. If one bores into a subject for several months, for one year or two years, perhaps three years or four years, it can eventually be mastered. . . .

The war of the People's Liberation Army is of a patriotic, just and revolutionary nature which must of necessity gain the support of the people. . . . the Communist Party seeks earnestly to unite the whole of the working class, the whole of the peasantry and the vast number of the revolutionary intelligentsia as the leading and foundation forces of this dictatorship. . . .

On the basis of the experience of these twenty-eight years, we have reached the same conclusions that Sun Yat-sen, in his will, mentioned gaining from "the experience of forty years." That is, "we must awaken the masses of the people and unite ourselves in a common struggle. . . ."

Internally, the people must be awakened. . . .

Basing itself on the science of Marxism-Leninism, the Chinese Communist Party clearly assessed the international and domestic situation. . . .

4

The Corruption of Absolute Power: The Testimony of Hermann Friedrich Graebe *

The great theologian, Reinhold Niebuhr, in a well-known passage, has suggested that, "Man's capacity for justice makes democracy possible, but man's inclination to injustice makes democracy unnecessary." History has repeatedly demonstrated the dangers of uncontrolled power. The following testimony is an eloquent reminder that efficiency can be utilized in the most barbarous ways, and that unchecked power has a price.

Before me, Homer B. Crawford, being authorized to administer oaths, personally appeared Hermann Fried-

rich Graebe, who, being by me duly sworn through the interpreter Elisabeth Radziejewska, made and subscribed the following statement:

I, Hermann Friedrich Graebe, declare under oath:

* *Nazi Conspiracy and Aggression* (Washington, D.C.: U.S. Government Printing Office, 1946), V, 696-99.

From September 1941 until January 1944 I was manager and engineer-in-charge of a branch office in Sdolbunow, Ukraine, of the Solingen building firm of Josef Jung. In this capacity it was my job to visit the building sites of the firm. Under contract to an Army Construction Office, the firm had orders to erect grain storage buildings on the former airport of Dubno, Ukraine.

On 5 October 1942, when I visited the building office at Dubno, my foreman Hubert Moennikes of 21 Aussenmuehlenweg, Hamburg-Haarburg, told me that in the vicinity of the site, Jews from Dubno had been shot in three large pits, each about 30 meters long and 3 meters deep. About 1500 persons had been killed daily. All of the 5000 Jews who had still been living in Dubno before the program were to be liquidated. As the shootings had taken place in his presence he was still much upset.

Thereupon I drove to the site, accompanied by Moennikes and saw near it great mounds of earth, about 30 meters long and 2 meters high. Several trucks stood in front of the mounds. Armed Ukrainian militia drove the people off the trucks under the supervision of an SS man. The militia men acted as guards on the trucks and drove them to and from the pit. All these people had the regulation yellow patches on the front and back of their clothes, and thus could be recognized as Jews.

Moennikes and I went directly to the pits. Nobody bothered us. Now I heard rifle shots in quick succession, from behind one of the earth mounds. The people who had got off the trucks —men, women, and children of all ages—had to undress upon the order of an SS man, who carried a riding or dog whip. They had to put down their clothes in fixed places, sorted according to shoes, top clothing and underclothing. I saw a heap of shoes of about 800 to 1000 pairs, great piles of underlinen and clothing. Without screaming or weeping these people undressed, stood around in family groups, kissed each other, said farewells and waited for a sign from another SS man, who stood near the pit, also with a whip in his hand. During the fifteen minutes that I stood near the pit I heard no complaint or plea for mercy. I watched a family of about eight persons, a man and woman, both about 50 with their children of about 1, 8, and 10, and two grown-up daughters of about 20 to 24. An old woman with snow-white hair was holding the one-year-old child in her arms and singing to it, and tickling it. The child was cooing with delight. The couple were looking on with tears in their eyes. The father was holding the hand of a boy about 10 years old and speaking to him softly; the boy was fighting his tears. The father pointed toward the sky, stroked his head, and seemed to explain something to him. At that moment the SS man at the pit shouted something to his comrade. The latter counted off about 20 persons and instructed them to go behind the earth mound. Among them was the family, which I have mentioned. I well remember a girl, slim and with black hair, who, as she passed close to me, pointed to herself and said, "23." I walked around the mound, and found myself confronted by a tremendous grave. People were closely wedged together and lying on top of each other so that only their heads were visible. Nearly all had blood running over their shoulders from their heads. Some of the people shot were still moving. Some were lifting their arms and turning their heads to show that they were still alive. The pit was already ⅔ full. I estimated that it already contained about 1000 people. I looked for the man who did the shooting. He was an SS man, who sat at the edge of the narrow end of the pit, his feet dangling into the pit. He had a tommy gun on his knees and was smoking a cigarette. The people, completely naked, went down some steps which were cut in the clay wall of the pit and clambered over the heads of the people lying there, to the place to which the SS man directed them. They lay down in front of the dead or injured people; some caressed those who were still alive and spoke to them in a low voice. Then I heard a series of shots. I looked into the pit and saw that the bodies were twitching or the heads lying already motionless on top of the bodies that lay before them. Blood was running from their necks. I was surprised that I was not ordered away, but I saw that there were two or three postmen in uniform nearby. The next batch was approaching already. They went down into the pit, lined themselves up against the previous victims and were shot. When I walked back round the mound I noticed another truckload of people which had just arrived. This time it included sick and infirm people. An old, very thin woman with terribly thin legs was undressed by others who were already naked, while two people held her up. The woman appeared to be paralyzed. The naked people carried the woman around the mound. I left with Moennikes and drove in my car back to Dubno.

On the morning of the next day, when I again visited the site, I saw about 30 naked people lying near the pit—about 30 to 50 meters away from it. Some of them were still alive; they looked straight in front of them with a fixed stare and seemed to notice neither the chilliness of the morning nor the workers of my firm who stood around. A girl of about 20 spoke to me and asked me to give her clothes, and help her escape. At that moment we heard a fast car approach and I noticed that it was an SS detail. I moved away to my site. Ten minutes later we heard shots from the vicinity of the pit—then they had themselves to lie down in this to be shot in the neck.

I make the above statement at Wiesbaden, Germany, on 10th November 1945. I swear before God that this is the absolute truth.

HERMANN FRIEDRICH GRAEBE

Subscribed and sworn to before me at Wiesbaden, Germany, this 10 day of November 1945.

HOMER B. CRAWFORD, Major, AC
Investigator Examiner,
War Crimes Branch

I, Elisabeth Radziejewska, being first duly sworn, state: That I truly translated the oath administered by Major Homer B. Crawford to Hermann Friedrich Graebe and that thereup he made and subscribed the foregoing statement in my presence.

ELIZABETH RADZIEJEWSKA
Interpreter

5

Comparative Politics — A Developmental Approach? *

GABRIEL A. ALMOND and G. BINGHAM POWELL, JR.

The argument for direction emphasizes efficiency and dispatch. The practical record, however, is ambiguous. There are many things that democracies seem to be capable of doing more expeditiously than their rivals—and not just the production of refrigerators. Why should this be so? In this discussion of developmental politics, Almond and Powell point to many of the contradictions and cross-purposes of dictatorial enterprise that may hamper progress.

In part the maintenance of law and order in a society centers around positive orientations toward governmental agencies. Often the citizens of the new nations are oriented only to the benefits of governmental outputs and, perhaps, to the channels through which demands can be made. They have not acquired a positive and supportive subject orientation—that is, they have not learned to obey the laws. Consequently, the political order has little support to draw upon in time of internal crisis. This problem, dramatically illustrated in the Congo, has been encountered in some degree in most of the new nations.

❁   ❁   ❁

In a comparative study of attitudes in five nations, the difference between attitudes in the United States and in the other nations illustrates this dimension.[1] Only in the United States did a very large proportion of the respondents say that when faced with a local political problem they would form a local political group and seek legitimate means of rectifying their grievances. Such expressions of competence and willingness to work actively through legitimate input channels were striking. All too often, as in Italy, the individual feels that he can have little influence as an individual on government actions. At best, this leads to passive acceptance where dissatisfactions are not overwhelming. At worst, resentments and frustrations will be submerged until the pressure is too great, and then will erupt in violence. Even in societies where interest groups and political parties have begun to develop, the emergence of an appropriate set of individual orientations to them is essential before they can be effectively employed.

It is also important to ascertain the general level of political trust in a society. Are political competitors and opponents viewed with suspicion? Does political interaction and discussion take place on a relatively free and easy basis, or are the channels of

---

* From *Comparative Politics: A Developmental Approach* by Gabriel A. Almond and G. Bingham Powell, Jr. Copyright © 1966, by Little, Brown and Company (Inc.). Reprinted by permission of the publisher.

[1] Gabriel A. Almond and Sidney Verba, *The Civic Culture* (Princeton: Princeton University Press, 1963), pp. 191ff.

communication regarding political matters constricted? In societies such as Italy and Germany the traumatic political experiences of the past half century have made politics a subject to avoid in personal interaction. This affects the cohesion of political groups and their willingness to interact with each other.

＊　　＊　　＊

In considering attitudes toward interpersonal relationships, we may also take note of the level of civility in political interaction—that is, the degree to which more or less formal norms of courtesy tend to dampen the harshness of political disagreement. The formal and informal customs of legislative bodies in Britain and the United States reflect such tendencies. It is perhaps doubly difficult for democratic politics to function in many of the new nations because they lack such moderating norms.

We have devoted considerable attention to the problem of interpersonal relationships because these constitute a crucial problem area in the political culture of the new nations. An ultimate test of a responsive and democratic system is its ability to transfer the power of government from one set of leaders to another. This may occur either between parties or within a single party. But if the level of personal trust is low, if the political process is viewed as a life-and-death conflict, and if little political courtesy mitigates the raw conflict, it will be very difficult for the incumbent elites to relinquish their roles in the political process and step aside for a new group of political actors. The stakes will seem too high; the opposition will seem too dangerous.

. . . The distorting effects of bureaucratic hierarchy may also create considerable problems of information for effective decision making. All large decision-making systems must depend to a considerable degree upon the bureaucracy to obtain and interpret information. In a bureaucracy, hierarchy and discipline are to some degree necessary for coordination of action. But a bureaucratic official is responsible to his superiors and is often dependent upon their favors for advancement. He often develops great sensitivity to the needs and wishes of his superiors. He has an inevitable tendency to tell powerful generals, cabinet ministers, or presidents that which they wish to hear or that which will reflect favorably on his own career. Active and innovating Presidents of the United States, such as Franklin Roosevelt, have been highly sensitive to this danger of distortion and have endeavored to supplement all formal information channels with vast networks of informal contacts with individuals at various points in the hierarchy.[2]

In open political systems, with many autonomous political structures and channels of communication, the elites can also utilize other information sources to help balance distortion by subordinates. Leaders read the newspapers, make personal appearances, and have polls conducted by autonomous organizations, in an effort to get an unbiased understanding of popular attitudes, and various sides of complex issues. However, in matters of security, in complex technological questions, and in times of crisis in particular, these normal channels may cease to operate or to be relevant. The United States' Cuban policy, for example, has tended to be shrouded in secrecy from the beginning, and many observers suggest that political

[2] Richard W. Neustadt, *Presidential Power* (New York: John Wiley & Sons, Inc., 1962), pp. 156 ff.; and Deutsch, *Nerves of Government, op. cit.*, pp. 224-25.

leaders have been dangerously dependent on such secret agencies and information channels as the CIA. Not only the desire to please, but also the special prejudices and orientations of any single agency, may distort information.

Although the differences are easy to exaggerate, the totalitarian systems face these problems of information distortion in a particularly complex fashion. Observers of closed political systems, such as Nazi Germany or Stalin's Russia, have remarked on the constant, but often unsuccessful, efforts made by the ruling elites to obtain information about what is happening throughout the system. The immense scale of government activities and the efforts to accomplish far-reaching goals of economic development and military victory, or simply to maintain top rank within the system in the face of changing and unstable conditions, create an insatiable need for information. Yet the communications patterns which tend to emerge in these systems are closed, nonautonomous patterns, because the elites wish to prevent the possibility of popular knowledge and activity which might lead to subversion, and because the lower officials are receptive only to pressures from above, and not from below.

These closed communication structures seem to have inherently pathological tendencies, particularly in stress situations. Such tendencies appear as a partial consequence of threats and use of violence and force in order to maintain control over lower officials and citizens. In such cases the lower officials who staff the communications line to the elite are confronted with a difficult set of alternatives. If they deliberately distort information and are discovered, the consequences are likely to be costly. But, reporting unpleasant facts is

likely to be nearly as dangerous. The man who dares hint that the leaders may have erred badly in their assessment of a situation is apt to have his career, if not his life, abruptly cut short in favor of those who convey more compatible news. The tendency of tyrants to surround themselves with "yes men," who confirm the existing beliefs of the ruler is well known. Boulding explains this phenomenon in the following terms:

The case is somewhat analogous to that of the schizophrenic or the extreme paranoid. His sense receptors are so much "afraid" of him that they merely confirm the products of his heated imagination. The terrorized information sources of the tyrant likewise tell him only what they think will be pleasing to his ears. Organizations as well as individuals can suffer from hallucinations. It is the peculiar dsease of authoritarian structures.[3]

Needless to say, the situation is reinforced by the average citizen's reluctance to tell even the lower officials anything but the formal "party line." Information about popular attitudes is likely to be distorted. So are reports of the inefficiency or ineffectiveness of the reporting subordinates. Even general "scientific" information may be heavily slanted as is apparent in the work of social scientists in the Soviet Union—and which has even been the case in the continuing support (until recently) of biological theories which have been long discredited in the West. It was through such tendencies that Hitler's conduct of the war in the last days become totally divorced from reality

Barrington Moore has emphasized the strenuous efforts made by totalitarian leaders to lessen their depen

[3] Kenneth Boulding, *The Image* (Ann Arbor: University of Michigan Press, 1956) p. 101.

dency on any single information source.[4] In the Soviet Union, Stalin used the secret police, the party, and the bureaucracy as checks on one another, relying on each separate organization to inform him of errors and deviations of the other two information channels. But, as Apter and others have suggested, in times of stress the multiple channels are apt to reinforce distorted information rather than to correct it.[5] In fact, this is likely even in much more autonomous systems.[6] If it is clear that the leadership is convinced of a set of facts, the information channels will find substantiations rather than denials.

These characteristic problems induced by closed communication systems suggest the limits on the performance of governmental functions in highly controlled authoritarian and totalitarian systems. The increase in control reaches a point of diminishing returns as the distortion of information and the costs of maintaining multiple information channels cut into effectiveness and efficiency.

[4] Barrington Moore, Jr., *Terror and Progress USSR* (Cambridge: Harvard University Press, 1954), pp. 176 ff.

[5] David Apter, *The Politics of Modernization* (Chicago: University of Chicago Press, 1965).

[6] See Ole Holsti, "The 1914 Case," *The American Political Science Review*, June, 1965, pp. 365-78.

6

Pluralist Democracy in the United States *

ROBERT A. DAHL

What is the American system like in practice? How does it truly operate? A leading student of power structures, both at the national and community level, is Robert Dahl, the author of Who Governs?, *a community study of New Haven, and* A Preface to Democratic Theory. *Dahl is the leading exponent of the pluralist model of American democracy. He is also probably the most influential political scientist of the current generation.*

. . . American political institutions, then, encourage political leaders to respond to severe conflicts in three ways:

1. By forming a new political coalition that can overpower the opposition.

* Robert A. Dahl, *Pluralist Democracy in the United States* (Chicago: Rand McNally & Company, 1967), pp. 291-95 and 325-26. Reprinted by permission of the publisher.

But this, as we shall see, is a difficult solution.

2. By incremental measures that postpone comprehensive change.

3. By enduring compromises that remove the issue from serious political conflict.

OVERPOWERING THE OPPOSITION. A severe conflict is sometimes moderated or even terminated when one political coalition gains enough power to overcome the resistance of its opponents. Instead of compromising, the winning coalition enacts its policies despite the opposition of the defeated coalition. If the opposition fights back, as it is likely to do, it finds itself too weak to prevail. Unable to reverse the main direction of policy imposed by the winning coalition, the opposition may in time accept the major policies enacted by the winners and settle down to bargaining for incremental adjustments; thus severe conflict gives way to a period of moderate conflict.

Probably the only effective way in American politics for one coalition significantly to reduce the bargaining power of an enemy coalition is to turn it into a visible and even isolated political minority by defeating it in national elections. However, because of the large number of positions where an embattled minority, unable to win the Presidency or a majority in either house of Congress, can dig in and successfully continue to challenge the policies of the majority coalition, a single electoral victory is ordinarily not necessarily enough, particularly if the contest is close. . . . Why, people often ask, don't elections settle things one way or the other? Why is it so difficult for a President and Congress ostensibly of the same party to terminate a severe conflict by overriding the objections of their opponents, carrying through their legislative program, and letting the country decide at the next election whether it likes the changes or disapproves of them?

By now it must be clear to the reader that American political institutions were never designed to operate in this fashion; nor do they. But in addition to the institutions themselves, several aspects of American beliefs, sentiments, or loyalties reduce still further the likelihood that elections can be decisive. For one thing,

party loyalties are, as we have seen incredibly persistent. It is uncom fortably close to being true that eithei of the two major parties could prob ably win twenty million votes for it: presidential candidate even if it nomi nated Ed the Talking Horse. The overwhelming electoral sweeps in the presidential elections of 1936, 1952 and 1964 left the defeated minority with a substantial share of popula votes (37 per cent in 1936, 44 pei cent in 1952, 39 per cent in 1964). Ir the twenty-six presidential election from 1864-1964, the defeated party received less than 40 per cent only seven times; it received 45 per cen or more in twelve elections, and from 40-45 per cent seven times. A party overwhelmed by a landslide is far in deed from being in a hopeless situa tion.

Then, too, the votes of a winning coalition are not uniformly distrib uted throughout the country; there are sizeable regional variations. A political minority in the nation ma be a political majority in a region, a with the New England Federalists in 1800 or the Democrats in the South in every election won by a Republican President from 1860 onward. A de feated minority with a powerful re gional base stands a good chance no only of surviving but of keeping mos of its senior political leaders in Con gress.

Finally, Americans are not agree on a single, definite, generally ac cepted rule for legitimate decision making in government. Although th legitimacy of rule by majorities is fre quently invoked, the majority prin ciple is not, among Americans, clear-cut rule of decision-making This principle invoked to support 'na tional' majorities (i.e., as revealed i national elections) is also used t support local, state, or regional ma jorities. . . .

POSTPONING COMPREHENSIVE CHANGES. .merican political institutions are xcellently designed for making in- remental changes. But they also oster delay in coming to grips with uestions that threaten severe con- ict. It is true that delay may provide recious time during which a seem- igly severe problem may change its hape, become more manageable, ven disappear. But postponement 1ay also inhibit leaders from facing a roblem squarely and searching for ecisive solutions—solutions that may e forced upon them many years later vhen they can no longer delay.

. . . In 1948, President Truman, act- ig on recommendations from his ad- isory Committee on Civil Rights, rec- mmended federal legislation against ynching, the poll-tax, segregation in ublic transportation, and discrimina- ion in employment. Although mild ivil rights legislation was passed in 957 and 1960, no major legislation on ivil rights cleared Congress until 964, almost two decades after Presi- lent Truman's recommendations. 'assage of American welfare and ocial security laws has followed the nactment of comparable laws in most luropean democracies by one to sev- ral generations. A national medical are program has been advocated for ;enerations. In 1945, President Tru- nan proposed to a Congress a com- rehensive medical insurance pro- ;ram for persons of all ages. The first aw establishing a national system of nedical insurance, though only for he elderly, was not enacted until 1965.

COMPROMISE. The existence of in- iumerable fortified positions from vhich an embattled but well organ- zed minority can fight off and wear lown an attack, combined with the ibsence of any *single* rule for making egitimate decisions on which the political activists are agreed, means that it is difficult to terminate a con- flict by the clear-cut victory of one side over another. Hence severe con- flicts are sometimes handled by reach- ing a compromise. Occasionally the result is a long-lasting compromise. . . .

Periods of Moderate Conflict

If you were to pick at random any year in American history since the Constitutional Convention to illus- trate the workings of the political system, you would stand a rather good chance of being able to describe American politics during that year as follows:

Important government policies would be arrived at through negotiation, bargain- ing, persuasion, and pressure at a con- siderable number of different sites in the political system—the White House, the bureaucracies, the labyrinth of committees in Congress, the federal and state courts, the state legislatures and executives, the local governments. No single organized political interest, party, class, region, or ethnic group would control all of these sites.

Different individuals and groups would not all exert an equal influence on deci- sions about government policies. The extent of influence individuals or groups exerted would depend on a complex set of factors: their political skills, how aroused and active they were, their numbers, and their access to such political resources as organiza- tion, money, connections, propaganda, etc. People who lacked even suffrage and had no other resources—slaves, for example—would of course be virtually powerless. But because *almost* every group has some political resources— at a minimum, the vote—most people who felt that their interests were sig- nificantly affected by a proposed change in policy would have some in- fluence in negotiations.

All the important political forces—particularly all the candidates and elected officials of the two major parties—would accept (or at any rate would not challenge) the legitimacy of the basic social, economic, and political structures of the United States. Organized opposition to these basic structures would be confined to minority movements too feeble to win representation in Congress or a single electoral vote for their presidential candidate.

Political conflict would be moderate.

Changes in policies would be marginal.

* * *

Why should this be so? Our paradigm of conflict . . . suggests four reasons:

The political institutions reward moderation and marginal change, and discourage deviant policies and comprehensive changes.

In the United States there is a massive convergence of attitudes on a number of key issues that divide citizens in other countries.

As one result, ways of life are not seriously threatened by the policies of opponents.

On issues over which Americans disagree, overlapping cleavages stimulate conciliation and compromise.

7

The Decline of Liberal Democracy *

HARVEY WHEELER

But does the system work as well as Dahl suggests? Harvey Wheeler, of the Center for the Study of Democratic Institutions, presents a critique in many ways typical of writers of the "New Left," finding that our system has degenerated. (This critique, though, is shared by many Rightists, although their program for the future "Restoration" of our real system of government differs.) Is our system of government today truly a departure from the past? Has participation in a meaningful sense grown or declined? Is it desirable that everybody has to participate fully and equally, whether they want to or not?

What are the theoretical assumptions underlying participational democracy?

1

There were assumptions that the average man was wise; he could find solutions to his and society's problems; he would participate actively in politics; and he was more incorruptible than those in authority.

2

Next was an implicit theory of common goals and how society should realize them. The better statement might be that participational democracy implied a theory of "anti-goals." For it was held that the best way to produce political goals was not through explicit governmental poli

* Harvey Wheeler, *The Rise and Fall of Liberal Democracy*, pp. 16-20, 25-26. Published by the Center for the Study of Democratic Institutions. Copyright, 1966, by the Fund for the Republic. Reprinted by permission of the Fund for the Republic.

cies but as a cumulative result of the people having been freed to develop, institute, and express goals individually and autonomously. This was the political counterpart of the unseen hand of classical economic theory. It yielded a counterpart of economic competition in the form of pressure-group politics. This was radical pluralism at the deepest level. If society refuses to make explicit its values and goals, the right ones are sure to appear as a result of free men and insitutions struggling against each other to achieve their own interests. Every conflicting interest and goal will somehow eventually be harmonized as organized groups battle it out in the legislative chambers and lobbies. Given this view, American political science, like other liberal institutions, reflected instead of prescribing, and its contribution to knowledge was the group theory of politics. The theory still dominates the academy.

3

Participational democracy also implied an assumption about recruitment and employment. The best way to get the public work done was to see that political offices were filled only by average Americans. The wisest governors would spring from and automatically reflect the wisdom of the people. This tenet became enshrined in the folklore of American politics as the Lincoln tradition of log cabin to White House. It was not long ago that politicians finally abandoned their belief that rich men were unsuitable condidates unless they had risen from humble origins.

4

Related to this was a proposition about public administration. It de-

rived from the ongoing struggle against a succession of power élites. The American doctrine was that politics and government were intrinsically simple from an administrative point of view. Nothing would have to be done in government that was above the comprehension or the ability of the average American. This was an attack on the European tradition of a professional civil service or administrative class, which Americans believed to be tainted by aristocratic or élitist principles. It was held that the average American was the most "professional" possible administrator of all governmental functions. Though this first appeared under the Jacksonians as the "spoils system," it persisted as the chief element distinguishing the American civil service from all others that had ever existed in history.

5

This in turn implied a theory about decision-making. Decisions should not be made by government officials except as a last resort and even then subject to severe restrictions. The ideal was that all decisions should be made by the sovereign people organized politically. Every possible governmental decision should be voted upon. Only with the fullest possible popular participation in the decision-making process could government function properly. . . .

8

. . . This also involved an anarchistic assumption about formal education or acculturation. Men should not take collective thought or action for the over-all shape or direction of their culture, their social institutions, or their system of values. Certainly the government should not be concerned with the nature of the family system, the economic order, the religious system, the direction of science, and so on. Everything would be done best if nothing were done about it. The result was a political system that was supposed to produce the common good in an automatic and unguided fashion. It entailed negative government: faith in the operation and efficacy of a kind of residual anarchist harmony. . . . This meant that the automaticity of the system was supposed to produce:

—Children well educated and made into good democratic citizens simply by leaving with each family the responsibility for controlling the acculturation process of its members.
—An economy efficient, equitable, and always tending to the public good.
—An officialdom staffed through the rotation of average citizens in and out of office, responsible to the people, and achieving the public good.
—A free flow of information through numerous private channels that would automatically discover the things the people ought to know and see that the appropriate information was available to them when it was needed.
—A country essentially isolated from the rest of the world and able to pursue its own interests without regard to the impact of those interests on others.
—Avoidance of the evils traditionally associated with European cities.
—Avoidance of the evils of aristocracy, oligarchy, and conspiratorial factions not in harmony with the public good.

. . . [D]uring the nineteenth century America made a great commitment to a special, and indeed a historically unique, form of democracy. It backed its gamble with some of the most ingenious governmental and political institutions known to history. Today, these institutions of populism and progressivism have been all but dismantled. They appear embarrassingly Victorian in restrospect as intricate gingerbread like those monuments of Victorian architecture we are now busily tearing down.

However, it is harder to eliminate beliefs and institutions than it is buildings. We still carry the participational commitment in two ways. First, a few of the institutional arrangements we developed to facilitate democratic participation are still with us, though often atrophied or modified. The direct primary is the most prominent example. Second and more important is the fact that even though in one part of our minds we realize that our participational experiment has failed, and even though we sometimes ridicule it, nonetheless, as a nation, we still hold to it, myth though it is. Participational democracy is the only really distinctive contribution we have made to politics and we seem fearful of admitting its failure. When we state the basis of our opposition to communism, it is that communism does not provide for democracy as we have understood it and therefore is not a "true" democracy. But the democracy we foist on others is one we ourselves no longer have. Despite our inner knowledge that our own participational forms no longer work, we continue to base our cold war on the claim that the non-Western world should adopt these forms forthwith, and when we look at the political systems of the newer democracies in the underdeveloped areas of the world, one of our chief criticisms is that they are not sufficiently participational in our special Victorian sense.

Participational democracy failed, but nothing was put in its place. We give ourselves numerous reasons for not redesigning our democratic institutions despite how badly they work in comparison with their original purposes. We reiterate defensively that though they may not achieve what they were designed for, what they do accomplish is pretty good; besides, things would be worse if any fundamentally new approach to democracy were attempted. Our immediate, visceral reaction to any current political issue continues to spring from an emotional commitment to participational democracy. We worry about the political apathy of the average voter. We disapprove of any public figure who does not announce his devotion to the innate political wisdom of the common man. We insist that the primary function of our elected representative is to reflect the desires of his constituency, their private interests rather than the dictates of the common good, and when we complain about him as a wheeler-dealer, we do not say that he is applying a corrupt view of democracy or of representation but that he is representing the desires of the wrong groups or is giving too much weight to certain groups over others. We assume that by keeping "his ear to the ground," by "not losing touch with the grass-roots," and by employing the most scientific public-opinion polling devices, our representative can make the original goals of participational democracy realizable.

*   *   *

We have already seen how the mass media have undercut democratic processes. They have also destroyed the mutuality of communication upon which community depends. What information we get and what communication takes place must come through the channels of the mass media. Yet there is no way of taking organized concern for our total informational needs and comparing them with what we actually produce. It is curious what happens to "communication" in a vast mass-media system. The word communication implies mutuality and reciprocation. But this is precisely what is missing.

We are familiar with the notion that the citizen is not in direct contact with

any crucial source of information. This is the nature of a mass medium; in being large enough and extensive enough to cover the mass of people, it must be distant from every person. The individual does not consume information from another "person" directly, but only from mass media "images" which have questionable status as "persons." For each functionary in the mass media must take concern, not for what he is as a person, but for his "image." What we see and hear are constructed "images." . . .

This has been the story of the rise and fall of American liberal democracy. . . . Throughout history democracy has been the most effective device for complex societies to coordinate the actions of masses of people performing a large variety of complex functions. But this quickly produces a dilemma. A complex society requires the participation of the people in the decision-making process, but popular participation in decision-making is possible only at relatively primitive levels of development and complexity. The participational feature of democracy becomes unworkable precisely at the point when complexity calls it forth and affluent masses demand it. The result is that the demand for participational democracy occurs for political reasons just at the time when it has been rendered dysfunctional for technological reasons. This has a further misfortune. The principle of democracy becomes so closely identified with the failings of participational devices that the critics of participational democracy are then able to discredit democracy itself and attribute to it the chief responsibility for the political failings of mass culture.

. . . Our times demand the development of new conceptions of legislation and new processes of deliberation. The theories of Jeremy Bentham and James Madison must be supplanted by new ones appropriate to the conditions of bureaucratic cultures and adequate to the challenges of the scientific revolution.

Are there any signs of such a development? Recently a new doctrine of democracy has appeared. It was developed initially by young people in their twenties but, despite its adament youth-centered bias, leadership of the movement is exercised by those already in their thirties. The "Port Huron Statement" of the Students for a Democratic Society, now only four years old, has already assumed the status of a holy text. Its framers, meaning to turn their backs on the ideological squabbles of the 1930's, seized upon a few simple propositions. Their overriding devotion was given to what they called *participatory* democracy. This not only

referred to anti-organization principles for conducting the business of the movement itself but also expressed a new approach to working with the unrepresented or dispossessed members of society. The Establishment, standing in the way of participatory democracy, is the announced enemy. There is no real difference between the Establishment liberals and the Establishment conservatives, between the civil and the corporate élites. Indeed, liberalism's unshakable hold on political and industrial power makes *it* the more formidable adversary. The solution? Organize the unrepresented, activate the poor and the Negroes, reconstitute the discontented, form a new coalition committed to the building of a new society dedicated to democracy, world order, and civil and economic justice.

8

Are Russia and the United States Converging? *

ZBIGNIEW BRZEZINSKI and SAMUEL P. HUNTINGTON

People speak of "the end of ideology." They suggest that the conflict of systems may decline as practical problems rather than philosophy become the foci of attention. We have already discussed the argument that industrial systems produce similar political structures. Here, two authoritative writers—one a major figure in the State Department on loan from academia—examine the possibilities and limits of convergence.

❋   ❋   ❋

Convergence or Evolution

The Communists believe that the world will converge, but into an es-

* Zbigniew Brzezinski and Samuel P. Huntington, *Political Power U.S.A./U.S.S.R.* (New York: The Viking Press, 1964), pp. 419-29. Copyright by the authors. Reprinted by permission of the authors.

sentially communist form of government. In the West, on the other hand, the widespread theory of convergence assumes that the fundamentally important aspects of the democratic system will be retained after America and Russia "converge" at some future, indeterminate historical juncture. Although probably there will be more

economic planning and social ownership in the West, the theory sees the Communist Party and its monopoly of power as the real victims of the historical process: both will fade away. Thus on closer examination it is striking to discover that most theories of the so-called convergence in reality posit not convergence but submergence of the opposite system. Hence the Western and the communist theories of convergence are basically revolutionary: both predict a revolutionary change in the character of one of the present systems. The Communists openly state it. In the West, it is implicit in the prevalent convergence argument.
. . . The argument . . . rests on the assumption of a cumulative impact on the political system, particularly the Soviet, of four factors: the industrial culture, the organizational and operational implications of the industrial system, affluence, and international involvement.

Undoubtedly certain universal traits inherent in the modern industrial and urban order affect the style and the values of contemporary mass culture and leisure. The Soviet leaders today are far more similar in clothing, in social behavior, even in some of their private aspirations, to their Western counterparts than was the case twenty-five years ago. The same is true of an average Soviet citizen. In that sense there has been, and there will be, a steady convergence of the West and the East, including China. Every factory built in some isolated Chinese town reduces the time, the cultural, the economic, and the social gap between, let us say, Chikurting and Chicago. But the question is, does it reduce the political difference? Is the form of leisure, mass culture, and working habits a determinant for political organization?
The archaic society was character

ized by the economic similarity and the political diversity of its institutions. A common economic "base" and a pastoral culture thus did not dictate the character of the political "superstructure." Today both China and India are at similar levels of development—yet no one would seriously argue that their political systems are becoming more alike. . . . The example of the archaic society indicates at the very least that not every common economic pattern dictates a common political structure. Perhaps the more complex, technological, and more socially impinging industrial economy does, but this proposition of causality remains to be proven.

Here, too, one can point to many examples which suggest that industrial complexity and maturity do not necessarily cause political uniformity and moderation. Essen under the Nazis was similar to Detroit in an economic and technological, as well as cultural, sense, yet the similarity did not preclude the Nazis from imposing on the society a relationship of mobilization and control quite unlike the one prevailing in Detroit. . . .

In analyzing the relationship between politics and economics in America and Russia it is, therefore, very important to look closely at *both* the character of the political system and the character of economic growth. If, in the Soviet and American cases, both the political systems and the character of economic growth are different, it is reasonable to conclude that the influence of economics on politics, and vice versa, is also likely to be quite different in the two societies. In the Soviet Union, a relatively backward society was to a degree industrialized and modernized (it is sometimes forgotten that the Soviet Union is still only a quasideveloped society) through total social mobilization effected by terroristic means wielded by a highly disciplined and motivated political elite. The very nature of this process is inimical to the emergence of political pluralism, while the liquidation of the private economic sector and of all informal leadership groups creates a social vacuum that must be filled through political integration on a national scale. In very broad terms, it would seem that in the Soviet case we are dealing with a process of very rapid industrialization which was politically directed and involved purposeful social "homogenizing." In the American case it was far more spontaneous, with national political coordination gradually emerging when social, economic, and political pluralism had already taken firm root.

These patterns of development have resulted in a strikingly different relationship between society and politics in each country. The American Revolution freed a society from the bonds of an irrelevant and restraining aristocratic order and made possible its subsequent, largely spontaneous, organic growth. The diversity, the pluralism, the fear of central control which characterized the early settlers, living in isolation not only from the world but also from one another, expressed itself in a political and social system designed to protect that diversity. One sees it in the segmented school system, in all the efforts to preserve regional and group autonomy, in the assertion of local community identity. The purposes of the political system were conservative insofar as society itself was concerned. This in turn inhibited the development of a political elite with a defined political outlook, since neither the social basis nor the consciousness of political purpose was present to sustain and justify the existence of such an elite. Today, in some respects, a modern American society, characterized by industrial dynamism and corporate efficiency, is governed by an anachronistic political system designed for the unique conditions of early-nineteenth-century America. This accounts for the weaknesses already noted.

In Russia, on the other hand, the Soviet political system came into being before the emergence of the Soviet society. Indeed, the political system was set up and organized for the specific purpose of creating a Soviet society. A power-motivated political elite was the *sine qua non* of the system, while the stupendous task of destroying the old social order and then of constructing a new one meant that power had to be centralized, wielded by professional political leaders, and exercised with sustained ruthlessness, skill, and ideological commitment. Governing a continental society, changing the way of life of 200 million people, consciously shaping the future of an entire social order is no mean task, and for this reason the emphasis of the leadership inevitably has been on the development of novel techniques of governing commensurate with this undertaking. Thus if it can be said that American politics can best be understood in terms of American society, Soviet society can best be understood in terms of Soviet politics. In the latter, political power preceded economic power; in the former, economic power preceded political. And it would be ironic indeed if a fading Marxism's last intellectual victory were to convince the West that economics shaped politics in the Soviet Union. Marxism cannot explain a communist state.

. . . [C]hanges in Soviet economic management and methods of planning and allocation need not challenge the ideological and power monopoly of the ruling Party. As Peter Wiles has argued, because of its introduction of computers, linear programming, and the various modern techniques usually associated with the concept of "economic rationality and maturity," "central planning or, better, the so-called command economy can now be rationally conducted. . . . The increasingly complex development of the economy no longer forces the Party to choose between the Marxist theory of value—which, in turn, prevents economic rationality—and the introduction of the market mechanism—which would threaten the ideological-political structure of the system. Indeed, the advance in techniques of economic control and coordination may make possible for the first time *both* further economic development and the retention of the ideological-political structure.

❋   ❋   ❋

It is here that the role and character of affluence come in. First of all, it is again essential to bear in mind the nature of the efforts used to attain that affluence. Affluence achieved by a mixed economic process, involving both the political system and independent individual and group activity, consolidates social diversity and creates new loci of social and political power. . . .

❋   ❋   ❋

The few available hints strongly suggest that the Soviet political leadership is concerned lest affluence take on an excessively individualistic character. To avoid that, cars will be pooled; so will the rest homes; people will live in "communal palaces," each housing about two thousand; they will eat together, enjoy almost fulltime education in the boarding schools starting shortly after birth, and will be provided by the state with free social facilities, such as transportation, housing, meals, social services, and even clothing. Affluent collectivism—this is to be the character of Soviet affluence.

These projections are seriously meant; the Soviet experts estimate that many aspects will be implemented roughly by 1975-2000. Should this come to pass, it is unlikely that such forms of affluence will impede the relationship of control and mobilization between the political system and the society. The political system will be characterized by greater rationality, less coercion, increased reliance on social self-control. The society will suffer less from the tensions originating in the lack of resources and, initially, from the absence of social consent for the new political-social system. A system combining self-sustaining popular control over social behavior, based on a highly collectivist affluence, with centralized managerial direction from above, will differ profoundly from the earlier Stalinist model but also from the existing Western affluent societies.

The current argument that communism cannot survive industrialization and affluence parallels eighteenth-century arguments about democracy. Democracy, it was assumed, could survive only in a poor, egalitarian, rural environment. It would be corrupted and undermined by affluence, urbanization, and industrialization. The "less luxury there is in a republic," Montesquieu argued, "the more it is perfect. . . . Republics end with luxury; monarchies with poverty." In a similar vein, Rousseau held that: "Monarchy . . . suits only wealthy nations; aristocracy, states of middling size and wealth; and democracy, states that are small and poor." So also it was argued that democracy required an agrarian society. This was, indeed, an old belief, dating back at least to Aristotle. Eighteenth-century democrats believed that the yeoman farmer was the backbone of democracy. Cities, said Jefferson, were "pestilential to the morals, the health, and the liberties of man." Governments in America will remain "virtuous . . . as long as they are chiefly agricultural. . . . When they get piled upon one another in large cities, as in Europe, they will become corrupt as in Europe." Jefferson's linking of farming and democracy became a dominant strain in American thinking. A century after Jefferson, the same argument reappeared in Turner's "frontier thesis" and the claim that American democracy came not from Europe but "out of the American forest. . . ." Despite these beliefs, however, affluence made democracy richer but not weaker, and industrialization strengthened democracy instead of corrupting it. They are having similar effects on communism. In all likelihood, the hopes of the contemporary advocates of convergence will be as unwarranted as the fears of the eighteenth- and nineteenth-century advocates of democracy.

A special factor influencing the development of political systems in our age is the unprecedented impact of international affairs and new, rapid means of communications. This is true particularly in the cases of the United States and the Soviet Union; both are most heavily involved in and committed to the present international rivalry. In assessing the impact of international affairs one must take note of several conflicting tendencies. The direct competition with the United States, especially the technical-economic one, has encouraged in the Soviet Union a tendency toward a more instrumental approach, highlighted by Professor Kapitsa's well-known statement to the effect that many of the Soviet space successes would have been impossible if the views of the "philosophers" (read: ideologues) had fully prevailed. In that, the leadership increasingly concurs. This has led it to accept scientific and scholarly exchanges with the

West in the expectation that Soviet technical progress will gain by them. At the same time, the exchanges have aroused the fears of some Party leaders, especially those charged with ideological matters, that Western humanists and philosophers, admitted in part as the necessary price for the scientific exchanges, will undermine the official ideology. It seems that by 1963 Soviet leaders had not resolved this issue and that there was an internal debate on the advantages and risks of the enterprise.

Similarly, the expansion of communism on the one hand has provided apparent proof for the correctness of the communist prophecy, but on the other hand has generated inter-Communist debates, thereby undermining somewhat the image of the doctrine as a universal creed. The expansion of communism from the Soviet Union into adjoining countries, furthermore, has meant that the Soviet Union is now exposed to the flow of competitive ideas from other communist states, more culturally akin to the West, which act as "transmission belts" for novel ideas, garbed in the common doctrine but reflecting a more European outlook. This, too, helps to weaken the control which the political system has maintained over the individual's exposure to ideologically undesirable views. Finally, the competition for the underdeveloped nation has involved a commitment of badly needed resources and the tacit acceptance of various regimes' claims to socialism, an acceptance that could eventually threaten domestic orthodoxy.

On the other hand, the very fact of the competition justifies the internal mobilization of resources, not to speak of armaments, and the related attempts to generate popular hostility to the United States. The new sense of Soviet nationalism is merged with the ideological interests of the ruling bureaucracy, and the competition with America is their natural expression. It is also important to bear in mind that the communist system was created as an institution of revolution and conflict and hence in some ways is less threatened by international tensions than by protracted international harmony. To be sure, both America and Russia may learn from each other ("codiscovery"), while the mutual balance of terror forces them to coexist. But this is not tantamount to becoming more alike, nor indeed is there much reassurance that their becoming more alike would necessarily diminish tensions between them. A common communist system has not prevented bitter hostility between China and Russia, and most European wars were fought by countries with very similar social and political structures.

This last point is particularly important because much of the emotional commitment to the convergence theory rests on the belief that it represents the only hope for peace. History shows that social-political uniformity and peace need not go hand in hand. In fact, the latter may be a more comforting conclusion than the

proposition—shared by both the Marxists and the "convergists"—that peace depends on uniformity. Such a premise is both curiously escapist and utopian. By now, the Communists particularly should realize that a communist America and a communist Russia would be likely to engage in a competition more intense than the relatively unequal struggle between Russia and China. Noncommunist believers in convergence also have no reason to assume that a noncommunist Russia, with its nationalist ambitions, would be less likely to strive to dominate the Eurasian continent that a communist Russia.

The theory of convergence thus minimizes or ignores the totality of the Russian and the American historical experience—political, social, and economic—and exaggerates the importance of one factor alone. It minimizes also the uniqueness of the historical process and forces it into a common pattern with fundamentally the same outcome for all. It asserts the repetitiveness of the historically familiar and ignores the probability that the future will see in both the United States and in the Soviet Union novel forms. . . .

CHAPTER THREE

The Constitution: Frame or Framework?

Forty years of crisis—a depression and a world war plus the cold war—have produced no major changes in the written American Constitution. Even the changes in interpretation, custom, and convention that have occurred have been shifts in relative power rather than differences in the total structure. The American Constitution, through the centuries, has proved exceedingly resilient and tough. Classifying the Bill of Rights as one group of changes and the Civil Rights Amendments as another, there have been perhaps a half dozen amendments in the entire history of the nation.

It seems fair to assume that the Constitution will continue to be the basis for American government for the foreseeable future. For this reason, many of the grandiose schemes for wholesale change seem unrealistic. There is no reason to believe that the American people have or will suddenly develop a genuine desire for parliamentary government or regionalism or, indeed, a new constitution.

The British writer, Walter Bagehot, suggested in a famous passage that a government must have two types of agencies—efficient instruments for carrying out actions and decorative branches of government for satisfying deep-felt human needs and emotions. In the British system, of course, this decorative or symbolic function is satisfied by the royal family.

THE CONSTITUTION: FLEXIBLE SYMBOL OR EMBODIMENT OF AN IDEOLOGY?

In the American system most of this symbolism has centered around the Constitution and the Court. By providing a decorative element, a tie with the past, and a set of mysteries, the Constitution enriches American life with a focus for unity.

But if the Constitution is a symbol, the question remains: what does it symbolize? There have been many interpretations—most, but by no means all, favorable.

In particular, the debate rages sporadically over the extent *to which* the Constitution should have a fixed symbolic content, or whether it should remain relatively flexible. Ideologues and pragmatists take opposite sides on the degree to which particular religious, economic, or class ideas are, or should be, enshrined in the document.

THE CONSTITUTION AS INSTRUMENT: WHO BENEFITS?

And the Constitution is not just a symbol but an operating instrument as well. As such, it is not just the written Constitution that counts but also the customs, patterns, and conventions that have grown around it. So, for example, the Vice President succeeds on the death of the President and becomes President, although the Constitution does not make clear whether this was to have been the case or whether he would merely become Acting President. It is, in other words, the Constitution in operation that is the working Constitution.

As an instrument, the Constitution is a source of political power, and is fought over because the wording of the Constitution is a form of strength or weakness for a particular group or program. The Constitution also provides a framework of operation which may accidentally or purposefully determine outcomes. It is also a method of governmental operations which either induces the solution of practical problems or hinders them.

1

American Society *

ROBIN M. WILLIAMS, JR.

How can the Constitution be a symbol of unity? If it is to have a definite symbolic content, wouldn't that divide the country much as political parties or specific measures would? The following reading by Robin Williams attempts to show that different groups can read into the Constitution entirely different interpretations. To him it is the ambiguities of the Constitution that are its strength.

The powers of the government of the United States are set by the some-

* Robin M. Williams, Jr., *American Society* (New York: Alfred A. Knopf, Inc., 1951), pp. 224-25. © 1951 by Alfred A. Knopf, Inc. Reprinted by permission of the publisher.

what elastic but definitely constricting bounds of a written constitution. Around that document has gradually accumulated a tremendous number of interpretations and commentaries, of court decisions, of beliefs and myths. The Constitution enjoys a veneration that makes it a substantial barrier against sudden or far-reaching changes in the structure of the states. There is a "psychology of constitutionalism," a widespread conviction that the Constitution is sufficient to cover all emergencies, that deviations from its provisions are unnecessary and dangerous, that a breach of the Constitution would bring down the whole structure of ordered and lawful government.

When it was written, the Constitution was a drastic innovation, not only in its content but in its basic idea that the form of government could be purposively determined. It was radical in the root sense of that word. Yet, in a similar root sense, it has had conservative consequences. During the period of consolidation of authority and partial return to prerevolutionary conditions that always follows the instituting of a new state, the Constitution was one of the few symbols of national scope available to the loose federation of weak and disunited provinces. Furthermore, it has been a rallying point for conserving (maintaining) the political and civil liberties of individuals. But it has been conservative in a more conventional sense, also, for it was actually adopted in a period of what was close to counterrevolution, and a major force in its drafting

and adoption was the desire to insure internal stability and the protection of property and trade. (The classical reference is Charles A. Beard: *An Economic Interpretation of the Constitution of the United States,* New York: 1913.) Undoubtedly the Constitution can be interpreted to conform to the interests of the more prosperous and propertied groups, and a stable legal order and venerated symbol of that order is advantageous to those interests.

This dual conservatism partly explains how it is that the Constitution can be defended with equal fervor by individuals whose motivations and interests are in most respects sharply opposed. The document has become almost a symbolic "sponge" that can absorb the allegiances of persons having amazingly diverse interests, values, ideas, political philosophies. Although the process by which this absorption occurs is not well understood (and is a research problem of first interest), its existence is probably of real importance to social stability. As with many other symbols of government, the very indefiniteness of the popularly imputed meanings facilitates a sense of order and integration not derivable from the specific applications of political doctrine. . . .

2

This Is a Republic, Not a Democracy *

THE JOHN BIRCH SOCIETY

The ambiguities that seem so valuable to Professor Williams strike others as a vacuum, as a symbol of national decay. Among groups calling for a revitalization of national purpose and for dedication to a defined political program, probably none has attracted the attention given the John Birch Society. This selection, which represents only a portion of a statement of basic beliefs, poses the question and challenge: Isn't there a fundamental form to American government which must be retained? Indirectly it suggests further problems: Just how much of the past must be kept? How do we arrive at such a determination? And who provides the answers?

We believe that a constitutional Republic, such as our Founding Fathers gave us, is probably the best of all forms of government. We believe that a democracy, which they tried hard to obviate, and into which the liberals have been trying for 50 years to convert our Republic, is one of the worst of all forms of government. We call attention to the fact that up to 1928 the U.S. Army Training Manual still gave our men in uniform the following quite accurate definition, which would have been thoroughly approved by the Constitutional Convention that established our Republic. "Democracy: A Government of the masses. Authority derived through mass meeting or any form of direct expression results in mobocracy. Attitude toward property is communistic —negating property rights. Attitude towards law is that the will of the majority shall regulate, whether it be based upon deliberation or governed by passion, prejudice, and impulse, without restraint or regard to consequences. Results in demagogism, license, agitation, discontent, anarchy." It is because all history proves this to be true that we repeat so emphatically: "This is a Republic, not a democracy; let's keep it that way."

We are opposed to collectivism as a political and economic system, even when it does not have the police-state features of communism. We are opposed to it no, matter whether the collectivism be called socialism or the welfare state or the New Deal or the Fair Deal or the New Frontier, or advanced under some other semantic disguise. And we are opposed to it no matter what may be the framework or form of government under which collectivism is imposed. We believe that increasing the size of government, increasing the centralization of government, and increasing the functions of government all act as brakes on material progress and as destroyers of personal freedom.

We believe that even where the size

---

* Statement of the principles of the John Birch Society, *Congressional Record,* June 12, 1962, p. A. 4293.

and functions of government are properly limited, as much of the power and duties of government as possible should be retained in the hands of as small governmental units as possible, as close to the people served by such units as possible. For the tendencies of any governing body to waste, expansion, and despotism all increase with the distance of that body from the people governed; the more closely any governing body can be kept under observation by those who pay its bills and provide its delegated authority, the more honestly responsible it will be. And the diffusion of governmental power and functions is one of the greatest safeguards against tyranny man has yet devised. For this reason it is extremely important in our case to keep our township, city, County and State governments from being bribed and coerced into coming under one direct chain of control from Washington.

We believe that for any people eternal vigilance is the price of liberty far more as against the insidious encroachment of internal tyranny than against the danger of subjugation from the outside or from the prospect of any sharp and decisive revolution. In a republic we must constantly seek to elect and to keep in power a government we can trust, manned by people we can trust, maintaining a currency we can trust, and working for purposes we can trust (none of which we have today). We think it is even more important for the government to obey the laws than for the people to do so. But for 30 years we have had a steady stream of governments which increasingly have regarded our laws and even our Constitution as mere pieces of paper, which should not be allowed to stand in the way of what they, in their omniscient benevolence, considered to be "for the greatest good of the greatest number." (Or in their power-seeking plans pretended so to believe.) We want a restoration of a "government of laws, and not of men" in this country; and if a few impeachments are necessary to bring that about, then we are all for the impeachments. . . .

3

Reading the Constitution Anew *

RICHARD HOFSTADTER

What kind of men were these Founding Fathers, who for many are symbolized by the Constitution? What did they intend by that document? Until the turn of the century they were uncritically admired in what one writer has called "the star-spangled manner." Under the impetus of the Progressive movement historians re-evaluated this. The works of Charles Beard provided a shocking interpretation. He saw the Constitution as the product of an upper class trying to preserve property. This Economic Interpretation of the Constitution was, until recently, the dominant approach to that period. Recent work has thrown this into real question. What consequences, if any, result from adoption of either view?

Every major turn in events seems to bring with it a turn in historical consciousness. . . . Such recent assessments of the American past as those made by Daniel Boorstin and Louis Hartz rest upon conceptions very different from those inherited by this generation from such of their forebears as Charles A. Beard or Frederick Jackson Turner. . . .

Beard had emphasized the social conflicts that gave rise to the Constitution and the political controversy that it caused. As he saw it, the Constitution was desired and created by a relatively small group of men who had a special interest in "personalty"— that is, not in land, but in property invested in commerce, shipping, manufacturing, and, above all, public securities. The framers of the Constitution, alarmed at the democratic tendencies of the state legislatures and at the fee-

bleness of the Articles of Confederation, drafted a stronger instrument of central government. . . . The new government, far from being an extension of democracy, was an effort to check the power of majorities by men whose political theory, as expressed in their deliberations, was antidemocratic. The presentation of the Constitution to the several states for ratification aroused a bitter conflict, which Beard traced to distinct social groupings. Although the document seemed to challenge the interests of agrarians generally, who constituted a majority of the population, and of debtors in particular, the proponents of the Constitution were able to win its acceptance because they were an aggressive elite, educated, concentrated in strategic places, keenly aware of their own interests; and because their agrarian opponents were scattered through the countryside, slow to move, ignorant of political affairs, or disfranchised by their inability to satisfy the property qualifications for voting.

In his *Charles Beard and the Con-*

* Richard Hofstadter, "Reading the Constitution Anew," *Commentary*, XXII, September 1956, 270-74. Reprinted by permission of the author and publisher.

stitution, Professor Brown, a student of Colonial history who has written an important book on *Middle Class Democracy and the Revolution in Massachusetts, 1691–1780,* dogs Beard chapter, page by page, and paragraph by paragraph through his classic work, challenging practically every significant assessment of the evidence. No review can do justice to the bulk of even the important criticisms Brown makes. I hope it is not unjust to select two differences that he seems to consider of particular importance. The first of these is over the relative role of real and personal property among the interests that made the Constitution. Brown has little trouble in showing that the preponderance of real property among the propertied interests of America in 1787–88 was so heavy (even among the very men designated by Beard as the important "personalty holders") as to give us grave cause indeed to doubt the validity of Beard's strong emphasis on personalty. . . .

Brown's second major criticism, however, raises fundamental questions about the interpretation of American political experience. He asks once again how democratic, or undemocratic, the society was which adopted the new Constitution in 1788. Where Beard emphasized the disfranchisement of adult males through the suffrage qualifications, Brown's own study of Massachusetts has done much to prove the wide availability of the right to vote in that province in Colonial times; and other recent studies dealing with other states tend to bear out his thesis. Brown properly points out that some of the efforts to minimize the breadth of the suffrage have rested upon the elementary fallacy of comparing the number of eligible voters, or even the number of actual voters in a given election, with the *total* population instead of with the whole number of *adult males.* Using the suffrage as his primary test of democracy, he argues that the Constitution must be understood not as the product of a class society with acute internal conflicts between the elite and the mass, but rather of a "democratic middle-class society." . . .

The whole effect of Beard's book is to suggest that a great many . . . opposed it bitterly, but that "the people," being disfranchised and outmaneuvered by "the interests," went down to defeat. . . . Although Beard believed that this was in large part because they were disfranchised by property qualifications, he conceded in one very revealing passage that "far more were disfranchised through apathy and lack of understanding of the significance of politics," and in another, gave away a great part of his case with the sweeping admission that "the wide distribution of property created an extensive electorate." The difference for our view of the period between disfranchisement by property qualifications and "disfranchisement" through apathy or ignorance is an enormous one. . . . Brown puts it well when he says:

One of the master keys to an understanding of the Constitution is not how many men could not vote, but why so many having the vote did not use it. . . . When we stop talking about the "mass of men" who *could not* vote on the Constitution and start talking about the "mass of men" who could vote but did not bother to do so, then, and only then, will we understand the Constitution and its adoption. . . . The Constitution was adopted with a great show of indifference. . . .

. . . The historiography of the future will be much closer to the argument of Brown's book than to Beard's. . . .

4

Yesterday's Constitution or Today's? *

CHARLES P. CURTIS

*This discussion by four leading authorities on the interpretation of the Consti-
tution pinpoints some of the different points of view about the responsibilities
of the Court. The late Charles Curtis, a Boston attorney and author, argues that
the judge should interpret the Constitution in the light of today's public opinion.
The other authorities are disturbed by this argument, and suggest other sources
for judicial standards. Their examples sum up some of the problems in this area.*

To whom is the Constitution addressed? To whom are we speaking?
Barring the egregious Dred Scott case,
up to 1868 all the acts of Congress
which the Supreme Court held unconstitutional related to the organization
of the courts. The Constitution was
speaking directly to the Court. Since
then, the Court has been concerned
with other parts of the Constitution
which are addressed to other agencies
of our government. Here the Court
has been exercising a secondary judgment, on a meaning which has already
been given to the Constitution by
someone who had likewise sworn to
support it and who therefore had also
a right to construe it.

To be sure, the Court has its own
opinion as to what the constitutional
words mean, but when they are addressed to someone else, the Court
uses its own meaning only for the purpose of comparing it with the meaning already given it by that other. The

Court is only a critic who compares a
picture for its likeness to the object.

This is one reason why only present
current meanings are pertinent. We
cannot have our government run as if
it were stuck in the end of the eighteenth century, when we are in the
middle of the twentieth. It is idle to
think that we shall become either
better or wiser than we are, or have
nobler aspirations than our best, just
because our forefathers hoped we
would or even intended we should.
"What's past is prologue, what to
come in yours and my discharge."

This . . . is also the reason why the
Court respects what the Congress, or
the governmental agency, or the official, thought the proper meaning to
be. As much deference is due as is deserved, and it is due as a matter of
fact, not as a presumption of law. The
deference depends on the dignity, the
local or expert knowledge, and the
known wisdom of the official, agency,
or legislative authority whose meaning
has been brought before the Court for
judgment. This makes it all the more
inappropriate, even offensive, to judge
their meanings by any but current
standards.

---

* Charles P. Curtis, "The Role of the
Constitutional Text," *Supreme Court and
Supreme Law*, ed. Edmond Cahn (Bloom-
ington, Ind.: Indiana University Press, 1954),
pp. 67-68, 72-75. Reprinted by permission
of the publisher.

It is plain, therefore, that any theory of the Court's interpretation of the Constitution must be the same theory on which the other government agencies act, consciously or unconsciously, when they interpret the Constitution for their purposes. The Court cannot fairly compare its own interpretation with theirs unless they are both made to the same pattern and based on the same principles. . . . It must be current, because the interpretations on which the Court is passing judgment are now and immediate. It must be practical, because these official interpretations concern our lives, and meaning and life are intertwined if not inextricable. At the same time and for the same reason, there is no possibility of its being easy to operate. Life is not simple nor do we really want it to be.

John P. Frank: I suspect that the audience like me finds Mr. Curtis an extraordinarily stimulating man. If he were as persuasive on the subject as he is stimulating, I would have nothing to say.

Solely, therefore, for definitional purposes, I would like to direct his attention to three concrete questions and ask him how, in his view of the proper approach to the matter, he would decide those questions or how he approaches them.

In order to test his technique, I will ask him to accept my assumptions as to what the law is or as to what the documents will show. First, take the cruel and unusual punishment clause in the Constitution. It is clear that the punishment of whipping was used almost universally in the eighteenth century and it was a common practice when that clause was adopted. However, at the present time only two states have whipping and only one has it for general purposes.

I would like to know whether in his view the practice of whipping should be held unconstitutional on the ground it may not have been a cruel and unusual punishment in the eighteenth century but it is now.

Curtis: Indeed, yes.

Frank: Let me give you all three because it is a comparison that I want to get. Secondly, let us suppose that we have on the face of the First Amendment an ambiguity which I think is clearly there, and that is: Does the protection of freedom of speech mean to allow for those exceptions which existed in English common law or doesn't it?

This is a disputable point. Let us assume that by no amount of analysis of the words of the First Amendment will we know for sure what was intended (if we care what was intended) in respect of the English common law exceptions. But we do have a complete, detailed, contemporary writing of Madison which shows without any doubt at all that the Amendment was intended not to allow for the English common law exceptions. Do we look to what Madison had to say and to what extent are we bound by it?

Finally, in connection with the impairment of contracts clause, let us suppose that a particular enactment of mortgage moratorium is offered and we know for sure that this is the kind of mortgage moratorium the Founding Fatners meant to preclude by the adoption of the contracts clause. Using Mr. Curtis' techniques, will he tell us what attention, if any, he will pay to intent and practice of the eighteenth century with regard to each?

Curtis: I think the first one is a very neat example of why I should discard original intention entirely. It is cruel as of the present, and it is unusual. There is no basis for restriction to what was unusual at that time. I should certainly hold whipping unconstitutional, looking for guidance to the present meaning of the word "unusual."

Take your second one, freedom of speech. I should ignore any restrictions put on it by the common law or the practices of the eighteenth century and look rather to what We believe now—I am using "We," as the Constitution does, with a capital W—and I should expect the Supreme Court to pick out the best views and try to give us their version of modern freedom of speech.

Answering your third question, I should ignore the contemporary practice. I would ignore any common law or eighteenth-century notions with respect to mortgage moratoriums.

Edmond Cahn: You would not feel a duty to consult what Madison said on the subject?

Curtis: I should be exceedingly interested in reading it in exactly the same way that I should be interested to read his biography or any other relevant history; but I was asked whether that bound the Supreme Court. To that I say no. . . .

Willard Hurst: I think some of this discussion is unduly abstract because it seems to ignore the fact that when you are talking about constitutional law, you are talking about the balance of power in the community and that the question of how you find meaning boils down concretely here to who finds the meaning.

I say that because I suspect in concrete cases Mr. Curtis and I would not find ourselves far apart, but I think a large part of the difference in formulation boils down to the fact that he is a greater friend of the Court than I am.

It seems to me that his approach is a way of practically reading Article V out of the federal Constitution. The men who wrote the Constitution, after all, included that Article as being as important a part as anything else. They provided a defined, regular procedure for changing or adapting it.

Many times what we are talking about here boils down to the question: Do you want your community policy choices to be made by judges, by legislators, by presidents, or by the electorate? And I stick to my basic distinction that you are dealing with language that sets up a standard. We have set up a way of doing business, which means we are willing to delegate adaptations and adjustments in certain realms to those who hold official power when the adjustment happens to become necessary. Nevertheless, a very basic principle of our constitutionalism is a distrust of official power. Hence I am not anxious to see the category of standards expanded.

We may not like everything to which the men of 1787 commit us. Of course, the world has changed. Nobody wants to run a twentieth-century society according to the eighteenth century. The real issue is who makes the policy choices in the twentieth century: judges or the combination of legislature and electorate that makes constitutional amendments. If you are dealing in an area (like the due process clause) which involves the matter of standards, there we have, for better or worse, committed our fortunes to the current holders of official power at the time the problem arises. So be it! If we are dealing with a question which is not in the realm of standards, we have a different way of dealing with it. Personally I am satisfied with the difference.

5

Constitutions: The Politics of Power *

HAROLD NORRIS

Constitutions, however, also fix power relationships between groups. The many different constitutions in the American system—we are prone to forget the state constitutions—sometimes have hidden consequences. Here a law professor, who was a delegate to his own state constitutional convention, analyzes the constitution of another state which was considering revision of its constitution. He shows how seemingly innocent changes might really decide the outcome of expected future disputes. Is his contention correct that the American public lacks understanding and concern over such longer-range issues or problems? If so, does that mean we have a system of majority rule only with regard to obvious disputes which catch the attention of the public, while more fundamental problems are decided by concealed power groups?

On April 4, 1967, the state of New York will convene its first constitutional convention since 1938. Early on the morning of September 29, Howard J. Samuels was on the platform of the White Plains railroad station, stopping commuters to tell them that he was running for delegate to the convention and to ask for their votes. As *The New York Times* reported next day: "He confirmed what he already suspected; people seemed to know little about the convention and to care less."
. . . [T]he national experience with state constitutional conventions is that the electorate does not adequately understand its sovereign role of constitution making . . . Emphasis on constitutional change has brought to light a new though not generally recognized stage in American politics and in the political education of the American

people. While the voter has an improved understanding of *issues*, he has generally less insight into *power*. He may be better informed about factors on the state level dealing with education, highways, taxation, civil rights, conservation, recreation, crime, pollution. He is much less aware of and sensitive to the more fundamental political question of who has the power, governmentally and factually, to deal with these issues. The voter and the student as well are confused by the echelons of government: on the vertical level, legislative, executive and judicial; and on the horizontal level, federal, state, county and municipal. In short, it is easier for the voter to sense the issue than to perceive the power behind that issue, or to hold that power accountable.

A constitution is a power document; it is a charter of power. Fundamental to a constitution is the governmental power it arranges and the political power it reflects. A state constitution,

* Harold Norris, "Constitutions: The Politics of Power," *The Nation*, Nov. 7, 1966, pp. 472-74. Reprinted by permission of the publisher.

deriving its character as a direct act of sovereignty—only the people of a state by direct vote can ordain and establish a constitution—is authority over authority. It states who shall do it.

But it is harder for people to get excited about the question of power (who shall do it?) than about issues and program (what shall be done?). Power has a greater reach into the future; program is more immediate. It takes more political insight and vision to understand power than program. To enlarge that insight and vision about power requires qualitatively improved political education. With more constitution making in the states, including the precedent making state of New York, national as well as state effort is needed. People, power, program and politics, pocketbook politics, have to be related in a new and more understandable way. Chief Justice Marshall's historic injunction is applicable here: "We must remember, it is a constitution we are expounding." a charter of government in which merge yesterday and tomorrow, principle and practice, means and ends. Making a constitution is the supreme act of government.

. . . [T]he sovereign people of New York (or any other state) will have to think about how to define state power in their constitution. What are the main power questions?

The one that dominates, animates and permeates all others at state constitutional conventions is apportionment. James Madison noted during the convention that founded this nation: "The great difficulty lies in the affair of representation; and if this could be adjusted all others would be surmountable." The pattern or formula of apportionment will decide who holds the legislative power in the state and can thus check and balance the governor and the courts. . . .

⁕   ⁕   ⁕

The allocation of power between the state and local governments will need careful definition. Home rule and fiscal matters—taxation, expenditures, the budget—often conflict. The real behind-the-scenes power struggle on home rule is between the urban interests and the rural legislators who control the state capitols over who shall tax, who shall receive and how much. The big cities, New York or Detroit, with budgets equal to that of the state itself, must go cap in hand to the state capitol to secure funds and authority to meet their multiplying problems. . . . As Frank Adams put it, "why should a resident of Niagara Falls have a determining voice on how much New York City should charge for a subway ride?"

One solution tendered by students of the problem is that cities be delegated power to legislate locally on all matters not specifically excluded in home-rule laws. . . . The problem is to grant cities power of the state to intervene to prevent misconduct. . . .

Constitutional conventions have generally not altered basically the Bill of Rights in the states. However, New York may consider eliminating literacy in English as a voting requirement, lowering the voting age to 18 and restricting wire tapping. . . . However, the dominant Bill of Rights issue in the New York convention will be church-state relations, particularly state aid to parochial schools. . . . Dean Mulligan of Fordham Law School called Article 11, Section 3 "an anachronism of the know-nothing era." That provision reads:

Neither the state nor any subdivision thereof shall use its property or credit or any public money . . . directly or indirectly, in aid or maintenance . . . of any school or institution of learning wholly or in part under the control or direction of any religious denomination.

If this provision is retained in New York, it will be a victory for those who want to protect religious freedom by keeping church and state separate. The national trend and Michigan's experience does not augur well for those who would confine the public treasury to public schools.

In a constitution, every sentence is important. Each line has relevance to the citizen's rights, liberty, property and power. . . .

6

Unwritten Rules of American Politics *

JOHN FISCHER

John Fischer, editor of Harper's, *points up the difficulties of changing the Constitution in his discussion of the unwritten rules of American politics. The American Constitutional system represents a legal distribution of powers built on a diversified series of power groups. The result, as Fischer points out, is all too often inaction in the face of crisis, and the lack of anyone who can speak for the nation as a whole. Thus, change, while always tantalizingly possible, is almost always out of political reach. What groups benefit from this reality?*

. . . Surprisingly little has been written about the rules of American politics during our generation . . . The most useful discussion of this tradition which I have come across is the work of John C. Calhoun, published nearly a century ago. . . .

Calhoun summed up his political thought in what he called the Doctrine of the Concurrent Majority. He saw the United States as a nation of tremendous and frightening diversity—a collection of many different climates, races, cultures, religions, and economic patterns. He saw the constant tension among all these special interests, and he realized that the central problem of American politics was to find some way of holding these conflicting groups together.

It could not be done by force; no one group was strong enough to impose its will on all the others. The goal could be achieved only by compromise—and no real compromise could be possible if any threat of coercion lurked behind the door. Therefore, Calhoun reasoned, every vital decision in American life would have to be adopted by a "concurrent majority"— by which he meant, in effect, a unanimous agreement of all interested parties. No decision which affected the interests of the slaveholders, he argued, should be taken without their consent; and by implication he would have given a similar veto to every other special interest, whether it be labor, management, the Catholic church, old-age pensioners, the silver miners, or the corn growers of the Middle West....

. . . [G]overnment by concurrent majority can exist only when no one power is strong enough to dominate completely, *and then only when all of the contending interest groups recognize and abide by certain rules of the game.*

These rules are the fundamental bond of unity in American political life. . . .

It is a rule which operates unofficially and entirely outside the Constitution—but it has given us a method by which all the official and constitutional organs of government can be made to work. It also provides a means of selecting leaders on all levels of our political life, for hammering out policies, and for organizing and managing the conquest of political power. . . .

The weaknesses of the American political system are obvious. . . . It is enough to note that most of the criticism has been aimed at two major flaws.

First, it is apparent that the doctrine of the concurrent majority is a negative one—a principle of inaction. A strong government, capable of rapid and decisive action, is difficult to achieve under a system which forbids it to do anything until virtually everybody acquiesces. In times of crisis, a dangerously long period of debate and compromise usually is necessary before any administration can carry out the drastic measures needed. The depression of the early Thirties, the crisis in foreign policy which ended only with Pearl Harbor, the crisis of the Marshall program all illustrate this recurring problem.

This same characteristic of our system gives undue weight to the small but well-organized pressure group—especially when it is fighting *against* something. . . .

An even more serious flaw in our scheme of politics is the difficulty in finding anybody to speak for the country as a whole. Calhoun would have argued that the national interest is merely the sum of all the various special interests, and therefore needs no spokesmen of its own—but in this case he clearly was wrong.

In practice, we tend to settle sectional and class conflicts at the expense of the nation as a whole—with results painful to all of us. . . .

CHAPTER FOUR

The Federal System:
Instrument of Liberty or Inefficiency?

The federal system is certainly one of the distinguishing characteristics of American government. The existence within the same territory of two sets of governments, both at least theoretically deriving their powers separately, creates problems and puzzles observers. When the former Russian dictator, Khrushchev, visited the United States, he was irritated by remarks of state and local officials, being convinced that they really were made at the behest of Washington. The federal system was really quite inexplicable to him, even though the Soviet Union is nominally a federal republic.

The independence of the states in many aspects of their activities has been held up as a bulwark to freedom. It has been described as the product of a people that want "unity without uniformity." They see it as a protection against any tyranny which could not control the diverse states. They find these separate governments "laboratories for experimentation" and chambers for new programs.

But there are clearly costs as well. The boundaries, sizes, and populations vary tremendously. The existence of 51 different legal systems means that American government is highly legalized. Businesses must deal with elaborate sets of laws. Individuals often are penalized by the existence of different systems of laws while those who make a study of the complexities can often use them to personal advantage at the expense of the community.

Because of the rapid growth of national economy and dissatisfaction with state government, observers for a long time have been predicting the demise of the states. But events belie these predictions. The states are as strong and as active as ever, growing in functions and in expenditures. The federal system seems to take on new patterns and meet new crises, but the American public appears to be very satisfied with the system as a whole.

STATES' RIGHTS: PRINCIPLE OR PRETEXT?

From the time of Jefferson, the issue of states' rights has been a key slogan in American politics. Many claims have been made for federalism and continue to be made.

The slogan of states' rights has two aspects. On the one hand, it may be a claim of divisions of power and abstract issues. Maintenance of the federal system is a desire of American public opinion, particularly in the name of freedom or diversity.

The claim that federalism fosters freedom has some very responsible backing. Roscoe Pound has observed that no government of continental size has been governed except as a federal system or as an autocracy. The American suspicion of power is a source of the support that states' rights can evoke. From Madison to Cahloun to modern writers, the argument is advanced that too much centralism is a threat to human liberty. While Nelson Rockefeller presents the traditional American viewpoint, the late Professor Neumann of Columbia University examines the historical record and suggests that the evidence for the identification of freedom with federalism is shakier than others argue.

States' rights, though, is often used as an argument in the course of debate to strengthen a particular issue. While the argument is in terms of abstract states' rights, the real purpose is to advance a particular cause. History seems to suggest that any party long out of power begins to stress states' rights, while the dominant party increasingly finds virtues in greater Federal activity. The classical example is Jefferson's purchase of Louisiana, but the reversal in our times of the positions of the Democratic and Republican parties is also suggestive.

FEDERAL AID TO THE STATES: HELP OR HINDRANCE?

This century has seen a shift of power to the national government. This has been a relative matter; all units of government have grown so far as the expenditures and personnel are concerned. But, the federal government's have grown faster than the states', and those of the states have grown more rapidly than those of the local governmental units. Today money is received from the national government and dispersed to local units or directly to the cities.

Some see these programs as weakening state governments. The states, they argue, have lost their power of independent choice. They follow along in the trail of federal grants and aid. Others see these programs not only as socially desirable but as fostering better state government. They recognize the problems of state government—regarded as the weakest link in our current American governmental structure—but find the fault to lie in their own internal problems —notably their failure to reapportion and to develop strong leadership in the governor's office and in the legislature. The shift of powers to the federal government then is seen as the result of state weakness rather than the cause.

NATION, STATE, CITIES: PARTNERS OR RIVALS?

Grants-in-aid are only part of a bigger picture. The essential point is the relationship between the two (or three) levels of government. How do they get along in our system? What should be an ideal relationship? Does the existence of the states create rivalries and conflicts that perplex the citizen?

In recent years, there has been an increasing tendency for the national government to deal directly with the cities and eliminate the "middle man" states. Is this a healthy development or an increasing emasculation of the federal system?

Some have hailed interpenetration of the various levels of government as a brand new development. Others find it simply an application of principles and practices that have been in existence since the nineteenth century. Depending on your point of view, the sharing of functions in American federalism can be seen as a new "creative federalism" or as simply an application of the basic principles of the Constitution.

1

Freedom and Federalism *

NELSON ROCKEFELLER

Nelson Rockefeller, while a serious candidate for presidential nomination, took time out to develop a series of lectures on the future of federalism. In this extract, he eloquently states the basis for identifying liberty and dispersion of power.

In the ominous spring of 1939, a bright and sunny May 3rd was a day marked by Adolf Hitler with another

* Nelson Aldrich Rockefeller, *The Future of Federalism* (Cambridge, Mass.: Harvard University Press, 1962), pp. 1-9. Copyright 1962 by The President and Fellows of Harvard College. Reprinted by permission of the publisher.

bellicose speech to the Reichstag calling for a showdown on Poland. On the same day, the League of Nations opened its "peace pavilion" at the World's Fair in New York City. And also on this same day, which seems so remote from the present instant, there was published a vigorous critique of American political life by a visitor from abroad, famed in intellectual and academic circles, who had just delivered a series of lectures on the American presidency. The visitor was Harold J. Laski. And the obituary he wrote upon an historic American political doctrine bore the title: "The Obsolescence of Federalism."

How did Professor Laski conclude that the age of federalism was languishing near death?

He did concede that "federalism is the appropriate governmental technique for an expanding capitalism." But, he declaimed, a "contracting capitalism cannot afford the luxury of federalism." Leaping from this premise, he insisted that the failure of the federal idea was unmistakably plain not only in the United States but also elsewhere in the world—in Canada, Australia, Germany. And he explained this universal failure in these words:

Whether we take the conditions of labor, the level of taxation, the standards of education, or the supply of amenities like housing and recreation, it has become clear that the true source of decision is no longer at the circumference, but at the center, of the state. For 48 separate units to seek to compete with the integrated power of giant capitalism is to invite defeat in almost every element of social life where approximate uniformity of condition is the test of the good life.

The two decades since have dealt a harsh retort to Professor Laski's pronouncement on federalism in the United States. It has been proven wrong in economic, social, and political terms. . . .

Private enterprise has become more vigorous, more creative. . . . The grim prognosis of 30 years ago has also been proven wrong in strictly political terms. For federalism—its ideas and its practice—has continued to show itself the adaptable and creative form of self-government that the Founding Fathers

of this nation conceived it to be. Decisions vital to national well-being have increasingly been made at the "circumference"—the states—as well as at the national "center," of political power.

These lectures are dedicated to the conviction that these basic political, social, and economic facts of life—and the lessons they carry for us—are crucial to the whole fate of freedom and of free men everywhere in this mid-twentieth century.

I do not use the word "freedom" casually. For nothing less than the historic concept of the free individual's worth and dignity, defined and attested by the whole Judeo-Christian tradition, is at stake in our world. . . .

The Federal Idea

The federal idea: what does this mean?

Let me first make it clear that I do not speak of the federal idea as merely a mechanical or technical or abstract formula for government operations. I refer to the federal idea broadly as a concept of government by which a sovereign people, for their greater progress and protection, yield a portion of their sovereignty to a political system that has more than one center of sovereign power, energy, and creativity. No one of these centers or levels has the power to destroy another. Under the Constitution, for example, there are two principal centers of government power—state and federal. As a practical matter, local government, by delegation of state authority under the principle of "home rule," is a third such key center of power. The federal idea, then, is above all an idea of a shared sovereignty at all times responsive to the needs and will of the people in whom sovereignty ultimately resides.

Our federal idea is complex and

subtle. It involves a balance of strengths. It puts into play a sharing of powers not only among different levels of government but—on each level—a separation of powers between the legislative, executive, and judicial branches of government. And it clearly signifies more than mere governmental structure. It demands faith in—and an environment for—the free play of individual initiative, private enterprise, social institutions, political organizations, and voluntary associations—all operating within a framework of laws and principles affirming the dignity and freedom of man.

A federal system, then, seeks stability without rigidity, security without inertia. It encourages innovation and inventiveness—governed by principle, and guided by purpose. It assures responsiveness more thoughtful than mere reflex—and liberty that does not lapse toward anarchy. In short, it seeks to hold the delicately precarious balance between freedom and order upon which depend decisively the liberty, peace, and prosperity of the individual. . . .

By providing several sources of political strength and creativity, a federal system invites inventive leadership—on all levels—to work toward genuine solutions to the problems of a diverse and complex society. These problems—whether they concern civil rights or urban development, industrialization or automation, natural resources or transportation—never arise at the same instant and in the same way throughout a great nation. A federal system, however, allows these problems to be met at the time and in the area where they first arise. If local solutions are not forthcoming, it is still possible to bring to bear the influence, the power, and the leadership of either the state or the national government.

2

Federalism and Freedom: A Critique *

FRANZ L. NEUMANN

Not all writers find the preceding argument conclusive. Franz Neumann examines the record of history and finds the case not proven. Freedom's link to federalism is vague, but the costs of federalism are clear.

The theoretical argument for federalism revolves around the potential

* Franz L. Neumann, "Federalism and Freedom: A Critique," in *Federalism Mature and Emergent*, ed. Arthur W. MacMahon. (New York: Doubleday & Company, Inc., 1955), pp. 45-49, 53-54. © by the Trustees of Columbia University in the City of New York. Reprinted by permission of the publisher.

of political power for evil. Federalism is seen as one of the devices to curb the evil use of power by dividing power among a number of competing power-units.

In its most radical form, this sentiment appears in the various anarchist schemes. It has been popular in the anarcho-syndicalist theories and prac tices of the Latin-speaking countries and with the IWW of the United States.

It is Lord Acton's statement on the corruptive effect of political power which appears to have today the greatest influence: Power tends to corrupt and absolute power corrupts absolutely. Great men are almost always bad men.[1] And Montesquieu [2] said this even more clearly. According to him [3] power could be checked only by power—a statement that few would be willing to quarrel with. Not ideologies and beliefs but only a counterpower can check power. In this he applies Cartesian principles and stands in the tradition of Spinoza who saw no way of limiting the state's absoluteness (which was a logical consequence of his assumptions and of his geometric method) except by a counterpower.

The Montesquieu generalization is, of course, designed to give his doctrine of the separation of powers an adequate theoretical base. But as little as the theory of separate powers follows from his sociological observation, as little does that of the preferability of the federal state. Bentham[4] rejected the separation of powers not only as incompatible with democracy but also because it could not really maximize freedom if the three organs of government were controlled by the same social group. A quite similar argument can be raised against federalism as a guarantee for liberty. Those who assert that the federal state through the dif-

fusion of *constitutional* powers actually diffuses *political* power often overlook the fact that the real cause for the existence of liberty is the pluralist structure of society and the multi-party (or two-party) system.[5] Federalism is not identical with social pluralism; and neither the two-party nor the multi-party system is the product of the federal state or the condition for its functioning.

Whether the federal state does indeed increase freedom[6] cannot be abstractly determined. We have some evidence that the federal state as such (that is, regardless of the form of government) has not fulfilled this role. The German Imperial Constitution certainly created a federal state but there is little doubt that politically it had a dual purpose: to be a dynastic alliance against the forces of liberalism and democracy,[7] and to secure the hegemony of Prussia.[8]

Perhaps more striking are the respective roles of federalism and centralism in the coming to power of National Socialism. Some believe, indeed, that the centralization under the Weimar Republic is wholly or at least partly responsible for the rise of National Socialism. But there is no evidence for this statement—nor indeed for the opposite one. It is certain that Bavaria, with the strongest states' rights tradition, gave shelter to the National Socialist movement and it is equally certain that the federal character of the Weimar Republic did not, after Hitler's appointment, delay the

---

[1] Quotations taken from G. Himmelfarb, *Lord Acton, A Study in Conscience and Politics* (Chicago: University of Chicago Press, 1952), p. 161.

[2] My edition of the *Spirit of the Laws* (New York: Hafner Library of Classics, 1949), XI, 4.

[3] See my Introduction, *ibid.*, pp. lvii-lviii.

[4] Bowring, ed., IX, 41ff.; and Elie Halevy, *The Growth of Philosophical Radicalism* trans. Mary Morris (New York: The Macmillan Company, 1928), pp. 258-59.

[5] See my Montesquieu Introduction, pp. lvii and lxiv.

[6] Cf. Carl J. Friedrich, *Constitutional Government and Democracy* (Boston: Ginn & Company, 1946), pp. 216-17.

[7] Rudolf Schlesinger, *Federalism in Central and Eastern Europe* (New York: Oxford University Press, Inc., 1945), p. 71.

[8] K. C. Wheare, *Federal Government* (New York: Oxford University Press, Inc., 1947), p. 15.

process of synchronization *(Gleich-schaltung)* of the various state governments. Nor is there any definable relation between democratic conviction and federalist (or unitary) sympathies. The National Socialists were both centralists and reactionary, as were the Nationalists. Democrats and Social Democrats were antifederalists and committed to the preservation of political freedom. The Catholic center was not wholeheartedly committed to any position, and the Communists were, in theory, for the unitary state but did not hesitate, during the revolution of 1918, to advocate the secession of Brunswick which they believed they had in their pocket.

The evidence is certainly too slight to be of great value in determining whether the federal system is preferable to the unitary state as an instrument to preserve or enhance civil liberties. Nor is it likely that convincing evidence can be obtained, since other factors—the plurality of the social structure, the functioning of a truly competitive party system, the strength of a favorable tradition, the intellectual level of the population, the attitude of the courts—do far more easily permit the formation of a counterpower against forces hostile to civil liberties than does the federal structure of the government.

If federalism, as such, has nothing in it that automatically guarantees the preservation of political freedom, American federalism may have features that have hindered the solution of pressing economic problems.[9] The impact of the American federal system, of the division of powers, on the condition of this country in the Thirties was not reassuring.

George C. S. Benson, in his book *The New Centralization,*[10] tried to show how federalism worked in the setting of the Great Depression.

First, he found federalism as an "obstruction of social legislation." The states hesitated to enact this legislation not only for fear of placing their manufacturers at a competitive disadvantage with manufacturers of states that did not regulate wages and hours and provide benefits, but also for fear of driving larger industries into these latter states.[11]

Secondly, there was great disparity among the states' financial resources. Not only were most states incapable of financing serious efforts at reform, but "Complete decentralization—complete local responsibility for governmental services—may then result in a 'spread' between the standards of different districts which would shock even the uncritical believer in a national 'American' standard."[12]

Thirdly, Benson found little evidence that the states were really the "experimental laboratories" they were pictured to be.[13]

Fourthly, the ability of the states to put programs into action in an efficient way was seriously questioned.

Lastly, the nature of the economic system is such that its workings were and are obviously not confined to the territory of any given city or state.

As our great business concerns grow more specialized and conduct larger scale operations, government cannot be expected to remain simple and pastoral.[14]

---

[9] For a discussion of this situation in Australia, see A. P. Canaway, *The Failure of Federalism in Australia,* London, Oxford University Press, 1930.

[10] New York, Farrar and Rinehart, 1941. On this problem see, in addition, Harold Laski, "The Obsolescence of Federalism," *The New Republic,* Vol. 98 (May 3, 1939) pp. 367-69.
[11] Benson, *op. cit.,* pp. 23-24.
[12] *Ibid.,* p. 30.
[13] *Ibid.,* p. 38.
[14] *Ibid.,* p. 40.

In sum, as Professor Key has written,

A characteristic of the federal system seems to be that entrenched interests in the long run can better protect themselves in dealing with state legislatures than with Congress or with federal administrators.[15]

---

[15] V. O. Key, Jr., *Politics, Parties, and Pressure Groups*, 3rd ed. (New York: Thomas Y. Crowell Company, 1952), p. 102.

3

How to Keep Our Liberty *

RAYMOND MOLEY

Advocates of states' rights have diagnosed their problem as in part constitutional and in part financial. They deplore Supreme Court decisions and actions by President and Congress forwarding national power. But they especially argue that it is the present system of taxation, which gives the federal government the lions' share of the tax dollar that ultimately makes it powerful. This has resulted in such proposals as the one to limit the income tax. Here is a sample argument by a leading columnist and political science professor, who was one of the first architects of the New Deal—the original head of Roosevelt's "Brain Trust"—and is currently a leading spokesman for conservative ideas.

The Federal Invasion of the States—Robbing Peter

The American Constitution was designed to preserve personal liberty by several means. Very important among these was the assurance of state sovereignty and, with it, local government. The ascendancy of the federal government is the deadly enemy not only of the states but of the citizens of the states. For socialism must seek its final objective on a national level.

To attain domination, the federal leviathan must first seize the sources of state and local revenue—revenue that is the life blood of government.

The extent of this seizure has already been most alarming.

The Hoover Commission's task force on federal-state relations points out that in 1890 the Federal government spent 36.2 per cent of all governmental outlays in the nation. In 1946, it spent 85.2 per cent. In 1890 local units spent 55.6 per cent. The state governments in 1946 spent 7.6 per cent.

The adoption of the federal income tax marked the beginning of a rapid rise of federal authority and the decline of state and local importance. Before the federal income tax was adopted, the federal government derived nearly all its revenue from customs, liquor, and tobacco taxes. The income tax immediately assumed major importance, but during World War I the federal government seized sev-

---

* Raymond Moley, *How to Keep Our Liberty* (New York: Alfred A. Knopf, Inc., 1952), pp. 109-13. © 1952 by Raymond Moley. Reprinted by permission of the publisher.

eral other sources of revenue, including various admissions taxes, stamp taxes, and manufacturers' excise taxes. Later it added motor fuel, gifts, and estates to its taxable sources. Other sources have been seized as they have been found, always with small regard for the prior possession of states and localities.

This money is not made in Washington. It comes from the states. The sources from which states have drawn their own revenue have been taken by the federal suction pump. Almost every productive source of taxation, except the property tax, has been lost to most of the states.

The result is utter confusion and overlapping of taxes. The same sources may be taxed several times, and taxpayers themselves have only the faintest notion of what they pay, what they pay for, and whom they are paying.

A large part of the collections of the federal government comes from such overlapping taxes. And the proportion of the federal "bite" from these sources is steadily getting larger. In 1934 its share of the taxes from these sources was 63 per cent. In 1946, it was 91 per cent.

Since all governments—federal, state, and local—follow the Donnybrook slogan, "Hit the heads you see!" obvious sources are hit hard, and more difficult but fair sources are neglected.

Since the greatest growth of federal power has taken place in the two wars and in the depression, it is easy to predict that in the great crisis created by the threat of communism this absorption of local sources of revenue will continue at an increasing rate. States are at a great disadvantage in this competition. The federal income tax is all-powerful. Moreover, an individual state has the handicap of trying to avoid driving individuals and businesses to other states that have more favorable taxes.

To Pay Paul

The grave danger of all this is that the state and local governments, which are close to the vital needs of the people and are under close observation by them, will become less competent to perform their proper functions. These protective divisions of our nation will wither for lack of nourishment.

Along with this progressive seizure of state and local sources of revenue, and on the overworked theory that under modern economic conditions the problems of government override state boundaries, the federal government has stolen from the states many of their traditional powers and functions. Assistance to the aged and unfortunate, highway building, the regulation of business and labor, the control of elections and primaries, the enforcement of criminal law, and many other activities of the states have been partially taken over by federal authority.

Under a constant enlargement of federal jurisdiction made possible by a more and more "liberal" interpretation of the Constitution by the Supreme Court, almost every aspect of competition and private business and labor is now subject to federal law. Consequently, state legislation in many of those fields has become meaningless. Regulation has loosed upon the states a horde of federal bureaucrats who have little sympathy for local customs, preferences, and protections, and who are responsible only to Washington. This condition has grown much worse during the war and in the subsequent cold war.

Great federal enterprises for defense and related purposes have grown up with payrolls so large that local communities have become increasingly dependent upon them. This has seriously impaired local independence.

Federal power has grown immensely through grants-in-aid to the states

Through such grants the federal government now influences or controls 75 per cent of state activities. Under the pretext of successive crises—the depression, the war, and the cold war—the size and variety of these grants have grown at a tremendous rate. Fifty years ago, only $3,000,000 was paid out of federal funds to the states. By 1912, grants had risen to $4,255,000. From then on, the march began in earnest, in part because the federal income tax with its unlimited power over incomes became operative, and in part because of the great requirements of World War I. . . . Under President Truman's administration, these grants have risen until in 1950 the sum was nearly $2,234,700,000. This is the most graphic way of describing the deterioration of a great constitutional system.

There has also been a parallel and consistent decline of local self-government through the increase of state grants to cities, counties, and other small units of government. In five years, state grants to localities have increased by a third.

A special evil in the development of federal power under President Roosevelt was the habit of by-passing the states in extending aid to cities and other local units of government. In the administration of relief under Harry Hopkins, this was a calculated political objective. The federal machine thus made a close alliance with city machines through the granting of relief money, to the political advantage of both.

Where money goes the bureaucrat follows. Money means power. And power begets control.

This trend, if continued, will ultimately erase local self-government and reduce the states to the status of mere agents or provinces of the federal government. The balance system created by the Constitution will be gone, and national socialism will have eliminated its most formidable barrier.

4

There Is No State Point of View *

EDWARD W. WEIDNER

States' rights, however, is not just an argument for state power. At its roots the argument stems from the claims and programs of groups seeking to advance some cause. As such, states' rights may be a valid argument or simply a mask for some privileged group.

It is a thesis of the present discussion that in the federal system in the United States there are relatively few direct clashes or compromises between

* Edward W. Weidner, "Decision-Making in a Federal System," *Federalism Mature and Emergent,* ed. Arthur W. MacMahon (New York: Doubleday & Company, Inc.,

1955), pp. 363, 365-69, 376-77. © by the Trustees of Columbia University in the City of New York. Reprinted by permission of the publisher.

state and national governments on large issues of national domestic policy. . . . The disagreements and conflicts that do arise and that may be encouraged by federalism's structural features are not basically clashes between much smaller groups of people, and the opposing groups are located within a single governmental level as often as not. . . .

While differences on public policy or values are to be expected in a country containing as many heterogeneous elements as are to be found in the United States, it does not necessarily follow that officials in the several states will take one policy position and those of the national government another. Indeed, . . . it would seem surprising if this were the case, given the diversity of conditions in the several states and the fact that the union is made up of all states. "States' rights" is only one of numerous values held by state officials, and it is relatively unimportant to many of them. The prime thing that the states have in common is their existence; it is possible that if an issue were presented that threatened the very existence of the states, their political officials might be brought together. In actual fact, a major issue of this kind has not been presented. Consequently, usually national government officials can find many of their state counterparts who support national policy objectives and many others who oppose. And among the states, differences in values are the rule. . . .

The states have been unable to follow a single course even in such comparatively noncontroversial areas as are covered by the so-called uniform state laws. If minimum standards are desired for the nation as a whole in a particular policy area such as health or welfare, it is the central government that must act to assure these ends. To leave the matter exclusively to the states means that there will be a variation in standards from very low to quite high. To set up a system of joint national-state participation means that standards and practices will vary much more than in a system of central action alone. It also means that some disagreement and conflict are inevitable because officials in various states will not all see eye-to-eye with those of the national government in terms of the objectives of the program.

This is not to blame the states in any way for their actions. Rather it is to recognize that public policy is in large part the result of the values that men hold and that these values vary from individual to individual and group to group. It would be unexpected and suprising if the several states followed identical or even similar courses of action on important public issues. The normal expectancy is that they will differ in greater or lesser degree among themselves in regard to policies they enact and in regard to the policies of the national government. . . .

The values that individuals hold are so diverse that there is no definable "state" point of view in intergovernmental relations as a whole. Even if the 48 governors were considered to be spokesmen for their entire states, there does not emerge a single state approach to intergovernmental relations. Occasionally all the governors will agree on a minor point or two but they have never agreed that a specific general reallocation of activities should take place between national and state governments. This is understandable since some of them are Democrats, some Republicans; some are liberals, others conservatives; some have national political ambitions, others do not; some come from poor states, others from well-to-do areas. These are only a few of the variables that affect the approach governors take on national-state relations. Much of the publicity arising from recent political events, Governors' Conferences, and the Council of State Governments tends to give the impression that all governors demand that certain functions and tax resources of the national government be turned over to the states. The impression is erroneous. It is true that the governors probably defend states' rights as vigorously as any other group of public officials; they tend to stress expediency values relative to state government. In part this is a function of their role as chief executive and chief party leader. Nevertheless, such a set of values may be subordinate to many other considerations, and consequently consensus is not easily forthcoming. . . .

Disagreement or conflict in national-state relations is limited. It is not a matter that normally determines election results or on which there is a clear public opinion. General issues of national-state relations have concerned only a small minority of individuals and groups in recent decades, usually a group of public officials at each level

and a few interest groups outside the framework of government. When an important new substantive policy for the national government is under consideration, national-state wide relations may take on a broader significance, as was the case in welfare and labor policy during the Thirties. As a whole, however, interest groups and public opinion have not found states' rights an attractive theme unless by the defense of states' rights they could defend some programmatic value. . . .

Administrative and legislative officials alike are of the opinion that the main clash of values occurs within a unit of government rather than between units. This is true even in regard to the issues arising from intergovernmental programs. . . . This is not to deny that there are some who defend states' rights or local self-government through a genuine concern for decentralism and not on the basis of expediency. . . . However, situations where the programmatic values of professional administrators are overridden by their expediency values are not frequent. . . .

5

Federalism and Political Culture: A View from the States *

DANIEL J. ELAZAR

Does the growth of federal aid, then, really mean the emergence of a national attitude, with only the functional disagreements remaining, as argued by Weidner? In this discussion Professor Elazar presents the contrary view. He sees the states as having proven themselves both more resilient and more vital than the federal government. States have been basically successful in altering federal programs to suit their own aims and to reflect their own patterns.

To develop his analysis, Elazar utilizes the concept of "political culture" developed by Almond in the study of comparative government, and found in our selections in Chapter Two. Does such a concept help or interfere with analysis?

The States as Systems within a System

The 50 American states, located between the powerful federal government and the burgeoning local governments in a metropolitanizing nation, are the keystones of the American governmental arch. This was the case when the Constitution was adopted in 1789 and remains true despite the great changes that have taken place in the intervening years.

This assertion runs counter to most contemporary perceptions of American government. If it were based upon an analysis of the present position of the states in light of formal *constitutional* interpretations alone, there would be great difficulty in substantiating it. In fact, the states maintain their central role because of their *political* position in the overall framework of the nation's political system, a position supported by the Constitution

but which transcends its formal bounds. Unlike the more or less visible constitutional status of the states, their political position is generally of low visibility, not only to the public at large but often even to those people involved in the day-to-day operations of American government.

*   *   *

Federalism and Political Culture

One of the observations coming out of the several studies of federal-state relations conducted in the 1950's was that the states themselves (or their local subdivisions) could virtually dictate the impact of federal-aided activities within their boundaries.[1] Take the

* Daniel J. Elazar, *American Federalism: A View from the States* (New York: Thomas Y. Crowell Co., 1966), pp. 1, 81-85. Reprinted by permission of the publisher.

[1] Governmental Affairs Institute, *A Survey Report on the Impact of Federal Grants-in-Aid on the Structure and Functions of State and Local Governments*, submitted to the Commission on Intergovernmental Relations (Washington: Government Printing Office, 1956). The statements in this and the following paragraphs are based in large part on the findings in the twenty-five states covered in that report.

case of the impact of federal aid on the administration of state government. In those states where administration is concentrated at the executive level and the governor is usually strong, federal aid has tended to strengthen executive powers by giving the governor more and better tools to wield. In those states where power is widely diffused among the separate executive departments, federal aid has tended to add to the diffusion by giving the individual departments new sources of funds outside of the normal channels of state control which can even be used to obtain more money and power from the legislature. In those states where earmarked funds reflect legislature or lobby domination over programs, earmarked federal funds have had the same effect. Despite many protestations to the contrary, only in rare situations have federal grant programs served to alter state administrative patterns in ways that did not coincide with already established state policies, though such grants have often sharpened certain tendencies in state administration.

Or, in the case of federal merit system requirements, states dominated by political attitudes conducive to notions of professionalization and the isolation of certain forms of government activity from the pressures of partisan politics have had little problem adjusting their programs to meet federal standards, since they had either adopted similar standards earlier or were quite in sympathy with the standards when proposed. . . .

A parallel situation exists in regard to the substance of the federal programs. Every state has certain dominant traditions about what constitutes proper government action and every state is generally predisposed toward those federal programs it can accept as consistent with those traditions. Many states have pioneered programs

that fit into their traditions before the initiation of similar ones at the federal level or on a nationwide basis through federal aid. This, too, tends to lessen the impact of federal action on the political systems of those states and also to lessen any negative state reaction to federal entrance into particular fields. . . . Today states like California accept federal aid for mental health programs not as an innovative device but as a reenforcement of existing programs. Professional mental health workers in states like New Jersey rely upon the same federal grants to keep their programs free of internally generated political pressures, arguing with the patronage-inclined legislatures that federal regulations demand that professional standards be maintained. Their colleagues in states like Illinois use federal aid to force the hands of their legislatures to expand state activities in new directions. Reformers interested in mental health in states like Mississippi are interested in federal aid to inaugurate new programs. In matters of national defense, the southern states have a long tradition of supporting state militia and National Guard units so that over the years they have taken greater advantage of federal subventions for the maintenance of military reserve units than most of their sisters have.

Many of these and other differences in state responses within the federal system appear to be stimulated by differences in political culture among the states. We have already defined political culture as the particular pattern of orientation to political action in which each political system is imbedded. Political culture, like all culture, is rooted in the cumulative historical experiences of particular groups of people. Indeed, the origins of particular patterns of political culture are often lost in the mists of time. Patterns of political culture frequently overlap several political systems, and two or more political cultures may coexist within the same political system.[2] Though little

[2] For a more complete definition of political culture, see Gabriel A. Almond, "Comparative Political Systems," *The Journal of Politics*, XVIII (1956), 391-409. Political culture is directly connected to historical phenomena. Specific elements of political culture frequently have their origins in historical events or situations which cause great and long-lasting changes among those who share the experiences they generate. These changes are then transmitted—and often intensified—through the process of acculturation to the descendants of the original group, including both "blood" and "galvanized" (those adopted into the group) descendants.

is known about the precise ways in which political culture is influential, it is possible to suggest some ways in which the differences in political culture are likely to be significant.

Perhaps because of the close relationship between political culture and historical phenomena, historians have done more to trace the ingredients that combine to create the patterns of political culture than have other social scientists. Though they have not done so to investigate political culture as such, they have provided the raw materials for such an investigation through their studies of other phenomena, such as migration patterns, political alliances and antagonisms, the historical roots of continuing social behavior, and the like. . . .

6

Creative Federalism *

MAX WAYS

Certainly the experience of the immediate past few years bears out Elazar's contention that state flexibility in implementing federal programs is growing. Has this independence of the states grown by chance? No, says Max Ways, who argues that the federal government is deliberately sponsoring local creativity, forgetting old slogans, and facing real problems. Some writers have indeed suggested that the federal government is sponsoring flexibility, not out of altruism or philosophy, but because Washington control has proven inefficient. A shortage of competent help at the national level also seems a possible factor. Recently Raymond Moley, whose position has appeared earlier in the chapter, has called "creative federalism" a slogan to mask a retreat from the Welfare State programs that have prevailed in recent decades. Is this or Max Ways' interpretation the more valid one?

. . . . U.S. history is making a major turn from the politics of issues to the politics of problems. . . .

. . . [S]ome observers try to force the present programs into the mold of yesterday's debates. They see the new

* Max Ways, "Creative Federalism and the Great Society," *Fortune*, January, 1966, pp. 121-23, 222-29. © 1966 Time Inc. Reprinted by permission of the publisher.

programs simply as another surge in the drive begun thirty years ago to expand the federal government's share of total power in order to right social wrongs. When the Johnson program is put into that context, liberals automatically applaud it and conservatives automatically denounce it. Both are missing the point.

With the new assumptions of vigor

in U.S. society came a new way of organizing federal programs. At Ann Arbor and on five public occasions since then Johnson has used a phrase, "creative federalism," that has not received the attention it deserves. Federalism means a relation, cooperative and competitive, between a limited central power and other powers that are essentially independent of it. In the long American dialogue over states' rights, it has been tacitly assumed that the total amount of power was constant and, therefore, any increase in federal power diminished the power of the states and/or "the people." Creative federalism starts from the contrary belief that total power—private and public, individual and organizational—is expanding very rapidly. As the range of conscious choice widens, it is possible to think of vast increases of federal government power that do not encroach upon or diminish any other power. Simultaneously, the power of states and local governments will increase; the power of private organizations, including businesses, will increase; and the power of individuals will increase.

Creative federalism as it is now developing emphasizes relationships between Washington and many other independent centers of decision in state and local government, in new public bodies, in universities, in professional organizations, and in business. This characteristic of the new programs is part of a rather belated application to government of the organizational habits developed by modern business. While everyone has been watching the influence of government policies on the economy, the impact of the economy's strength and its mode of organization have been quietly altering the way the government works. Tens of thousands of professional and managerial types, in and out of government service, are shaping and executing

Great Society programs. This is as it should be, for professional and managerial men are preeminently oriented toward direction choosing and problem solving within a complex framework of many centers of decision.

This new outlook in Washington is the deepest reason for the rapprochement, during the Johnson Administration, between government and business. The two still have and will always have different responsibilities and aims. But they are beginning to use the same working language, depend on the same kinds of people, and get at tasks and decisions in the same way. More than administrative style is involved in this Washington shift. The whole framework of U.S. politics is changing.

*   *   *

Most issues of the 1930's had this same characteristic of taking from group A to give to group B. Indeed, a class redistribution of income and power was one of the stated aims of the New Deal. Thirty years ago belief was widespread that the U.S. economy was "mature," that a large and increasing proportion of all social initiative would have to be exercised through the federal government, that the hope of progress lay in the enlarged federal power to take from the "economic royalists" and give to the under-privileged. In the struggle arising from such beliefs the political positions called "radical," "liberal," and "conservative" jelled into their present meanings.

The Johnson program does not fit any of these molds. Except for the special case of the Negro, every group is now believed capable of advancing under its own steam. Consequently, the old welfarist arguments for government intervention lose some of their force and urgency while the newer problem-solving approach comes to the fore.

❊   ❊   ❊

Will the Partner Stay Junior?

Those Washington officials now busily setting up the programs like to describe the new roles for the federal government with the phrase "junior partner." An easy cynicism, bred of past conditions, is quick to suspect that this junior partner means to enlarge his scope until he takes over the shop. But an examination of the new programs in detail shows this cynicism is misplaced. These programs are so designed that they will work only if the "senior partners"—i.e., elements of the society other than the federal government—continue to grow and innovate vigorously. If that hope is disappointed, the federal "junior partner," instead of increasing his power, will be in trouble with the electorate.

Because the Washington junior partners are aware of this danger, "creative federalism" includes a deliberate policy of encouraging the growth of institutions that will be independent of and, in part, antagonistic to the federal government power. Almost every part of every new program transfers federal funds to some outside agency. Nothing will be achieved if the recipients—universities, state and local educational authorities, hospitals, medical schools, and poverty-program councils—merely become subservient arms directed by the central federal power. Tension between Washington and other independent centers is required by the whole body of experience out of which the notion of "creative federalism" comes.

This way of doing things entered the government by osmosis from corporate management. Big corporations have been getting bigger, but executives are increasingly and justifiably impatient of outside criticism that, using the language of fifty years ago, attacks corporations as "monolithic" concentrations of power in a few hands. From the inside of any great corporation it is obvious that top management spends a great deal of its time trying to enlarge the responsibilities and strengthen the initiative of other power centers within the corporation. Such policies are pursued in the face of certain knowledge that the multiplied and strengthened power centers will develop troublesome tensions with top management and with one another. Top management does not pursue this "polycentric" policy out of altruism or masochism. It does so because the complexity of modern knowledge, reflected in the complexity of organized action, demands that much of the decision making be decentralized.

❊   ❊   ❊

The new patterns first entered Washington at the point where the connection between government, advanced business, and science is most intense— the Defense Department. . . .

Many Great Society programs are marked by an emphasis, similar to that of the Defense Department, on "cost effectiveness". . . .

❊   ❊   ❊

The New Limits Are Practical Ones

It is as true today as it ever was that a free society must be vigilant against concentration of power in a few hands. It is also true that in the twentieth century many national governments, using humanitarian slogans, have tended to squash the sphere of local government and constrict the scope of private organizations and individuals. The U.S.

has not been immune to this trend. Twenty-five years ago state and local government in the U.S. *was* anemic, and predictions—some approving, some despairing—were widely made that the federal political system must be transformed into a unitary national system on the British or French model. Twenty-five years ago the dispersed and competing power centers of private enterprise *were* being cramped by the encroaching power of Washington.

As resistance to this trend developed, the U.S. seemed to be in a struggle between what was politically practical and what was, by traditional interpretation, constitutional. The traditionalists lost ground steadily until it became much harder to see the tidy pigeonholes into which Americans used to separate what was private, what was governmental, what was state, what was federal. Today the scope of federal action cannot be specifically defined by categories (e.g., defense and foreign affairs). The federal government may have a proper function in almost any field of action. This change raises a question: can a central government that has massive roles in business agriculture, schools, health, and even, perhaps, garbage collection truly be described as a "limited" federal government?

The answer, oddly, is yes. The new limits on federal power have been imposed by political practicality. Ironically, the popular hunger for progress that seemed to generate a threat to limited government has come to the rescue of limited government. An electorate that began to expect real results —and would not be fobbed off by such psychological titillations as "soaking the rich"—pressed political leaders toward more effective modes of action. These modes turned out to put a heavy *practical* emphasis on state and local government, on business freedom, on the market as a way of making economic decisions.

*   *   *

. . . In a way that was hardly conceivable twenty-five years ago, U.S. democratic institutions have proved flexible and adaptable and are becoming, once again, the objects of envy and admiration by discerning men in other countries. The American political genius is moving through creative federalism toward new ways of expanding individual choice while maintaining social cohesion.

7

Whistlin' Dixie: Creative Federalism in Action *

JESSIE HILL FORD

Not all who advocate more extensive programs—that is to say, those who disagree with Mr. Moley in the direction that government should take on welfare—share Mr. Ways' admiration for the new creative federalism. They see it as a form by which the states corrupt the purpose of the federal government, but leave the nation to pay the bill. This vignette of a Southern Governors' Conference suggests that the eternal ingratitude of aid recipients is not limited to the area of foreign affairs.

While the governors of the seventeen states represented are heads of state for several million Americans of African descent, there are no Negroes present at the Southern Governors' Conference save for the single instance of a "Jug Band," which will be playing old Southern and ragtime melodies on board the *Belle of Louisville* when she cruises to Kenlake State Park Sunday evening, September 18, for the Old Western Kentucky Barbecue.

Creative Federalism

Demonstrations of "creative Federalism" will be held at the press conferences granted by Governors Faubus of Arkansas, Wallace of Alabama, McKeithen of Louisiana, and others.

"Creative Federalism" is a process by which a Southern governor kicks hell out of the Washington Adminis-

* Jessie Hill Ford, "Whistlin' Dixie," *Atlantic Monthly*, Dec. 1966, pp. 87-88, 90. Copyright © 1966, by The Atlantic Monthly Company, Boston, Mass. 02116. Reprinted by permission of Harold Ober Associates, Inc., and the publisher.

tration with both feet while holding out both hands for federal aid. It is a neat trick calling for acute balance and considerable verbal dexterity. The press will want to attend these demonstrations.

Wallace Demonstrates

"Well, course if they rule against us they rule against us, and we just lost the case in the federal court. I'll say this—uh—that they have picked a panel to try the case in the Fifth Circuit. It's a stacked panel—and the ruling—and the judge who—federal judge —who picks the panels to decide cases involved in *our* state, he picks a panel that he knows will be at least two-to-one against us.

"So I wouldn't doubt but what the decision hasn't already been written because the federal court system [*pounding the desk*] in most instances has its mind made up in advance [*pounding desk*], and I tell you what —people are gettin' tired of federal courts and HEW *trifling* with their children. And in this destroying of the neighborhood school system they're trifling with your chillun and mine. And I say that the federal courts and HEW had better watch out! Because the ultimate law in this country is the people themselves, and not me as a governor, nor the President, nor HEW, nor federal courts!"

A few questions later he struck out again from the springboard of "local control."

"If you don't think local control will improve the quality—what you're saying is that some fellow a thousand miles away with a beard in Washington, and that's what most of 'em got in that department up in HEW. You sayin' that they have more ability to determine what is in the interest of the schoolchildren than do the people who live here in this, uh—uh—section of Kentucky. And I b'lieve the people in this section of Kentucky know better what is in the interest of their children than somebody a thousand miles away—and if they *don't* know, and they're not able to do it, they just oughtta abolish the state of Kentucky, and they just oughtta abolish the local governing body, and they just oughtta abolish the city governing bodies: because in effect you're saying that those in Washington are the only ones that have intelligence enough and integrity enough to do right about schools—and now we got the federal government a thousand miles away, *two* thousand miles away, telling every school board what water fountain they can have over here, where the school can be located, who can ride on what bus, and who can teach—!"

Governor Wallace's tirade continued with references to editorials in the Chicago *Tribune* and then: "The New York *Times* wrote an editorial in their New York *Times* magazine about six months ago about the quality of education deteriorating in New York because of this very thing I'm talking about."

*   *   *

Reporter: "Do you think the federal government ought to withdraw some of the money it's spending in Huntsville, Alabama?"

Visibly affronted and angered, Wallace seemed to swell. He puffed out his chest and angled his dark chin line in the reporter's direction as he replied:

"Well, of course what you're trying to say is that if you don't—er—if you take any federal money which is *taxpayers' money!* And the members of the press ought to emphasize that. IT'S TAXPAYERS' MONEY! It's not federal money. It's not state money. It's not county money. It comes from the pockets of the taxpayers. And just because some area of government puts some money into a location gives them no right then to tell ya who you kin sell-ya house to, or tell ya who you kin employ.

"So, ah, when you are sayin' that if you accept money, uh, in Alabama, which is yore money too—uh—that then you should subject yourself to every whim and caprice and regimentation, then that's—ah, poor government!"

8

*Why Cities Are Turning to Washington for Cash**

MAYOR JEROME CAVANAGH

While state programs have been made more flexible by the federal government, the federal government has also moved to "eliminate the middle man" and deal directly with the cities. Mayor Jerome Cavanagh of Detroit, who has been a spokesman for several major organizations of municipal officials, here explains why the cities view this as a desirable trend in most instances.

Q Mayor Cavanagh, is the Federal Government offering more and more money to the nation's cities?

A Yes. There is an increasing number of tools supplied from Washington that are available to cities.

The poverty program is the most obvious one right now. Then there are such things as job-training programs, public housing—that's one of the older ones—urban renewal. Some cities have participated in Area Redevelopment Administration programs. The Juvenile Delinquency Control Act is another program cities have participated in. There are others that could be mentioned.

I don't want to imply, though, that I think these federal aids to cities are adequate. I think the tools available to help us with our problems are definitely inadequate.

Q How much federal money has Detroit received?

A Since I've been in office—the past

3½ years—the federal aid has amounted to more than 60 million dollars.

Q What is that in relation to your total budget?

A It comes to less than 9 per cent of the total money spent by the city. Almost all the rest is local money.

Q Is it getting so a city can't afford to refuse money from Washington?

A Well, I think a city is very foolish if it does refuse. I feel the money belongs principally to the people from whom it was collected—and that means people in the cities.

Q Will this trend to direct aid for cities alter the traditional relationship of city, State and federal governments?

A It has been changing for years—particularly in the last five or six years—and it is going to be accelerated.

It's a rather new and unique relationship in America—the federal-city relationship. And I say, thank goodness it has happened.

Q Why do you say that?

A Because, traditionally, the States have not exhibited enough concern about the urban areas. In fact, often they have turned their backs on urban problems. That's why this federal-city relationship has developed.

* "Why Cities Are Turning to Washington for Cash," Interview with Mayor Jerome Cavanagh, *U.S. News & World Report*, Aug. 23, 1965, pp. 44-45. Copyright © 1965, U.S. News and World Report, Inc. Reprinted by permission of the publisher.

I'd hate to contemplate the face of America—particularly its cities—had we not had a program such as urban renewal, for example.

The cities are the real unfinished domestic business of this country. Crime, delinquency, dropouts, you name it— these are city problems, and the cities are expected to cope with them. Well, they can't do it alone.

We hear Governors say, "Oh, that's a local problem. That's got to be handled locally."

The sources of local revenue—of a city government's revenue—have been gradually pre-empted by States and by the Federal Government.

So here we have this unique situation in America: the agonizing problems of the cities without those cities being able to do enough about it financially, on their own. There is an almost total lack of interest, lack of help, on the part of the State. Then, along comes the Federal Government and, almost apologetically, gives a little bit of help.

Q How do you mean, apologetically?

A Well, at times, totally unreasonable things are done—for example, the provision for a Governor's veto stuck in the middle of the Poverty Act.

Here is a federal-city program in which the States aren't spending one nickel—and a Governor's-veto provision is stuck into it. I know why it was done, of course. It was done to appease some people in Congress who were concerned, they said, about States' rights.

Q Is there any chance that this federal-to-city trend will result in a real breakdown of the federation of States, and we'll end up with a fully centralized Government where everything is run from Washington?

A No, I don't think so.

You know, the biggest share—the vast percentage—of these programs and the revenues for them are either local or State right now. Only a small percentage, really, is federal. And I'm sure it will continue to be that way.

Q Mayor Cavanagh, is money the overriding reason why the cities have turned to the Federal Government?

A Money and understanding—and by "understanding" I mean this: Federal Governments, both Democratic and Republican, have been much more oriented toward the real problems that exist in this country, and those problems exist in the urban areas. State governments, with their traditionally rural domination, have not shown that same concern.

Voice in Cabinet for Cities—

Q You said earlier these federal programs for cities are still inadequate. What more needs to be done?

A Well, I think the Congress is taking a gigantic step this year with this new Department of Urban Affairs that will give the cities of America a voice at the highest level of Federal Government—right in the Cabinet.

I do feel that most of the urban aids that are enacted by Congress are inadequate. I don't know of one totally adequate program.

Now, I know this puts me in a position of saying, "Money, money, money —that's all we want."

Q Are you saying it's really not that simple?

A The fact of the matter is that the people in this country—principally those who live in cities, and that's where most of us live—want, demand and need help and services.

They want and need better schools, better education, all the things we could talk about. And the only way you provide these things is to spend money on them.

It seems to me that a country that accepts without too much question the expenditure—rightful expenditure—of billions of dollars in a space program ought to accept the expenditure of billions of dollars on the great unfinished task of America, and that is the urban problem.

It's really an urgent problem—how we learn to live with dignity next door to each other on these 40 or 50-foot lots we have, or in an apartment building. We're attempting to learn how to live in space, and this is important. I won't say let us first learn how to live in the cities before we learn how to live in space, but at least let's pay the same kind of attention to both problems. This has a meaning that goes far beyond the United States.

U.S. Aid and Influence

Q Mr. Mayor, to get back to the subject of federal aid for cities, does any pressure go along with this money?

A Very candidly, I have not found any pressure, and I think I've been as active in the federal-city relationship as any mayor in America. Now, there have been suggestions made to us in some programs, but I don't consider that pressure. Others might, but I don't.

You remember there was all this furor a few months ago about the necessity of having poor people participate to the maximum in the administration of the poverty program? Well,

we have never had in this city, directly or indirectly, any suggestions, calls or anything else from the Office of Economic Opportunity in relation to this issue. Maybe it's happened in some sections of the country, I don't know. But it hasn't happened here. I should add that the poor have been involved in Detroit's poverty program.

Q Well, are there cases where local practices are being influenced by Washington because of these programs?

A I'd be less than realistic if I said there isn't some indirect influence on policy and programming. The same is true of State-city relationships.

Q Is this good or bad?

A I consider it a good thing because it so happens that I'm in agreement with the federal administrators, philosophically, on the need for the programs and the approach to the problems.

I have never found any federal administrator, from the Cabinet level on down, who has ever said, directly or indirectly, "The money is available if you do this or that."

To me, the interesting thing about this federal-city relationship is the truly co-operative climate that exists between the two. I know some people decry the federal-city relationship for the very reasons that you're questioning me about "undue influence"—but the cities with which I'm familiar haven't found that to be a fact.

9

Minority Views on S. 1633 *

During his administration, President Kennedy suggested legislation creating a Department of Housing and Urban Affairs, a proposal which became politically controversial and explosive and which was approved only after his death. The following excerpts from the minority views of the Senate Committee dealing with the bill question not only the proposal, but the whole nature of relationships between the nation and the cities.

The introduction of legislation to create a Department of Urban Affairs and Housing carries this Nation toward the dangerous policies of political spending which hits hard at self-reliance. There has been a growing tendency to begin programs which aggressively make larger and larger segments of our population dependent on the federal system, solely on the theory that local government cannot handle these special problems.

* * *

Every pressure group in the nation, looking for federal funds, wants to have its representative crowding to the President's Cabinet table, not to advise and guide him on the problems of government, but to push for special favors for special interests.

The eventual demolition of power and authority of lesser levels of government such as city, county, or state, can be seen in the blueprints and the plans for a department of government which will take over the handling of problems which are, in a large part, entirely local responsibilities. A line of communication will be set up directly from the city mayor's office to the center of the federal government. County commissioners, state legislatures, governors will be ignored since they will be asked to contribute nothing.

It should not be necessary to stress the value of keeping local controls over local problems, but, with the increased tendency to diminish the authority of governors, state legislatures, and other levels of local government, such warnings must be sounded whenever the opportunity arises.

The Advisory Commission on Intergovernmental Relations, in a letter to the chairman of the Government Operations Committee, warned—

. . . the Commission believes that activities of the Federal Government with respect to urban problems should be conducted in such a way as to give free rein and encouragement to the initiative of the States in exercising leadership with respect to the solution of problems involving their political subdivisions.

The representative of the National Association of County Officials said in his testimony—

. . . such a Department may well em-

* Committee on Government Operations, United States Senate, Report No. 879, 87th Cong., 1st Sess. September 6, 1961 (Washington, D.C.: Government Printing Office, 1961), pp. 24-25, 27-28, 30.

power large metropolitan cities to deal directly with the Federal Government, bypassing not only the States, but local communities as well. Those of us at the local government level have grave concern the proposed Department . . . might strengthen the hand of the metropolitan core city to the extent that it would be in a position to dominate, because of its close association with the Federal Government, other local municipalities who operate contiguously to or within the periphery of the core city's metropolitan area.

Enactment of this legislation will not encourage the initiative of states or of cities, but will violate the principles of the federal system, usurp authority vested in state governments, crumble the walls of self-determination, demolish local leadership, and build ever higher the stronghold of central government.

The people who live in the cities of this nation, themselves, should be warned that the espousal of such a cause will eventually demean their own stature in a political sense. If Washington pays the bill, Washington will direct the action. It has been ever thus. We are, more and more, moving toward a directed economy in this country. The theory of those who support more federal intervention is that Washington knows best, works best, pays best, and all lesser segments of government must change, they must reshape their concepts of self-determination, and accept the blueprints of the planners.

More than hopscotching over the state and county governments, this new department can eventually nullify local city government.

A department of government, which will carry out the functions envisioned by the supporters of the plan, will be the most powerful cabinet post, and it will be the most expensive. There is a steady stream of pious protestations in

government that we need to cut down the deficit and the public debt, but we will, in one sweeping gesture, create a goliath which will drain our treasury and which will keep a watchful, police eye on every urban community and its citizens, planning, spending, directing until citizens will not call city hall when streets need repair, or a water main needs replacing, but will notify their congressman to contact the cabinet member handling such problems, seeking repairs and services.

More than losing control over local city government, these citizens of urban areas may find corrupt administrations in certain city governments perpetuated. The attention of Congress should be called to the many scandals currently being aired, which involve the city governments of some of our largest cities, where, as one columnist expressed it, "there is a municipal system that is shoddy, incredibly inefficient, and complacently corrupt." Congress should consider carefully before making federal funds available for the corrupt administrators to dispense for their own political gain.

*   *   *

The assumption by proponents of this legislation is that the majority of our people, because they live in urban areas, have no Cabinet-level representation. The fact is that they are served in a variety of ways by every department of government, including the Department of Agriculture.

The concept of a Department of Urban Affairs applies the principle of creating a department to assist people because of their location and not because of functions which need to be performed in their behalf. In other words, this would be the only department whose services would be denied some people merely on a geographic basis. It does not, as other departments do, have "something in it for everyone."

* * *

Supporters of the bill admit that nearly 70 per cent of our population and nearly 80 per cent of our productive capacity are in urban areas. Further, the areas of needed slum clearance, blight, and other big city problems are in our most populous, and wealthiest states and cities.

Statements before the committee suggested that cities had not yet utilized their own resources to solve their problems and it was pointed out that many cities had failed to continue to use existing programs when information was circulated that a Depart-

ment of Urban Affairs was to be created.

* * *

There have been charges made that cities have been "sitting on their hands," allowing problems to accumulate, or to remain unattended, in order to make a more impressive showing of need.

Surely this subject matter needs more study and consideration than it has thus far received. It is therefore our view that this measure should be rejected.

Respectfully submitted.

JOHN L. MCCLELLAN
KARL E. MUNDT
CARL T. CURTIS
SAM J. ERVIN

10

The Politics of Tax-Sharing *

WILLIAM V. SHANNON

This newspaper article and the following one by John Herbers deal with one of the most widely talked about issues in American federalism today. A surprising coalition of conservatives and liberals have been urging tax-sharing—that is, the provision of funds by the federal government for the states without specifications for its use. The opposition is a different coalition from the one that has prevailed in the past. The disagreement also raises questions about the relationship of the three levels of government to the patterns of conflict and cooperation that might emerge in the future.

It is one of the small ironies of politics that the "Heller Plan" devised by a former chairman of the Council of Economic Advisers in the Kennedy

and Johnson Administrations is well on its way to becoming the chief Republican idea for the Presidential campaign of 1968.

The plan envisages the Federal Government setting aside and distributing to the states each year a small percentage of the Federal individual income-

* William V. Shannon, "The Politics of Tax-Sharing," *New York Times*, Jan. 9, 1967, p. 38. Reprinted by permission of the publisher.

tax base with no strings attached as to how the money would be used. It takes its name from Dr. Walter W. Heller. He first proposed it in a little-noticed speech in 1960, nearly sold it to President Johnson in late 1964 and has now developed it cogently and persuasively as part of his book, "New Dimensions of Political Economy."

Understandably Popular

There is no mystery as to why the plan is popular with governors, regardless of party. On the assumption that the individual income-tax base—the amount reported as net taxable income by all individuals—will reach $300 billion in 1967, the distribution of 1 per cent of it to the states would mean an infusion of $3 billion. On a per capita basis, New York would receive $280 million.

Six days before the 1964 election, the White House in a public statement said the Johnson Administration was giving "intensive study" to fiscal policies that would "strengthen state and local governments."

The very next day Senator Goldwater, in one of the campaign's rare displays of bipartisan agreement, urged that the Federal Government "give back to the states a share of the taxes collected from them."

Several weeks after the election, however, President Johnson told reporters at a background briefing that he was laying aside the plan for the time being. He appeared to be irritated by "leaks" to the press. But two other factors also played a big part in his negative decision.

One was that Mr. President foresaw the possibility that the Vietnam war might swallow up all of the anticipated increase in personal income-tax revenues. That possibility has materialized. No action will be taken on the Heller plan until the war ends.

The other reason was the squall of protest from within the Federal bureaucracy. Agencies which administer Washington's grant-in-aid programs according to strict regulations are dubious about passing large sums of money to the states without any standards or controls. Influential trade unions and liberals in Congress who share this distrust of state governments backed up these bureaucratic objections.

But while the Heller plan has languished within the Administration for the past two years, it has found increasing favor among Republicans. In July 1965 the Ripon Society, a group of young G.O.P. intellectuals, and the Republican Governors' Association joined in issuing a study paper endorsing the idea.

Positive Content

The appeal of the plan for Republicans is easy to understand. They have long been identified with the championing of state and local government and opposition to big government in Washington, but these arguments have become stale and tiresome. Too often, state's rights sound like an excuse for doing nothing. Tax-sharing would revitalize the states by providing fresh revenue. It gives a traditional conservative argument a positive content.

At the same time, as Dr. Heller points out in his book, the Supreme Court's decisions requiring the reapportionment of the legislatures are making the states much more responsive to urban needs. The old Democratic party antipathy to the states as strongholds of rural reactionaries is dying out.

Yet the complexities of revenue sharing are real. It might alter substantially the way in which grant-in-aid programs are administered. Many critics believe that it would, in effect, reward states such as New Jersey that have no income tax and be less fair to states that are doing a responsible job of taxing themselves.

Representative Henry Reuss, Wisconsin Democrat, favors tying revenue sharing to an incentive plan for the modernization of state governments and the wider acceptance of regional government. There have been suggestions for diverting some of the money directly to metropolitan areas rather than to the states. Some favor block grants for broad purposes such as health or education.

For Careful Appraisal

Since these complexities do exist and since the Heller plan—or any Republican variation of it—is not going to be put into effect while the Vietnam war continues, now would seem the time for a careful, detailed appraisal by a study commission. . . .

11

Mayors Oppose U. S. Tax-Sharing with the States *

JOHN HERBERS

WASHINGTON, Feb. 6—A group of Mayors told Congress today they were unalterably opposed to the idea of the Federal Government's sharing its tax revenue with the states.

"Tax sharing is the most dangerous idea in America today," Mayor John F. Collins of Boston told a Senate subcommittee on intergovernmental relations.

Harold Tollefson, Mayor of Tacoma, Wash., president of the National League of Cities, said state governments could not be trusted to respond to urban needs. He spoke for the league.

Last week several governors, including Governor Rockefeller of New York, urged the subcommittee to endorse some plan of sharing tax revenue with the states, which have been bypassed

under many Federal grant-in-aid programs. The Governors said the states were showing new responsibility and initiative in meeting the needs of their citizens and their help was needed to make the Federal system work more efficiently.

Republican leaders in Congress have endorsed the concept of the Federal Government's giving the states a percentage of its revenue and have given the idea top priority in the Republican legislative program. A number of Democrats have also introduced tax-sharing bills, in an effort to strengthen the states and decentralize some domestic services.

Confusion on All Levels

The subcommittee is investigating the confusion, inefficiency and delay that have obtained on all levels of the Federal system in the administration

---

* John Herbers, *New York Times,* Feb. 7, 1967, p. 1. Reprinted by permission of the publisher.

of grants, which this year will total about $15-billion.

Senator Edmund S. Muskie, Democrat of Maine, the chairman, said before hearing from the Mayors that he was "encouraged by the optimism of the Governors."

"They are trying to generate new life into this level of government, and I want to support them in this endeavor," Mr. Muskie, a former Governor, said. "But they still need legislative and constitutional reform, and they have a long way to go to establish their own leadership over the planning and administration of state programs."

Until they do, Mr. Muskie said, the Federal Government must continue to "fill the void and provide more direct assistance to local communities." He added that "the most important domestic problem today is the deterioration of our central cities."

Mayor Collins said that if the states were given Federal grants with no strings attached, as some of the bills in Congress prescribe, the money would stop at the statehouses.

"The sooner we get away from this and back to the idea of block grants [for specific programs] the better," Mr. Collins said.

Suburbs Criticized

Mr. Tollefson said cities would welcome help from the states but "the past leaves too many doubts."

"In those cases where programs are channeled through the states, we believe provisions should be made for local escape or appeal," he said.

Suburban communities also came in for criticism. Senator Muskie said that between urban deterioration and rural blight "there are the affluent suburban and exurban dwellers who seem to have forgotten that the other half of America needs help."

"Suburbanites," Mayor Collins said, "come into the city every day, make their living, then go home to a couple of acres of land, drink a couple of martinis and chuckle over urban problems.". . .

12

The Political Side of Urban Development: Fragmentation *

SCOTT GREER and DAVID W. MINAR

Theories and ideology are one thing, practice another. In this study of the urban development program two authorities on the problems of metropolitan life attempt to assay the consequences of our political arrangements upon a particular program. As they indicate, divided responsibility does not always maximize efficiency.

The oldest and most fixed dimension of fragmentation is that created by the

federal system, written deep into the American political culture and into

* Scott Greer and David W. Minar, "The Political Side of Urban Development and Redevelopment," *Annals of the American* *Academy of Political and Social Science,* March, 1964, pp. 63-67. Reprinted by permission of the authors and publisher.

the nation's constitutional ground rules. Its division of effective operating powers has always been a source of some difficulty, but, with the extension of scale, it has been even more a strait jacket on the processes of political response to social change. Urban problems have become national problems, and metropolitan social space has flowed over all sorts of geographic confinements. Still, the federal system is such that nation, states, and local governments remain as often rival and to some extent independent centers of problem identification and policy-making.

*   *   *

A second type of fragmentation with similar consequences is that produced by the multiplication of local units of government, particularly evident in the metropolitan area. It takes no special knowledge to realize that the metropolis does not even fit together like a complicated jigsaw puzzle. It is nothing so rational. The very title of Robert Wood's study of government in the New York area, *1400 Governments,* tells a good part of the story of the condition of that metropolitan scene. The spot on which this article is written falls within nine governmental jurisdictions from the county level down. The Chicago standard metropolitan area has nearly a thousand such units. And this picture is duplicated not only in the great centers of population but in most of the smaller ones as well.

Here again the consequences have to do with abilities for action. . . . Tradition ties action programs to the legal structures of municipalities while problems overrun jurisdictional boundaries. Supplies of leadership and revenue are distributed differently from the stock of urban problems, such as standard housing, crime, and intergroup tensions. Most often, the

problems of physical and social decay are seen as the central city's problems, and, even when their broader implications are understood long-standing legal and ideological boundaries prohibit all but the most feeble of broad-scale remedies. In many places the division of jurisdiction is not only spatial but also functional so that education and recreation and transit and sewage disposal and a host of other aspects of the urban development picture are charged to distinct units of government. Whatever the particular picture for a metropolitan area, its main blank spots are similar: no co-ordination, no power, no responsibility.

*   *   *

The present urban-renewal program is, historically, one of our most ambitious efforts to intervene with public power in community development. With its goals of decent housing for all American families, central business district redevelopment, and comprehensive planning for the metropolis, it is a radical program of urban reform. The logic of the program is simple. The police power is used to enforce housing codes, bringing the existing stock up to standard and destroying what cannot be profitably made standard; on the cleared land resulting, new development will replace the lost units.

The true shape of the program, as it works out in the hundreds of participating cities, is something again.

*   *   *

Although the urban-renewal program can acquire land, by negotiation or eminent domain, displace the present owners and users and destroy existing structures, it cannot build any buildings except public facilities on the cleared land. Thus it is completely dependent upon the private market in real estate for its "renewal" effects.

This means that the local public authority must either gamble on its knowledge of the private land market or prenegotiate sales. In either event, renewal occurs not where it might benefit the community directly but where it must do so indirectly through benefiting the private investors. . . .

Urban renewal is also committed to the government of the local municipality. Because action can be taken only through a local public authority, it must be underwritten in terms of political and fiscal responsibility by the city government. While the federal agency has a veto power on the city's program, the city in turn may refuse to co-operate with the agency. Thus, many of the politically unpalatable aspects of the working program are honored in the breach: housing codes are enforced selectively or not at all, the local contribution in the shape of school buildings, street paving, and the like may be far out of phase with the urban-renewal efforts to improve neighborhoods, and a sudden revolt of the voters through referendum, initiative, or recall may throw out the entire program—in Springfield, Oregon, all three deities of the secular trinity were invoked: the referendum necessary to the program was lost, the housing code was repealed through initiative, and proponents of urban renewal in the city council had to face a recall election. Under the circumstances, the federal agency is notably chary about too rigid insistence upon the letter of the law.

Many federal programs other than urban renewal have massive impacts on most of the cities where urban-renewal efforts are being made. Co-ordination among the federal agencies affecting a given city is almost nil; this may result from the use of the state as a middleman, as in the case of the federal highway program, or it may result from simple lack of concern, as in the

hiatus between the administration of Federal Housing Administration (FHA) mortgage insurance and the planners of urban renewal. In any event, urban renewal may be at the mercy of powerful federal agencies over which it has no control. The federal highway program may site a cloverleaf in the middle of the urban-renewal area, may displace thousands of householders and completely disrupt the urban-renewal relocation operations, and may hold up the sale of urban-renewal land for months while officials decide where excess ramps should go. Meanwhile FHA may co-operate with the highway program in stimulating dispersion to the suburbs while urban renewal struggles to revivify the central city.

At the metropolitan level, the multitude of jurisdictions—cities, towns, suburbs, special districts, counties, even states—makes any over-all planning of the city a farce. Weak as most planning commissions are in effecting development and redevelopment, their power is further curtailed by city boundaries; few of them exercise jurisdiction outside the municipality. And because there is no other local municipal body with power to underwrite the program, urban renewal is similarly limited—usually to a central city and separately, one or two larger suburbs. . . . Yet the governmental log jam at the local level, preventing *metropolitan* planning and development, results in serious distortions of the program. The central city-suburb schisms turn urban renewal into a holy war to recapture the suburban, white, middle class—a war the central city is doomed to lose—and distract attention from the major clientele of the central city: the working class, the ethnics, the disprivileged.

Thus, the implications of these various divisions of power for urban development and redevelopment are basic: they produce the dilemmas of the programs. Destructive as they seem to those committed to changing the shape of our cities, they are per-fectly understandable in view of the political culture of Americans as it is now translated, through governmental structure, into the local polity.

13

The Federal System: Overcoming Fragmentation *

MORTON GRODZINS

This provocative reinterpretation of our federal past by Morton Grodzins suggests that there has been rather more continuity in the American system than is usually assumed. It also points to an optimistic prediction of the future of American federalism.

The Sharing of Functions

The American form of government is often, but erroneously, symbolized by a three-layer cake. A far more accurate image is the rainbow or marble cake, characterized by an inseparable mingling of differently colored ingredients, the colors appearing in vertical and diagonal strands and unexpected whirls. As colors are mixed in the marble cake, so functions are mixed in the American federal system. Consider the health officer, styled "sanitarian," of a rural county in a border state. He embodies the whole idea of the marble cake of government.

The sanitarian is appointed by the state under merit standards established by the federal government. His base salary comes jointly from state and federal funds, the county provides him with an office and office amenities

* President's Commitee on National Goals, *Goals for Americans* (Englewood Cliffs, N.J.: Prentice-Hall, Inc., 1960), pp. 265-66, 268-9, 271-78, 280-81. Reprinted by permission of the publisher.

and pays a portion of his expenses, and the largest city in the county also contributes to his salary and office by virtue of his appointment as a city plumbing inspector. It is impossible from moment to moment to tell under which governmental hat the sanitarian operates. His work of inspecting the purity of food is carried out under federal standards; but he is enforcing state laws when inspecting commodities that have not been in interstate commerce; and somewhat perversely he also acts under state authority when inspecting milk coming into the county from producing areas across the state border. He is a federal officer when impounding impure drugs shipped from a neighboring state; a federal-state officer when distributing typhoid immunization serum; a state officer when enforcing standards of industrial hygiene; a state-local officer when inspecting the city's water supply; and (to complete the circle) a local officer when insisting that the city butchers adopt more hygienic methods of handling their garbage. But he cannot and does not think of himself as acting in these separate capacities. All business in the county that concerns public health and sanitation he considers his business. Paid largely from federal funds, he does not find it strange to attend meetings of the city council to give expert advice on matters ranging from rotten apples to rabies control. He is even deputized as a member of both the city and county police forces.

The sanitarian is an extreme case, but he accurately represents an important aspect of the whole range of governmental activities in the United States. Functions are not neatly parceled out among the many governments. They are shared functions. It is difficult to find any governmental activity which does not involve all three of the so-called "levels" of the federal system. In the most local of local functions—law enforcement or education, for example—the federal and state governments play important roles. In what, a priori, may be considered the purest central government activities—the conduct of foreign affairs, for example—the state and local governments have considerable responsibilities, directly and indirectly.

❖   ❖   ❖

A Point of History

The American federal system has never been a system of separated governmental activities. There has never been a time when it was possible to put neat labels on discrete "federal," "state," and "local" functions. Even before the Constitution, a statute of 1785, reinforced by the Northwest Ordinance of 1787, gave grants-in-land to the states for public schools. Thus the national government was a prime force in making possible what is now taken to be the most local function of all, pri-

mary and secondary education. More important, the nation, before it was fully organized, established by this action a first principle of American federalism: the national government would use its superior resources to initiate and support national programs, principally administered by the states and localities.

The essential unity of state and federal financial systems was again recognized in the earliest constitutional days with the assumption by the federal government of the Revolutionary War debts of the states. Other points of federal-state collaboration during the Federalist period concerned the militia, law enforcement, court practices, the administration of elections, public health measures, pilot laws, and many other matters.

The nineteenth century is widely believed to have been the pre-eminent period of duality in the American system. Lord Bryce at the end of the century described (in *The American Commonwealth*) the federal and state governments as "distinct and separate in their action." The system, he said, was "like a great factory wherein two sets of machinery are at work, their revolving wheels apparently intermixed, their bands crossing one another, yet each set doing its own work without touching or hampering the other." Great works may contain gross errors. Bryce was wrong. The nineteenth century, like the early days of the republic, was a period principally characterized by intergovernmental collaboration.

❖   ❖   ❖

A long, extensive, and continuous experience is therefore the foundation of the present system of shared functions characteristic of the American federal system, what we have called the marble cake of government. It is a misjudgment of our history and our present situation to believe that a neat separation of governmental functions could take place without drastic alterations in our society and system of government.

＊　　＊　　＊

The constitutional restraints on the expansion of national authority are less important and less direct today than they were in 1879 or in 1936. But to say that they are less important is not to say that they are unimportant.

The nation's politics reflect these decentralizing causes and add some of their own. The political parties of the United States are unique. They seldom perform the function that parties traditionally perform in other countries, the function of gathering together diverse strands of power and welding them into one. Except during the period of nominating and electing a president and for the essential but nonsubstantive business of organizing the houses of Congress, the American parties rarely coalesce power at all. Characteristically they do the reverse, serving as a canopy under which special and local interests are represented with little regard for anything that can be called a party program. National leaders are elected on a party ticket, but in Congress they must seek crossparty support if their leadership is to be effective. It is a rare president during rare periods who can produce legislation without facing the defection of substantial numbers of his own party. (Wilson could do this in the first session of the 63rd Congress; but Franklin D. Roosevelt could not, even during the famous hundred days of 1933.) Presidents whose parties form the majority of the congressional houses must still count heavily on support from the other party.

The parties provide the pivot on which the entire governmental system swings. Party operations, first of all,

produce in legislation the basic division of functions between the federal government, on the one hand, and state and local governments, on the other. The Supreme Court's permissiveness with respect to the expansion of national powers has not in fact produced any considerable extension of exclusive federal functions. The body of federal law in all fields has remained, in the words of Henry M. Hart, Jr. and Herbert Wechsler, "interstitial in its nature," limited in objective and resting upon the principal body of legal relationships defined by state law. It is difficult to find any area of federal legislation that is not significantly affected by state law.

In areas of new or enlarged federal activity, legislation characteristically provides important roles for state and local governments. This is as true of Democratic as of Republican administrations and true even of functions for which arguments of efficiency would produce exclusive federal responsibility. Thus the unemployment compensation program of the New Deal and the airport program of President Truman's administration both provided important responsibilities for state governments. In both cases attempts to eliminate state participation were defeated by a crossparty coalition of pro-state votes and influence. A large fraction of the Senate is usually made up of exgovernors, and the membership of both houses is composed of men who know that their reelection depends less upon national leaders or national party organization than upon support from their home constituencies. State and local officials are key members of these constituencies, often central figures in selecting candidates and in turning out the vote. Under such circumstances, national legislation taking state and local views heavily into account is inevitable.

Second, the undisciplined parties affect the character of the federal system as a result of senatorial and congressional interference in federal administrative programs on behalf of local interests. Many aspects of the legislative involvement in administrative affairs are formalized. The Legislative Reorganization Act of 1946, to take only one example, provided that each of the standing committees "shall exercise continuous watchfulness" over administration of laws within its jurisdiction. But the formal system of controls, extensive as it is, does not compare in importance with the informal and extralegal network of relationships in producing continuous legislative involvement in administrative affairs.

Senators and congressmen spend a major fraction of their time representing problems of their constituents before administrative agencies. An even larger fraction of congressional staff time is devoted to the same task. The total magnitude of such "case work" operations is great. In one five-month period of 1943 the Office of Price Administration received a weekly average of 842 letters from members of Congress. If phone calls and personal contacts are added, each member of Congress on the average presented the OPA with a problem involving one of his constituents twice a day in each five-day work week. Data for less vulnerable agencies during less intensive periods are also impressive. In 1958, to take only one example, the Department of Agriculture estimated (and underestimated) that it received an average of 159 congressional letters per working day. Special congressional liaison staffs have been created to service this mass of business, though all higher officials meet it in one form or another. The Air Force in 1958 had, under the command of a major general, 137 people (55 officers and 82 civilians) working in its liaison office.

The widespread, consistent, and in many ways unpredictable character of legislative interference in administrative affairs has many consequences for the tone and character of American administrative behavior. From the perspective of this paper, the important consequence is the comprehensive, day-to-day, even hour-by-hour impact of local views on national programs. No point of substance or procedure is immune from congressional scrutiny. A substantial portion of the entire weight of this impact is on behalf of the state and local governments. It is a weight that can alter procedures for screening immigration applications, diverting the course of a national highway, changing the tone of an international negotiation, and amending a social security law to accommodate local practices or fulfil local desires.

The party system compels administrators to take a political role. This is a third way in which the parties function to decentralize the American system. The administrator must play politics for the same reason that the politician is able to play in administration: the parties are without program and without discipline.

In response to the unprotected position in which the party situation places him, the administrator is forced to seek support where he can find it. One ever-present task is to nurse the Congress of the United States, that crucial constituency which ultimately controls his agency's budget and program. From the administrator's view, a sympathetic consideration of congressional requests (if not downright submission to them) is the surest way to build the political support without which the administrative job could not continue. Even the completely task-oriented administrator must be sensitive to the need for congressional support and to the relationship between case work requests, on one side, and budgetary and legislative support, on the other. "You do a good job handling the personal problems and requests of a Congressman," a White House officer said, "and you have an easier time convincing him to back your program." Thus there is an important link between the nursing of congressional requests, requests that largely concern local matters, and the most comprehensive national programs. The administrator must accommodate to the former as a price of gaining support for the latter.

One result of administrative politics is that the administrative agency may become the captive of the nation-wide interest group it serves or presumably regulates. In such cases no government may come out with effective authority: the winners are the interest groups themselves. But in a very large number of cases, states and localities also win influence. The politics of administration is a process of making peace with legislators who for the most part consider themselves the guardians of local interests. The political role of administrators therefore contributes to the power of states and localities in national programs.

Finally, the way the party system operates gives American politics their over-all distinctive tone. The lack of party discipline produces an openness in the system that allows individuals, groups, and institutions (including state and local governments) to attempt to influence national policy at every step of the legislative-administrative process. This is the "multiple-crack" attribute of the American government. "Crack" has two meanings. It means not only many fissures or access points; it also means, less statically, opportunities for wallops or smacks at government.

If the parties were more disciplined, the result would not be a cessation of the process by which individuals and groups impinge themselves upon the central government. But the present state of the parties clearly allows for a far greater operation of the multiple crack than would be possible under the conditions of centralized party control. American interest groups exploit literally uncountable access points in the legislative-administrative process. If legislative lobbying, from committee stages to the conference committee, does not produce results, a cabinet secretary is called. His immediate associates are petitioned. Bureau chiefs and their aides are hit. Field officers are put under pressure. Campaigns are instituted by which friends of the agency apply a secondary influence on behalf of the interested party. A conference with the President may be urged.

To these multiple points for bringing influence must be added the multiple voices of the influences. Consider, for example, those in a small town who wish to have a federal action taken. The easy merging of public and private interest at the local level means that the influence attempt is made in the name of the whole community, thus removing it from political partisanship. The Rotary Club as well as the City Council, the Chamber of Commerce and the mayor, eminent citizens and political bosses—all are readily enlisted. If a conference in a senator's office will expedite matters, someone on the local scene can be found to make such a conference possible and effective. If technical information is needed, technicians will supply it. State or national professional organizations of local officials, individual congressmen and senators, and not infrequently whole state delegations will make the local cause their own. Federal field officers, who service localities, often assume local views. So may elected and appointed state officers. Friendships are exploited, and political mortgages called due. Under these circumstances, national policies are molded by local action.

In summary, then, the party system functions to devolve power. The American parties, unlike any other, are highly responsive when directives move from the bottom to the top, highly unresponsive from top to bottom. Congressmen and senators can rarely ignore concerted demands from their home constituencies; but no party leader can expect the same kind of response from those below, whether he be a President asking for congressional support or a congressman seeking aid from local or state leaders.

❉   ❉   ❉

In a governmental system of genuinely shared responsibilities, disagreements inevitably occur. Opinions clash over proximate ends, particular ways of doing things become the subject of public debate, innovations are contested. These are not basic defects in the system. Rather, they are the system's energy-reflecting life blood. There can be no permanent "solutions" short of changing the system itself by elevating one partner to absolute supremacy. What can be done is to attempt to produce conditions in which conflict will not fester but be turned to constructive solutions of particular problems.

A long list of specific points of difficulty in the federal system can be easily identified. No adequate congressional or administrative mechanism exists to review the patchwork of grants in terms of national needs. There is no procedure by which to judge, for example, whether the national government is justified in spending so much more for highways than for education. The working force in some states is inadequate for the effec-

tive performance of some nation-wide programs, while honest and not-so-honest graft frustrates efficiency in others. Some federal aid programs distort state budgets, and some are so closely supervised as to impede state action in meeting local needs. Grants are given for programs too narrowly defined, and over-all programs at the state level consequently suffer. Administrative, accounting and auditing difficulties are the consequence of the multiplicity of grant programs. City officials complain that the states are intrusive fifth wheels in housing, urban redevelopment, and airport building programs.

❉   ❉   ❉

The geography of state boundaries as well as many aspects of state internal organization, are the products of history and cannot be justified on any grounds of rational efficiency. Who, today, would create major governmental subdivisions the size of Maryland, Delaware, New Jersey, or Rhode Island? Who would write into Oklahoma's fundamental law an absolute state debt limit of $500,000? Who would design (to cite only the most extreme cases) Georgia's and Florida's gross underrepresentation of urban areas in both houses of the legislature?

A complete catalogue of state political and administrative horrors would fill a sizeable volume. Yet exhortations to erase them have roughly the same effect as similar exhortations to erase sin. Some of the worst inanities—for example, the boundaries of the states themselves—are fixed in the national constitution and defy alteration for all foreseeable time. Others, such as urban underrepresentation in state legislatures, serve the overrepresented groups, including some urban ones, and the effective political organizatio of the deprived groups must precede reform.

Despite deficiencies of politics and organizations that are unchangeable or slowly changing, it is an error to look at the states as static anachronisms. Some of them—New York, Minnesota, and California, to take three examples spanning the country—have administrative organizations that compare favorably in many ways with the national establishment. Many more in recent years have moved rapidly towards integrated administrative departments, state-wide budgeting, and central leadership. The others have models-in-existence to follow, and active professional organizations (led by the Council of State Governments) promoting their development. Slow as this change may be, the states move in the direction of greater internal effectiveness.

The pace toward more effective performance at the state level is likely to increase. Urban leaders, who generally feel themselves disadvantaged in state affairs, and suburban and rural spokesmen, who are most concerned about national centralization, have a common interest in this task. The urban dwellers want greater equality in state affairs, including a more equitable share of state financial aid; nonurban dwellers are concerned that city dissatisfactions should not be met by exclusive federal, or federal-local, programs. Antagonistic, rather than amiable, cooperation may be the consequence. But it is a cooperation that can be turned to politically effective measures for a desirable upgrading of state institutions.

If one looks closely, there is scant evidence for the fear of the federal octopus, the fear that expansion of central programs and influence threatens to reduce the states and localities to compliant administrative arms of the central government. In fact, state and local governments are touching a larger proportion of the people in more ways than ever before; and they are spending a higher fraction of the total national product than ever before. Federal programs have increased, rather than diminished, the importance of the governors; stimulated professionalism in state agencies; increased citizen interest and participation in government; and, generally, enlarged and made more effective the scope of state action.[1] It may no longer be true in any significant sense that the states and localities are "closer" than the federal government to the people. It is true that the smaller governments remain active and powerful members of the federal system.

*   *   *

The American federal system exhibits many evidences of the dispersion of power not only because of formal federalism but more importantly because our politics reflect and reinforce the nation's diversities-within-unity. Those who value the virtues of decentralization, which writ large are virtues of freedom, need not scruple at recognizing the defects of those virtues. The defects are principally the danger that parochial and private interests may not coincide with, or give way to, the nation's interest. The necessary cure for these defects is effective national leadership.

The centrifugal force of domestic politics needs to be balanced by the centripetal force of strong presidential

[1] See the valuable report, *The Impact of Federal Grants-in-Aid on the Structure and Functions of State and Local Governments*, submitted to the Commission on Intergovernmental Relations by the Governmental Affairs Institute (Washington, D.C.: Government Printing Office, 1955).

leadership. Simultaneous strength at center and periphery exhibits the American system at its best, if also at its noisiest. The interests of both find effective spokesmen. States and localities (and private interest groups) do not lose their influence opportunities, but national policy becomes more than the simple consequence of successful, momentary concentrations of nonnational pressures: it is guided by national leaders.[2]

[2] Messrs. Perkins and Redford state:
Professor Grodzins has made a significant contribution. The federal system has contributed to a "mild chaos" both administratively and financially. He accurately assesses the several quite futile attempts to disentangle the administrative and fiscal relationships of the states and the national government. . . .

CHAPTER FIVE

Civil Liberties:
The Bill of Rights

"All declare for liberty," former Justice Reed once suggested, "and proceed to disagree among themselves as to its true meaning." Americans assume that he legacy of the Constitution not only assures freedom but solves all problems with regard to their interpretation as well. But each day presents new problems in the field of human freedom. Reconciling liberty and authority, freedom and rder, and the rights of the individual with the needs of the community are continuous and demanding tasks.

History helps in understanding some of our civil liberties problems, but no mount of historical knowledge will completely solve such questions as how to reat our giant new mass media—movies, radio, television. Traditional notions f freedom of the press have to be adjusted to deal with these new resources. National defense and national security in the modern world present problems ifferent at the very least in size and scope from the situations of 1789.

In this chapter we shall try to approach some of the basic questions in civil berties. This is an area with many ramifications and where events change apidly, and only highlights can be discussed. The rapid pace of developments in this area means that the treatment and even the terms used in discussing ivil liberties are not as standardized as those used in some of the other areas f American government. We discuss the issues under three major headings.

How Free Can We Be Without Chaos?

First we will consider political rights and the rights of expression and association. These rights are, in a very real sense, basic to the democratic system. But not everything done in the name of these freedoms can be allowed. "The most stringent protection of civil liberties," wrote Justice Holmes, "could not protect a man in falsely shouting 'Fire!' in a crowded theatre." But how do we divide what is to be protected from that which should be regulated? Drawing the line in practice has been one of the most difficult problems of our times —and the issues of communism and subversion have made the public, philosophers, and judges think hard and long, and yet end up in sharp disagreement.

A second category—almost equally debated—concerns the rights of the individual in his individuality—his right to privacy, to individual opinions, procedural rights in criminal trials and religious freedom. In a society that pushes people together into giant cities and involves each with the other to an increasing degree, the problem gets greater year by year. It is because conformity is the easy way to get along in an organized society that the need for individual rights is so great. But not every claim can be recognized.

Finally, there is the problem of the treatment of individuals and groups by the government—the problem of equal protection of the laws. This question of equality under the law also blends into the problem of equality through the law and the responsibility by government for the maintenance of equality.

In short, American democracy has to face the problem of maintaining its freedom in a cold war situation hostile to liberty. At the same time, we must face the problem of adjusting liberty to modern conditions and of creating and establishing new rights where changing conditions and the conscience of the community demands them.

The Right to Be Let Alone Versus the Need to Organize Society

In the novel *1984*, George Orwell paints a startling picture of life in a society where almost every move is spied upon and controlled by the government. Readers have found this more blood-curdling and terrifying a story than many a thriller. Instinctively we all feel that there is some corner of our world that is our own and should be untouched by other humans. In recent years an "activist" Court has attempted to protect such individuality. To a large extent this has resulted in a race between the effectiveness of legal procedures and the developments of modern technology. With the perfection of "snooping devices" and methods of recording and analyzing, it is hard to say that technology has been losing any ground.

Another issue that has plagued society through history and over which wars have been fought is the problem of separation of church and state. American society has emphasized the essentially secular nature of the government and has left religion largely to operate in its own sphere. But, the talk of a "wall of separation" between church and state is partly belied by our insistence upon religious ceremonies in connection with government on the one hand, and governmental support, at least indirectly, on the other. We exempt churches from taxation, and we have chaplains in the army. In recent years, the line of separation has become fuzzy in the area of education. On the one hand, claims have been pressed for aid to parochial schools on the grounds that it is discriminatory not to help children in religious schools get an education through public funds. At the same time, the argument is advanced as to whether religious education should be allowed in the schools at all. The Supreme Court has taken the position that a state may not hold religious instruction on school grounds, or require ceremonial prayers, but may release children to go to religious instruction on school time. A number of such questions have caused court rulings and public controversy.

Negroes and Whites: The Challenge of Equal Protection of the Laws

It may not be literally true that "one-half of the Constitution is to be found in the Commerce Clause and the other half in the Fourteenth Amendment." Still, a good deal of constitutional litigation and questions of power have centered around these two provisions. Particularly in recent years, the Fourteenth Amendment has come into its own.

Among the provisions of that post-Civil War-Reconstruction amendment is the prohibition that "nor shall any State . . . deny to any person within its jurisdiction the equal protection of the laws." As with some other parts of the Fourteenth Amendment, the language is not self-explanatory. In 1896 the Supreme Court, in the well-known case of *Plessy v. Ferguson,* held that laws requiring Negroes to board separate cars of a railroad train did not violate this provision so long as the accommodations were "equal but separate." The majority opinion held that there was no implication of inferiority in such segregation, although Justice John Marshall Harlan of Kentucky questioned this argument, insisting that the Constitution was "colorblind," and that the "thin disguise of separate accommodations will fool no one nor atone for the wrong this day done."

The reasoning of the majority in *Plessy v. Ferguson* was dominant in the upholding of most segregation laws in the early part of the century. However, in 1923 zoning laws requiring Negroes to live in separate sections of towns were declared unconstitutional. Beginning in 1937 a series of cases undermined the principle of "separate but equal" in the field of graduate education. Finally, in 1954, the Supreme Court ruled that "in the field of education 'separate but equal' has no place." The Court called for progress with "deliberate speed." Since that time slow and painful progress has been made toward school integration in every state which formerly had segregation. In some instances this has involved only a handful of Negro students in a whole state, a process of token integration.

Recently, however, the issue of southern school integration has receded to the background. Jobs, housing, and personal respect for the Negro as an individual have now come to the fore. These issues are necessarily raised in the North as well as the South, and have aroused more controversy as the demands involve changes next door rather than in another section of the country.

In this new atmosphere the tactics of the civil rights leaders have remained relatively static, involving mass demonstrations and the like. Some argue that such tactics were appropriate in demanding basic rights of participation in a situation in the South where the Negro was denied effective political power, and inappropriate where the political process is, in fact, open. Not only the goals but also the tactics of the civil rights movement have therefore aroused controversy, and some of its adherents are now its questioners. Only time will tell whether this is a temporary phenomenon leading to renewed progress or a permanent and perhaps disastrous reversal.

1

Free Speech and Free Government *

ALEXANDER MEIKLEJOHN

Probably the strongest defense of free speech is that made by a little book of about 100 pages by one of the most respected of American philosophers and educators, a man known for maintaining the courage of his convictions where personal sacrifice was involved. Professor Meiklejohn maintains that all speech in the public domain, without exception, is to be allowed and actions alone proscribed. This he sees not as an individual right, a privilege owed by the community to a citizen, but rather as a social right. When we allow an idea to be expressed we are benefiting ourselves and not the expresser. In recent years Justice Black has openly come about to a similar form of "absolute" free speech, arguing even that libel laws are unconstitutional.

. . . What do we mean when we say that "Congress shall make no law . . . abridging the freedom of speech . . .?" . . .Are we, for example, required by the First Amendment to give men freedom to advocate the abolition of the First Amendment? Are we bound to grant freedom of speech to those who, if they had the power, would re-

fuse it to us? The First Amendment, taken literally, seems to answer, "Yes," to those questions. It seems to say that no speech, however dangerous, may, for that reason, be suppressed. But the Federal Bureau of Investigation, the un-American Activities Committee, the Department of Justice, the President, are, at the same time, answering "No" to the same question. Which answer is right? What is the valid American doctrine concerning the freedom of speech? . . .

. . . Here . . . the town meeting suggests an answer. That meeting is

* Alexander Meiklejohn, *Free Speech and Its Relation to Self-Government* (New York: Harper and Row, Publishers, 1948), pp. vi-xii, 24-27, 49-50. Copyright 1948 by Harper and Row, Publishers, Incorporated. Reprinted by permission of the publisher.

called to discuss and, on the basis of such discussion, to decide matters of public policy. For example: Shall there be a school? Where shall it be located? Who shall teach? What shall be taught? The community has agreed that such questions as these shall be freely discussed and that, when the discussion is ended, decision upon them will be made by vote of the citizens. Now, in that method of political self-government, the point of ultimate interest is not the words of the speakers, but the minds of the hearers. The final aim of the meeting is the voting of wise decisions. The voters, therefore, must be made as wise as possible. The welfare of the community requires that those who decide issues shall understand them. They must know what they are voting about. . . .

The First Amendment, then, is not the guardian of unregulated talkativeness. It does not require that, on every occasion, every citizen shall take part in public debate. Nor can it even give assurance that everyone shall have opportunity to do so. If, for example, at a town meeting, twenty like-minded citizens have become a "party," and if one of them has read to the meeting an argument which they have all approved, it would be ludicrously out of order for each of the others to insist on reading it again. No competent moderator would tolerate that wasting of the time available for free discussion. What is essential is not that everyone shall speak, but that everything worth saying shall be said. To this end, for example, it may be arranged that each of the known conflicting points of view shall have, and shall be limited to, an assigned share of the time available. But however it be arranged, the vital point, as stated negatively, is that no suggestion of policy shall be denied a hearing because it is on one side of the issue rather than another. . . . When men govern themselves, it is they—and

no one else—who must pass judgment upon unwisdom and unfairness and danger. And that means that unwise ideas must have a hearing as well as wise ones, unfair as well as fair, dangerous as well as safe, un-American as well as American. Just so far as, at any point, the citizens who are to decide an issue are denied acquaintance with information or opinion or doubt or disbelief or criticism which is relevant to that issue, just so far the result must be ill-considered, ill-balanced planning for the general good. *It is that mutilation of the thinking process of the community against which the First Amendment to the Constitution is directed. . . .*

If, then, on any occasion in the United States it is allowable to say that the Constitution is a good document it is equally allowable, in that situation, to say that the Constitution is a bad document. If a public building may be used in which to say, in time of war, that the war is justified, then the same building may be used in which to say that it is not justified. If it be publicly argued that conscription for armed service is moral and necessary, it may likewise be publicly argued that it is immoral and unnecessary. If it may be said that American political institutions are superior to those of England or Russia or Germany, it may, with equal freedom, be said that those of England or Russia or Germany are superior to ours. These conflicting views may be expressed, must be expressed, not because they are valid, but because they are relevant. If they are responsibly entertained by anyone, we, the voters, need to hear them. When a question of policy is "before the house," free men choose to meet it not with their eyes shut, but with their eyes open. To be afraid of ideas, any idea, is to be unfit for self-government. . . .

. . . Holmes' . . . formula tells us that

whenever the expression of a minority opinion involves clear and present danger to the public safety it may be denied the protection of the First Amendment. And that means that whenever crucial and dangerous issues have come upon the nation, free and unhindered discussion of them must stop. . . . Under that ruling, dissenting judges might, in "dangerous" situations, be forbidden to record their dissents. Minority citizens might, in like situations, be required to hold their peace. No one, of course, believes that this is what Mr. Holmes or the court intended to say. But it is what, in plain words, they did say. The "clear and present danger" opinion stands on the record of the court as a peculiarly inept and unsuccessful attempt to formulate an exception to the principle of the freedom of speech. . . .

2

Heresy, Yes: Conspiracy, No *

SIDNEY HOOK

Here we have a statement by a leading anti-Communist philosopher, himself a great admirer of civil liberties, who condemns what he regards as soft-headed thinking among many defenders of these liberties. He distinguishes between freedom in the realm of ideas and the menace of the conspiratorial element in Communism.

The failure to recognize the distinction between heresy and conspiracy is fatal to a liberal civilization, for the inescapable consequence of their identification is either self-destruction, when heresies are punished as conspiracies, or destruction at the hands of their enemies, when conspiracies are tolerated as heresies.

A heresy is a set of unpopular ideas or opinions on matters of grave concern to the community. The right to profess publicly a heresy of any character, on any theme, is an essential ele-

* Sidney Hook, *Heresy, Yes: Conspiracy, No* (New York: The John Day Company, Inc., 1953), pp. 21-22, 25-26, 30, 32. © 1953 by Sidney Hook. Reprinted and adapted by permission of the author.

ment of a liberal society. The liberal stands ready to defend the honest heretic no matter what his views against any attempt to curb him. It is enough that the heretic pays the price of unpopularity which he cannot avoid. In some respects each of us is a heretic, but a liberal society can impose no official orthodoxies of *belief*, disagreement with which entails loss of liberty or life.

A conspiracy, as distinct from a heresy, is a secret or underground movement which seeks to attain its ends not by normal political or educational processes but by playing outside the rules of the game. Because it undermines the conditions which are required in order that doctrines may freely compete for acceptance, because where successful it ruthlessly destroys all heretics and dissenters, a conspiracy cannot be tolerated *without* self-stultification in a liberal society.

A heresy does not shrink from publicity. It welcomes it. Not so a conspiracy. The signs of a conspiracy are secrecy, anonymity, the use of false names and labels, and the calculated lie. It does not offer its wares openly but by systematic infiltration into all organizations of cultural life, it seeks to capture strategic posts to carry out a policy alien to the purposes of the organization. There is political conspiracy, which is the concern of the state; but there may also be a conspiracy against a labor union, a cultural or professional association, or an educational institution which is not primarily the concern of the state but of its own members. In general, whoever subverts the rules of a democratic organization and seeks to win by chicanery what cannot be fairly won in the process of free discussion is a conspirator.

Communist *ideas* are heresies, and liberals need have no fear of them where they are freely and openly expressed. They should be studied and evaluated in the light of all the relevant evidence. No one should be punished because he holds them. The Communist *movement*, however, is something quite different from a mere heresy, for wherever it exists it operates along the lines laid down by Lenin as guides to Communists of all countries, and perfected in great detail since then. . . .

. . . Liberals in the twentieth century are confronted by a situation quite unfamiliar to their forbears. For they must contend not with fearless heretics, indigenous elements of the community who, like the abolitionists and revolutionists of old, scorn conceal-ment, and who make no bones about their hostility to the principles of liberalism. They find themselves in the unique historical predicament of having to deal with native elements who, by secrecy and stratagem, serve the interests of a foreign power which believes itself entitled to speak for all mankind, and whose victory spells the end of all liberal civilization and with it the right to heresy. . . .

The problems which underground conspiracy creates for a liberal society are of tremendous magnitude. They cannot be dismissed by a quotation from Jefferson. . . .

. . . "Association" by way of membership in the Communist party is not innocent or coincidental but is a *form of active cooperation and collaboration* in carrying out the purposes of a conspiratorial organization. The Communist party sees to it that all members are instructed about the purposes as soon as they join. Continued membership is possible only in virtue of a series of continued *acts* of obedience to instructions. Those who dub the active cooperation required of all members of the Communist party "guilt by association" coyly suggest by that phrase the innocuous association of chance or occasional encounters with Communists in social gatherings. They simply ignore the fact that all members of the Communist party must "associate" by active cooperation with its purposes or be expelled. . . .

David Lilienthal, a realistic not a ritualistic liberal, has warned us against the "Scare-the-dopes!" method of discussing nuclear energy. There is also a "Scare-the-dopes!" method of discussion of the problem of communistic conspiracy. It is used by those who employ the term "communist" with scandalous looseness as a synonym for any economic or political heresy, and who shout conspiracy where there is only heresy. It is also used by those who do not tell us how to meet the real dangers of Communist conspiracy but shout "Hysteria!," "Fascism!," or "Police State!" when the first faltering efforts are made to cope with dangers hitherto unprecedented in the history of American democracy. . . .

3

The President's Crime Commission Meets the Press *

MEET THE PRESS

The use of police authority is a peculiarly delicate and vital part of government because it involves thousands of tiny, crucial, and sensitive decisions. In an increasingly sophisticated society the exercise of authority must also become more sophisticated. But this requires new patterns of thought, and not only on the part of policemen. In 1967 President Johnson's Crime Commission presented the public with new evidence on the nature of crime and social control, new patterns of thinking about dealing with such problems, and some statement of old, yet provocative, disagreements. Is crime fundamentally a socially created phenomenon or a reflection of individual failures? Do we "get tough" or work on ameliorating slums? Has there been moral decay in our society?

Mr. Spivak: Professor Vorenberg, how would you like America to think about crime?

Mr. Vorenberg: I think the first step is to move beyond the slogans and the scapegoats that people have used so long to think about crime: claims that police are handcuffed or that the young people are going to hell and that all criminals are really sick or misunderstood, that the courts are coddling criminals. These are not only deceiving, they are one of the main reasons so little progress has been made in dealing with the problems of crime, something like a witch doctor chants to avoid facing the fact that the system really needs major surgery or

transfusion of money, people and new ideas.

*   *   *

Mr. Spivak: Mr. Young, do you conclude that the crime situation in the United States at the present time is a dangerous threat to our society from what you have seen of the Commission report—findings?

Mr. Young: I wouldn't say a dangerous threat. I would say it is a serious problem, and I think the great contribution of this Commission is in putting this problem in its proper perspective. I think there has been a tendency to relate crime and Negroes all too often. I think this report really puts it in the proper focus, pointing out as it does with facts and figures, that crime is a phenomena of socio-economic

---

* "Meet the Press," The National Broadcasting Company, February 19, 1967. Reprinted by permission of "Meet the Press."

conditions and not of race, pointing out how the inner-city slums always produce higher crime rates whether they are occupied during a certain period by the Negro or by Italians or by Germans or Poles or Irish, whatever the group might be. In pointing out the implications and the ramifications of poverty and poor housing and its impact upon crime, I think now it puts it in its proper perspective. This is one of the real contributions.

      ❖   ❖   ❖

Mr. Spivak: Professor Wechsler, a recent article in the Saturday Evening Post says, "The American way of dealing with crime, and the people accused of crime, is an unholy and inexcusable mess."

Based on the Commission's findings, will you give us your opinion on that? Do you think it is a mess?

Mr. Wechsler: I think that is a bit of an overstatement, Mr. Spivak. There are good things about it and bad things about it, but insofar as the article points to the general idea that there is one way to deal with crime and that is to hit it hard, with tough prosecution, major penalties, boil the culprits in oil—this general attitude is stupid, ineffective and this report shows why.

      ❖   ❖   ❖

Mr. Rowan: Talking about public attitudes again, do you think the public is prepared to accept this rather broad and compassionate view of crime and criminals?

Mr. Vorenberg: I don't think the most optimistic person thinks there will ever be a time when social conditions will eradicate all crime, but I think the combination of trying to deal with the roots of the problem at the same time we are trying to strengthen the operations and the technology of the police and the courts and correc-

tions, I think this is something the people will accept.

Mr. Rowan: But isn't it true that what this report boils down to is a request for massive expenditures for social welfare, for education, for race relations? In short, isn't it a ringing appeal for a greater Great Society?

Mr. Vorenberg: I think it is a combination of that, plus an appeal for more resources and ideas in people in the area of law enforcement and corrections themselves. It is both.

      ❖   ❖   ❖

Mr. Frankel: There is a great debate around the country though on these questions, with many people in law enforcement saying, "We can't do the job if we have to coddle these people and can't even ask a question without a lawyer being around, can't get confessions from people."

Others say, "No, this doesn't really injure the job of the police departments if they were to do it right," and so on. Why didn't the Commission investigate these problems and come up with some studies on whether or not the court has really hampered police enforcement?

Mr. Cahill: Of course I think you have brought up a very good point, Mr. Frankel, because the courts are continually changing our concepts in the field of law enforcement, because of the fact that whether we agree or disagree with the decision, as long as this is the law, we in the field of law enforcement will abide by it. Then we can only change our concepts, elevate our standards and develop new techniques to meet the new challenge.

The Commission actually just did not have the time to go into these particular types of studies in many areas that we would like to. . . .

Mr. Rogers: Mr. Young, as a civil rights leader yourself you are acutely aware that the civil rights movement preaches civil disobedience, sit-ins, lie-ins, refusals to move on and so on.

In your studies with the Commission, did you find that this might have fostered disrespect for the police and thereby add to the rate of crime?

Mr. Young: No. I think again one of the great contributions of this Commission was to draw a sharp distinction between legitimate civil rights activity and riots, for example. I think that the attitude of the Negro community which the Commission documented, attitudes of suspicion and hostility in a greater degree than among the white community, was not related to what happened in connection with civil disobedience but was more related to their day-to-day experiences and the fact that the policeman was accessible and a symbol of authority and in many cases many Negroes living in the South, or those who have lived in the South, have suffered at the hand of the policeman who oftentimes was an instrument of maintaining injustice and the status quo.

⁂   ⁂   ⁂

Mr. Spivak: Professor Wechsler, crime, according to the Commission's report, has been increasing at the rate of about 46 percent during the period, I think, of about five years, while the population itself has increased at a much slower rate. Do you think that this rapid increase of crime compared to the growth of the population is due to a growing disrespect for law? . . .

Mr. Wechsler: As you know, this report presents the most detailed and sophisticated analysis of this problem of increased rates of crime to be presented ever, I think, in the literature of criminology, and there is nothing in the picture that would lead one to be willing to accept any single simplistic explanation of the sort that you ask about.

The report in great detail shows

changes in the percentage of the population represented by people of different age levels. People of different age levels are prone to a greater or lesser degree to commit crimes of particular kinds. It points to factors like the increase in the number of automobiles, for example, which everybody knows about, effects necessarily the number of cars that are stolen.

On the basis of all of this and on the basis of very careful calculations the staff came up with, a conclusion that I think is right, that there has been an appreciable increase in the incidence of crime. Something more than 50 percent of it is probably mainly attributable to increases in the number of youngsters—relative number of youngsters in the population and the drift to the central cities that has occurred during the period you have in mind. Something less than 50 per cent of the increase is inexplicable in any terms that data can suggest. . . .

Mr. Spivak: You don't believe then there has been a growing disrespect for law due to the sitdowns, due to the civil rights demonstrations, due to the protest meetings and all the rest? You think that during this past decade there has been no breakdown at all in respect of law?

Mr. Wechsler: This is entirely a personal opinion, but my recollection of the 1920's, when I went to college was that my generation, the class of 1928 in college, hadn't the slightest respect for law indeed. Indeed, we didn't even believe there was a legal system. As a matter of fact, we were almost right about that.

Mr. Rowan: Secretary Katzenbach, let's talk a bit about fighting organized crime.

The Commission says, "The present status of the law with respect to wiretapping and bugging is intolerable. It serves the interests neither of privacy nor of law enforcement. In one way or the other, the present controversy with respect to electronic surveillance must be resolved."

The truth was, the Commission couldn't resolve it, could it?

Mr. Katzenbach: Oh, yes, I think the Commission did resolve it. It said there should be a federal law on this subject, and the Commission unanimously said that federal law should restrict—either abolish or restrict—most rigorously the use of wiretapping or electronic eavesdropping and it should absolutely confine this, if not abolishing it entirely, to the most important category of organized crime-type cases and then in a very limited way with court approval and so forth. So really, there was very little dissention in the Commission in this respect.

The question was whether you cut it out entirely or cut it out almost entirely.

Mr. Rowan: The way I read the report, it says it should be abolished or placed under rigid control when referring to private use. But when talking about fighting crime, it says, "A majority of the members of the Commission believe that legislation should be enacted granting carefully circumscribed authority for electronic surveillance." This implies that a minority didn't feel this way.

Mr. Katzenbach: The minority felt it should be abolished entirely for police officials and for others. The majority felt that police officials might have some occasional use for this, but that should be strictly and rigidly controlled. So the area of difference, Mr. Rowan, between members of the Commission was very, very small, indeed, on this subject.

* * *

Mr. Stern: Mr. Young, on page 115 of the report it states, "The Commission does have evidence from its own studies and from police officials themselves that in some cities a significant percentage of policemen assigned to high crime areas do treat citizens with disrespect and sometimes abuse them physically."

* * *

You have indicted all cities though by this general statement. Don't you think it would be fair to those cities not engaged in this practice to indicate which cities do?

Mr. Young: No, I think we might have alerted all cities to do a little soul-searching to see whether they were included.

Mr. Stern: Chief Cahill, you have sat here silently as Mr. Katzenbach has suggested the recent Supreme Court decisions have not hindered law enforcement. You have sat here silently as Mr. Vorenberg has suggested that the police might stop pointing their fingers at the Supreme Court and get on with the job of law enforcement by themselves.

It is no breach of decorum on this program to disagree with them.

Mr. Cahill: My position has been made very clear on many programs I have appeared on locally in my own city, and my position, I think, is very clear here too. I have made it very clear that progressive police departments, progressive police officers are not going to sit and cry baby shoes. I don't think law enforcement has to make excuses to anybody for the efforts that they have put forth to elevate their standards, to develop the educational background of the persons they are bringing into the field of law enforcement, the proper training, the development of techniques, hardware and all of the uses that we put newfound communications to at the present time.

I still say that I am the one who is closest to the picture. I, as a police officer—I am the man down on the street working with the person. As far as the rulings being handed down by the courts today are concerned, I go back to the same question. I think that in some cases we have forgotten the victim, and the victim also is a member of society. We in law enforcement are attempting to maintain that very delicate balance between the rights of the individual and the rights of society.

If the rights of the individual are so built around, and a fortress of rights are built all around him, then I think society as a whole is going to suffer. . . . [T]he police do have a concern, but again I go back to whatever the law is. We will live with it.

❋   ❋   ❋

Mr. Spivak: Do a large percentage of the poor people, a vast majority of the poor people commit crimes?

Mr. Young: No, but most of the crime is committed by poor people. In fact, a study in Washington made by the Stanford University team showed that ninety per cent of the crimes of assault and violence were committed by people making under $5,000.

Mr. Spivak: But what about the other people who didn't commit crime, did the Commission try to find out why so many people who were poor, decent, self-respecting, hard-working, trying to get out of poverty? Did they look into that at all?

Mr. Young: We have to distinguish here between crime. It made quite clear that crimes against property were far greater than crimes against persons, and that in fact crimes of embezzlement and attempts to evade one's tax payments and fraud, that these are crimes that in many cases are much greater in number, and these occur among the very wealthy. But the public reaction is largely to crimes of violence and here again this is greatly

overplayed because less than 13 per cent of the crimes in Washington, D.C., for example, are crimes against the person. They are crimes against property.

Mr. Spivak: Now, I know you are especially interested in the Negro problem. Can you give us any idea why the percentage of crime among the Negroes has been so much higher than among the whites? I think that some of the figures I have seen say that is almost four times as high as among the whites. Thirteen times as high for murder and robbery.

Mr. Young: It goes right back to the fact that crime is committed largely by people who are poor, who are circumscribed in their living, who are denied opportunities. These figures are almost identical with what they were with the Poles, the Irish, the Italian, the German, when they were similarly situated.

But the Negro has had greater difficulty in moving out of the ghetto. I think it is also equally important to point out that the truth of the thing is that much of this crime is directed against the Negro himself. That crime is not inter-racial; it is intra-racial and that the Negro is the greatest victim of that crime, that, actually, in a city like Chicago, the Negro stands six times as much opportunity of being robbed and assaulted as a white person. A Negro whom in Chicago has eight times as much chance of being raped as a white person, so the Negro is also the greater victim, and it is very interesting and disturbing to me that all too often we don't get disturbed about the crime among Negroes unless that crime is directed toward white people. Then we get disturbed about it.

❋   ❋   ❋

Mr. Frankel: Professor Wechsler, as I read this material, it seems to me that you were saying something very intriguing that I am not sure the Commission then dealt with explicitly; namely, that although a great deal of the crime in this country is in fact done by the better-off people and they are punished less or able to defend themselves better while committing it, on the other hand, you do have the problem of the attitudes of the poorest of people toward law enforcement, the feeling they are not getting a fair shake at the hands of the law.

Doesn't these two things together cite one of the major problems, namely, that our system of punishment and our system of dealing with criminals is cockeyed, that the embezzler and the tax evader gets a few months in jail, whereas the petty larcenist gets sent up for a few years?

Mr. Wechsler: This is a problem, and one of the great needs of the system is to get it looked at afresh and sufficiently objectively so that inequalities and absurdities of this kind are laid on the table and dealt with. I think one of the optimistic features of the present situation is that there is now such a strong disposition to do exactly that. Lawyers who 20 years ago wouldn't soil their hands with criminal law problems are now working at these things. The American Law Institute, the American Bar Association, and judges who handled these matters routinely, 20 or 30 years ago, are really suffering with these problems now, and I sense that we are making progress.

❋   ❋   ❋

Mr. Rogers: Secretary Katzenbach, the Commission surveyed ten thousand households, and you came up with twice as many crimes as the FBI's Uniform Crime Reports, published every year.

Since the FBI report is the best available, how in the world are we going to know what is going on in the world of crime if this is only 50 per cent right?

Mr. Katzenbach: I think the Uniform Crime Reports of the FBI are excellent. They depend on what is reported to them by the police and, of course, the police depend on what is reported to them by the citizens. The significance of that is not so much in the measurement of crime in my judgment as suggesting a new technique which police forces can use to find out whether new measures that they are taking are or are not having any impact within an area. A survey technique, I think we showed, would be feasible in determining this.

Mr. Rogers: Do you think that the public is unduly concerned about crime? There is a note of that in the whole report, that crime is not really bad for you—that you can live with crime.

Mr. Katzenbach: No, not at all. I think quite the opposite. I think what we are saying in here is that the public isn't nearly enough concerned about crime and not nearly enough involved in it and, on the other hand, the public is much too much concerned about the wrong kind of crime; that they are concerned about interracial crime that rarely takes place; that they are concerned about what a stranger is going to do to them. Most crimes, at least of violence, are committed by people they know. They have an incorrect picture of crime, but surely they should be concerned about it. I hope this report will help them be more concerned about it.

Mr. Spivak: Chief Cahill, you are the practical man on this panel of Commission members. I understand that one boy in six is referred to a juvenile court, and that 40 percent of all male children in the United States will be arrested for non-traffic offenses during their lives. Do you put those figures that high?

Mr. Cahill: I was surprised myself that they were that high. We recognized the fact, because of our statistics in our own department and from the Federal Bureau of Investigation, that it was high. I didn't realize that it was going to be this high, but it certainly does point up to us and to the entire nation that one of the solutions to crime and the area where we are going to have to attack crime in the future is in the area of our youth, because this is a growing segment of our population.

✿   ✿   ✿

Mr. Spivak: I'd like to ask you one more question on a practical line. Mr. Vorenberg has been reported as saying—and I don't know whether he did, but I will quote it anyhow, "Prison is a lousy place to prepare a guy to live outside a prison."

From your experience would you say that prison, or the fear of prison, plays much of a part in preventing crime?

Mr. Cahill: Again you have to look at the two types of persons we are talking about. You have the hard-core criminal that God above couldn't straighten out. Then you have the other individual who is receptive to proper rehabilitation. These are the persons that we have to work on very, very seriously . . . but then there is the other individual who has to be singled out and recognized, and he is the one who has to be removed from society.

✿   ✿   ✿

Mr. Rogers: Professor Wechsler, the Commission makes a number of sweeping recommendations with respect to the courts, including bringing a lot of sub-rosa practices out in the open like plea bargaining. Do you have any real expectation that the courts will reform themselves along these lines?

Mr. Wechsler: Yes, I have some such expectation. As a matter of fact, there is a very important project going on now in the American Bar Association, the so-called Minimum Standards of Criminal Justice Project, in which committees are examining precisely these types of problems and coming up with standards. These are committees of judges and lawyers, and I have great confidence that these standards, as they get to be approved, will be translated into action.

The one on plea bargaining I think is particularly one where the need for formalization is recognized and where something will happen.

✿   ✿   ✿

Mr. Spivak: One last tough one: If you could only put one recommendation in force, what would it be?

Mr. Vorenberg: I think if I could put only one recommendation into effect, it would be the recommendation that the states and cities start tomorrow morning to do the planning that the report talks about.

4

The First Amendment Has Served Us Well *

ROBERT F. DRINAN, S.J.

For years, if not centuries, American schools have emphasized some aspects of religious ceremony in small ways. In a series of Supreme Court decisions, it was held that Bible reading or public prayer in the course of the school day was improper, violating the First Amendment. Protesting this denial of "the prayer throb of the American people," Senator Everett Dirksen of Illinois sought a constitutional amendment to permit "voluntary prayer." In hearings before the Senate Judiciary Committee in 1966, the most effective witness against the proposal was probably Robert Drinan, a Catholic priest, a law school dean, and an authority on constitutional law. Senator Roman Hruska, however, had a few tough questions.

Father Drinan: It is difficult to overstate the significance of the fact that the Bill of Rights has never been amended in all of American history. The 10 amendments to the Constitution which spell out the fundamental guarantees have existed there now in a remarkably durable way under the oldest written operative constitution in the world.

The one partially successful attempt in American history to change the first amendment's provisions was the Blaine amendment in 1896, and that proposal, which all but passed the Senate except for one vote, which had been passed by the House of Representatives, would have simultaneously done two things. It would have required Bible reading in the public schools while simultaneously denying any Federal aid or State support for church-related schools. The Blaine amendment reflected the mood at that time and sought somehow to capture

the mood and seek the apotheosis of a public school with Bible reading.

Justification therefore for amending the Bill of Rights in the nature of things should be very, very serious. And especially it seems to me, should it be grave when we consider that the 16 words about religion in the first amendment have served us well in this country. . . .

*   *   *

Let me speak first about the secularization of the public schools.

Since the end of World War II the student population in church-related elementary and secondary schools has more than doubled. These schools—operated by Catholic, Lutheran, Orthodox Jewish, and other groups—now enroll every seventh child who goes to school in America. The unprecedented growth of these institutions in the last 20 years is both the cause and the effect of the secularizing process which has been going on over a long period of time in the public schools.

The private sectarian school seeks to

---

* Statement of Robert F. Drinan, S.J., Dean of the Boston College Law School. *School Prayer,* Hearings Before the Senate Judiciary Committee, 1967, pp. 7 ff.

create a religious orientation within its curriculum which will combine with secular learning the essential elements of the Scriptural, sacred, and spiritual values of the Judaeo-Christian culture. The nonpublic church-related school is built on the premise that the orientation of the public school is and must continue to be secular; some advocates of denominational schools would in fact claim that the public school is secularistic—even to the point of unconstitutionally "establishing" a secular or nonreligious philosophy of education.

Whatever one might think about the need or wisdom of private, church-related schools, it is undeniable that the public school has become an institution where religious values may be referred to or taught only in the most general way. It is a school whose only religious orientation is that it has no religious orientation.

The public school has in fact been an institution of this character for a long time; the banning of Bible reading and of prayer by the Supreme Court in 1963 merely stripped away the widespread illusion that the American public school somehow combined piety and learning in an eminently satisfactory way. The various constitutional amendments proposed by Congressmen and Senators to restore to the public schools the last vestiges of their piety—Bible reading and prayer —constitute an almost irrational refusal to surrender one of the most persistent myths in American life—the illusion that the public school can train future citizens in morality and piety.

❋   ❋   ❋

Now, as a Catholic and as an educator, I more than most Americans concede and lament the thunderous silence about religion in the public schools. Along with an ever-increasing number of critics of the public schools, I note with regret that virtually all public school administrators have failed to give any leadership or exercise any initiative in establishing courses about religion. . . . And I say categorically that the absence of objective teaching about religion in the public school is one of the most serious educational limitations of public education in this country. Now no one pretends that the structuring of courses about religion or the selection of personnel to teach these courses are easy tasks. But educators would concur that religion should have its place in a public school curriculum which teaches every subject from art to zoology.

There are several feasible and constitutional ways by which the secularization of the public school can be lessened. No one pretends that any of these methods is entirely satisfactory but clearly they offer a more realistic way by which students can actually learn about religion than is offered by the so-called voluntary prayer. Among the clearly available and perfectly constitutional options open to the public school are the following:

1. Released or dismissed time off the school premises, clearly validated in 1952 by the *Zorach* opinion.
2. Teaching about religion. The U.S. Supreme Court went out of its way in the majority and concurring opinions to point out that the Supreme Court in its 1962 and 1963 opinions was not saying anything against the constitutionality of teaching about religion.
3. A study of the Bible. Once again the Court expressly stated that the Bible as literature, the Bible as one of the world's most influential books, certainly can and should be studied.

In view, therefore, of the options that are available to public school educators, which to be sure they have neglected, but why is it that anyone can think that a "voluntary" prayer can have any significant effect in neutralizing the impact of 30 hours every week of religionless teaching on the mind and heart of a child? I was requested and strongly urged to testify here today by Catholic, Protestant, and Jewish individuals and organizations, and the overwhelming majority of leaders in all of these three religious bodies is strongly opposed. . . . Why is it then, I ask, that 40 Members of the U.S. Senate introduced in March 1966 a resolution seeking to do that which is directly opposed to the best judgment of virtually all of the religious leaders and denominational groups in the Nation? . . . For what reasons do 40 Senators seek to appear more pious than the churches and more righteous than the Supreme Court?

It is also distressing to me to note that no professional organization of educators, to my knowledge, would endorse an amendment to the Constitution which would permit the recitation of prayers. By what process of reasoning, therefore, do 40 Senators think that they can or should propose an addition to the curriculum of the public schools of this Nation which has not been requested and indeed has been rejected by the vast majority of public school educators in America?

Experts on constitutional law who will support Senate Resolution 148 are as scarce as the religionists and educators who will endorse it. The vast legal literature about the *Engel* and *Schempp* decisions has in general tended to join the consensus among religionists and educators to the effect that an amendment of the Bill of Rights is not the way to bring religion into the public school.

* * *

Senator Hruska: . . . Would you elaborate on this "truly pathetic de-

sire" of the elected representatives to reflect the thinking and the voices and the desires of those who are responsible for their being in public office?

Father Drinan: It seems to me that Congressmen should decide this on basic constitutional principles, regardless of what the masses or the vast majority or people who write letters say, that they should decide this on educational, religious, constitutional grounds, regardless of how many individuals want more godliness in the schools.

Senator Hruska: Well, that is an anomaly, really, when you suggest that these elected representatives of the people should decide this on the basis of truly constitutional principles. You see, this is one step of remaking the Constitution. This is not a matter of interpreting the Constitution. This is one of the many steps necessary to change the Constitution.

Now, to what source should these representatives repair in that desire to represent their people? Should they go to the Founding Fathers who said, "Congress shall make no law," should they go back that far or should they go to the present interpretation and say, "No, we will make no change," or should they go to the people? That is the question, should they go to the people they represent?

Father Drinan: You are assuming, Senator, that the people, according to a scientific Gallup poll, are opposed to *Schempp* and *Murray*, and I do not think that that is so. That was a 6-to-1 decision, you know, and there was a good deal of controversy about it. But the dust has settled, and I would say that individuals who understand the issues more and more feel that those decisions were correctly decided.

* * *

Senator Hruska: . . . If there is a substantial difference of opinion, why not let the people decide whether they agree with your view or Senator Dirksen's view as subscribed to by 47 other Senators, and resolve it in that way? Is that an unreasonable request?

Father Drinan: Senator, it can be resolved by litigation. They can bring subsequent cases, as they did in *Stein* —in the *Stein* case in New York. . . .

* * *

Senator Hruska: Of course, they can litigate and they have litigated, and each time the line gets pushed farther and farther back. But they can also amend the Constitution, can they not?

Father Drinan: Yes, Senator.

5

"Absolute Is in the Dark" *

ERWIN N. GRISWOLD

A quite different point of view is developed by another Dean, Erwin Griswold of the Harvard Law School. He sees the question of separation of church and state as much more flexible and the political tradition of America as favoring some sort of religious tone in our daily life. He characterizes the approach followed by the Court as both inflexible and dangerous. Minorities as well as majorities must be tolerant, he argues, and religion in schools can play a positive role in the development of pluralism in American society.

* * *

I venture the thought, quite seriously, that it was unfortunate that the question involved in the *Engel* case was ever thought of as a matter for judicial decision, that it was unfortunate that the Court decided the case, one way or the other, and that this unhappy situation resulted solely from the absolutist position which the Court has taken and intimated in such matters, thus inviting such litigation in its extreme form.

What do I mean by this? I have in mind at least two separate lines of

thought. One is the fact that we have a tradition, a spiritual and cultural tradition, of which we ought not to be deprived by judges carrying into effect the logical implications of absolutist notions not expressed in the Constitution itself, and surely never contemplated by those who put the constitutional provisions into effect. The other is that there are some matters which are essentially local in nature, important matters, but nonetheless matters to be worked out by the people themselves in their own communities, when no basic rights of others are impaired. It was said long ago that every question in this country tends to become a legal question. But is that wise? Is it inevitable? Are there not questions of detail, questions of give and take

* Erwin N. Griswold, "Absolute Is in the Dark—A Discussion of the Approach of the Supreme Court to Constitutional Questions," 8 *Utah L. Rev.* 167 (1963). Reprinted by permission of the author and publisher.

questions at the fringe, which are better left to nonjudicial determination?

First, as to the long tradition. Is it not clear as a matter of historical fact that this was a Christian nation? . . . It is perfectly true, and highly salutary, that the First Amendment forbade Congress to pass any law "respecting an establishment of religion or prohibiting the free exercise thereof." These are great provisions, of great sweep and basic importance. But to say that they require that all trace of religion be kept out of any sort of public activity is sheer invention. Our history is full of these traces; chaplains in Congress and in the armed forces; chapels in prisons; "In God We Trust" on our money; to mention only a few. God is referred to in our national anthem, and in "America," and many others of what may be called our national songs. Must all of these things be rigorously extirpated in order to satisfy a constitutional absolutism? What about Sunday? What about Christmas? Must we deny our whole heritage, our culture, the things of spirit and soul which have sustained us in the past and helped bind us together in times of good and bad?

Does our deep-seated tolerance of all religions—or, to the same extent, of no religion—require that we give up all religious observance in public activities? Why should it? It certainly never occurred to the Founders that it would. It is hardly likely that it was entirely accidental that these questions did not even come before the Court in the first hundred and fifty years of our constitutional history. . . . Now let me turn to the other point—that there are some matters which should be settled on the local level, in each community, and should not become great Supreme Court cases. . . . The prayer involved in the *Engel* case was not compulsory. As the Supreme Court itself recited, no pupil was com-

pelled "to join in the prayer over his or his parents' objection." [1] This, to me, is crucial. If any student was compelled to join against his conviction, this would present a serious and justiciable question, akin to that presented in the flag salute case.[2]

No pupil is compelled to participate. Must all refrain because one does not wish to join? This would suggest that no school can have a Pledge of Allegiance to the flag if any student does not wish to join. I heartily agree with the decision in the Barnette case [3] that no student can be compelled to join in a flag salute against his religious scruples. But it is a far cry from that decision to say that no school district can have a flag salute for those who want to participate if there is any student who does not wish to join. This is a country of religious toleration. That is a great consequence of our history embodied in the First Amendment. But does religious toleration mean religious sterility? . . . Does the fact that we have officially adopted toleration as our standard mean that we must give up our history and our tradition? The Moslem who comes here may worship as he pleases, and may hold public office without discrimination. That is as it should be. But why should it follow that he can require others to give up their Christian tradition merely because he is a tolerated and welcomed member of the community?

Though we have a considerable common cultural heritage, there have always been minority groups in our country. This, I am sure, has been healthy and educational for all concerned. We have surely gained from having a less homogeneous population.

[1] *Engel v. Vitale,* 370 U.S. 421, 423 (1962).
[2] *West Virginia Board of Education v. Barnette,* 319 U.S. 624 (1943).
[3] *West Virginia Board of Education v. Barnette,* 319 U.S. 624 (1943).

Of course, the rights of all, especially those of minorities, must be protected and preserved. But does that require that the majority, where there is such a majority, must give up its cultural heritage and tradition? Why?

Let us consider the Jewish child, or the Catholic child, or the nonbeliever, or the Congregationalist, or the Quaker. He, either alone, or with a few or many others of his views, attends a public school, whose school district, by local action, has prescribed the Regents prayer. When the prayer is recited, if this child or his parents feel that he cannot participate, he may stand or sit, in respectful attention, while the other children take part in the ceremony. Or he may leave the room. It is said that this is bad, because it sets him apart from other children. It is even said that there is an element of compulsion in this—what the Supreme Court has called an "indirect coercive pressure upon religious minorities to conform." [4] But is this the way it should be looked at? The child of a nonconforming or a minority group is, to be sure, different in his beliefs. That is what it means to be a member of a minority. Is it not desirable, and educational, for him to learn and observe this, in the atmosphere of the school—not so much that he is different, as that other children are

different from him? And is it not desirable that, at the same time, he experiences and learns the fact that his difference is tolerated and accepted? No compulsion is put upon him. He need not participate. But he, too, has the opportunity to be tolerant. He allows the majority of the group to follow their own tradition, perhaps coming to understand and to respect what they feel is significant to them.

Is this not a useful and valuable and educational and, indeed, a spiritual experience for the children of what I have called the majority group? They experience the values of their own culture; but they also see that there are others who do not accept those values, and that they are wholly tolerated in their nonacceptance. Learning tolerance for other persons, no matter how different, and respect for their beliefs, may be an important part of American education, and wholly consistent with the First Amendment.[5] . . .

---

[4] *Engel v. Vitale,* 370 U.S. 421, 431 (1962).

[5] "Acquainting the student with religious pluralism is part of democratic public education's duty to introduce future citizens to pluralism of all types: economic, political, ethnic, racial and others. Schooling should enable the student to face the actualities of free society. If instead it gives him only silly, sentimental notions concerning the unity of all Americans he will be an incompetent citizen." R. M. Healey, *Jefferson on Religion in Public Education* (New Haven, Conn.: Yale University Press, 1962), p. 270.

6

The Supreme Court Enunciates
a Constitutional Right of Privacy *

U.S. SUPREME COURT

Because the issue of birth control involves on the one hand convictions as to the very nature of mankind, and on the other economic and physical imperatives that press upon us throughout the world, it has created bitter political antagonisms and deep soul searching. In Griswold v. Connecticut, a case involving this issue, the Supreme Court held, for the first time, that there was a constitutional right of privacy. This, it was held, extended to the marriage relationship. Since every man has a different view of what is essential to privacy, how much help does the opinion of Justice Douglas provide in actually protecting that right? Is it a coincidence that the Justices should decide to try to protect privacy at a time when it is so deeply threatened by mass society?

GRISWOLD v. CONNECTICUT

> 381 U.S. 479, 14 L.Ed.2d 510,
> 85 S.Ct. 1678 (1965).

Mr. Justice DOUGLAS delivered the opinion of the Court.

Appellant Griswold is Executive Director of the Planned Parenthood League of Connecticut. . . .

*   *   *

They gave information, instruction, and medical advice to *married persons* as to the means of preventing conception. They examined the wife and prescribed the best contraceptive device or material for her use. . . .

The statutes whose constitutionality is involved in this appeal are §§ 53-32 and 54-196 of the General Statutes of Connecticut (1938). The former provides:

"Any person who uses any drug, medicinal article or instrument for the purpose of preventing conception shall be fined not less than fifty dollars or imprisoned not less than sixty days nor more than one year or be both fined and imprisoned."

Section 54-196 provides:

"Any person who assists, abets, counsels, causes, hires or commands another to commit any offense may be prosecuted and punished as if he were the principal offender."

The appellants were found guilty as accessories and fined $100 each, against the claim that the accessory statute as so applied violated the Fourteenth Amendment. . . .

*   *   *

The association of people is not mentioned in the Constitution nor in the Bill of Rights. The right to educate a child in a school of the parents' choice—whether public or private or parochial—is also not mentioned. Nor is the right to study any particular subject or any foreign language. Yet

---

* Griswold v. Connecticut, 381 U.S. 479, 14 L.Ed.2d 510, 85 S.Ct. 1678 (1965).

the First Amendment has been construed to include certain of those rights.

By Pierce v. Society of Sisters, supra, the right to educate one's children as one chooses is made applicable to the States by the force of the First and Fourteenth Amendments. . . .

In NAACP v. State of Alabama, . . . we protected the "freedom to associate and privacy in one's associations," noting that freedom of association was a peripheral First Amendment right. Disclosure of membership lists of a constitutionally valid association, we held, was invalid "as entailing the likelihood of a substantial restraint upon the exercise by petitioner's members of their right to freedom of association." In other words, the First Amendment has a penumbra where privacy is protected from governmental intrusion. In like context, we have protected forms of "association" that are not political in the customary sense but pertain to the social, legal, and economic benefit of the members. . . .

*   *   *

. . . The right of "association," like the right of belief (West Virginia State Board of Education v. Barnette, . . . is more than the right to attend a meeting; it includes the right to express one's attitudes or philosophies by membership in a group or by affiliation with it or by other lawful means. Association in that context is a form of expression of opinion; and while it is not expressly included in the First Amendment its existence is necessary in making the express guarantees fully meaningful.

The foregoing cases suggest that specific guarantees in the Bill of Rights have penumbras, formed by emanations from those guarantees that help give them life and substance. . . .

*   *   *

. . . Various guarantees create zones of privacy.

The present case, then, concerns a relationship lying within the zone of privacy created by several fundamental constitutional guarantees. And it concerns a law which, in forbidding the *use* of contraceptives rather than regulating their manufacture or sale, seeks to achieve its goals by means having a maximum destructive impact upon that relationship. Such a law cannot stand in light of the familiar principle, so often applied by this Court, that a "governmental purpose to control or prevent activities constitutionally subject to state regulation may not be achieved by means which sweep unnecessarily broadly and thereby invade the area of protected freedoms." NAACP v. Alabama.

*   *   *

Would we allow the police to search the sacred precincts of marital bedrooms for tell-tale signs of the use of contraceptives? The very idea is repulsive to the notions of privacy surrounding the marriage relationship.

We deal with a right of privacy older than the Bill of Rights—older than our political parties, older than our school system. Marriage is a coming together for better or for worse, hopefully enduring, and intimate to the degree of being sacred. It is an association that promotes a way of life, not causes; a harmony in living, not political faiths; a bilateral loyalty, not commercial or social projects. Yet it is an association for as noble a purpose as any involved in our prior decisions.

Reversed.

*   *   *

Mr. Justice BLACK, with whom Mr. Justice STEWART joins, dissenting.

. . . In order that there may be no room at all to doubt why I vote as I do, I feel constrained to add that the law is every bit offensive to me as it is my Brethren of the majority and my Brothers HARLAN, WHITE and GOLDBERG who, reciting reasons why it is offensive to them, hold it unconstitutional. . . .

*   *   *

The Court talks about a constitutional "right of privacy" as though there is some constitutional provision or provisions forbidding any law ever to be passed which might abridge the "privacy" of individuals. But there is not. There are, of course, guarantees in certain specific constitutional provisions which are designed in part to protect privacy at certain times and places with respect to certain activities. Such, for example, is the Fourth Amendment's guarantee against "unreasonable searches and seizures." But I think it belittles that Amendment to talk about it as though it protects nothing but "privacy." To treat it that way is to give it a niggardly interpretation, not the kind of liberal reading I think any Bill of Rights provision should be given. . . .

*   *   *

I realize that many good and able men have eloquently spoken and written, sometimes in rhapsodical strains, about the duty of this Court to keep the Constitution in tune with the times. The idea is that the Constitution must be changed from time to time and that this Court is charged with a duty to make those changes. For myself, I must with all deference reject that philosophy. The Constitution makers knew the need for change and

provided for it. Amendments suggested by the people's elected representatives can be submitted to the people or their selected agents for ratification. That method of change was good for our Fathers, and being somewhat old-fashioned I must add it is good enough for me. . . .

*   *   *

[My concurring brethren] would reinstate the Lochner, Coppage, Adkins, Burns line of cases, cases from which this Court recoiled after the 1930's, and which had been I thought totally discredited until now. Apparently my Brethren have less quarrel with state economic regulations than former Justices of their persuasion had. But any limitation upon their using the natural law due process philosophy to strike down any state law, dealing with any activity whatever, will obviously be only self-imposed.

*   *   *

Mr. Justice GOLDBERG, whom THE CHIEF JUSTICE and Mr. Justice BRENNAN join, concurring. . . . To hold that a right so basic and fundamental and so deep-rooted in our society as the right of privacy in marriage may be infringed because that right is not guaranteed in so many words by the first eight amendments to the Constitution is to ignore the Ninth Amendment . . . which specifically states that "[t]he enumeration in the Constitution, of certain rights shall not be *construed* to deny or disparage others retained by the people." . . .

*   *   *

7

Letter from Birmingham City Jail *

MARTIN LUTHER KING, JR.

Nobel Prize winner Martin Luther King composed a rebuttal to white clergymen of Birmingham who protested his leadership of demonstrations while actually imprisoned. This remains the fullest exposition of Reverend King's philosophy of nonviolence, and an eloquent demonstration of why he emerged as the spokesman of the civil rights movement. In recent years, questions have developed as the philosophy has been applied to concrete situations with regard to both civil rights and the Vietnamese war. Are demonstrations which involve force legitimate where Negro political disadvantage is a product of apathy, rather than a consequence of intimidation of legal disability? Does the fact that Negro apathy is a product of discriminatory education and political experience denied them in the past mean that they should have the right to use extraordinary tactics in the present? What if a minority has full access to the political process, but—as in the case of the Vietnamese war—regards the majority policy not just as mistaken but as immoral? And why should minority tactics stop with non-violence, if indeed immorality is being condoned?

While confined here in the Birmingham City Jail, I came across your recent statement calling our present activities "unwise and untimely." Seldom, if ever, do I pause to answer criticism of my work and ideas. . . . But since I feel that you are men of genuine good will and your criticisms are sincerely set forth, I would like to answer your statement in what I hope will be patient and reasonable terms.

I think I should give the reason for my being in Birmingham, since you have been influenced by the argument of "outsiders coming in." I have the honor of serving as president of the Southern Christian Leadership Conference, an organization operating in every Southern state with headquarters in Atlanta, Georgia. . . .

Moreover, I am cognizant of th interrelatedness of all communitie and states. I cannot sit idly by in At lanta and not be concerned abou what happens in Birmingham. Injus tice anywhere is a threat to justic everywhere. We are caught in an in escapable network of mutuality tie in a single garment of destiny. . . Never again can we afford to live wit the narrow, provincial "outside agita tor" idea. Anyone who lives inside th United States can never be considere an outsider anywhere in this countr

You deplore the demonstratior that are presently taking place i Birmingham. But I am sorry that you statement did not express a simila concern for the conditions tha brought the demonstrations into be ing. I am sure that each of you woul want to go beyond the superfici social analyst who looks merely at e fects, and does not grapple with u

* Martin Luther King, Jr., "Letter from Birmingham City Jail," *The New Leader*, June 24, 1963, pp. 3-11. Reprinted by permission of the author and publisher.

derlying causes. I would not hesitate to say that it is unfortunate that so-called demonstrations are taking place in Birmingham at this time, but I would say in more emphatic terms that it is even more unfortunate that the white power structure of this city left the Negro community with no other alternative.

In any nonviolent campaign there are four basic steps: 1) collection of the facts to determine whether injustices are alive; 2) negotiation; 3) self-purification; and 4) direct action. We have gone through all of these steps in Birmingham. There can be no gainsaying of the fact that racial injustice engulfs this community. Birmingham is probably the most thoroughly segregated city in the United States. Its ugly record of police brutality is known in every section of this country. Its unjust treatment of Negroes in the courts is a notorious reality. There have been more unsolved bombings of Negro homes and churches in Birmingham than any city in this nation. These are the hard, brutal, and unbelievable facts. On the basis of these conditions Negro leaders sought to negotiate with the city fathers. But the political leaders consistently refused to engage in good faith negotiation. . . .

You may well ask, "Why direct action? Why sit-ins, marches, etc.? Isn't negotiation a better path?" You are exactly right in your call for negotiation. Indeed, this is the purpose of direct action. Nonviolent direct action seeks to create such a crisis and establish such creative tension that a community that has constantly refused to negotiate is forced to confront the issue. It seeks so to dramatize the issue that it can no longer be ignored.

I just referred to the creation of tension as a part of the work of the nonviolent resister. This may sound rather shocking. But I must confess that I am not afraid of the word "tension." I have earnestly worked and preached against violent tension, but there is a type of constructive nonviolent tension that is necessary for growth. Just as Socrates felt that it was necessary to create a tension in the mind so that individuals could rise from the bondage of myths and half-truths to the unfettered realm of creative analysis and objective appraisal, we must see the need of having nonviolent gadflies to create the kind of tension in society that will help men rise from the dark depths of prejudice and racism to the majestic heights of understanding and brotherhood. So the purpose of the direct action is to create a situation so crisis-packed that it will inevitably open the door to negotiation. We, therefore, concur with you in your call for negotiation. Too long has our beloved Southland been bogged down in the tragic attempt to live in monologue rather than dialogue.

One of the basic points in your statement is that our acts are untimely. . . . We know through painful experience that freedom is never voluntarily given by the oppressor; it must be demanded by the oppressed. Frankly I have never yet engaged in a direct action movement that was "well timed," according to the timetable of those who have not suffered unduly from the disease of segregation. For years now I have heard the word "Wait!" It rings in the ear of every Negro with a piercing familiarity. This "wait" has almost always meant "never." It has been a tranquilizing Thalidomide, relieving the emotional stress for a moment, only to give birth to an ill-formed infant of frustration. We have waited for more than 340 years for our constitutional and God-given rights. The nations of Asia and Africa are moving with jet-like speed toward the goal of political independence, and we still creep at horse and buggy pace toward the gaining of a cup of coffee at a lunch counter.

I guess it is easy for those who have never felt the stinging darts of segregation to say wait. But when you have seen vicious mobs lynch your mothers and fathers at will and drown your sisters and brothers at whim; when you have seen hate-filled policemen curse, kick, brutalize, and even kill your black brothers and sisters with impunity; when you see the vast majority of your 20-million Negro brothers smothering in an air-tight cage of poverty in the midst of an affluent society; when you suddenly find your tongue twisted and your speech stammering as you seek to explain to your six-year-old daughter why she can't go to the public amusement park that has just been advertised on television . . . and see the depressing clouds of inferiority begin to form in her little mental sky . . . when you take a cross-country drive and find it necessary to sleep night after night in the uncomfortable corners of your automobile because no motel will accept you; when you are humiliated day in and day out by nagging signs reading "white" men and "colored"; when your first name becomes "nigger" and your middle name becomes "boy" (however old you are) and your last name becomes "John," and when your wife and mother are never given the respected title "Mrs."; when you are harried by day and haunted by night by the fact that you are a Negro, living constantly at tip-toe stance never quite knowing what to expect next, and plagued with inner fears and outer resentments; when you are forever fighting a degenerating sense of "nobodiness"—then you will understand why we find it difficult to wait. . . .

You express a great deal of anxiety over our willingness to break laws. This is certainly a legitimate concern. Since we so diligently urge people to obey the Supreme Court's decision o 1954 outlawing segregation in the pub lic schools, it is rather strange an paradoxical to find us consciousl breaking laws. One may well asl "How can you advocate breakin some laws and obeying others?" Th answer is found in the fact that ther are two types of laws: There are *jus* laws and there are *unjust* laws. On has not only a legal but a moral re sponsibility to obey just laws. Cor versely, one has a moral responsibilit to disobey unjust laws. I would agre with Saint Augustine that "An unju; law is no law at all."

Now what is the difference betwee the two? How does one determin when a law is just or unjust? A ju; law is a man-made code that squar€ with the moral law or the law of Go< An unjust law is a mode that is out (harmony with the moral law. . . .

I hope you can see the distinction am trying to point out. In no sense d I advocate evading or defying the la as the rabid segregationist would d€ This would lead to anarchy. One wh breaks an unjust law must do it *openl; lovingly* (not hatefully as the whi† mothers did in New Orleans whe they were seen on television screamin "nigger, nigger, nigger") and with willingness to accept the penalty. submit that an individual who breal a law that conscience tells him is u1 just, and willingly accepts the penal by staying in jail to arouse the cor science of the community over its ii justice, is in reality expressing tl very highest respect for law. . . .

You spoke of our activity in Birr ingham as extreme. At first I w rather disappointed that fellow clerg men would see my nonviolent effor as those of the extremist. . . . I stand the middle of two opposing forces the Negro community. One is a for€ of complacency made up of Negro who, as a result of long years of o pression, have been so completely drained of self-respect and a sense of "somebodiness" that they have adjusted to segregation, and of a few Negroes in the middle class who, because of a degree of academic and economic security, and because at points they profit by segregation, have unconsciously become insensitive to the problems of the masses. The other force is one of bitterness and hatred and comes perilously close to advocating violence. It is expressed in the various black nationalist groups that are springing up over the nation, the largest and best known being Elijah Muhammad's Muslim movement. This movement is nourished by the contemporary frustration over the continued existence of racial discrimination. It is made up of people who have lost faith in America, who have absolutely repudiated Christianity, and who have concluded that the white man is an incurable "devil."

I have tried to stand between these two forces saying that we need not follow the "do-nothingism" of the complacent or the hatred and despair of the black nationalist. There is the more excellent way of love and nonviolent protest. I'm grateful to God that, through the Negro church, the dimension of nonviolence entered our struggle. If this philosophy had not emerged I am convinced that by now many streets of the South would be flowing with floods of blood. And I am further convinced that if our white brothers dismiss us . . . and refuse to support our nonviolent efforts, millions of Negroes, out of frustration and despair, will seek solace and security in black nationalist ideologies, a development that will lead inevitably to a frightening racial nightmare. . . .

I must close now. But before closing I am impelled to mention one other point in your statement that troubled me profoundly. You warmly commended the Birmingham police force for keeping "order" and "preventing violence." I don't believe you would have so warmly commended the police force if you had seen its angry, violent dogs literally biting six unarmed, nonviolent Negroes. . . .

I wish you had commended the Negro sit-inners and demonstrators of Birmingham for their sublime courage, their willingness to suffer, and their amazing discipline in the midst of the most inhuman provocation. One day the South will recognize its real heroes. . . . One day the South will know that when these disinherited children of God sat down at lunch counters they were in reality standing up for the best in the American dream and the most sacred values in our Judeo-Christian heritage, and thus carrying our whole nation back to great wells of democracy which were dug deep by the founding fathers in the formulation of the Constitution and the declaration of Independence. . . .

If I have said anything in this letter that is an overstatement of the truth and is indicative of an unreasonable impatience, I beg you to forgive me. If I have said anything in this letter that is an understatement of the truth and is indicative of my having a patience that makes me patient with anything less than brotherhood, I beg God to forgive me. . . .

Let us all hope that the dark clouds of racial prejudice will soon pass away and the deep fog of misunderstanding will be lifted from our fear-drenched communities and in some not too distant tomorrow the radiant stars of love and brotherhood will shine over our great nation with all of their scintillating beauty.

Yours for the cause of
Peace and Brotherhood

M. L. KING, JR.

8

Civil Rights Must Not Destroy Liberty *

WILLIAM F. BUCKLEY, JR.

How far should the national government go in this implementation of the Supreme Court's decision? An editor of the National Review, *a leading organ of American conservatism, here argues that the course suggested by* Brown v. Board of Education *will lead to the destruction of liberty for the white and Negro community alike. The advantages of integration are problematic, Buckley suggests; but the costs of federal power are clear and decisive.*

. . . Let us take the word of the predominating school of social scientists and stipulate that segregation is the cause of personality disturbances. And—mark this—not only against the Negro, but also against the white. The argument is not new; it has often been used against corporal punishment. It is not only the victim who is damaged, psychiatrists report, but also the executioner, in whom sadistic impulses are dangerously encouraged. No one who has contemplated a man brandishing a fiery cross and preaching hatred needs help from social science to know that the race problem has debasing effects on black and white alike.

Assume all this to be true. Assume, also, that the legal and political power is wholly at the disposal of the society to effect its point of view in the South. Assume, in other words, that *Brown v. Board of Education* and the supporting decisions of the Supreme Court deconstitutionalized segregated public schooling beyond the point of argu-

ment. Then assume that the raw power necessary to enforce that decision is available to the present administration, and that the will of the nation is such as to insure that Congress will supply power where power is lacking. Should the federal government then proceed?

The list of sanctions available to the government is endless. The economic power of the federal government has in our time reached the point where it cannot be denied; cannot, in fact, be defied. If Congress can seriously entertain the question whether to spend money to aid public schooling in any state whose public schools are segregated, why can't Congress debate the question whether it is prepared to spend money for road-building in a segregated state? Or for unemployment? Or for farmers' subsidies? Already the Attorney General has hinted he is considering (for purely punitive reasons) recommending to his old friend the Commander-in-Chief the removal of our large military installations from segregated areas.

In a word, the federal government is in a position to visit intolerable economic sanctions against the defiant

* William F. Buckley, Jr., "Civil Rights Must Not Destroy Liberty," *Saturday Review,* November 11, 1961, pp. 21-22. Reprinted by permission of the author and publisher.

state. Not to mention the government's arsenal of legal weapons. Why cannot the Congress (assuming always a purposive mood on the subject of segregation) pass laws increasing the penalties for those held guilty of contempt of court in a certain category of cases? And why can't the courts rule—as Professor Auerbach of the University of Wisconsin has recommended—that any state which, having fought to the end of the legal road, sets out to close down its public schools rather than integrate them, be forbidden to do so on the grounds that such action, under such circumstances, becomes not the free exercise of the state's power, but an act of defiance of a federal court? By such reasoning the federal government could take over the operation of the schools. . . .

What would be accomplished by turning the legislative, judicial, and executive resources of this country over to a crash program of integration? Let us suppose the program were so successful as to make South Carolina like New York City. This spring a distinguished New York Negro told the audience of the television program "Open End" that he did not know three white people in all of New York with whom he felt genuinely comfortable, such is the prevalence of prejudice even in this cosmopolitan center. Louis Lomax may be more sensitive, and hence more bitter, than the average New York Negro, and so unrepresentative of the state of Negro serenity in the North; but then, too, Dr. Martin Luther King is more sensitive, and so more bitter, than the average Southern Negro, and hence unqualified as a litmus of the Southern Negro's discontent. . . .

The deep disturbances isolated by the social scientists are not, I think, of the kind that are removed by integrating the waiting rooms and the schools. It has even been revealed (*Villanova* *Law Review,* Fall 1960) that the very tests cited by the Supreme Court in *Brown* as evidence that Southern Negro children were suffering personality damage, when administered in the North yielded not merely similar results, but results that seemed to indicate a greater psychic disturbance in integrated Northern Negroes than in segregated Southern Negroes! I believe that the forms of segregation, which so much engross us at the moment and which alone are within the reach of the law to alter, are of tertiary importance, and of transitory nature; and under the circumstances the question arises even more urgently: *Should* we resort to convulsive measures that do violence to the traditions of our system in order to remove the forms of segregation in the South? If the results were predictably and unambiguously successful, the case might be made persuasively. If a clean stroke through the tissue of American mores could reach through to the cancer, forever to extirpate it, then one might say, in due gravity: let us operate. But when the results are thus ambiguous? Use the federal power to slash through the warp and woof of society in pursuit of a social ideal which was never realized even under the clement circumstances of a Chicago or a New York or a Philadelphia?

I say no. A conservative is seldom disposed to use the federal government as the sword of social justice, for the sword is generally two-edged ("The government can only do something for the people in proportion as it can do something to the people," Jefferson said). If it is doubtful just what enduring benefits the Southern Negro would receive from the intervention of government on the scale needed to, say, integrate the schools in South Carolina, it is less doubtful what the consequences of interposition would be to the ideal of local government and the sense of community, ideals which I am not ready to abandon, not even to kill Jim Crow.

What, meanwhile, are the Negroes actually losing that they would not lose if the government took over in the South? One thing alone, I think, and that is the institutional face of segregation. That is important; but it is in the last analysis only a form. What matters is the substance of segregation. The kind of familiarity that might lessen racial consciousness is outside the power of the government to effect. I would even argue that it is outside the power of the government to accelerate. . . .

It is true that the separation of the races on account of color is nonrational, then circumstance will in due course break down segregation. When it becomes self-evident that biological, intellectual, cultural, and psychic similarities among the races render social separation capricious and atavistic, then the myths will begin to fade, as they have done in respect of the Irish, the Italian, the Jew; then integration will come—the right kind of integration. But meanwhile there *are* differences between the races which surely will not be denied by an organization

explicitly devoted to the advancement of colored people. The Negro community must advance, and is advancing. The Reverend William Sloane Coffin of Yale University, returning from his whirl with the Freedom Riders, rejected the request of Mr. Robert Kennedy that the Riders withdraw to let the situation cool off with the words: "The Negroes have been waiting for ninety years." Mr. Coffin spoke nonsense, and showed scant respect for the productive labors, material and spiritual, of three generations of Negroes. A sociologist at Brooklyn College only a few weeks before had observed that never in the history of nations has a racial minority advanced so fast as the Negroes have done in America. How far will they go on to advance? To the point where social separation will vanish?

I do not know, but I hope that circumstance will usher in that day, and that when the Negroes have finally realized their long dream of attaining to the status of the white man, the white man will still be free; and that depends, in part, on the moderation of those whose inclination it is to build a superstate that will give them Instant Integration.

9

Which Way for the Negro? *

THE EDITORS OF NEWSWEEK

Success itself can engender new and tougher problems. The Civil Rights movement has witnessed this bittersweet experience. Today Negroes and whites are reassessing the meaning of equality and the limits of protest techniques.

Never has a long, hot summer dawned quite so early in spring—and never has the Negro leadership approached it in so deep a state of disarray. The civil-rights movement stands at the brink of another riot season, its black constituency more restive than ever, its white allies increasingly disaffected, its own command hopelessly divided over means and even basic ends. "The Movement is dead," one of its best and most knowledgeable Washington friends said last week. And, if the obituary is premature, it is no less certain that the Negro American has come to an hour of quickening crisis.

The Movement won its memorable victories marching in unison, the reformers side by side with the revolutionaries, the nation and the government behind them. But those triumphs over Southern segregation now seem suddenly pale against the shadows of poverty and despair in the ghetto, and neither leaders nor followers are certain which way to go next. Reformers like the NAACP's Roy Wilkins, the Urban League's Whitney Young and free-lance idea man Bayard Rustin

argue a politics of coalition—but the coalition began crumbling long ago as marches, riots and antiwhite sloganeering moved ever closer to home. SNCC's Stokely Carmichael preaches "black power" without a program; CORE's Floyd McKissick tries to practice it without a bankroll. And most critically of all, Martin Luther King, a man synonymous with civil rights for many whites, has wandered at least part-time into the peace movement—a diversion scarcely calculated to win friends or influence public policy. The old ecumenical spirit that bound the leaders one to another, and to white America, is plainly a thing of the past. "The glue," a government man says dolefully, "isn't there."

Worse still, the babel of voices is mixed with the gathering portents of violence. . . .

   * * *

. . . "There is no city in the U.S. in the summer of 1967 that's really free from the possibility of violence," one leading civil-rights figure warned last week.

'TARGET CITY': The real tragedy is that, after three violent summers, the riot has become an accepted if not acceptable fact of American life. The

Movement has neither the reach nor the resources to enforce peace in the ghetto: . . .

* * *

The Movement, at this critical moment, is not even agreed on precisely what the problems are. By Stokely Carmichael's lights—and he is increasingly the style-setter for the militants —black America is the white man's colony, held in thrall by its fear of the master class and by its paralyzing doubts about itself. Carmichael, accordingly, has cast himself as a sort of itinerant shock therapist. "We're all caught up in rhetoric, we don't have a program," frets one SNCC staffer. But Carmichael's program is rhetoric, and his language today is, if anything, more inflammatory than it was when he and his black-power preachments burst on the national consciousness a year ago.

He shrills at the whole pantheon of American heroes, from Christopher Columbus ("a dumb honky")* through George Washington ("a honky who had slaves") and Abe Lincoln ("another honky") to Lyndon Johnson ("a buffoon"). He urges Negroes watching Tarzan on TV to "yell for the black people to come together and beat the hell out of him." "To hell with the laws of the United States," he tells black audiences. He characterizes riots as "rebellions," insists that the black man need not apologize for them, and exhorts: "If a honky tries to shoot you, kill him before God gets the news." At the drop of a slogan, he will set a crowd chanting endlessly against the Vietnam war: "Hell no, we won't go!"

* "Honky" is Stokelyese, of uncertain origin, for the white man. One guess is that the term derives from "hunky"—a derogatory term for a Hungarian or any East European. Carmichael shrugs off etymology and offers a synonym instead: "cracker."

'IN THE RED'. And he has found an audience: a generation of Negro college students who were kindergartners when the Supreme Court struck down school segregation in 1954, not yet teen-agers when the sit-ins of 1960 sparked the Negro revolt—and are bitterly impatient today. Carmichael has spent the past two months touring campuses, soaking whites $1,000 for a rather tame exposition of black power, charging Negro colleges $500 for the gloves-off treatment. The circuit ride is partly an act of fiscal desperation: SNCC's fund sources are drying up ("We're gloriously in the red," enthuses one staff monastic) and some field men have not been paid in five months. Even more, it is an effort to captivate the young, some as prospective recruits (SNCC hopes to field 300 Negro students in Alabama this summer), others as black-power activists on their campuses or in their hometowns.

Carmichael is not entirely happy in his work. . . . He talks among friends as though he had accomplished his mission: "We've been making men out of Negroes—men who aren't afraid of honkies whether they're wearing sheets or badges . . . Now, black power is legitimate, and we can begin to challenge white institutions." Yet he has little more to show . . . than an unmeasurable impact on the black man's psyche and the white man's nerves. . . .

ANGRY TALK: CORE's McKissick is a good deal more programmatic, despite a taste for angry talk and a nomadic instinct for ultimately profitless causes. (His latest: Adam Clayton Powell and Cassius Clay.) Movement insiders say that he is really a constructive sort—that he embraced black power partly under pressure from some black nationalists in his high command, partly to rescue CORE from folding under a $500,000 mountain of debts. He still defends the choice: CORE, he says, has halved its debts and lifted the mortgage from its future. ("One year ago we were about to close," he told *Newsweek's* Ruth Ross. "Not now.") Yet he acts rather like a man who has painted himself into a corner. "You would like us to stand in the streets and chant black power for your amusement," he lectured a recent meeting of U.S. newspaper editors. "You'd rather know us by black power than by our program."

*   *   *

McKissick's programs are scarcely more radical than the NAACP's or the Urban League's. But he and Carmichael represent a romantic, even a millenarian strain in the Movement: they call on Negroes to give up on the System and make do by themselves. It is precisely this that divides them from the Youngs, the Wilkinses and the Rustins. The moderates have no illusions about the depths of altruism within the System. "The history of America has been response to tragedy and crisis," says Whitney Young. "You have five accidents at a street corner and you put up a stoplight." But, as they move into the long, twilight struggle for decent jobs, housing and schools, they recognize that they need the System more than ever before.

CHANGES: And their grand strategy has changed accordingly. "Before," says Movement intellectual Rustin, "it was dreams and courage: sit in a bus and go to jail. We need much more than that now. Then, we had Bull Connor, hoses and dogs—I doubt that we'll have that again. Now, economics becomes the crucial issue, and you have to go to Congress to get the billions you need. The center of gravity has moved from protest to politics." Roy Wilkins, a graying old soldier of 65 who has dealt in both techniques, quite agrees. The drama of the sit-ins and the big parades has given way, in

his view, to "the infighting, the subtleties, stopping the effort to cut off what has been gained. How do you deal with those from whom you've won half a loaf when they maneuver to make it a quarter-loaf—or if it's a whole loaf and they try to delay it? You study first what it's all about, then you buttonhole congressmen, you hold seminars to spread the word to the voters . . . Threatening techniques will not fill the bill."

The moderates are a good deal less certain about how to reconstruct the old civil-rights consensus—if, indeed, it can be reconstructed at all. The NAACP lobbies and educates and registers voters; Young proselytizes businessmen; Rustin works toward Negro-labor-clergy liberal coalitions on single issues. Yet the war and the white backlash have sapped Congress's will to act. "Rent supplements, demonstration cities, the poverty program, aid to education—these are the civil-rights issues today," says Young—and all are in varying degrees of money trouble. . . .

MONOLITHIC: And so pessimism underlies the professed optimism of the moderates. The cycle of black anger and white backlash has run beyond their control. "Out of 19 million Negroes," says Young, "18,990,000 didn't throw a Molotov cocktail or shout 'black power'—they suffered patiently as they always have." Yet Negroes are still a monolithic "they" to many whites, and "they" seem fitted to be judged on the excesses of a minority within a minority. . . .

For moderates and militants alike, the crucial figure is Martin Luther King—and both have energetically paid him court. Neither side comes to King with any deep, enduring love. The moderates rate him a poor tactician; the militants still mockingly call him "De Lawd," and one SNCC worker says sourly: "He's got one foot in the cotton field and one in the White House." Yet both sides recognize him as the Movement's most powerful icon, and King wavers between them.

'PIED PIPER': Some of the moderates wish King had remained in his native South leading "pied piper" voter-registration campaigns instead of carrying his Dixiefied protest techniques north to Chicago. His campaign there, indeed, is floundering. It has so far produced no more than marginal victories: a paper fair-housing treaty that has yet to be effectively implemented, and at least a piece of the backlash that helped unseat liberal U.S. Sen. Paul Douglas. . . . Yet, if the moderates were privately upset by the Chicago campaign, they are openly dismayed by King's drift into the peace movement. Whitney Young argued against the idea in a marathon phone talk with King that ran till 3:30 one March morning; Rustin, an old and trusted friend with his own deep roots in antiwar crusading, argued in vain that King at least ought to get out of the leftist-organized Spring Mobilization march on the United Nations Plaza last month.

But King appeared at the Spring Mobilization, and, though he cautiously left the platform before Carmichael's flammable speech, he accepted Stokely's embrace of welcome to the fold. Next day, King showed up at a secret strategy caucus of civil-rights leaders, government men and foundation angels, convened by the Field Foundation in New York. The elders of the Movement were preoccupied with the nitty-gritty issues: finding jobs, registering voters and implementing programs already on the books.

SUMMIT: King listened in, vowed that he would be spending no more than 3 to 5 per cent of his time on peace and asked the Movement mainliners for a second date nine days later to talk about their problems some more. But, two days before that session, King and Dr. Benjamin Spock announced a "Vietnam Summer" project to put 10,000 recruits in the field drumming up opposition to the war. King subsequently insisted he had no intention of going as far as leading a third-party "peace ticket" for 1968. But the scheduled civil-rights summit suddenly seemed pointless; it never came off. "The Movement is back where it began," one Urban Leaguer remarked joylessly. "It's us and the NAACP."

"The tragedy," one moderate elder said, "is not that King is going to the peace issue but that he's leaving civil rights. Instead of providing the inspirational leadership, the magnetism, he's diverting energy and attention from the basic problems of poverty and discrimination. . . .

*   *   *

Yet King, during a two-month winter retreat in Jamaica, appeared to have locked himself into his new course. . . . He considered his role as a Nobel peace laureate, a clergyman, even a prophet. And he reached his decision: "Most of my time will still be spent in the civil-rights movement . . . but I refuse to segregate my principles. I cannot limit my moral concern to only one area, civil rights."

And he drifted, in the process, a shade closer to the Carmichael view of the world. "I can't unite [with him] around violence and black separation," King told *Newsweek's* Marvin Kupfer. But a soupcon of SNCC's anti-establishment line found its way into a little-publicized position paper King delivered to his own Southern Christian Leadership Conference: "Our nettlesome task is to discover how to organize our strength into compelling power so that government cannot elude our demands . . . SCLC must now undertake a massive job of organization to gain economic and political power for Negroes." And he has decreed a new set of militant techniques toward that end; an escalated Chicago marching and organizing campaign (perhaps including a new fair-housing assault on bellicose Cicero), a twenty-city boycott campaign against companies with discriminatory hiring policies, an effort to remobilize white college students for work in political-education campaigns.

'THOUGHT-OUT DEMONSTRATIONS': Most of all, King has decided that the war is not only morally wrong in itself but a barrier to further progress for the Negro. "Many of the very programs we're talking about," he says, "have been stifled because of that war in Vietnam. I am absolutely convinced that the frustrations are going to continue to increase in the ghettos of our nation as long as the war continues." He insists he will pick his peace activities with care, march only in "well-planned, thought-out demonstrations." But he will weave Vietnam into his civil-rights speeches as well. "I have been in the ghettos and talked to many people," he says. "The one time they rise to their feet is when I speak out on Vietnam." If his new voice of protest had precisely the opposite effect on many white moderates who once were part of the civil-rights consensus, so be it. "The damage to the Movement," King insists, "is just not a question. I don't think anybody supporting the civil-rights movement with the right point of view will drop their support."

So King, more than any single figure, stood for the confusions besetting the deeply divided Movement in its critical hour. The marches and the sit-ins and the triumphs of the past had sealed the Negro American's dignity into law—without materially altering the hard, bread-and-butter conditions of his life. Yet a decade and more of protest—and three summers scarred by violence—had left white tempers ragged; even those whites still disposed to listen were uncertain whom to listen to. . . .

CHAPTER SIX

Public Opinion and Interest Groups: Who Speaks for Me?

Few concepts in democracy are more widely held and more fluently ex
pressed than the belief in the validity of public opinion. The American literar
tradition is full of lyrical references to "the sovereignty of the people," and ou
everyday language contains such aphorisms as "You can't fool all of the peopl
all of the time," or "Know the truth and the truth shall make you free."

In the middle of the nineteenth century, Abraham Lincoln said, "Publi
sentiment is everything," and a few years later James Bryce referred to ou
political system as "government by popular opinion." This idealistic appraisal o
public opinion was rudely shattered after World War I by the opinion theorist
who, using the tools and findings of some of the new social sciences, tended t
discount or to deglamorize the earlier exaltations. New concepts of mass an
individual psychology, many emphasizing the irrational and emotional bases o
opinion, refuted or at least modified some of the previous assumptions.

In the 1920's Walter Lippmann published *Public Opinion* and *The Phan
tom Public*. Both of these books reappraised the nature of public opinion an
the role of the average man in the process of self-government. In the 1950'
there were alarming concerns that the passive persuasiveness of mass medi
and the "engineering of consent" would do serious damage to the integrity an
critical power of public opinion. Today there is still great solicitude regardin
the impact of mass media and the danger of manipulation by public opinio
experts. However, there may well be a trend toward more confidence in publi
opinion or, at least, a greater feeling of the importance of public opinion. A

V. O. Key, Jr., points out, "Unless mass views have some place in the shaping of public policy, all the talk about democracy is nonsense."

From a consideration of public opinion it is just one short step to a discussion of lobbying activity and interest groups. Public opinion, like all forms of social interaction, has a group basis. Groups meet. They have opinions. They take public positions. Their views are expressed frequently with great skill and great effectiveness.

The following chapter discusses the role of public opinion and lobbying activity in representative government. The material is presented in the framework of two issues—"Public Opinion—The Voice of the People or the Echo of the Makers of Opinion?" and "Lobbying: Pressure Politics or Communication and the Right of Petition?"

THE VOICE OF THE PEOPLE OR THE ECHO OF THE MAKERS OF OPINION?

Do the people have the same opportunity to be heard as they had a century ago? Is public opinion becoming merchandized and manipulated? How powerful is the public relations industry? Some students of contemporary trends see great danger in the combination of electronic communication and "the engineering of consent." Other writers take a more relaxed view of the present scene. These individuals point out that there are protections built into the system. For example, there are many publics and subpublics and we know the things that sway one public will alienate another. We also know there is a difference between the "attentive" public and the public at large and that public opinion may be silent as well as active. The latent public, however, serves as a check upon irresponsible and unrestrained leadership. Finally, there is a system of interaction between democratic leadership and the mass, and in this interaction public opinion rules an area within which permissive governmental discussion and action may occur.

Eugene Burdick discusses the new underworld of psychologists, sociologists, pollsters, and survey experts who appear to be playing an increasing role in American politics. Following this, Herbert Blumer analyzes public opinion in terms of its composition and effect. The section ends with a case study on change in public opinion.

LOBBYING: PRESSURE POLITICS OR COMMUNICATION AND THE RIGHT OF PETITION

Probably no other process in American government is more debatable and subject to more subjective interpretation than is lobbying activity. Not only are the techniques of lobbying increasing faster than our knowledge and understanding, but its role and influence are highly controversial. In the section on lobbying and pressure politics, James Deakin discusses lobbying from the vantage point of a Washington correspondent. Lester W. Milbrath analyzes it from the perspective of a political scientist. The section ends with a short case study.

1

The New Underworld *

EUGENE BURDICK

Who are the people in the "new underworld"? Why does Eugene Burdick use the phrase, the "new underworld"? Do you agree that the advent of the "new underworld" will mean the "end of politics as Americans have known it in the past"?

There is a benign underworld in American politics. It is not the underworld of cigar-chewing pot-bellied officials who mysteriously run "the machine." Such men are still around, but their power is waning. They are becoming obsolete though they have not yet learned that fact.

The new underworld is made up of innocent and well-intentioned people who work with slide rules and calculating machines and computers which can retain an almost infinite number of bits of information as well as sort, categorize, and reproduce this information at the press of a button. Most of these people are highly educated, many of them are Ph.D.'s, and none that I have met have malignant political designs on the American public. They may, however, radically reconstruct the American political system, build a new politics, and even

modify revered and venerable American institutions—facts of which they are blissfully innocent. They are technicians and artists; all of them want, desperately, to be scientists.

The American public believes that it "chooses" the Party candidates for the Presidency and then makes a free and sovereign choice between the two candidates. This is hardly an accurate description of what happens. The American public believes it is sovereign. It is not. The American public believes that its views "trickle up" to the halls of the Congress and the White House and become law. This is rarely so. The American public believes in some vague and undefined way that its opinion is a fundament of our democracy. Too often this is not the case.

This situation is not evil. There is no conspiracy against the American public. There is only a great gap in knowledge. A few know a great deal, the great mass know very little. The few that know decide the shape and character of American politics.

* Eugene Burdick, Preface to *The 480* (New York: McGraw-Hill Book Company, 1964), pp. vii-ix. Copyright © 1964 by Kamima, Inc. Reprinted by permission of the publisher.

The Presidential candidate will say, publicly, often, and with a profound hypocrisy that he believes in the "common man" and is appealing to him. It is a form of Plato's Royal Sie: there are plenty of common men about and all the candidates know them well. They will vote out of habit for the party they voted for at the last election, and the one before. The "uncommon man" is the person the candidates are trying to find, identify, analyze and appeal to. The victorious Presidential candidate is the one who is most successful in appealing to the uncommon voter.

The "uncommon voter" is not, alas, always a superior person. His "uncommonness" sometimes consists of being bloody minded, hostile, ignorant, frightened and prejudiced.

The Presidential candidate will make the form appearances before the "bosses" and the political rallies, but he knows these are not important. Political dinners at $100 a plate will not affect the election. The Presidential candidates this year care very little whether the major newspapers or *Time* or *Newsweek* indorse them. They will be courteous to editors and publishers, but they know that newspapers and magazines comment significantly after an election not before. Most of the newspapers opposed F.D.R. each time he ran and it did not hurt him. It would appear that the American voters do not necessarily trust the political views of their newspapers.

Who will the Presidential candidates listen to? They will attend most carefully to the views of their invisible underworld, usually quite small. There is every reason to believe that President Kennedy defeated Vice-President Nixon in 1960 in great part because President Kennedy had put together a perceptive, quick, and "scientific" group from the new underworld. Nixon tried but was not as successful as Kennedy in his recruiting.

Every Presidential aspirant must say "I believe that the American people when they have all the facts will make the right decision." But he knows it is not true. The average American voter has neither the interest nor the information to make a rational decision between the two major Presidential candidates. The average voter votes the way his father did. He tells his wife to vote the way he does ... and usually she obeys. Furthermore, these American voters are exposed to words and slogans which have been carefully researched to make sure they have exactly the desired effect. The candidates listen to these expert, a-political, neutrals much more closely than to any boss from Boston or Chicago or the Far West.

Why the phrase "new underworld"? Because these people operate in happy anonymity. This underworld, made up of psychologists, sociologists, pollsters, social survey experts and statisticians, cares little about issues. That is one reason the candidates keep them invisible. The *romantic* heart of politics is partisan rather than neutral and deals with issues rather than statistics.

There is nothing un-American in all of this. On the contrary, it is in the best American tradition to use new facts, new discoveries, new insights. But there is a potential here which is ominous. First, the existence and mode of operation of the new underworld should be made known to the people. Much of the information given to President Kennedy in 1960 was handled at the time as if it were "top secret" classified information. Copies of reports were numbered and the information was seen only by those who had to see it. This was not casual reading, this was armament for a major battle.

Slavish adherence, to such advice might mean the end of statesmanship. Candidates often do not say what they believe: they say what they know the people want to hear. And if farmers want to hear something which is contradictory to what trade unionists want to hear, two speeches will be written. One will be delivered in Des Moines and the other in Detroit. The new techniques could make a science out of this hypocrisy.

"The public temperature" is taken. If the pulse is feverish, the public is told "fever is good. I support it." The "public pulse" is taken and if it is low the public is told "passivity is good. I stand four-square behind it."

This may or may not result in evil. Certainly it will result in the end of politics as Americans have known it in the past. . . .

2

The Nature of Public Opinion *

HERBERT BLUMER

What is meant by the "universe of discourse"? Is public opinion a unanimous opinion? Is it the opinion of the majority? Why must an issue exist before we can have a public? Does the author feel that public opinion is irrational, emotional, and unreasoned?

Public opinion should be viewed as a collective product. As such, it is not a unanimous opinion with which everyone in the public agrees, nor is it necessarily the opinion of a majority. Being a collective opinion it may be (and usually is) different from the opinion of any of the groups in the public. It can be thought of, perhaps, as a composite opinion formed out of the several opinions that are held in the public; or better, as the central tendency set by the striving among these separate opinions and, consequently, as being shaped by the relative strength and play of opposition among them. In this process, the opinion of some minority group may exert a much greater influence in the shaping of the collective opinion than does the view of a majority group. Being a collective product, public opinion does represent the entire public as it is being mobilized to act on the issue, and as such, does enable concerted action which is not necessarily based on consensus, rapport, or chance alignment of individual choices. Public opinion is always moving toward a decision even though it never is unanimous.

* Herbert Blumer, *Principles of Sociology*, ed. Alfred McClung Lee, rev. ed. (New York: Barnes and Noble, Inc., 1951), pp. 191-93. Reprinted by permission of the publisher.

The Universe of Discourse

The formation of public opinion occurs through the give and take of discussion. Argument and counter-argument become the means by which it is shaped. For this process of discussion to go on, it is essential for the public to have what has been called a "universe of discourse"—the possession of a common language or the ability to agree on the meaning of fundamental terms. Unless they can understand one another, discussion and argumentation are not only fruitless, but impossible. Public discussion today, particularly on certain national issues, is likely to be hampered by the absence of a universe of discourse. Further, if the groups or parties in the public adopt dogmatic and sectarian positions, public discussion comes to a standstill; for such sectarian attitudes are tantamount to a refusal to adopt the point of view of one another and to alter one's own position in the face of attack or criticism. The formation of public opinion implies that people share one another's experience and are willing to make compromises and concessions. It is only in this way that the public, divided as it is, can come to act as a unit.

Interest Groups

The public, ordinarily, is made up of interest groups and a more detached and disinterested spectator-like body. The issue which creates the public is usually set by contesting interest groups. These interest groups have an immediate private concern in the way the issue is met and, therefore, they endeavor to win to their position the support and allegiance of the outside disinterested group. This puts the disinterested group, as Lippmann has pointed out, in the position of arbiter and judge. It is their align-ment which determines, usually, which of the competing schemes is likely to enter most freely into the final action. This strategic and decisive place held by those not identified with the immediate interest groups means that public discussion is carried on primarily among them. The interest groups endeavor to shape and set the opinions of these relatively disinterested people.

Viewed in this way, one can understand the varying quality of public opinion, and also the use of means of influence, such as propaganda, which subvert intelligent public discussion. A given public opinion is likely to be anywhere between a highly emotional and prejudiced point of view and a highly intelligent and thoughtful opinion. In other words, public discussion may be carried on different levels, with different degrees of thoroughness and limitation. The efforts made by interest groups to shape public opinion may be primarily attempts to arouse or set emotional attitudes and to provide misinformation. It is this feature which has led many students of public opinion to deny its rational character and to emphasize instead, its emotional and un-reasoned nature. One must recognize, however, that the very process of controversial discussion forces a certain amount of rational consideration and that, consequently, the resulting collective opinion has a certain rational character. The fact that contentions have to be defended and justified and opposing contentions criticized and shown to be untenable, involves evaluation, weighing, and judgment. Perhaps it would be accurate to say that public opinion is rational, but need not be intelligent.

The Role of Public Discussion

It is clear that the quality of public

opinion depends to a large extent on the effectiveness of public discussion. In turn, this effectiveness depends on the availability and flexibility of the agencies of public communication, such as the press, the radio, and public meetings. Basic to their effective use is the possibility of free discussion. If certain of the contending views are barred from gaining presentation to the disinterested public or suffer some discrimination as to the possibility of being argued before them, then, correspondingly, there is interference with effective public discussion.

As mentioned above, the concerns of interest groups readily lead them to efforts to manipulate public opinion. This is particularly true today, when public issues are many and the opportunities for thorough discussion are limited. This setting has been conducive to the employment, in increasing degree, of "propaganda"; today most students of public opinion find that their chief concern is the study of propaganda.

3

A Case Study in Change in Public Opinion *

ANGUS CAMPBELL, PHILIP E. CONVERSE, WARREN MILLER and DONALD E. STOKES

What does the following selection tell us about the intensity with which voters hold their views? To what extent does time alter or distort public opinion? In your judgment, how realistic is the public's view of men, events, and the political environment?

At the beginning of the Eisenhower years our interviews with a cross section of the electorate explored the public image of Eisenhower himself, of his Democratic opponent, of the Republican and Democratic Parties, and of the groups and issues that the parties and candidates were thought to affect. These materials were duplicated by interviews with a new sample of the electorate in the campaign of 1956, at the end of Eisenhower's first term.[1] By comparing interview responses at these two points in time we have a remarkable portrait of public feeling toward the elements of politics in this period and of changes in its content through an interval of four years. Percept and affect are freely mixed in the view

---

* Angus Campbell, Philip E. Converse, Warren Miller, and Donald E. Stokes, "A Case Study in Change in Public Opinion," THE AMERICAN VOTER, ab. ed., (New York: John A. Wiley and Sons, Inc., 1964), pp. 16-26. Reprinted by permission of the publisher.

[1] For this purpose a standard set of eight free-answer questions was used in the pre-election interviews of 1952 and 1956. For each of the parties, one question sought favorable responses and one unfavorable responses, and for each of the candidates, one question sought favorable comment and one unfavorable comment.

of parties and candidates held by the electorate, and the qualities attributed to these objects evoke strong evaluative feeling.

The first historical period to leave an unmistakable imprint upon these responses is that of the Great Depression. Three marks of the depression experience and its political aftermath are discernible in the responses given in the first Eisenhower-Stevenson election. First of all, the Democratic Party was widely perceived in 1952 as the party of prosperity and the Republican Party as the party of depression. Great numbers of responses in that year associated the Democrats with good times, the Republicans with economic distress. Secondly, there was in 1952 a broad measure of approval for the domestic policies of the New Deal and Fair Deal. Favorable references to the domestic policies arising out of the Roosevelt and Truman Administrations were quite frequent. And as a third legacy of the depression experience, there was in 1952 a strong sense of good feeling toward the Democratic Party and hostility toward the Republican Party on the basis of the groups each was thought to favor. The Democratic Party was widely perceived as the friend of lower status groups; the Republican Party in opposite terms.

We do not know to what extent these attitudes had lessened in force from the mid-Depression years. Yet it is remarkable how strongly they carried over into the 1950's despite the efforts of Republican presidential candidates in every election since 1936 to create a more liberal image of the party. With a Republican President elected at last, the events of 1952 to 1956, however, challenged several of the assumptions on which the attitudes of an earlier era had rested. In the first place, a Republican occupied the White House in these years without a serious break in the nation's good times. With the recession of 1957-1958 yet to be experienced, the influence on public attitude of the nation's high nonfarm prosperity during the first Eisenhower Administration is suggested by Table 1. References to prosperity and depression declined 50 per cent from 1952 to 1956. And four years of Republican good times destroyed most of a 14-1 margin the Democrats had had in the partisanship of these responses. After haunting every Republican candidate for President since 1932, memories of the Hoover Depression had receded,

Table 1. References to Prosperity and Depression

	1952 [a]	1956
Pro-Democratic and Anti-Republican	974	316
Pro-Republican and Anti-Democratic	70	213
Totals	1044	529

[a] In this and subsequent tables the number of responses in 1952 has been increased by the ratio of the size of the 1956 sample to the size of the 1952 sample to make possible a direct comparison of frequencies in the two years. The effect of the adjustment is to equate frequencies whose size relative to the size of their respective samples is the same. In reading these tables it should be kept in mind that one respondent could make more than one reference; hence the number of references may be larger than the number of individuals mentioning a given subject.

Table 2. References to Social Welfare Policies [a]

	1952	1956
Pro-Democratic and Anti-Republican	421	259
Pro-Republican and Anti-Democratic	96	101
Totals	517	360

[a] This tabulation is limited to domestic policies clearly in the area of social welfare. References to farm policy, civil rights legislation, etc., are not included.

at least temporarily, as a direct force in American politics.

A second aspect of this four-year interval that might be expected to challenge the attitudes of the past was the willingness of the Eisenhower Administration to embrace most of the reforms of the New Deal. This disposition to accept and even extend the social welfare policies of the previous twenty years undoubtedly lessened an important difference the public had perceived between the parties. The extent of this change is suggested by the summary of references to social welfare policies in Table-2. The references of policies of this sort was reduced by a third between these election campaigns, and the proportion of responses associating the Democrats favorably or the Republicans unfavorably with any of these policies declined substantially. As a token of this shift, the Democratic advantage on social security was reduced by two-thirds from 1952 to 1956.

The Eisenhower Administration was not equally successful, however, in dispelling the popular belief that the

Republicans were the party of the great and the Democrats the party of the small. Despite the change in public attitude toward the Republican Party on matters of economic and social welfare, the years 1952 to 1956 did not lessen this aspect of the image of the parties fixed in the Depression era. A large number of responses in 1956 still approved of the Democratic Party and disapproved of the Republican Party on the basis of the groups each was felt to support as may be seen in Table 3. The Democrats were still thought to help groups primarily of lower status: the common people, working people, the laboring man, Negroes, farmers, and (in 1956 only) the small business man. The Republicans, on the other hand, were thought to help those of higher status: big businessmen, the upper class, the well-to-do.

Changes in these parts of the popular view of the parties show the impact that changes in the external world can have on political attitudes. The forces underlying these changes may be more sharply defined if we consider the farm sector of the economy

Table 3. References to Groups

	1952	1956
Pro-Democratic and Anti-Republican	1438	1659
Pro-Republican and Anti-Democratic	256	294
Totals	1694	1953

omy. The prosperity of the Eisenhower years was felt only uncertainly on the nation's farms, and the posture of the Administration toward farm problems aroused widespread opposition. As a result, the moderation of public attitude toward the economic and social welfare record of the Republican Party did not extend to matters of farm policy. References to farm policy increased markedly between 1952 and 1956 and were strongly Democratic in partisanship. Moreover, references linking the Republicans unfavorably or the Democrats favorably with the welfare of farmers as a group were much more frequent in the latter year.

Other elements of the historical setting from which the attitudes of these years evolved are apparent in the responses given in these campaigns. Events more recent than the Great Depression had received wide attention in the years preceding the 1952 election. The worldwide struggle with the Soviet Union had culminated in a limited war that was widely seen as having exposed the nation to a humiliating defeat without having gained any essential end. The years preceding the 1952 election were also marked by increasing publicity about evidences of corruption in the federal government. Each of these more contemporary sets of events left an impression clearly discernible in the responses of 1952. References to foreign policy and the Korean War were of high frequency and strongly Republican in partisanship. And great

numbers of responses cited misdeeds of the Democratic Administration and the need for a change in party control of the executive branch.

The attitudes, too, were modified by the unfolding of events from 1952 to 1956. Several changes in the external political world are reflected in the perceptions of the parties and candidates held by the electorate. In the first place, the ending of the Korean War enhanced the impression that the Republicans were better able than the Democrats to assure peace. Mr. Eisenhower and his party were widely supported in 1952 in the belief that they might end the Korean conflict. Their success in doing so and in preventing the outbreak of hostilities involving the United States elsewhere in the world added to public confidence that the cause of peace would be better served if the Republicans were continued in office. References to war and peace in 1952 were pro-Republican or anti-Democratic by a ratio greater than seven to one. By 1956 the ratio had increased five times, owing to the virtual disappearance of comments favorable to the Democrats or unfavorable to the Republicans.

Through the first Eisenhower administration, moreover, the Republican advantage in foreign affairs publican advantage in foreign affairs came to center much more completely on questions of war and peace. The finding of fault with the Democratic handling of the early cold war conflict, particularly in eastern Eu-

Table 4. References to War and Peace

	1952	1956
Pro-Democratic and Anti-Republican	68	15
Pro-Republican and Anti-Democratic	514	595
Totals	582	610

Table 5. References to Other Foreign Issues

	1952	1956
Pro-Democratic and Anti-Republican	143	145
Pro-Republican and Anti-Democratic	567	342
Totals	710	487

rope and China, seemed to lessen with the passage of time. And there was apparently a greater sense that what a Republican Administration might be able to do in these troubled areas was not widely different from what had been done by a Democratic Administration. The trend of these responses is shown in Table 5.

It is noteworthy that the total volume of comment about war and peace and other issues of foreign affairs was small relative to the level of other sorts of responses in these years. The Second World War as well as the Korean War had intervened between the experience of the Depression and the years 1952 to 1956. Yet the number of responses reflecting the Great Depression and its political aftermath was much greater than the number referring to issues raised by these wars or any other aspect of foreign affairs. Neither conflict seems to have had a great and lasting impact on popular political attitudes. By comparison with the impact of the Civil War, the effect of the wars of the twentieth century seems slight indeed.

Public concern about the corruption issue subsided rapidly with the Democratic Party out of power. However strong the sense of Democratic sin four years earlier, the party's loss of power seems to have accomplished its expiation by 1956. The swift decline of comment of this sort suggests that mismanagement and corruption are not issues that are easily kept alive after a change in control of the government.

At least one aspect of our recent political history is notable for the relatively slight extent to which it influenced public attitude toward parties and candidates in these years. In view of the enormous furor over internal subversion and the conduct of Senator McCarthy, it is astonishing to discover that the issue of domestic Communism was little mentioned by the public in 1952. The third element of the slogan reminding the electorate of "Corruption, Korea, and Communism" apparently was wide of the mark. Corruption and Korea were salient partisan issues for the electorate in that year. Communism, in the sense of domestic subversion, was not. Fewer responses touched the issue of domestic Communism in 1952 than referred to such esoteric subjects as the Point Four program and

Table 6. References to Corruption and "Time for a Change" Theme

	1952	1956
Pro-Republican references to corruption	546	93
Pro-Republican references to need for a change	490	. . .
Pro-Democratic references to corruption	. . .	20
Pro-Democratic references to need for a change	. . .	23

Table 7. References to Groups

	1952	1956
Associated with the Republican Party	563	663
Associated with the Democratic Party	855	886
Associated with Eisenhower	112	219
Associated with Stevenson	164	185
Totals	1694	1953

foreign economic aid and Mr. Stevenson's marital problems. By 1956 the issue had virtually disappeared.

Of the elements of politics that had emerged relatively recently as objects of partisan feeling, none was of greater importance in these years than the presidential candidates. The fact that the great prize of American politics is won by popular endorsement of a single man means that the appearance of new candidates may alter by a good deal an existing balance of electoral strength between the parties. An inspection of popular response to the candidates in these years suggests the correctness of the Republican strategy of using a figure who had won immense public esteem outside politics to overturn a long-established Democratic majority. The content of this response tells something, too, about the changes that may occur in public reaction to the figures of presidential politics.

An inspection of references to matters of group interest and to domestic issues in 1952 and 1956 makes clear that response of this sort was associated more with the parties than it was with either of the candidates. A summary of these references strongly suggests that the attitudes they reflect were for the most part formed prior to the entry of Mr. Eisenhower and Mr. Stevenson into the political arena. In 1952 neither of these men was perceived in these terms to any significant degree. Although each candidate evoked somewhat more responses of this sort four years later, the numbers of responses connecting either with group interest or issues of domestic policy were still small by comparison with the volumes of comment on these matters associated with the two parties. With respect to Mr. Eisenhower, this result was due in part to a moderation in domestic controversy during his first Administration. But it must also be an extraordinary comment on the way Mr. Eisenhower had interpreted his office. In view of the enormous responsibilities for legislative, partisan, and executive leadership that attach to the presidency, it is difficult to believe that a man could serve four

Table 8. References to Domestic Issues

	1952	1956
Associated with the Republican Party	1276	898
Associated with the Democratic Party	1825	1001
Associated with Eisenhower	164	322
Associated with Stevenson	162	357
Totals	3427	2578

Table 9. References to Foreign Issues

	1952	1956
Associated wtih the Republican Party	336	329
Associated with the Democratic Party	420	183
Associated with Eisenhower	546	481
Associated with Stevenson	62	58
Totals	1364	1051

years in this office and yet be associated with domestic issues to as slight a degree as an opponent who was wholly without public office in the same period.

Mr. Eisenhower was of course much more widely associated with issues of foreign affairs. Owing to his background, somewhat more than a third of all references to war and peace and to other foreign issues in 1952 were associated with Eisenhower. In 1956, with a smaller volume of total comment about foreign affairs, this fraction was increased to nearly one-half. Both major parties were frequently linked with foreign issues in the first of these elections, but with the Democratic Party's record receding in time, relatively fewer of these comments referred to the Democrats in the second campaign. In neither year did Mr. Stevenson make any marked impression on the electorate in relation to foreign affairs. In view of his great concern with foreign policy, the attention he gave to foreign issues in his campaign addresses, and his travels abroad between these elections, this fact suggests how deep may be the gulf that separates the public's view of a candidate and the image he seeks to project. Mr. Stevenson probably had had more contact with foreign affairs than most presidential candidates. Yet his contact failed to cross the threshold of public awareness.

We have already called attention to the likelihood that a new figure in national politics will be evaluated by the public partly in terms of his connection with his party. This was true of both Mr. Eisenhower and Mr. Stevenson in these years. In each campaign, references were made to the fact that a candidate was the representative of his party and bore the party symbol. The extent to which Eisenhower and Stevenson were evaluated in these terms may be seen in Table 10. These figures make clear that the tendency to evaluate the candidates in terms of party was less pronounced in the second of these elections.

Although a candidate is likely to be seen partly in terms of his connection with party and with issues of public policy and matters of group

Table 10. References to Candidates in Terms of Party

	1952	1956
Favorable to Eisenhower	121	57
Unfavorable to Eisenhower	220	162
Favorable to Stevenson	264	202
Unfavorable to Stevenson	360	64
Totals	965	485

Table 11. References to Personal Attributes of the Candidates

	1952	1956
Favorable to Eisenhower	2256	2226
Unfavorable to Eisenhower	906	854
Totals	3162	3080
Favorable to Stevenson	1416	1045
Unfavorable to Stevenson	555	1184
Totals	1971	2229

interest, he will be evaluated as well in terms of personal attributes. In the presidential elections of the 1950's most references to the candidates dealt with their record and experience, their abilities, and their personal characteristics. Since General Eisenhower entered politics as an established public figure, it is not surprising that his personal attributes were much more fully described in public response than were those of Governor Stevenson. In the campaign of 1952 references of this sort to Eisenhower exceeded in number references to personal qualities of Stevenson by more than sixty per cent. The figures of Table 11 indicate that at the end of Eisenhower's first term his personal characteristics were far better known to the public than were those of Mr. Stevenson. Nonetheless, a profound change in public attitude toward Stevenson is evident in these data. The perception of Stevenson's personal characteristics was less full in 1952 than that of Eisenhower's; but it was warmly favorable. By 1956 the response to Stevenson was much less approving. More than half the references to his personal attributes in the latter year were unfavorable.

A finer analysis of response to the candidates brings to light a number of changes in their public images between the two campaigns.

The character of these changes suggests several clues to the forces shap-

ing perceptions of the candidates in these years. A full classification of references to Eisenhower suggests that his appeal, already strongly personal in 1952, became overwhelmingly so in 1956. In the earlier campaign, Eisenhower's military experience and record in Europe were clearly remembered. By 1956 these themes had receded, without the substitution of nearly as many references to his record and experience as president. Moreover, references to his skills as leader and administrator were fewer in 1956 than before. It was the response to personal qualities—to his sincerity, his integrity and sense of duty, his virtue as a family man, his religious devotion, and his sheer likeableness—that rose substantially in the second campaign. These frequencies leave the strong impression that in 1956 Eisenhower was honored not so much for his performance as President as for the quality of his person.

The flaws in the Eisenhower image were few, and in neither campaign were they matters for which the candidate could be held entirely accountable. In 1952 a large number of references cited Eisenhower's background as a military man (446) and his lack of experience in civil government (198). Presumably his induction as President and subsequent nonmilitary bearing quieted most of these doubts (only 16 references to lack of experience in 1956), though

Table 12. Favorable References to Eisenhower and Stevenson [a]

	Eisenhower		Stevenson	
	1952	1956	1952	1956
Generally good man, capable, experienced	301	330	200	190
Record and experience				
Military experience	202	111	–	–
Record in Europe	250	94	–	–
Political and other experience	57	106	354	115
Qualifications and abilities				
Good leader, knows how to handle people	138	107	19	20
Good administrator	64	26	36	10
Strong, decisive	53	32	7	11
Independent	70	17	32	21
Educated	97	62	149	180
Good speaker	31	42	141	100
Personal qualities				
Integrity, ideals	271	291	111	77
Sense of duty, patriotism	70	74	25	20
Inspiring, inspires confidence	53	39	14	4
Religious	19	85	7	2
Kind, warm	11	41	11	8
Sincere	63	126	33	33
Likeable, nice personality, I like him	220	363	91	77
Good family life	26	57	9	4

[a] Since a number of minor categories have been omitted from Table 2-12, the totals are somewhat smaller than the entries of Table 2-11.

comments on his military background were still given in 1956 (63 references). Critical response in the latter year dealt primarily with the issue of his health (386) and his capacity to be a full-time president (64). Other than this the only unfavorable reference of any frequency was the doubt that Eisenhower as President was wholly his own man (73).

The popular response to Stevenson showed a general lessening of enchantment in his second appeal to the electorate, but several details of this loss in esteem stand out. The benefit to Mr. Stevenson of having been Governor of Illinois, as measured by references to his record and experience, seems largely to have

been dissipated after four years. References to his experience in public service dropped quite low in 1956, and comments about his lack of experience increased over the four-year period from 25 to 72. Also, references to Stevenson's personal qualities, which had been substantially favorable in his first campaign, were much less so in his second. Responses like "I don't like him" increased from 34 to 159. Surprisingly, Stevenson's divorce seemed more on the public's mind in the latter year (from 85 to 137 references). Finally, the response to Mr. Stevenson's campaign performance was much more critical in 1956 (261 references) than in 1952 (103 references).

4

*A Washington Correspondent Looks at Lobbying**

JAMES DEAKIN

Why is the popular image of lobbying misleading? Is it true that "he who pays the piper calls the tune" in American politics? How does the author justify his contention that if there were no Washington lobbyists we would have to create some?

Politicians come and politicians go, as the public chooses. But the lobbyist —the hardy, resourceful agent of the non-public interest—goes on forever.

Lobbyists have been called a secret, invisible arm of government. Washington's lobbying corps has been nicknamed "the third house of Congress" and "the fourth branch of government." Both labels attest to the intimate relationship between lobbying and government. Often the nicknames have been less complimentary: "influence peddlers," "fixers," "five percenters" and, in an earlier day, "boodlers."

To apply these epithets indiscriminately to all lobbyists today is both inaccurate and unfair. The modern lobbyist is more likely to be a technician, competent and well informed in his field. He performs a vital function in furnishing Congress with facts and information. But he is more than a technician of facts. He is a technician of pressure. He exerts pressure on those who make the laws.

Washington swarms with lobbyists.

It always has and probably always will. More than 1,100 individuals and organizations are currently registered as lobbyists, which means that, on the face of things, they outnumber the 535 members of Congress by two to one. But the real ratio is much higher than that. Because the law regulating lobbying is virtually a dead letter, a horde of company representatives, public relations men, lawyers and organizations engaged in influencing government in one way or another do not register as lobbyists. There are at least 8 to 10 lobbyists for every member of Congress.

No group in Washington is more controversial than these gentlemen. Their operations are scrutinized occasionally—and usually unfavorably— by Congress, the President and the press. But remarkably little is known about the lobbyists themselves and what they do.

They are an immensely diverse crew.

A lady named Margo Cairns has been gently pressuring Congress for years to adopt the corn tassel as the national floral emblem. She is a lobbyist.

* James Deakin, *The Lobbyists* (Washington, D.C.: Public Affairs Press, 1966), pp. 1-8, 12-15. Reprinted by permission of the publisher.

Attorney Charles Patrick Clark represents Franco Spain and various well-heeled clients to the tune of $200,000 a year, about twice the salary of the President of the United States. He is a lobbyist.

A group of Washington teen-agers organized a campaign to persuade Congress to vote more money for the capital's dilapidated schools. Several of the students registered under the lobbying law. They were lobbyists.

Frank Ikard, a former Texas Congressman, registered as a lobbyist shortly after he became executive vice president of the American Petroleum Institute at a salary of $50,000 a year. While in Congress, Ikard was a member of the House Ways and Means Committee, which has jurisdiction over such matters as oil depletion allowances. At the present time he is president of the institute.

A "retired" couple, Harry and Ruth Kingman, pound the marble corridors of Congress in unceasing, selfless pursuit of votes for public interest legislation, including civil rights and federal aid to education. Kingman, a former Y.M.C.A. executive in his seventies, and his wife, in her sixties, are the entire staff of the Citizens' Lobby for Freedom and Fair Play. Their organization has an annual budget of just over $8,000, most of which comes from Kingman's pension. They are lobbyists.

Stephen G. Slipher, an assistant vice president of the powerful United States Savings and Loan League, is in the $40,000 to $50,000-a-year bracket. His assistant, Glenwood S. Troop; makes more than $25,000 a year. So does Sidney Zagri, legislative counsel for the International Brotherhood of Teamsters. Former Congressman Andrew Biemiller, head of the AFL-CIO's legislative department, draws about $20,000 per year. All these men are lobbyists. . . .

If there were no lobbyists, as Voltaire said of God, we would have to invent some. In effect the founding fathers authorized lobbying. As a result of some frustrating experiences with George the Third, they decided the American people must have a guaranteed right of access to their new government. Lobbying followed, inevitably.

Today lobbying is so inextricably bound up with the governmental process that it is often hard to tell where the legislator leaves off and the lobbyist begins.

Lobbyists draft much of the legislation introduced in Congress. Some lobbyists estimate that fully half of the bills dropped in the hopper are written in whole or part by pressure groups. Lobbyists write and present much of the testimony heard by Congressional committees. Lobbyists and special interest spokesmen ghostwrite many of the speeches given in Congress.

The public relations firm of Selvage and Lee, Inc., representing the Overseas Companies of Portugal, admitted writing speeches on Portuguese policy in Angola for 14 legislators. One of them was Representative Joseph W. Martin Jr., Massachusetts Republican and former Speaker. Selvage and Lee boasted that Martin "used [our] stuff without change, apart from abbreviation."

Lobbyists have been known to use Congressmen's offices as their own, sometimes with long-distance telephone calls and stenographic help thrown in, all at the taxpayers' expense.

Lobbyists take an intimate part in the continual wheeling and dealing, the conferring, negotiating and compromising that go on in the formation of laws.

Not surprisingly, there are some distasteful connotations to the word lobbyist. In the minds of a good many Americans it conjures up disreputable images. It suggests a sinister character slinking through the halls of Congress, trailing behind the faint aroma of thousand-dollar bills. To the cringing Congressman, desperately in need of ready cash to meet his alimony, the overhead on his yacht and the demands of his Lolita, this crafty traducer dispenses the long green from a handy little black bag. In return for which the fawning legislator cheerfully sells the Republic down the river. After the vote, of course, there is the nightly orgy at the palatial manse of the beautiful Washington hostess who is having an illicit affair with this or that prominent Senator, and all clink glasses in a toast to another good day's work.

Bribes, blondes and booze—these are the durable ingredients in the popular image of lobbying and an everlasting boon to writers for slick magazines and Sunday supplements. The changing nature of American politics, however, has reduced the importance of all three as elements in pressure and power.

There are no reliable statistics on cash bribery and outright corruption, since the participants seldom advertise and cannot be depended upon to answers questionnaires truthfully. But students of government agree that the direct bribe—once a standard lobbying technique—is not a major factor today. The campaign contribution, perfectly legal and absolutely vital to most members of Congress, is another matter. The campaign donation, not the out-and-out bribe, is an important weapon in modern lobbying. But even it is far from being the only way in which money is used to influence the course of government.

Some authorities caution that the campaign contribution can be overrated as a means of gaining influence and exerting pressure. Professor Alexander Heard, who made a thorough study of money in American politics, concluded that "he who pays the piper does not always call the tune, at least not in politics. Politicians prize votes more than dollars."

Nevertheless, many Washington lobbyists, are heavy contributors to the national party committees and to individual Congressmen. Furthermore, their contributions frequently go to members of Congressional committees which handle legislation directly affecting the interests of their clients. To interpret all campaign gifts by lobbyists as altruistic donations, as contributions given purely out of desire for good government, would be risky. But to view them only as bribes is to ignore the realities of government. They fall somewhere in between.

Sex is, if anything, a more dubious factor in lobbying today than the bribe. Sex is nice, but it doesn't necessarily swing votes.

There are several reasons for this. Extramarital dalliance is politically dangerous for the married Congressman. And if he is a chaser despite his vows, he does not have to depend on the lobbyist as a source of supply. Washington is freshly furnished each year with a new stock of callipygian young things eager to work on Capitol Hill. The amateurs always outnumber the pros.

This is not to say that Washington is sexless. The amatory proclivities of some lawmakers are an endless source of gossip at the equally endless cocktail parties. But the lobbyist who uses girls in his work is more likely to find himself obtaining them for his out-of-town clients and employers on their trips to Washington than for Congressmen. There are exceptions, but generally speaking, bedroom gymnastics have little real impact on the business of making laws. For one thing, the older legislators who dominate Congress, and who are the objects of the lobbyist's tenderest concern, are not easily swayed by women. They have other vices, other rheums. Their main and enduring vice is power.

There are differences of opinion about the third item in the popular lobbying trilogy—entertainment (including, of course, liquor). When political scientist Lester W. Milbrath interviewed 100 Washington lobbyists, he found that they gave entertaining a very low rating. On an effectiveness scale of 0 to 10, entertainment scored a median of 1.17. The lobbyists explained that members of Congress and other top officials are deluged with invitations, that some of these are "required" social events which they feel they must attend, and that they are under such pressure to go to parties that an evening spent at home with the family "seems like a gift."

Nevertheless the lobbyists do a lot of entertaining. It has been estimated that 1,500 large cocktail parties complete with receiving line and music— "alcoholic mass meetings," one reporter has called them—take place in Washington each year. Besides these are numberless at-home dinners and parties, large and small. Not all of these affairs are given by lobbyists. The diplomatic corps, the military and the Mmes. Mesta and Cafritz are unflagging. But lobbyists are among the most indefatigable party-givers.

A veteran staff member of a Senate subcommittee subject to intense lobbying pressures advised:

"Don't leave out the parties. They're damned important, especially with the new Congressmen. . . .

Washington is a very practical town, and money and votes mean more than liquor. In the final analysis, this is why bribes, blondes and booze don't rank as high as they once did in the lobbyist's scheme of things. They just aren't as important to the Congressman (to his political survival, which is his first law) as votes, and the money with which to get votes. The legislator may accept the lobbyist's entertainment, and gladly, but he is far more likely to do what the lobbyist wants if votes are involved.

Entertainment remains an important lobbying technique, but its principal function is to create and maintain good will. It is not usually a major determining factor in the legislative process. Some lobbyists explain that they wine and dine the lawmakers primarily because their clients expect them to, not because they believe it will have a direct impact on legislation. Many businessmen, they say, assume that what works corporately will work governmentally. The experienced lobbyist may consider this naive, but to tell the client would be to jeopardize the expense account, so the partying goes on.

There are always, of course, the sleazy, fly-by-night operators, holding forth over drinks in the crowded hotel bars on Capitol Hill, talking big, and willing, for a price, to try to "reach" a Congressman with a thinly-veiled campaign contribution, a drinking bout or a party girl. These are the shady, not-so-clever gentry who end up in the headlines. It makes spicy reading, but the point to remember is that this kind of thing seldom affects the course of government in any significant degree.

After an extensive investigation of lobbying, a House committee headed by the late Representative Frank Buchanan of Pennsylvania discussed the changed character of lobbying. "In the 1870's and 1880's, 'lobbying' meant direct, individual solicitation of legislators, with a strong presumption of corruption attached," the committee said. But in the middle of the twentieth century, the Buchanan report went on, it means something quite different.

"Modern pressure on legislative bodies is rarely corrupt... it is increasingly indirect, and [it is] largely the product of group rather than individual effort," said the committee. The key words are "indirect" and "group."

Indirect pressure consists of campaigns to whip up public opinion for or against a piece of legislation. These campaigns almost always are organized and directed by lobbyists or lobbying groups. Indirect pressure, also known as grassroots lobbying, is one of the prime techniques of modern lobbying. In terms of the money spent and the impact on the public interest, it is the most important technique. It has the greatest effect on the legislator simply because it involves a large number of actual or potential votes.

Group pressure, as the Buchanan committee pointed out, means that large organizations, possessing the financial resources required to organize grassroots pressure, and commanding substantial blocs of votes, are the most significant factor in lobbying today. The massive, heavily-financed grassroots campaign is the trademark of modern lobbying, not the cash-under-the-table, babes-in-the-bedroom approach of the nineteenth century entrepreneur.

The individual lobbyist is, of course, still with us and always will be. He is as important as ever, but these days he usually operates with a big corporation, a trade association or a labor union behind him. He regularly combines direct lobbying and persuasion of Congressmen with organized indirect pressure from the legislators' constituents back home....

* * *

The conventional image of lobbying unfortunately misses both the good and the bad sides of the subject. Conceiving of the lobbyist only as tempter and corrupter, it ignores his very real contribution to the process of making laws. The Congressman confronted with an annual mountain of complicated legislation and distracted by the problems of his constituents, must rely on the lobbyist for facts, statistics and information. This is the informational side of lobbying, and it is essential.

The immense complexities of the American economy make it impossible for Congress to legislate without informed, expert assistance. It must know, as accurately as possible, how a law will affect the diverse elements of the economy. One means of transmitting this information is the lobbyist.

In the case of federal highway legislation, for example, the late Senator Richard L. Neuberger of Oregon commented that three substantial segments of the economy felt that their interests were directly at stake: the truck lines, the railroads because the truck lines are their principal competitors for freight, and the American Automobile Association because the motorist pays most of the cost of building the highways.

"Lobbyists for these groups paraded to my office constantly," Neuberger reported. "They presented vast quantities of facts and figures—some of which I challenged, but a lot of which were accurate and impressive. No improper inducement ever was ventured. Without the data made available by railroads and truckers and the A.A.A., I doubt if I would have felt fully qualified to reach a decision on the kind of highway bill which was best for the nation."

From the founding days of the Republic it has been recognized that special interest groups must be represented in some way in the councils of government. . . .

. . . Professor Heard has observed that "no popular government in history has yet survived that did not in some way permit such interests to exercise effective means of petition."

The interplay of special interests in the formation of laws is considered one of the strengths of democracy. It is vital to the survival of the democratic system that groups with well-defined interests—business and industry, labor, farmers, veterans, teachers, professional men, women's groups and so on—have a way of communicating with the legislature. Many devices are used to make this communication possible. The lobbyist is one of them. He is an agent of the special interest group, the nonpublic interest.

5

A Political Scientist Looks at Lobbying *

LESTER W. MILBRATH

How does the author support the position that "the overall impact of lobbying is relatively minor"? What are the best safeguards against irresponsibility and possible corruption in lobbying activity? What positive contribution does lobbying make to the political process"?

The weight of the evidence that this study brings to bear suggests that there is relatively little influence or power in lobbying per se. There are many forces in addition to lobbying which influence public policy; in most cases these other forces clearly outweigh the impact of lobbying. Voters set the broad trends of public policy which all the other influences on policy must follow. It is for this reason that so many forces battle to manipulate public opinion. Public opinion is a factor which sets the boundaries for the policy struggle. On certain questions the boundaries are closely restricted, and the policy decisions of officials must closely follow public demands. On other questions the boundaries may be broader, leaving wider discretion to decision-makers and more possibility for lobbyists to influence their decisions. Questions of large public attention and import are chiefly determined by considerations of political success and winning the next election. The chief executive, through his political leadership, his ability to mold public opinion, and his command of the resources and imagination of the executive bureaucracy, has the greatest single impact on the shape of public policy. Questions of small technical nature, which attract little public attention, are more subject to lobbying influence.

* Lester W. Milbrath, *The Washington Lobbyists* (Chicago: Rand McNally and Company, 1963), pp. 354-58. Reprinted by permission of the publisher.

The growth of one lobby group or coalition generally stimulates the development of an opposing group. Most careful observers of governmental decision-making have concluded that the overall impact of lobbying is relatively minor. This point was made by both lobbyist and congressional respondents and agrees with the observation of other writers on the subject.[1]

If the conclusion that lobbying has a relatively weak impact on policy is added to the conclusions that system controls and legal controls are adequate, that public decisions cannot be bought or stolen, and that the lobbying process is relatively clean, the result is clear: lobbying as we see it today in Washington presents little or no danger to the system. This does not mean that a dangerous situation could not arise or that lobbyists would not engage in unethical or unfair tactics if they believed these would be to their special advantage. The best insurance against danger and corruption in the process is an alert citizenry which elects responsible officials to public office. A wide-open communications system and viable and responsible public media are important preconditions to maintaining public alertness.

* * *

Eckstein raises the most fundamental question about lobbying and pressures groups: "What contributions do pressure groups make to the political system as a whole, and do these contributions tend to make the system more or less viable (stable and effective)? Are their consequences 'dysfunctional' or 'eufunctional' for the larger systems in which they operate?"[2] Though this study focuses on lobbying rather than pressure groups, the question is essentially the same; however, the contribution of these data to an answer is relatively limited.

In this context it is relevant to point out again that lobbying is inevitable and is likely to grow in scope. One lobbyist says it is analogous to automobile drivers: there are a few bad drivers, but people continue to drive, and more cars are added to the road each year. Lobbying is protected by the First Amendment to the Constitution, and government officials are not disposed to hamper its growth or activities.

Granted the inevitability of lobbying, what are its positive contributions to the political process? Lobbyists provide information and other services which are welcomed by governmental decision-makers. These services are costly and somewhat wasteful; the public or the consumer pays for them ultimately; congressional officials even claim they could function quite adequately without them. In another sense, however, they are indispensable. If information from lobbyists and lobby groups was, for some reason, unavailable to government officials, they would be largely dependent on their own staff for information and ideas. Since the Congress is reluctant to staff itself adequately, it would have to turn primarily to the Executive for information. This would create an even further imbalance between Congress and the Executive in policy-mak-

[1] William S. White, *Citadel: The Story of the U.S. Senate* (New York: Harper & Row, Publishers, 1956), pp. 145, 149; Donald R. Mathews, *U.S. Senators and Their World* (Chapel Hill: University of North Carolina Press, 1960), pp. 195-96; V. O. Key, Jr., *Public Opinion and American Democracy* (New York: Alfred A. Knopf, Inc., 1961), chap. xx.

[2] Harry Eckstein, *Pressure Group Politics: The Case of the British Medical Association* (London: George Allen & Unwin, 1960), p. 152.

ing.[3] More important, cutting off lobbying communications would eliminate a valuable, even indispensable, source of creativity. There is no assurance that government institutions can turn up all the possible alternative solutions to policy problems. A decision-maker who has his mind made up may well have to have new points of view forcefully thrust upon him before he can perceive and accept them. The clash of viewpoints between contesting groups is not only informative; it also is creative. Formerly unperceived alternatives may arise from the challenge to previously accepted possibilities.

Eckstein (1960, p. 162) suggests that *lobby groups perform* two other indispensable functions in the political system: *integration and disjunction.* Officials must know very specifically what the effects of a given policy will be and how citizens will react to that policy. Lobby groups and lobbyists define opinion for government with a sense of reality and specificity which political parties, the mass media, opinion polls, and staff assistants seldom, if ever, can achieve. Aggregating and defining specialized opinions have both integrative and disjunctive aspects. The function is integrative in that persons with special interests or problems need group action to aggregate their views and communicate the positions to officials. The aggregation process requires some compromise on the part of group members and therefore is integrative. Group opinion is a more manageable consideration for officials than scattered individual opinions.

Specialized opinion is disjunctive as well, in that it encourages multiple group demands. Political parties (especially in a two-party system) strive for a very broad integration in order to win elections. That kind of integration can be achieved only by reaching a very low and vague denominator which may not be very functional for making policy. If special interests were confined to vague representation through political parties, they might begin to feel alienated from a political system which persistently distorts their goals.[4] Affording disparate interests special representation through their own lobby group probably contributes to the stability of the system. There is reason to suppose, then, that the policy-making system produces wiser or more intelligent decisions and functions with more stability than might be the case if lobby groups and lobbyists were not present. If we had no lobby groups and lobbyists we would probably have to invent them to improve the functioning of the system.

---

[3] The author is indebted to James A. Robinson for suggesting this point.

[4] The Washington representatives at the Brookings round table all represented corporations. They expressed dissatisfaction with general business organizations such as the National Association of Manufacturers and the National Chamber of Commerce and even with their own trade associations for compromising too much on policy, being too vague, and being too slow to take action. Paul W. Cherington and Ralph L. Gillen, *The Business Representatives in Washington* (Washington, D.C.: The Brookings Institution, 1962).

6

*Pressure Politics: A Case Study**

JAMES DEAKIN

*How do the older techniques of lobbying activity differ from the new "styles"?
What is meant by "lobbying at the grassroots"? Is it not probable that Telstar
would have passed on its own merits without the behind-the-scenes maneuvering?*

Stately, plump Alexander Wiley
seemed pleased with himself as he
came out of the committee room.

Although his Wisconsin constituents
were soon to replace him, Wiley at this
time was the senior Republican member of the United States Senate, with
almost 24 years tenure. He was the
ranking G.O.P. member of three important committees—Foreign Relations, Judiciary, and Space Sciences.
The last-named committee was considering a bill to put the communications satellite (Telstar) program in the
hands of a private corporation dominated by the American Telephone and
Telegraph Company.

Waiting for the Senator as he
emerged from the space committee
meeting was a younger man, well-
dressed and extremely personable. He
was a lobbyist for A.T. and T. The two
men walked down the hall to Wiley's
office, chatting amiably.

Months before the Telstar bill came
to a vote, the lobbyist became a regular visitor to Wiley's office. He dropped

in at least once a day, and sometimes
twice, for a period of several months.
"He called on Wiley constantly," said
a former member of the Senator's staff.
"He was a very pleasant person, very
sophisticated. He made himself useful
to Wiley in a multitude of ways."

The lobbyist assigned to Wiley was
one of a team of A.T and T. men who
fanned out quietly and efficiently
through the halls of Congress to help
smooth the passage of the Telstar
measure through an already-complai-
sant legislature.

From the home states and districts
of members of Congress came vice
presidents and managers of local telephone companies, solid men of good
standing in the community, often long-
time friends or acquaintances of the
Senators and Representatives. Virtually every member was visited at least
once.

Within a week after the Telstar bill
was introduced in the House, a Texas
Congressman was contacted by every
important businessman in his district,
with only three exceptions. Curious
about the three, he checked and found
they were on a fishing trip. The calls
and letters from the businessmen,
urging him to support the Telstar

* James Deakin, *The Lobbyists* (Washing-
on, D.C.: Public Affairs Press, 1966), pp.
26-28. Reprinted by permission of the publisher.

measure, were prompted by a telephone company executive in his district.

Much of the lobbying in this connection was on a geographic basis. Southern Senators, for instance, were visited by an executive of the Southern Bell Telephone Company. Often he brought along a vice president of the Bell System located in the Senator's area. The conversations were invariably cordial. Most of the time, said a participant in several such conferences, the telephone officials simply probed, pleasantly but persistently, into the Congressman's stand on the Telstar measure. Their visits served, of course, to remind the legislator of the political and economic importance and pervasive influence of a corporation whose operations extend into almost every hamlet in the land and whose assets total some 26 billion dollars.

In arguing for private ownership of the burgeoning space communications industry, the A.T. and T. men emphasized that their corporation had spent $50,000,000 on space communications research between 1957 and 1962. Rarely did they mention the amount contributed in the same period by the American taxpayer—$175,000,000 on space communications technology specifically and a staggering 25 billion dollars on the general space program, many aspects of which were closely related to communications.

The A.T. and T. lobbyists were discreet, unobtrusive—"They always used a soft sell approach," a committee staff aide commented—and [were] unfailingly helpful. They were particularly attentive to Senators who appeared to be wavering on the Telstar bill.

Did the Senator want information about Telstar? The lobbyists supplied it promptly, sometimes instantly, and then followed up with telephone calls several days later to see if any more statistics were desired. "The most striking thing about the A.T. and T. material," said one Senator, "was that it almost completely ignored everybody else who had contributed to the space communications program."

A.T. and T.'s blanket lobbying for the Telstar bill paid off handsomely. The space committee reported out the measure unanimously, and later the Senate approved it by a vote of 66 to 11. Amendments offered by a small band of liberals to protect the public interest were defeated by similarly lopsided margins. A filibuster effort by the liberals was brushed aside contemptuously. For the first time since 1927 cloture was voted to cut off debate.

CHAPTER SEVEN

Political Parties and Political Philosophies: The Will and the Way

Both the critics and the supporters of the American party system strongly believe that political parties are essential to a modern democracy. The two groups divide over whether the two major parties should be stronger, should develop more party discipline, and should adopt distinguishing principles and distinctive tenets. Within each political party there are liberal and conservative groups which make themselves heard on every national issue. In this chapter we propose to examine political parties in the first problem, "Do American Political Parties Mean Anything?" Then we turn to a discussion of conservatism and liberalism in the section, "Which Way America—Right, Left, Neither?"

Do American Political Parties Mean Anything?

The problem posed in this section is in a sense twofold: (1) What are the differences, if any, between the Democratic and Republican parties? (2) should political parties in America sharply oppose each other, take programmatic positions, and develop more party discipline?

Critics of the present condition frequently argue that the two major political parties are as alike as two peas in the same pod. Further, since the two parties do not differ over things that matter, the entire body politic suffers. In short,

American political parties are flabby, weak, and unable to provide the necessary responsibility in government.

Supporters of the American political party system assert that there are both psychological and actual differences between the parties. Both Democrats and Republicans see their party as different from the opposition party and many voters *believe* there are significant differences. Beyond this, it is pointed out that there *are* actual differences in orientation, philosophy, and the general stance of the two parties. Proponents of the existing system insist that the flexible, resilient, and compromising character of American political parties is the real genius of American government.

In the following section Will Stanton humanizes and humorizes about the two parties. Clinton Rossiter analyzes sociological, psychological, historical, and economic differences between the parties. Stephen K. Bailey discusses the present status and future of both parties.

WHICH WAY AMERICA—LEFT, RIGHT, NEITHER?

There is a fairly widespread assumption that political parties in America have no discernible differences but that the terms "conservative" and "liberal" are solid words with fixed dictionary meanings. This may be true to some extent in the abstract. However, it is confusing and sometimes utterly misleading to apply the conservative and liberal label to individuals and groups on the contemporary political scene. Here one finds a range of views, a complexity of loyalties, and a whole spectrum of personal convictions.

In his book, *Conservatism in America: The Thankless Persuasion*, Clinton Rossiter classifies American conservatives into three main groups—ultra-conservatives, middling conservatives, and liberal conservatives. He dramatizes the difficulties of definition by distinguishing between "conservative" (a generic heading for those who believe in a philosophy based upon order and tradition) and "Conservative" (a precise term for those who hold a philosophy reaching back to Edmund Burke). Nor is the problem of the conservatives a singular one. Liberals face the same dilemma in attempting to encompass the views of all who march under their banner. In fact, liberalism has been referred to as a "wild deuce" that can fit in any hand.

All of this makes categorical statements hazardous. As an alternative to definitive explanations, we present the views of two distinguished Americans, one a noted conservative; the other an eloquent liberal. Barry Goldwater states his views in "The Conscience of a Conservative" and Senator Eugene McCarthy of Minnesota sets forth his convictions in "The Conscience of a Liberal." To add to the picture, a noted scholar, Daniel Bell, comments on the radical right and the politically dispossessed, while a *Time* essay discusses "The New Left—What Is It"?

1

How to Tell a Democrat from a Republican *

WILL STANTON

Are there real differences between Democrats and Republicans or does everything depend upon picking the right kind of parents, choice of residence, occupational status, educational attainment, and financial position? How many of the social and psychological characteristics between the two parties do you regard as valid?

To the casual observer of turtles, it is pretty hard to tell the difference between a male and a female. Fortunately, this doesn't present any problem to turtles. So it is in politics. It takes no more than a glance for a Republican to spot a Democrat and vice versa, although to the outsider they may appear to be almost indistinguishable. It is true that their platforms and points of view do overlap—to about the extent that a dime covers a penny. However, there does remain this narrow border of difference, and this is the area I should like to explore.

The Democrats tend to think of themselves as the more openhanded party. Surprisingly, the Republicans agree. You have to have an open hand, they say, in order to reach into somebody else's pockets. They, in turn, think of themselves as more tightfisted. Again there is agreement. They already have theirs, the Democrats

point out, and they're not going to let anyone take it away.

Although Republicans are traditionally the party of wealth, some extremely rich families are Democrats. A similar situation exists in England, where a few families are so unbelievably ancient that they don't have to send their children to the proper schools. Here, these people are so loaded they don't have to be Republicans. When one of them runs for high office, the argument is that he is so rich he can afford to run the country as a sort of hobby. The Republicans are more likely to represent their candidate as a sober sort of chap who could use the job.

This brings up a curious facet of our economy. Bankers, being Republican, would prefer to lend their money to other Republicans. The catch here is that other Republicans already have money. So bankers must daily undergo the traumatic experience of handing over money to people they consider irresponsible and untrustworthy at best.

During a recent survey in an Eastern university, it was discovered that whereas the faculty were predomi-

* Will Stanton, "The View From the Fence, or How to Tell a Democrat From a Republican," *Ladies Home Journal*, November, 1962, pp. 58-59. Reprinted by permission of the author.

nantly Democrats, the students were, for the most part, Republicans. The only significant exception to this pattern was the football team, whose members had been recruited mainly from Democratic families. It was felt that these athletes would not change their political views until their bowling alleys had started paying off.

Republicans are often pictured as solemn or even pompous—Democrats are more frivolous. That is to say, Democrats are the sort who go around pushing one another into swimming pools on which a Republican holds the first mortgage.

In general, Democrats are people trying to get someplace—Republicans are people trying to stay where they are. Both feel the Government should help them do it. It may help to picture them as Jack Sprat and his wife, with the country being represented by the platter.

Critical observers are fond of referring to the Democrats as the War Party and to the Republicans as the Depression Party. No one has ever explained who started all the wars and depressions before there were Republicans and Democrats. It is as though the Russians should accuse the United States of having started athlete's foot. It wouldn't do anyone any harm and might have a therapeutic effect on the Russians—helping them to relieve tension and anxieties.

Perhaps if we pay a visit to an imaginary small town, the differences between the two factions can be noted more specifically. The first things we notice as we approach are the signs erected by the chamber of commerce and the various service and business organizations. These will be manned mostly by Republicans. Perhaps the town has a little-theater group; here you will find nothing but Democrats— at least on the stage. There are two explanations for this. The Democrats maintain that Republicans make poor actors. The other viewpoint is that actors make poor Republicans.

At any rate, all the Republicans you will find in a little-theater group will be in the box office or on the board of directors. Then when the actors demand fancier costumes or more greasepaint, the board says, "No, you can't have it." Most people feel that is the natural order of things.

Incidentally, the plays they put on will be written by Democrats. Republicans do their share of writing, but not plays. They write letters to the editor. Democrats circulate more petitions and carry more signs. Republicans do biographies of other Republicans. They feel these are the only fit subjects for a literary work. Republican women usually write about their grandfathers.

It has been suggested that a man best reveals himself by the things he throws away. Let us suppose, for example, that in exploring our imaginary small town we come upon a trash can containing an empty sour-mash whiskey bottle and some sprigs of sodden mint. A Democrat lives here. Moving on, we find a bottle that has contained a fine brand of Scotch. A Republican this time. But now we find not one but several empty Scotch bottles of various brands. This one is tricky. Not, as you might first suppose, a number of Republicans sharing a common trash can. This would be greatly out of character. Much more likely, I think, a Democrat wishing to impress the trashman.

Continuing our exploratory walk along a tree-shaded street we see a house. It is two and a half stories high, painted tan with brown trim.

In front there are matching ba with built-in seats, a bed of rhubarb door are panels of stained glass. In th center of the door is a bell with handle that turns. At one corner is hexagonal tower with a cupola. Ther is a lilac bush in front of this, some what root-bound, and along the side is a row of peonies.

In the backyard is a grape arbor with built-in seats, a bed of rhubarb, and by the back door a trumpet vine. The garage was formerly a carriage house. In it is a three-year-old dark-blue sedan of the medium-price field. If you examine the inside of the rear window, you will discover the remains of a Nixon sticker.

A month later we pass the house again. There is a red-and-cream station wagon in the driveway with one door open. It is last year's model, but looks considerably older. Directly in back of one rear wheel is a toy steam shovel. In the backyard a badminton net trails from a single, listing pole. There is a case of empty tonic bottles beside the front door. From the hi-fi in the living room comes the voice of Dylan Thomas. A family of Democrats has moved in. The former owners have gone to Pasadena.

In this account I have attempted to feel my way along, stepping on the same number of toes on either side of the fence. I have tried to avoid singling out any one person or group as an object of ridicule. The only fair and just way—indeed the American way in my opinion—is to offend everybody equally.

To Be Read Aloud by a Democrat To a Republican or by a Republican to a Democrat

Although to the casual glance Republicans and Democrats may appear to be almost indistinguishable, here are some hints which should result in positive identification:

Democrats seldom make good polo players. They would rather listen to Béla Bartók.

The people you see coming out of white wooden churches are Republicans.

Democrats buy most of the books that have been banned somewhere. Republicans form censorship committees and read them as a group.

Republicans are likely to have fewer but larger debts that cause them no concern.

Democrats owe a lot of small bills. They don't worry either.

Republicans consume three fourths of all the rutabaga produced in this country. The remainder is thrown out.

Republicans usually wear hats and almost always clean their paintbrushes.

Democrats give their worn-out clothes to those less fortunate. Republicans wear theirs.

Republicans post all the signs saying NO TRESPASSING and THESE DEER ARE PRIVATE PROPERTY and so on. Democrats bring picnic baskets and start their bonfires with the signs.

Republicans employ exterminators. Democrats step on the bugs.

Republicans have governesses for their children. Democrats have grandmothers.

Democrats name their children after currently popular sports figures, politicians and entertainers. Republican children are named after their parents or grandparents, according to where the most money is.

Large cities such as New York are filled with Republicans—up until 5 P.M. At this point there is a phenomenon much like an automatic washer starting the spin cycle. People begin pouring out of every exit of the city. These are Republicans going home.

Democrats keep trying to cut down on smoking, but are not successful. Neither are Republicans.

Republicans tend to keep their shades drawn, although there is seldom any reason why they should. Democrats ought to, but don't.

Republicans fish from the stern of a chartered boat. Democrats sit on the dock and let the fish come to them.

Republicans study the financial pages of the newspaper. Democrats put them in the bottom of the bird cage.

Most of the stuff you see alongside the road has been thrown out of car windows by Democrats.

On Saturday, Republicans head for the hunting lodge or the yacht club. Democrats wash the car and get a haircut.

Republicans raise dahlias, Dalmatians and eyebrows. Democrats raise Airedales, kids and taxes.

Democrats eat the fish they catch. Republicans hang them on the wall.

Democrats watch TV crime and Western shows that make them clench their fists and become red in the face. Republicans get the same effect from the presidential press conferences.

Christmas cards that Democrats send are filled with reindeer and chimneys and long messages. Republicans select cards containing a spray of holly, or a single candle.

Democrats are continually saying, "This Christmas we're going to be sensible." Republicans consider this highly unlikely.

Republicans smoke cigars on weekdays.

Republicans have guest rooms. Democrats have spare rooms filled with old baby furniture.

Republican boys date Democratic girls. They plan to marry Republican girls, but feel they're entitled to a little fun first.

Democrats make up plans and then do something else. Republicans follow the plans their grandfathers made.

Democrats purchase all the tools—the power saws and mowers. A Republican probably wouldn't know how to use a screwdriver.

Democrats suffer from chapped hands and headaches. Republicans have tennis elbow and gout.

Republicans sleep in twin beds—some even in separate rooms. That is why there are more Democrats.

2

Democrats or Republicans: What Difference Does It Make *

CLINTON ROSSITER

Does the author assert that there are strong differences between Democrats and Republicans? What generalizations does he make regarding the character of the two parties? Where would Professor Rossiter place the heart of each party?

. . . My answer, I fear, will prove unsatisfactory to many, because in some important respects there is and can be no real difference between the Democrats and the Republicans, because the unwritten laws of American politics demand that the parties overlap substantially in principle, policy, character, appeal, and purpose—or cease to be parties with any hope of winning a national election. Yet if there are necessary similarities between the Democrats and the Republicans, there are also necessary differences, and we must have them clearly in mind before we can say that we understand the politics of American democracy. [The classic statement of the point of view that there is no real difference between the parties was made by Bryce in *The American Commonwealth:*

There are now two great and several minor parties in the United States. The great parties are the Republicans and the Democrats. What are their principles, their distinctive tenets,

their tendencies? Which of them is for free trade, for civil service reform, for a spirited foreign policy, for the regulation of telegraphs by legislation, for a national bankrupt law, for changes in the currency, for any other of the twenty issues which one hears discussed in the country as seriously involving its welfare?

This is what a European is always asking of intelligent Republicans and intelligent Democrats. He is always asking because he never gets an answer. The replies leave him in deeper perplexity. After some months the truth begins to dawn upon him. Neither party has anything definite to say on these issues; neither party has any principles, any distinctive tenets. Both have traditions. Both claim to have tendencies. Both have certainly war cries, organizations, interests enlisted in their support. But those interests are in the main the interests of getting or keeping the patronage of the government. Tenets and policies, points of political doctrine and points of political practice, have all but vanished. They have not been thrown away but have been stripped away by Time and the progress of events, fulfilling some policies, blot-

* Clinton Rossiter, *Parties and Politics in America* (Ithaca, N. Y.: Cornell University Press, 1960), pp. 108-118, 148-149. © 1960 by Cornell University. Reprinted by permission of the publisher.

ting out others. All has been lost, except office or the hope of it.[1] [2]

The parties themselves—the leaders, organizers, propagandists, and "card carriers" of our two enduring coalitions—seem to have a number of differences clearly in their minds, or should I say firmly in their viscera? Emotion, after all, is a vital ingredient of politics, and our parties are about as divided on emotional grounds as we would want them to be. Scratch a real Republican and you will find a man with a deep suspicion of the Democrats. Scratch a real Democrat and you will find a man at least as ready to assault the Republicans as he is to bicker with his own colleagues. Perhaps the best way to measure the emotional gap between the two parties is to talk in terms of images. What image does each party have of itself? What image does it have of the other party? These are admittedly vague questions to which one can give only vague answers that are derived largely from a process best described as "intuitive empiricism." Yet the questions are important; they deal with some of the essential considerations of party allegiance and party division in this country. We must answer them as best we can.

Certainly the Democrats have a fairly clear self-image of themselves, and one need not read far at all in their platforms, speeches, and appeals to learn that the image is, altogether naturally, colorful and flattering. Those Democrats who raise their eyes occasionally above the consuming, two-act spectacle of the struggle for victory and the division of its spoils make much, perhaps too much, of their fabulous past. They celebrate the achievements of the party, paying special attention to its domestic and diplomatic leadership in the twentieth century and, in addition, insisting that it is

preminently "the party of the most liberty and opportunity for the most people." They salute its heroes, of whom four—Jefferson, Jackson, Wilson, and Roosevelt—loom over the landscape of memory like giants, which they were. They delight in the whole sweep of American history, certain that they have been the "movers and shakers" and their opponents, whether Federalists or Whigs or Republicans, the "stick-in-the-muds." Sometimes their enthusiasm gets the better of their sense of proportion, as when they, having laid claim to Jefferson, lay claim to the Declaration of Independence; but for the most part they have spun their self-congratulatory myths out of the substance of fact—spun nylon out of coal, as it were.

The Democrats, being primarily a party and only incidentally a lodge, are really much more concerned with the present and future than with the past. It is the image of themselves they project into the American future that moves them to their best efforts. They pride themselves as "the party of progress," as the men most willing to experiment boldly with new methods for achieving welfare, security, and prosperity. They pride themselves as "the party of the people," as the men most concerned to scatter the fruits of progress widely among all ranks and classes. They are beginning to pride themselves as "the party of the world," as the men best fitted to carry forward the work of Wilson, Roosevelt, and Truman and to negotiate benevolently and prudently with men of all nations. And deep down inside, where feelings are cherished but not openly flaunted, they pride themselves as "the party of the professionals." They are the men who have brought order to politics; they are the men who have taught the nation its lessons in meaningful compromise. Amateurism is all very well in its place, which is on the fringes of

[1] James Bryce, *American Commonwealth,* II, 20.   [2] Footnote Rossiter.

the Democratic party or at the core of the Republican party; but professionalism, be it the professionalism of Southern county bosses or Northern precinct bosses, is the essence of the kind of politics that most Democrats like to practice. The Democrats, in their own opinion, are the "old pros" of American politics. . . .

To the Republicans this self-molded image of achievement, heroism, liberty, progress, democracy, worldliness, and professional competence appears as a caricature of reality. Even when we make allowance for the natural mistrust of one band of politicians for the other band across the street, we are struck by the intensity of the Republican image of Democratic weakness, wickedness, and false counsel. Republicans usually begin their assessment of the Democratic party by throwing out everything that took place before the Civil War. Jackson is only a name out of a misty past; Jefferson would be happier with the Republicans today than with the Democrats. Whatever services the Democrats performed before the Republicans came upon the scene in 1856, their record ever since has been one of which modern Democrats, if they would ever look up from the anxious toil of keeping a brawling family from breaking up completely, would hardly choose to boast.

The plain fact is that the Republicans, for all the friendly contacts they keep with their counterparts in the Democratic party, look upon that party as a vehicle of demagoguery, radicalism, plunder, socialism, unsound economics, bossism, corruption, subversion, and ill repute. Even the stanchest Republican will boast that some of his "best friends" are Democrats, but even the mildest finds something off-color in the party as a whole. There have been too many patrician demagogues like Roosevelt and too many vulgar ones like Huey Long, too

many addlepated "pinks" like Henry Wallace and dangerous ones like R. G. Tugwell, too many big spenders like Harry Truman and big lenders like Dean Acheson and big plunderers like Frank Hague. It is a party much too willing to hazard inflation in the interest of false prosperity and real votes. It is a party racked since time out of mind by big and little bosses who have no principles save that of victory and no interest in victory save that of the spoils. The morals of party politics are never exactly dainty, the Republicans admit, but the morals of Democratic politics are downright shoddy.

Worse than all this, it is a party that cannot be trusted to maintain a patriotic front against the assaults of the nation's acknowledged enemies and the blandishments of its self-styled friends. It has harbored a shocking number of heretics, subversives, and traitors; it has surrendered our freedom of maneuver to the leaders of a dozen other countries, some of them not even friendly; it has squandered American lives and treasure in a vain search for peace and world order. As it was the party of Clement Vallandigham in the 1860's, it was the party of Alger Hiss in the 1940's. "Not all Democrats were rebels," Republican orators shouted as they "waved the bloody shirt" after the Civil War, "but all rebels were Democrats." "Not all Democrats were pinks and subversives," I heard a Republican remark just the other day, "but all pinks and subversives were Democrats—and they still are."

And as it was the party of the Boston Irish in the 1850's, it is the party of the New York Puerto Ricans in the 1960's. This is the last and most repelling element in the total image of the Democratic party held by many good Republicans: it speaks with an accent; it is not quite American; it is just not respectable. And if the accent of the Pole or the Jew or the Puerto Rican is music to the friendly ears of other, perhaps more broad-minded Republicans, there is always the accent of the Southern racist to remind them to stay put in the ranks behind Lincoln and McKinley.

This is, admittedly, a harsh image, not all of whose harshness can be explained as a simple, corrective reaction to the pretensions of the Democrats themselves. It is not an image, fortunately, on which many Republicans dwell obsessively or most Republicans are prepared to act. In the real world of politics, lawmaking, and administration it presents no insurmountable barrier to the bipartisan jockeying and co-operation that makes our system livable and workable. The image is there, nonetheless, carried sturdily in millions of Republican bosoms, and it is perhaps a more important force in the total pattern of our politics than the positive image carried by the Democrats themselves. The latter does not forbid loyal Democrats to go off the reservation; the former makes it an act of heresy for loyal Republicans to embrace the sweaty Democrats.

Let that be the essential image of the Democratic party in which both Democrats and Republicans put stock. It is indeed a sweaty army—heavy with the sweet sweat of toil for the American people, according to the Democrats themselves; reeking with the sour sweat of corruption and "80 per cent Americanism," according to the Republicans.

Democrats will say angrily that, in my review of the achievements and failures of the Republicans . . . , I was much too kind to the Grand Old Party. Republicans will say even more angrily that I was much too cruel. They, too, carry a flattering self-image in their minds, which, because of their fewer years and less motley composition, is a good deal sharper than the self-image of the Democrats. They, too,

celebrate their historic achievements, painting them in far brighter colors than the scholarly pastels I have used. Consider these claims in the *Republican Fact-Book* of 1948:

The Republican Party has a long and honorable history of majority control of this country during the most expansive period of its development. Between 1861 and 1933, Republican Presidents were in office three-fourths of the time. They shaped governmental policy which encouraged the development of the country's vast resources; built up its defenses; created its national banking system; established a currency which circulated throughout the world on a par with gold; made the credit of the country the most stable in the world; formulated economic policies which made this country the leader among all nations in agriculture, mining, and manufacturing—in short, made the United States first among the nations.

Having broken the slave bonds of the Negro and made him a free man; having bound up the deep wounds of a nation divided against itself; the Republican Party continued to proceed on a program of adherence to the principles of Constitutional Government which the genius of the founding fathers had laid down. Within the framework of justice and law, the Republican Party built up the confidence of the people in the American Way of Life.[3]

They, too, salute their heroes joyfully. If the Democrats have four giants, they have one, Abraham Lincoln, who is more than a match all by himself for these four and all others the opposition can muster. Lincoln belongs to all Americans, indeed to all men of good will everywhere in the world, but he belongs first of all to the Republicans. He is an essential myth without whom no Republican orator or organizer or platform writer would know just how to proceed. It is pos-

---

[3] *Republican   Fact-Book*   (Washington, 1948), 5.

sible that Dwight D. Eisenhower is a similar myth in the making.

The *Fact-Book* makes this short, happy statement of "Republican Principles," and catches almost perfectly the feeling millions of Republicans have about their party:

The Republican Party was originated in 1854 as the political group dedicated to the freedom of the individual and the safeguard of his inalienable rights. It has since remained steadfastly devoted to these basic American principles—free initiative, free enterprise, and the dignity of the average man. More than ever the deep significance of the Republican stand for Constitutionalism, States' Rights, encouragement of American enterprise and a minimum of Government interference with freedom of opportunity becomes apparent today when the extent to which these principles have been whittled down by the Democratic Party is realized.

Here is the essence of true Republicanism, even in these days of the modern, domesticated, politely New Dealish party: individualism as opposed to collectivism, free enterprise as opposed to "socialistic meddling," constitutionalism as opposed to "one-man rule," states' rights as opposed to centralization. It is, indeed, the party of "the American Way of Life." It took the lead in building the Way; it has defended it patriotically against subversion and radicalism; it is, in a real sense, the Way Incarnate. I do not mean this at all facetiously when I say that the average Republican is much readier than the average Democrat to identify his own party with the nation and its household gods—home, mother, the flag, and free enterprise.

A final ingredient in the Republican self-image is the warm feeling of respectability that characterizes the record, principles, operations, and tone of the party. It is businesslike without being coldly professional, sound without being callous, steady without being stale. It is "100 per cent American," not only in the stout fight it puts up for American principles, but in the mood in which it thinks, the temper in which it acts, the accent in which it speaks. Here, in particular, the image the Republicans have of themselves needs the image they have of the Democrats to bring it into sharp focus. The Democrats are plainly a disreputable crowd; the Republicans, by contrast, are men of standing and sobriety. Many a middle-class American in many a small town has had to explain painfully why he chose to be a Democrat. No middle-class American need feel uneasy as a Republican. Even when he is a minority—for example, among the heathen on a college campus—he can, like any white, Anglo-Saxon Protestant, warm himself before his little fire of self-esteem. [The situation described by Brand Whitlock in the Ohio of his youth still exists in many parts of America:

In such an atmosphere as that in the Ohio of those days it was natural to be a Republican; it was more than that, it was inevitable that one should be a Republican; it was not a matter of intellectual choice, it was a process of biological selection. The Republican party was not a faction, not a group, not a wing, it was an institution like those Emerson speaks of in his essay on Politics, rooted like oak trees in the center around which men group themselves as best they can. It was a fundamental and self-evident thing, like life, and liberty, and the pursuit of happiness, or like the flag or the federal judiciary. It was elemental like gravity, the sun, the stars, the ocean. It was merely a synonym for patriotism, another name for the nation. One became, in Urbana and in Ohio for many years, a Republican just as the Eskimo dons fur clothes. It was inconceivable that any self-respecting man should be a Democrat. There were, perhaps, Democrats in Lighttown; but then there were rebels in Alabama, and in the Ku Klux Klan, about which we read in the evening, in the Cincinnati *Gazette*.[4]] [5]

The Democrats find all this talk of the American Way of Life a sham and a bore. The Republican party with which they have to contend is a pompous, superpatriotic, self-centered, hypocritical band of hard-minded men with a unique penchant for serving themselves while insisting that they are serving all America. Who are they, ask the Democrats, to shout about individualism when they fought so bitterly against all attempts to rescue helpless individuals in the 1930's? Who are they to wave the bloody shirt of treason against the administrations of Roosevelt and Truman when they yapped and snarled at almost every constructive step toward leadership of the free world? Who are they to shout the glories of free enterprise when they have always banked so heavily on the government for friendly support of their schemes? Who are they to strike a posture of purity and wag their finger at the corruption of the city machines when they took favors from this government—protective tariffs, subsidies, land grants—that were worth billions rather than millions? The Republicans may rejoice in the memory of Lincoln, but if Lincoln were here today he would have a hard time warming to a single man in Eisenhower's Cabinet.

The essence of the Democratic image of the Republican party is the certain knowledge that, for all its protestations about liberty and justice for every American, it is the party of the few, of the rich, of the interests, of the upper classes. It is constitutionally incapable of looking out over the whole

of America and, in the skillful, purposeful manner of the Democrats, of caring for the legitimate needs of all ranks and callings. It takes no broad view; it thinks no big thoughts; it has no warm heart. It is not creative in domestic affairs, for the best it has been able to do throughout a generation of Democratic innovation and progress is first to shout "Good God! No!" and then "Me, too!" It is not reliable in foreign affairs, for it has repeatedly confused our friends and neighbors with its threats and boasts and changes of mind. It is not even what a conservative party is supposed to be: sound and prudent and steady. The Republicans, not the Democrats, produced the wildest demagogue in American history and backed him with zeal. The Republican party is indeed a minority, the Democrats conclude, in the range of its interests as well as in numbers. It is a minority, that is to say, because it deserves to be a minority.

If we can discount the natural excesses of admiration and abuse that are present in these pairs of images, we can come up with some fairly useful generalizations about the character of our two parties. To speak of the character of a group of human beings as numerous and formless as an American party is an exercise in illusion, for it is to personalize the impersonal and individualize the collective. Yet one cannot spend much time in the clubhouses and convention halls in which the parties do their political business without becoming aware of certain vague but substantial differences in character or, as I prefer, style. A gathering of Democrats *is* more sweaty, disorderly, offhand, and rowdy than a gathering of Republicans; it is also likely to be more cheerful, imaginative, tolerant of dissent, and skillful at the game of give-and-take. A gathering of Republicans *is* more respectable, sober, purposeful, and businesslike

[4] *Forty Years of It* (New York, 1914), 27.
[5] Footnote Rossiter.

than a gathering of Democrats; it is also likely to be more self-righteous, pompous, cut-and-dried, and just plain boring. In a Republican office one hears much talk of programs and policies; at a Republican convention the color and excitement, such as they are, seem labored and staged. In a Democratic clubhouse one hears much talk of votes and voters; at a Democratic convention the color and excitement are generated by the delegates themselves. Republicans seem to lean to the ideological side of politics, Democrats to the practical. The most famous of all "smoke-filled rooms" (Colonel Harvey's at the Blackstone in Chicago in 1920) was, to be sure, inhabited by Republicans, but I have the distinct impression—distinct as only the impressions of a nonsmoker can be—that the air is bluer and thicker and yet somehow softer in any room where Democrats have gathered to do their immemorial business.

Taken all-in-all, the two parties show two of the familiar faces of America, much alike in respects that would catch the attention of the foreign observer, somewhat different in those for which an American with a sharp sociological eye would be looking. A writer who has been, in his time, to many political conventions and to even more business luncheons once summed it up for me by remarking, "The Republicans look to me like Rotarians at the speakers' table, the Democrats like Rotarians at table 16, back near the entrance to the kitchen." Those at the speakers' table, we agreed, are just a little bit stiff, correct, falsely hearty, and conscious of their eminence. No angry voice is raised to mar their unity of principle and purpose. They all wear vests, they all smile brightly, they all sing the familiar songs with fervor. They are leaders of the community, and they know it. Meanwhile, back at table 16, things are more relaxed and

less self-conscious. Arguments are aired with abandon and settled (or forgotten) with a shrug. Dress is more casual, salutes are more boisterous, jokes are more earthy. They may be leaders, too, but at the moment they are just the boys at table 16. The respectable Republicans who delight in their polite unity, the relaxed Democrats who cherish their rowdy variety—they are all good Americans together, but there is a difference in their styles. That difference is caught vividly in the choice of beastly emblems that was made for all of us long ago: the slightly ridiculous but tough and long-lived Donkey—the perfect symbol of the rowdy Democrats; the majestic but ponderous Elephant—the perfect symbol of the respectable Republicans. Can anyone imagine the Donkey as a Republican or the Elephant as a Democrat? . . .

Where, then, is the heart of each party, and what is the distance between dead-center Republicanism and dead-center Democracy? The answer, I think, is that the heart of the Republican party is that position where Senator Taft pitched his famous camp—halfway between the standpattism of "the unreconstructed Old Guard" and the me-tooism of "the disguised New Dealers." The heart of the Democratic party, at least in thirty-nine states of the Union, is that position where Adlai Stevenson raised his famous standard—halfway between the aggressive reformism of "the laboristic liberals" and the moderate opportunism of "the Texas brokers." Neither of these notable men could win through to the Presidency and thus put his mark indelibly on his party. Taft, indeed, was too good a Republican even to win the nomination. Yet each in his own way and at his best moments came as close to being the beau ideal of his party as did any man in the postwar years.

The distance between the well-known positions of these two men on domestic and international affairs is a pretty accurate measure of the distance between the two parties and as reasonable an answer as one can make to those who still demand to know "the difference between the Democrats and the Republicans." The difference, I repeat, is one of tendencies rather than principles. In most parts of this country it comes down to a difference between an urban, working-class, new-stock, union-oriented party with a penchant for reform and spending, and a rural-suburban, middle-class, old-stock, business-oriented party with a penchant for the status quo and saving. Look deep into the soul of a Democrat and you will find plans to build 400,000 units of public housing and to ship 300 tractors to Ghana (whether Ghana wants them or not); look deep into the soul of a Republican and you will find hopes for a reduction in taxes and for a balanced budget.

There are those who will insist that this is not enough of a difference. Each of the parties is a permissive coalition within which the basic urges of the heart are too often sacrificed on the altar of a specious unity. Each overlaps the other excessively in principle, aspiration, and appeal; each abandons its alleged identity in the scramble for votes. And in each may be found, even in states where the Republican-Democratic split is sharpest, important men who seem to vote more often with the other party than with their own, for example, Senator Lausche of Ohio and Senator Javits of New York. To persons who complain on all these scores I can say only that those are the facts of life in a two-party system that operates under a constitution of divided authority. A party that presumes to be a majority must of necessity be a coalition; two parties that are locked in equal struggle must of necessity overlap. Let the critics of the American parties go to any other country with two-party politics, even to relatively homogeneous Britain, and there, too, they will see evidences of internal compromise and external overlap; there, too, they will hear complaints about the lack of clear-cut differences between the parties. This is the burden of the citizen of such a country, and especially of the United States: never to be sure of the "real difference" between the two parties, never to be certain that his vote will "count," always to be on the alert for maverick candidates, always to look beneath party labels at the men who wear them. . . .

3

American Political Parties *

STEPHEN K. BAILEY

A close student of American political parties, Professor Stephen K. Bailey suggests reasons why our political parties should be strengthened. He also analyzes some of the social changes which are currently taking place in American society, and ventures an opinion on how these changes are affecting our party system.

One reason why it is safe to suggest that the national party system must be strengthened in order to bring sustained power in our government is that the safeguards of the Constitution will continue to discourage any force that becomes so unified as to threaten our freedom. The American people hold firm to the sanctity of the Constitution. It is inconceivable that they would countenance a wholesale revision of the Constitution in the foreseeable future. No model of a new or improved party system that rests on substantial constitutional change is realistic.

In suggesting new directions for our national party system, therefore, the British parliamentary model is ruled out. But it is not ruled out simply because its wholesale adoption here is unthinkable. It is ruled out because it has shortcomings which do not warrant emulation. The relative independence of the legislature in the American system of government is, within limits, a powerful asset. At its best, it assures continuing social criticism and

review of the bureaucracy without which big government might easily become lethargic and unresponsive or officious and dangerous.

What we are after is a national two-party system that will continue to have room for diversity and compromise but will nevertheless bring about more coherent and responsible programming by the executive and legislative branches and more coherent and responsible criticism of policy and administration. We are after a system that will make parties compete vigorously to find the right answers; that will organize political power at the national level so that it is adequate to carry out those answers; and that will make this power ultimately accountable to popular majorities.

This neither presumes nor suggests ideological or highly disciplined parties, although it does presume differences in the ideological propensities of each party and also presumes that party members who vote consistently against their own party's majority will not be favored with positions of party power inside or outside the Congress.

Various changes in state primary laws, in methods of choosing national convention delegates and national

* Stephen K. Bailey, *The Condition of Our National Parties* (New York: The Fund for the Republic, 1959), pp. 12-13, 17-21. Reprinted by permission of the publisher.

committee members, and in grass-roots political organization could have a profound influence on national party behavior. But, in my opinion, changes of this sort will come about rapidly only if prior attention is given to the following political reforms (some of which are already under way):

One: To create mass-based, long-range, and (in part) tax-supported national party financing—not only to underwrite and extend present functions but to increase national committee services and financial aid to congressional campaign committees and to individual candidates running in primary as well as general elections;

Two: To expand two-party competition into all congressional districts and states;

Three: To create, by formal action of the two national conventions, permanent advisory councils and staffs to both national committees;

Four: To provide social and office facilities for each national party along the Mall, between the White House and Capitol Hill, to serve as symbolic and practical links between the executive and legislative branches of government, as well as between the party and its membership across the country;

Five: To provide, by constitutional amendment, for the simultaneous election every four years of the President, the House of Representatives, and half the members of the United States Senate—all Senators to serve for eight years;

Six: To establish or strengthen party policy committees in the House and Senate to guide congressional business; hold reasonably frequent party caucuses; nominate members for committee assignments, who would then be elected in the caucuses; and receive, hold joint hearings, and report on all general presidential messages;

Seven: To find a mathematical formula for computing congressional seniority which will give added weight to those legislators who come from competitive two-party districts and states;

Eight: To repeal the 22nd Amendment;

Nine: To develop machinery for keeping an active roster of talented people for the important executive posts in the national government.

. . . The national parties have become what they are because of these historical conflicts which they have had to settle, hide, or gloss over. In some cases they have been the master brokers between rich and poor, country and city, butter and oleo, capital and labor, Italian and Irish, new and old. At other times, they have hidden certain conflicts in order to satisfy powerful economic interests which have stood to gain by exploiting conflict locally and disguising it nationally. Each party has been caught in the dilemma, on the one hand, of trying to forge an image of harmony in the interests of the majority in order to win the Presidency, and, on the other hand, of being unable to eradicate the very different kind of image which generations of conservative log-rolls and bipartisan "innerclubism" in the Congress have created in the public eye.

But what happens when the conditions of conflict change? For they are changing, and rapidly, in the United States.

The Social Changes

Take the struggle between the old and the new. We used to be able to tell the difference between old and new settlers by their accent, or dress, or occupational level. But we are fuller of hundred per cent Americans every day and are rapidly reaching the time when nationality politics will be as anachronistic as the trolley car. Samuel Lubell has set the beginning of the end of this traditional conflict in the late Thirties with the coming of age of those whose parents and grandparents had arrived in the great immigration surge at the turn of this century. With the acceptance of the stranger as a person has come acceptance of his ways and his beliefs. A Jew is Governor of Connecticut; a Catholic is almost certain to be on the national ticket of at least one of our two national parties in 1960.[1] Matters which once split us and made us fearful are now absorbed almost without question as our population becomes increasingly homogenized.

Or take sectional and class conflict. The heart has been cut out of sectionalism by vast changes in technology and communications which have dispersed industry and revolutionized agriculture. Where are the one-crop "Cotton Ed" Smiths of a few years back? The fact is that there are precious few one-crop areas left in America. And even where there are, as in some of the great agricultural regions of the Great Plains, technology is bringing a revolution of another kind. In the last five years almost four million people have left the farm. The forecast for reapportionment of congressional seats after the 1960 census suggests a dramatic decrease in rural representation in the United States Congress, and this trend will continue as the rise in population throws more and more people into metropolitan areas.

The movement in urban politics tends to be toward class rather than regional politics. But even class politics has changed. It is no longer a kind of rabble vs. gentry rivalry. Rather, among other things, it is national industry against highly bureaucratized and wellpaid national labor. Senator Barry Goldwater of Arizona is not a regional figure. In the congressional elections of 1958, national giants contended in that sparsely populated desert state, and for national stakes.

What bothers the auto worker in Detroit bothers the auto worker in Los Angeles. What worries the businessman in Chicago worries his competitor in Boston. With transcontinental jet planes, the political or labor or industrial leader whose home is in San Francisco is almost more accessible to his counterpart in New York than is a train traveler from Boston; and, in any case, distance has been obliterated by electricity, electronics, and the direct-dial telephone.

And what is happening to the Negro issue? It, too, is becoming nationalized. Today there are more Negroes in New York than in New Orleans; more in Detroit than in Birmingham, Alabama; more in Pittsburgh than in Little Rock; more in Los Angeles than in Richmond; more in Chicago than in Atlanta. The Negroes' locustlike migration to northern metropolitan centers may have brought new problems to city governments, but it has aroused a critical competition between the two major parties in the North and West to capture the Negro vote. In heavily populated, evenly divided states, a bloc shift of a few votes can mean thirty or forty electoral college votes for a presidential candidate.

Perhaps more than any one other factor, the northern migration of the Negro is working tremendous transformation in our political life. The South no longer can exercise a veto in either presidential convention. Some diehards may walk out in 1960, but the result will only be that they will risk losing what waning power they have in the Congress. For, in more than sixty congressional districts in the North and West, the Negro holds the political balance of power if he decides to bloc-vote; and in the South his po-

---

[1] John F. Kennedy destroyed the prevailing political myth that a Catholic could not be elected President of the United States by winning that highest elective office in 1960.

litical power is likely to increase steadily despite the present tensions.

As for the clash of personal political ambitions in the United States, they are being completely submerged by the international and domestic concerns of the American public. War and peace, inflation and depression, are both personal and universal issues; tariffs, taxes, foreign aid, military spending, federal reserve policies, and hosts of other national policies affect local economic activities across the land. Politicians who wish to become statesmen must be able to talk intelligently about issues that concern people in *all* constituencies. The extraordinary social and economic changes now going on are absorbing and transcending the old conflicts of personal ambitions.

The Party Changes

The shifts in the nature of the conflicts are reflected in the changes that are already taking place in our party system:

(1) The number of one-party states and one-party congressional districts is dramatically declining.

In less than twenty years, the number of one-party delegations in Congress (in which the two Senators and all members of the House from a single state are of one party) has dropped more than 50 per cent—from twenty-four in 1942 to eleven in 1958.

The number of Southern congressional districts which had contested elections increased from forty-eight to sixty in the brief period from 1952 to 1956. In the same period of time, the total Republican vote in the South for members of the House rose from 1,872,000 in 1952 to 2,371,000 in 1956.[2]

(2) The permanent staffs of the national party committees and the variety of committee functions have grown greatly during the past decade. Until World War II both national committees were served by skeletal staffs, except for the few months before national presidential elections. Today both of them maintain year-round staffs of between seventy-five and a hundred people. In election years this number doubles or triples. The annual budget of each committee amounts to almost a million dollars—a figure which skyrockets during election years.

(3) Both national committees are doing everything within their power to spread their financial base. The evolution has been from fat-cats and expensive fund-raising banquets to mass appeals and direct-mail solicitation.

(4) Almost unnoticed, a revolution has occurred in the "nationalization" of off-year senatorial and congressional campaigns. As recently as 1938, the press and the public criticized President Roosevelt for campaigning in an off-year election. But in 1954, when both the President and the titular leader of the Democrats actively campaigned in their parties' congressional elections, both the newspapers and the voters seemed to accept the fact that it was perfectly all right for the executive wings of the parties to interest themselves actively in the outcome of the legislative contests. In 1958, both national committees sent out representatives to help develop party strength in various regions and to give services to local campaigns. The campaign committees on Capitol Hill also provided services to these campaigns

---

[2] The Republican Nixon-Lodge ticket polled around a half million more votes in the South than Eisenhower-Nixon received in 1956. It is said that in 1960 there were

4.6 Republican votes cast in the South for every 5 Democratic votes. See O. Douglas Weeks, "The Presidential Election of 1960— Texas and the South," *Public Affairs Comment,* University of Texas, VII. No. 1 (January 1961), 1.

as a matter of course, and, in spite of occasional frictions, worked in closer cooperation with the national committees than in any previous off-year election in history.

(5) Since 1937, the presidents have met regularly with party leaders in the Congress on matters of legislative priority and strategy. This has elevated the prestige and power of these men, particularly on matters of foreign policy and national defense. The passage of the Legislative Reorganization Act of 1946 further recognized the need for party leadership in the Congress, and succeeded to some degree in institutionalizing the leadership function in the Senate which established party policy committees with paid staffs.

(6) The creation of the Democratic Advisory Council and the recent appearance of an embryonic Republican counterpart show a new concern in both parties for clarifying the party image. There is little doubt that, eventually, pronouncements of these "executive wings" of the parties will be more effective than similar attempts by congressional leaders or individual party spokesmen excepting the president.

The Conclusion

This far from exhaustive list of the responses of our political system to nationalizing forces represents only the beginnings of adaptation and adjustment. Our basic political institutions, and their relationships to each other and to the public, are in a state of flux. If we want a political system designed to give full play to America's political energies and to hold them within bounds set by a popular majority, we are obligated to modify the system still further.

The reforms outlined in these pages will not obviate America's continuing need for personal force and political virtuosity in the office of the presidency and in top positions in the Congress. Nor will these or any other party reforms dispel the terrifying military, diplomatic, and social problems of our age. But they will help the parties toward stronger leadership in a more responsible framework than has been traditional. To paraphrase Emerson, they can help us to perceive the terror of life and to man ourselves to face it. In this apocalyptic age, can we ask for greater service from our political parties? We must not ask for less.

4

The Conscience of a Conservative *

BARRY GOLDWATER

The most interesting phenomenon in recent American politics has been the rise of a very articulate conservative movement, and the most noted of the political conservative spokesmen is Barry Goldwater, of Arizona. In the following paragraphs Mr. Goldwater sets forth his beliefs on the meaning of conservatism and the steps that should be taken to translate these beliefs into action.

I have been much concerned that so many people today with conservative instincts feel compelled to apologize for them. Or if not to apologize directly, to qualify their commitments in a way that amounts to breast-beating. "Republican candidates," Vice-President Nixon has said, "should be economic conservatives, but conservatives with a heart." President Eisenhower announced during his first term, "I am conservative when it comes to economic problems but liberal when it comes to human problems." Still other Republican leaders have insisted on calling themselves "progressive" conservatives.[1] These formulations are tantamount to an admission that conservatism is a narrow, mechanistic economic theory that may work very well as a bookkeeper's guide, but cannot be relied upon as a comprehensive political philosophy.

The same judgment, though in the form of an attack rather than an admission, is advanced by the radical camp. "We liberals," they say, "are interested in people. Our concern is with human beings, while you conservatives are preoccupied with the preservation of economic privilege and status." Take them a step further, and the liberals will turn the accusations into a class argument: it is the little people that concern us, not the "malefactors of great wealth."

Such statements, from friend and foe alike, do great injustice to the conservative point of view. Conservatism is not an economic theory, though it has economic implications. The shoe is precisely on the other foot: it is socialism that subordinates all other considerations to man's material well-being. It is conservatism that puts material things in their proper place—that has a structured view of the human being and of human society, in which economics plays only a subsidiary role.

The root difference between the conservatives and the liberals of today is that conservatives take account of the whole man, while the liberals tend

---

* Barry Goldwater, *The Conscience of a Conservative* (Shepherdsville, Kentucky: Victor Publishing Company, 1960), pp. 9-14. Reprinted by permission of the publisher.

[1] This is a strange label indeed: it implies that "ordinary" conservatism is opposed to progress. Have we forgotten that America made its greatest progress when conservative principles were honored and preserved?

to look only at the material side of man's nature. The conservative believes that man is, in part, an economic, an animal creature; but that he is also a spiritual creature with spiritual needs and spiritual desires. What is more, these needs and desires reflect the superior side of man's nature, and thus take precedence over his economic wants. Conservatism therefore looks upon the enhancement of man's spiritual nature as the primary concern of political philosophy. Liberals, on the other hand—in the name of a concern for "human beings"—regard the satisfaction of economic wants as the dominant mission of society. They are, moreover, in a hurry. So that their characteristic approach is to harness the society's political and economic forces into a collective effort to compel "progress." In this approach, I believe they fight against nature.

Surely the first obligation of a political thinker is to understand the nature of man. The conservative does not claim special powers of perception on this point, but he does claim a familiarity with the accumulated wisdom and experience of history, and he is not too proud to learn from the great minds of the past.

The first thing he has learned about man is that each member of the species is a unique creature. Man's most sacred possession is his individual soul—which has an immortal side, but also a mortal one. The mortal side establishes his absolute differentness from every other human being. Only a philosophy that takes into account the essential differences between men, and, accordingly, makes provision for developing the different potentialities of each man can claim to be in accord with nature. We have heard much in our time about "the common man." It is a concept that pays little attention to the history of a nation that grew great

through the initiative and ambition of uncommon men. The conservative knows that to regard man as part of an undifferentiated mass is to consign him to ultimate slavery.

Secondly, the conservative has learned that the economic and spiritual aspects of man's nature are inextricably intertwined. He cannot be economically free, or even economically efficient, if he is enslaved politically; conversely, man's political freedom is illusory if he is dependent for his economic needs on the state.

The conservative realizes, thirdly, that man's development, in both its spiritual and material aspects, is not something that can be directed by outside forces. Every man, for his individual good and for the good of his society, is responsible for his own development. The choices that govern his life are choices that he must make: they cannot be made by any other human being, or by a collectivity of human beings. If the conservative is less anxious than his liberal brethren to increase social security "benefits," it is because he is more anxious than his liberal brethren that people be free throughout their lives to spend their earnings when and as they see fit.

So it is that conservatism, throughout history, has regarded man neither as a potential pawn of other men, nor as a part of a general collectivity in which the sacredness and the separate identity of individual human beings are ignored. Throughout history, true conservatism has been at war equally with autocrats and with "democratic" Jacobins. The true conservative was sympathetic with the plight of the hapless peasant under the tyranny of the French monarchy. And he was equally revolted at the attempt to solve that problem by a mob tyranny that paraded under the banner of egalitarianism. . . .

5

The Conscience of a Liberal *

EUGENE J. McCARTHY

Senator McCarthy examines the term "liberalism" and points out what it is and what it is not. He shows some of the strengths and some of the pitfalls into which liberals are prone to fall, but most of all Senator McCarthy explains what it means to be a liberal at this point in the twentieth century.

Politics in the United States is non-doctrinaire and nonideological. Two terms, however, applied to politics seem to have doctrinal or ideological content for those who use them. These are the words "liberal" and "conservative." In states which do not have party designation for legislators—like my own state, Minnesota—it is a practice to hold organizing caucuses of "liberals" and of "conservatives." Americans for Democratic Action, a "liberal" organization, regularly calls for the purification of the Democratic party by the elimination of the "conservative" members. The Conservative Citizens Committee, in companionship with a new organization called simply the New Party, is trying to purge the Republican party of its "liberal" tendencies.

The clarification of the terms liberal and conservative, at least as they are applied to politics, is made more difficult because many explanations and definitions of liberals and liberalism have been offered by conservatives, and on the other hand, many explanations and definitions of conservatives and of conservatism have been offered by liberals.

In line with this practice William F. Buckley, Jr., admitted conservative and editor of the *National Review*, makes his case against the liberals by saying that "there is an enormous area in which the liberal does not know how to think. More specifically," says Buckley, "he is illogical, he is inconsistent, and he cannot assess evidence."

Liberals on the other hand are inclined to be less direct and harsh, but rather given to more subtle or sophisticated explanations of their conservative opponents. Witness Arthur Schlesinger, Jr.'s analysis of the new conservatism as having strong interior tendencies toward schizophrenia.[1] He asserts that it is out of touch with reality. There are less sophisticated liberals, I admit, who are satisfied to call conservatives "medieval" or "Neanderthal."

Life would certainly be made much easier for liberals if it were possible to define carefully the word "liberalism" and limit its use according to

---

* Eugene J. McCarthy, *Frontiers in American Democracy* (New York: World Publishing Company, 1960), pp. 63-70. Reprinted by permission of the publisher.

[1] "The New Conservatism: Politics of Nostalgia," *The Reporter*, June 16, 1955, p. 11.

this restricted definition. Until such a definition can be worked out, it would be helpful if the word "liberal" were used only as a modifier. If this were general agreement, no one would be merely a liberal, or a "pseudo-liberal" in the terminology of J. Edgar Hoover. Anyone to whom the word was applied would have to be a liberal something. In politics he would not be merely a liberal, but a liberal Republican, a liberal Democrat, or a liberal Vegetarian, or a liberal something else. There no longer would be religious liberals, but liberal Methodists, liberal Presbyterians, liberal Catholics, and so on. The word "intellectual" and the word "liberal" would no longer be considered synonymous. There would henceforth be liberal intellectuals and illiberal intellectuals, and when *Time* magazine's phrenological distinctions were applied, liberal eggheads and illiberal eggheads—or turnip-heads, if you prefer.

The truth is that American liberalism is not a twentieth-century manifestation of nineteenth-century liberalism. It is not even a development from that earlier liberalism.

Liberalism in the United States is not a system of philosophy, or a religion, or a school of political, economic, or social thought. It is not a way of life, as some of its proponents claim and as some of its opponents charge. It is not a "demanding faith" as Americans for Democratic Action say; nor is it on the contrary an "undemanding faith" as Professor William Leuchtenburg of Harvard University critically described it; nor is it without faith, or at least without a home for "faith," as Frederich K. Wilhelmsen of Santa Clara University wrote in *Commonweal*.

I believe it fair to say that American liberalism is no more materialistic in its metaphysics than is American conservatism. It is no more rationalistic in its psychology than is American conservatism. It cannot be described as more utilitarian, more positivistic, or relativistic in its ethics and in its value judgments than can conservatism. Nor can it be described as more opportunistic or Machiavellian in its politics.

To the extent that the liberal movement in the United States in this century can be given historical position and positive content, it must be identified and associated with the New Deal of the first two Roosevelt administrations. The New Deal involved political and economic changes which were the results of a response to urgent practical demands, rather than a fulfillment or an advancement of an ideology or a doctrinaire theory of political, economic, or social organization.

The total program provided for the pooling of social risks, as in the case of the social security program, and the pooling of economic risks, as in the case of the Federal Deposit Insurance program. It included such projects as the Tennessee Valley Authority and the hydroelectric developments in the Far West. In each case, the decision to include the specific program or project was based on practical considerations—the development and distribution of power, for example, or the related problems of navigation and flood control, rather than to an ideological demand for social ownership or collectivization. At the same time that the above-mentioned programs were advanced, or projects begun, along with others providing for greater control by government over such things as the investment market and the wages and hours of workingmen, efforts were made to protect the small independent business and the independent family-size farm.

As the general economic well-being of the people of the United States improved, the positive content of the liberal movement narrowed and popular support fell away. When there is a call for volunteers to make and carry the bricks of domestic economic reform, the liberal response is strong. The Marshall Plan and Point IV programs too—foreign-aid programs closely akin in spirit to our domestic programs—were strongly endorsed by liberal groups.

In short, if American liberalism has one mark it is its economic emphasis. Yet few if any liberal thinkers really believe the "belly" communist argument, or believe that communism can be overcome by dropping Montgomery Ward catalogues from airplanes flying over communist countries.

The lack of ideological unity among American liberals, beyond agreement on economic programs and civil rights, explains in part their attachment to individual leaders manifest in their enthusiasm for President Roosevelt, their short-lived courtship of General Eisenhower in the Eisenhower-and/or-Douglas campaign of 1948, and since then their enthusiastic support of Adlai Stevenson. The attachment to one person eliminates or at least moderates the division, reduces the uncertainties and conflicts, and provides in the person a unity of cause.

If the bond among American liberals today is not one of ideas or even of program, how can we distinguish them? The common trait, I believe, is one of method or manner of approach to human problems. It is this manner of approach that distinguishes the liberal from the illiberal and establishes the characteristics of modern liberalism and the modern liberal.

The liberal is ideally and characteristically an optimist, not blindly so as one who fails to understand or to comprehend the reality of the times, but rather as one who, with full awareness of the difficulties of a situation and with full awareness also of the potentiality for failure of man and his institutions, remains hopefully confident that improvement and progress can be accomplished. This does not mean that he believes that things are necessarily getting better and better, nor does it require any belief in the inevitability of progress.

The ideal liberal is normally progressive, willing both to advocate and to accept change—really a safe general position since no individual person or human institution can ever claim perfection. But he need not always advocate something wholly new; he can support elements of the status quo, or he may even advocate a return to conditions known in the past. He does not necessarily believe in change for the sake of change or, as some critics of liberals insist, in historical determinism and the inevitability of collectivization.

The liberal is normally tolerant of the opinions and actions of others, yet he exercises this tolerance without abjectly denying the certainty of his own position, without conceding that another's position may be right, without agreeing to disagree, and certainly without accepting that one man's opinion is as good as that of another. The basis for his tolerance must be a genuine humility arising from the awareness of the limitations of the human person and from a sense of the dignity of every man.

There are, of course, dangers in the liberal approach. Optimism can become self-delusion, change an obsession. Because the future is not the past, the liberal may be led, as Vincent McNabb points out, to think that it must be something entirely different from the past. He may therefore neglect or take lightly the lesson of history and underestimate the value of custom and of tradition. He may accept that there must be an absolute break between past and present, and again between present and future. His tolerance gone too far may lead him to accept unsound positions of religious indifferentism, of intellectual pluralism, and of subjective morality. However, such excesses are not inherent in liberalism.

In his concern for freedom, the liberal is in danger of forgetting the obligations and restraints that are the price of freedom and of discounting the importance of institutions and their function in the perfecting of individual persons.

The liberal of today cannot be satisfied in the belief that his approach to human problems is the better one, but must clarify his ideas as to the nature of man and the meaning and goal of human existence. The liberal of today must do more than "feel free." He must concern himself not only with claiming freedom, but with understanding it, since time has worked significant changes in the meaning of this word.

The liberal who speaks much of freedom must stop to consider its meaning. He should recall that the free man of the Greek philosophers is the man who has achieved freedom, who has overcome ignorance and acquired a measure of self-mastery. In this classical philosophical tradition, the concept of freedom is applied principally to the state of being, rather than to the conditions under which man lives and works in order to attain that state. In our time the emphasis has been upon the condition of the striving, rather than upon the status which might be reached. The meaning which we give to the term "freedom," either in the static sense or as it relates to the condition of man's living and seeking for fulfillment, depends basically upon our concept of the nature of man and the purpose of his existence.

It is not enough to want freedom for its own sake. Freedom is not baseless or relative, but desired and pursued to make man more responsible, more in control of his life and his time. Thus freedom from want makes a man more surely free to choose poverty if he wishes. Freedom from oppression or domination leaves a man more truly free to choose the object of his allegiance, or to whom he will give obedience.

The complexity of modern problems, the quickened pace of historical change, the involvement with people of other races and cultures—all call for a liberal response. American liberalism as a force bearing on American politics can be a positive force for good only if it clarifies its positive content and becomes something more than the liberalism of the immediate past. Optimism, generosity, tolerance, and even humility, good and necessary as they are, are of little use unless there can be some agreement as to what is good.

American liberals today are faced with the pluralistic society they once only dreamed and talked about. There is no longer a dominant group in our American culture, although it will take time for the popular mind to cast off the image of the American prototype, to whose loyalties and mores all other groups conformed and were American in so far as they conformed. The liberal's task is to secure this individualistic society with his tolerance and generosity and at the same time in the words of Woodrow Wilson, "to make sure of the things which unite."

6

Our Radical Right—The Dispossessed *

DANIEL BELL

A phenomenon of the 1960's has been the rise throughout the country of various radical–right groups—the John Birch Society, Christian Crusade, and White Citizen Councils, to name a few. Although they may differ in detail, on many points these disparate groups are united. Most political, social, military, and economic trends are viewed with alarm. They also exhibit something of a nostalgia for an earlier age. What groups are a fertile recruiting ground for the radical right? Why do these people feel dispossessed? Is this rebellion a transitory movement, or does it have deep roots?

Most of the political changes that have transformed American life, the changes that have aroused such notable right-wing rancor today, originated in legislative measures passed thirty years ago and before—the income tax, social security, welfare measures, and the like. In many instances, the changes have been irrevocably built into the structure of American society. Why then have the consequences of these changes become manifest only at this very late date? And what is the nature of the right-wing rancor? . . .

Over the years since 1932, then, there has been a steady erosion of conservative influence. The expansion of the executive agencies of government in the past three decades, drawing key personnel largely from the major universities, has given the middle and (later) top echelons of government a predominantly liberal coloration; and this is one of the factors

that accounts for the tension between the Executive and the Congress which has been so marked in the last decade and a half. More slowly, the personnel of the life-time federal judiciary began to change through appointments by Democratic presidents.

The right-wing Republicans hoped that the election of Dwight Eisenhower would reverse this massive trend. But it did not—perhaps could not. Eisenhower's Labor Secretary courted the unions; social security benefits increased; duing the 1957-59 recession, unemployment benefits were extended; and to reverse the economic slowdown, the government in good Keynesian style, ran $12,000,000,000 budgetary deficit. Only Congress, reflecting the disproportionate power of the small-town areas and the established seniority system, has remained, practically speaking, under conservative control. For the Radical Right, then, eight years of "moderation" proved as frustrating as twenty years of New Dealism.

To this extent, the meaning of the

* Daniel Bell, "The Dispossessed—1962," *Columbia University Forum* (Fall, 1962), pp. 4-12. Reprinted by permission of the author.

Kennedy victory for the members of the Radical Right was the gnawing realization that as a social group they were becoming dispossessed of their power in American society. But more than a generational change has taken place. Until thirty years ago, the source of "visible" political and social power in American life was predominantly the small-town leaders: lawyers, real estate dealers, bankers, merchants, and small manufacturers. Their political hegemony in the states was virtually complete; nationally, the values of the society reflected the influence of the business community.

The first challenges to this dominance came from the ethnic groups in the large urban centers and from the trade union movement. Only after considerable friction were these challenges absorbed; power became more diffused. But the newer threat does not arise from any direct political competition, as was true in the case of the urban political machines. It arises from the fact that the complex problems of contemporary economic and political and military management require a technical expertise which is far beyond the understanding of the dispossessed groups for whom the "simple virtues" and the "traditional moralities" were the only guides that were felt to be necessary to the formulation of public policy. It arises from the fact that social change now has to be directed and planned. For the ramifications of many major changes—whether it be space exploration, counterforce military strategy, urban renewal, or medicare—are widespread and produce a whole series of secondary effects whose consequences have to be anticipated lest chaos result. (The passage of medicare, for example, would require a widespread hospital-building program and a stepped-up recruitment of nurses to meet the shortages

that would certainly ensue.) As a corollary to these general conditions, it is a new "technocratic" elite—scientists, mathematicians, economists, sociologists, with their new techniques of decision-making: input-output matrices, systems analysis, linear programming—that now becomes essential if not to the wielding of power, then to the formulations and analyses on which political judgments have to be made. It is these complexities and the rise of the new skill groups which pose the real threat of dispossession to those who once held power by virtue of their wealth or property or gerrymandered political control.

The Small-Town Mind

In identifying "the dispossessed" it would be misleading to apply economic labels. It is not economic interest alone that elicits their anxieties. A small businessman may have made considerable amounts of money in the last decade (in part, because he has wider scope in masking profits than a large corporation), and yet . . . strongly resent the regulations in Washington, the high income tax, or, more to the point, the erosion of his own political status. Indeed, to the extent that any such economic location is possible, one can say that the social group most threatened by the structural changes in society is the "old" middle class: the independent physician, farm owner, small-town lawyer, real estate promoter, home builder, automobile dealer, small businessman, and the like. But the common denominator of such groups is the life-style and value of Protestant Fundamentalism—the nativist nationalism, the good-and-evil moralism through which they see the world. Theirs are the values of the dominant thought of the nineteenth century; and they have been defending these values—in what is now a rear-guard action—for the last forty years.

The present upsurge of American nativism on the Radical Right is most directly paralleled, in fact, in the virulent assaults on teachers' loyalty which were levied in the 1920's by fundamentalist churchmen in the name of God and by patriotic organizations like the American Legion in the name of country. Such conflicts—most vividly the Scopes trial and the bellicose efforts of Mayor "Big Bill" Thompson in Chicago to expunge favorable references to Great Britain from the school textbooks—were between "fundamentalists" and "modernists, between "patriots" and "internationalists." These skirmishes in the 1920's were the first defensive reactions of the nativist and the old middle-class elements to the entry into society of formerly "disenfranchised" elements, particularly the children of immigrants and members of minority ethnic groups—an entry made through the only major route open to them, the urban political machines. In short, theirs was a reaction to the rise of a mass society. . . .

The social ideas of fundamentalism are quite familiar—a return to the "simple" virtues of individual initiative and self-reliance. In political terms, this means a dismantling of much of the social security program, the elimination of the income tax, the reduction of the role of the federal government in economic life, and the return to the state and local governments of the major responsibilities for welfare, labor, and similar legislation. Now from any realistic political view, the dismantling of social security, income tax, etc., is quite hopeless, as elections since 1936 have proved. But what gives the fundamentalist Right its political momentum today is its effort to hitch these attacks on "collectivism" to a high-powered anti-

communist crusade, which identifie *any* extension of government powe: as communism. What in effect it seek: to do is identify the welfare state with socialism and equate liberalism with communism. In this respect, it repre sents a crude but powerful effort t resist *all* social change, to use th emotions generated by foreign policy conflicts to confuse domestic issues.

Until now, much of the politica strength of the small-town right win; has stemmed from its ability to bloc the reapportionment of seats in th state legislatures and to gerrymande seats for Congress; the result is heavily disproportionate representa tion of the small towns and rura areas in both assemblies. In the U.S House of Representatives, for exam ple, 260 of the 435 seats—or almos 60 per cent of all the seats—are i districts dominated by small town and rural areas. In thirteen state: fewer than a third of the voters—and these are primarily in small towns— can elect a majority of the state legis lators; in forty-four states, less tha 40 per cent can elect a majority. Th Supreme Court decision of Apri 1962, ordering a redistricting of seat in the Tennessee legislature (whic had blocked all reapportionment sinc 1901) may be the most important pc litical act of the decade. Certainly will break the hold of the small tow on many state legislatures and reduc its influence in Congress—but ho soon remains to be seen.

The Managerial Dispossessed

To list the managerial executive class as among "the dispossessed seems strange, especially in the ligl of the argument that a revolutio which is undermining property as th basis of power is enfranchising a ne class of technical personnel, amon whom are the business executives. Y the managerial class has been under immense strain all through this period, a strain arising, in part from the discrepancy between their large power and prestige within a particular enterprise and their lesser power and esteem in the nation as a whole.

The modern corporation, even though it holds its legitimation from the institution of private property, is vastly different from the family firm which it has succeeded. The family firm of old was securely rooted in the legal and moral tradition of private property. The enterprise "belonged to" the owner, and was sanctioned, depending on one's theological tastes, by God or by Natural Right. The modern manager clearly lacks the inherited family justifications: increasingly he is recruited from the amorphous middle class. He receives a salary, bonus, options, expense accounts, and "perks" (perquisites, like the use of company planes [and] memberships in country clubs), but his power is transitory and he cannot pass on his position; the manager needs an ideology. In no other capitalist order but the American—not in England, or Germany, or France—has this drive for ideology been so compulsive. . . .

Already in 1960, the efforts of a number of corporations led by General Electric, to go "directly" into politics by sending out vast amounts of propaganda to their employees and to the public, by encouraging right-to-work referendums in the states—indicated the mood of political dispossession in many corporations. Since then, a significant number of corporations have been contributing financially to the seminars of the Radical Right evangelists. The National Education Program, at Harding College in Arkansas, which prepares films on communism and materials on free enterprise, has been used extensively by General Electric, U.S. Steel, Olin Mathieson Chemical, Monsanto Chemical, Swift & Co., and others. Boeing Aviation and the Richfield Oil Co. has [sic] sponsored many of the anticommunism seminars on the West Coast. The Jones and Laughlin Steel Company has a widespread propaganda program for its employees. One of the most politically active companies is the Allen Bradley Co. of Milwaukee, which makes machine tools and electrical equipment. The Allen Bradley Co. advertises in the John Birch Society magazine and reprinted the testimony before the House Un-American Activities Committee on Fred Schwarz, a reprint which Schwarz claims had "wider distribution than any other government document in the history of the United States, with the possible exception of the Bill of Rights, the Declaration of Independence, and the Constitution." Ironically, the Allen Bradley Co., which continually extols the virtue of free enterprise, was one of the electrical companies convicted of collusive bidding and illegal price-rigging.

Despite the failure of the corporations to affect significantly the 1960 elections—their failure on the right-to-work issue being one key indicator—it is likely that the Kennedy-Blough imbroglio of 1962 will provide an even greater impetus for corporations to finance right-wing political activity in the coming years.

The Military Dispossessed

The irony for the American military establishment is that at a time when the military in the new states overseas has emerged as one of the ruling forces of those states (often because it is the one organized group in an amorphous society), and while at this time in United States history the amount of money spent for military purposes (roughly 50 per cent of the federal budget) is the highest in peacetime history, the U.S. military is subject to grave challenges in its very own bailiwick. The problems of national security, like those of the national economy, have become so staggeringly complex that they can no longer be settled simply by military common sense or past experience. . . .

In the last decade, most of the thinking on strategic problems, political and economic has been done in the universities or in government-financed but autonomous bodies like the RAND Corporation. A new profession, that of the "military intellectual" has emerged, and men like Kahn, Wohlstetter, Brodie, Hitch, Kissinger, Bokie, Schelling "move freely through the corridors of the Pentagon and the State Department," as the TLS writer observed, "rather as the Jesuits through the courts of Madrid and Vienna three centuries ago."

In structural terms, the military establishment may be one of the tripods of a "power elite," but in sociological fact the military officers feel dispossessed because they often lack the necessary technical skills or knowledge to answer the new problems confronting them. Since the end of World War II, the military has been involved in a number of battles to defend its elite position, beginning in 1945 with the young physicists and nuclear scientists, down to the present action against the "technipols" (the military's derisive term for technicians and political theorists) whom Secretary McNamara has brought into the Department of Defense. For in present-day decision-making the nature of strategy involves a kind of analysis for which experience alone is insufficient. Consider the complex problem of choosing a "weapons system": the long lead time that is necessary in planning and testing—let alone producing—such weapons com-

pels an analyst to construct mathematical models as almost the only means of making rational choices. The recent controversy over the desirability of the RS-70 bomber is a case in point. The systems analysts in the office of the Secretary of Defense, led by Charles Hitch, an economist from RAND who has become the comptroller in the Pentagon, decided on the basis of computer analysis that the manned RS-70 bomber would be outmoded by the time it could come into full production, and that it would be wiser to concentrate on missiles. . . .

The traditional services, and their chiefs, have reacted to all this with dismay. As a recent article in *Fortune* put it:

It was at this point that the military professionals began to exhibit real alarm. McNamara did not ignore them; they had their say, as usual, in defense of their service budgets. But his drive, his intense preoccupation with figures and facts, left the Chiefs and their staffs with the feeling that the computers were taking over.

And the *Fortune* article, reflecting the dismay of the service Chiefs, was also a veiled attack on McNamara's penchant for "quantification," for his failure to respect "the uncomputable that had made Curtis Le May (the head of the big bomber command) the world's finest operational airman," for his "inexperience" in military strategy and for his reliance on the technipols, "the inner group of lay experts who were dispersed through State, the White House, and Defense." The import of the article was clear: the traditional military professionals were being dispossessed. . . .

One can already see, in the behavior of retired officers, the rancor of an old guard that finds its knowledge outdated, its authority disputed or ignored, and that is beginning argue, bitterly, that if only its advice had been followed, America would not be on the defensive. A surprising number of high-ranking officers on active duty, as well as high-ranking retired officers, have become active in extreme Right organizations. A few—Major General Walker is an example—may feel that all intellectuals are involved in a "plot" against the nation. No doubt most of the military men will be forced—a number have already plunged—into the more complex and bureaucratic game of recruiting particular groups of scientists for their own purposes (in part through the power of the purse) or attempting to make alliances. In the long run, the military profession may itself become transformed through new modes of training, and a new social type may arise.

The Southern Dispossessed

In his primer on "one-upmanship," Stephen Potter observed that one could destroy any political generalization by asking, "but what about the South?" The American South contains many of "the dispossessed," and partakes of the Radical Right, but, to be sure, the reasons for this evolution may be of a somewhat different order.

For many decades, there has not been one South but two Souths, that of myth and that of reality, and the fact is that for the past hundred years the South has lived more by its myth than its reality. . . .

At the heart of the myth is this idea of a community, of an organic way of life, which is morally superior to the deracinated, vulgarized, tinseled North. Mr. Davidson's words merely reiterate the note struck by George Fitzhugh, in his *Sociology for the South* (1854), when he attacked the North for instituting an industrial wage slavery which was worse than the direct master-slave relationship in the South. ("There can never be among slaves a class so degraded as is found about the wharves and suburbs of cities.") The pastoral society of the South ("quiet and contented . . . has suffered so little from crime or extreme poverty") was contrasted with the brutish system of industrial laissez-faire (which only promoted selfishness [and] indifference to community and to liberty itself).

But any "traditional" view of the Southern past usually ignores, in the most extraordinary way, not only the direct economic exploitation of the Negro slave, but the *unrestrained* way in which the Negro could be dehumanized—unrestrained as Stanley Elkins has pointed out in his book *Slavery,* because of the lack of any moral agency, such as existed in Catholic countries, which could impose a set of limits through a conception of the Negro as a human soul.

All this has left its mark. One rarely finds in other former slave-holding societies the fear of color and especially the sense of guilt (deriving in considerable measure from unconscious sexual fantasies and fears) over the treatment of the Negro as subhuman, a buffoon, or a child that one finds in the American South. To say of the post-Civil War South, as Mr. Davidson does, that its difficulty lies in having lived with Negroes as "technical citizens, endowed with their citizenship without Southern consent," is a nicety that begs the question whether the South is indeed a part of the larger American polity and its moral code (or only a "defeated union"), and to ignore altogether the exploitative economic and social nature of the "organic community."

If a huge portion—in some areas the majority—of a population has to be exempted from the Southern "community," so, too, must one subtract the large stratum of "poor whites." For a society that, in myth at least, describes itself as reproducing the "constitutional order of the early Republic," the existence of Southern populism, with its raw appeals to violence, with its rant and swagger, with its contempt for culture, must be most embarrassing. It is much too easy—and simply false—to ascribe Southern populism to "northern theories of egalitarianism." Tom Watson, Tom Heflin, Gene Talmadge, Cole Blease, James K. Vardaman, Theodore Bilbo, Huey Long, John Rankin, and Orville Faubus (Snopeses that they may be)—are as indigenous to the South as John C. Calhoun, George Fitzhugh, Thomas R. Dew, or any other genteel intellectual and potitical figures. . . .

The Revolt Against Modernity

In the broadest sense, the attitude of the Right in the United States is a revolt against modernity and the requirements of planned social change in the society. (By "planned social change" I mean the attempt to be aware of the ramified consequences of any social action and to plan accordingly; a modern corporation could not exist without planning its future; neither can a society.) Often, as in the jibe of Senator Goldwater against the "whiz kids in the Pentagon" or the heavy-handed attack by former President Eisenhower against the "theorists" in government, these attitudes are part of an anti-intellectualism which is a defensive posture against the complexities of modern problems.

But more is at stake for the Right There is a deeper threat which they correctly perceive—the threat of dis placement.

The new nature of decision-making its increasing technicality, forces a dis placement of the older elites. Within a business enterprise, the newer tech niques of operations research and linear programming almost amount to the "automation" of middle manage ment and its displacement by mathe maticians and engineers, working either within the firm or as consultants In the economy, the businessman find himself subject to price, wage, and in vestment criteria laid down by the economists in government. In the pol ity, the old military elites find them selves challenged in the determination of strategy by scientists, who have th technical knowledge on nuclear capa bility—missile development and the like—or by the "military intellectuals whose conceptions of weapon system and political warfare seek to guid military allocations.

In the broadest sense, the spread of education, of research, of administra tion and government creates a new constituency, the technical and profe sional intelligentsia. While these ar not bound by the common ethos tha would constitute them a new class, no even a cohesive social group, they ar the products of a new system of re cruitment for power (just as propert and inheritance represented the ol system) and those who are the prod ucts of the old system understandabl feel a vague and apprehensive di quiet—the disquiet of the dispossesse

7

*"The New Left—What Is It?"**

How would you explain the statement, "At best, the New Left is all heart. At worst, it is no mind."? On what issues does the New Left join the New Right? In your opinion, what is the probable future of the "New Left"?

Only five or six years ago, to call someone a radical in America seemed quaint and was largely meaningless. Most of the radical proposals of a generation before had become Government policy, and even Communism seemed to have turned relatively conservative. Today, thanks to that amorphous band known as the New Radicals, the word has at least some measure of fresh meaning.

The Old Left had a program for the future; the New Left's program is mostly a cry of rage. The Old Left organized and proselyted, playing its part in bringing about the American welfare state. But it is precisely big government, the benevolent Big Brother, that the New Left is rebelling against. Says Author Paul Jacobs, an Old Leftist himself: "We were rejecting a depression; they're rejecting affluence."

The New Radicals have no power base. Their number, while indeterminate, is obviously small. Still, they are a presence and a voice—partly because of the sheer energy of their commitment, which demands not just parlor protest but physical inconvenience as expressed in the sit-in, the demonstration, the march. They speak for the

beleaguered individual in an impersonal society—whether Negro sharecropper, white welfare recipient, or campus dropout. Above all, they speak, or shout, against the Viet Nam war. Says Sociologist Daniel Bell: "At best, the New Left is all heart. At worst, it is no mind." They changed the temper, the tone and to some extent the terms of political debate. The question is what function or future they have beyond that.

You Can Always Hate Dad

Who are they? Given their almost anarchist horror of formal organization, they are difficult to identify. They are mostly young, bright, from well-to-do, often liberal families. They are creatures of conscience, the children of men of conscience, and they regard their patrimony as a reproach. The largest and most permanent of the shifting New Left groups is the Students for a Democratic Society (some 30,000 members by rough count), whose president changes every year, and whose members once even considered abolishing the office. Originally part of the left-wing but anti-Communist League for Industrial Democracy, the s.d.s. soon began to strike out in its own. In 1962, at a meeting at Port Huron, Mich., 43

---

* "The New Radicals," *Time*, April 28, 1967, pp. 26-27. Reprinted by permission of the publisher.

representatives of more than a dozen universities and colleges adopted a lengthy manifesto attacking the quality of American life and the direction of U.S. foreign policy. Besides S.D.S., the New Left includes other small groups, largely consisting of individuals with a surrounding cluster of followers. There is, of course, Mario Savio, of the Berkeley Free Speech Movement, but his stature has faded along with the issue. The more stable heroes in the New Left's pantheon are Staughton Lynd, 38, a pacifist and professor of American history at Yale between speaking engagements, and Tom Hayden, 27, an S.D.S. founder who now heads the independent Newark Community Union Project, a small but energetic program to help the poor. Both attracted a lot of attention a year ago when they went on a self-appointed peace mission to Hanoi. While the New Left scorns conventional politics, it has set up an ambitiously titled National Conference for New Politics, which has backed candidates in local elections, and helped win a seat in the Georgia legislature for Julian Bond, a founder of S.N.C.C.

The movement has spawned some dozen magazines and newspapers, including the sensationalist *Ramparts* and the more intellectual *Studies on the Left*. The lesser publications appear erratically, when the editors happen to have the money, and tend to be studded by advertisements for psychedelic happenings and underground movies and interviews with Allen Ginsberg or Timothy Leary. They also offer lots of free verse on the joys of copulation, distinguished from John Donne's comparable rhapsodies by a self-conscious injection of four-letter words doggedly intended to shock. The movement's bard is Bob Dylan (when in doubt, New Leftists always sing). But on the whole the New Left distrusts the hippies and the beats, who want to drop out of society.

The New Left label is applied to various organizations that do not necessarily accept it. While most New Leftists still embrace S.N.C.C. and CORE, the embrace is one-sided; the leaders of those organizations, with their new drive for black power, have frozen whites out. Most New Leftists claim as their spiritual ancestors Thoreau, Emerson and Whitman rather than Marx or Lenin. Thus they are distinct from the various Communist and socialist groups descended from the old, pre-World War II left, though they share many of their aims and indiscriminately welcome their presence in any sit-in, teach-in or be-in. Chief among these Marxist-oriented groups are the W.E.B. DuBois Clubs (membership 3,000), who still chatter about the class struggle and, unlike S.D.S., believe in working through coalitions with liberal forces to achieve their aims. A sympathetic historian of the New Left, Author Jack Newfield, declares sweepingly: "DuBois members are just not hung-up by the same things S.D.S.ers are. They don't make embarrassing speeches about how we must love each other. They are not viscerally outraged by the moral deceits of society in the way S.D.S. members are; they are not in total rebellion. The key difference is that the DuBois Club members don't hate their fathers. S.D.S.ers do."

The New Left is determined not to cooperate with groups that have ever slightly bowed to the status quo. When Civil Rights Leader Bayard Rustin suggested that the New Left shift from protest to coalition politics and work with labor and liberals, he was berated as a cop-out who was threatening its moral purity. Michael Harrington, who put poverty on the map in his book *The Other America*, is now similarly denounced; he calls the New Leftists "mystical militants."

The New Left's chief enemy, so declared, is not the far right but rather what it calls "the liberal Establishment" or "corporate liberalism." Hayden argues that the social legislation of the New Deal has enslaved the poor and left them worse off than they were before. Demands Farrel Broslawsky, professor of history at Los Angeles Valley College and recent candidate for the state legislature: "Who are the judges who participate in legal lynchings? The appointees of flaming liberals like President Kennedy. Who perpetuates racism? The unions. Who votes for war? The good liberal Congressmen. Who perpetuates alienation? The liberal administrators like Clark Kerr. The liberals are gutless, pusillanimous and totally lacking in sincerity." He adds: "Listening to them is like being beaten to death with a warm sponge."

Some Call It Rape

The liberals return the compliment. As Critic Irving Howe puts it, the New Leftists show "an unconsidered enmity toward something vaguely called the Establishment, an equally unreflective belief in the 'decline of the West,' a crude, unqualified anti-Americanism, drawn from every source."

The New Leftists often act as if they had no memory and had read no history; they seem unaware of the Communist-organized rebellions in Greece and Malaya, the invasion of South Korea, the repression of the Hungarian uprising, the Berlin Wall. While they are theoretically opposed to any dictatorship they endlessly make allowances for Communist regimes; they feel outraged by U.S. leaders while either apologizing for or extolling Castro and Mao, and of course they want instant, unilateral U.S. withdrawal from Viet Nam, heedless of the consequences. "We refuse to be anti-Communist," declared Lynd and Hayden in a statement written for Studies on the Left, since the term is

used "to justify a foreign policy that is no more sophisticated than rape."

The recurrent theme is that there must be purity at home first, that the U.S. must heal its own sick society before it can presume to treat others. What, then, do the New Leftists prescribe for the U.S.? They know what they do not want, but not necessarily what they want. Typical is a statement by Clark Kissinger, 26, a former S.D.S. national secretary who ran for alderman in Chicago (and won 864 votes out of 18,970): "You can imagine the system as a table. Lyndon Johnson sits at the head of the table, labor has a place at the table, industry has a place, the building industry, the grape growers, the State Street merchants—they all have places. Right now, the poor don't sit at the table; they get some crumbs thrown down to them. Well, we don't want a place at the table. We want to turn it upside down."

When asked what they would do once the table is overturned, the New Radicals mostly reply that this does not concern them. They have no program, and they do not want one. The immediate problem is to discredit and destroy the old society. Let others worry about the details of rebuilding later. But, when pressed, many of the New Left members do state their expectations. These ideas are not systematized and come from many different spokesmen; still, something like a New Left vision of the future emerges.

Yearning for the Past

The vision is utopian and full of inner contradictions. In a general way, the New Radicals would nationalize basic industry, although some would only tax it more heavily. "The rich" would also be taxed to the point of doing away with big private fortunes. "We must abolish the competitive ethic," says S.D.S. President Nick Egleson. "Do we want to make 8,000,000 cars a year if we are ruining the lives of the people who are making them?" But, while New Leftists loathe capitalism, they assume that the miraculous U.S. economy will go right on turning out wealth no matter what is done to it. Everyone, in the phrase of a New Leftist, will "have money or credit, whether he is able to work or not." Everyone will be guaranteed medical care and education; some suggest 24-hour schools, for children by day, for the parents by night.

Some see the Federal Government as the chief source of all the necessary funds—though they detest the government and, with almost states'-righters' fervor, would curb the federal role in society. Here, as well as in its hostility toward liberals, is where the New Left joins the New Right, including the Young Americans for Freedom (membership: 30,000). They both distrust big government, want to curb its interference in local and private affairs. Individual spokesmen for both right and left have even suggested abolishing the draft, though for very different reasons. (Some New Leftists want to eliminate armies altogether.) They both favor voluntary activities, including private or neighborhood-controlled education, police and social services. But there are differences. The New Left thinks of the poor as victims and believes that the conservatives think of them only as failures. The New Leftists have a mystical faith in the purity and wisdom of the poor, "uncorrupted" by the Establishment— an idea that the New Right rejects as nonsense.

The New Leftists resemble Russia's 19th century *narodniks* (populists), mostly middle-class students, who idealized the peasants and went to live among them, trying to rouse them to action. The overriding dream of the New Left is "participatory democracy," which means, among other things, that workers should have a vote on the running of their plants, students on what they should be taught, and the poor (as long as there are any) on welfare programs. To make this possible, life must center on small communities, cities must be broken up. Scratch utopia and you find nostalgia: the New Leftists really look backward, to a time of small social units and close personal relations. With yearnings for an almost medieval setting, they want to repeal bigness—which some men have been hankering to do ever since the Industrial Revolution. In *News from Nowhere*, William Morris visualized a new London broken up into idyllic villages. Charles Fourier and Robert Owen envisioned small self-sufficient communities, inspiring such American utopian experiments as Brook Farm and New Harmony. Sometimes the New Left's vision sounds like New Harmony computerized. Says James Weinstein, an editor of *Studies on the Left*: "People will meet in little communities and decide what they want. All their desires will be fed into the computers, which will pass their needs on to the industries." Many of the New Left's current projects are surprisingly small-scale, such as the "free universities" and other "parallel institutions" which it has improvised as alternatives to existing ones. Hayden lists his top aims as "rent control, play streets, apartment repairs, higher welfare payments, jobs."

Something else the New Leftists have in common with other utopians is a remarkably detailed concern for the physical environment. They dream of "the total beautiful society" with smogless air, unpolluted rivers, swift and clean public transportation and, in the phrase of Atlanta Lawyer Howard Moore, "airlines carrying the people all over the country to the great museums." Paul Goodman, 55, one of the aging gurus of the New Left, spends much time visualizing how city streets could be turned into playgrounds or parks, and how motor cars could be barred from Manhattan (the last being an idea that should do a lot to win friends for the New Left).

Ultimately, the New Leftists, like all utopians, not only want to reform society: they really want to reform human nature. They want men to work not for gain or glory but for the satisfaction of contributing to the general good. In a broad sense, the movement is not political at all but religious. "We want to create a world in which love is more possible," says an s.d.s. leader, Carl Oglesby. For all their rant and naivete, the New Radicals can sound strongly appealing. The fact that many of their proposals are impractical and that they lack a program is not an ultimate argument against them. Critics may perform a service to a society by pointing out evil and injustice without necessarily offering alternatives. Some of the things the New Left says about modern American life need to be said and evoke certain echoes in anyone who has ever been in white-hot anger over a slum, or a traffic jam, or a piece of blatant official hypocrisy, or a TV commercial, or has felt alone in a big organization.

Wanted: Middle-Aged Leftists

The trouble is that even in the role of merely negative or gadfly critics, the New Radicals are too mindless. In the words of one New Left manifesto, they want to remain "permanently radical"—which is about as possible as remaining permanently young. Their refusal to make common cause with liberals and other reformers, their dedication to action rather than thought, emotion rather than reason, will almost surely

destroy what influence they have. Some are already disillusioned: protest demonstrations are not changing the Viet Nam situation, and the civil rights movement is not only stalled but increasingly hostile to them. Their leaders say that they will now concentrate on community action, and wistfully speak of a coalition of the universities and the poor—but that will not work either. The poor are not radical. What they really want to be is middle-class, and once they buy a car and make a down payment on a house, they will ignore the New Left and stick with their unions or political parties.

Says Staughton Lynd: "The key question is whether the movement will grow beyond its student base and produce men who will carry their radicalism into middle age and beyond." The New Left leaders are afraid of the American talent for assimilating dissent—and this is already happening to some of their ideas. Practically everybody has a kind word for decentralization, in the interests of efficiency if not humanity; the war on poverty, while now bogged down, will be carried on. Even the guaranteed annual wage is not beyond the capacity of modern industrial society. Thus quite a few of the New Left proposals, in modified form, will be taken over by the liberals and by the managers. As for the New Left's anger at the human condition, its yearning for love, these will, as always, be taken over by the poets, the preachers, and perhaps a few minor saints. The present New Left will undoubtedly fade without producing many middle-aged radicals. But it will have performed a function. There should always be a New Left—to drive conventional society to a constant, sometimes painful review of its own values.

CHAPTER EIGHT

Nominations and Elections:
Can Great Men Get Elected?

Without question the most recognizable and generally accepted hallmark of popular government is the free election. Obviously a free society requires additional safeguards, but without regular, unshackled elections, popular rule as we understand it cannot exist. Not all countries with elections are free, but no country can be free without elections. Indeed, our judgment of the democratic character of nations, states, and even local communities frequently hinges upon the integrity of the ballot box, contested elections, and public participation in the political process. Elections are a way in which power can be maintained or transferred in an orderly manner. In many respects, free societies achieve their finest hour when the governed elect their governors

The following chapter poses the question, "Can Great Men Get Elected?" Almost a century ago Lord Bryce considered this question and answered it negatively when he wrote, "Why Great Men Are Not Chosen President" in *The American Commonwealth.* The hazards to great men in politics are different today, but they do exist.

The section begins with the problem of recruitment, "The Ideal Candidate Availability vs. The Man of Stature." Part of the recruitment process on the presidential level is the nominating convention. Some of the problems involved are presented in the section, "National Nominating Conventions: Prefabricated Pageantry or Underrated Political Institutions?" A third test that all candidates must face is the campaign. The overriding question here is "Do Campaigns Change Votes?" What Does An Election Mean?"

THE IDEAL CANDIDATE: AVAILABILITY VS. THE MAN OF STATURE?

The Constitution sets forth in clear language the legal qualifications for the Presidency. Yet it would be inaccurate to assume that the terms stated in the Constitution completely determine the recruitment of presidental candidates. Some of the most important prerequisites for the office are political considerations; that is, conditions which go beyond constitutional requirements. The first section of this chapter explores the problem of whether the laws of availability impose too heavy a burden on first-rate candidates. Art Buchwald writes on the self-denying responses which running for office imposes on a candidate, and Paul T. David, Ralph M. Goldman, and Richard C. Bain take an authoritative look at presidential types.

THE NATIONAL NOMINATING CONVENTION: PREFABRICATED PAGEANTRY OR UNDERRATED POLITICAL INSTITUTION?

Foreign visitors are often amazed and sometimes offended by the manner in which Americans nominate their Chief Executive. They regard the national convention as something of a circus, "disgustingly wasteful of time, lacking in taste and seriousness." And almost everyone, both foreign and domestic observers alike, agrees that the campaigning before and after a national convention is an exhaustive physical and emotional marathon.

The national convention, however, is not without merit. As a political institution, it helps to build party morale, regenerates loyalty and allegiance, and brings the insignificant party worker in contact with the party leaders. Since the advent of radio and television, the national convention has brought the candidates closer to the people, many of whom would not listen to political speeches at any other time. Thus the convention stimulates interest in the candidates and serves as a good method of advertising the party.

Clinton Rossiter notes, "We see our follies as a people in the follies of the convention, and unless we reform ourselves, which I know we will not and I suspect we dare not do, the convention will continue to disturb the reasonable, shock the fastidious, and fascinate all of us." Other authorities see both good and bad in the convention, and, like Dwight D. Eisenhower, urge reform.

DO CAMPAIGNS CHANGE VOTES?

Jim Farley once said people make up their minds in September on how they will vote in November. To a certain extent this idea is reinforced by earlier voting studies which seriously questioned the popular assumption that campaigning caused widespread vote switching. On the contrary, these studies seemed to say that the major effect of a campaign was to unite the faithful, activate the voter, and spur party workers on to greater effort rather than to persuade the average voter to change his mind.

On the other hand, there is always the example of Harry S. Truman's presidential campaign in 1948, in which significant shifts in voter preference during the closing weeks of the campaign resulted in his election. Furthermore, we still do not know what the ultimate impact of mass media, mass money, and mass psychology will be. In the article, "The Almost Perfect Campaign," James M. Perry discusses a recent gubernatorial campaign in New York in which large amounts of money, skillful use of new media, and masterful talent in public relations played a major role.

ELECTIONS: WHAT DOES AN ELECTION MEAN?

Elections in this country are never absolute mandates. The United States does not have party government as it exists in Great Britain, and further, we do not vote for the President and all of the members of Congress at one time. As a consequence, elections are general guidelines rather than finished house-plans. Moving beyond these considerations, however, there is still room for debate as to: (1) the significance of elections, and (2) the extent to which an election represents an individual's decision on political issues.

In the last section of this chapter, Bernard R. Berelson, Paul F. Lazarsfeld and William M. McPhee report part of their research on the 1948 campaign in the city of Elmira, New York. A somewhat different point of view is suggested by Arthur Maass in "Voters Are Not Fools."

1

The Ideal Candidate *

ART BUCHWALD

How well observed is the unwritten law in American politics, "The office should seek the man; the man should not blatantly seek the office."? Can you cite examples of privately active but publicly shy candidates? Are there any law breakers?

This is the time of year when everyone is checking on the 1968 Republi-

* Art Buchwald, "Non-Candidates' Bandwagon Roll," St. Louis *Post-Dispatch, Washington Post,* April 12, 1967. Reprinted by permission of the author.

can nominees for President. It isn't easy when you speak to them to guess their intentions, as I discovered talking to one politician whose name has been bandied about.

"Sir," I said, "your name has been

mentioned as a possible presidential candidate for 1968. What do you have to say about this?"

"It's absolute nonsense. I have enough to do serving the good people of my state for the next four years and I have no presidential aspirations at this time."

"But there have been 20 Glotz for President offices opened up around the country," I said.

"Twenty-three, to be exact. There are two more opening next week. I would like to say I strongly disapprove of these activities started by many well-meaning supporters. I have repeatedly told them at fund-raising dinners, rallies and press conferences that I am not interested in running for the presidential office in 1968. Unfortunately, I cannot control what any private citizen wants to do on his own."

"Yes, sir. I went to your campaign headquarters at 1750 Pennsylvania Avenue."

"You mean 1755, don't you? The phone number is ARizona 2-3456. What about it?"

"Well, they seemed to indicate that you had no objection to their starting the bandwagon rolling at this time."

"Well, they're wrong. I told them at a strategy meeting the other night that I did not wish to be considered a candidate and I would hope they'd respect my wishes in this respect. I further told them I would only accept nonpolitical speeches to GOP delegates and Young Republican clubs. I reminded them there were so many better candidates than myself." "Whom did you mention?"

"Governor Klonk, for example. You know, the one who bankrupted his state. I think he'd make a fine candidate."

"Who else?"

"Senator Zap. He's young, attractive, has tremendous sex appeal and I don't think his inexperience in government should be held against him."

"That's very fair of you."

"Then there's Senator Zilch, who certainly has a great deal of strength in the Black Power areas. I could support Senator Zilch with a clear conscience, even though I would hate the religious issue to come up in 1968."

"What about former Vice President Zimmer?"

"Zimmer has worked very hard for the Republican party since he was Vice President and should be given another shot at the big job. The fact he hasn't even been able to get elected to Blue Cross in the last four years should not be considered. He's just had a series of bad breaks."

"Sir, there's some talk that Governor Rhubarb might be a dark horse candidate."

"I've known Governor Rhubarb and I have the highest respect for him. I also feel strongly that a man who has been divorced three times would make as good a candidate as a man who has only been married once, so I hope no one will bring that up at the convention."

"Well, it appears you're really working for other candidates rather than for yourself."

"You bet I am. I promised Ray Bliss that no matter what I did, I would not attack any Republican publicly and endanger our chances in 1968."

"In case of a deadlock, would you consider a draft for yourself?"

"I think I've made my position clear that I am not interested in the job. Of course, if President Eisenhower asked me to run. . . ."

2

Is There a Presidential Type? *

PAUL T. DAVID, RALPH M. GOLDMAN, and RICHARD C. BAIN

What office seems to be the best "springboard" to the Presidency? Can you cite an example of a "typical" nominee? An "untypical" nominee?

* * *

What political offices have been most important as the final stepping stone to a presidential nomination? To success in the election that followed? If the information basic to these questions is organized for the two time periods on an in-party basis, out-party basis, as in Table 9, the result is at least thought-provoking, even though the figures to be considered are too few and too small to provide statistical evidence of any simple pattern of one-way, one-factor causation.

One striking feature is the small total number (six) of first-time nominees for President from 1896 to 1960 in the party in power, and the even smaller number (two) of these who won election. The two winners—William Howard Taft and Herbert Hoover —came directly out of the administration of the party in power; when an in-party administration went outside of its own ranks for a new nominee (Cox and Stevenson) or was unable to control the choice (Bryan), it lost the

election and went out of power. One can speculate that a party too weak or too divided internally to deal smoothly with the problems of succession in the headship will also find its competitive problems difficult until its leadership situation has again become stablized.

For the out-party the relative predominance of governors among the thirteen first-time nominees of the period 1896-1960 is clear. Six out-party governors won nomination; three won election (McKinley, Wilson, and F. D. Roosevelt, three lost (Smith, Landon, and Dewey). In the earlier period the out-party nominated only two governors; one was elected.

The record of the six generals in winning election was merely average. Of the in-party nominees, Grant won and Scott was a specacular loser. Hancock lost as the out-party nominee, as did McClellan. The out-party winners were Taylor and Eisenhower, one in each period.

All the incumbent senators nominated for President prior to 1896 lost their elections (Clay, Cass, and Douglas). In the period 1896-1960, the two senators nominated (Harding and Kennedy) were both out-party winners.

As for candidates holding no governmental position when first nom-

* Paul T. David, Ralph M. Goldman and Richard C. Bain, *The Politics of National Nominating Conventions* (New York: Random House, Inc., 1964). Condensation by Kathleen Sproul of the Brookings Institution Study, 1960, pp. 157-65. Reprinted by permission of the publisher.

inated, the respective in-parties lost elections with Blaine in 1884 and Bryan in 1896, and thereafter made no such nomination. Out-parties did relatively well before 1892 with former holders of public office (the two Harrisons, Polk, Pierce, and Lincoln). Between 1896 and 1960 an out-party candidate with only previous governmental experience (Davis) and one with no government experience (Wilkie) lost; the showing further illustrates the apparent need for incumbency in some high office in seeking the Presidency under modern conditions.

Is There a Type That Emerges?

Popular writing in every presidential election year always includes efforts to define the personality characteristics and other qualifications of "the perfect President" or "the ideal nominee." The data we have presented do not lend themselves easily to this kind of judgment—except to suggest that there *is* no single pattern of characteristics that the conventions will invariably choose. A convention may be guided to some extent by an unconscious ideal that has already screened out those clearly unavailable, but it is mainly seeking to choose among those who are still available. The system seems to throw up a wide range of types for choice, although not always very wide in any one year.

The early Presidents from Washington to John Quincy Adams were all well known from their previous participation in national affairs, and had many qualities in common. The con-

Table 9. Sources of First-Time Nominees and Their Electoral Success, by Party Status, 1832-1892 and 1896-1960 [a]

Governmental Position of Nominee	Party In Power		Party Out of Power	
	1832-1892	*1896-1960*	*1832-1892*	*1896-1960*
PRESIDENTIAL NOMINEES				
Governor	1/1	0/2	1/2	3/6
Federal Official [b]	1/1	2/2	–	–
Army General	1/2	–	1/3	1/1
Senator	0/2	–	0/1	2/2
Other [c]	2/2	0/1	–	0/2
None	0/1	0/1	5/8	0/2
Total	5/9	2/6	7/14	6/13
VICE-PRESIDENTIAL NOMINEES				
Senator	1/3	4/5	2/3	2/5
Representative	3/3	1/1	0/1	1/1
Governor	–	1/1	1/2	2/5
Federal Official [b]	1/2	1/3	0/1	–
Other [d]	0/1	–	1/1	–
None	3/6	2/3	4/7	1/4
Total	8/15	9/13	8/15	6/15

[a] In each cell of the table, the denominator is the total number of nominees in the category and the numerator is the number who won in the ensuing general election.

[b] Appointive officials in the Executive Branch.

[c] Two Vice Presidents, one representative in Congress, and two judges.

[d] One army general and one state official.

gressional nominating caucus in most cases stayed within the circle of its own observation and acquaintance-ship. When Andrew Jackson came to power as a people's hero, the earlier channels of advancement were disregarded and the convention system soon effectively prevented their restoration. Within a decade the field was open to state officials as well as federal, to legislators as well as executives, and to persons with no government experience who had somehow developed that intangible quality known as availability. . . .

*   *   *

Among the eight first-time Democratic nominees for President from 1896 through 1956, for instance, Bryan, Parker, and Davis all seem notably untypical in major respects. Bryan was young, inexperienced, and from a small, predominantly Republican state. Parker, a high court judge long withdrawn from active politics, was a vigorous supporter of the gold standard opposed earlier by majorities of his party. Davis was a Wall Street lawyer, who had previously been elected twice to the House of Representatives from West Virginia and held appointive positions under Wilson.

Each of the other Democrats—Wilson, Cox, Smith, F. D. Roosevelt, and Stevenson—was the active and able incumbent governor of a populous, hard-fought, two-party state. Their ages respectively were 55, 50, 55, 50, 52. Relatively new to the national scene, each had already achieved distinction in a public-service type of career. Cox was somewhat untypical in being a businessman and publisher, and Smith was certainly untypical in being highly urban and of the Roman Catholic faith. But all five were typical of much that has seemed best in the American political system; the rapid elevation,

through elective executive office in states where politics is vigorous and competitive, of able leaders still in the prime of life who have not necessarily yet taken on the characteristics of a "father image." This appears to be the type recently preferred by the Democratic party in its first-time presidential nominations, when the type was available. And the two elected—Wilson and Roosevelt—were highly exemplary of that preference.

The Republican party seems to have had a fondness for "untypical" nominees— of whom Willkie was probably the most outstanding example, with his total lack of governmental experience. Eisenhower, with his eminence as a five-star general, was a reversion to an earlier pattern of American politics—and thus one of the most untypical of the choices offered. Hughes, remote and Olympian, was untypical—despite his experience as a successful governor of New York State —as the only Supreme Court Justice in history nominated for President. Harding, the only nominee from the Senate between Douglas in 1860 and Kennedy in 1960, was untypical in a sufficient number of other respects.

Of the other five Republican nominees of 1896-1956, McKinley, Landon, and Dewey were incumbent governors, and Taft and Hoover served in the Cabinets of the Presidents that they succeeded. They seem to offer a composite pattern of the Republican preference in first-time presidential nominees. All were able executives, well known to be closely affiliated with the business community. Their ages respectively were 53, 49, 42, 51, and 54. Their careers had included distinguished public service and evidence of capacity to cultivate the electorate. With the exception of Landon, their origins were the populous, two-party states that often decide presidential elections. None of them, except per haps Dewey, was characterized by the kind of dynamism in approaching public problems that appeared to be a collective characteristic of the five Democrats deemed typical. They were therefore less likely to become the kind of "strong" President that, since Lincoln, seems to have been regarded by the Republican party as objectionable in the White House.

Table 10. The Presidents up to 1945 as Rated by Historians [a]

(adapted here to categories of nominating systems and political parties)

Category Assigned by Poll of 55 Historians	Presidents Selected Prior to Convention System	Presidents Nominated in National Party Conventions	
		Democratic	Republican [b]
Great	2. G. Washington 5. T. Jefferson 6. A. Jackson	3. F. D. Roosevelt 4. W. Wilson	1. A. Lincoln
Near Great	9. J. Adams	8. G. Cleveland 10. J. K. Polk	7. T. Roosevelt
Average	11. J. Q. Adams 12. J. Monroe 14. J. Madison	15. M. Van Buren	13. R. B. Hayes 16. W. H. Taft 17. C. A. Arthur 18. W. McKinley 19. A. Johnson 20. H. Hoover 21. B. Harrison
Below Average		26. J. Buchanan 27. F. Pierce	22. J. Tyler 23. C. Coolidge 24. M. Fillmore 25. Z. Taylor
Failure			28. U. S. Grant 29. W. G. Harding

[a] Arthur M. Schlesinger, "The U.S. Presidents," *Life* (Nov. 1, 1948). Professor Schlesinger explained that he conducted the poll informally among his "colleagues in American history and government. . . . There was a large measure of agreement among the 'experts' within the important categories of great, near great, and failures. The six greats . . . had no close runners-up, although Lincoln was the only one to get all 55 votes for the top rank." Harrison and Garfield were omitted because of the brevity of their life in office. Truman was omitted because his record was not complete at the time. (Rating material used by courtesy of Professor Schlesinger and *Life*.)

[b] Includes Whig (Tyler, Fillmore, and Taylor) and War Democrat (Johnson).

The type that has been most frequently preferred by the conventions of the two parties when they had an adequate opportunity for choice has provided the more successful Presidents of recent decades—Wilson and F. D. Roosevelt, McKinley, Taft, and Hoover. In a poll of fifty-five historians conducted in the late 1940's by Arthur M. Schlesinger, the two Democrats were rated as "greats," the three Republicans as at least average. The poll rated the only "untypical" nominee of either party to win election—Harding —as an outright failure as President. The set of ratings (published in *Life* in 1948) is here classified in Table 10, according to the political party of the Presidents and the system which nominated them. (The ratings express one form of authoritative opinion. The reader may disagree with some of them—as do the authors of this book.)

One must remember that either party at any given time can choose only from those who are available. If the preferred type, especially in a party out of power, is a vote-getting governor with a distinguished record in an important two-party state the number is seldom large. There have been times in out-party history when no such candidate was available, and some of the odd nominations that have been made were the result.

The picture given in this chapter has been one based mainly on the long historical record. It remains to be seen whether the nominations of 1960 reflect some permanent change. Kennedy was an incumbent senator when nominated, as Nixon had been before becoming Vice President. Neither had ever been a governor and neither had ever headed a large executive organization. In other respects, however, both men conformed to the type that has been identified: both had risen rapidly and with great distinction in a public service career, both were relatively young—43 and 47—and each was the product of vigorous competition in the campaigns and elections of a populous, two-party state.

It is possible that the Senate may become the most important source of presidential candidates in the future; the growing importance of the issues of national policy and of American involvement with the world at large are shifting the political spectrum in that direction. But it is much too early to conclude that governors are finished as presidential candidates, and especially so on any permanent or long-term basis.

3

Our National Nominating Conventions Are a Disgrace*

DWIGHT D. EISENHOWER

Why does former President Dwight D. Eisenhower reject a national primary as a substitute for the national nominating convention? What activities in the convention especially contribute to disorder? How can the problems of the national nominating convention be solved?

In my opinion—and I think most Americans will agree—our Presidential nominating conventions have become a thoroughly disgraceful spectacle which can scarcely fail to appall our own voters and create a shockingly bad image of our country abroad. Now that we are midway between the conventions of 1964 and 1968, it seems time to discuss this matter frankly. We can view the events of two years ago with some perspective, and there is still time to adopt reforms before the summer of 1968 is upon us.

First, I want to make it clear that I am not among those who wish to abolish the nominating conventions in favor of a national primary. Over the years, the conventions have done a reasonably good job of choosing men of ability and honor. There are, moreover, compelling arguments against a national primary. In most Presidential years at least two primary elections would be necessary. With perhaps four or five men seeking the nomination in

each party, it is unlikely that any one of them—except an incumbent President—could win a majority vote on the first round. Unless we nominated by plurality, which certainly is not desirable, a runoff would be necessary. All this would prolong the selection of candidates almost unbearably and wear down the interest of voters long before the main event.

Furthermore, if we nominated by primary, only wealthy men could normally run for the Presidency. Any campaign which attempts to cover this big country is enormously expensive. Once a candidate is nominated, of course, he is backed by the resources of his party. But in a primary campaign the aspirant must find a way to pay his own expenses—and I certainly do not think we should close the door of the Presidency to any man of integrity and ability simply because he cannot afford to run. Therefore I feel that the nominating conventions must be retained.

Point of Disorder

There is, however, no reason under heaven why these conventions must be exercises in chaos and tumult—unmannerly, undignified, ridiculous. Here we have men and women meeting to perform a vital task. The same atmosphere of dignity should prevail that we find in Congress or in any other major deliberative body. Yet our conventions now resemble a rioting mob of juvenile delinquents.

The floor often becomes a scene of milling humanity, and the din is such that delegates frequently cannot hear what is said on the podium. The thumping of the chairman's gavel, as he futilely tries to restore order, is an endless refrain to television viewers, many of whom turn off their sets in frustration.

Press, radio and television reporters roam the aisles at will, and often work their way into the center of a delegation for an interview. Reporters and delegates alike chatter into walkietalkies, thereby increasing the hubbub. The confusion becomes so frustrating that it is almost impossible for a delegation to hold a caucus on the floor.

The ultimate in mob scenes occurs, of course, after each candidate is placed in nomination. The band plays the candidate's theme song *ad infinitum*, and the parade of demonstrators begins. The doors at the rear of the halls are opened, and imported shouters—who have no official status whatsoever—swarm in with their banners and placards and noisemaking devices. The moment the uproar begins to diminish a bit, the candidate's managers whip up the frenzy of the faithful and prod the mercenaries into new feats of raucous clamor. The theory seems to be that the man who gets a 20-minute ovation would make twice as good a candidate as the 10-minute man.

Besmirched by Travesty

Sometimes the artificiality of these demonstrations is so ludicrous as to be acutely embarrassing. I recall one such instance some years ago. The hour was late, and most of the delegates had left the hall. But one more name remained to be placed in nomination—the name of a distinguished American who had served his country long and well. Finally, the speeches were ended, and the time had come for the joyous ovation. With few delegates left to participate, a motley assortment of characters from the city streets—obviously hired for the occasion—came in. Their performance, in a hall littered with wastepaper and debris, was lifeless and pathetic. Yet all this went out on television. As an American, I was embarrassed for my country. As a human being, I was outraged that the name of a prominent citizen should have been besmirched by such a travesty.

In times past, bad manners at our conventions—such as talking and visiting during a speech—have been largely due to thoughtlessness and the delegates' preoccupation with their own affairs. At the 1964 Republican convention in San Francisco, however, a new note of deliberate rudeness was injected. Booing and hissing were common, and insulting remarks were exchanged. The low point of the convention—perhaps of all conventions—came when New York's Gov. Nelson Rockefeller found it virtually impossible to deliver his speech. Chairman Thurston Morton furiously tried to quell the shocking display of bad manners, but without much success.

I suppose that this rudeness at San Francisco was the outgrowth of the sharp conflict between opposing camps. Whatever the reason, it was unpardonable—and a complete negation of the spirit of democracy. I was bitterly ashamed. I wish to add most emphatically that none of this was caused or condoned by the principal figures of the convention. It resulted from the lack of machinery for firm control of the unruly.

The Road to Reform

Until recent times, the spectacle of our nominating conventions was strictly for domestic consumption, and even in our own country few people ever *saw* a convention. Now, with television coverage, these riotous proceedings go into virtually every home. Worse, millions of TV viewers in foreign countries see the conventions, either live by satellite communication or from tapes flown across the oceans.

Now, I am all for television, radio and press coverage of the conventions. It is one way to bring home to our own people the issues and problems of government and to make them conscious of their duties as citizens. It is a way to show the workings of our brand of democracy—which is still the best form of government on earth—to our friends overseas. But certainly we should show all these people, at home and abroad, a dignified deliberative body at work, not "Operation Chaos."

I am happy to say that my own party is now making a determined start toward reform. Our national chairman, Ray Bliss, has appointed a committee of distinguished Republicans to study convention procedures and make recommendations. Somewhere along the way, I am told, the committee may ask for my suggestions, and I shall be most happy to coöperate.

My recommendations will be about as follows:

1. The permanent chairman should have better means for controlling convention procedure. If a violation of the rules occurs—a disturbance, an exhibition of rudeness—he should have the power to eject the disorderly or even to clear the hall and reconvene the convention at a later hour. If this were done even once, I think that people would soon get the idea that dignified and courteous deportment is obligatory.

2. No one except delegates and those with official convention business should be permitted on the floor. Even the alternate delegates should be seated in the gallery; when needed they could descend to the floor.

3. The above rule should apply to all reporters—television, press and radio. They could be provided with ample facilities *off the floor*. This recommendation may bring loud protest from some of our public media, but I think it is highly necessary. Congress wouldn't think of letting reporters come onto the floor of the House or Senate to interview members. The business of a convention is just as important as that of Congress, and the convention should have the same right to reach its decisions undisturbed. I have discussed this problem with one top network official, and I gather that at least some of the broadcasting people would be happy and relieved to operate under more orderly rules.

4. Walkie-talkies should be banned from the floor. Closed telephone circuits should be set up in the hall *for the delegates*, so that they could reach anyone in the hall quickly and easily, but these phones should not be connected with outside circuits. If a delegate wished to talk with someone outside the hall, he could go to a telephone elsewhere in the building.

5. All noisemaking devices should be banned from the hall, and any delegate or spectator using one of these abominations should be ejected. Moreover, there should be only one band inside the building—the official one. It could play some rousing music at the beginning and end of sessions, and play the theme song of each candidate during his demonstration—but at no other time.

6. Demonstrations should be restricted to ten minutes—ample time for a display of genuine enthusiasm. Participation in demonstrations should

be limited to delegates and alternates —no hired hands from the streets, no pretty high-school girls in cheerleader costumes.

7. Any booing or hissing or other disorderly conduct from spectators in the galleries should be quelled instantly and firmly, and the culprits should be evicted from the hall.

8. Although the convention should in no way interfere with protest demonstrations by legitimate groups *outside the hall*, it should have the right to expect that its business will not be impeded by them. Demonstrators who try to prevent the entry or departure of delegates by lying down in streets or doorways should be removed by the police. Any city unwilling to give a firm guarantee of such protection should be avoided as a convention site.

These are my recommendations. If they were adopted and enforced, I am sure that they would make our conventions respectable exhibits of democracy at work. It may be objected that such rules would be so inhibiting as to take all the steam and enthusiasm out of party procedure. I believe that the opposite is true. I am aware that genuine emotion—loyalty to a candidate, deep conviction on issues, patriotism—is an essential ingredient of political gatherings. But I believe that, within the framework of these rules, there would still be full scope for honest emotion and the kind of enthusiasm that makes party wheels turn.

The Urgent Need

There is one other suggestion which I think merits careful consideration by both parties. Each of the two conventions now lasts four days. That is much too long. If the recommendations I have offered were adopted, and if speeches were reduced in number and duration, the entire business of a convention could easily be accomplished in two days. This would be highly desirable for virtually everyone concerned, including the long-suffering public.

In any case, the urgent job before us now is to reform convention procedures—so that the summer of 1968 will not find us once more presenting to the world an inept, inane interpretation of the democratic process. As a Republican, I am delighted that my party is diligently studying the problem. As an American, I ardently hope that *both* parties will take the proper steps as soon as humanly possible.

4

The Hiring of Presidents *

CLINTON ROSSITER

What does Clinton Rossiter mean when he states that criticisms of the national nominating convention are really criticisms of our civilization? Has any national nominating convention ever passed over a first-rate candidate or ignored the wishes of the people? What is meant by the statement that the convention is "part and parcel of the magic by which men rule"?

*   *   *

The case against the nominating convention is almost too familiar to bear repeating. I doubt that I need rehearse the cultural sins of which it is accused by sensitive observers. It should be enough to remind ourselves that this windy, vulgar circus is met to nominate a candidate for the most powerful office on earth, and to wonder if there could be any gathering of men that seems less in character with its high purpose, that seems more unhappily to express what Henry James called "the triumph of the superficial and the apotheosis of the raw." The convention is certainly a gross distortion of that picture of intelligent men reasoning together which we carry in our heads as the image of free government. It was the sight of an American convention that led a famous European scholar (Ostrogorski) to observe, first, that "fifteen thousand people all attacked at once with Saint Vitus' dance" was not his idea of democracy;

and, second, that God in His infinite wisdom watches benevolently over drunkards, little children, and the United States of America.

And yet the case against the convention as a cultural abomination is itself a distortion. It is, indeed, a barrage directed through clouded sights at the wrong target. For the plain truth is that most criticisms of this noisy, plebeian, commercial institution are really criticisms of the noisy, plebeian, commercial civilization within which it operates. We see our follies as a people in the follies of the convention, and unless we reform ourselves, which I know we will not and suspect we dare not do, the convention will continue to disturb the reasonable, shock the fastidious, and fascinate all of us. In any case, it is yet to be proved that men who act like deacons can make a better choice of candidates for the Presidency than men who act like clowns, and that—the kind of choice the convention makes—is the meaningful test of its value as an institution of American life.

The more technical charges against the nominating convention are that it is undemocratic, since it cuts the rank

---

and file of the party out of the process of selecting a candidate; unreliable, since it ignores or distorts the real sentiment of the party in making the selection; and corrupts, since it puts a premium on the kind of horse trading in which men cannot expect to succeed unless they unlearn every rule of public and private morality. The convention, we are told, offers us a man we neither want nor deserve, and it offers him on a platter of corruption and cynicism. Those who make these charges usually go on to advocate some sort of nationwide presidential primary. The convention would become a pep rally to shout approval of the people's choice or quite possibly, would be abolished altogether.

These charges, it seems to me, are a caricature of reality. The first and third might just as easily be leveled at Congress as at the nominating convention, while the second, which is most often and earnestly advanced, simply cannot stand up under the scrutiny of history. When in the twentieth century, except perhaps in the Republican convention of 1912, has a majority of the voters of either great party been handed a candidate it did not want? When, except in the nomination of Harding in 1920, did a convention pass over several first-rate men to choose an acknowledged second-rater? Quite to the contrary of accepted legend, the convention has done a remarkable job over the years in giving the voters of each party the man whom they, too, would have selected had they been faced with the necessity of making a responsible choice. The convention is anxious to satisfy, not frustrate, the hopes of the members of the party; if the latter give an unmistakable sound, the former will echo it gladly and faithfully. If they speak in a babble of voices, if they cannot agree on a clear choice, the convention will choose their man for them, even if it takes a hundred ballots, and the choice, more-

over, will be made finally with near or complete unanimity. One of the undeniable merits of the convention, as opposed to the primary, is that it heals most of the wounds that are inevitably laid open in the rough process of making so momentous a political decision.

There is something to be said, I suppose, for the efforts of Senator Douglas and his friends to encourage the growth of presidential-preference primaries. In more than one-third of the states of the Union the voters of each party are now given some chance to elect or instruct their delegation to the convention, and no one would argue that professional politicians should be protected against such expressions of the public mood or choice. Yet it would be a mistake to make these exercises in public opinion much more uniform in pattern or binding in effect than they are at present. Reformers should be careful not to upset the nice balance that history has struck between the hard responsibilities of the professionals at the convention and the vague wishes of the voters at home. The real question about our presidential primaries, it seems to me, is not whether they should take over completely the key role of the convention, which is an academic question at best, but whether they are worth all the fuss they cause in the minds of the public and all the strain they put upon even the most hard-shelled candidates. The active campaign for the Presidency becomes much too long drawn out a process; money becomes much too decisive a factor in the hopes and plans of any one candidate; some of the best candidates are torn between the responsibility of the important position they already fill and the lure of the one after which they hunger and thirst. Under the system as it now operates, even the most popular candidates are hostages to whim and accident, especially to the whim of the "favorite sons" who sprout quadrennially and to the accident of the timetable of the primaries. The Democrats of New Hampshire, where the first primary is usually held, are all fine people, I am sure, but neither so fine nor so wise that they should be able to make or break a presidential aspirant all by themselves. I am inclined to agree with Adlai Stevenson, who speaks to the point with matchless authority, that the presidential primaries are a "very, very questionable method of selecting presidential candidates." Rather than have a handful of primaries spread carelessly over the months between February and July, it might be the wiser and even more democratic thing to have none at all. I for one would be happy to see our strongest candidates take the advice of the publisher of the *Adirondack Daily Enterprise*, James Loeb, Jr., and join in boycotting the present system entirely. It is, by almost any standard, one of the failures of our political system.

The convention, to the contrary, is a clear if not brilliant success. It meets the one test to which we like to put all our institutions: it does the job it is asked to do, and does it remarkably well. Indeed, one can be more positive than this in defense of the convention, for it performs several tasks that no other institution or arrangement can perform at all. Not only does it serve as the major unifying influence in political parties that are decentralized to the point of anarchy; it is, as Professor V. O. Key has written, "part and parcel of the magic by which men rule." And Americans, I again insist, are far from that enlightened condition in which political magic has lost its usefulness. The nominating convention fills a constitutional void; it unites and inspires each of the parties; it arouses interest in the grand plebiscite through which we choose our President. We will have to hear more convincing charges than have hitherto been pressed against the convention before we tamper with this venerable instrument of American democracy.

5

The Almost Perfect Campaign *

JAMES M. PERRY

After reading this case study, would you say that anyone, given sufficient money, television time, and proficiency in public relations, can be elected? Can you give an example of a candidate's failure despite money, television, and expert advice? What, in the author's opinion, can prevent the exploitation of campaign techniques by a dangerous and sinister man?

Nelson A. Rockefeller, the happiest multimillionaire, repeated those magic

* James M. Perry, "The Almost Perfect Campaign," *The National Observer*, January 9, 1967. Reprinted by permission of the publisher.

words last week: "I do solemnly swear that I will . . . faithfully discharge the duties of the office of governor according to the best of my ability."

Sweet words for a man no one ever thought could be elected to a third term. Costly words. To win re-election, some $260,000 was spent for each lovely little word. Nelson Rockefeller's winning campaign was far and away the most expensive state-wide effort ever put together in this country. Not only the most expensive, but the most professional, the most astute, the most imaginative, and perhaps the most ruthless. It was, in fact, the closest thing to a perfect political campaign this democracy has ever seen.

Some supporting evidence:

No state-wide candidate has ever used television so much, so well. A National Observer survey indicates that 3,027 commercials were shown on New York State's 22 commercial television stations in behalf of Mr. Rockefeller. The actual figures, given the inconsistency of reporting methods, might run as high as 4,000.

No state-wide candidate has ever distributed so much literature and campaign paraphernalia. The Rockefeller forces distributed 27,000,000 buttons, brochures, and broadsides. That's about 4½ items for every person who turned out to vote.

The candidate himself, traveling by bus, by jet, by helicopter, even by seaplane—and constantly in radio touch with his 84-room headquarters at the New York Hilton—visited all 62 counties in the state. In August alone, he shook hands at 17 county fairs in upstate New York. Mr. Rockefeller spent his energy with just as much abandon as he and loyal members of his family spent their cash. . . .

❋   ❋   ❋

And for the ordinary voter, living anywhere, the Rockefeller campaign is significant. After all, this campaign, like any other, was ultimately directed at that lone voter, buffeted by personal problems and petty concerns and hardly willing or able to devote more than peripheral attention to politicians

or to political issues. In this campaign, new techniques were used to win that lone voter's attention and his support. Some of these techniques—if improperly used by sincere men or properly used by insincere men—may be dangerous. They at least should be understood.

Here then is the story—told in detail for the first time—of how the almost-perfect campaign was planned and waged.

To start at the beginning, there was Nelson Rockefeller. A very unpopular Nelson Rockefeller. At his side was a heavy-set man named William J. Ronan, one-time dean of the New York University Graduate School of Public Administration and Social Services. . . .

❋   ❋   ❋

"We had a problem," Dr. Ronan recalls. "In January of 1966 the position of the governor in the polls was not very good. Indications were that almost anyone could beat him. There were so many negatives. He had been in office for almost eight years and he had made a lot of decisions that irritated some people; other people just thought they were aggrieved. He'd raised taxes twice in a major way. One was a sales tax. And he got full credit for all these new taxes. . . .

❋   ❋   ❋

"On the other side, Rockefeller had accomplished more in eight years than any other governor. But these positives weren't apparent. He'd done so much it was all kind of a blur—the state university, highways, aid to local governments, health, parks, right across the board.

"Adding it all up, the governor just wasn't popular. People didn't like him any more."

That's almost an understatement. The Rockefeller problem was so serious that some Republican leaders actually were calling for him to step aside in favor of U.S. Sen. Jacob Javits. Even some of the people closest to Rockefeller were privately saying that defeat was inevitable. But things weren't quite as bad as they looked. As Dr. Ronan says, "Fortune favors the brave."

One of the secrets of the Rockefeller campaign's success was its early start. First, there was Dr. Ronan, ready to go on issues. Then there was "the other Bill"—William L. Pfeiffer, an old professional who had worked for Mr. Rockefeller before. This time, he actually went to work for Rockefeller on Dec. 1, 1964. His assignment was to organize the 1966 campaign—to pick the personnel, to open a headquarters, to lay out a schedule. Bill Ronan was the ideas man; Bill Pfeiffer was the organization man. Ultimately, Mr. Pfeiffer put together a "paid staff" of 307 people, 190 of them working out of headquarters at the New York Hilton. In a more traditional way, his operation was just as brilliant as Dr. Ronan's. And almost as costly.

Yet, with all credit to Mr. Pfeiffer and the professionals working for him, the major assignment was Dr. Ronan's. He had to sell Nelson Rockefeller just as Miles Laboratories sells Alka-Seltzer. He had to make an unpopular governor an acceptable product.

And so he formed a small committee, himself at its head, grandiloquently called the Substantive Issues Group. Like Dr. Ronan himself, this elite group—never numbering more than five—was exclusively intellectual.

"We undertook a pre-campaign approach," says Dr. Ronan. "We wanted to improve the governor's position before the state convention (the ticket in New York is chosen by party convention, not by direct primary). Since people were down on the governor, we decided to sell his accomplishments without using him at all."

The key decision was the choice of an advertising agency. "We wanted to depart from the usual political approach," Dr. Ronan notes. "We moseyed around the field and we found Jack Tinker & Partners, part of the Interpublic complex. We liked their different approach. It was offbeat and it had been successful in restoring some products." One of those restored products was Alka-Seltzer; another, Braniff Airways, Inc. . . .

* * *

The creation of good television takes time. Mr. Rockefeller, because he was an incumbent and because of his own farsightedness, had the time. His ultimate Democratic opponent, Frank W. O'Connor, never did have the time, and the quality of his television showed it.

"Advance planning is so damn important," says Tinker's Mr. Conroy. "I don't see why a lot of incumbents don't start planning a lot sooner. And, in fact, I don't see why the out-party couldn't start early too. The state committee could easily put together a program attacking the incumbent and his record, even without having a candidate of their own."

And so the work began, Dr. Ronan and his team deciding on the issues to be stressed, the agency people developing these issues into brilliant television commercials. As Bill Pfeiffer puts it: "We had to sell the record, associate it with the governor. And it had to be done so subtly it crept up on you before you knew what the hell had happened to you."

Tinker commercials are prepared by teams. Each team is composed of a copywriter and an art director. Unlike most agencies, the two members of the team follow the commercial all the way through the production process, from writing the script to directing the filming to editing the sound. Two of these teams were assigned to the Rockefeller account. . . .

The first commercials produced by these teams all were 60 seconds in length. Each was done in a process called sound-on-film; it's slower to produce but the quality is better. Moreover, a creative team can do more with film than with tape. It is not surprising that most of the Rockefeller commercials were sound-on-film; that all of the Democratic commercials were videotape.

The first Tinker commercial set the whole tone of the early phase of the campaign. The title of the commercial is "Fish Interview." Stage directions read: "Open on hand wearing a press hat and microphone to resemble a reporter talking to a fish puppet."

The script reads, in part:

Reporter: You, sir.

Fish: Uh huh.

Reporter: How do you feel about Governor Rockefeller's Pure Waters Program?

Fish: His pure what?

Reporter: Pure waters.

Fish: Oh, oh yeah.

Reporter: This program, sir, is wiping out water pollution in New York within six years.

Fish: Well, it was pretty smelly down here.

Reporter: By the end of summer, the governor will have called in every major polluter for a hearing.

And so on, for an exchange or two more.

Bill Pfeiffer remembers looking at the first Tinker commercials with a number of political leaders. "The politicos," says Mr. Pfeiffer, "said it was no damn good. They're so used to the staged stuff, to the candidate standing there talking. You had to wait out these Tinker commercials to find out what they were all about. But the politicos thought they were just a waste of time. That's when I knew we had done the right thing.

Each commercial dealt with a single subject, directly and imaginatively. The commercials were amusing and they were interesting. And each of them contained a germ or two of truth.

The second Tinker commercial was classic in its utter simplicity. A camera was mounted on a hood of a car, and the commercial showed what the camera photographed as the road slipped by. The script reads: "If you took all the roads Governor Rockefeller has built, and all the roads he's widened and straightened and smoothed out . . . if you took all these roads, and laid them end to end, they'd stretch all the way to . . . Hawaii."

At that point—the Hawaii bit—the sound swells; it's all crashing breakers and hula music. Then the car obviously backs up and turns around. The road starts to slip by again. The voice returns: "All the way to Hawaii . . . and all the way back."

Then came "Butterfingers" (about state scholarships). . . . Nelson Rockefeller didn't appear in any of these commercials. His voice wasn't ever used. The Tinker agency picked a professional—actor Ed Binnis—to read the scripts. It is the same Ed Binnis that millions of Americans hear on television every day—talking about Alka Seltzer and Gillette razors.

The first of the soft-sell Tinker commercials began popping up on screen in July. Just as Bill Pfeiffer says, they "crept up" on the viewer. Long before the commercials began to appear, the Rockefeller and Tinker people had worked out a schedule based on a detailed analysis of the voters' market.

They had found, for example, that 86.7 per cent of the registered voters lives in 22 of the 62 counties. Conclusion from that: Saturate the television markets serving those 22 counties. Thus, the 60-second commercials were

```
N. Y. REPUBLICAN STATE COMMITTEE            Film Number:   R-60-5
Estimate #R-6-2530                          Title:         Butterfingers
8/4/66                                      Length:        :60
FINAL AS PRODUCED
```

	VIDEO		AUDIO
1.	OPEN ON FULL SHOT OF KID APPROACHING CAMERA DRIBBLING BASKETBALL. CUTS OF A PICK-UP BASKETBALL GAME IN A LOWER CLASS NEIGHBORHOOD. THERE ARE ABOUT FIVE TALL, FAST, GOOD BALLPLAYERS AND ONE SHORT, FAT INEPT KID.	1.	(MUSIC)
2.	THE CAMERA FROM TIME TO TIME DRAWS THE VIEWER'S ATTENTION TO THE INEPT KID. HE IS THE ONE THE MESSAGE IS ADDRESSED TO.	2.	(MUSIC UNDER) ANNCR: (V.O.) Hey kid. Want to go to college? Maybe you catch the eye of some coach; get yourself a scholarship. No, you don't have to be nine foot tall to get a scholarship, or a blooming genius either. Why, if you can get _into_ college, you can get the money to help you _go_ to college. From New York State. Two hundred thousand new state scholarships and grants are sitting there waiting, every year. Two hundred thousand new chances to make it, every year, even for you, shorty..., tubby..., butterfingers. The man responsible for those new scholarships is Governor Rockefeller. Who was no Bob Cousy himself.
		3.	Jack Tinker & Partners, Inc.

cheduled for the six stations in New York city and for television stations erving Albany, Binghamton, Buffalo, Rochester, and Syracuse.

The television campaign was divided into three phases. Phase 1 covered the period July 5 to Sept. 12. In that period, the schedule called for running 37 Rockefeller 60-second commercials every week in New York City and 18 every week in each of the five upstate markets.

The result was that the Rockefeller commercials, stressing the administration's accomplishments but never the candidate himself, were shown 700 times before the state convention ever began.

That, of course, was only part of the pre-convention strategy. The governor himself quietly toured the state all during August, shaking hands and trying to make friends. Personal emissaries—men like George Hinman, who had done so much for Mr. Rockefeller in his Presidential efforts—toured the state, talking to "opinion makers." An indication of the success of this effort may be the fact that only two daily newspapers in the state—the Adirondack Enterprise and the Syracuse Herald-Journal—ultimately decided to support a candidate opposed to Mr. Rockefeller. In New York City, both the liberal Post and the conservative Daily News, which rarely agree about anything, endorsed Mr. Rockefeller. . . .

*   *   *

"First," says Dr. Ronan, "we wanted to reach the opinion makers, for we were afraid we had lost them. They just weren't articulate for us and I mean the legislators, the newspaper people, the leaders of various special groups. So we decided to approach them on a clientele basis. We prepared eye-getting stuff in each category--a brochure for the people in the field of mental retardation, another for labor, another for the fine arts." Salty Bill Pfeiffer puts it in somewhat different terms. "It was out of this world," he says. "We had something for every group except the Times Square prostitutes."

Preparing the literature is one thing; distributing it is another. In most campaigns, thousands of brochures are still lying around headquarters the day after election. This time, a paid worker was assigned to each kind of brochure with instructions to make sure the literature got to the people it was written for. Thus, if there was a meeting anywhere in the state of people interested in higher education, there was a Rockefeller staffer there to make sure everyone got a brochure dealing entirely with what the governor had done for higher education in New York.

Another Ronan innovation was the preparation of a series of brochures aimed at individual regions in the state. Every major region had a Rockefeller brochure, and the text in each told precisely what the Rockefeller administration had done for that part of the state. Getting the facts out of the bureaucracy was the tough part of that job; it was accomplished only be-

cause the fact-gathering had begun months earlier. . . .

*   *   *

Because they had started so early, the Rockefeller people had the time—and, to be sure, the cash—to anticipate the issues. Polls were taken regularly. They showed that one of the major criticisms of the governor was that he was arrogant. "So," says Dr. Ronan, "we flipped that over to the positive. The positive of arrogance is leadership. So we said, 'This is leadership and let's keep it in Albany.' It came through again and again in what we did. It was summed up by the phrase, 'He Cares.'"

The polls had also shown the voters were angry about high taxes. The answer to that was to show where the money had gone. All the Rockefeller material emphasized the amount of money that had been returned to local jurisdictions in the form of state aid.

The Rockefeller people also tried to anticipate their opponent. They guessed right that Frank D. O'Connor, president of the New York City Council, would be the Democrats' choice. He was chosen at the Democratic State Convention in Buffalo on Sept. 7-8. By then, the Republicans had a fat file on his career and almost everything he had ever said.

Thus, after both conventions were over, the Rockefeller campaign moved into a new—and tougher—phase. Gradually, radio and TV commercials (radio was used to supplement television) began to zero in on Mr. O'Connor. Finally, Mr. Rockefeller appeared full-face, using his own voice, to attack with extraordinary ruthlessness his gentle and bumbling Democratic opponent.

Mr. O'Connor had no meaningful reply. The Democrats, up to the time of their convention, had done almost nothing about preparing a campaign. They had no literature, no television hardly any organization. The entirely predictable result was chaos in their camp. Worse, they were constantly on the defense. Troubling the waters, too, were the additional candidacies of Franklin D. Roosevelt, Jr., on the Liberal ticket, and Paul L. Adams, on the Conservative.

The Tinker agency returned to the battle, preparing 10- and 20-second commercials attacking Mr. O'Connor and his record. Typical was the script; "Frank O'Connor, the man who led the fight against the New York State Thruway, is running for governor. Get in your car. Drive down to the polls, and vote."

Of necessity, all spot commercials are oversimplifications. After all, no one can say very much even in 60 seconds. In the first phase, though, most of the Rockefeller commercials were reasonably truthful. Now, however, in the second and third phases, they became distortions. Take the thruway commercial. Mr. O'Connor, as a state legislator, didn't actually oppose a thruway. What he did oppose—taking his own party's position—was a toll road. He and the Democrats wanted a free road. That refinement, naturally, never was explained.

Or take this Rockefeller 20-second commercial. The script reads: "Frank O'Connor from New York City is running for governor. He says the New York subways should be free. Guess who he thinks should pay for them?"

It is interesting that this commercial was only run in *upstate* New York; never in New York City. Moreover Mr. O'Connor never meant to say that he wanted the New York subways free now or even at any time in the next few years. He had been musing about long-term goals when he made his proposal, and he had been thinking about subways in all cities. Again, Mr. O'Connor never was able to explain the refinements involved.

In every campaign, smart politicians look for the "gut issue," an emotional, supercharged issue that can be battered home to almost every voter. The Rockefeller people, months before the campaign began, anticipated just such a gut issue. When it came time, they were ready.

The issue was, specifically, narcotics; more broadly, crime. Mr. Rockefeller as governor, had proposed a sweeping narcotics program. It involved getting all of the addicts off the street—mandatory treatment, in other words—and jailing all of the pushers. It was strong stuff, so strong that it worried many civil libertarians. Yet, for voters generally, it was popular enough, for every poll taken in New York State recently rates crime as the leading concern of the citizenry.

The Rockefeller people expected that Mr. O'Connor would take a position against the Rockefeller narcotics program. Mr. O'Connor did take such a position, perhaps to win back dissident liberals to the Democratic line (many of them were flocking to the Liberal Party and its candidate, Mr. Roosevelt). Or perhaps Mr. O'Connor, as his aides suggest, just thought the program, as outlined by Mr. Rockefeller, was unworkable.

Whatever the reason, Mr. O'Connor was vulnerable, and he was clobbered by every device available to his opposition. The television commercials were eerie, frightening. A police car, lights flashing, cruises down a dark street. There's the sound of footsteps in the background. A disembodied voice begins talking: "If you walk home at night or if there's a teen-ager in your family, you should be worried. Governor Rockefeller's worried. As much as half the crime in New York is caused by addicts. That's why the governor has sponsored a tough new law that can get addicts off the streets for up to three years. . . ."

At first, the commercials made no mention of Mr. O'Connor. Then they noted that, as district attorney of Queens, he had been alone among all prosecutors in the state in opposing a tough narcotics law. Finally, Mr. Rockefeller himself—speaking into a battery of microphones in a television studio—took the fight directly to his opponent. "If you want to keep crime rates high," he concluded, "O'Connor is your man."

It was devastating. Its effect was heightened by a local issue in New York City—the police civilian-review board. The Conservative Party and the police themselves had managed to get a referendum on the ballot challenging Mayor John Lindsay's review board. It was, by itself, the most emotional issue in the city. And the narcotics issue dovetailed neatly with it.

In the final weeks of the campaign, the Rockefeller people simply overwhelmed the opposition. And television was the battering ram.

Consider these figures.

On television station WNBC, in New York City, the Rockefeller forces ran 208 commercials. They paid $237,000 to do it. The O'Connor forces ran on this same station 23 commercials. They paid $41,000. On WCBS, Rockefeller outspent O'Connor $231,-105 to $35,920. On WABC, the third network station in the city, it was $137,000 for Rockefeller and $25,100 for O'Connor.

The disparity upstate was sometimes even more remarkable. On WBEN in Buffalo, Rockefeller spent $27,762; O'Connor, $2,465. Little WWNY in Watertown ran 99 Rockefeller commercials, at $3,067.50, against 18 O'Connor commercials, at $1,307.50.

Rockefeller strategists hasten to point out that they began their television campaign 'way back in July. They're right, of course—but they had to start that early to make a campaign. That early spending was just as crucial as the final spending. It was, in fact, one campaign. And when it was all over Rockefeller outspent O'Connor by almost 10 to 1.

What were the actual figures? It's hard to say. Democrats and even some Republicans insist that Rockefeller spent as much as $10,000,000. The National Observer's sampling of campaign costs would indicate a lower figure, perhaps something over $6,000,-000. The official figure filed by Mr. Rockefeller and his people is $4,800,-000. Hardly anyone doubts, however, that the O'Connor people are reasonably accurate when they say they spent $600,000. It just couldn't have been much more.

Even with this lopsided spending, Mr. Rockefeller didn't win by very much. The final count was: Rockefeller, 2,690,626; O'Connor, 2,298,363; Adams, 510,023; Roosevelt, 507,234. Almost surely, Mr. Rockefeller could have been beaten. He won because he had the money and the talent to wage a brilliant campaign. And, to be sure, he had luck on his side—luck in having the Democrats pick the bumbling Mr. O'Connor, luck in having Mr. Roosevelt and Mr. Adams splintering the vote. . . .

*　　*　　*

The Lessons?

——Money and more money. Money wisely, even ruthlessly, spent. A candidate or a party must have it early and spend it often.

——Television. It's the premier instrument for political campaigning. It penetrates into almost every home; it sways and angers and converts. Item: During the week of Oct. 18, Rockefeller ran 74 television commercials in New York City. They were seen in 9 per cent of all television homes in the city (and 5,600,000 of 6,000,000 New York homes have television). Not seen just once—but seen an average of 9.8 times in each home.

——Experts. No one wins any more with amateurs. Good television means people like Dr. Ronan and the copywriters and art directors at Jack Tinker. Good organization requires innovators like Bill Pfeiffer.

——Time. It takes time to put together a campaign. Mr. Rockefeller had the time, Mr. O'Connor didn't. It was as simple as that.

But what about candidates? Is there a lesson in New York that almost any-

one can be elected, given money, television, experts, and time? Perhaps not. Mr. Rockefeller, after all, is a great campaigner, and he has been, many people think, a strong and effective governor. There was, in all the confusion and bitterness, a product to be sold, albeit in a battered and dusty package.

Yet, a note of doubt remains. These new techniques are so overwhelming, so terribly effective. Some day, maybe they will elect a truly dangerous and sinister man to high public office.

The preventive, perhaps, is a general understanding of what it's all about.

6

Voting *

BERNARD R. BERELSON, PAUL F. LAZARSFELD and WILLIAM N. McPHEE

The following selection is taken from a study of Elmira, New York, during the presidential campaign of 1948. What do the authors mean when they say, "His vote is formed in the midst of his fellows in a sort of a group decision"? Do you agree with the quotation, "the decisions of men, when they come to choose their governors, are influenced by considerations which escape all scientific analysis"? How do the authors relate traditional democratic theory to their findings in voting research?

*   *   *

The Social Group and the Political System

Underlying the influence of the social group is the ambiguity of political stimuli. The individualistic

* Bernard R. Berelson, Paul F. Lazarsfeld, William N. McPhee, *Voting* (Chicago: University of Chicago Press, 1954), pp. 114-15, 20-23. Reprinted by permission of the publisher.

tradition of thinking about politics, as typically expressed in democratic theory, implies that it is possible and reasonably convenient for the voter to see clearcut alternatives: to judge the differences between candidates, weigh the relevance of the issues to his own needs, and then rightly or wrongly "decide" what to do. The scheme implied in this tradition of thinking about politics requires a reasonably clear political choice that can be responded to directly by the individual, but this is not always, or even usually, the case.

Suppose we think of two polar types of modern elections. An unusual type of election (e.g., 1936) presents a clear-cut and easily understood program that had major consequences for a large number of voters, that was highlighted by dramatic events, and that was symbolized by a magnetic candidate. At the opposite pole there is an election period (e.g., 1948) in which voters can find no clear programs, no simple picture of what is at stake, no visible consequences win or lose for the average citizen, no appealing and dramatic candidates—in short, a thoroughly ordinary period against the backdrop of reasonably stable times during which the citizen would prefer to be left undisturbed in the normal pursuit of job and family activities.

In situations of high ambiguity, according to the evidence of psychological experiments, two kinds of behavior occur that we have encountered in this political analysis. First, with no clear directives from stimuli outside themselves, people are likely to fall back on directive forces within themselves. This means that voters are likely to fall back on early allegiances, experiences, values, and norms—for example, those associated with being raised as a member of the working class or a minority group. Second, voters are likely to be especially vulnerable to less relevant influences than direct political stimuli. If voters cannot test the appropriateness of their decisions by reference to political consequences, then they are especially likely to be influenced by other, nonpolitical facts— for example, what trusted people around them are doing. As a result, old interests and traditions of class and minority blocs are brought to bear upon the determination of today's vote.

In this process the principal agencies are not Machiavellian manipulators, as is commonly supposed when bloc votes are delivered at the polls, but the ordinary family, friends, co-workers, and fellow organization members with whom we are all surrounded. In short, the influences to which voters are most susceptible are opinions of trusted people expressed to one another. . .

*   *   *

Lord Bryce pointed out the difficulties in a theory of democracy that assumes that each citizen must himself be capable of voting intelligently:

Orthodox democratic theory assumes that every citizen has, or ought to have, thought out for himself certain opinions, i.e., ought to have a definite view, defensible by argument, of what the country needs, of what principles ought to be applied in governing it, of the man to whose hands the government ought to be entrusted. There are persons who talk, though certainly very few who act, as if they believed this theory, which may be compared to the theory of some ultra Protestants that every good Christian has or ought to have . . . worked out for himself from the Bible a system of theology.

In the first place, however, the information available to the individual voter is not limited to that directly possessed by him. True, the individual casts his own personal ballot. But, as we have tried to indicate throughout this volume, that is perhaps the most individualized action he takes in an election. His vote is formed in the midst of his fellows in a sort of group decision—if, indeed, it may be called a decision at all—and the total information and knowledge possessed in the group's present and past generation can be made available for the group choice. Here is where opinion-leading relationships, for example, play an active role.

Second, and probably more important, the individual voter may not have a great deal of detailed information, but he usually has picked up the crucial *general* information as part of his social learning itself. He may not know the parties' positions on the tariff, or who is for reciprocal trade treaties, or what are the differences on Asiatic policy, or how the parties split on civil rights, or how many security risks were exposed by whom. But he cannot live in an American community without knowing broadly where the parties stand. He has learned that the Republicans are more conservative and the Democrats more liberal—and he can locate his own sentiments and cast his vote accordingly. After all, he must vote for one or the other party, and, if he knows the big thing about the parties, he does not need to know all the little things. The basic role a party plays as an institution in American life is more important to his voting than a particular stand on a particular issue.

    *   *   *

How can our analysis be reconciled with the classical theory of liberal political democracy? Is the theory "wrong"? Must it be discarded in favor of empirical political sociology? Must its ethical or normative content be dismissed as incompatible with the nature of modern man or of mass society? That is not our view. Rather, it seems to us that modern political theory of democracy stands in need of revision and not replacement by empirical

sociology. The classical political philosophers were right in the direction of their assessment of the virtues of the citizen. But they demanded those virtues in too extreme or doctrinal a form. The voter does have some principles, he does have information and rationality, he does have interest—but he does not have them in the extreme, elaborate, comprehensive, or detailed form in which they were uniformly recommended by political philosophers . . . [T]he typical citizen has other interests in life, and it is good, even for the political system, that he pursues them. The classical requirements are more appropriate for the opinion leaders in the society, but even they do not meet them directly. Happily for the system, voters distribute themselves along a continuum:

And it turns out that this distribution itself, with its internal checks and balances, can perform the functions and incorporate the same values ascribed by some theorists to each individual in the system as well as to the constitutive political institutions!

Twentieth-century political theory —both analytic and normative—will arise only from hard and long observation of the actual world of politics, closely identified with the deeper problems of practical politics. Values and the behavior they are meant to guide are not distinctly separate or separable parts of life as it is lived; and how Elmirans choose their governors is not completely unrelated to the considerations of how they are *supposed* to choose them. We disagree equally with those who believe that normative theory about the proper health of a

SOCIABLE MAN	POLITICAL MAN	IDEOLOGICAL MAN
(Indifferent to public affairs, nonpartisan, flexible . . .)		(Absorbed in public affairs, highly partisan, rigid . . .)

democracy has nothing to gain from analytic studies like ours; with those who believe that the whole political tradition from Mill to Locke is irrelevant to our realistic understanding and assessment of modern democracy; or with those like Harold Laski who believe that "the decisions of men, when they come to choose their governors, are influenced by considerations which escape all scientific analysis."

We agree with Cobban: "For a century and a half the Western democracies have been living on the stock of basic political ideas that were last restated toward the end of the eighteenth century. That is a long time. . . . The gap thus formed between political facts and political ideas has steadily widened. It has taken a long time for the results to become evident; but now that we have seen what politics devoid of a contemporary moral and political theory means, it is possible that something may be done about it." . . .

7

Voters Are Not Fools *

ARTHUR MAASS

Do the findings of V. O. Key, Jr. support the thesis that voting is a group experience rather than an individual decision? What does Key conclude about the Switch Voter? How much importance does Key attach to the cult of personality in presidential elections? How important are policy preferences in influencing vote decisions?

. . . "The perverse and unorthodox argument of this little book," says V. O. Key, Jr., "is that voters are not fools."

Such an argument is unorthodox because some social scientists, using data and analytical techniques similar to Key's, have for years been teaching us something different.

From his analysis of presidential campaign data of recent decades, Key finds that the American voter and electorate are neither "strait-jacketed by social determinants" nor "moved

by subconscious urges triggered by devilishly skillful propagandists." The portrait that emerges is rather that of "an electorate moved by concern about central and relevant questions of public policy, of governmental performance, and of executive personality."

When V. O. Key in April 1963 was struck by an illness from which he was unable to recover, he was working with intense urgency on this manuscript, in part, as his close friends have testified, because he knew that the "perverse" findings were of basic importance for both the theory and the practice of democracy in America.

Broadly, Key's method is to classify voters in presidential elections as standpatters (those who vote for the

* Arthur Maass, Foreword to V. O. Key, Jr., *The Responsible Electorate* (Cambridge, Mass.: The Belknap Press of Harvard University Press, Copyright, 1966, by the President and Fellows of Harvard College), pp. vii-xv. Reprinted by permission of the publishers.

candidate of the same party in successive elections), switchers, and new voters, and to determine whether there are significant correlations between the presidential choice of these three types of voters and their opinions of the issues, events, and candidates of the campaigns.

From the data on the actions and attitudes of the shifting voters, Key concludes that they move from party to party in a manner that is broadly consistent with their policy preferences, and that switchers are far more numerous than is commonly supposed. The data on those voters who stand pat with their party from election to election do not lead to a very different conclusion, however. On the average, "the standpatters do not have to behave as mugwumps to keep their consciences clear; they are already where they ought to be in the light of their policy attitudes."

The major conclusions to be drawn from Key's findings are first, that political man is rational, and second, that the political institutions that he has developed, at least those for election of the president, are rational too.

In elaborating his argument Key shows certain characteristics that are familiar to those who have followed his work closely over the years. His deep commitment to democratic and human values and his optimism about the human race are combined with superb craftsmanship, a fine sensitivity to the relevance and irrelevance of political data and arguments, and a hardheadedness that ensures that moral purpose never passes as a cover for sloppy analysis. Thus Key is unsympathetic with, and distrustful of, political and behavioral theories that degrade the rationality of man and of the institutions that man creates freely; and with a great mastery and inventiveness of technique, he is able to prove that many such theories are

false. I can illustrate this with several examples.

(1) It has been popular among political scientists and commentators to analyze election returns according to the voting behavior of large groups of persons with like attributes: occuption, religion, residence, education; and to imply that the imperatives of these economic and demographic factors guide the voting. Despite recent efforts of some political scientists to discourage this use of group imperatives, an astonishing number of people persist in doing so. Key is unsympathetic to the unflattering, deterministic implications of this analytic technique, and he shows that the technique is faulty. Gross characteristics of groups of individuals serve as an adequate indication of attitudes only when the issues of the campaign affect directly and clearly the members of the group. "The fact that a person is, say, a Negro serves as an index to what he believes and to why he votes as he does only when an election concerns Negroes as Negroes and when the members of the group are aware of the issue and see it as basic among their concerns of the moment." Where gross data indicate, for example, that 70 per cent of businessmen voted one way, Key invariably asks the question why 30 per cent did not vote their apparent economic interests; and the answer not infrequently is that the classification provided by the gross data is irrelevant. Furthermore, he finds that even where group attitudes are present, voters' individual policy preferences are important. To understand elections, the investigator should examine directly the voters' attitudes about issues and other questions of the campaign. This is precisely what Key does in this book.

(2) Some political commentators have found a significant factor of irrationality in the way we elect the president. This they derive from the

frequency of elections in which the same party retains power, and from their assumption that this is the consequence of simple repetitive voting. Key inquires, as most others have not, about the process by which a majority party maintains its dominance, and he finds that its apparently stable majority may be in fact highly changeful. The popular majority does not hold together like a ball of sticky popcorn; no sooner has it been constructed than it begins to crumble. "A series of maintaining elections occurs only in consequence of a complex process of interaction between government and populace in which old friends are sustained, old enemies are converted into new friends, old friends become even bitter opponents, and new voters are attracted to the cause." Electoral majorities, then, although they may have a stable base, are frequently majorities of the moment, *ad hoc* majorities created by the voters' responses to the actions and policies of government.

(3) Some voting studies have concluded that the standpat voter is on the average more interested and more intelligent than the switchers; that those who most readily change their party voting preferences are the least interested and the most inconsistent in their beliefs. Since switchers contribute the necessary flexibility to our political system, this means that the system's rationality depends on the "least admirable" voters. Confronted with this pessimistic conclusion for democratic government, Key is impelled to a careful re-examination and reinterpretation of the evidence. First he develops a different, and for his purposes more reliable, definition of a switching voter as one who changes his party vote from one election to another, rather than one who changes his views during a campaign. He then finds that although the characteristics of the switchers can vary from election

to election, they are not necessarily either less informed or less involved than the standpatters. In some elections, at least, they do not differ significantly from standpatters in their average level of education, in the frequency of their "don't know" or "no opinion" answers to public policy questions, or in their level of interest in politics. The major factors that distinguish switchers from standpatters are those of issues and opinions of presidential candidates' qualities "Those who switch do so to support governmental policies or outlook with which they agree, not because of subtle psychological or sociological peculiarities." Thus the political system is not held together by a buffer function of the uninterested voter.

(4) Some political writers have made much of an irrational cult of personality in presidential elections While granting that personality play a role in voting and that our data and analytical tools do not permit completely satisfactory appraisals of this role, Key rejects the cult of personality with its disturbing implications about the motivation of voters and the rationality of the political system. With respect to the claim that personality cult accounts for Roosevelt's re-elections he says poignantly that "it become ridiculous immediately if one contemplates what the fate of Franklin Delano Roosevelt would have been had he from 1933 to 1936 stood for those policies which were urged upon the country by the reactionaries of the day." And as for the pretended power of the father image of Eisenhower Key doubts the necessity of resorting to such "dubious hypotheses" to explain the response of the electorate.

(5) Key's study confirms earlier findings that the electorate judges retrospectively. Voters respond more clearly to those events that they have experienced and observed; proposal

for the future, being hazy and uncertain, neither engage the voter nor govern his actions in the same degree. From this evidence some commentators conclude that voters are playing a largely irrelevant role, for their choices in a presidential election should be based on the candidates' positions on new issues and future policies and programs.

Key does not hesitate to draw attention to the limiting consequences of the evidence. He notes that the minority party cannot play the role of an imaginative advocate, for it is captive of the majority. It gains votes principally from among those who are disappointed by, or disapprove of, the Administration. "Thus, as a matter of practical politics, it must appear to be a common scold rather than a bold exponent of innovation." But Key is also quick to point out that a combination of the electorate's retrospective judgment and the custom of party accountability enables the electorate in fact to exercise a prospective influence; for governments, and parties, and candidates "must worry, not about the meaning of past elections, but about their fate at future elections." The most effective weapon of popular control in a democratic system is the capacity of the electorate to throw a party from power.

To uncover the true nature of American voting behavior and the functions that the electorate and elections perform in the system as a whole, Key wanted to study a series of presidential elections extending over a considerable period of time and including campaigns and results of considerable variety, as did those of 1936, 1948, 1952, and 1960. To do this he had to tap data sources (largely Gallup polls) that previously had been eschewed by many analysts of voting behavior, in part because the data were considered to be soft. (There were questions

about the methods used to select the samples, construct and test the questions, conduct the interviews, test the reliability of a voter's recall of his vote four years earlier, etc.) To use these data, therefore, Key had to improvise techniques of analysis as well as apply tests of significance and reliability. At these tasks he was, of course, expert, but nonetheless he corresponded with several professional associates to get their reactions to what he was doing. After a careful examination of this correspondence, of Key's comments on it, of the dating of the correspondence in relation to that of successive drafts of the chapters, and above all of the text itself, Professor Cummings and I have no doubt that Key was satisfied that his data were of sufficient quality to support his analytical techniques and that the techniques were adequate to support his findings.

Key anticipated two possible objections to his attribution of significance to the parallelism of policy preferences and the direction of the vote. It might be claimed that when voters are interviewed they improvise policy views that seem to be consistent with the way they plan to vote for other reasons entirely. Key believed that although this doubtless occurs to some unknown extent, its importance should be discounted, for a voter must be fairly well informed if he is able to simulate a pattern of policy preferences that is consistent with his intended vote. A second objection might be that policy preferences are merely views that voters who are identified with a political party perceive as the orthodox party line. Key affirms that the doctrines of the party leadership can shape the policy preferences of many persons, but here too he discounts the significance of the phenomenon for his argument. Although this type of formation of policy attitudes may occur among standpatters, it is not even relevant for the millions of switching voters at each presidential election who can play a decisive role in the outcome. Finally, and with regard to both of these objections, Key points out that it is the parallelism of vote and policy that is significant, not its origin. However the opinions come into being, their supportive function in the political system should be the same.

V. O. Key died a year before the 1964 election, and before most observers thought that Barry Goldwater had a real chance to become the Republican presidential nominee. The relationships between the voters' policy preferences and their votes in 1964 are still being studied by the analysts. Yet the broad pattern of the 1964 results appears to confirm Key's thesis that voters on the average base their vote decisions on the issue positions of the candidates and on their expectations concerning how the candidates would perform as president.

Compared with 1960, and with most other presidential elections in recent years, the candidates were poles apart in 1964. The oft-noted absence of a meaningful dialogue on issues in the campaign only masked the fact that there was a wide gap between the policy positions the two candidates espoused on such vital matters as civil rights, domestic welfare legislation, and, many voters thought, on the restraint the candidate would exercise as president on questions involving war or peace.

There is evidence that many Republicans voted for Barry Goldwater despite misgivings about many of his policy positions. But Goldwater's determination to give the voters "a choice, not an echo" seems also to have wrenched an extraordinarily large number of voters from their traditional party loyalties. An election in which the State of Mississippi votes 87 per cent Republican, while nationwide, one Republican in every five supports the Democratic presidential nominee points up the importance that policy considerations can assume when the choice given the voters on issues is sharply drawn.

CHAPTER NINE

The Presidency:
The Hardest Job in the World?

The American Presidency is a product of growth as much as creation. The office was "made" not only by the framers at the Constitutional Convention but by virtually every strong president who has occupied the White House. Today the Presidency is described as "the nerve center of the nation," "our main contribution to democratic government," and "the great glue factory that binds the party and the nation."

The dramatic increase in presidential power and responsibility has spotlighted certain institutional and operational problems. The office places enormous burdens upon one man. Unlike the British monarch who merely reigns and the British Prime Minister and his cabinet who rule, the American president must both "reign and rule." Furthermore the President has no strong party system to help him steer a program through an independent and sometimes hostile legislature. It is not at all curious that a number of scholars urge reform and regeneration of the office. On the other hand, equally strong and more numerous voices caution, "Leave Your Presidency Alone."

This chapter deals with two problems: (1) the nature of the Presidency and its strengths and weaknesses as a political institution; and (2) the character and limits of presidential power in relation to Congress.

THE PRESIDENCY: TRANSITION OR MAJOR TRANSFORMATION?

The problems of the Presidency are manifold. Woodrow Wilson, who knew the office during a stress period in American history, warned "Men of ordinary physique and discretion cannot be presidents and live, if the strain be not somehow relieved. We shall be obliged always to be picking our chief magistrates from among wise and prudent athletes—a small class."

The sprawling Executive Office still defies complete presidential direction and control. There is a wide gap between the president's responsibility and his authority to administer. At times the breech between President and Congress seems to grow larger rather than smaller. There is no strong party or cabinet system to give the President needed help. In short, it appears as though intolerable burdens were placed upon one man.

The question remains; is the Presidency simply adjusting to contemporary events or is it, as an institution, undergoing a major transformation? John F. Kennedy urges an invigorated office. Professor Aaron Wildavsky notes the contrast of presidential power in domestic and foreign affairs. James MacGregor Burns comments on the problems arising out of the success of presidential government, while Clinton Rossiter urges only minor readjustments.

The Dilemma of Power: A Debate—The Presidency vs. Congress

Every commentator has observed the significant changes that have taken place in the office of the Chief Executive through the years. These changes have come about as the result of domestic and world crises, technological developments, growing urbanization, and the increasing complexity of our society.

To some the changes which have taken place in the Presidency have been logical and necessary. However, the steady growth of presidential power and influence has not met with universal approval and acceptance. There are those who believe that the concentration of power in the office of the President is a threat to our basic freedoms. They decry "One Man Rule" and "Presidential Government." These individuals favor a limited Presidency.

The two viewpoints on presidential power frequently clash over the proper role of the President in relationship to Congress. Should the President be a "lobbyist for the people" or should he play a restrained and limited role? Is the President becoming too powerful and overshadowing Congress? Should Congress be regenerated?

In the second section of this chapter, Arthur M. Schlesinger, Jr. makes a case for the Presidency while Alfred de Grazia argues for a stronger Congress.

1

John F. Kennedy Looks at the Presidency *

JOHN F. KENNEDY

John F. Kennedy made the following comments when he was still a member of the United States Senate. He was at the time a presidential hopeful. What is meant by the statement that the White House "must be the center for moral leadership"? What models does John F. Kennedy cite as effective Presidents? Which Presidents does Kennedy reject as inadequate?

❋ ❋ ❋

Whatever the political affiliation of our next President, whatever his views may be on all the issues and problems that rush in upon us, he must above all be the Chief Executive in every sense of the word. He must be prepared to exercise the fullest powers of his office—all that are specified and some that are not. He must master complex problems as well as receive one-page memorandums. He must originate action as well as study groups. He must reopen the channels of communication between the world of thought and the seat of power.

Ulysses Grant considered the President "a purely administrative officer." If he administered the Government departments efficiently, delegated his functions smoothly, and performed his ceremonies of state with decorum and grace, no more was to be expected of him. But that is not the place the Presidency was meant to have in American life. The President is alone, at the top—the loneliest job there is, as Harry Truman has said.

If there is destructive dissension

among the services, he alone can step in and straighten it out—instead of waiting for unanimity. If administrative agencies are not carrying out their mandate—if a brushfire threatens some part of the globe—he alone deserves the blame, not his Secretary of Agriculture.

"The President is at liberty, both in law and conscience, to be as big a man as he can." So wrote Professor Woodrow Wilson. But President Woodrow Wilson discovered that to be a big man in the White House inevitably brings cries of dictatorship.

So did Lincoln and Jackson and the two Roosevelts. And so may the next occupant of that office, if he is the man the times demand. But how much better it would be, in the turbulent sixties, to have a Roosevelt or a Wilson than to have another James Buchanan, cringing in the White House, afraid to move.

Nor can we afford a Chief Executive who is praised primarily for what he did not do, the disasters he prevented, the bills he vetoed—a President wishing his subordinates would produce more missiles or build more schools. We will need instead what the Con-

* From *The Congressional Record,* January 18, 1960, pp. 711-12.

stitution envisioned: a chief Executive who is the vital center of action in our whole scheme of Government.

This includes the legislative process as well. The President cannot afford—for the sake of the office as well as the Nation—to be another Warren G. Harding, described by one backer as a man who "would, when elected, sign whatever bill the Senate sent him—and not send bills for the Senate to pass." Rather he must know when to lead the Congress, when to consult it and when he should act alone.

Having served 14 years in the legislative branch, I would not look with favor upon its domination by the Executive. Under our government of "power as the rival of power," to use Hamilton's phrase, Congress must not surrender its responsibilities. But neither should it dominate. However large its share in the formulation of domestic programs, it is the President alone who must make the major decisions of our foreign policy.

That is what the Constitution wisely commands. And, even domestically, the President must initiate policies and devise laws to meet the needs of the Nation. And he must be prepared to use all the resources of his office to insure the enactment of that legislation —even when conflict is the result. . . .

But, however bitter their farewells, the facts of the matter are that Roosevelt and Wilson did get things done—not only through their Executive powers but through the Congress as well. Calvin Coolidge, on the other hand, departed from Washington with cheers of Congress still ringing in his ears. But when his World Court bill was under fire on Capitol Hill he sent no messages, gave no encouragement to the bill's leaders, and paid little or no attention to the whole proceeding—and the cause of world justice was set back.

To be sure, Coolidge had held the usual White House breakfasts with congressional leaders—but they were aimed, as he himself said, at "good fellowship," not a discussion of "public business." And at his press conferences, according to press historians, where he preferred to talk about the local flower show and its exhibits, reporters who finally extracted from him a single sentence—"I'm against that bill"—would rush to file tongue-in-cheek dispatches, proclaiming that: "President Coolidge, in a fighting mood, today served notice on Congress that he intended to combat, with all the resources at his command, the pending bill. . . ."

But in the coming years we will need a real fighting mood in the White House—a man who will not retreat in the face of pressure from his congressional leaders—who will not let down those supporting his views on the floor. Divided Government over the past 6 years has only been further confused by this lack of legislative leadership. To restore it next year will help restore purpose to both the Presidency and the Congress.

The facts of the matter are that legislative leadership is not possible without party leadership, in the most political sense—and Mr. Eisenhower prefers to stay above politics (although a weekly news magazine last fall reported the startling news, and I quote, that "President Eisenhower is emerging as a major political figure"). When asked, early in his first term, how he liked the "game of politics," he replied with a frown that his questioner was using a derogatory phrase. "Being President," he said, "is a great experience . . . but the word 'politics' . . I have no great liking for that."

But no President, it seems to me, can escape politics. He has not only been chosen by the Nation—he has been chosen by his party. And if he insists that he is "President of all the people" and should, therefore, offend none of them—if he blurs the issues and differences between the parties—if he neglects the party machinery and avoids his party's leadership—then he has not only weakened the political party as an instrument of the democratic process—he has dealt a blow to the democratic process itself.

I prefer the example of Abe Lincoln, who loved politics with the passion of a born practitioner. For example, he waited up all night in 1863 to get the crucial returns on the Ohio governor-ship. When the Unionist candidate was elected, Lincoln wired: "Glory to God in the highest. Ohio has saved the nation."

But the White House is not only the center of political leadership. It must be the center of moral leadership—a "bully pulpit," as Theodore Roosevelt described it. For only the President represents the national interest. And upon him alone converge all the needs and aspirations of all parts of the country, all departments of the Government, all nations of the world....

2

The Two Presidencies *

AARON WILDAVSKY

Would you agree that Presidents no longer "play politics" with foreign aid and defense policies? How great a role does the military play in policy-making? Do our relations with Red China fit into the author's thesis that Presidents always get their way in foreign policy matters?

The United States has one President, but it has two presidencies; one presidency is for domestic affairs, and the other is concerned with defense and foreign policy. Since World War II, Presidents have had much greater success in controlling the nation's defense and foreign policies than in dominating its domestic policies. Even Lyndon Johnson has seen his early record of victories in domestic legislation diminish as his concern with foreign affairs grows.

* Aaron Wildavsky, "The Two Presidencies," *Trans-Action* (St. Louis, Mo.: Washing University, December, 1966), pp. 7-14. Reprinted by permission of the publisher.

What powers does the President have to control defense and foreign policies and so completely overwhelm those who might wish to thwart him?

The President's normal problem with domestic policy is to get congressional support for the programs he prefers. In foreign affairs, in contrast, he can almost always get support for policies that he believes will protect the nation—but his problem is to find a viable policy.

Whoever they are, whether they begin by caring about foreign policy like Eisenhower and Kennedy or about domestic policies like Truman and Johnson, Presidents soon discover they have more policy preferences in domestic matters than in foreign policy. The Republican and Democratic parties possess a traditional roster of policies, which can easily be adopted by a new President —for example, he can be either for or against Medicare and aid to education. Since existing domestic policy usually changes in only small steps, Presidents find it relatively simple to make minor adjustments. However, although any President knows he supports foreign aid and NATO, the world outside changes much more rapidly than the nation inside—Presidents and their parties have no prior policies on Argentina and the Congo. The world has become a highly intractable place with a whirl of forces we cannot or do not know how to alter.

The Record of Presidential Control

It takes great crises, such as Roosevelt's hundred days in the midst of depression, or the extraordinary majorities that Barry Goldwater's candidacy willed to Lyndon Johnson, for Presidents to succeed in controlling domestic policy. From the end of the 1930's to the present (what may roughly be called the modern era), Presidents have often been frustrated in their domestic programs. From 1938, when conservatives regrouped their forces, to the time of his death, Franklin Roosevelt did not get a single piece of significant domestic legislation passed. Truman lost out on most of his intense domestic preferences, except perhaps for housing. Since Eisenhower did not ask for much domestic legislation, he did not meet consistent defeat, yet he failed in his general policy of curtailing governmental commitments. Kennedy, of course, faced great difficulties with domestic legislation.

In the realm of foreign policy there has not been a single major issue on which Presidents, when they were serious and determined, have failed. The list of their victories is impressive: entry into the United Nations, the Marshall Plan, NATO, the Truman Doctrine, the decisions to stay out of Indochina in 1954 and to intervene in Vietnam in the 1960's, aid to Poland and Yugoslavia, the test-ban treaty, and many more. Serious setbacks to the President in controlling foreign policy are extraordinary and unusual.

Table I, compiled from the Congressional Quarterly Service tabulation of presidential initiative and congressional response from 1948 through 1964, shows that Presidents have significantly better records in foreign and defense matters than in domestic policies. When refugees and immigration—which Congress considers primarily a domestic concern—are removed from the general foreign policy area, it is clear that Presidents prevail about 70 percent of the time in defense and foreign policy, compared with 40 percent in the domestic sphere.

World Events and Presidential Resources

Power in politics is control over governmental decisions. How does President manage his control of foreign and defense policy? The answer does not reside in the greater constitutional power in foreign affairs that Presidents have possessed since the founding of the Republic. The answer lies in the changes that have taken place since 1945.

The number of nations with which the United States has diplomatic relations has increased from 53 in 1939 to 113 in 1966. But sheer numbers do not tell enough; the world has also

Table 1. Congressional Action on Presidential Proposals From 1948-1964

Policy Area	Congressional Action % Pass	% Fail	Number of Proposals
Domestic policy (natural resources, labor, agriculture, taxes, etc.)	40.2	59.8	2499
Defense policy (defense, disarmament, manpower, misc.)	73.3	26.7	90
Foreign policy	58.5	41.5	655
Immigration, refugees	13.2	86.0	129
Treaties, general foreign relations, State Department, foreign aid	70.8	29.2	445

Source: Congressional Quarterly Service, *Congress and the Nation*, 1945-1964 (Washington, 1965)

become a much more dangerous place. However remote it may seem at times, our government must always be aware of the possibility of nuclear war.

Yet the mere existence of great powers with effective thermonuclear weapons would not, in and of itself, vastly increase our rate of interaction with most other nations. We see events in Assam or Burundi as important because they are also part of a larger worldwide contest, called the cold war, in which great powers are rivals for the control or support of other nations. Moreover, the reaction against the blatant isolationism of the 1930's has led to a concern with foreign policy that is worldwide in scope. We are interested in what happens everywhere because we see these events as connected with larger interests involving, at the worst, the possibility of ultimate destruction.

Given the overriding fact that the world is dangerous and that small causes are perceived to have potentially great effects in an unstable world, it follows that Presidents must be interested in relatively "small" matters. So they give Azerbaijan or Lebanon or Vietnam huge amounts of their time. Arthur Schlesinger, Jr., wrote of Kennedy that "in the first two months of his administration he probably spent more time on Laos than on anything else." Few failures in domestic policy, Presidents soon realize, could have as disastrous consequences as any one of dozens of mistakes in the international arena.

The result is that foreign policy concerns tend to drive out domestic policy. Except for occasional questions of domestic prosperity and for civil rights, foreign affairs have consistently higher priority for Presidents. Once, when trying to talk to President Kennedy about natural resources, Secretary of the Interior Stewart Udall remarked, "He's imprisoned by Berlin."

The importance of foreign affairs to Presidents is intensified by the increasing speed of events in the international arena. The event and its consequences follow closely on top of one another. The blunder at the Bay of Pigs is swiftly followed by the near catastrophe of the Cuban missile crisis. Presidents can no longer count on passing along their most difficult problems to their successors. They must expect to face the consequences of their actions—or failure to act— while still in office.

Domestic policy-making is usually based on experimental adjustments to an existing situation. Only a few decisions, such as those involving large dams, irretrievably commit future generations. Decisions in foreign affairs, however, are often perceived to be irreversible. This is expressed, for example, in the fear of escalation or the various "spiral" or "domino" theories of international conflict.

If decisions are perceived to be both important and irreversible, there is every reason for Presidents to devote a great deal of resources to them. Presidents have to be oriented toward the future in the use of their resources. They serve a fixed term in office, and they cannot automatically count on support from the populace, Congress, or the administrative apparatus. They have to be careful, therefore, to husband their resources for pressing future needs. But because the consequences of events in foreign affairs are potentially more grave, faster to manifest themselves, and less easily reversible than in domestic affairs, Presidents are more willing to use up their resources.

The Power to Act

Their formal powers to commit resources in foregin affairs and defense are vast. Particularly important is their power as Commander-in-Chief to move troops. Faced with situations like the invasion of South Korea or the emplacement of missiles in Cuba, fast action is required. Presidents possess both the formal power to act and the knowledge that elites and the general public expect them to act. Once they have committed American forces, it is difficult for Congress or anyone else to alter the course of events. The Dominican venture is a recent case in point.

Presidential discretion in foreign affairs also makes it difficult (though not impossible) for Congress to restrict their actions. Presidents can use executive agreements instead of treaties, enter into tacit agreements instead of written ones, and otherwise help create *de facto* situations not easily reversed. Presidents also have far greater ability than anyone else to obtain information on developments abroad through the Departments of State and Defense. The need for secrecy in some aspects of foreign and defense policy further restricts the ability of others to compete with Presidents. These things are all well known. What is not so generally appreciated is the growing presidential ability to *use* information to achieve goals.

In the past Presidents were amateurs in military strategy. They could not even get much useful advice outside of the military. As late as the 1930's the number of people outside the military establishment who were professionally engaged in the study of defense policy could be numbered on the fingers. Today there are hundreds of such men. The rise of the defense intellectuals has given the President of the United States enhanced ability to control defense policy. He is no longer dependent on the military for advice. He can choose among defense intellectuals from the research corporations and the academies for alternative sources of advice. He can install these men in his own office. He can play them off against each other or use them to extend spheres of coordination.

Even with these advisers, however, Presidents and Secretaries of Defense might still be too bewildered by the complexity of nuclear situations to take action—unless they had an understanding of the doctrine and concepts of deterence. But knowledge of doctrine about deterrence has been widely diffused; it can be picked up by any intelligent person who will read books or listen to enough hours of conversation. Whether or not the doctrine is good is a separate question; the point is that civilians can feel they understand what is going on in defense policy. Perhaps the most extraordinary feature of presidential action during the Cuban missile crisis was the degree to which the Commander-in-Chief of the Armed Forces insisted on controlling even the smallest moves. From the positioning of ships to the methods of boarding, to the precise words and actions to be taken by individual soldiers and sailors, the President and his civilian advisers were in control.

Although Presidents have rivals for power in foreign affairs, the rivals do not usually succeed. Presidents prevail not only because they may have superior resources but because their potential opponents are weak, divided, or believe that they should not control foreign policy. Let us consider the potential rivals—the general citizenry, special interest groups, the Congress, the military, the so-called military-industrial complex, and the State Department.

Competitors for Control of Policy

THE PUBLIC. The general public is much more dependent on Presidents in foreign affairs than in domestic matters. While many people know about the impact of social security and Medicare, few know about politics in Malawi. So it is not surprising that people expect the President to act in foreign affairs and reward him with their confidence. Gallup Polls consistently show that presidential popularity rises after he takes action in a crisis—whether the action is disastrous as in the Bay of Pigs or successful as in the Cuban missile crisis. Decisive action, such as the bombing of oil fields near Haiphong, resulted in a sharp (though temporary) increase in Johnson's popularity.

The Vietnam situation illustrates another problem of public opinion in foreign affairs: it is extremely difficult to get operational policy directions from the general public. It took a long time before any sizable public interest in the subject developed. Nothing short of the large scale involvement of American troops under fire probably could have brought about the current high level of concern. Yet this relatively well developed popular opinion is difficult to interpret. While a majority appear to support President Johnson's policy, it appears that they could easily be persuaded to withdraw from Vietnam if the administration changed its line. Although a sizable majority would support various initiatives to end the war, they would seemingly be appalled if this action led to Communist encroachments elsewhere in Southeast Asia (See "The President, the Polls, and Vietnam" by Seymour Martin Lipset, *Trans-action,* Sept/Oct 1966).

Although Presidents lead opinion in foreign affairs, they know they will be held accountable for the consequences of their actions. President Johnson has maintained a large commitment in Vietnam. His popularity shoots up now and again in the midst of some imposing action. But the fact that a body of citizens do not like the war comes back to damage his overall popularity. We will support your initiatives, the people seem to say, but we will reserve the right to punish you (or your party) if we do not like the results.

SPECIAL INTEREST GROUPS. Opinions are easier to gauge in domestic affairs because, for one thing, there is a stable structure of interest groups that covers virtually all matters of concern. The farm, labor, business, conservation, veteran, civil rights, and other interest groups provide cues when a proposed policy affects them.

Thus people who identify with these groups may adopt their views. But in foreign policy matters the interest group structure is weak, unstable, and thin rather than dense. In many matters affecting Africa and Asia, for example, it is hard to think of well-known interest groups. While ephemeral groups arise from time to time to support or protest particular policies, they usually disappear when the immediate problem is resolved. In contrast, longer-lasting elite groups like the Foreign Policy Association and Council on Foreign Relations are composed of people of diverse views; refusal to take strong positions on controversial matters is a condition of their continued viability.

The strongest interest groups are probably the ethnic associations whose members have strong ties with a homeland, as in Poland or Cuba, so they are rarely activated simultaneously on any specific issue. They are most effective when most narrowly and intensely focused—as in the fierce pressure from Jews to recognize the state of Israel. But their relatively small numbers limits their significance to Presidents in the vastly more important general foreign policy picture—as continued aid to the Arab countries shows. Moreover, some ethnic groups may conflict on significant issues such as American acceptance of the Oder-Neisse line separating Poland from what is now East Germany.

THE CONGRESS. Congressmen also exercise power in foreign affairs. Yet they are ordinarily not serious competitors with the President because they follow a self-denying ordinance. They do not think it is their job to determine the nation's defense policies. Lewis A. Dexter's extensive interviews with members of the Senate Armed Services Committee, who might be expected to want a voice in defense policy, reveal that they do not desire for men like themselves to run the nation's defense establishment. Aside from a few specific conflicts among the armed services which allow both the possibility and desirability of direct intervention, the Armed Services Committee constitutes a sort of real estate committee dealing with the regional economic consequences of the location of military facilities.

The congressional appropriations power is potentially a significant resource, but circumstances since the end of World War II have tended to reduce its effectiveness. The appropriations committees and Congress itself might make their will felt by refusing to allot funds unless basic policies were altered. But this has not happened. While Congress makes its traditional small cuts in the military budget, Presidents have mostly found themselves warding off congressional attempts to increase specific items still further.

Most of the time, the administration's refusal to spend has not been seriously challenged. However, there have been occasions when individual legislators or committees have been influential. Senator Henry Jackson in his campaign (with the aid of colleagues on the Joint Committee on Atomic Energy) was able to gain acceptance for the Polaris weapons system and Senator Arthur H. Vandenberg played a part in determining the shape of the Marshall Plan and so on. The few congressmen who are expert in defense policy act, as Samuel P. Huntington says, largely as lobbyists with the executive branch. It is apparently more fruitful for these congressional experts to use their resources in order to get a hearing from the executive than to work on other congressmen.

When an issue involves the actual use or threat of violence, it takes a great deal to convince congressmen not to follow the President's lead.

James Robinson's tabulation of foreign and defense policy issues from the late 1930's to 1961 (Table II) shows dominant influence by Congress in only one case out of seven—the 1954 decision not to intervene with armed force in Indochina. In that instance President Eisenhower deliberately sounded out congressional opinion and, finding it negative, decided not to intervene—against the advice of Admiral Radford, chairman of the Joint Chiefs of Staff. This attempt to abandon responsibility did not succeed, as the years of American involvement demonstrate.

THE MILITARY. The outstanding feature of the military's participation in making defense policy is their amazing weakness. Whether the policy decisions involve the size of the armed forces, the choice of weapons systems, the total defense budget, or its division into components, the military have not prevailed. Let us take budgetary decisions as representative of the key choices to be made in defense policy. Since the end of World War II the military has not been able to achieve significant (billion dollar) increases in appropriations by their own efforts. Under Truman and Eisenhower defense budgets were determined by what Huntington calls the remainder method: the two Presidents estimated revenues, decided what they could spend on domestic matters, and the remainder was assigned to defense. The usual controversy was between some military and congressional groups supporting much larger expenditures while the President and his executive allies refused. A typical case, involving the desire of the Air Force to increase the number of groups of planes is described by Huntington in *The Common Defense:*

The FY [fiscal year] 1949 budget provided 48 groups. After the Czech coup, the administration yielded and backed an Air Force of 55 groups in its spring rearmament program. Congress added additional funds to aid Air Force expansion to 70 groups. The Administration refused to utilize them, however, and in the gathering economy wave of the summer and fall of 1948, the Air Force goal was cut back again to 48 groups. In 1949 the House of Representatives picked up the challenge and appropriated funds for 58 groups. The President impounded the money. In June, 1950, the Air Force had 48 groups.

The great increases in the defense budget were due far more to Stalin and modern technology than to the military. The Korean War resulted in an increase from 12 to 44 billions and much of the rest followed Sputnik and the huge costs of missile programs. Thus modern technology and international conflict put an end to the one major effort to subordinate foreign affairs to domestic policies through the budget.

It could be argued that the President merely ratifies the decisions made by the military and their allies. If the military and/or Congress were united and insistent on defense policy, it would certainly be difficult for Presidents to resist these forces. But it is precisely the disunity of the military that has characterized the entire postwar period. Indeed, the military have not been united on any major matter of defense policy. The apparent unity of the Joint Chiefs of Staff turns out to be illusory. The vast majority of their recommendations appear to be unanimous and are accepted by the Secretary of Defense and the President. But this facade of unity can only be achieved by methods that vitiate the impact of the recommendations. Genuine disagreements are hidden by vague language that commits no one to anything. Mutually contradictory plans are strung together so everyone appears to get something, but nothing is decided. Since it is impossible to agree

Table 2. Congressional Involvement in Foreign and Defense Policy Decisions

Issue	Congressional Involvement (High, Low, None)	Initiator (Congress or Executive)	Predominant Influence (Congress or Executive)	Legislation or Resolution (Yes or No)	Violence at Stake (Yes or No)	Decision Time (Long or Short)
Neutrality Legislation, the 1930's	High	Exec	Cong	Yes	No	Long
Lend-Lease, 1941	High	Exec	Exec	Yes	Yes	Long
Aid to Russia, 1941	Low	Exec	Exec	No	No	Long
Repeal of Chinese Exclusion, 1943	High	Cong	Cong	Yes	No	Long
Fulbright Resolution, 1943	High	Cong	Cong	Yes	No	Long
Building of the Atomic Bomb, 1944	Low	Exec	Exec	Yes	Yes	Long
Foreign Services Act of 1946	High	Exec	Exec	Yes	No	Long
Truman Doctrine, 1947	High	Exec	Exec	Yes	No	Long
The Marshall Plan, 1947-48	High	Exec	Exec	Yes	No	Long
Berlin Airlift, 1948	None	Exec	Exec	No	Yes	Long
Vandenberg Resolution, 1948	High	Exec	Cong	Yes	No	Long
North Atlantic Treaty, 1947-49	High	Exec	Exec	Yes	No	Long
Korean Decision, 1950	None	Exec	Exec	No	Yes	Short
Japanese Peace Treaty, 1952	High	Exec	Exec	Yes	No	Long
Bohlen Nomination, 1953	High	Exec	Exec	Yes	No	Long
Indo-China, 1954	High	Exec	Cong	No	Yes	Short
Formosan Resolution, 1955	High	Exec	Exec	Yes	Yes	Long
International Finance Corporation, 1956	Low	Exec	Exec	Yes	No	Long
Foreign Aid, 1957	High	Exec	Exec	Yes	No	Long
Reciprocal Trade Agreements, 1958	High	Exec	Exec	Yes	No	Long
Monroney Resolution, 1958	High	Cong	Cong	Yes	No	Long
Cuban Decision, 1961	Low	Exec	Exec	No	Yes	Long

Source: James A. Robinson, *Congress and Foreign Policy-Making* (Homewood, Illinois 1962)

on really important matters, all sorts of trivia are brought in to make a record of agreement. While it may be true, as Admiral Denfield, a former Chief of Naval Operations, said, that "On nine-tenths of the matters that come before them the Joint Chiefs of Staff reach agreement themselves," the vastly more important truth is that "normally the *only* disputes are on strategic concepts, the size and composition of forces, and budget matters."

MILITARY-INDUSTRIAL. But what about the fabled military-industrial complex? If the military alone is divided and weak, perhaps the giant industrial firms that are so dependent on defense contracts play a large part in making policy.

First, there is an important distinction between the questions "Who will get a given contract?" and "What will our defense policy be?" It is apparent that different answers may be given to these quite different questions. There are literally tens of thousands of defense contractors. They may compete vigorously for business. In the course of this competition, they may wine and dine military officers, use retired generals, seek intervention by their congressmen, place ads in trade journals, and even contribute to political campaigns. The famous TFX controversy—should General Dynamics or Boeing get the expensive contract?—is a larger than life example of the pressures brought to bear in search of lucrative contracts.

But neither the TFX case nor the usual vigorous competition for contracts is involved with the making of substantive defense policy. Vital questions like the size of the defense budget, the choice of strategic programs, massive retaliation vs. a counter-city strategy, and the like were far beyond the policy aims of any company. Industrial firms, then, do not control such decisions, nor is there much evidence that they actually try. No doubt a precipitous and drastic rush to disarmament would meet with opposition from industrial firms among other interests. However, there has never been a time when any significant element in the government considered a disarmament policy to be feasible.

It may appear that industrial firms had no special reason to concern themselves with the government's stance on defense because they agree with the national consensus on resisting communism, maintaining a large defense establishment, and rejecting isolationism. However, this hypothesis about the climate of opinion explains everything and nothing. For every policy that is adopted or rejected can be explained away on the grounds that the cold war climate of opinion dictated what happened. Did the United States fail to intervene with armed force in Vietnam in 1954? That must be because the climate of opinion was against it. Did the United States send troops to Vietnam in the 1960's? That must be because the cold war climate demanded it. If the United States builds more missiles, negotiates a test-ban treaty, intervenes in the Dominican Republic, fails to intervene in a dozen other situations, all these actions fit the hypothesis by definition. The argument is reminiscent of those who defined the Soviet Union as permanently hostile and therefore interpreted increases of Soviet troops as menacing and decreases of troop strength as equally sinister.

If the growth of the military establishment is not directly equated with increasing military control of defense policy, the extraordinary weakness of the professional soldier still requires explanation. Huntington has written about how major military leaders were seduced in the Truman and Eisenhower years into believing that they should bow to the judgment of civilians that the economy could not stand much larger military expenditures. Once the size of the military pie was accepted as a fixed constraint, the military services were compelled to put their major energies into quarreling with one another over who should get the larger share. Given the natural rivalries of the military and their traditional acceptance of civilian rule, the President and his advisers—who could claim responsibility for the broader picture of reconciling defense and domestic policies—had the upper hand. There are, however, additional explanations to be considered.

The dominant role of the congressional appropriations committee is to be guardian of the treasury. This is manifested in the pride of its members in cutting the President's budget. Thus it was difficult to get this crucial committee to recommend even a few hundred million increase in defense; it was practically impossible to get them to consider the several billion jump that might really have made a difference. A related budgetary matter concerned the planning, programming, and budgeting system introduced by Secretary of Defense McNamara. For if the defense budget contained major categories that crisscrossed the services, only the Secretary of Defense could put it together. Whatever the other debatable consequences of program budgeting, its major consequence was to grant power to the secretary and his civilian advisers.

The subordination of the military through program budgeting is just one symptom of a more general weakness of the military. In the past decade the military has suffered a lack of intellectual skills appropriate to the nuclear age. For no one has (and no one wants) direct experience with nuclear war. So the usual military talk about being the only people to have combat experience is not very impressive. Instead, the imaginative creation of possible future wars—in order to avoid them—requires people with a high capacity for abstract thought combined with the ability to manipulate symbols using quantitative methods. West Point has not produced many such men.

THE STATE DEPARTMENT. Modern Presidents expect the State Department to carry out their policies. John F. Kennedy felt that State was "in some particular sense 'his' department." If a Secretary of State forgets this, as was apparently the case with James Byrnes under Truman, a President may find another man. But the State Department, especially the Foreign Service, is also a highly professional organization with a life and momentum of its own. If a President does not push hard, he may find his preferences somehow dissipated in time. Arthur Schlesinger fills his book on Kennedy with laments about the bureaucratic inertia and recalcitrance of the State Department.

Yet Schlesinger's own account suggests that State could not ordinarily resist the President. At one point, he writes of "the President, himself, increasingly the day-to-day director of American foreign policy." On the next page, we learn that "Kennedy dealt personally with almost every aspect of policy around the globe. He knew more about certain areas than the senior officials at State and probably called as many issues to their attention as they did to his." The President insisted on his way in Laos. He pushed through his policy on the Congo against strong opposition with the State Department. Had Kennedy wanted to get a great deal more initiative out of the State Department, as Schlesinger insists, he could have replaced the Secretary of State, a man who did not command special support in the Democratic party or in Congress. It may be that Kennedy wanted too strongly to run his own foreign policy. Dean Rusk may have known far better than Schlesinger that the one thing Kennedy did not want was a man who might rival him in the field of foreign affairs.

Schlesinger comes closest to the truth when he writes that "the White House could always win any battle it chose over the [Foreign] Service; but the prestige and proficiency of the Service limited the number of battles any White House would find it profitable to fight." When the President knew what he wanted, he got it. When he was doubtful and perplexed, he sought good advice and frequently did not get that. But there is no evidence that the people on his staff came up with better ideas. The real problem may have been a lack of good ideas anywhere. Kennedy undoubtedly encouraged his staff to prod the State Department. But the President was sufficiently cautious not to push so hard that he got his way when he was not certain what that way should be. In this context Kennedy appears to have played his staff off against elements in the State Department.

The growth of a special White House staff to help Presidents in foreign affairs expresses their need for assistance, their refusal to rely completely on the regular executive agencies, and their ability to find competent men. The deployment of this staff must remain a presidential prerogative, however, if its members are to serve Presidents and not their opponents. Whenever critics do not like existing foreign and defense policies, they are likely to complain that the White House staff is screening out divergent views from the President's attention. Naturally, the critics recommend introducing many more different viewpoints. If the critics could maneuver the President into counting hands all day ("on the one hand and on the other"), they would make it impossible for him to act. Such a viewpoint is also congenial to those who believe that action rather than inaction is the greatest present danger in foreign policy. But Presidents resolutely refuse to become prisoners of their advisers by using them as other people would like. Presidents remain in control of their staff as well as of major foreign policy decisions.

How Complete Is the Control?

Some analysts say that the success of Presidents in controlling foreign policy decisions is largely illusory. It is achieved, they say, by anticipating the reactions of others, and eliminating proposals that would run into severe opposition. There is some truth in this objection. In politics, where transactions are based on a high degree of mutual interdependence, what others may do has to be taken into account. But basing presidential success in foreign and defense policy on anticipated reactions suggests a static situation

which does not exist. For if Presidents propose only those policies that would get support in Congress, and Congress opposes them only when it knows that it can muster overwhelming strength, there would never be any conflict. Indeed, there might never be any action.

How can "anticipated reaction" explain the conflict over policies like the Marshall Plan and the test-ban treaty in which severe opposition was overcome only by strenuous efforts? Furthermore, why doesn't "anticipated reaction" work in domestic affairs? One would have to argue that for some reason presidential perception of what would be successful is consistently confused on domestic issues and most always accurate on major foreign policy issues. But the role of "anticipated reactions" should be greater in the more familiar domestic situations, which provide a backlog of experience for forecasting, than in foreign policy with many novel situations such as the Suez crisis or the Rhodesian affair.

Are there significant historial examples which might refute the thesis of presidential control of foreign policy? Foreign aid may be a case in point. For many years, Presidents have struggled to get foreign aid appropriations because of hostility from public and congressional opinion. Yet several billion dollars a year are appropriated regularly despite the evident unpopularity of the program. In the aid programs to Communist countries like Poland and Yugoslavia, the Congress attaches all sorts of restrictions to the aid, but Presidents find ways of getting around them.

What about the example of recognition of Communist China? The sentiment of the country always has been against recognizing Red China or admitting it to the United Nations. But have Presidents wanted to recognize Red China and been hamstrung by opposition? The answer, I suggest, is a qualified "no." By the time recognition of Red China might have become a serious issue for the Truman administration, the war in Korea effectively precluded its consideration. There is no evidence that President Eisenhower or Secretary Dulles ever thought it wise to recognize Red China or help admit her to the United Nations. The Kennedy administration viewed the matter as not of major importance and, considering the the opposition, moved cautiously in suggesting change. Then came the war in Vietnam. If the advantages for foreign policy had been perceived to be much higher, then Kennedy or Johnson might have proposed changing American policy toward recognition of Red China.

One possible exception, in the case of Red China, however, does not seem sufficient to invalidate the general thesis that Presidents do considerably better in getting their way in foreign and defense policy than in domestic policies.

The World Influence

The forces impelling Presidents to be concerned with the widest range of foreign and defense policies also affect the ways in which they calculate their power stakes. As Kennedy used to say, "Domestic policy . . . can only defeat us; foreign policy can kill us."

It no longer makes sense for Presidents to "play politics" with foreign and defense policies. In the past, Presidents might have thought that they could gain by prolonged delay or by not acting at all. The problem might disappear or be passed on to their successors. Presidents must now expect to pay the high costs themselves if the world situation deteriorates. The advantages of pursuing a policy that is viable in the world, that will not blow upon Presidents or their fellow citizens, far outweigh any temporary

political disadvantages accrued in sup porting an initially unpopular policy Compared with domestic affairs, Presi dents engaged in world politics are immensely more concerned with meet ing problems on their own terms. Whe supports and opposes a policy, though a matter of considerable interest, doe not assume the crucial importance tha it does in domestic affairs. The bes policy Presidents can find is also the best politics.

The fact that there are numerou foreign and defense policy situation competing for a President's attentio means that it is worthwhile to organiz political activity in order to affect hi agenda. For if a President pays mor attention to certain problems he ma develop different preferences; he ma seek and receive different advice; hi new calculations may lead him to de vote greater resources to seeking solution. Interested congressmen ma exert influence not by directly deter mining a presidential decision, but in directly by making it costly for President to avoid reconsidering th basis for his action. For example citizen groups, such as those con cerned with a change in China policy may have an impact simply by keer ing their proposals on the publi agenda. A President may be compelle to reconsider a problem even thoug he could not overtly be forced to alte the prevailing policy.

In foreign affairs we may be ap proaching the stage where knowledg is power. There is a tremendous re ceptivity to good ideas in Washingtor Most anyone who can present a cor vincing rationale for dealing with hard world finds a ready audience The best way to convince Presidents t follow a desired policy is to show tha it might work. A man like McNamar thrives because he performs; he come up with answers he can defend. It i to be sure, extremely difficult to devis

good policies or to predict their consequences accurately. Nor is it easy to
convince others that a given policy is
superior to other alternatives. But it is
the way to influence with Presidents.
For if they are convinced that the current policy is best, the likelihood of
gaining sufficient force to compel a
change is quite small. The man who
can build better foreign policies will
find Presidents beating a path to his
door.

3

The Presidency at the Crossroads *

JAMES MacGREGOR BURNS

*What are some of the specific crises or crossroads which the Presidency faces and
will continue to face in the foreseeable future? Why is presidential power so unacceptable to many when historically the Presidency has been the instrument of expanding civil rights and civil liberties? What does Professor Burns mean when he
writes, "it is hard to see the Presidency as personalized today"?*

The Presidency is the most paradoxical agency of American government.
For one thing, it was the least planned
part of our carefully laid out governmental system. The Founding Fathers
defined the power of the President
vaguely; said nothing about a cabinet
or staff assistants; and, of course, had
little conception of the vast bureaucracy over which the President would
come to preside.

A second paradox of the Presidency
is the refusal of the people—and of
political scientists—to come to grips
with the colossal power that now reposes in the White House. We solemnly analyze the niceties of the

checks and balances among President,
Congress, and Courts, and the ultimate
check of the voters, at a time when the
President can unleash a nuclear holo-
caust that would obliterate the checks
and balances, the Constitution, and the
voters. We have given power to the
President precisely in the area where
his rash action might be uncheckable
and irreversible—that is, in foreign and
military policy—and we carefully
fence him in in those areas where
Presidential errors could be limited
and reversed—notably in domestic fiscal policy.

The President has always been the
practical agency that American leaders have used, and voters have endorsed, to cope with urgent demands
for governmental action. From Jefferson's purchase of Louisiana—unconstitutional by his own admission—to
Lincoln's conduct of the war, to Franklin Roosevelt's provision of destroyers

* James MacGregor Burns, "The Presidency at the Crossroads," in *The Crossroads
Papers, A Look into the American Future*,
ed. and with an Introduction by Hans J.
Morgenthau. Copyright © 1965 by W. W.
Norton & Company, Inc. Reprinted by permission of the publisher.

to Great Britain, to Kennedy's dispatch of troops to Oxford, Mississippi, the President has supplied an infinitely expandable and flexible reservoir of governmental power.

It is Congress that has lagged in confronting the major domestic and foreign policies of our century; the very branch that the Founding Fathers had expected to be the more active and creative department of government has come to be assessed mainly in terms of its effectiveness in passing the President's program. We hear a great deal of criticism of the President in this country but not very much criticism of the Presidency. Certainly the President has been allowed to organize the top level of his executive department pretty much as he wishes. Congress, however, proceeds under a continuous barrage of criticism as an institution, and the crucial question raised about our national legislature is less its effectiveness than its capacity to reform itself—or at least to put its two houses into some kind of order.

For some years, many of us have preached the need for Congressional reform, while—at least in my case—lacking much confidence in the power of Congress to reform itself. I had hoped that John Kennedy might have won in 1964 in such a heavy sweep that he would have brought into Congress enough Kennedy Democrats not only to enact his program, but to reorganize Congress to make it a more democratic, responsible, and effective body. The tragedy in Dallas marked the end of this possibility for Kennedy. Lyndon Johnson assumed his legislative responsibilities with a sure and skilled hand. He put his personal standing with Senators behind the Kennedy-Johnson program. He also benefited from popular identification of the program with the fallen President.

Unless Johnson can bring about sweeping Congressional reform, we

are headed back to a period of politic as usual as the two conservative Con gressional parties combine to block o stall Presidential programs, especiall programs requiring the heavy spend ing of money. But how long can poli tics as usual serve us, or even survive in a time of heavy and persistent de mands on our political system? I ca think of no situation that better ex emplifies Hans Morgenthau's commen that "we are living in a world tha is characterized by unprecedentec change both in quantity and quality and our modes of thought and actio are limping far behind what thos changes require of us." We are, I be lieve, approaching a crossroads in th organization of national power and crossroads also in our thinking abou the shape of our national government

The point is this: since the very be ginning, the American people hav tended to embrace the Madisonia formula as the orthodox and legitimat model for organizing our national gov ernment (and our state governments a well). We have tended to ignore an other, competing model, which I hav labeled the Jeffersonian model. Unde this second model, strong leaders tr to carry out their programs with th cooperation of their party in Congres the majority party is well enoug organized to serve as a bridge betwee the President and his majority in Con gress; the majority party does not hav the power to obstruct the President legislation but only the right to carr the issue to the people; and the issue resolved at the next election. The Je fersonian model, in short, is that c strong leadership, responsible partie majority rule, fair elections (whic assumes a healthy atmosphere of free press and civil liberties), and vigorous opposition eager not only t win power at the next election but t present an alternative program o which it would govern if elected.

Central to the Jeffersonian model

the concept of strong Presidential leadership. This must be emphasized, for as a result of a long dalliance of political scientists with the dream of responsible political parties, the crucial role of leadership has tended to be subordinated to the concept of a democratically operated two-party system. Let me repeat—leadership is central to the Jeffersonian model (as Jefferson himself demonstrated); without leadership, all the rest of the model collapses.

In pursuit of the dominant Madisonian model, Americans have tended to see audacious uses of Presidential power as "exceptions to the rule"—something that has to be resorted to in emergency situations, but is intrinsically dubious and dangerous. Only because of repeated emergencies has the Presidency emerged as the crucial instrument of power it is. It is clear, however, that for the rest of this decade, and probably for the rest of this century, the United States will confront a series of crises at home and abroad. The question I pose is: will the Jeffersonian model become the exception or the rule? If chronic crisis indeed faces us, and if this means a further enhancement of Presidential power, and if this becomes the common pattern of the next few years or even decades, should we continue to look on Presidential power as an exceptional and questionable activity?

Perhaps we should revise our concepts, perhaps we should reassess our thinking, and see Presidential power as really is—a wholly democratic way of dealing with the problems and crises of government, assuming that the rest of the Jeffersonian model stands intact—a strong party supporting and restricting the President, an effective opposition party, and a pluralistic society protecting civil liberties.

Americans are slowly coming to recognize the fact that the Presidency has been historically a vital weapon for protecting and expanding individual civil liberties and civil rights, rather than a threat to them. Here again is a place where we must revise our orthodox thinking. The framers of the Constitution feared a strong executive as a possible engine of tyranny. They were thinking in terms of historical figures who had seized governments and dictated to the people. The farmers also still smarted under the executive authority, often exaggerated, of colonial governors and other minions of the Crown. They expected that Congress would be the great bulwark of the people's liberties, because Congress was so directly representative of the people. But things have turned out much differently. Again and again it has been the President who has acted to defend civil liberties and civil rights —most notably in this century. It has been Congress that has either threatened minority rights and individual liberties through legislation, or has tolerated such onslaughts against civil liberties as were represented by Mc-Carthyism and the Un-American Affairs Committee. Above all, the President has symbolized the fact that freedom needs to be protected against both arbitrary governmental and arbitrary private power, and that freedoms can be expanded both through private action and through public action.

The most relevant case in point is civil rights. In the last thirty years it has been five Presidents, from Roosevelt to Johnson, who have pressed ahead on a program of broadening civil rights through legislation. It has been Congress that has resisted such an effort, largely because of the influence of Southerners in the power structure of both Houses. The startling reversal of what was expected of these two branches of Government is due to circumstances too complex to go into here, but the fact of the reversal can hardly be disputed.

The conventional wisdom has it that, even though the President may take leadership on such matters as civil rights, the very power of the Presidency represents an ominous threat to the maintenance of the people's liberty. The arguments are fourfold:

First, the contention that the Presidency may be filled by either an incompetent of the Harding type, or a demagogue of the Huey Long or the Joe McCarthy type. Perhaps the best answer to this double-barreled argument is the simplest one: in the twentieth century we have had only one Harding in the White House, and no Huey Longs or Joe McCarthys. Indeed, either because of the caliber of the men elected to the White House, or because of the influence of the Presidency on the incumbent, this has been a century of strikingly effective Presidents, or at least of highly capable "near-greats." Even the three Vice-Presidents who have been elevated to the Presidency during this century have turned out to be unusually able men—and this is doubtless true of Lyndon Johnson as well.

A second conventional concern about the American President is that, as Professor Edward Corwin said in 1941, the Presidency might become dangerously personalized, in two senses: overly dependent on the accident of personality and lacking independent advice from organs of Government over which the President had no control. But, with the enormous development of the staff system since Corwin's time, it is hard to see the Presidency as personalized today. Certainly Presidents would deny it; men like Roosevelt and Kennedy have felt the restraints and limitations of the bureaucracy as a whole and of the cluster of permanent civil servants who go on from Presidency to Presidency. We hear much about the "lonely President"—and doubtless in certain crucial hours he does feel very alone. But actually the President is surrounded by men and, even more, responds to the advice of the many men with whom he has had to work to gain his office and to administer it. The President cannot take day-to-day action without operating through a bureaucracy that has been built up over many years, and which embraces a whole set of restraints and safeguards in itself.

A third traditional charge against the Presidency is that it is an unrepresentative office. The President, said, simply represents popular majorities—and, indeed, popular majorities that are distorted by the workings of the Electoral College. Congress, on the other hand, it is held, represents the great consensus of the nation because of its ability to respond to the special needs and pressures of a tremendous variety of Congressional districts in fifty states. Whether or not the President is unrepresentative and Congress representative depends of course on one's definition of democratic representation. Congress does tend to represent more of a consensus, though a consensus greatly distorted because of its overrepresentation of rural and conservative interests. The President does perhaps overrepresent the urban, liberal, labor, ethnic minority groups in the nation, both because of their sheer number and because of the winner-take-all impact of the Electoral College.

To attempt to resolve the question of the Presidency as a representative institution would take us beyond the confines of this essay. Actually, however, representation as viewed by the conventional wisdom is essentially irrelevant to the issue. The greatness of a President has not been his mirrorlike representation of the people but his responsibility to the future. The great Presidents, like Theodore Roosevelt

ith his conservation policies, or
Voodrow Wilson with his belief in
nternational organization, or Franklin
Roosevelt with his dedication to West-
rn unity against the Axis, or John
ennedy with his vision of a grand
ew design, have looked beyond im-
ediate majorities to the place they
ould like to hold in history. Or per-
aps they discerned that one way to
chieve majorities in elections would
e to keep an eye on the likely hind-
ght of history.

Our conventional thinking about the
residency will be tested and chal-
nged even more in the future than in
e past, because of the tests that lie
head. The simultaneous impact of
eightened civil rights struggles at
ome and repeated cold war crises
broad, combined with our failure to
solve the Congressional deadlock,
eans that the Presidency will become
ore embattled than ever during the
te 1960's. We have seen the White
ouse turned into a command post
uring the two Cuban crises and dur-
g civil rights crises; we will see much
ore of this kind of thing during the
mainder of the decade.

Because the Presidency cannot in
e long run endure this kind of al-
ost continual crisis, the President—
me President—will eventually try, I
resee, to get a grip on his domestic
oblems at least, so that he can plan
ainst the coming of crisis, instead of
ways having to cope with the fact of
isis. The great domestic demands on
e Presidency in this decade—to the
tent that he tries to anticipate crises
will be fiscal. The question will be,
ven a continuing stalemate in Con-
ess, whether the President will be
le to act out of some power of his
vn, or innovate some power of his
vn, that will enable him to plan
ainst chronic crisis—for example, to
rry out a successful war against
verty, and to take steps to tackle
the economic and social malaise that
lies at the root of the civil rights problem.

There are some omens of this kind of
struggle. President Roosevelt told Congress during World War II to take a
certain action in the fiscal field, and
warned that otherwise he would—and
Congress avoided a showdown. President Kennedy asked for authority to
change tax rates within certain limits;
Congress, of course, denied him this
authority, but the question would be
very acute in a recession. Lyndon B.
Johnson favored civil rights legislation
that would give the President the authority to withhold Federal funds
from any program or activity receiving
Federal assistance directly or indirectly. Even if Congress should withdraw this authority at a later time, this
is one situation where the President
may have the whip hand. For, by cus-
ton, he has exercised the power not to
spend money appropriated by Congress for certain projects (especially
military). What if he should leave
unspent money—let's say highway
money—dearly wanted by the states
pursuing segregationist policies or
failing to cooperate with Federal civil
rights measures?

The outcome may well be a power
fight between Congress and the President, with each using its fiscal power
to put pressure on the other branch.
And such a fight would precipitate the
gravest Constitutional struggle since
the Civil War. The outcome of such a
fight cannot be predicted. But one
thing is clear. The more embattled the
Presidency becomes in the years ahead,
the more Americans will cling to it as
their central instrument for guarding
national security and expanding the
people's freedoms. But they can cling
to this great engine of democracy only
if our modes of thought anticipate the
pace of change rather than limping
behind it.

4

Leave Your Presidency Alone *

CLINTON ROSSITER

As a governmental institution, Clinton Rossiter finds the American Presidency to be not without fault. In fact, he urges reforms and corrections. In the main, however, he concludes that the office may be tinkered with for minor adjustments but that it should not be radically changed. As it now stands, the Presidency is "one of our chief bulwarks against decline and chaos."

. . . I detect a deep note of satisfaction, although hardly of complacency, with the American Presidency as it stands today. A steady theme seems to have run all through this final review of its weaknesses and problems, a theme entitled (with apologies to the genius of Thurber) "Leave Your Presidency Alone!" This feeling of satisfaction springs, I am frank to admit, from a political outlook more concerned with the world as it is than as it is said to have been by reactionaries and is promised to be by radicals. Since this outlook is now shared by a staggering majority of Americans, I feel that I am expressing something more than a personal opinion. If we accept the facts of life in the 1960's, as we must, and if we shun the false counsels of perfection, as we do, then we are bound to conclude that we are richly blessed with a choice instrument of constitutional democracy. Judged in the light of memory and desire, the Presidency is in a state of sturdy health, and that

is why we should not give way easily to despair over the defects men of too much zeal or too little courage claim to discover in it. Some of these are not defects at all; some are chronic in our system of government; some could be cured only by opening the way to others far more malign.

This does not mean that we should stand pat with the Presidency. Rather we should confine ourselves to small readjustments—I have noted a dozen or more that might be worth a try—and leave the usual avenues open to prescriptive change. We should abolish the electoral college but leave the electoral system to pursue its illogical but hitherto effective way. We should plan carefully for mobilization in the event of war but take care that the inherent emergency power of the president—the power used by Lincoln to blockade the South, by Wilson to arm the merchant men, and by Roosevelt to bring off the Destroyer Deal—be left intact and untrammeled. We should experiment with a joint executive-legislative council and the item veto but be on our guard against the urge to alter radically the pattern of competitive coexistence between Congress and President

---

* Clinton Rossiter, *The American Presidency*, rev. ed. (New York: Harcourt, Brace & World, Inc., 1960), pp. 258-61. ©1956, 1960 by Clinton Rossiter. Reprinted by permission of the publisher.

We should give the president all the aides he can use but beware the deceptively simple solution of a second and even third vice-president for executive purposes. And we should tinker modestly with the president's machinery but wake from the false dream of perfect harmony in high places, especially in the highest place of all. For if the Presidency could speak, it would say with Whitman:

Do I contradict myself?
Very well then I contradict myself.
(I am large, I contain multitudes.)

"Leave Your Presidency Alone": that is the message of this chapter, and I trust I have made clear . . . why I transmit it so confidently. To put the final case for the American Presidency as forcefully as possible, let me point once again to its essential qualities:

It strikes a felicitous balance between power and limitations. In a world in which power is the price of freedom, the Presidency, as Professor Merriam and his colleagues wrote in 1937, "stands across the path of those who mistakenly assert that democracy must fail because it can neither decide promptly nor act vigorously." In a world in which power has been abused on a tragic scale, it presents a heartening lesson in the uses of constitutionalism. To repeat the moral of an earlier chapter, the power of the Presidency moves as a mighty host only with the grain of liberty and morality. The quest of constitutional government is for the right balance of authority and restraint, and Americans may take some pride in the balance they have built into the Presidency.

It provides a steady focus of leadership: of administration, Congress, and people. In a constitutional system compounded of diversity and antagonism, the Presidency looms up as the countervailing force of unity and harmony. In a society ridden by centrifugal forces, it is, as Sidney Hyman has written, the "common reference point for social effort." The relentless progress of this continental republic has made the Presidency our one truly national political institution. There are those who would reserve this role to Congress, but as the least aggressive of our presidents, Calvin Coolidge, once testified, "It is because in their hours of timidity the Congress becomes subservient to the importunities of organized minorities that the president comes more and more to stand as the champion of the rights of the whole country." The more Congress becomes, in Burke's phrase, "a confused and scuffling bustle of local agency," the more the Presidency must become a clear beacon of national purpose.

It is a priceless symbol of our continuity and destiny as a people. Few nations have solved so simply and yet grandly the problem of finding and maintaining an office of state that embodies their majesty and reflects their character. Only the Constitution overshadows the Presidency as an object of popular reverence, and the Constitution does not walk about smiling and shaking hands. "The simple fact is," a distinguished, disgruntled Briton wrote at the end of the "Royal Soap Opera" of 1955, "that the United States Presidency today is a far more dignified institution than the British monarchy." In all honesty and tact we must quickly demur, but we can be well satisfied with our "republican king."

5

The Case for Today's Presidency*

ARTHUR M. SCHLESINGER, JR.

Would you agree that in recent history an activist Presidency has been "the most effective way of overcoming the tendencies toward inertia" inherent in our system? Why have liberals tended to advocate Presidential power while conservatives have tended to support Congressional power? How has Presidential power been limited by bureaucracy, Court, and Congress?

* * *

It has been a turbulent century, marked by war, depression, and a fantastic increase in the tempo of social change; and one result of the accelerating demands on government has been the growing centrality of the President. For a system of coordinate checks and balance tends toward stalemate; and history supports those who have seen in an activist presidency the most effective way of overcoming the tendencies toward inertia inherent in our polity. Even a President like Eisenhower, nominally devoted to a limited view of the presidency, found himself setting the congressional agenda as a matter of routine and exercising powers of initiative and pressure in relation to the Congress which would have horrified Senator Hoar and his colleagues of the late nineteenth century. It was Eisenhower, indeed, who first established an office of congression liaison in the White House.

Nor did this evolution of president authority justify the classic fear— copiously expressed a century earli by Webster and Clay—that a stro President would become an engine despotism and tyranny. "We are in t midst of a revolution," Clay had urg against Jackson,

. . . hitherto bloodless, but rapidly ter ing toward a total change of the p republican character of the Governme and to the concentration of all power the hands of one man. . . . If Congr does not apply an instantaneous and fective remedy, the fatal collapse v soon come on, and we shall die—ignol die—base, mean, and abject slaves; t scorn and contempt of mankind; pitied, unwept, unmourned!

This fearful prophecy had hardly be sustained by events, even though t delusion of persecution lingers in t shape of the political myth that national government is the enemy the people. History, on the contra would seem to show that the natio government is a valuable means which a free people pursues its go

* Arthur M. Schlesinger, Jr., "The Case for Today's Presidency," in Arthur M. Schlesinger, Jr. and Alfred de Grazia, *Congress and the Presidency: Their Role in Modern Times* (Washington, D.C.: American Enterprise Institute for Public Policy Research, 1967), pp. 13-19, 27-29. Reprinted by permission of the publisher.

The increase in national authority has thus far not destroyed individual freedoms—except such freedoms as those to hire children for a few cents to labor from dawn to dusk in the mills, or to run sweatshops, or to market fraudulent securities, or to operate extortionate monopolies, or to deny one-tenth of the American people their legal and constitutional rights—all freedoms with which one supposes our country can happily dispense. Indeed, the national government has greatly strengthened the freedoms of the First and Fourteenth Amendments and assured the individual American new liberty to speak his mind, follow his conscience, and exercise his lawful rights.

I trust you will forgive this extended historical introduction. But I think it is more than simply the occupational reflex of a professional historian. The backward glance is justified in my mind by several things. It reminds us that the question of the relationship between the President and the Congress has received a good deal of thoughtful attention through our history. It reminds us that it involves practical questions of power rather than abstract questions of principle. And it reminds us that while nearly every increase in presidential power has produced a reaction in favor of the limitation of that power—thus the posthumous punishment of Franklin Roosevelt through the Twenty-second Amendment for having committed the offense of winning four elections to the presidency—the reaction has never quite cut the power back to its earlier level.

Yet it would be wrong to conclude that the President has irrevocably triumphed in the unending guerrilla war. For, while the presidency is a good deal stronger today than it was, say, 5 years ago, it is not notably stronger than the presidency imagined in the Federalist Papers. Moreover, in significant respects the presidency in recent years has lost power—by which I mean freedom of decision and action—to the executive bureaucracy, to the Supreme Court, and to the Congress.

Since the relationship to Congress is our theme tonight, I shall only touch briefly on the other challenges to presidential authority. I have written at length elsewhere about the tension within the executive branch between the presidential government and the permanent government—a tension now so deep in the system as to suggest that we now have four rather than three branches of government, and that an activist presidency may encounter almost as much opposition from the permanent government as from the Congress or the Court. During the New Deal, conservatives had bemoaned the expansion of the national government as a threat to freedom. They might more wisely have hailed the bureaucracy as a bulwark against change. For the permanent government develops its own stubborn vested interests in policy, its own fraternal alliances with committees of the Congress, its own ties to the press, its own national constituencies. It tends toward the belief that Presidents come and Presidents go, but it goes on forever. As such, the permanent government is politically neutral; its essential commitment is only to doing things as they have been done before. This frustrated the enthusiasts who came to Washington with Eisenhower in 1953 zealous to dismantle the New Deal, as it frustrated the enthusiasts who came to Washington with Kennedy in 1961 zealous to get the country moving again. It will confront every President who wants to change things with a series of long and exasperating problems.

The loss of power to the Court has come about partly as a result of the judicial veto of presidential actions—

as in the steel seizure case of 1952—
and even more as a result of the failure
of the presidency and the Congress to
meet national obligations—as in the
cases ending the national shame of
segregation and discrimination.

The loss of power to the Congress
is a more complicated matter. Wilson in *Congressional Government*
deplored the tendency of late nineteenth century Congress to get "into
the habit of investigating and managing everything." No one can say
that this habit has particularly languished in modern times. In the hands
of Senator McCarthy a dozen years
ago the congressional investigation
displayed its considerable capacity
to harass and sabotage presidential
policy—as a score of more benign investigations have displayed a capacity to fortify and improve presidential
initiative. As for the increase in congressional attempts to manage the
executive branch, one has only to
compare the latitude and discretion
permitted the President in the Works
Progress Act of 1935 with the tight
and detailed administrative control
imposed by Congress in a not dissimilar piece of legislation, the Economic Opportunity Act of 1964. Some
observers concluded a trifle hastily
from the experience of the 89th Congress that a secular change of some
sort had taken place, and that Congress hereafter would be in a state of
permanent subordination to the executive. I recall, for example, a fashion of deriding the thesis set forth by
James MacGregor Burns in his book
The Stalemate of Democracy. But I
fear that the 90th Congress will only
show how transient was the situation
produced for the Democratic executive by the Republican nomination of
Goldwater in 1964.

If Congress has lost ground against
the main-line forces of the President,
it has retained its capacity for daring

forays into the heart of presidentia[l]
power. Let me hasten to add tha[t]
in thus describing the ebb and flo[w]
of the guerrilla war, I intend no ge[n]-
eral value judgments. There can b[e]
no greater fallacy than to suppos[e]
every accretion to presidential powe[r]
good and every accretion to congressional power bad—or vice versa. A[t]
the risk of repetition, let me sugge[st]
again that the judgment must b[e]
made case by case on specific practical effects. The struggle among th[e]
branches of government is part o[f]
the health of the American polity, an[d]
its continuation makes democracy po[s]-
sible by enabling the electorate t[o]
shift the weight of decision in on[e]
direction or another according to th[e]
results desired.

Thus I am not persuaded by th[e]
recent proposal that members of th[e]
House of Representatives be electe[d]
for four-year terms concurrently wit[h]
the President. While this idea wou[ld]
clearly strengthen the presidency, [it]
would also deprive both the Pres[i]-
dent and the country of the plebi[s]-
citary value of mid-term election[s]
and for this periodic sounding of th[e]
national mood the public opinion po[ll]
is no substitute. On the other han[d]
I do feel that the President is entitled to have his legislative progra[m]
go to the floor of both houses f[or]
debate and vote. The present abili[ty]
of the Congress to impound pres[i]-
dential recommendations in commi[t]-
tee and keep them from consideratio[n]
by the whole is a dangerous frail[ty]
of our system. Let presidential recommendations, after a specified perio[d]
be voted up or voted down—but ma[ke]
sure they come to a vote. This obje[c]-
tive could be rather simply attaine[d]
by a modification of congressio[nal]
rules and agreement with the leade[r]-
ship in both houses.

My discussion thus far has ce[n]-
tered on the relationship between t[he]

President and the Congress in the field of domestic policy. While this has been the most significant part of the relationship through most of our history, it is by no means the entire relationship—nor perhaps is it any longer today even the most significant. For the field of foreign affairs confronts the relationship between the executive and the legislative with its most difficult and delicate problems. Here the Constitution has given the President certain powers bearing on foreign affairs—day-to-day conduct of foreign policy, command of the armed forces, treaty-making authority, reception of ambassadors, and so on—while it has given other powers to Congress—appropriations, the commerce power, maintenance of armed forces, treaty veto, and so on. . . .

＊　　＊　　＊

Yet the congressional role has been by no means negligible. Indeed, in certain respects, as a consequence particularly of the increasing dependence of foreign policy on appropriations, Congress has more means of influencing the conduct of foreign affairs than ever before. Consider, for example, our Latin American policy. Franklin Roosevelt, in committing the nation to the Good Neighbor policy, could do so by unilateral decision, just as Monroe had handed down his doctrine on his own recognizance a century earlier. But President Kennedy, his Alliance for Progress, was pretty much at the mercy of Congress every step along the way. On the other hand, Congress can use the appropriations power to control foreign policy only when the issues lack visible urgency; a member of Congress, no matter how deeply he opposes the war in Vietnam, would hardly be well advised to oppose that war by refusing support to the troops fighting in the field.

Once again, I will not apologize for this historical review; and once again I must emphasize that the question of the distribution of power between the President and the Congress, in foreign as well as domestic affairs, is a matter not of right or wrong but of practical results. Thus some of us in the past who have been all-out supporters of the presidential prerogative have been forced to think again as a consequence of the present involvement in Vietnam. Since activist Presidents want to change things, since domestic policy has been the main field of presidential action through our history, and since Congress, partly for its own institutional reasons, tends in due course to oppose presidential activism, liberals, in general, have argued for the presidency and conservatives for the Congress. But this has been the result of circumstance, not of principle—as suggested by the fact that today, for perhaps the first time in our history, a strong President proposes to use presidential powers (in Vietnam) for purposes which liberals, in general, question and conservatives, in general, approve. Conceivably this, if protracted here and applied to other issues, could result in an exchange of positions comparable to that between the Federalists and the Jeffersonians from 1800 to 1814.

My own feeling is that, while the Congress should give the President more administrative discretion in the execution of statutes, something must be done to assure the Congress a more authoritative and continuing voice in fundamental decisions in foreign policy. The President must have wide tactical flexibility, but not so wide that he can impose by himself the decisions which may make the difference between peace and war in the nuclear age. But I do not see that this voice can be assured by structural or procedural changes in the legislative-executive relationship. And, since the efficacy of our policy depends on the presidency, it remains vital, while guarding against presidential excesses, to protect the essential prerogatives.

The answer, I think, lies not in the mechanics of government but in the dynamics of politics. The ambiguities of the relationship correspond to the complex and shifting realities of American political folkways. Our past history gives us a variety of possible combinations; our present obligation is to seek that combination which best serves what we conscientiously regard as the national interest. The answer, in short, lies ultimately with the electorate itself and the pressures it can bring to bear on both the presidency and the Congress. . . .

6

The Case for Congress *

ALFRED DE GRAZIA

According to the author, what are some of the myths of the Presidency? Would you agree that the President has become an "elected Emperor"? What four recommendations does Professor de Grazia make toward cutting the Presidency down to size? Which recommendations would you support? Which would you reject?

. . . I have dealt in other places with the lush verdure of myth that surrounds the presidency in America and prevents both scholars and laymen from clear-cutting analysis of the office and its operations. Nonetheless neither I nor anyone has put the issues sharply enough. Here I mean to name these myths of the presidency, and to point out from what psychological sources they emanate. Then I would attempt to say who

provokes and promotes the myth, and what are its effects.

By a myth I mean a belief based upon a distortion of reality that is caused by subconscious wishes and that unconsciously guides mental and physical activity. One does not need to be a psychologist to understand the operation of myth in politics, though my colleagues in psychology have launched many an assault upon the mysteries of the subject, the latest under the formidable name of "cognitive dissonance." Myth is good or bad depending upon our view of its effects. An ancient playwright had a phrase that covers our interest well enough: "Those whom the gods would destroy, they first make mad."

* Alfred de Grazia, "The Case for Congress" in Arthur M. Schlesinger, Jr. and Alfred de Grazia, *Congress and the Presidency: Their Role in Modern Times* (Washington, D.C.: American Enterprise Institute for Public Policy Research, 1967), pp. 38-44, 87-89. Reprinted by permission of the publisher.

The myth of the President ascribes to him unusual qualities, most often good, occasionally bad, but whether saintly or diabolical they are far in excess of those he had before he took office or beyond the average of those around him no matter who they may have been or are. Just about every miracle assigned by folk tales to kings and emperors of far off lands and times has been replicated by recent American Presidents.

The President is believed to represent the people, not in any ordinary sense but in the most remarkable of ways, involving psychic waves, psychological projections, and even the statistical proofs of scientoid professors who feel themselves immune from vulgar obsessions. With the expansion of the presidential constituency to include the world there is no possibility of a competitor short of the Universal Pope or a Stalin or Mao Tse-tung.

The hard core of representation, the practical everyday rational representation, whose absence once drove American colonials to revolt against the English Crown, is left to congressmen and sundry officials to enjoy. There is an irony in the conduct of some people: on the one hand they are saying that it is terribly important for one man to have 1/200,000th of the right to elect his representative if another man has 1/200,000th of the right; on the other hand they are ready to consign all powers to a central figure in the belief that this central person stands in an intimate relationship to them and 200,000,000 others, far more intimate than the strict representatives.[1]

A third myth is that the President the source of good administration in government. If you called for favorable witnesses to this myth, you could line up most management experts and political science professors. It happens that there is a coincidence between the vulgar magic of one-man rule and the primitive science of administration. This executive or military concept of administration deductively subscribes to any system of administration no matter how complicated, how vast, how intended for divergent purposes, so long as it premises a concentration of authority at the top of the pyramid.

A Committee on Economic Development report on U.S. budget reorganization,[2] issued earlier this year, can be fished out of the annual tides of hundreds of similar so-called studies. They all start with the same premises and end with the same conclusions. Typically, Congress is "given the wrong end of the stick" for blocking "efficient budget practice." It is widely assumed, too, that the President can handle an unlimited number of activities, both ceremonial and executive.

It is moreover contained in the myth of the President that he has a monopoly of the public interest. (To be sure he delegates it to the executive establishment, of which, more later.) This reputation stems naturally from the way in which he personalizes the nation for all people, and from the doctrines of administration that have been shaped to suit his twin role as national hero and national executive. All in all, he is, as Dennis Brogan and other foreigners have called him, "an elective emperor" of considerable power, probably greater than that of Louis XIV, famous Sun-King of France.

This mythical figure, whose depic-

[1] Reference here is, of course, to the movement for "one-man, one-vote" which burst bounds triumphantly in the sixties.

[2] *Budgeting for National Objectives,* January, 1966.

tion here can be supplemented by thousands of details, represents of course little of reality. From a purely historical point of view or from a time-and-motion analysis, the President would not behave according to the myth: he is not hero, nor miracle-worker, nor efficient executive, nor privy to the public interest. Or, to put it another way, he is when he is, and he isn't when he isn't.

But the myth has a profoundly psychological basis in the popular mind. The President is a father figure, not a jobholder. This "fact" is most actively displayed upon the death of a President. When President Lincoln died, Walt Whitman chanted,

For you they call, the swaying mass,
their eager faces turning,
Here Captain! Dear Father!

When President Roosevelt died, doctors observed the dreams of their patients to be suffused with the character of their fathers. Dr. Martha Wolfenstein and others have investigated the psychological response to President Kennedy's death.[3] Extraordinary depths were plumbed. Intellectual college students wept, while athletes envisioned tortures for Lee Oswald. Adults displayed more emotion, prolonged longer, than children. Reactions were of grief, disbelief, anger towards people and groups, internal turmoil, blanking out, infantile reversions, somatic disturbances, and obsession with the question "How could it happen?", an illogical obsession since the Vice President is created to become President "when, as, and if" it happens. "Anxiety and apprehension of other bad things happening were widespread." There was fear of aggression at home, abroad, and within the family, and

self-destructive impulses were felt. There was a great deal of posthumous "obedience" to the murdered leader, who, as you will recall, was pursuing some unpopular programs and was having much trouble in persuading Congress of his ideas. The President's chief opponent suffered a precipitous decline in popularity.

The President is a symbol of social unity, and the more unruly living and split up a society is, the more do people yearn for a central person to stand for what is wanting. The President is a symbol of power. His mail is full of the most outlandish requests; he is Santa Claus, Batman, 007, Big Brother, Smoky the Bear, and a host of other wonder-workers. He is human, comprehensible; his complications, which are never allowed to appear excessive, are better understood than those of the impersonal bureaucracy or the Congress. Even cynical and hardened newsmen print only half the truth about the President. Reluctantly they let it leak out through private conversations or let one or two exceedingly tough (or should the word be "dedicated") characters expose the ordinary, the conflictful, the incompetent, the sick, the wrong, the distasteful side that most men must have.

In fact, the myth of the President is provoked and promoted by the opposition. "Every knock is a boost" goes the saying. No newspaper in the country attacked President Franklin Roosevelt as continuously and sharply as did the *Chicago Tribune*. Yet Professor Harold Gosnell had to resort to multiple correlation techniques to discover any relation between *Tribune* circulation and the Roosevelt vote.[4] At that, Gosnell proved what most experts no longer had believed

[3] *Children and the Death of a President* (1965).

[4] Cf. *Machine Politics: Chicago Model* (1937).

namely that newspapers *do* influence elections.

Pro or *con*, the newspapers keep the President in the headlines, on TV, and radio, and especially as the newspapers grow thin the presidential proportion grows higher. Even the *New York Times*, the world's bulkiest newspaper, carries as much material on the presidency as on the Congress and the executive branch combined. The proportion is so huge that not even the most naive person could imagine that it would correspond to the actual power of the President. Indeed, the flood of publicity continues when the President is resting or being operated upon for an affliction.[7] And of course, after he dies, fame completely outstrips power. Or, we should say, fame acts as the precipitator and promoter of power.

Most congressmen are by no means resentful of the paramountcy of the chief, and will often compete fiercely, regardless of party, to bask in his sunshine. They must do so, for the increasingly centralized press services and nationalized columnists can only afford to carry items on national figures. The American nation is not growing smaller; it is expanding. Its image makers are contracting, however, and whatever is local, personally meaningful, and quietly effective is ignored. The individual grows miniscule while the figures on the national scene grow more entrancing and grotesquely huge.

Howard K. Smith has coined a term for those who oppose the President's policies in Vietnam only until the chips are down. He calls them the "undissenters". They give the public the impression that a great debate may be shaping up, and then 'cut out for the tall grass." Constitutional provisions having to do with Congress' power to declare war are disregarded; no one thinks to fashion out of the junked proviso some new machinery that will at least stop a war from being a one-man war.

Many voices in Congress and on the outside call for ways to help the President carry his burdens. Rarely do they think to take a burden entirely. Or if they do, they turn invariably to the bureaucracy as the storage tank of executive authority....

You see, it does appear to me that Professor Schlesinger's Congress and presidency are painted upon some canvas of ages gone by. They are skiffs on a brisk little sea. They seem one taller than the other depending on whether you look at them from one angle or from another. The onrushing tides of change that he alludes to almost casually in his paper have apparently left almost undisturbed this nice little yachting scene.

To my view, on the other hand, all of America is a dynamic system in which the freedom of all the parts depends upon the type of unity that is maintained throughout the system. All social change has to be compensated for within the system. All the republican institutions of the nation, including the supreme legislature, are losing their energy within the system because we have discovered only one way to do things, and have discovered no way to undo them.

I hope that I may in conclusion repeat the major propositions that I have put forward in this debate.

The first is that the office of the President will not cure itself of its tendencies towards a cult of personality and rampant activism. We should therefore attempt, by our votes, by establishing the proper attitudes in high places and the press, and by structural adjustments, to maintain the office of the President as a humanly proportioned, legislatively effective, and administratively competent office. Four recommendations point the way to this:

1. Restrict presidential tenure to one term of six years.
2. Relieve the President of his continuous and total political responsibility for being "the nuclear trigger."
3. Reorganize the administrative authority of the chief executive so that other powerful representative officials can help him control and fashion the establishment.
4. Reorganize Congress and the bureaucracy with a revised presidential concept in mind.

With respect to parties, I recommend continued decentralization. With respect to the administrative establishment, I suggest a complete representative structure with relation to the outside world, ending in a juncture with Congress. I also suggest a built-in, continuous system of Congressional Tribunes to bring about contraction, devolution, and termination of the powers and activities of government agencies. And I would urge Congress to create a more vibrant and coherent image before the country by addressing itself to the country in the same manner as the President does. Congress requires a new myth for the future.

Other recommendations have been made in my paper and elsewhere. They are all predicated upon the desire to fulfill those ideals that were originally suggested: to promote group and personal autonomy and creativity, to provide equality of opportunity under a rule of law, and to practice an openmindedness towards the world.

CHAPTER TEN

Congress:
The New, Old, or Last Frontier?

Since representative government has such a high place in our value system, it is rather curious that Congress should have such a poor public image. The droll story and the humorous anecdote frequently satirize the national legislature while the Senators Phogbounds and Claghorns in the mass media tend to stereotype the average congressman.

Part of the problem stems from a failure to understand the critical function of Congress in compromising controversial issues and achieving a degree of consensus among disparate interest groups. At the same time the substantial committee work in Congress is seldom seen. Instead the public eye falls upon a listless, half-empty chamber ignoring a prepared speech by an equally disinterested colleague or a newspaper headline describing the circus-like performance of a reckless investigating committee.

Congress has its shortcomings—inertia and delay, conservatism, and a tendency at times, to intervene in the province of the Executive. The system, nevertheless, does work and it works despite a congressman's lack of systematic information, his overburdening committee duties, and the endless demands of constituents who regard a congressman as something of a cross between a Capitol guide and a glorified bell boy. In a nation where 70 per cent of the people do not know the name of their senator or congressman, it is highly probable that the national legislators do a better job than most apathetic citizens realize, or perhaps, deserve.

The following section explores two major issues relating to Congress as a political institution. The first of these, "Congress: Alteration or Adaptation?"

deals with the response of Congress to the twentieth century. The second problem, "Power in Congress: Three Views of the 'Hill,'" relates to the problem of leadership, roles, and power in the national legislature.

CONGRESS: ALTERATION OR ADAPTATION?

Most of the suggestions which one hears for the reform of Congress are procedural changes. Such proposals as joint committee hearings or the installation of electronic voting equipment in the House might save time, money, and energy, but these innovations would probably not drastically alter present patterns. On the other hand, there are other possible changes which would affect the basic power structure of Congress. The question raised in this section is, "Which way should Congress move?" Should the changes be procedural or substantive, or should there be no changes whatsoever? All three points of view are expressed here. Samuel P. Huntington suggests that unless Congress undertakes fundamental reform it will find it increasingly difficult to perform some of its historic functions. However, Congress could adapt itself to the current trends, modify traditional patterns and expand other functions. Hubert H. Humphrey argues for immediate and practical alterations. David B. Truman points out ways in which many of the suggested reforms would after or fail to alter the power structure.

POWER IN CONGRESS: THREE VIEWS OF THE "HILL"

Fundamental to an understanding of Congress is an awareness of the patterns of influence and of power within each house. It is important to know something of the leadership and followship, the concentration and distribution of power, and the role of the individual congressman in the legislative process. In fact, without this background it is impossible to understand or to properly evaluate Congress as a governmental institution.

Woodrow Wilson was one of the first political scientists to examine the internal operation of Congresss. His *Congressional Government* remains a classic account of the power of the leadership in the House and Senate and the influence of committees and committee chairmen. In recent years, other writers have analyzed the power of informal groupings, such as the inner club of the Senate, as well as the place of the "outsider" and other individuals who refuse to go along with the system but who by force of character and personality frequently become highly effective legislators.

The second section of this chapter presents some observations on the exercise of power in Congress. Senator Joseph S. Clark discusses the congressional establishment. Clayton Fritchey evaluates the "inner club" of the Senate and assesses the influence of the nonmember. The late Congressman Clem Miller writes with clarity and insight on the exercise of power in the House of Representatives.

1

Congressional Responses to the Twentieth Century *

SAMUEL P. HUNTINGTON

Would you agree with the author that Congress has conceded both the initiative in lawmaking and the dominant influence in determining the final content of legislation? Does it follow that Congress has lost its future? What possible directions does Professor Huntington see for Congress?

... Eighty per cent of the bills enacted into law, one congressman has estimated, originate in the executive branch. Indeed, in most instances congressmen do not admit a responsibility to take legislative action except in response to executive requests. Congress, as one senator has complained, "has surrendered its rightful place in the leadership in the lawmaking process to the White House. No longer is Congress the source of major legislation. It now merely filters legislative proposals from the President, straining out some and reluctantly letting others pass through. These days no one expects Congress to devise the important bills." [1] The President now determines the legislative agenda of Congress almost as thoroughly as the British Cabinet sets the legislative agenda of Parliament. The institutionalization of this role

was one of the more significant developments in presidential-congressional relations after World War II. [2]

Congress has conceded not only the initiative in originating legislation but —and perhaps inevitably as the result of losing the initiative—it has also lost the dominant influence it once had in shaping the final content of legislation. Between 1882 and 1909 Congress had a preponderant influence in shaping the content of sixteen (55 per cent) out of twenty-nine major laws enacted during those years. It had a preponderant influence over seventeen (46 per cent) of thirty-seven major laws passed between 1910 and 1932. During the constitutional revolution of the New Deal, however, its influence declined markedly: only two (8 per cent) of twenty-four major laws passed between 1933 and 1940 were primarily the work of Congress. [3] Certainly its record after World War II was little

* Samuel P. Huntington, "Congressional Responses to the Twentieth Century," in *The Congress and America's Future*, ed. David B. Truman, © 1965 by The American Assembly. Reprinted by permission of Prentice-Hall, Inc., Englewood Cliffs, New Jersey.

[1] Abraham Ribicoff, "Doesn't Congress Have Ideas of Its Own?" *Saturday Evening Post*, 237 (March 21, 1964), 6.

[2] Richard E. Neustadt, "Presidency and Legislation: Planning the President's Program," *American Political Science Review*, 49 (December 1955), 980-1021.

[3] Lawrence H. Chamberlain, *The President, Congress, and Legislation* (New York: Columbia University Press, 1946), pp. 450-52.

better. The loss of congressional control over the substance of policy is most marked, of course, in the area of national defense and foreign policy. At one time Congress did not hesitate to legislate the size and weapons of the armed forces. Now this power—to raise and support armies, to provide and maintain a navy—is firmly in the hands of the executive. Is Congress, one congressional committee asked plaintively in 1962, to play simply "the passive role of supine acquiescence" in executive programs or is it to be "an active participant in the determination of the direction of our defense policy?" The committee, however, already knew the answer:

> To any student of government, it is eminently clear that the role of the Congress in determining national policy, defense or otherwise, has deteriorated over the years. More and more the role of Congress has come to be that of a sometimes querulous but essentially kindly uncle who complains while furiously puffing on his pipe but who finally, as everyone expects, gives in and hands over the allowance, grants the permission, or raises his hand in blessing, and then returns to the rocking chair for another year of somnolence broken only by an occasional anxious glance down the avenue and a muttered doubt as to whether he had done the right thing.[4]

In domestic legislation Congress's influence is undoubtedly greater, but even here its primary impact is on the timing and details of legislation, not on the subjects and content of legislation. . . .

Adaptation or Reform

Insulation has made Congress unwilling to initiate laws. Dispersion has made Congress unable to aggregate individual bills into a coherent legislative program. Constituent service and administrative overseeing have eaten into the time and energy which congressmen give legislative matters. Congress is thus left in its legislative dilemma where the assertion of power is almost equivalent to the obstruction of action. What then are the possibilities for institutional adaptation or institutional reform?

Living with the Dilemma

Conceivably neither adaptation nor reform is necessary. The present distribution of power and functions could continue indefinitely. Instead of escaping from its dilemma, Congress could learn to live with it. In each of the four institutional crises mentioned earlier, the issue of institutional adaptation came to a head over one issue: the presidential election of 1824, the House of Commons Reform Bill of 1832, the Lloyd George budget of 1910, and the Supreme Court reorganization plan of 1937. The adaptation crisis of Congress differs in that to date a constitutional crisis between the executive branch and Congress has been avoided. Congress has procrastinated, obstructed, and watered down executive legislative proposals, but it has also come close to the point where it no longer dares openly to veto them. . . . If Congress uses its powers to delay and to amend with prudence and circumspection, there is no necessary reason why it should not retain them for the indefinite future. If Congress, however, did reject a major administration measure, like tax reduction or civil rights, the issue would be joined, the country would be thrown into a constitutional crisis, and the executive branch would mobilize its forces for a showdown

---

[4] House Report 1406, Eighty-seventh Congress, Second Session (1962), p. 7.

over the authority of Congress to
veto legislation.

Reform Versus Adaptation: Restructuring Power

The resumption by Congress of an
active, positive role in the legislative
process would require a drastic re-
structuring of power relationships,
including reversal of the tendencies
toward insulation, dispersion, and
oversight. Fundamental "reforms"
would thus be required. To date two
general types of proposals have been
advanced for the structural reform of
Congress. Ironically, however, neither
set of proposals is likely, if enacted,
to achieve the results which its principal proponents desire. One set of
reformers, "democratizers" like Senator Clark, attack the power of the
Senate "Establishment" or "Inner
Club" and urge an equalizing of
power among congressmen so that a
majority of each house can work
its will. These reformers stand four-
square in the Norris tradition.
Dissolution of the Senate "Establishment" and other measures of demo-
cratization, however, would disperse
power among still more people, multiply the opportunities for minority
veto (by extending them to more
minorities), and thus make timely
legislative action still more difficult.
The "party reformers" such as Professor James M. Burns, on the other
hand, place their reliance on presidential leadership and urge the
strengthening of the party organization in Congress to insure support by
his own party for the President's
measures. In actuality, however, the
centralization of power within Congress in party committees and leadership bodies would also increase the
power of Congress. It would tend to
reconstitute Congress as an effective
legislative body, deprive the President

of his monopoly of the "national interest," and force him to come to terms
with the centralized congressional
leadership, much as Theodore Roosevelt had to come to terms with Speaker
Cannon. Instead of strengthening
presidential leadership, the proposals
of the party reformers would weaken
it.

The dispersion of power in Congress has created a situation in which
the internal problem of Congress is
not dictatorship but oligarchy. The
only effective alternative to oligarchy
is centralized authority. Oligarchies,
however, are unlikely to reform themselves.... Reform of Congress would
depend upon the central leaders'
breaking with the oligarchy, mobiliz-
ing majorities from younger and less
influential congressmen, and employing these majorities to expand and to
institutionalize their own power.

Centralization of power within
Congress would also, in some measure, help solve the problem of
insulation. Some of Congress's insulation has been defensive in nature, a
compensation for its declining role in
the legislative process as well as a
cause of that decline. Seniority, which
is largely responsible for the insulation, is a symptom of more basic institutional needs and fears. Greater
authority for the central leaders of
Congress would necessarily involve a
modification of the seniority system.
Conversely, in the absence of strong
central leadership, recourse to seniority is virtually inevitable. Election of
committee chairmen by the committees themselves, by party caucuses,
or by each house would stimulate
antagonisms among members and
multiply the opportunities for outside forces from the executive branch
or from interest groups to influence
the proceedings. Selection by seniority is, in effect, selection by heredity:
power goes not to the oldest son of

the king but to the oldest child of the institution. It protects Congress against divisive and external influences. It does this, however, through a purely arbitrary method which offers no assurance that the distribution of authority in the Congress will bear any relation to the distribution of opinion in the country, in the rest of the government, or within Congress itself. It purchases institutional integrity at a high price in terms of institutional isolation. The nineteenth-century assignment of committee positions and chairmanships by the Speaker, on the other hand, permitted flexibility and a balancing of viewpoints from within and without the House. . . . The resumption of this power by the Speaker in the House and its acquisition by the majority leader in the Senate would restore to Congress a more positive role in the legislative process and strengthen it vis-à-vis the executive branch. Paradoxically, however, the most ardent congressional critics of executive power are also the most strenuous opponents of centralized power in Congress.

Congressional insulation may also be weakened in other ways. The decline in mobility between congressional leadership positions and administration leadership positions has been counterbalanced, in some measure, by the rise of the Senate as a source of Presidents. This is due to several causes. The almost insoluble problems confronting state governments tarnish the glamor and limit the tenure of their governors. The nationalization of communications has helped senators play a role in the news media which is exceeded only by the President. In addition, senators, unlike governors, can usually claim some familiarity with the overriding problems of domestic and foreign policy.

Senatorial insulation may also be weakened to the extent that individuals who have made their reputations on the national scene find it feasible and desirable to run for the Senate. . . .

. . . In 1964 Robert Kennedy would probably have been the strongest candidate in any one of a dozen northeastern industrial states.

Recruitment of senators from the national scene rather than from local politics would significantly narrow the gap between Congress and the other elements of national leadership. The "local politics" ladder to the Senate would be replaced or supplemented by a "national politics" line in which mobile individuals might move from the Establishment to the administration to the Senate. This would be one important step toward breaking congressional insulation. The end of insulation, however, would only occur if at a later date these same individuals could freely move back from the Senate to the administration. Mobility between Congress and the administration similar to that which now exists between the establishment and the administration would bring about drastic changes in American politics, not the least of which would be a great increase in the attractiveness of running for Congress. Opening up this possibility, however, depends upon the modification of seniority, and that, in turn, depends upon the centralization of power in Congress.

Adaptation and Reform: Redefining Function

A poltiically easier, although psychologically more difficult, way out of Congress's dilemma involves not the reversal but the intensification of the recent trends of congressional evolution. Congress is in a legislative dilemma because opinion conceives of it as a legislature. If it gave up the effort to play even a delaying role in the legislative process, it could, quite conceivably, play a much more positive and influential role in the political system as a whole. Representative assemblies have not always been legislatures. They had their origins in medieval times as courts and as councils. An assembly need not legislate to exist and to be important. Indeed, some would argue that assemblies should not legislate. "[A] numerous assembly," John Stuart Mill contended, "is as little fitted for the direct business of legislation as for that of administration." [5] Representative assemblies acquired their legislative functions in the 17th and 18th centuries; there is no necessary reason why liberty, democracy, or constitutional government depends upon their exercising those functions in the twentieth century. Legislation has become much too complex politically to be effectively handled by a representative assembly. The primary work of legislation must be done, and increasingly is being done, by the three "houses" of the executive branch: the bureaucracy, the administration, and the President.

Far more important than the preservation of Congress as a legislative institution is the preservation of Congress as an autonomous institution. When the performance of one function becomes "dysfunctional" to the workings of an institution, the sensible course is to abandon it for other functions. In the 1930s the Supreme Court was forced to surrender its function of disallowing national and state social legislation. Since then it has wielded its veto on federal legislation only rarely and with the greatest discretion. This loss of power, however, has been more than compensated for by its new role in protecting civil rights and civil liberties against state action. . . .

The redefinition of Congress's functions away from legislation would involve, in the first instance, a restriction of the power of Congress to delay indefinitely presidential legislative requests. Constitutionally, Congress would still retain its authority to approve legislation. Practically, Congress could, as Walter Lippmann and others have suggested, bind itself to approve or disapprove urgent Presidential proposals within a time limit of, say, three or six months. If thus compelled to choose openly, Congress, it may be supposed, would almost invariably approve presidential requests. Its veto power would become a reserve power like that of the Supreme Court if not like that of the British Crown. On these "urgent" measures it would perform a legitimizing function rather than a legislative function. At the same time, the requirement that Congress pass or reject presidential requests would also presumably induce executive leaders to consult with congressional leaders in drafting such legislation. Congress would also, of course, continue to amend and to vote freely on "non-urgent" executive requests.

Explicit acceptance of the idea that legislation was not its primary function would, in large part, simply be recognition of the direction which change has already been taking. It would legitimize and expand the functions of constituent service and administrative oversight which, in practice, already constitute the principal work of most congressmen. Increasingly isolated as it is from the dominant social forces in society, Congress would capitalize on its position as the representative of the un-

---

[5] John Stuart Mill, "On Representative Government," *Utilitarianism, Liberty, and Representative Government* (London: J. M. Dent), p. 235.

organized interests of individuals. It would become a proponent of popular demands against the bureaucracy rather than the opponent of popular demands for legislation. It would thus continue to play a major although different role in the constitutional system of checks and balances.

A recent survey of the functioning of legislative bodies in forty-one countries concludes that parliaments are in general losing their initiative and power in legislation. At the same time, however, they are gaining power in the "control of government activity." [6] Most legislatures however,

are much less autonomous and powerful than Congress. Congress has lost less power over legislation and gained more power over administration than other parliaments. It is precisely this fact which gives rise to its legislative dilemma. If Congress can generate the leadership and the will to make the drastic changes required to reverse the trends toward insulation, dispersion, and overseeing, it could still resume a positive role in the legislative process. If this is impossible, an alternative path is to abandon the legislative effort and to focus upon those functions of constituent service and bureaucratic control which insulation and dispersion do enable it to play in the national government.

[6] Inter-Parliamentary Union, *Parliaments: A Comparative Study on Structure and Functioning of Representative Institutions in Forty-One Countries* (New York: Frederick A. Praeger, 1963), p. 398.

2

To Move Congress Out of Its Ruts *

HUBERT H. HUMPHREY

How practical are the suggestions put forth by Vice-President Humphrey for Congressional reform? Which of his proposals would alter the current power structure of Congress? Which of the proposed reforms could be achieved quickly?

Most members of Congress are dedicated and conscientious legislators and public servants, aware of the power they hold over the dollars and destiny of the American people

* Hubert H. Humphrey, "To Move Congress Out of Its Ruts," *The New York Times Magazine*, April 7, 1963, pp. 130-31. © 1962/1963 by The New York Times Company. Reprinted by permission of the publisher.

and so many others throughout the world. If they are given extra time— or rather freed from unnecessarily time-consuming duties—they will spend most of it tackling the huge task of informing themselves.

Several steps can be taken to give them that extra time. These are not the final answers to the time problem of members of Congress, but they would help.

First, more joint meetings of congressional committees. A legislative question involving disarmament and arms control, for example, normally requires consideration by the Foreign Relations and Armed Services Committees of the Senate and the House and the Joint Committee on Atomic Energy. Joint meetings would save the time of members serving on more than one of these committees.

Second, more standing joint committees including members of both the House and the Senate. Such committees would save time, particularly toward the end of each congressional session, by paving the way to speedier conference agreements between the Senate and the House on controversial issues.

Third, more efficient scheduling of the work days of Congress. Certain days could be scheduled specifically for floor debate and action by the full House or Senate. Other days could be restricted exclusively for hearings and action by the congressional committees.

In the early months of the session, the full House or Senate would meet only a few days each week. As committees completed their action in the later months of the session, the Senate and House would meet more often. This pattern would save time for members, and end the absurd necessity of members literally running from committee room to Senate or House chamber when issues in which they are involved are up for action at different places at the same time.

Fourth, modification of the "Morning Hour" in the Senate, in which members read miscellaneous speeches of marginal or undated importance and insert various articles into the *Congressional Record.* Instead, members would be permitted to send their "morning hour" speeches and articles to the clerk for insertion in the *Record,* without taking their own time and the time of other senators to read them word-for-word.

Fifth, a requirement in the Senate that members restrict their remarks to the issue formally listed as the business of the Senate. In a debate over agricultural programs, for example, a senator would not be able to spend an hour discussing a totally unrelated subject. This "Rule of Germaneness" now applies only to debate in the House of Representatives.

Sixth, a summer recess of Congress of at least three weeks. This would take time away from legislative duties, but ultimately, I am convinced, would save time. The immediate value would be the opportunity for members of Congress to spend some time with families and constituents in a period (June or July) when schools are closed and citizens are not tied at home because of weather.

The indirect value would be the change of pace and rest such a recess would give to each member. He would return for the final busy weeks of the session refreshed for more efficient performance of his legislative duties. Congressmen are human beings; they get tired and their nerves can become frayed from long months of pressure and hard work. A summer recess would probably reduce the inevitable tensions and bickering so common in the final weeks of congressional sessions.

Seventh, modification and adoption of the British "Question Period," in which administration leaders would report on and answer questions of general importance before the full Senate and House. This would save time, help to keep members of Congress better informed on administration programs and policy and sustain the necessary frequent contact between the Executive and Legislative branches of government.

This final suggestion—and some of the others—would have a valuable side-effect; it would save the time of high administration leaders who have their own crucial problems of too many duties for too few hours.

It is not unusual for the Secretary of State and the Secretary of Defense and other Cabinet officers to give basically the same testimony and answer basically the same questions for several different congressional committees. The Secretary of State, for example, might be called early in the session to outline the foreign aid program—including military aid—to the Senate Committee on Foreign Relations. He will then repeat the same testimony to the Senate Armed Services Committee, and again to the House Armed Services Committee.

The result, I believe, is an excessive demand on the time of these officials. Secretary of State Dean Rusk made 54 personal appearances before congressional committees during the 87th Congress—29 in 1961 and 25 in 1962. Secretary of Defense Robert McNamara spent a total of 203 hours before congressional committees during the 87th Congress—88.75 in 1961 and 114.25 in 1962.

Standing Joint Committees, more joint meetings of committees and a "Question Period" for the full House or Senate would save the time of congressmen and these high officials—and serve to inform all members of Congress more thoroughly.

Another congressional defect which tends to waste time—and to cause confusion and occasional conflict between members—rests with the line-up of Senate and House committees. New problems and programs created by a world transformed by nuclear power and the space age are being handled by a congressional committee system which has changed little in 50 years.

There were two weeks of confusion following introduction of my bill in 1961 to establish a United States Arms Control and Disarmament Agency. This measure was first assigned to the Foreign Relations Committee, then switched to the Government Operations Committee, then back to the Foreign Relations Committee. At one point, it almost went to the Armed Services Committee. (The bill finally remained with Foreign Relations, was approved and signed into law.)

The Communications Satellite Act bounced from committee to committee before it was finally processed and sent to the floor last year. At one time or another, this bill involved the Interstate and Foreign Commerce Committee, the Foreign Relations Committee, the Government Operations Committee, the Space and Astronautics Committee and, of course, the Appropriations Committee.

Is a more up-to-date committee line-up, responsive to modern problems and modern opportunities, needed? I believe it is, and that a thorough review of the present committee and subcommittee line-ups and jurisdictions is necessary.

That review would be one of the prime responsibilities of a "Joint Committee on the Organization of Congress," which would be established by a resolution sponsored by Senator Joseph S. Clark (D., Pa.) and 31 other senators representing both parties. A companion measure in the House agrees that this committee of seven senators and seven representatives should conduct a complete review—the first since 1946—of Congress and produce recommendations for its improvement.

I expect this "Joint Committee on the Organization of Congress" to be established. Its work will be one of the most significant efforts of the 88th

Congress. And its task will be difficult, because there is little popular interest or direct political advantage in the tedious effort for procedural reform within Congress.

But the American people want good government, and sense that the legislative branch has not been performing its functions with the order and effectiveness the nation deserves. The waning weeks of the 87th Congress included fights over such petty issues as what room the Appropriations Conference Committee should meet in, and long delays over minor details of legislation.

Displays of bickering and pettiness tend to obscure the real record of achievement written by recent Congresses and to diminish the respect and confidence of the people in their own representative government. Perhaps the greatest need in Congress today is not so much for studies, procedural changes and committee modernization. It may rather be a more thoroughly responsive attitude by members of Congress, who need to realize that the rules and traditions of Capitol Hill are not sacred, and that the national interest and public service are more important than individual or committee powers and prerogatives.

3

The Prospects for Change *

DAVID B. TRUMAN

How do the ideas in Professor Truman's article square with those advanced by Vice-President Humphrey? What does the author mean when he states "'waste' is after all a relative term . . ."? Comment on the quotation, "The Congress and its power structure cannot profitably be viewed as something separate and isolable from the remainder of the government and the society."

    ❖   ❖   ❖

The Congress today is more nearly a legislature in the strict sense than is the national assembly in any other major country of the world. One may, however, question whether it is in any

* David B. Truman, "The Prospects for Change," *The Congress and America's Future*, ed. David B. Truman, © 1965 by The American Assembly. Reprinted by permission of Prentice-Hall, Inc., Englewood Cliffs, New Jersey.

realistic sense possible, under the technical conditions of an industrialized and interdependent society, for the Congress more fully to exercise the legislative function. The point is raised not in order to propose an answer but rather to introduce the third problem to be confronted in assessing proposals for change, the problem of feasibility: Can it be done?

Discussions of reform frequently are carried on with the unstated assumption that anything is possible, that the question of feasibility is essentially irrelevant. Yet proposals for change that would require major alterations in the Constitution almost certainly are beyond the bounds of feasibility. . . .

＊　　＊　　＊　　＊

Many suggestions for revision, of course, would have no appreciable effect on dispersion, whatever else they might accomplish. In turn, a number of these could be adopted without major difficulty simply because they do not significantly affect the power structure or the political risks of the individual members. In this category would fall most of the suggestions for altering the "workload" of the Congress, such as providing separate days for committee and floor work, delegating to some special tribunal the handling of additional private bills—since 1946 chiefly bills dealing with the immigration and naturalization problems of individuals —and adding to the personal staffs of representatives and senators. They might well lighten the burdens of members, but none of them would touch the power structure at all closely. Some of them would, of course, promote efficiency in the sense that they would save time, but "waste" is after all a relative term, to be measured by what might have been done with what was saved. What appears as a "waste" of time, moreover, may, in a chamber in which power is diffused, be a source of some control by leaders, as the adjournment rush in most legislatures demonstrates.

Also in the neutral category probably should be placed proposals that Congress divest itself of the somewhat anachronistic duty of being the legislature for the District of Columbia. The change would reduce the power

and perquisites of two committees; and it would be at least a symbolic loss for those who fear self-government in a city in which white citizens are not a majority, but the effects on Congress would be slight. Equally nominal, for the Congress, would be a requirement of joint hearings by House and Senate committees. If the change could be made, which is doubtful, some time of administration witnesses would be saved, which would be a gain, but the congressional effects would be insubstantial. Unless it were given power over revenue and appropriations, the creation of a joint committee on fiscal policy would likely go the way of the 1946 reorganization's legislative budget or at best become a vehicle for instruction, such as the Joint Economic Committee. (If it were given such power, which is unlikely, it would become a formidable rival to any other points of control in the Congress.)

Finally, it seems likely that proposals in the realm of congressional "ethics"—chiefly conflict-of-interest and "moonlighting" activities—would have a neutral effect as long as they went no farther than disclosure. They might reduce the utility of some Congressmen to outside interests, and they would tend to increase public respect for the Congress—clearly an advantage, especially if they resulted in eliminating the double standard for the legislative and executive branches —but their power implications would otherwise be slight.

A considerable number of suggestions, especially some that are urged in the name of "democratizing" the House or Senate, would have the effect of further weakening the power of the central "elective" leadership, the Speaker and the floor leaders. Thus the suggestion, recurrent over the years, that the number of signatures required in the House to make effective a petition discharging a committee from further consideration of a bill be reduced from the present 218 to something like 150 would transfer control from one minority to another (and shifting) one equally inaccessible to control by the elective leaders. Similarly, as noted earlier, under a twenty-one-day rule for calling a bill out of the House Rules Committee in which authority so to act were granted to the standing committees, the effect would be to weaken the Speaker's control of the agenda if he "owned" the Rules Committee. In any case it would in this form enhance the powers of the chairmen of the legislative committees.

In both House and Senate several proposed modifications of the seniority rule, however unlikely of adoption, would tend toward further dispersion. For example, caucus election of committee chairmen by secret ballot or the choice of chairmen by majority vote of the committee members would at best give nothing additional to the central leadership and at worst would strengthen the autonomy of chairmen, especially if an incumbent were regularly re-elected.

Further increasing the professional staffs of the standing committees, whatever its benefits in other respects, would tend to strengthen committee autonomy. Similarly, the elimination of remaining jurisdictional ambiguities among committees would, as did the "reforms" of 1946, reduce further the discretion of the elective leaders in both houses.

Finally, the introduction of electronic voting equipment, frequently recommended by outsiders as a time-saver, especially in the House, would strengthen minority control by facilitating snap votes. Further, it probably would take from the central leadership the time it now has during a long roll call to muster max-imum support from the waverers or the negotiators.

A great many devices can be imagined that would directly increase central control from within the House and Senate or do so indirectly by reducing the opportunities for a minority to block or seriously to delay congressional action. These would in varying degrees assault the collective powers of the present oligarchy, and their prospects are therefore correspondingly limited. In a body where risks are individual and localized, decentralized authority is likely to have a broad base of support, especially among those who have been re-elected at least once. Such decentralization puts within a member's reach the means of helping himself politically—an entirely worthy motive—and it is the more attractive because he cannot clearly see the capacity of any central leadership, in or out of Congress, to do the equivalent for him. A successful assault, therefore, would require a crisis severe enough to isolate the members of the oligarchy and to solidify the rank and file around central leaders willing to spearhead a serious shake-up.

The most promising, though not necessarily feasible, means all would have one feature in common, namely, increased leadership control of the timetable, not only in the chambers, but also in the committees. In the Senate a simpler and more easily invoked rule for limiting debate than the present two-thirds of those present and voting would control the most serious and most notorious threat to the timetable in that chamber, the filibuster. In the House a reinstituted twenty-one-day rule, but one that placed the authority to call up a bill blockaded by the Rules Committee in the hands of the Speaker or the majority leader, would strengthen the position of at least the Democratic leaders in the chamber.

In both houses some alternatives to or modifications in the seniority rule would aid the leaders in relation to the committees and in the chambers generally. A return to the practice under which the Speaker designated committee chairmen in the House and a granting of comparable power to the majority leader in the Senate would of course contribute to centralized control. The circumstances that would have to exist in order to make such a change possible, moreover, would assure use of the power, at least for several years. The less drastic proposal for caucus election of chairman from among the three most senior members of a committee would have the same tendency only if the Speaker and majority leader were able and willing to make their preferences prevail. If they were not, the result would be a reinforcement of dispersion.

A striking fact about the Congress in this century is that most, if not all, of those developments that have tended toward reducing or restraining the dispersion of power in the separate houses and in the Congress as a whole have come from outside the legislature and chiefly from the White House. In some instances the Congress has been formally a partner in the changes, where legislation has provided the occasion for them, and in some instances not. But in either case, the anti-dispersion effects have been secondary, and largely unintended, consequences of lines of action taken by the President primarily to discharge his own responsibilities and to meet the needs of his role.

Thus the Budget and Accounting Act of 1921, which established the executive budget in pursuit of the goal of fiscal efficiency, created for the first time a government-wide fiscal program and gave the President responsi-

bility for its formulation and, equally important, its public presentation. The act did not achieve quite the integration of the appropriating and revenue activities in the Congress that some sponsors hoped for, but it did lead to the setting of rational, if not inflexible, proportions in expenditure. In the course of time, moreover, it created something of a counterbalance to the agency-committee relation that could be useful in as well as outside the Congress. The Employment Act of 1946, though it created no comparable operating functions, placed on the President the responsibility for developing and pronouncing the requirements of the economy as a whole and the government's part in meeting them. Although little more than an agenda-setting device, it is at least that and as such is a check on complete committee freedom in setting the congressional program.

Alongside and reinforcing these formal and legislatively created activities, at least three less conspicuous practices have developed since the 1930s. In the first place, the President's legislative program, as Neustadt has demonstrated . . . developed from the needs of a succession of chief executives, but it acquired vigor and, in all probability, permanence because it also met the needs of others—the agencies and, more important, the Congress, including its committees. It has provided the latter with not merely a "laundry-list" but a set of priorities. Its priority-setting qualities, moreover, have been strengthened in consequence of the increased and continuing prominence of foreign policy-national security problems. Presidential priorities are not coincident with congressional ones, but in these areas limits have grown up around committee autonomy and hence around congressional disjunction.

In the second place, as a likely consequence of the President's stake in his program, the growth of a White House staff specialized in legislative liaison has introduced an element of coherence and coordination into congressional deliberations, especially at the committee stage. Again, although it has been little studied, one suspects that its viability depends not merely on presidential desire but also in its utility in *general*, and not necessarily for identical reasons, to committee chairmen, to elective leaders, and even to some agencies. It clearly is not and cannot be a legislative high command, but it seems to have acquired informational and secondary influence capabilities that are centripetal in tendency.

Thirdly, the now well-established practice of regular presidential consultation with his party's principal elective leaders in the Congress works in the same direction. Like the two developments already mentioned, it was initially an outgrowth of presidential needs, but apparently it also has utility for elective leaders, especially if they head a nominal majority in Congress. Particularly if these leaders in name see themselves potentially as leaders in fact—and they need not do so—their relations with the President seem useful. The President's program and priorities are not necessarily theirs, and they do not, if they are prudent, attempt to operate simply as his lieutenants. But they may share with him the handicaps of power dispersion in the Congress, and their collaboration with him may—again if they see themselves as more than the servants of the congressional oligarchy—place limits on its effects, to their joint advantage.

A possible implication of these developments for the further restriction of dispersion is that they may offer something of a pattern for the future. Needs in the Presidency, if they are at least consistent with needs in Congress

and among its central leaders, may lead to new practices whose consequence, in all likelihood unintended, could be some further limit on the dispersion of power. One such need, as yet not clearly felt, is suggested by Neustadt . . . in his discussion of the common stakes of elective politicians against career officials.

A next step, though it would be a long and difficult one, might be, as Walter Lippmann and Huntington . . . have suggested, toward a commitment in Congress to bring to a vote, at least by mid-session, any legislation carrying top priority from the administration. The prospect of such a commitment would require more care in the construction of the President's program, since some means would be needed explicitly to distinguish urgent needs from trial balloons, and the invidious judgments that this would require might be too costly politically. It also would require a collegial commitment from the congressional oligarchy that might prove impossible of achievement. But the attempt would at least follow logically from the trends of several decades.

Prospects of strengthening central leadership through jointly acceptable leverage from outside Congress have at least the semblance of feasibility, and not only because of the developments already identified. Evidence suggests that reforms that would rest largely on the initiative of the Congress itself do not command requisite majorities. For example, a random sample of the House in 1963 found a majority supporting only fourteen of thirty-two specific proposals of reform. Of the proposals enjoying such support, only two were ones likely to be of major consequence—reinstatement of the twenty-one-day rule and a four-year term for representatives (which senators certainly would not favor).

The remainder . . . appealed only to a minority.[1]

Whether or not outside leverage leads to a reduction in dispersion, the examples discussed here underscore a

central point: The Congress and its power structure cannot profitably be viewed as something separate and isolable from the remainder of the government and the society. They affect and are affected by needs and changes in the society, and in the government as a whole. They must, therefore, be looked at within this context.

---

[1] Michael O'Leary, ed., *Congressional Reorganization: Problems and Prospects* (Hanover, N.H., 1964), pp. 18-21, 58-63.

4

The Congressional Establishment *

SENATOR JOSEPH S. CLARK

What relationships does Senator Clark see between the American and Congressional Establishments? Who belongs to the Congressional Establishment? Does the Congressional Establishment always win? Why or why not?

An intelligent reader's guide to the Congressional Establishment must begin with a definition of the ruling clique in both Houses. Richard Rovere, one of the ablest Washington correspondents, defines "The American Establishment" as "a more or less closed and self-sustaining institution that holds a preponderance of power in our more or less open society." [1] His definition, applied to the more limited Congressional field, remains accurate.

The two Establishments, American and Congressional, have much in common. For example, the members of each constantly deny there is such a

thing. In both cases experts disagree on exactly what the Establishment is and how it works; but, as Mr. Rovere points out, they disagree also about the Kingdom of God—which doesn't prove *it* doesn't exist. Within both Establishments there is a good deal of tolerance for doctrinal divergence so long as the members stand solidly together when the chips are down and the Establishment's power, prestige and prerogatives are under attack.

John Kenneth Galbraith aptly defined members of any Establishment as "the pivotal people." Most writers on the subject, including the present one, exclude themselves when defining the Establishment and even consider themselves its victims. Douglas Dillon and John McCloy are the prototypes of Mr. Rovere's American Establishment. Richard Russell and Judge Howard Smith are patriarchs of the Congressional Establishment.

---

* Senator Joseph S. Clark, *Congress: The Sapless Branch* rev. ed. (New York: Harper and Row, Publishers, 1965), pp. 111-15. © 1964 by Joseph S. Clark. Reprinted by permission of the publisher.

[1] Richard H. Rovere, *The American Establishment* (New York: Harcourt, Brace & World, Inc., 1962).

The Congressional Establishment is organized in the same easygoing way as its broader national big brother. There are no written bylaws, no conventions, no overt determination of a program. The essential difference is that the Congressional Establishment defends the status quo and views majority rule with distaste, while the American Establishment is content to abide by the principles of democracy along the more liberal lines suggested by the editorial page of its house organ, the *New York Times*.

Within broad limits and subject to some exceptions the Congressional Establishment consists of those Democratic chairmen and ranking Republican members of the important legislative committees who, through seniority and pressures exerted on junior colleagues, control the institutional machinery of Congress. They use this control to prevent a fair hearing and a vote on the merits of the President's program. The official "leadership" group of the Congress—Speaker of the House, Senate Majority Leader, *et al.*—are usually captives of the Establishment, although they can sometimes be found looking out over the walls of their prison, plotting escape.

The Establishment does not always win. It frequently does not use all the parliamentary tools which are available to it. In the Senate it has lost strength consistently since the election of 1958. Its members, almost without exception, are charming and amiable gentlemen, popular with their colleagues, who sincerely believe that the safety of the Republic depends on defeating the "dangerous innovations" in our social life and political economy which are constantly being proposed by the President of the United States.

It is important to note that the views of the Congressional Establishment are not shared by a majority of their own colleagues, who, left to their own devices, would be prepared to bring the Congress into line to cope with the necessities of our times.

In an earlier work I described the Senate Establishment as "almost the antithesis of democracy. It is not selected by any democratic process. It appears to be quite unresponsive to the caucuses of the two parties, be they Democratic or Republican. It is what might be called a self-perpetuating oligarchy with mild, but only mild, overtones of plutocracy." [2]

There are plenty of rich men in the Senate, but only a few of them are high in the ranks of the Establishment; and none of them would admit to a belief that the accumulation of great wealth is a principal object of life. This is another distinction between the American and the Congressional Establishments. The former has, despite its slightly liberal orientation, definite overtones of plutocracy, although its tolerance is much more for inherited than for recently acquired wealth.

The bonds which hold the Congressional Establishment together are: white supremacy; a stronger devotion to property than to human rights; support of the military establishment; belligerence in foreign affairs; and a determination to prevent Congressional reform. The high-water marks of the Senatorial Establishment in 1963 were the two votes on limiting debate in the Senate in order to change the filibuster rule. In response to a question posed by the Vice President, "Does the Senate have the right, notwithstanding its rules, to terminate debate at the beginning of a new Congress by majority vote in order to pass upon a change in its rules?" there were 44 ayes and 53 nays. The Establish-

---

[2] Joseph S. Clark, *The Senate Establishment* (New York: Hill and Wang, 1963), p. 22.

ment, knowing it had finally rallied enough votes to assure a negative result, permitted a vote on January 21 after a desultory filibuster lasting nine days. On February 7 a cloture petition which would have cut off further debate on the proposed changes in Rule XXII and which required a favorable vote of two-thirds of those present was lost 54-42. Including the announced position of the four absentees, the Senate stood 56-44 in favor of limiting debate (and therefore almost certainly in favor of a more liberal rule of terminating debate), nine short of the necessary two-thirds. But the majority did not prevail.

A low-water mark of the Establishment was the Test Ban Treaty, which came to a vote on September 24, 1963, after more than a month of desultory debate. Under the Constitution two-thirds of those present and voting were required for ratification. The affirmative vote was 80-19. The hard core of the Establishment with the exception of Senator Mundt voted "no."

The most crushing defeat ever suffered by the Establishment was when cloture was applied to the Civil Rights Bill on June 10, 1964, by a vote of 71 to 29.

A typical Establishment line-up occurred on the Mundt bill to block the sale of wheat to Russia (by prohibiting the Export-Import Bank from guaranteeing loans to finance the sales) when all but two of the "anti-test ban" Senators supported Senator Mundt and opposed Presidents Kennedy and Johnson—the vote was on November 26, 1963—in their attempt to further relax the tensions of the Cold War. The Mundt proposal was tabled by a vote of 57 to 35.

Every member of the Senate, except one, Senator Lausche, who voted against the Test Ban Treaty, also voted

Democrats	Rules Change and Closure thereon	Test Ban Treaty	Wheat Sale to Russia	Cloture on Civil Rights	Reappor tionmen
Russell of Georgia	no	no	no	no	no
Stennis of Mississippi	no	no	no	no	no
Eastland of Mississippi	no	no	no	no	no
Long of Louisiana	no	no	yes	no	no
Byrd of Virginia	no	no	no	no	no
Byrd of West Virginia	no	no	yes	no	no
Robertson of Virginia	no	no	no	no	no
Talmadge of Georgia	no	no	no	no	no
McClellan of Arkansas	no	no	no	no	no
Thurmond of South Carolina *	no	no	no	no	no
Republicans					
Curtis of Nebraska	no	no	no	yes	no
Goldwater of Arizona	no	no	no	no	no
Mundt of South Dakota	no	yes	no	yes	no
Simpson of Wyoming	no	no	no	no	no
Jordan of Idaho	no	no	no	yes	no
Smith of Maine	no	no	no	yes	yes
Bennett of Utah	no	no	no	no	no
Tower of Texas	no	no	no	no	no

* Senator Thurmond became a Republican in the fall of 1964.

n the negative on the question posed by the Vice President regarding the ight of the Senate to change its rules, and on the motion for cloture on rules change. The eighteen Senators listed on the following page represent the hard core of the Establishment and its loyal followers.

Note the absence on this list of several staunch card-carrying members of the Establishment: Ellender of Louisiana, Hayden of Arizona, Holland of Florida, Johnston of South Carolina, Hill and Sparkman of Alabama, Can-

non of Nevada; and on the Republican side Cotton of New Hampshire, Williams of Delaware, Mundt of South Dakota and Dirksen of Illinois. They all voted *against* cloture but *for* the Test Ban Treaty. Note also that, unlike Wilson's "twelve willful men" in 1917, the hard core of the Establishment did not utilize the filibuster to prevent a vote on the treaty or on the wheat deal. It seems clear that it is only in opposition to Congressional reform and civil rights that the Establishment will play all its cards. . . .

5

Who Belongs to the Senate's Inner Club *

CLAYTON FRITCHEY

How do you account for the fact that the Senate rather than the House is known for its "inner club"? What are the qualifications for membership? How influential is the "club"?

Nearly all Washingtonians as well as many citizens elsewhere know about the Club (that sovereign Inner Club of the U.S. Senate), but nobody knows who belongs to it. This column is intended to correct that strange and long-enduring oversight.

There is a growing tendency to refer to the Club as the Establishment, or the latter perhaps describes more precisely the increasingly tenuous nature of the group. But by either name

* Clayton Fritchey, "Who Belongs to the Senate's Inner Club," *Harpers Magazine*, May, 1967, pp. 104, 106, 108. Copyright © 1967, by Harper's Magazine, Inc. Reprinted by permission of the author.

it remains a unique force, difficult to define, and even more difficult to identify in terms of individual Senators. It is not always seen; it often is not heard—but the Captial knows it is there; and, without much fuss, it functions when it counts.

Yet after all these years it remains as mysterious as ever. It is a Club without a clubhouse; there are no directors and no membership lists. There are no meetings and no minutes. It casts blackballs, but even Senators themselves can't explain how, when, or where. There is only one feature on which all agree: the "President" of the Club is Senator

Richard Russell (Democrat, Georgia),* chairman of the powerful Armed Services Committee, which presides over the vast Defense Department, also an establishment but of another kind.

Some Senators think the Club collectively can be described in a sentence. One said to me, "Get out the *Congressional Directory* and look up the chairmen of the standing committees. That's the Club." Another said, "Go look up the Appropriations Committee. They're all there." Still another said. "The simplest way to go about this is just to get up a list of those who support the oil-depletion allowance." There is much to be said for all these characterizations, but they still don't provide a satisfactory definition.

Who Is In?

Broadly, the Senate may be divided into four groups: (1) members of the Inner Club; (2) potential or would-be members; (3) non-members; and (4) anti-members. In trying to determine which Senators fit into each category, I sought the views of a cross section of Senators and their wives, as well as the opinions of Senate staff workers, lobbyists, newspaper correspondents who cover the Hill, and Administration people. It turned out to be possible to draw up a list on which there was general agreement, although, of course, with shadings and reservations.

First come the relatively small number of full-fledged members. In alphabetical order (with Republicans in italics) they are:

Clinton Anderson	New Mexico
Alan Bible	Nevada
Robert C. Byrd	West Virginia

Howard Cannon	Nevada
Everett Dirksen	Illinois
Allen Ellender	Louisiana
Sam J. Ervin, Jr.	North Carolina
Carl Hayden	Arizona
Bourke Hickenlooper	Iowa
Lister Hill	Alabama
Spessard Holland	Florida
Roman L. Hruska	Nebraska
Henry M. Jackson	Washington
B. Everett Jordan	North Carolina
Russell Long	Louisiana
Warren Magnuson	Washington
Mike Mansfield	Montana
John L. McClellan	Arkansas
Thruston Morton	Kentucky
Karl E. Mundt	South Dakota
Edmund Muskie	Maine
John Pastore	Rhode Island
Richard B. Russell	Georgia
George Smathers	Florida
John Sparkman	Alabama
John Stennis	Mississippi
Stuart Symington	Missouri

This list includes the Minority Leader (Dirksen), the Majority Leader (Mansfield), the Assistant Majority Leader (Long), and—a newcomer—Robert Byrd, who has been promoted to the No. 3 slot in the Democratic hierarchy. Some of those polled had reservations on Symington and Sparkman because both once had outside ambitions: one was a candidate for the Democratic Presidential nomination and the other was Stevenson's running mate in 1952. Also they are often more independent than some of their colleagues, but the consensus was that they should be included. Thus, the inner-core group totals 27, of which 22 are Democrats and 12 are from the South.

The remaining members of the Club might be described as half or three-quarters fledged: they belong but are not charter members, so to speak, because of limited seniority or, more often, because they seem a little "different" and are sometimes given to ge-

* See "Russell of Georgia: The Old Guard at Its Shrewdest," by Douglas Kiker (*Harper's,* September 1966).

ing off on their own. This list is composed of:

George Aiken	Vermont
Gordon Allott	Colorado
Frank Carlson	Kansas
Norris Cotton	New Hampshire
James Eastland	Mississippi
Thomas H. Kuchel	California
Mike Monroney	Oklahoma
Joseph M. Montoya	New Mexico
Gaylord Nelson	Wisconsin
Jennings Randolph	West Virginia
Abraham Ribicoff	Connecticut
Hugh Scott	Pennsylvania
Herman E. Talmadge	Georgia
Milton R. Young	North Dakota

Some of those polled thought Eastland should be listed as a full-fledged member because he is chairman of the Judiciary Committee, but others felt he was too often an embarrassment to the Senate. The total for this group is 14, seven of them Democrats, and two from the South. Thus the total membership of the Club is 41, dividing as 29 Democrats (14 from the South) and 12 Republicans.

Not yet in the Club but possibly on the way to membership are these potentials:

E. L. Bartlett	Alaska
Birch Bayh	Indiana
Daniel B. Brewster	Maryland
Harry F. Byrd, Jr.	Virginia
Fred R. Harris	Oklahoma
Daniel K. Inouye	Hawaii
Gale W. McGee	Wyoming
Lee Metcalf	Montana
Walter F. Mondale	Minnesota
George Murphy	California
Joseph Tydings	Maryland
Harrison Williams, Jr.	New Jersey

Who Is Out?

In the non-member group there are some who would like to belong, and a few who couldn't be dragged in, but most of them simply have other fish

to fry. They get along well enough with the Establishment, and are generally well liked in return, but prefer to pursue independent lines of their own. Republicans John Sherman Cooper (Kentucky), Clifford Case (New Jersey), Jacob Javits (New York), and Democrats Claiborne Pell (Rhode Island), Frank Church (Idaho), Albert Gore (Tennessee), Philip Hart (Michigian), Vance Hartke (Indiana), Eugene McCarthy (Minnesota), William Proxmire (Wisconsin), and Ralph Yarborough (Texas) are notable examples of the Senators in this category. Another would be Joseph S. Clark (Pennsylvania Democrat), but his is a special case. The non-member group also includes all the new Senators elected last fall, as well as most of the first-termers. They simply aren't eligible yet.

The Kennedy brothers are, of course, also a special case. They are involved in a super fish fry, as was brother Jack. On his own, the amiable Teddy might some day have become at least a fringe member of the Club, but he is associated with Robert F., who, like John F., is the archetype of the national kind of politician that the Club regards with suspicion. It believes (correctly) that the Kennedy family has always looked on the Senate as a means to an end, but not an end in itself.

And then there are a few very outspoken Senators like Wayne Morse (Oregon), Stephen Young (Ohio), and Ernest Gruening (Alaska), three Democrats who don't care a bit whether the Club keeps or not. They seem to be wholly indifferent to what the Institution thinks or feels about them. And finally there is the singular case of Senator J. W. Fulbright (Arkansas Democrat), a remarkable example of how a Senator can have nearly all the attributes of a full-fledged charter member, and yet not belong. He is a Southerner, he has great seniority, he is the chairman of the august Foreign Relations Committee; moreover, he is often an economic conservative, and he has voted with the segregationists. Finally, he is a staunch supporter of the filibuster, and has the distinction of having been called an "overeducated SOB" by Harry Truman. Not even the pillars of the Club can top those credentials. But in the final analysis Fulbright is an individualist and a thinker. His reputation rests not on his seniority but on such contributions as the Fulbright Resolution, the Fulbright Scholarships, and the Fulbright scrutiny of Vietnam. His intellectualism alone alienates him from the Club, and makes him suspect. It is possible the Senator might once have cared about this, but it is quite clear these days that all he presently cares about is trying to make the country and, if possible, the Senate give serious thought to war and peace.

What the Club Does

For decades the Club's principal achievement, if it can be called that, has been putting various Presidents in their place, chiefly liberal ones like Franklin Roosevelt and Harry Truman. It didn't have to do this to the modest Eisenhower, for he knew his place and kept it. When young John F. Kennedy left the Senate (where he had never been a member of the Inner Club) and went to the White House he learned more about the power of this group than when he had his office on the Hill. The New Frontier's legislation simply withered on the Club's vines.

The recent notion that the Club itself had begun to wither was based on three developments which occurred more or less simultaneously. First, a super member of the Club (Lyndon Johnson) suddenly became

President, and so for a time enjoyed an indulgence on the Hill that is seldom granted Chief Executives. Then the Democratic landslide of 1964 enhanced the ranks of the nonmembers, and, finally, death, defeat, and retirement eliminated some of the Club's charter members, including such stalwarts as Byrd and Robertson of Virginia, and Saltonstall of Massachusetts. Yet the legislative record of 1966 and the opening maneuvers of 1967 demonstrate that the flag of this peculiar Establishment still waves.

Aside from its quiet satisfaction in squelching activist Presidents, the influence of the Club is mainly felt on important (sometimes all-important) matters affecting the Senate as an institution. The true member never permits ideology, party loyalty, or even personal conviction to supersede his dedication to promoting the Senate's primacy in the American constitutional system, whether the Constitution calls for it or not.

The Constitution, for instance, provides that most legislation shall be passed by majority vote, but the Senate amended that, in effect, by inventing the filibuster, which makes it necessary to get a two-thirds vote whenever the Club so chooses. Few Presidents have been able to overcome that obstacle. A classic and revealing example of how the Inner Club operates is provided by the struggle this year over changing Rule 22, which requires a two-thirds vote to shut off unlimited debate. Last year the civil-rights act of 1966 would easily have passed if it had not been filibustered to death. There was a clear majority for it, but not two-thirds for closure of debate.

When the 90th Congress convened in January it was apparent that new legislation on civil rights and labor would again be defeated in the same way later on in the session if Rule 22 was not changed so that closure could be invoked by less than a two-thirds vote. The liberal leaders thought they had a definite majority for modifying the rule, but in the showdown they lost badly. The Majority Leader, Senator Mansfield, and the Minority Leader, Senator Dirksen, speaking for the Club, simply argued that a vote for the proposed change was a vote against the Senate. The implication was that a member who supported the change was no better than a traitor to the Institution. This was pretty intimidating for new and junior Senators who hope in time to become members of the Inner Club themselves. It also put on the spot Senators who are not members but like to remain on good terms with the Inner Group. In any case, the effect was devastating. Thirteen Senators defected from the liberal ranks, although nearly all of the thirteen will probably vote later on for the civil-rights legislation that was doomed by their failure to help modify Rule 22. In short, when they had to choose between loyalty to their ideological convictions and loyalty to the Senate (as defined by the Club) they saluted the latter.

Another illuminating example this year of how the Club unobtrusively asserts itself is the momentary resolution of the long fight over broadening and tightening Senate supervision of the Central Intelligence Agency. A majority has been in favor of this for years (especially since the Bay of Pigs and U-2 fiascoes and the disclosure this February of CIA's links with students and other "private" organizations), but it has been opposed by Senator Russell, the "president" of the Club. Russell is the informal head of an informal group of Senators and Representatives who have been acting as so-called watchdogs over the CIA, but without notable results. Nevertheless, Russell has successfully resisted all efforts to establish a new standing committee

(like the Joint Atomic Energy Committee) to oversee the CIA. Last year when Senator Fulbright and a majority of the Foreign Relations Committee recommended broader supervision, Russell accused them of trying to "muscle in" on his authority. The fight was taken to the floor of the Senate (although behind closed doors) and Russell won hands down. He did not argue the merits of the case. Again it was put on the basis of loyalty to the Institution and its way of doing things. Thus, a vote against Russell was transformed into a vote against the Club, and once more a number of Senators were willing to subordinate their convictions on the real issue rather than go against the Establishment.

Having publicly put his challengers in their place, Senator Russell has now moved to head off renewed agitation at this session by quietly inviting three members of the Foreign Relations Committee to sit in on meetings of his private watchdog group. Besides Fulbright, he invited Senators Mansfield and Hickenlooper, both members of the Club. The presence of Fulbright will help some, so the concession is better than nothing but it is no substitute for the kind of systematic supervision of the CIA that is needed. Nevertheless, the president of the Club has prevailed for the time being.

Still another revealing instance of the Club at work occurred when Senator Joseph Clark sought election as secretary of the Democratic Senate Conference, a post that ranks No. 3, just back of Majority Leader Mansfield and the Assistant Majority Leader, Senator Long, another member of the Inner Club. Clark is a constructive, creative Senator, but above all he is independent, and has not even hesitated to question publicly the rules (both written and unwritten) of the Senate. So it was perhaps foolish of him to aspire to the hierarchy, but he thought he had enough support to win and thus went ahead. If he ever had the votes, they melted away when the Club turned thumbs down on his candidacy. As if to rub it in, they elected Senator Robert Byrd of West Virginia, who is anathema to most liberals because he is a former organizer for the Ku Klux Klan and a consistent opponent of civil-rights legislation. As a member of the Club he is on the fringe, but as against Clark that was good enough. So now the Club occupies all three of the leadership positions on the Democratic side.

Qualifications for Membership

Since there is unanimous agreement that Russell is the quintessential Senator, perhaps the simplest way to describe a full-fledged member of the Club is to describe *him,* although few others of the Inner Group have all of his characteristics. Russell has immense seniority, he is the chairman of a potent committee, he is a Southerner. That's a big start, but still only a start. Personally, he is courtly and unostentatious; his word is good; he lives and lets live; his dignity is both seen and felt. All of these qualities are important, too, but not always necessary for admission. The critical requirement that he fulfills so grandly—the *sine qua non* for real membership—is a lifetime of never putting anything ahead of the Senate. There was a very fleeting apostasy in 1952 when for a few weeks he reached out for the Democratic Presidential nomination that went to Adlai Stevenson. His fellow members correctly sensed this was only a brief aberration. Never before or since has his personal ambition exceeded the ambience of the Senate. He is the Great Conformer, the Guardian of the Institution's traditions (bad, good, or indifferent), the exemplar of non-free-wheeling. He is little known to the national public (a matter of indifference to him) and there is little in the way of positive achievement to show for his 33 years in the Senate—but that does not reduce his stature within the Institution. In the eyes of many Senators he stands for something bigger the Senate itself. The reason so many non-members often go along with the Club is that they realize their own importance derives from the importance the Club has managed to give the Senate over the years. After all, the U. S. Senate is the only upper body in the world of any significance: it has not only preserved its constitutional powers, but magnified them by standing together in asserting privilege and restraining the executive branch. The chief basis of this is the seniority system, which automatically prevent Presidents from playing off Senator against each other in the struggle for power. While numerous non-member including liberals, often deplore the conservative, obstructionist nature of the Club, they secretly enjoy the prestige and perquisites which they have inherited because of the Club's relentless pursuit of power over the years. That's why some of the Senators who voted for changing Rule 22 were privately glad the filibuster was preserved This is the ultimate weapon—the power to wring great tribute and concessions from the Administration—an Administration. No other upper house in the world can do it.

Now, if examining Russell is one clue to the Club, another, in reverse would be a brief look at John F. Kennedy before he became President. He was in Congress fourteen years, including election to two terms in the Senate, but he was never at any time a member of the Club. It was quite clear to his colleagues from the first that he was not going to spend a life time gradually working his way up in the Senate by dutifully adhering to the Club rules of self-effacement, routine chores, routine thoughts, and cultivation of his elders. He was bent on a national constituency from the outset, and that alone disbarred him from the inner circle. Kennedy couldn't have cared less. He was told he would need his old colleagues if he ever got to be President, but he was already sophisticated enough to perceive that the Club generally will not even play ball with a former member except on its own terms. Lyndon Johnson can confirm this assessment. He and others can also testify that, while the power and prestige of the Club may not be quite as pervasive as in the past, the opening months of the 90th Congress show that it is still very much in business.

6

*Power in the House**

CLEM MILLER

The late Congressman Clem Miller wrote a series of letters to a group of friends in which he conveyed some of his impressions and personal observations of Congress at work. These letters have since been published in a book entitled Member of the House, *from which the following letter is taken.*

What popular ideas on the way in which a bill becomes a law are challenged in this letter? Who sets voting lines? How powerful are individual Congressmen in determining the fate of a bill?

Dear Friend:

In recent weeks we have been talking about the locus of congressional power. Let us now relate it to the Floor of the House. Previously, we have seen that as an issue mounts in importance, ability to influence on the Floor of the House lessens.

We have also seen that debate changes few votes. Now let us consider how votes *are* changed. Members do change the votes of other Members and Members do switch from vote to vote. This is done on a personal basis. But shifts of this kind seldom change a final result. Final results are almost always changed only by a hierarchic shift. Even in these instances, substantial hierarchic changes can be made without immediately altering the final result. For example, the South is shifting from a pro-mutual security position to one opposed. There was a shift of thirty-four votes between 1958 and 1959. However, the influx of northern Democrats cancelled the effect this shift might otherwise have had.

Now, to understand the manner in which an individual might be induced

* Clem Miller, *Member of the House,* ed. John W. Baker (New York: Charles Scribner's Sons, 1962), pp. 107-109. Copyright © Charles Scribner's Sons. Reprinted by permission of the publisher.

to change his vote, let us first examine the seating arrangements in the House Chamber. Republicans arrange themselves on the Speaker's left, Democrats on his right. Attendance is a chancy affair. Democrats outnumber Republicans generally, but the latter are there when they have to be.

There are no assigned seats in the Chamber. There are characteristic groupings. Illinois always sits in a back corner. Massachusetts has a steady little knot in the center aisle. The southerners arrange themselves in a boot-shaped group behind the majority tables. Kentucky is a solid row, center aisle. And immediately behind them sit Brock and McGinley of Nebraska in what you might call the left-field bleachers. Connecticut sits together but the place changes from day to day. I could go blindfolded to the seats many Members habitually sit in. Others stand behind the rail, in the rear. Others stand along the sides, and never sit at all. Others walk in one door to respond to their names at roll calls and immediately exit by another. Others inhabit the cloakroom.

Then there are the floaters, going from group to group, taking soundings, reporting rumors. "How are you going to vote on the _____ Bill?" The floaters link the sub-blocs to establish a consensus.

Let's see how this works out in practice. Let us refer to a bill relatively devoid of party overtones—for example, the Auto Safety Bill. Some representatives seemed to be against it because it might cost some money in the Department of Commerce. Other congressmen were for it because it promised to save lives, and thus, they argued, would save money in the long run. But by and large, there was doubt and hesitation. Everywhere the call was, "How are you going to vote?" State delegations sent representatives around to do private polling. No one

appeared to be following the debate. There was banter back and forth. "Are you against *saving lives*?" "What are you, a *spender*?" Little knots of conversation, much of its seeming idle or irrelevant, actually signified a working out of opinions. The roll begins, "Abbitt, Abernathy, Adair, Addonizio . . ." Some wait for bellwethers. They pass over the first call, listening for key votes.

I saw one influential Democrat listening to a friend who wants him to vote "no." He does so. Then, later, he taps another friend on the shoulder. "How'd you vote?" The other friend voted for it. Sheepishly, and amid some kidding, "influential" gets up at the call's end to change his vote. A small incident, but this is the working out of power. "Another friend" had power because he was consulted by one with power.

The most interesting roll call of the session, in my mind, was on the so-called Vault Cash Bill. This was designed, among other things, to lower reserves of Federal Reserve member banks. It was regarded as a giveaway of billions by some. To others, it constituted a small but significant addition to inflation. To most, it was a confusing bill, almost incomprehensible and not very significant.

Some Members asked friends, "Is it a giveaway?" "No, but . . ." The floaters scurried back and forth. At the end, in frustrated confusion, many Members went with the committee chairman who had reported the bill favorably. The fact that it gave advantages to banks stirred the embers of the old Populist sentiment and fanned the sparks of a young group. These congressmen were aroused and they were convinced on a personal basis. The leadership of the committee chairman was not persuasive to them. However, the tradition of following the chairman was strong enough to hold a maority to his side, so the revolt failed.

What may be learned from these examples is that voting lines are set by the committee chairmen (and by each committee's senior minority member) and hence by the Leadership; that generally this is sufficient to carry the day; and finally, that individuals may shift back and forth within this framework in response to personal appeals and deeply ingrained prejudices. The total effect is a series of decisions inspired by committee leaders, but lacking coordinated, overall policy direction.

Very sincerely,

Clem Miller

CHAPTER ELEVEN

The Supreme Court:
Supreme in What?

The United States Supreme Court puzzles not only foreigners but Ameri-cans as well. Its combination of powers and functions is one source of con-fusion, the limits of its power another. In one sense the Court can do so much yet in another sense it can do very little. And a clear picture of this situation is difficult even for lawyers to understand, because, as we shall see, the Court is a legal institution but not merely a legal body.

The Court can only hear cases—that is, issues must come before them in the form of arguments between two individuals or groups of individuals where one party genuinely claims something from the other. The something at issue may be, but doesn't have to be, monetarily valuable; one of the parties may want to imprison the other or interfere with what is claimed as the other one's freedom of religion, for example. (This limits what the Court can do right there, for it cannot create cases from whole cloth.)

Controversies may reach the Supreme Court on appeal from decisions of lower federal courts and (through these courts) from federal administrative de-cisions. The second great stream of cases comes directly from the highest state court having jurisdiction (not necessarily the state supreme court) in cases where a right is claimed under the federal Constitution or a federal law or a treaty of the United States. This, of course, means that most state cases cannot be appealed to the Supreme Court; only a very small number involve a federal right. It also means that very often the Supreme Court does not review the whole case involved but only that part of the controversy dealing with the federal right. There are a few cases that start right in the Supreme Court cases involving ambassadors and suits between states, but these are comparatively unimportant most of the time.

The important thing to remember in these cases that come up on appeal is that the Court can pretty well decide whether it wants to hear a case. Over three-quarters of the cases yearly come up by grant of the writ of *certiorari*, which is just a Latin way of saying the Court wants to hear the case and is ordering the lower court to send up the record. The judges must rule on a number of other cases, usually about 15 per cent of their total, where, for example, a state court rules a federal law unconstitutional or upholds its own law against a claim that it violates the federal Constitution. This is to keep the laws in the various states as uniform as possible. Even in these cases, however, the Court may reach a decision after a fairly cursory examination of the issue, and so keep a large measure of control over its docket.

What makes the United States Supreme Court the most important court in the world? It is the fact that: (1) it has all of the powers that most high courts have to overrule the lower courts of the same judicial system; (2) it has many powers of review over federal administrative agencies; (3) it has power to interpret the words of Congress subject, of course, to "correction" of this interpretation by Congress; (4) it has the power to interpret the Constitution subject only to correction by the very difficult method of amendment; (5) it has the power exercised successfully at least since 1803 and *Marbury v. Madison* to declare congressional and presidential actions out of bounds as having violated the Constitution; (6) it can declare state laws unconstitutional as violating rather vague provisions (particularly of the due process and equal protection clauses of the Fourteenth Amendment and the interstate commerce clause, which the Court in the absence of any words at all has held to be a limit on what states can do).

It is those last two powers that make the difference. Here the Court not only tries cases; in the course of hearing cases it can put on trial the very laws passed by the legislature or the acts of the Executive and the administration on the national level and all parts of the state governments. This means that within certain limits it is a censor of the actions of all other branches of government, and in many cases has the last say (short of amendment of the Constitution). Major laws and programs, then, in the United States may and have been brought to a standstill as a result of lawsuits involving a corner chicken dealer or drugstore owner. Important issues may hinge on a legal technicality. The judge is caught between worrying about the technicalities and seeing the greater issues behind them. The power to discard laws as unconstitutional presents problems different in very real and obvious ways from a traffic court case or a divorce or a suit in an automobile collision.

There are some who claim that this power makes the Court the real ruler of America—one critic spoke of the United States as an example of "government by the judiciary." Others see in the Court a defense of free government. Some would like the Court to be tightly bound by the rules of the past; others call for a Court with statesmanlike vision to fashion the Constitution to the future.

In order to help you understand and choose from these positions this chapter will focus on several questions. We will first take a quick look at the operations of the Court and attempt to get a vision of the Court's place in our governmental system—to see what kind of institution we have here and to see how it is conceived of by different writers. Our second problem will be one of recruitment—where do the judges come from and where should they come from? What is the experience that qualifies them for their position of power? Our third problem is also a question of sources, but of the sources of the law. Is the law a "fixed" discoverable thing like the laws of physics used to be thought of or is it the last guess of the fifth member of the Court or the prejudices of the majority of the Court? Finally, what is the place of the Court with regard to making policy? Can it lead the country and should it try to? Running throughout these problems there is an underlying issue which virtually all of the readings inevitably try to answer—how do you reconcile the power of these nine men with majority rule and democracy?

What Manner of Institution?

What does the Court do? This simple question has many different answers depending on how you want to view it. We will first look at what the Court does in the simplest way—the day-to-day routines of the Court. Then in a broader view we will consider its role in our political system. Finally, we will consider several different views of its basic meaning. By first understanding the operations of the Court and of its position in the system we can approach this deeper question. Does the Court represent the finest in American thought, a gyroscope keeping the system on an even keel, doing things no other institution can do? Or does it represent a strange and un-American oligarchy, more powerful than the men in the Kremlin?

Where Do the Judges and the Law Come From?

How should judges of the Supreme Court be selected? One former president has described his way of choosing:

> When I was president I always tried to have the cabinet and advisors around me interested in a whole cross-section of the country's economy and political thought, and I think the highest court in the land should be so constituted that every viewpoint is expressed in the opinions of the court.[1]

Other presidents have followed much the same pattern. One thing they have been consistent in is choosing the vast majority from their own party. In this century, according to the American Bar Association, every president has chosen well over 80 per cent of all federal judges from his own political party.

Does this of itself suggest that the Supreme Court is a political body? Is it perhaps wrong to choose judges to represent parts of the country, points of view, or political affiliation? In recent years there has been a cry for more judi

---

[1] Harry S. Truman to Samuel Krislov, May 20, 1954.

cial experience on the part of appointees to the Court. Some have suggested promotion from the lower courts with previous experience being a prerequisite. Still others call for a more radical approach—perhaps the replacement of our present system of appointment by the president and ratification by the Senate.

What Can the Court Do?

The ultimate test of a political institution is its ability to satisfy the people on whose behalf it acts. The Supreme Court is no exception to this rule. The Court must serve some useful function or go under. Another test of institutions is accountability; unchecked power is a source of danger both to the community and to the wielders of it. What is the function the Court serves? As we shall see, there are jobs in our system it alone does and which, some argue, it alone can do.

There are also definite limitations on the power of the Supreme Court. Some of these exist in law, others in fact. There is the power that other branches of government wield over the Court. There is also the simple fact that public acceptance is necessary to enforce decisions of the Court. As the desegregation controversy reflects so well, the arsenal of weapons of the judicial system is not unlimited in the face of popular hostility. This, in turn, raises questions: How far can the Court go in defying public opinion? When should it attempt to do so and when should it not?

Yet another problem exists in the field of civil liberties. Can the Court lead in requiring freedom of speech and other political freedoms? In so doing will it serve democracy or perhaps weaken it by diluting majority rule and the responsibility of the community? The Supreme Court does not have tight self-defined limits to guide it in defining its total position in our government. For that reason the judges often disagree among themselves on this question. Ex-Justice Frankfurter argued that the Court should interfere almost never with laws of Congress. Black and Douglas represent a group that argues that where basic freedoms are concerned the Court should be less tolerant of majority rule. Because these freedoms are the heart of the political process of a democracy and are necessary to maintain political parties and the whole system of responsible scrutiny of policies, the judges argue that these require special protection. This argument has spilled over into popular discussion; it is one of the major problems now facing the Court and which will continue to face it in the years to come.

1

How the Supreme Court Reaches Decisions *

ANTHONY LEWIS

The following is a detailed step-by-step breakdown of Supreme Court routine as described by The New York Times' *Supreme Court reporter. The Times has a great tradition in careful coverage of the Court, which has usually been poorly covered by the press because of the intricacies of the legal process. Mr. Lewis was given legal training as preparation for his reportorial role.*

The first step in any case is for the Court to decide whether it will decide. Congress has given the justices almost complete discretion to say what cases they will hear and the volume of business requires stringent exercise of that discretion.

To help get through the approximately 1,500 petitions filed each term, most of the justices have their law clerks prepare a short memorandum on each case. But the justices make the decision, and their grounds will of course vary. A class of cases which seems vitally important to one member of the Court may appear to another one entirely unworthy of Supreme Court review. The issue of what cases to take has provoked bitter public argument among the justices.

The Court's formal choice of cases to be heard is made in a weekly conference which is the heart of the processes of decision in the Court. The conference meets each Friday at 11 o'clock during or preceding the weeks the Court is in session. It usually runs on until evening and may go over to

Saturday. By tradition each justice shakes hands around the table as he enters the room. (That is thirty-six handshakes altogether.) By another tradition, designed to assure secrecy, no one but the nine is ever allowed in the room during the conference. When clerks bring messages, the junior justice goes to the door to get them.

The late Justice Robert H. Jackson noted in 1954 that conference time would allow on the average only five minutes of discussion per item. He wrote: "All that saves the Court from being hopelessly bogged down is that many of the items are so frivolous on mere inspection that no one finds them worthy of discussion and they are disposed of by unanimous consent."

The Chief Justice has a special responsibility for making the conference work, for disposing of its heavy case load. He announces each case on the list in turn and then leads the discussion. On a "frivolous" petition for review he may do no more than remark that he will put it with the rejects unless someone objects. Or he may indicate other reasons for not taking the case. Justice Frankfurter in a 1955 talk to Illinois lawyers gave an example of what a Chief Justice may say:

* Anthony Lewis, "How the Supreme Court Reaches Decisions," *The New York Times Magazine*, December 1, 1957, pp. 51-54. Reprinted by permission of the author.

"This is a very interesting and important question . . . , but we can't do any better than Judge Julian Mack (late judge of the United States Court of Appeals) did with it below. He really knows more about this field of law than the rest of us. I suggest we deny this petition for *certiorari*."

It takes the votes of four justices to grant a petition for *certiorari*, the formal device usually used to bring a case up for review. Those cases which the Court does agree to hear are put on the calendar. The clerk of the Court picks a date for oral argument, usually several months after the decision to hear the case and sometimes now—because of a clogged calendar—more than a year.

Before oral argument begins, both sides submit printed briefs giving their versions of the facts in detail and their legal positions. A printed record is also prepared. This includes all, or significant portions, of the transcript made in the trial of the lawsuit, exhibits and previous judicial opinions in the case. This record may run to thousands of pages.

* * *

The critical moment in the process of decision is in all likelihood the oral argument of a case. And here the ways of decision—often, indeed, the minds of the justices—are open to public view. For anyone who wants to understand the workings of the Court, the printed text of an opinion is a poor substitute for listening to argument.

The Court hears argument two weeks out of each month during the October-June term. It sits Monday through Thursday from 12 to 4:30, with a half-hour out for lunch. Each side is usually limited to an hour, in some simpler cases to a half hour.

In the marble-pillared courtroom the justices look down at the speaker's stand from their raised seats. The lawyer for the party which lost in the lower courts begins: "Mr. Chief Justice, may it please the Court . . ." Speaking preferably without a prepared text, he states the facts briefly, then moves on to his legal positions. The other side has its turn; then there is a brief rebuttal.

Before he gets very far, the lawyer is likely to be interrupted by questions from one or more of the justices: Will he clarify such-and-such a fact? Does the case he just cited really stand for what he said? Will he agree that the Court cannot find for him unless . . .?

The Court sees itself not "a dozing audience for the reading of soliloquies," Justice Frankfurter has said, "but as a questioning body, utilizing oral argument as a means for exposing the difficulties of a case with a view to meeting them." The questions show the attorney the doubts he must put at rest if he is to carry the Court. They may forecast the decision of the Court.

The conference discussion of cases just argued begins with the Chief Justice. The senior associate, now Justice Black, speaks next, and so on down the line of seniority. Voting follows, but in reverse order—from the junior justice up.

As presiding officer, the Chief Justice shapes the character of the conference by deciding, for example, how long to let debate continue before calling for a vote.

Immediately after the conference, and the resulting vote, the job of writing opinions in the decided cases is divided among the justices. The Chief Justice assigns the majority opinion if he is in the majority; if not, the senior associate in the majority makes the assignment. The writer of the dissent, if any, is selected the same way. And, of course, any justice may write a concurring or dissenting opinion on his own. Thomas Jefferson thought every member of the Court ought to publish his views on every case—to be sure they weren't just blindly following John Marshall.

Assigning opinions is an art all its own, and an important one. To prevent fragmentation of the Court, for example, it may be wise to pick as the writer the justice who takes the middle view in a case. Hughes was said to pick "liberal" justices to write opinions in "conservative" decisions, and vice versa, so as to hold the Court as near as possible to a centrist position. Assigning the opinion to a member of the majority who holds an extreme view of the case may make other justices break away and write concurring opinions, giving their own reasons for the results. . . .

Underlying the opinion-writing process is the great problem of producing a collective judgment from the labors of individuals. It goes without saying that the result in a Supreme Court case may be less important than the reasons for it. And it may not be easy to agree on the reasons.

As opinions are drafted, copies are circulated among the other members of the Court. The copies come back with comments. Further drafts follow. One justice's price for adherence may be enough to send another into dissent. The writer may have to squelch some of his own views to carry the Court.

In contrast to the caution of the writer for the majority, the dissenter frequently indulges in exaggeration, painting the majority's view blacker than it really is. Majority opinions are revised to answer draft dissents which have been circulated. A notorious example of this was the Dred Scott case; the statements in Chief Justice Taney's majority opinion which most infuriated the North were added in answer to the furious dissent by a minority of the Court.

The drafting and redrafting of opinions may take months. Some Monday the last corrections will have been made in the Court's basement print shop. Shortly after noon one of the justices will begin reading, pneumatic tubes will carry copies of the opinion to the press room, and the process of decision in another case will be ended

2

Powerful, Irresponsible, and Human *

FRED RODELL

Not all people see the Court in the admiring way Mr. Lewis seems to. Oldline Democrats and Progressives like Robert LaFollette and even Teddy Roosevelt were suspicious of the Court. These and others thought the power of the judges was a denial of majority rule. This point of view still persists, and has much logic behind it. Another example—is Fred Rodell, a professor at Yale Law School and, incidentally, a close friend of Justice William Douglas. Whether any of the justices, including Douglas, would agree with the rather strong statements that follow seems doubtful.

At the top levels of the three branches of the civilian government of the United States sit the Congress, the President plus his Cabinet, and the Supreme Court. Of these three—in this unmilitary, unclerical nation—only one wears a uniform. Only one carries on its most important business in utter secret behind locked doors—and indeed never reports, even after death, what really went on there. Only one, its members holding office for life if they choose, is completely irresponsible to anyone or anything but themselves and their own consciences. Only one depends for much of its immense influence on its prestige as a semi-sacred institution and preserves that prestige with the trappings and show of superficial dignity rather than earning it, year after working year, by the dignity and wisdom of what it is and does. Under our otherwise democratic form of government, only one top

ruling group uses ceremony and secrecy, robes and ritual, as instruments of its *official* policy, as wellsprings of its power.

The nine men who are the Supreme Court of the United States are at once the most powerful and the most irresponsible of all the men in the world who govern other men. Not even the bosses of the Kremlin, each held back by fear of losing his head should he ever offend his fellows, wield such loose and long-ranging and accountable-to-no-one power as do the nine or five-out-of-nine justices who can give orders to any other governing official in the United States—from the members of a village school board who would force their young charges to salute the flag, to a president who would take over the steel industry to keep production going—and can make those orders stick. Ours may be, for puffing purposes, a "government of checks and balances," but there is no check at all on what the Supreme Court does—save only three that are as pretty in theory as they are pointless in practice. (These are the Senate's

---

* Fred Rodell, *Nine Men: A Political History of the Supreme Court from 1790 to 1955* (New York: Random House, 1955), pp. 3-6. © 1955 by Fred Rodell. Reprinted by permission of the publisher.

power to reject a newly named justice, used only once this century, and in the past usually unwisely; the power to impeach a justice, only once tried and never carried through; the power of the people to reverse a Supreme Court decision by amending the Constitution, as they have done just three times in our whole history.) The nine justices sit secure and stand supreme over Congress, president, governors, state legislatures, commissions, administrators, lesser judges, mayors, city councils, and dog-catchers—with none to say them nay.

Lest these words sound like arrant overstatement, here are what three of the most thoughtful men who ever held high national office said about the Supreme Court's flat and final power of government. Thomas Jefferson, who was president when the court first fully used this power, exploded, prophetically but futilely:

Our Constitution . . . intending to establish three departments, coordinate and independent, that they might check and balance one another . . . has given, according to this opinion, to one of them alone the right to prescribe rules for the government of the others, and to that one, too, which is unelected by and independent of the nation. . . . The Constitution, on this hypothesis, is a mere thing of wax in the hands of the judiciary which they may twist and shape into any form they please.

Jefferson was talking of the Court's then brand-newly wielded power to override Congress and the president. More than a century later, Justice Holmes revealingly in dissent, berated his brethren for freely using their judicial power to upset *state* laws:

As the decisions now stand I see hardly any limit but the sky to the invalidating of those rights ['*the constitutional rights of the states*'] if they happen to strike a majority of this Court as for any reason undesirable. I cannot believe that the [Fourteenth] Amendment was intended to give us carte blanche to embody our economic or moral beliefs in its prohibitions.

And a few years after, Justice Stone, he too in dissent, exclaimed: "The only check upon our own exercise of power is our own sense of self-restraint."

In Stone's same angry protest against the Court's six-to-three veto of the first Agricultural Adjustment Act —a protest that helped spark Franklin Roosevelt's "Court-packing" plan and later led FDR to reward its author with the Chief Justiceship—he also said: "Courts are not the only agency of government that must be assumed to have capacity to govern." This statement, while true on its face, is essentially and subtly—though of course not deliberately—misleading. No "agency of government" governs; no "court" governs; only the men who run the agency of government or the court or the Supreme Court do the governing. The power is theirs because the decisions are theirs; decisions are not made by abstractions like agencies or courts. Justice Stone, who knew what he meant, might a little better have said: "Five or six of the nine men who make up this Court are not the only men in our government who must be assumed to have the capacity to govern." And he might have added: "Nor are they necessarily the wisest in their judgements; I work with them and have reason to know."

3

Are Judges Politicians? *

CHARLES A. BEARD

What do the presidents look for in selecting a candidate? Are there politics involved in the selection? The following discussion by Charles A. Beard in his The Republic *puts these questions in historical perspective. Professor Beard, always a realist, had little use for the myth that most judges were chosen for legal ability alone without knowledge of any efforts on their behalf. He also puts into perspective the sense in which justices of the Court can be said to be partisan.*

* * *

Dr. Smyth: What about Judge Ranyin's statement that Supreme Court justices are above partisanship? I presume he meant that they ought to be above partisanship, for he has been vociferous in contending that President Franklin D. Roosevelt's judges are just New Deal judges. Perhaps he thinks that until the New Deal all justices were above partisanship. If so, that is a question of historical fact which a study of history can answer.

Beard: If partisanship is taken in the narrow sense to mean that judges of the Supreme Court have perverted the Constitution and the law to serve some low interests of party managers, I think it would be true to historical facts to maintain that the Supreme Court has been remarkably free from partisanship. There have been a few cases in which traces of political jobbery have appeared, but they are so few that they may be discarded and

the Supreme Court acquitted of partisanship in this sense.

But in the larger sense of grand public policies espoused by political parties, the Supreme Court has not been above and indifferent to the great conflicting interests of parties. On the contrary, the justices on that bench have reflected those interests in the momentous cases of American history—such as the Dred Scott case of 1857, the Legal Tender cases of 1872, the income tax case of 1895, the Insular cases after the Spanish war, and some of the New Deal cases. This is not to say that the justices of the Court in such cases always divide according to their party labels. They do not. Nor indeed do hot partisans in general divide sharply over such issues. There are Republicans sympathetic to the New Deal, and there are Democrats who have fought it from the beginning.

Dr. Smyth: I should think that one test would be whether, in selecting Supreme Court justices, presidents have been indifferent to party considerations and chosen freely or equally from both parties. If it is just a mat-

---

* Charles A. Beard, *The Republic* (New York: The Viking Press, Inc., 1943), pp. 229-34. Copyright 1943 by Charles A. Beard. Reprinted by permission of the publisher.

ter of getting a competent lawyer who knows the Constitution, then presidents might choose men outside their party about as often as they do men inside. For instance President Roosevelt appointed Harlan Stone Chief Justice after the resignation of Mr. Hughes, and Mr. Stone is a Republican. How many such cases of such cases of such nonpartisanship have there been in our history?

Beard: Not many. I recall only two offhand. Let us look at the roll: . . .

President Taft elevated Edward D. White, of Louisiana, a Democrat, to the place of Chief Justice. White was a good, sound, conservative like Taft, but a party Democrat, no Bryan Democrat.

The next Chief Justice was William H. Taft, nominated by President Harding. As to their party politics, no comment is necessary.

After Taft's resignation, President Hoover selected Charles E. Hughes. No comment on party politics is needed here.

With the elevation of Justice Harlan Stone to the Chief Justiceship by President Roosevelt came the second break. . . .

Dr. Smyth: But all of President Roosevelt's other appointees to the Court were good, sound New-Deal Democrats—Black, Reed, Murphy, Douglas, Frankfurter, Jackson, Byrnes, and Rutledge. Stone had often been favorable to the New Deal in his opinions. . . . Give me that list of Chief Justices. I want to show it to Judge Ranyin and ask him whether he still thinks that the Supreme Court is above partisanship. As a doctor of medicine I do not know a thing about jurisprudence, but I need only common sense to see through a hole in a millstone.

Beard: Here is the list and also a list of all the other Supreme Court justices since the creation of the

Court under President Washington, with annotations relative to their politics and their appointments. Look it over.

Dr. Smyth (dryly, after running through the list): This very string of facts indicates to me that there has been a lot of partisanship in the narrow sense of the term.

Beard: In some appointments, perhaps so, but my rule still holds good, namely, that even partisan judges have seldom, if ever, sunk to the level of petty politics, although they have often sustained or struck at actions involving grand national politics. It is right here that they have displayed their power, for good or ill. Yet I would warn you that the work of the Court is not all on dramatic cases. What it does by decisions and opinions relative to routine matters, in the aggregate may well outweigh in terms of national interest and welfare its actions in highly controversial cases. . . .

Dr. Smyth: Innocently no doubt, I have always thought of that membership as an honor which went to great lawyers, with no seeking or political maneuvering on their part.

Beard: There are of course a number of cases in which the honor has apparently gone to men who have not sought it or perhaps even permitted their friends to seek it for them. . . .

For many of the . . . justices the records are ample and convincing. They permit us to say that ambitious men, usually though not always active politicians, have zealously sought membership on the Court and employed great ingenuity in their own behalf. William Howard Taft's early ambition was to be a justice of the Supreme Court. After the election of Harding in 1920, as Pringle shows in his *Life and Times of William Howard Taft*, Mr. Taft made a point of visitnig Harding, enlisted the interest of

Harry Daugherty in his behalf, and, with great trepidation of spirit, pulled wires to secure the Chief Justiceship. His labors were successful, thanks partly to Daugherty's sympathetic cooperation. And no man in the United States was more concerned than Taft with getting the right kind of justices for the Court—that is, good, sound conservatives who held his own views respecting the powers and functions of the Court.... Presidents have recognized the fact that the Supreme Court is a center of great power and have tried to select justices in general sympathy with their policies. This rule applies to Republicans and Democrats alike.

And why not? The Supreme Court is not a group of disembodied spirits operating in a vacuum on logical premises that express or affect none of the powerful interests over which party conflicts rage. In a refined but none the less real way, its members express these conflicts of interest. It would be preposterous for a president who believes that his policies are sound and constitutional to nominate judges who hold opposite views— judges who would declare his policies unconstitutional. Presidents are sometimes disappointed in details but in the general run they get what they expect.

Dr. Smyth: I remember hearing that Theodore Roosevelt was disappointed—yes, angry—because Justice Holmes did not decide some cases to suit him.

Beard: That is true. But one of the reasons Theodore Roosevelt assigned for nominating Holmes was the progressive views on labor and social legislation Holmes had expounded as judge in Massachusetts. These views Holmes continued to expound as a

justice of the Supreme Court throughout his entire career in that tribunal....

Dr. Smyth: But justices of the Supreme Court abstain from politics after they are appointed, however active they have been previously?

Beard: Though in general they abstain from active participation in party politics, here again there have been exceptions. A number of justices during the past hundred years have actively, if quietly, carried on underground campaigns to get the nomination for the presidency. I know of no evidence that Justice Charles E. Hughes worked to get the Republican nomination in 1916; still he got it and resigned from the Court to run for president. Many justices while in service on the bench have maintained intimate relations with their party brother in the White House, and have advised him in law, tactics, and strategy. There is some popular resentment at this, but the practice has been common to the latest hour.

Dr. Smyth: At least they do not make political speeches for their party brother in the White House.

Beard: Campaign speeches, no. At all events I never heard of any case under that head, although justices have occasionally been accused of injecting campaign speeches into their opinions, sometimes with an eye to their own political prospects. Yet justices of the Supreme Court have gone around making speeches in support of presidential policies. Speaking more politely, we should perhaps call them addresses. They are usually delivered on ceremonial occasions, such as the Fourth of July, or at commencements when justices receive honorary degrees from colleges and universities....

4

A Political Approach to the Courts *

MARTIN SHAPIRO

*In recent years political scientists and other social scientists, as well as legal theo-
rists, have examined more closely the relationship between law and politics. Reflecting the trends in political science, this has taken two broadly conceived modes
of analysis. In the first instance, attention has been given to theoretical ways of
conceptualizing legal action. In the second, a quantitative or statistical approach
has become more dominant. Both, but especiallu the second, have proven to be
controversial, particularly among traditional legalistic writers.*

. . . [A] new approach to the study
of courts is in the making. . . .

Professor David Truman has been
a catalyst for this new jurisprudence.
It may be argued that his brief section on the judiciary in *The Governmental Process* is little more than an
assertion that courts can be just as
conveniently handled within his system of analysis as other government
bodies can. Truman attempts to analyze all government in terms of the
influence and interactions of interest
groups, measuring influence largely in
terms of "access." He admits that there
is little of the kind of direct access to
the courts that pressure groups have to
legislative bodies. The Supreme Court
is after all not subject to the same
types of pressure as the Congress. He
emphasizes indirect access through
such means as influencing the selection of judges. . . .

*   *   *

. . . Truman does mention that organized groups do gain direct access to the
courts by engaging in litigation, and
he emphasizes that litigation, like
war, is the conduct of politics by
other means.

Furthermore, Truman's rather general suggestions about group access
to the courts have been followed up
in terms of both pressure-group lobbying and the "constituency" of the
Court. Lobbying techniques like the
amicus brief, the test case, and the
writing of law-review articles favorable to certain causes have been described, and the long-range judicial
campaigns of such groups as the
N.A.A.C.P. have been analyzed. . . .

*   *   *

. . . This approach leads us away
from broad generalizations about the
role of Congress or the Presidency or
the Supreme Court in American government and into the problem of
exactly what parts certain agencies of
government, including the Supreme
Court in the hierarchy of courts has

* Martin Shapiro, "Political Jurisprudence," in *Law and Politics in the Supreme
Court* (New York: The Free Press, 1964),
pp. 8-14. Copyright © by The Free Press
of Glencoe, a Division of The Macmillan
Company, 1964. Reprinted by permission
of the publisher.

also begun to receive some attention in terms of the political relationships between superior and subordinate in a highly bureaucratized governmental structure.

❊ ❊ ❊

Particular attention has been paid to the bar as a group that has constant access to the Court through the arguments and briefs of its members, their academic and polemic writing, and their recruitment as justices. Lawyers are no longer viewed simply as contestants before an impartial referee or as officers of the Court. They form a constellation of political forces that play upon a political agency.

Indeed the whole discussion of lobbying and constituency inevitably leads to the question of whether or not the Court is a "clientele" agency. This expression is usually associated with those regulatory agencies that have become spokesmen for the interests they were established to regulate. It has often been argued that the I.C.C. has served as a clientele agency for the railroads. The viewed as a spokesman for uphold-Court has, of course, always been ing "The Constitution" against the hostile sentiments of the moment. If, however, the Court is visualized as caught in reciprocal relations of service and support with various special interests or constituencies, then the concept of clientele agency may be applicable to the Supreme Court, as well as to the I.C.C.

❊ ❊ ❊

. . . The "political" attacks on the Court in the late '30s and early '50s have inspired considerable commentary, much of which inevitably, and some deliberately, describes and evaluates the political power of the Court in terms of its ability to protect itself in the clinches.

❊ ❊ ❊

Supreme Court justices, of course, vote, and their individual votes determine the general outcomes of the cases. Their votes, or more precisely the internal alignments or arrangements of their votes, shift from case to case. The opinions of the justices in individual cases also add up to a kind of over-all record for the term, in the way that the sum of a given Congress's legislative decisions allows us to generalize about its legislative behavior. It is not surprising therefore that the same voting analysis techniques that have been used to describe how legislatures and electorates arrive at decisions have now been applied to the Supreme Court. Much of this statistical analysis is strictly descriptive, an attempt to show the relation of one Justice's votes to another's, the presence of blocs, the possibility that certain Justices vacillate, or the direction in which the Court is moving on particular issues.

Behind the gross description of voting patterns, however, lies an attempt to understand the motivation of judges. The foundation of behavioral psychology is the proposition that we may discover the way men think by observing how they behave. One, perhaps the crucial, aspect of a justice's behavior is how he votes. The study of his voting may therefore tell us how he thinks. Two basic techniques have been used in this approach. In the first, the level of agreement between each possible pair of Justices is recorded, and those Justices with the highest level of agreement, in terms of voting the same way in the same cases, are grouped. Justices belonging to the same bloc, that is, voting together in a relatively large number of cases, are assumed to share a common attitude around which the bloc clusters. A group of

Justices who constantly vote for the individual and against the government in civil-rights cases may be described as having a procivil-rights attitude. The other basic method is scalogram analysis, which also measures behavior on the basis of votes with or against the majority. If certain cases "scale," that is, show symmetrical voting patterns among the Justices, then it is assumed that voting on those cases was determined by a single attitude dimension, for instance, sentiment toward labor unions or business.

The general assumption of both group and scale analysis has been that attitudes toward the various socioeconomic and political interests presented by the cases are an important factor in determining at least some of the decisions of some of the Justices. Attitudinal-statistical research has not only sought to isolate and measure attitudes toward social values like freedom of speech or free enterprise, but it has also sought to measure the Justices' attitudes toward other government agencies and toward the Court itself, that is, toward judicial self-restraint, spheres of competence, and so forth.

❖   ❖   ❖

Parallel to attitudinal research and using much of the same data is an approach that treats the Court as a small group and subjects it to the general modes of analysis and measurement that psychologists and sociologists have devised for examining such groups. The nine Justices then become the subject of studies in small-group psychology, which aim at discovering patterns of leadership, deference, and so forth. The role of the Chief Justice as political leader has been described and attempts have been made to assess the relative power and influence of the Justices *vis-à-vis* one another. While much of bloc analysis is aimed at identifying operative political attitudes, it can also be employed to chart the group politics of the court itself. The existence of relatively firm blocs may ensure the power of "swing Justices" and the need for compromise in order to gain a majority. Conversely, it may explain the intransigent and absolutist opinions of Justices caught in a minority bloc that has no hope of gaining a majority and therefore no motivation to compromise.

Also closely related to attitudinal studies are some research results that may be labeled crudely "behavioral." Although statistics may demonstrate that Justice X always votes probusiness, they offer no proof that he does so because he allows strongly probusiness sentiments to shape his decisions. Indeed, there is a kind of basic circularity in statistical approaches to the problem of judicial attitudes. Consistency in voting behavior is used to infer the attitude, and then the attitude is used to explain the consistency. This circularity can be at least partially broken by seeking for information on attitudes in materials other than voting records or by manipulating the case samples to reduce the possibility of incursions by stray variables. Even with their circularity, however, statistical studies are useful to political jurisprudence. If we find that Justice X or, more important, Justices X, Y, Z, A, and B always vote prolabor, we may still not have learned why, but we have discovered something about the impact of the Supreme Court on labor policy and the nature of its relations with other labor policy-makers. A simple description of what happened, that is, who won, may be quite useful in assessing the political role of the Supreme Court. . . .

5

Elect Supreme Court Justices? *

DAVID LAWRENCE

If the Supreme Court is political shouldn't it be subject to political controls? This is the position taken in the following article by David Lawrence, who is a political columnist, publisher of U.S. News and World Report, *and one of the leading and most vocal critics of the Court's desegregation decision. The suggestion he makes, however, is one that has been discussed several times in our history, and, he argues, has precedent and logic behind it.*

Now that the Supreme Court has transformed itself into what is being termed "another legislative body," a movement has started to bring about the election of the high court justices by the people. It would require a constitutional amendment.

The idea, of course, is not novel. This happens to be the custom in the several states with few exceptions. Thirty-six states elect their highest court judges at the polls, four states elect their top judges by vote of the state legislatures, and only eight states follow the federal custom of appointment by the Executive with the consent of the Legislature.

Since the Supreme Court of the United States has set itself up as having the right to tell Congress how to run its committees and the executive departments that they must retain employees they don't like, the ques-

tion of how the Supreme Court, itself, shall be held accountable for its acts has arisen. This has happened several times before in American history.

The late President Franklin D. Roosevelt thought the answer to an arbitrary or capricious court was to increase the number of justices so he could appoint those who would decide cases as he thought they should be decided. This scheme was called "courtpacking." It required legislation and was frowned on by Congress in 1937. Former President Theodore Roosevelt, as a candidate for the presidency in 1912, urged that there be a system of "recall of judicial decision" so the people, by referendum, could affirm or reverse decisions, especially in state courts.

Today the Supreme Court of the United States has rendered so many conflicting and confusing decisions that many lawyers throughout the country are perplexed and bewildered. The issue was succinctly stated by a member of the Supreme Court itself, the late Justice Robert H. Jackson,

* David Lawrence, "Elect Supreme Court Justices?" *Washington Evening Star*, June 20, 1957. © 1957 by the New York Herald Tribune, Inc. Reprinted by permission of the author and publisher.

who, in the course of an opinion in 1953, wrote:

Rightly or wrongly, the belief is widely held by the practicing profession that this court no longer respects impersonal rules of law, but is guided in these matters by personal impressions which from time to time may be shared by a majority of justices. Whatever has been intended, this court also has generated an impression . . . that regard for precedents and authorities is obsolete, that words no longer mean what they have always meant to the profession, that the law knows no fixed principles.

For the last 20 years many of the professors of law in the university law schools, particularly in the East, have raised a whole generation of so-called "liberals" who believe the Supreme Court should make "policy" and that to adhere to historic principles is out of keeping with the spirit of the times. This is the type of thinking which has bred throughout the country a feeling that the court pays more attention to sociology or political science or ideological considerations nowadays than it does to fundamental interpretation of the Constitution and to the enduring principles of jurisprudence.

If, therefore, the Supreme Court is to make "policies," to whom should it be responsible? It now places itself above both the Congress and the Executive, which are themselves accountable to the people. The justices, however, are accountable to no one but themselves. Such an autocracy was never envisioned by the Founding Fathers when they authorized life tenure for justices. The several states have wisely written into their constitutions that judges must go before the people—sometimes after six-year and sometimes after twelve- or fourteen-year terms. But there is a check by the people.

Criticism of the Supreme Court is mounting. Unfortunately, it is a criticism that attributes political or ideological motives to the justices. Many Republicans and Democrats, moreover, are blaming President Eisenhower for the peculiar attitude Chief Justice Warren has taken since being on the high court. "Why was Warren ever appointed?" is asked repeatedly in political circles. He was known as a middle-of-the-roader for many years. Eisenhower, however, is reported to be as much surprised as the general public that Warren has become enamored of the Douglas-Black philosophy and consistently follows the radical line without the slightest show of independence.

Justice Black wrote extensively on the rights of congressional investigating committees when he was a United States Senator, and so did Justice Frankfurter before he came to the court. They both thought investigating committees shouldn't be restricted in gathering information and in browbeating recalcitrant witnesses. They wrote approvingly of the harassment of the businessmen of those days. But when the harassment now turns to persons who have had "past associations" with Communists and who conceal their connections, both Justices Frankfurter and Black seem to become champions of the very individual rights which they once urged should be denied as businessmen sought to exercise them against the witch-hunting and fishing expeditions of congressional committees.

So, since it is all so obviously political, there are many persons here in Congress who are coming reluctantly to the conclusion that election of judges for fixed terms, with the right to run for re-election, is the only way out of the political dilemma which the present court has created by its "legislative" decisions.

6

We Must Go Back in Order to Go Forward *

JOHN T. FLYNN

Here we have a sample of the position most of our writers have suggested is out of fashion—namely that the law and the Constitution have a definite meaning which the judges should enforce. Where they don't do so they are clearly violating the Constitution, and should be called to account. Mr. Flynn was a critic of the New Deal and of decisions of the Supreme Court since 1937. He suggests a simple remedy for the decisions he regards as erroneous, a suggestion which itself should raise some questions about the meaning and nature of law. (Not everyone, of course, would agree with Mr. Flynn's historical statements, but they represent a definite point of view.)

The Supreme Court is empowered, under the Constitution, to "interpret" the meaning of the Constitution where questions of judicial differences appear. It had, according to its time-honored practice, interpreted the Constitution to mean what its framers wanted it to mean, and declared Roosevelt's first-term acts unconstitutional—in the most important case by unanimous decision. . . .

Once a Supreme Court subservient to the president and the new collectivist revolution was installed, the job was easy. It was simply necessary for the Supreme Court to give new and utterly different meanings to *four words* in the Constitution—meanings those words had never had in the preceding 148 years. The four words are comprised in the terms "general welfare" and "interstate commerce." The term "general welfare" was

clearly understood for a century and a half. I have listed the specific powers conferred upon Congress. Congress was empowered to collect taxes, etc., "to provide for the common defense and *general welfare of the United States.*" That did not mean that Congress could tax for any project which might seem good to Congress to "promote the general welfare." It did not refer to general welfare in the sense the word "welfare" is now used—as a system of handouts to the indigent, etc. . . .

The Courts never wavered, throughout our history, in their clear understanding of the term "commerce" and of "interstate commerce." It meant trade; and it included transportation as an inevitable function of trade. They understood precisely what the Constitution meant and why the terms were used. . . . In 1871 an attempt was made to show that commerce included manufacture. Justice Field rejected that theory and held that interstate commerce in a commodity begins *"whenever a commod-*

---

* John T. Flynn, *The Decline of the American Republic: And How to Rebuild It* (New York: Devin-Adair Co., 1955), pp. 99, 101, 105-107, 165-66. Reprinted by permission of the publisher.

ity has begun to move as an article of trade from one state to another."

Of course, the subject became troublesome when large corporations began to spread their activities over many states, and when the growing evil of corporate monopoly began to make itself felt. Communities and smaller interests clamored for action by the federal government against the growing power of the trusts, and for every abuse there was a band of organized reformers calling for action against their own pet abuse. They all overlooked the fact that while there was the problem of curbing predatory or antisocial man on one side, there was also the continuing great adventure, attempted in America, of keeping in leash the abuses of too-powerful antisocial government.

But the Courts always, to their credit, kept foremost in mind the meaning of the Constitution and in decision after decision on questions involving "interstate commerce" kept to the true meaning of the clause. . . .

. . . *We must go back in order to go forward. We must return to the great highway of the American Republic.*

Obviously the nation faced a tremendous reconstruction job on our mutilated Constitution and on our sadly battered Republic.

The first, the most challenging enterprise is to return the federal Constitution to its historic limits as contrued by the Supreme Court for 145 years. No proof is necessary of the bold design of President Roosevelt, guided by the audacious crew of socialist and communist revolutionaries who surrounded him. That design was to alter the Constitution by judicial interpretation. The amend-

ment of the Constitution can be legally effected by only one method—and that is set out in the instrument itself. Unable to carry out this revolutionary alteration of the government by lawful methods, Roosevelt turned to an outrageous assault upon the judges of the Supreme Court for the purpose of driving them off the bench and replacing them with compliant political judges—some of them social revolutionists—who could be depended on to torture the words of the Constitution into such meanings as would literally alter the whole shape and nature of our federal system. This assault was made possible by the lawless mind of the President, the boldness of the conspirators who surrounded him, and the disturbed and troubled state of the public mind under the influence of the depression.

The escape from the consequences of this great crime against our society is perhaps the most difficult of all the problems that confront us. The infamy which characterizes this adventure, however, justifies a bold counterstroke to correct it. But it is a stroke that can be carried out within the clear meaning of the Constitution. I urge a constitutional amendment, and suggest the following wording:

The decisions of the Supreme Court between 1937 and the date of the final adoption of this amendment, rendered by a Court designedly packed to alter by interpretation the clear meanings of the Constitution, are hereby declared to have no force and effect as precedents in judicial or other proceedings in determining the meaning of the words, sections and provisions of the Constitution of the United States.

7

A Tenant at Sufferance *

CHARLES P. CURTIS

Charles Curtis calls the Court "tenant at sufferance"—one that must remember that the other branches of government can limit its power. President Roosevelt's famous "Court-packing" plan is one example of a method by which the Court can be brought to heel; in 1958 Senator Jenner and Senator Butler introduced bills that would have limited the Court's jurisdiction over matters involving state powers and internal security. These weapons are always there, and the Court cannot forget it.

... The first fact to be recognized is that the Court exercises the doctrine at the sufferance of Congress. To begin with, the very jurisdiction of the Court in all important cases is subject to "Such exceptions and under such regulations as the Congress shall make." That is the language of the Constitution, Article III. To be sure, its original jurisdiction as a court of first instance cannot be taken away from it, but that covers only cases affecting ambassadors, ministers, consuls, and between the states themselves. None of them bring suit very often and when they do it is more important to them than to us. If that were all the business the Court had, the place would be an honorable sinecure for tired lawyers and others, and nobody but themselves would want to write a book about it. It is the Court's appellate jurisdiction that counts, and that is held and exercised at the pleasure of Congress. Con-

gress can even take away the Court's jurisdiction in a case already pending before it. Once Congress did just that, and the Court unanimously agreed that Congress had power to do it.

That was the McCardle case in 1869. McCardle was a Mississippi editor who was arrested and held for trial before a military commission under one of the Reconstruction Acts. After McCardle's case had been argued, Congress apprehended the Court might interfere in a matter of personal liberty. So Congress repealed the section which gave McCardle a right to appeal to the Court. Johnson, stouthearted fellow, vetoed the repeal right in the middle of his impeachment trial but Congress passed it over his veto. And the Court acquiesced. With dry dignity—the grapes were sour—Chief Justice Chase, for a unanimous court, said, "Judicial duty is not less fitly performed by declining ungranted jurisdiction than in exercising firmly that which the Constitution and the laws confer." The Court, he said, was "not at liberty to inquire into the motives of the Legislature." B. R. Cur-

* Charles P. Curtis, *Lions Under the Throne* (Boston, Mass.: Houghton Mifflin Company, 1954), pp. 35-38. Reprinted by permission of the publisher.

tis, the ex-justice, who had dissented in the Dred Scott case, remarked, "Congress, with the acquiescence of the country, has subdued the Supreme Court, as well as the President."

Congress sets the times when the Court is to sit. Once, long ago now, in Marshall's time, the Seventh Congress forced the Court to adjourn for over a year. Senator Bayard asked, "May it not lead to the virtual abolition of the Court?" Yet Marshall acquiesced. "The office still remains," he said, "to receive and exercise any new judicial powers which the Legislature may confer."

Congress has complete power over the enforcement of the Court's judgments. The president might use the army to prevent their enforcement, just as he can use the army to enforce the law. . . . If the use of the army against embattled deputy marshals is too fanciful, the power of Congress to cut off appropriations is not. It could do to the Court what it has done to any other department of the government.

Congress has complete authority under the Constitution to fix the number of justices. It has changed the members more than once. Even the American Bar Association admitted that Roosevelt's proposal to Congress in 1937 to increase the Court to fifteen would be constitutional. They denounced it, and the bar cried out, four to one, that it would be "constitutionally immoral." Immoral or not, you will agree, as they did, that it was within the constitutional power of Congress to do it.

Bryce called this "a joint in the court's armour." The Fathers of the Constitution, he said, studied nothing more than to secure the complete independence of the judiciary. The president was not permitted to remove the judges, nor Congress to diminish their salaries. One thing only was either forgotten or deemed undesirable, because highly inconvenient, to determine—the number of judges in the Supreme Court. Here, he said, was a weak point, a joint in the court's armor through which a weapon might some day penetrate. . . .

Bryce asks what prevents such immoral assaults on the fundamental law. Not the mechanism of government, he answers himself, for all its checks have been evaded. Not the conscience of the legislature and the president, for heated combatants seldom shrink from justifying the means by the end. Nothing but the fear of the people, whose broad good sense and attachment to the great principles of the Constitution may generally be relied on to condemn such a perversion of its forms. Yet if excitement has risen high over the country, a majority of the people may acquiesce; and then it matters little whether what is really a revolution be accomplished by openly violating or by merely distorting the forms of law. To the people we come sooner or later, said Bryce, and it is upon their wisdom and self-restraint that the stability of the most cunningly devised scheme of government will in the last resort depend. . . .

8

The High Court's Role in Policy *

The news clipping reprinted below summarizes a study by Robert Dahl of Yale University attempting to assess the political conditions under which the Court may flourish. The point of view here is an interesting supplement to the idea that a political conflict determines the question of Court influence.

Washington, Sept. 30—Two questions that have arisen in the minds of many Americans, particularly in the South, about the Supreme Court these past few years are:

1. Can the court really make new national policy, and make it stick even if it is widely disapproved?
2. What can a disapproving citizenry do to reverse or modify new policies set by the court? And with what chance of success?

Question number 1 has been studied of late by an expert, and his findings have been published in the Journal of Public Law, issued by the Emory University Law School in Atlanta.

In this study, Dr. Robert A. Dahl, a Yale University Professor of Political Science, analyzed what had happened in the seventy-eight cases in which the high tribunal, in its history up to 1957, had struck down as unconstitutional eight-seven (sic) provisions of federal law.

There were instances in which the

court was changing policy fixed by Congress and, in nearly every case, approved by the President.

Decisions Modified

No fewer than twenty-six times Congress passed new legislation that had the effect of reversing the court. In other instances the situation itself changed, and the new court policy was unimportant. Or, several times, the court modified its own earlier decisions.

This led Dr. Dahl to the conclusion that the policy views of the court never remain for long out of line with the policy views of the lawmaking majority. And he noted that to have a strong lawmaking majority, Congress and the White House must be controlled by the same party.

He found that, on rare occasion, the court could "delay the application" of policy up to twenty-five years. But, he said, it is most likely to be successful when faced with a "weak" lawmaking majority. And, he added, "by itself the court is about powerless to effect the course of national policy."

Dr. Dahl said he felt the court had got by so far with its school segregation decision of 1954 because of an unusual situation in political leader-

---

* "High Court's Role in Policy Studied: Bench and Congress Never Split Permanently on an Issue, Survey Finds," *The New York Times,* October 5, 1958. Copyright 1958 by The New York Times Company. Reprinted by permission of the publisher.

ship. He said, in effect that advocates of school integration while "not strong enough to get what they wanted enacted by Congress, still were and are powerful enough to prevent any successful attack on the legislative powers of the court."

This leads to the second question: What can be done?

If Dr. Dahl is right about pro-integration strength, present attempts to limit the appellate jurisdiction of the court are doomed to failure.

In certain limited areas—such as spelling out that Congress must specify that a new federal law is to supersede state laws on the same subject before the High Court can rule that Congress intended to do so—Congress may well curb the court.

History shows that presidents over a period of years have exerted powerful influence over the court. This is due, obviously, to their power of nomination (which usually amounts to appointments) of new High Court justices.

9

Is the Supreme Court Attempting Too Much? *

ROBERT G. McCLOSKEY

The Warren Court has been a most active one with many accomplishments to its credit in the fields of civil rights and civil liberties. Some, indeed, think it has taken on more than a court should. There are two sides to this question. What is proper in a democracy for such a body to attempt? Another is the problem of what is practical for an agency that has no troops or finances available to effectuate its decisions. This provocative study by Robert McCloskey attempts to analyze the potential assets and liabilities of the Court, and ways of viewing legal power.

* * *

Historical generalizations are almost always either contestable or obvious. The first one offered here may strike some readers as open to doubt and others as self-evident. It is that the Court of the past dozen years has developed "judicial activism" to a degree that at least matches the record of the "Old Court" of the

---

* Robert McCloskey, "Reflections on the Warren Court," *Virginia Law Review,* 1965, pp. 1233, 1247, 1249, 1263. Reprinted by permission of the publisher.

1920's and 1930's and that certainly exceeds the record of any other Court in our constitutional history. When we reflect that the American Supreme Court has, since Marshall, been by long odds the most potent court in the world, this statement about modern judicial tendencies can be seen in all its implications. We might say, paraphrasing Mr. Churchill, that only once before in history has a judicial tribunal tried to influence so many so much.

. . . [T]he Warren Court appears to

have succeeded impressively in freeing itself from the self-doubts that deterred consitutional development during the 1940-1953 period. With a zeal that seemed to increase as the years went by, the Justices have advanced boldly along the civil rights front. A variety of new subjects—e.g., libel and censorship laws, the right to travel, the postal power—have been brought within their purview. Old doctrines that offered a pretext for judicial inaction, like the doctrine of "political questions" or the "privilege doctrine," have been jettisoned or greatly eroded. . . . The 1920-1936 Court invalidated nearly 200 state acts: its batting average is distinctly the higher, although the Warren Court's performance in this category has improved—if that is the word—in very recent years. . . .

Yet it is arguable that the role of the Warren Court is in some ways still more imposing, that it has attempted even more than its famous predecessor. . . . No Court ever challenged the national will as boldly as did the "Old Court" when it struck at the New Deal, but no Court ever so sharply and hastily backed down as that same tribunal did in 1937. A sequence in which a throne is audaciously claimed in one moment and abdicated in the next can hardly be viewed on the whole as an example of judicial intrepidity. . . .

Beyond that, there is another difference between the nature of the Warren Court's undertakings and those of any Court of the past; and the difference may be crucial to our comparison. Traditionally the Supreme Court has been chiefly concerned with preserving the cake of custom, with telling the people of the nation that they must continue to operate as they were already used to operating. The modern Court has assumed the more affirmative task of breaking old habits, of telling the nation that it must stop doing what it was accustomed to and must start doing something else. It has been trying, that is, not only to forbid certain kinds of governmental and social action, but to bring a different state of affairs, and even a different state of mind, into being.

. . . [W]hat are its prospects for maintaining that claim successfully? This is not, be it noted, the question whether the Court has the *right* so to command America, that is, whether constitutional text and tradition can warrant such regality. Nor is it the somewhat different question whether in terms of democratic theory the judiciary *ought* to be entrusted with such an important part in the moulding of public policy. The issue is a narrower one. . . . Does the Supreme Court have enough such power to play its modern self-assigned role as a major initiative-supplying agency of modern government?

There are in the current scene some legitimate grounds for doubt about the Court's power to play the momentous part it has chosen, and there have been some danger signals. For one thing it may be that "judicial realism" has eroded the traditional mystique that often lent support to Court authority in other days. For more than half a century scholars and judges have been repudiating the mythology that the Court is merely the impersonal voice of indisputable constitutional verities, and have been emphasizing that the judicial process involves an element of free choice based on policy judgments. . . . [T]he modern Court is bereft of another kind of backing which historically sustained it: the active support of the business community and related elements such as commercial lawyers and the conservative press. . . . [F]or the past twenty-five years the Justices have been making it abundantly plain that the Constitution is no longer a refuge for disgruntled property holders, and have turned their sympathy to other objects—to Negroes and other disadvantaged minorities, to religious and political dissenters, to persons accused of crime. However morally justifiable this shift may be, it has meant that the business community no longer rises to the Court's defense with its old enthusiasm, and this loss of a powerful traditional ally is not a small matter in an assessment of the present Court's capabilities.

. . . [T]he Court, like other governing bodies, must maintain a favorable balance between the forces that bolster its authority and those that oppose it—between friends and enemies, to put the matter bluntly. No doubt its capital of public support, deriving from the American tradition of respect for the judiciary, is sufficient to counterbalance the disaffection evoked by a certain number of commands that vex those who are commanded. Though the Justices drew very heavily on that capital in the desegregation decisions, this alone was not too heavy a withdrawal for the Court's prestige to stand. But since then the Warren Court has gathered in a whole series of further commitments in fields like criminal procedure, school religious practices, censorship and the rest; and it is arguable that each commitment has strained the capital a little further. Each one, that is, has augmented the accumulating mass of judicial enforcement problems, has created a new and additional body of critics and adversaries.

❋   ❋   ❋

Yet there is an argument to be made on the other side: there are considerations lending some support to a belief that the modern Court's power

is equal to its aspirations. In the first place it is of course possible that the balance between friends and adversaries has been redressed on both sides. . . . Perhaps the losses are partially compensated by an increase of amicability among those who approve recent judicial policies—that is, Negroes and Northern liberals of various types. . . .

Ironically enough, their ranks seem to have been strengthened at least temporarily by the 1964 election. Not for many years has a presidential candidate criticized the Court as sharply as Mr. Goldwater did. He chose to make the judiciary a secondary but significant campaign issue, and Mr. Johnson's overwhelming victory could thus be interpreted, rightly or wrongly, as an implied vindication of the Court. . . . Sometimes the right enemy is as valuable as a friend.

In still another way the march of recent political events may have improved the Court's position. In the analysis above I have emphasized the scope and the cumulative weight of the tasks which the Warren Court has assumed. . . . [T]he heaviest load the Court has borne throughout most of this time was the responsibility for coping with the issue of racial discrimination. For almost ten years this arduous matter, surely the most formidable of modern domestic problems, was left virtually untouched by presidents and congresses; insofar as a national governmental policy was developing, it was being fashioned by the judiciary alone. But in very recent years, the other two branches have at length bestirred themselves to take the problem in hand, and the result has been a lightening of the Court's total burden. . . .

These considerations favoring an optimistic prognosis bring to mind another, more general speculation about the nature of current American political opinion and the relationship of the Court to American public attitudes. In reviewing the factors that might give pause to judicial activists, I have assumed *arguendo* that the Court's power to command America is in the nature of a capital fund which is diminished by each expenditure of power; and further that the potential alignment of supporters and opponents for a given judicial policy is relatively fixed. But this reckons without the possibility that the Court's political environment is more dynamic than static. It may not be true that power is automatically depleted in proportion to its exertion. Not only is it likely, as already mentioned, that a policy judgment will make friends as well as enemies in the short run. There is also the possibility that the analogy of a capital fund is faulty, that in the long run the assertion of power will to some extent augment power. Perhaps a sweeping judicial claim of authority helps generate a disposition to accept that authority; perhaps the habit of command tends to produce a habit of obedience.

10

Can the Supreme Court Defend Civil Liberties? *

EDMOND CAHN

Edmond Cahn was one of the leading authorities on American law. His work is regarded as among the most brilliant and profound writings on the American legal order. He was also a firm defender of the "preferred freedoms" wing of the Court. Here he discusses the propriety of Court intervention, the nature of democratic theory in our political system.

In recent years, innumerable speeches and articles, not to mention Justice Robert H. Jackson's posthumous book, have been devoted to contending that the Supreme Court can do little or nothing. Most of this literature sounds like the querulous excuses of a hypochondriac. Back in 1935 and 1936, the court drank some raw wine and woke up with a bad

* Edmond Cahn, "Can the Supreme Court Defend Civil Liberties?" Pamphlet No. 9, Sidney Hillman Foundation, n.d., pp. 7-8, 15-18. Reprinted by permission of the author and publisher.

headache in 1937. You would think the hangover would have ended by now, but such is not the case. On the contrary, the memories of the 1930s still haunt many of the justices. They keep wringing their hands over the court's impotence, while they tell us that unlike Congress, it must sit and wait for cases to come before it, that unlike Congress it cannot launch its own investigations, and that it must depend on other branches of the government to define its appellate jurisdiction and enforce its decrees. Justice Jackson said that no court decree could have stopped the downfall of the French monarchy or the onslaught of the French Revolution, as though he believed that our conditions were similar to those of Paris in 1789 and as though our Secretary of Agriculture had looked unsympathetically at some starving employees of General Motors and said "Let them eat cake."

Of course, the Supreme Court must function like a court; it cannot perform the operations of a legislature. Of course, like all governmental institutions, there are limits to its powers. But Congress and the President do not refuse to perform their duties just because they cannot also act like a court. We know and the court knows it *can* act forcefully and courageously when it wills to. It has done so on many occasions, for example, in the steel seizure case and very recently in the school segregation cases.

Four Ways to Say No

A hypochondriac can gradually convince himself that day by day he is able to do less and less. Then, if he is a really imaginative hypochondriac, he will find a complicated variety of ways to say "No, I can't." There are at least four technical ways for the Supreme Court to say "no" without appearing to do so. (1) It can say the party who is trying to present the question to it has no standing to sue. In other words, the question may be an important question, but the party who poses it is not the right party. (2) The court can say the proceeding is not a true "case or controversy" and is, therefore, not within its power under the Constitution. (3) It can say the question in the case is a "political question," which means that the executive or legislative or perhaps the electorate must find the answer, not the courts. (4) In the majority of instances, the Supreme Court can sim-

ply refuse to take the case at all, without publishing any explanation. Most of the Supreme Court's appellate jurisdiction is taken or refused at the justices' option by granting or denying a writ of *certiorari*. . . .

The Clash on the Supreme Court

On the present Supreme Court, there is comparatively little disagreement about the constitutionality of federal economic and social legislation; that is no longer the problem. But when a case involves freedom of personal and political expression, that is to say, a right under the First Amendment, then philosophy clashes against philosophy. The majoritarian justices acknowledge that the First Amendment is couched in absolute and categorical terms, forbidding *any* abridgement of free expression, whether reasonable or unreasonable. Nevertheless, majoritarian justices take a neutral, laissez-faire attitude toward laws abridging free expression if they can find some "reasonable" ground for the legislation.

The libertarians emphasize the absolute language of the First Amendment, which says that Congress shall make "no law" abridging these freedoms. They say that there are three basic reasons why language is so very absolute: (1) Some of the rights of free expression, such as worshipping God and forming one's private opinions, cannot become the proper business or concern of any government; (2) without active exchange of information and ideas, a society stagnates and ultimately loses its freedom and (3) representative government needs the criticism of a free press and free debate so that the people may be able to make informed decisions. This is the libertarian philosophy.

In one important field of constitutional law, the Supreme Court's majoritarians do follow the principles of the libertarians. I refer, of course, to the rights of Negroes to equal protection of the laws. We have made such magnificent, though—Heaven knows—belated, strides toward racial equality in the past generation because on this front the *whole* court has adopted a libertarian view. As libertarian justices see it, this record shows that the court need not surrender fundamental American ideals, or follow a laissez-faire policy, or exhibit an abject humility when it comes to deal with the enemies of freedom. If, in the teeth of prejudice and passion, the court can uphold equal protection of the laws, why is not the Jeffersonian philosophy likewise applicable when First Amendment liberties are attacked, or when security procedures violate elementary standards of fairness?

The U.S. and England

There is another string to the majoritarian bow. They like to point to the superiority of the English system, under which Parliament is supreme and the courts possess no right of constitutional review. The majoritarians claim that Americans rely too much on the Supreme Court to protect their liberties, and thus become lazy and flaccid. In England, we are told, they order these things better. Since Englishmen cannot turn to the courts to invalidate an act of Parliament, the newspapers speak up more actively and the House of Commons is peculiarly sensitive to any infringement of liberty or miscarriage of justice. Thus, it is claimed, the English system reposes genuine trust in the people. . . .

Half a Loaf

The difficulty with the majoritarians is that they are trying to graft an incomplete slice of the English system on ours. They don't say, "Let us change to a parliamentary government, headed by a prime minister who will be subject, along with the other heads of departments, to regular scrutiny at a 'question hour.'" They don't say that, if the legislature censures a minister's action, the whole government will resign. Thus the majoritarians are proposing to take away one of our major protections—the Supreme Court's intervention—without putting anything in its stead. After a century and a half of relying on the Supreme Court as one, though of course not the only, means of defense, why should we acquiesce in its abandoning the function unless we are provided with some equivalent shield for our rights?

Finally, which philosophy puts more trust in the people? The majoritarians claim it is theirs, because they follow a policy of laissez-faire toward the people's elected representatives, and refuse to accord a preferred position to First Amendment freedoms. Here I think is the very nucleus of their error. When a problem arises under the First Amendment, it may appear on the surface as though the majoritarians favor deferring to the people and the libertarians favor defying the people.

On deeper analysis, we discover precisely the contrary. For what happens when a majoritarian court yields to legislative excitement in a First Amendment case? The restrictive law or administrative order becomes effective and reduces the people's access to information and opinion. What happens when a libertarian view prevails and such a law is struck down? Then the channels of information and persuasion are kept open, and the people remain free to examine, evaluate, and decide for themselves. Real confidence in the people will give them credit for capacity to reject Communist propaganda and Communist advocacy. If the mass of Americans were so myopic that they could not be trusted to see the conspicuous folly and falsity of Communist advocacy, the republic would indeed be in a hopeless state. It is the libertarians who have a genuine and robust faith in the people and in the republic. . . .

CHAPTER TWELVE

United States Foreign Policy

This book has thus far treated the United States as a nation living in isolation. We have considered the philosophical assumptions around which American government is organized; we have examined its structure and institutions; we have looked at its informal government devices. But however effective this approach may be for classroom purposes, true perspective is greatly distorted by such a treatment.

For the United States is only one nation among many. We live in a world which has over 100 sovereign nations and only fragments of international government. In such a chaotic international scene, national survival itself is at stake. Furthermore, the possibility of withdrawing from the turbulence of world affairs diminishes steadily because of intercontinental ballistic missiles, TV programs, scheduled air flights, and competing probes into outer space. Over 10 per cent of our gross national product is spent each year for national defense.

In the international arena the United States has an uneven balance sheet: in terms of population we are but pygmies, with less than 6 per cent of the world's people; in terms of wealth and power we loom as the world's leading nation. Our standard of living is the world's highest, our productive plant is the world's largest, and our military strength, thanks to an advanced technology, is the greatest single force in world affairs.

With such power goes responsibility. Obviously, if our diplomats are committed to the preservation of American interests in the contemporary world, those interests need definition. Also, the fate of many other nations is tied to American policy. It has been said that "when the United States sneezes, Europe gets a cold." What is true of Europe is also true for Asia, Africa, and islands of the sea.

WHICH APPROACH TO WORLD AFFAIRS: REALISTIC, LEGALISTIC, HUMANISTIC, OR MILITARISTIC?

Prior to World War II the "great debate" in American foreign policy centered around "isolation" or "intervention." Isolation was discarded by the march of events in favor of intervention.

Today some foreign-policy spokesmen are described as "hard-liners," "soft-liners," "hawks," "doves," or "chickens." Some Americans believe that the United States has a mission in the world—to spread the doctrine of individual worth and integrity. Other Americans dismiss this as gross sentimentality and insist that the chief role of foreign policy is to protect us from predatory neighbors. Some spokesmen plead for a clear-eyed realism, divorced from ideology. Others insist that the basic United States commitment should be to treaties, alliances, and the growing body of international law.

Such a sample does not exhaust the conflicting philosophies. But the spokesmen and viewpoints presented here are in the mainstream of present United States debates over foreign policy.

THE UNITED STATES AND THE COMMUNIST BLOC: PERMANENT HOSTILITY OR DECREASING TENSIONS?

One approach to the Communist bloc rests heavily on ideology and the historical record. Marx, Lenin, and Stalin agreed that there could be nothing except a strategic truce with world capitalism. Communism is dedicated to the overthrow of other economic-political systems and is only temporarily diverted from such long-range goals. The foreign policy records of the USSR and Red China confirm this ideological analysis.

Another approach denies the preceding analysis. It posits that the Communist world is not a single massive entity with a single true faith. Rifts and dissension are apparent everywhere. Many third-generation Russian Communists seem willing and eager to grasp the good life of the present, rather than to pursue world revolution.

The conflict between these schools of thought is direct and sharp. Who is right? Can we or should we negotiate with the Soviet leaders? Are the American "hard-liners" actually creating the situation they most fear by refusing to negotiate? Is the Soviet Union an unstable, scheming conspiracy, or do Russian leaders simply work for the best interests of the Soviet Union as they define them?

THE UNITED STATES AND WESTERN EUROPE: AN ATLANTIC COMMUNITY OR TWO SEPARATE ENTITIES?

Western Europe has been of special concern to the United States since World War II. American wealth distributed under the auspices of the Marshall Plan rehabilitated these countries in the years between 1948 and 1955. American armed might was the foundation of the North Atlantic Treaty Organization, which protected the continent against Russian aggression. The European Free Trade Association and the European Economic Community (European Common Market) was created under the benign eye of the United States.

All of these developments seemed to move ahead within an uncoordinated but reasonable plan. Western Europe would grow stronger, more unified, and more closely allied to the United States. But the script as thus written has been revised in recent years. European nations have criticized United States policy in the Far East; they have made their own approaches to the Soviet Union; they have been increasingly restive in NATO. Is this a passing phase? Or is it the end of an era? Should the United States accept a changing Europe and recast its approach, or should it try to preserve the older arrangement?

1

*In Search of a Realistic Foreign Policy**

SENATOR J. W. FULBRIGHT

Senator Fulbright has played a questioning, critical role as Chairman of the Senate Foreign Relations Committee during the past dozen years. His great concern, expressed in the following selection, has been that the United States would adopt a moralistic, unswerving course in world affairs. According to Fulbright, what are some "old myths?" and "new realities?" What are some "unthinkable thoughts?" Can a nation survive when it is cut loose from moral commitments?

There is an inevitable divergence, attributable to the imperfections of the human mind, between the world as it is and the world as men perceive it. As long as our perceptions are reasonably close to objective reality, it is possible for us to act upon our problems in a rational and appropriate manner. But when our perceptions fail to keep pace with events, when we refuse to believe something be-cause it displeases or frightens us, or is simply startlingly unfamiliar, then the gap between fact and perception becomes a chasm, and action becomes irrelevant and irrational.

There has always—and inevitably—been some divergence between the realities of foreign policy and our ideas about it. This divergence has in certain respects been growing rather than narrowing, and we are handicapped, according, by policies based on old myths rather than current realities. The divergence is dangerous and unnecessary—dangerous because it can reduce foreign policy to a fraudu-

* From J. W. Fulbright, *Old Myths and New Realities* (Random House, 1964), pp. 3-4, 6-8, 70-73, 76-77. © Copyright 1964 by J. William Fulbright. Reprinted by permission of Random House, Inc.

lent game of imagery and appearances, unnecessary because it can be overcome by the determination of men in high office to dispel prevailing misconceptions through the candid dissemination of unpleasant but inescapable facts.

*   *   *

These astonishing changes in the configuration of the postwar world have had an unsettling effect on both public and official opinion in the United States. One reason for this, I believe, lies in the fact that we are a people used to looking at the world, and indeed at ourselves, in moralistic rather than empirical terms. We are predisposed to regard any conflict as a clash between good and evil rather than as simply a clash between conflicting interests. We are inclined to confuse freedom and democracy, which we regard as moral principles, with the way in which they are practiced in America—with capitalism, federalism, and the two-party system, which are not moral principles but simply the preferred and accepted practices of the American people. There is much cant in American moralism and not a little inconsistency. It resembles in some ways the religious faith of the many respectable people who, in Samuel Butler's words, would be equally horrified to hear the Christian religion doubted or to see it practiced."

Our national vocabulary is full of "self-evident truths," not only about "life, liberty, and happiness," but about a vast number of personal and public issues, including the cold war. It has become one of the "self-evident truths" of the postwar era that, just as the President resides in Washington and the Pope in Rome, the Devil resides immutably in Moscow. We have come to regard the Kremlin as the permanent seat of his power and

we have grown almost comfortable with a menace which, though unspeakably evil, has had the redeeming virtues of constancy, predictability, and familiarity. Now the Devil has betrayed us by traveling abroad and, worse still, by dispersing himself, turning up now here, now there, and in many places at once, with a devilish disregard for the laboriously constructed frontiers of ideology.

We are confronted with a complex and fluid world situation, and we are not adapting ourselves to it. We are clinging to old myths in the face of new realities, and we are seeking to escape the contradictions by narrowing the permissible bounds of public discussion, by relegating an increasing number of ideas and viewpoints to a growing category of "unthinkable thoughts." I believe that this tendency can and should be reversed, that it is within our ability, and unquestionably in our interests, to cut loose from established myths and to start thinking some "unthinkable thoughts"— about the cold war and East—West relations, about the underdeveloped countries and particularly those in Latin America, about the changing nature of the Chinese Communist threat in Asia, and about the festering war in Vietnam.

*   *   *

When all is said and done, when the abstractions and subtleties of political science have been exhausted, there remain the most basic unanswered questions about war and peace and why we contest the issues we contest and why we even care about them. As Aldous Huxley has written: "There may be arguments about the best way of raising wheat in a cold climate or of re-afforesting a denuded mountain. But such arguments never lead to organized slaughter. Organized slaughter is the result of arguments about such questions as the following: Which is the best nation? The best religion? The best political theory? The best form of government? Why are other people so stupid and wicked? Why can't they see how good and intelligent we are? Why do they resist our beneficent efforts to bring them under our control and make them like ourselves?"[1]

In our search for answers to the complex questions of war and peace, we come ultimately to the paradox of man himself, which I have never heard better expressed than in a one-page essay called "Man," written by an American hill-country philosopher whose writings suggest strongly the style and thought of Mark Twain. It reads as follows:

Man is a queer animal, like the beasts of the fields, the fowls of the air, and the fishes of the sea, he came into this world without his consent and is going out the same way.

At birth he is one of the most helpless creatures in all existence. He can neither walk, talk, swim nor crawl, and has but two legs while most other animals have four legs. Unlike other animals he has no covering for his body to protect it against the bite or sting of poisonous insects, tooth or claw of ferocious beasts save a little hair which appears about his body only in patches.

With all his limitations he yet has one advantage over animals—the power of reason, but history shows that he often discards that for superstition. Of all the animals on earth, man has shown himself to be the most cruel and brutal. He is the only animal that will create instruments of death for his own destruction.

Man is the only animal on all the earth that has ever been known to burn its young as a sacrifice to appease the wrath of some imaginary deity. He is the only

one that will build homes, towns and cities at such a cost in sacrifice and suffering and turn around and destroy them in war.

He is the only animal that will gather his fellows together in creeds, clans, and nations, line them up in companies, regiments, armies, and get glory out of their slaughter. Just because some king or politician told him to.

Man is the only creature in all existence that is not satisfied with the punishment he can inflict on his fellows while here, but had to invent a hell of fire and brimstone in which to burn them after they are dead.

Where he came from, or when, or how, or where he is going after death he does not know, but he hopes to live again in ease and idleness where he can worship his gods and enjoy himself, watching his fellow creatures wriggle and writhe in eternal flames down in hell.

The root question, for which I must confess I have no answer, is how and why it is that so much of the energy and intelligence that men could use to make life better for themselves is used instead to make life difficult and painful for other men. When the subtleties of strategy and power and diplomatic method have all been explained, we are still left with the seemingly unanswerable question of how and why it is that we *care* about such things, which are so remote from the personal satisfactions that bring pleasure and grace and fulfillment into our lives.

The paradoxes of human nature are eternal and perhaps unanswerable, but I do think we know enough about elemental human needs to be able to apply certain psychological principles in our efforts to alleviate the tensions of the cold war.

❖   ❖   ❖

We must bring to bear all the resources of human knowledge and invention to build viable foundations

---

[1] Aldous Huxley, "The Politics of Ecology" pamphlet, published by The Center for the Study of Democratic Institutions, Santa Barbara, California, 1963), p. 6.

of security in the nuclear age—the resources of political science and history, of economics and sociology, of psychology and literature and the arts. It is not enough to seek security through armaments or even through ingenious schemes of disarmament; nor is it enough to seek security through schemes for the transfer of territories or for the deployment and redeployment of forces. Security is a state of mind rather than a set of devices and arrangements. The latter are important because they contribute, but only to the extent that they contribute, to generating a *psychological process* in which peoples and statesmen come increasingly to think of war as undesirable and unfeasible.

It is this *process* that has critical importance for our security. Whether we advance it by seeking a settlement on Berlin or a new disarmament agreement, by the opening of consulates or by a joint enterprise in space, is less important than that the process be advanced. Our emphasis at any one time should be on those issues which seem most likely to be tractable and soluble. As long as we are by one means or another cultivating a world-wide state of mind in which peace is favored over war, we are doing the most effective possible thing to strengthen the foundations of our security. And only when such a state of mind is widely prevalent in the world will the kind of unprecedented political creativity on a global scale which has been made necessary by the invention of nuclear weapons become possible as well.

2

Our Foreign Policy Is Based on International Law *

DEAN RUSK

One tradition that dominates American foreign policy is that of legalism and the sanctity of international law. We justify our actions in terms of treaty obligations. We encourage international conferences. We point hopefully toward an eventual world order based on law. All of these ideas are woven into the following address delivered by United States Secretary of State Dean Rusk.

How realistic is such an approach? Does force always take precedence over law in international affairs? Are most existing arrangements imposed by the strong on the weak? Will international law spread and eventually have the authority of national law? Is there danger that an emphasis on legalism will encase our foreign policy in an intellectual straitjacket?

❊　❊　❊

. . . Current United States policy arouses the criticism that it is at once

too legal and tough. Time was when the criticism of American concern with the legal element in international relations was that it led to softness—to a "legalistic-moralistic" approach to foreign affairs which conformed more to the ideal than to the real.

* Dean Rusk, "The Control of Force in International Relations," *Department of State Bulletin*, May 10, 1965, pp. 695-96, 699-701.

Today, criticism of American attachment to the role of law is that it leads not to softness but to severity. We are criticized not for sacrificing our national interests to international interests but for endeavoring to impose the international interest upon other nations. We are criticized for treating the statement of the law by the International Court of Justice as authoritative. We are criticized for taking collective security seriously.

This criticism is, I think, a sign of strength—of our strength and of the strength of international law. It is a tribute to a blending of political purpose with legal ethic.

American foreign policy is at once principled and pragmatic. Its central objective is our national safety and well-being—to "secure the Blessings of Liberty to ourselves and our Posterity." But we know we can no longer find security and well-being in defenses and policies which are confined to North America, or the Western Hemisphere, or the North Atlantic community.

This has become a very small planet. We have to be concerned with all of it—with all of its land, waters, atmosphere, and with surrounding space. We have a deep national interest in peace, the prevention of aggression, the faithful performance of agreements, the growth of international law. Our foreign policy is rooted in the profoundly practical realization that the purposes and principles of the United Nations Charter must animate the behavior of states if mankind is to prosper or is even to survive. Or at least they must animate enough states with enough will and enough resources to see to it that others do not violate those rules with impunity.

The preamble and articles 1 and 2 of the charter set forth abiding purposes of American policy. This is not surprising, since we took the lead in drafting the charter—at a time when the biggest war in history was still raging and we and others were thinking deeply about its frightful costs and the ghastly mistakes and miscalculations which led to it.

The kind of world we seek is the kind set forth in the opening sections of the charter: a world community of independent states, each with the institutions of its own choice but cooperating with one another to promote their mutual welfare, a world in which the use of force is effectively inhibited, a world of expanding human rights and well-being, a world of expanding international law, a world in which an agreement is a commitment and not just a tactic.

We believe that this is the sort of world a great majority of the governments of the world deserve. We believe it is the sort of world man must achieve if he is not to perish. As I said on another occasion:[1]

If once the international rule of law could be discussed with a certain condescension as a utopian ideal, today it becomes an elementary practical necessity. *Pacta sunt servanda* now becomes the basis of survival.

Unhappily, a minority of governments is committed to different ideas of the conduct and organization of human affairs. They are dedicated to the promotion of the Communist world revolution. And their doctrine justifies any technique, any ruse, any deceit, which contributes to that end. They may differ as to tactics from time to time. And the two principal Communist powers are competitors for the leadership of the world Communist movement. But both are committed to the eventual communization of the entire world

[1] For an address by Secretary Rusk before the American Law Institute on May 22, 1964, see BULLETIN of June 8, 1964, p. 886.

The overriding issue of our time is which concepts are to prevail: those set forth in the United Nations Charter or those proclaimed in the name of a world revolution.

Charter Prohibitions on Use of Force

The paramount commitment of the charter is article 2, paragraph 4, which reads:

All Members shall refrain in their international relations from the threat or use of force against the territorial integrity or political independence of any state, or in any other manner inconsistent with the Purposes of the United Nations.

This comprehensive limitation went beyond the Covenant of the League of Nations. This more sweeping commitment sought to apply a bitter lesson of the interwar period—that the threat or use of force, whether or not called "war," feeds on success. The indelible lesson of those years is that the time to stop aggression is at its very beginning.

The exceptions to the prohibitions on the use or threat of force were expressly set forth in the charter. The use of force is legal:

—as a collective measure by the United Nations, or
—as action by regional agencies in accordance with chapter VIII of the charter, or
—in individual or collective self-defense.

When article 2, paragraph 4, was written it was widely regarded as general international law, governing both members and nonmembers of the United Nations. And on the universal reach of the principle embodied in article 2, paragraph 4, wide agreement remains.

Thus, last year, a United Nations Special Committee on Principles of International Law Concerning Friendly Relations and Cooperation Among States met in Mexico City. All shades of United Nations opinion were represented. The Committee's purpose was to study and possibly to elaborate certain of those principles. The Committee debated much and agreed on little. But on one point, it reached swift and unanimous agreement: that all states, and not only all members of the United Nations, are bound to refrain in their international relations from the threat or use of force against the territorial integrity or political independence of any state. Nonrecognition of the statehood of a political entity was held not to affect the international application of this cardinal rule of general international law.

❖   ❖   ❖

A "Common Law of Mankind"

Before closing I should like to turn away from the immediate difficulties and dangers of the situation in Southeast Asia and remind you of the dramatic progress that shapes and is being shaped by expanding international law.

A "common law of mankind"—to use the happy phrase of your distinguished colleague Wilfred Jenks—is growing as the world shrinks and as the vistas of space expand. This year is, by proclamation of the General Assembly, International Cooperation Year, a year to direct attention to the common interests of mankind and to accelerate the joint efforts being undertaken to further them. Those common interests are enormous and intricate, and the joint efforts which further them are developing fast, although perhaps not fast enough.

In the 19th century the United States attended an average of one international conference a year. Now we attend nearly 600 a year. We are party to 4,300 treaties and other international agreements in force. Three-fourths of these were signed in the last 25 years. Our interest in the observance of all of these treaties and agreements is profound, whether the issue is peace in Laos, or the payment of United Nations assessments, or the allocation of radio frequencies, or the application of airline safeguards, or the control of illicit traffic in narcotics, or any other issue which states have chosen to regulate through the lawmaking process. The writing of international cooperation into international law is meaningful only if the law is obeyed—and only if the international institutions which administer and develop the law function in accordance with agreed procedures, until the procedures are changed.

Everything suggests that the rate of growth in international law, like the rate of change in almost every other field these days, is rising at a very steep angle.

In recent years the law of the sea has been developed and codified, but it first evolved in a leisurely fashion over the centuries. International agreements to regulate aerial navigation had to be worked out within the period of a couple of decades. Now, within the first few years of man's adventures in outer space, we are deeply involved in the creation of international institutions, regulations, and law to govern this effort.

Already the United Nations has developed a set of legal principles to govern the use of outer space and declared celestial bodies free from national appropriation.

Already nations, including the United States and the Soviet Union, have agreed not to orbit weapons of mass destruction in outer space.

Already the Legal Subcommittee of the United Nations Committee on Outer Space is formulating international agreements on liability for damage caused by the reentry of objects launched into outer space and on rescue and return of astronauts and space objects.

Already the first international sounding-rocket range has been established in India and is being offered for United Nations sponsorhip.

To make orderly space exploration possible at this stage, the International Tele-communication Union had to allocate radio frequencies for the purpose.

To take advantage of weather reporting and forecasting potential of observation satellites, married to computer technology, the World Meteorological Organization is creating a vast system of data acquisition, analysis, and distribution which depends entirely on international agreement, regulation, and standards.

And to start building a single global communications satellite system, we have created a novel international institution in which a private American corporation shares ownership with 45 governments.

This is but part of the story of how the pace of discovery and invention forces us to reach out for international agreement, to build international institutions, to do things in accordance with an expanding international and transnational law. Phenomenal as the growth of treaty obligations is, the true innovation of 20th-century international law lies more in the fact that we have nearly 80 international institutions which are capable of carrying out those obligations.

It is important that the processes and products of international cooperation be understood and appreciated; and it is important that the broader significance of the contributions of international problems of an economic, social, scientific, and humanitarian character not be overestimated. For all the progress of peace could be incinerated in war.

Thus the control of force in international relations remains the paramount problem which confronts the diplomat and the lawyer—and the man in the street and the man in the rice field. Most of mankind is not in an immediate position to grapple very directly with that problem, but the problem is no less crucial. The responsibility of those, in your profession and mine, who do grapple with it is the greater. I am happy to acknowledge that this Society in thinking and debating courageously and constructively about the conditions of peace, continues to make its unique contribution and to make it well.

3

The Anglo-American Traditional Policy Is Humanistic *

SIR PATRICK DEAN

The modern world has stressed comprehensive ideologies as a foundation for foreign policy. Probably the most widely advertised ideology has been that of Communism, which pictures the inevitable destruction of capitalism and the world-wide triumph of the International Soviet. Almost intuitively, many Americans have urged a counter-ideology that anticipates the ultimate destruction of Communism.

At best this ideological approach is negative. The British ambassador to the United States, Sir Patrick Dean, here advances another ideological concept of foreign policy—that of humanistic concern for individual rights. Can such an idea be dignified with the name ideology? Is it actually a public relations phrase divorced from the real world? Or is it a valid description of our goals on the world scene? For instance, does it explain United States policy in Asia? Europe? Latin America?

❖   ❖   ❖

The vast and unprecedented political reorganization which has taken place right across the globe in the last twenty years requires us to study anew what we might call the ideology of our foreign policy. In this comparatively brief period some fifty new nation states have been created with a total population of over one billion.

Before the second world war most of these states were members of half a dozen great imperial systems whose rulers could effectively and exclusively answer for them and discuss with each other, in terms of the reality of world power, the problems of ensuring peaceful relations and economic and commercial cooperation among them all within an inter-imperial world community. Now all that is changed, and we must now ask ourselves what sort of international society, what sort of world-wide pat

* Sir Patrick Dean, "The Ideology of Foreign Policy," *Vital Speeches of the Day*, 32, No. 6 (January 1, 1966), 173-75. Reprinted by permission of the publisher.

tern of relationships should now be our objective. The problem is how best can we organize, not only from government to government, but from people to people, relationships involving human beings of all races, cultures and creeds, divided as they are into so many states and so different as are those states in size, population, resources and economic capacity. I am not now referring to an international society in terms of an organization such as the United Nations or the many other international organizations which have special functions to perform, particularly in the preservation of peace. These have their place and are, indeed, essential. I use the word "society" in its first dictionary sense, as "association with one's fellow men" in whatever political or economic groups they are organized.

There are at first sight two very easy ways to answer this question.

One is that offered by a succession of Communist "Internationales." The Communists believe in the inevitability of the Communist way of life, and that their political and economic organization will one day triumph all over the world because of the internal contradictions of capitalism, and irrespective of the dictates of individual and personal morality and aspirations. The Communists conform to this almost mystical doctrine of inevitability, and in their Communist anthem look confidently to the day when "the internationale" will, as they put it, "unite the human race."

*   *   *

Another apparently simple way to answer this question is that taken by many who most strongly oppose Communism. For them the nations of the world are unfortunately, but irrevocably, divided into two groups composed of Communist and anti-Communist nations, with the so-called

non-aligned countries as both a buffer and a field between them for peaceful penetration by both sides. The proponents of this view then identify the anti-Communist nations as champions of democracy and declare that the first objective of foreign policy should be the discrediting and the defeat of the Communists.

For both the extreme Communist and the extreme anti-Communist the mainspring of political existence is an ideology according to which all international relationships must primarily be evaluated. For the reasons which I have given, I believe that neither of these extremes can provide a basis for international society, and that both must be rejected.

There is a third viewpoint which focuses neither upon an ideology nor upon the individual. According to this, the center of the political universe is the nation-state, the triumphant glory of which is the highest achievable goal of its citizens, transcending the rights and aspirations of the individuals within the state. Except in the most superficial way, no concession is made to the idea of any larger community of nations, including the community of mankind itself. A nation's existence, from this standpoint, requires certain relationships with other countries, but international agreements, obligations and institutions and every form of international collaboration between peoples and governments are to be evaluated only in terms of their effectiveness as instruments for fulfilling the purposes of the nation and the state.

This concept of national independence and self-sufficiency ignores altogether the economic and political facts of modern international society. It is incompatible, too, with the practical needs and methods of modern industrial production and distribution and of modern science and technology. It unhappily resembles the ultra-nationalism which produced the Great Depression of the 1930's, and ultimately led to the second world war. In terms of an enduring international society this concept, which has been tried and failed before, bears no real hope for the future, and is as unacceptable as the extremes of a world united under international Communism and a world uncompromisingly divided by the cold war.

Is there yet another choice? I think there is. It is the concept of an international society, in which national pride and personal characteristics are not derogated, but the rights of individual men are the foundation of coexistence. In this society it is recognized that the individual must be the master and not the slave of his ideological and national environment, and that the only true fulfillment can come from his being able to choose in freedom, and satisfy in dignity, his own personal, spiritual and material aspirations.

The concept of the rights of the individual in a context larger than the national environment was, of course, basic to your own American Revolution. The great step forward made by Jefferson and the founders of this Republic was that they took the rights which they had been brought up to regard as theirs as Englishmen under King James' Charter—the right of equality under the law and of representative self-government through the rule of the majority—and solemnly declared that these were valid not only for Englishmen, not only for Americans, but for all men everywhere. Quite apart from the internal development of the United States Constitution, their attitude has ever since provided an idealistic element in United States foreign policy which observers in other counrties have frequently failed to understand or allow for—with, for some of them, disastrous results.

The same humanistic attitude towards human rights and self-government greatly influenced British political thought throughout the 19th century, both at home and in our attitude to colonies of native Africans and Asians, as well as of British settlers. It is possible, and sometimes popular, to be cynical about British colonial policy, and I do not claim that it was at all times and in all places completely humane or disinterested. But I do think that even the most critical would now have to acknowledge that the view, which in the end has prevailed, has been that of those who believed that we held our colonies in trust for native populations who were equally entitled, with the British settlers, to all the rights of human beings, to equality under the law and to representative self-government under majority rule.

* * *

The most obvious barrier to co-operation between peoples is the threat of the use of illegal force in the settlement of international disputes and the attempts of ambitious nationalists to dominate their neighbors by various forms of aggression, disguised and undisguised, as, for example, has occurred in recent years in Korea, in Hungary, in Tibet, in Vietnam and in Malaysia. The concept of the kind of international society I have attempted to define is implicit in the Articles of the Charter of the United Nations. The United Nations and the numerous international agencies associated with it must be our primary resort in our efforts to establish a pattern of dealing between nations and peoples in which differences can be settled peaceably and legitimate national aspirations can be fulfilled. But we should also seek to define in an even broader and more positive sense the kind of international society in which we as individuals would like to live. For at best, international institutions, however wisely constituted and directed, can only embody and express relationships between groups of individuals which have at least begun to grow naturally between peoples.

At a time when champions of old style nationalism and competing ideologies are extremely vocal in the world, it is worth noting that Britain and the United States, because of their shared devotion to the ideals of humanity, law and personal freedom, have achieved a harmonious and vigorous partnership without sacrificing any national ideal or compromising any deeply revered ideology. Is it too much to hope that a similar sort of relationship might one day be established first, let us say, between Europe, the Commonwealth and North America, then between the industrialized and the developing nations and eventually between all peace-loving nations everywhere?

Let me conclude by quoting to you some words, not of a profound professional political scientist, nor of a professional diplomat, but of E. B. White of the "New Yorker" in the imaginary instructions which he wrote for the American delegates to the first General Assembly of the United Nations Organization in London nearly twenty years ago. I cannot answer for every one of them but I think that they have a wisdom and a truth which is relevant to my theme today. Here are his words:

When you rise to speak, get up like a man anywhere.

Do not bring home any bacon; it will have turned rancid on the journey. Bring home instead a silken thread, by which you may find your way back.

Bear in mind always that foreign policy is domestic policy with its hat on. The purpose of the meeting, although not so stated anywhere, is to replace policy with law, and to make common cause.

Make common cause.

Think not to represent us by safeguarding our interests. Represent us by perceiving that our interests are other peoples, and theirs ours.

When you think with longing of the place where you were born, remember that the sun leaves it daily to go somewhere else.

If you would speak up for us, speak up for people, for the free man. We are not despatching you to build national greatness. Unless you understand this, believe it, you might better be at the race track, where you can have a good time simply by guessing wrong.

Peace is to be had when people's antagonisms and antipathies are subject to the discipline of law and the decency of government.

Do not try to save the world by loving thy neighbor; it will only make him nervous. Save the world by respecting thy neighbor's rights under law and insisting that he respect yours under the same law. In short, save the world. . . .

To some of you these words may smack too much of evangelism. But they are practical instructions, and, as I began this address by saying, in this uneasy and tumultuous world we need more confidence in ourselves and our beliefs, more faith in our neighbors and their humanity, and greater determination to fashion our relations with all our fellow-men in conditions of equality, justice and human dignity.

4

Military Power Is the Foundation of Foreign Policy *

BARRY GOLDWATER

Many Americans find all talk of a foreign policy based on ideology, negotiation, or law so much gibberish. They are convinced that our goals in the world are directly related to our military strength. If we are strong, our voice will be clear and decisive. If we are weak, no one will heed us.

This concept was presented forcefully by Barry Goldwater during the 1964 presidential campaign. His defeat did not end the debate over the place of military power in foreign affairs.

Somehow, in some way, a relationship does exist between military strength and foreign policy. But is the Strategic Air Command's motto "Peace Is Our Profession" an overstatement? Are all maneuvers toward disarmament a disaster? What of the Nuclear Test Ban treaty? Should military leaders exercise a decisive voice on foreign policy? Or should they be but one component in a complicated mix of ideas?

* * *

What peace there is in the world today is the result of our strength. The conflict that breaks out is the result of our weakness. Wherever and whenever we have moved from strength, we have moved closer to peace. Wherever we have moved from fear or weakness, we have moved closer to war.

On the dark day when Nikita Khrushchev sabotaged the 1960 Paris Conference, President Eisenhower's Secretary of Defense alerted the Strategic Air Command. We moved from resolution and strength. And Nikita Khrushchev backed down. *He* moved from fear. He returned to Moscow, via East Berlin, and warned the Communist world to avoid further

* Barry Goldwater, *Where I Stand* (New York: McGraw-Hill Book Company, Inc., 1964), pp. 68-69, 71, 73-75, 77-78. Copyright © 1964 by Barry Goldwater. Reprinted by permission of the publisher.

provocations, to be patient—in effect, to back down.

Again, under President Eisenhower, our first move in the Berlin crisis of 1958-59 was to move an extra aircraft carrier to the Sixth Fleet as a clear warning to the Communists. Khrushchev cooled down again, far more quickly and with far less cost to us than when Robert McNamara called up the reserves in 1961. That was a chaotic and costly maneuver that did nothing but perpetuate the now apparently permanent crisis in Germany.

When our Marines moved into Lebanon, when we moved our naval and air power in the Formosa Straits, we moved closer to peace, not war. It was when our nerve failed at the Bay of Pigs that we moved closer to war by opening the door for the missile crisis.

During the missile crisis, briefly, we moved from strength—and the Communists had to retreat. But since then the balance has been tipping away from us again. Indecision and lack of follow-through have shored up Communism's outpost in our hemisphere and have permitted it to expand its influence. A blockade of Cuba would not risk war. It is the blockade against common sense in this Administration that risks war by letting problems fester rather than resolving them.

But let us be very clear on the crucial point: the national power which has permitted us to move from strength in the past and which even today *could* permit us to do so—*this power is not perpetual or automatic.* It cannot be maintained at a standstill. There is another side to the power equation—the Communist side. If our power remains at a standstill while theirs grows we shall be, in effect, disarming ourselves. And this, I charge, is what we are now doing.

If the Communists make a major weapons breakthrough while we sit on our plans, burn our bombers, and permit free-world alliances to crumble, there can be no peace in the world. Communism would have the tools of nuclear blackmail and would use them. And this mighty nation, mighty no longer, would be ringed by crisis, hemmed in by threats, and pressed closer and closer to the fateful choice of war or surrender.

There are four fatal flaws in our defense posture which foreshadow that grim time. These flaws will not be repaired by the men who created them. They have a vested interest in their own mistakes. Let me list the flaws and then elaborate upon them.

First: we are building a Maginot Line of missiles.

Second: we are failing to introduce rapid technological advances, sometimes because of false economy, sometimes because of misguided steps toward disarmament.

Third: we are permitting our defense policies to disrupt NATO and our other alliances.

Fourth: we are downgrading the armed services, ignoring professional military advice, and substituting one man's bookkeeping technique for national policy.

* * *

Manned systems have many characteristics lacking in ballistic missiles—the ability to hit unanticipated targets, to perform post-attack reconnaissance, to do the jobs of mopping up, to allow margins for the errors of missile targeting, to permit maneuver, to be *re-used* and *recalled* if desired. The motto of the Strategic Air Command is "Peace Is Our Profession." Let us make sure that they have the tools to practice that profession.

* * *

God help us if we can't have American leadership that thinks as forcefully and devoutly of America—that thinks as forcefully of the cause of freedom all over the world and seeks to re-unite the free world, not divide it.

The more our defense policies move toward a one-weapon system, toward major reliance on missiles based in the United States, toward denial of real nuclear partnership with our allies—so long as we move that way, NATO will decline and eventually fall apart. There may be no NATO after 1970 if the politics of this Administration are permitted to continue.

Is that what Americans want? To be isolated, to be friendless, to be prepared to defend freedom only by the devastation of intercontinental nuclear war? . . .

The shield of peace is the power of the peace-loving nations. The day that shield drops is the day that bombs may drop. Today, the preponderant strength we have carried over from the Eisenhower years gives us the capability to rebuff and roll back Communism, and also the power to deter war. Today it is the *will to win* that we lack.

Tomorrow, if we do not change our course and our commanders, we may not have the capability even if we should find the will. I do not want to risk the security of this nation, of the entire free world, by replacing the real shield of peace with vain hopes and misplaced faith. *This is no computer-room game we are playing.*

This is freedom's time on the line of history. And if we cannot or will not defend ourselves it might well be freedom's *last* time for dark centuries to come. Let our arms match our cause. Let our men match the times. This is the way to peace through strength. This is the way freedom's cause can win, *without war*, but with honor and justice. This is the victory that we must seek.

❊   ❊   ❊

We have not adequately tested our missiles. We have not accumulated the sort of data which the Soviets may well have accumulated in their big-blast tests. We have not fully tested the hardness of our missile silos. We have not fully tested the effects of nuclear-generated blackout, of gamma pulses, or other blast phenomena. The reliability of these weapons is simply not great enough. Nor is the weapon itself versatile enough, or flexible

enough, so that we can afford to put all of our eggs in this single basket.

This is not war talk. This is peace talk. This is how we can keep the peace. This Administration is moving toward a rigid and weak position—the way to tempt our enemy to war, the way to tempt him to mistakes, to *stumble* toward war.

Peace can be kept through strength. And that is what I am talking about. This is what military leaders like Curtis LeMay are talking about. Let me quote his testimony, in the same hearings that have got him into such hot water with this lukewarm Administration. He said this:

I am trying to defend the country ten years from now . . . I firmly believe the right answer is to have a mix of weapons systems and not depend on one . . . I say to you if you were President of the United States and had only missiles to fire, when are you going to press that button? I say that you are going to think a long time before you do it.

If you have anything else to show your will, you are going to use it . . . The big use of these manned systems comes before the war ever starts, to show the will to fight. You have flexibility . . . I think this is a very important part of our defense. If we can prevent a war from happening, we will have succeeded in our mission. If the war happens, I think we have failed.

Is that war-mongering? It is not. That is *peace*-mongering—the *right* way.

5

The United States Must Not Negotiate with the Soviet Union *

SLOBODAN M. DRASKOVICH

One position with respect to United States–Communist relations is clear-cut. It advocates regarding Communism as a world-wide conspiracy, undeviatingly committed to our destruction. Any negotiation is futile. Any hope that the passage of time will soften orthodox Marxism only reveals American muddleheadedness. A vigorous summary of that position appears below.

If this concept is accepted, certain questions regarding United States foreign policy follow. Faced with an implacable enemy, should we not wage preventive war? Is there any chance that the Communist world will eventually fall because of its own inner contradictions? Can any segments of the Communist bloc be split off through adroit diplomacy?

Implementing the various points of our non-political approach to the problems of our foreign policy, as I suggested last month, America has spent all its energy in attempts to attain non-political goals. The purpose of this article will be to briefly examine some of these goals:

THE RELAXATION OR LESSENING OF TENSION. Here is a Soviet propaganda device which means that anybody who resists the Communist conquest of the world is, obviously, a warmonger, who is creating tension. Tensions, as everybody knows, lead to war. Thus this slogan makes sense only from the Communist point of view and within the framework of Communist political warfare. It does not make any sense from our viewpoint. Our efforts for lessening tensions can be judged honest, sincere, and ef-

ficient by the USSR only if, and in the degree to which, we surrender.

* * *

NEGOTIATION has been a basic ingredient of our foreign policy. But negotiations make no sense under the circumstances. What can antipodes—when one is waging total political war with the aim of destroying the other, while the other is imploring the one for a little understanding of her peaceful soul, to "give us a fair shake"—negotiate about. About ways and means to avoid war? But that is precisely the Communist aim. Why should they negotiate about that? And their atom-rattling is no threat of war, since Communists do not threaten to take action when they are ready. They take it, without warning. If the Communists indulge in negotiations, and very long and wearisome ones, it is because negotiations have an important place in their strategy and arsenal. They serve to blackmail us, expose us to the world

---

* Condensed from Slobodan M. Draskovich, "American Foreign Policy," *American Opinion*, December, 1962, pp. 37–42. Reprinted by permission of the publisher.

as unyielding warmongers, to ridicule us, and to force us to retreat and prepare further retreats. Negotiations pave the way for the Communist conquest of the world, without war. That is why the Communists negotiate. But what have we ever won from our negotiations with the Communists?!?

WORKING TO REACH AGREEMENTS. The Communists have a unique record of disregarding obligations and violating agreements. To them such things are scraps of paper, or pie crusts whose only function is to be broken, in the witty explanation of Nikita Khrushchev. Where is the agreement that the Communists have respected!?!

DISARMAMENT. From the Communist point of view, this is of supreme importance. They know their superiority in political warfare, just as they are fully aware of their irremediable inferiority in military strength and capacity. Therefore the Communists are interested in seeing the United States disarm, as much as possible, as soon as possible, and as unilaterally as possible. We have gone a long way to accommodate them. We have imposed on ourselves a three-year moratorium in nuclear testing, which made it possible for the Soviets to gain a little on us in the meantime. They then put more pressure behind their propaganda that the United States was threatening the health of mankind and the sanity of future generations.

* * *

CULTURAL CONTACTS WITH THE COMMUNISTS WORLD. Great importance is attributed to cultural contacts with the Communists. These are supposed to show how erudite we are and to establish strong links in the non-controversial fields of art, literature, theater, and ballet. However; the theoreticians of the cultural exchange programs regret that Communist "culture" is permitted to exist only to serve the political sphere. Every Communist ballet ensemble or troupe has its political commissar, who does not come to dance but to accomplish those subversive missions assigned to him. Even the artistic performance of the *Bolshoi* or*Moyseyev* accomplishes the important political task of compelling our naive eyes to look the other way—away from the Communist reality of terror, subversion, subhuman treatment of citizens, ruthless fomenting of civil war throughout the globe, and hunger riots in the land of the victorious proletariat.

And, finally, we have strong doubts regarding the importance, for the fate of mankind, of establishing whether Jasha Heifetz is a better violinist than David Oistrakh, or Van Cliburn has a more elegant touch on the piano than Emil Gilels, or whether Danny Kaye can crack funnier jokes than his Soviet counterparts. As a newspaperwoman aptly remarked after a review of the travels of a group of American entertainers, "the world will not be impressed and attracted to our country if we prove that we are the most entertaining nation on earth, they want to know if we are the strongest and most determined to defend freedom."

TRADE AND ECONOMIC AID. If the Communists simply held different views on economic problems, without any imperialist ambitions and criminal notions about men and nations, it would be conceivable to trade with them and teach them modern methods in agriculture, or industry, or communications. But—once more—the Communists want to conquer the world and use everything, especially economics, to that end. A rather well-known Communist, Vladimir Ulyanov-

Lenin reportedly stated that "When the capitalist world starts trade with us, on that day it will begin to finance its own destruction." The Communists force their people to produce under slave labor conditions, which makes the production costs much lower. They are interested in buying only what is useful for the purposes of strengthening their total revolutionary strength. Finally, and this belongs in this chapter as well as in the next, they are squeezing all of the knowledge and profit from us which they possibly can. At the same time they are working at the realization of their mammoth plan of capturing all former Western colonies, so as to deprive the economy of the Free World of vital raw materials (uranium in Katanga, for instance), and markets.

By trading with the Communist countries, we are strengthening them economically, we are saving the most irresponsible and incapable clique ever to wield power anywhere, at any time, to escape certain and deserved doom. And, we are financing our own destruction.

ANTI-COLONIALISM. In the view of our foreign policy makers and planners, the main problem today is not Communism: It is poverty and the new emerging nations of the world (which are poor because—so runs the explicit or implicit theory—the nations of the Free World have exploited them for centuries). And, it is only natural and right that the free nations, and above all the United States, go about feeding and freeing. First, and before anything else, we must give to the Watussi his political independence, because such is the "irresistible force" of history, the "rising expectation," the "Wind," the "trend."

The problem has many aspects. Most of these so-called nations are centuries or millenia away from possessing the requirements for nationhood and independence. The favorite theme about the alleged analogy between the "winds of freedom" in Africa and the same winds in America in 1776 betray either abysmal ignorance and lack of judgment or—much worse—deliberate distortion. It is true that in these days the techniques of governing masses have been perfected to such an extent that anybody, any group of ambitious men can, provided that they have enough international support or political influence, diplomatic and financial pressure, and brute force, rule anywhere. For, on the world market, human lives are cheaper than ever. So, you do not need to have a nation, meaning national identity, to proclaim "national independence." But then the revolutionary forces behind the movement are not those of nationalism. The best proof of this shameless fraud is the fact that everything has been done by the Communists to enslave 100 million Europeans and 500 million Chinese with old traditions of nationhood and independence. Yet not one of the great readers of the tea leaves of history detects any sign or need for restoring national independence to *those* nations. To grant "national independence" to Uganda or Tanganyika is the sacred duty of mankind. But where is the sacred duty to restore the independence of Poland, or Latvia, or Rumania, or China?!

* * *

ACTIVE AID TO COMMUNISTS. But the real core of the thinking of our foreign policy experts is probably best exemplified in the case of Communist Yugoslavia and Joseph Broz-Tito. There is no example where the facts of the matter have been so clear and unequivocal, and where the sup-

porters of a Communist dictator and his regime have been bolder in defiance of the most elementary truth, logic, and decency. A well-known Washington columnist has called this the law of "investment in error."
... The harm which the Tito "defection" has done to world Communism can be taken seriously only by those who entertain a superstitious fear and awe of Communism, so that the slightest sign of internal Communist difficulties is taken as a valid substitute for the non-existent struggle of the Free World to destroy Communism by creating real trouble for the Communists.

While it is nonsense to speak of Tito breaking up the Communist monolith, the Tito phenomenon has been used to revolutionize American political thinking. And, it has split American unity regarding Communism. Until 1948 the prevalent idea among Americans was that Communism was bad, that it was irreconcilably opposed to everything America represents and stands for. Titoism put forth and promoted the idea of "good," and therefore acceptable, Communism. The most important consequence is that it has permitted the most sinister maneuvers against freedom to pass as "antiCommunism." For if Tito is an enemy of Moscow and Communist Internationalism (which he is not and never has been) then, logically, helping Tito is hurting Moscow. Yes, only anti-Communists aid good old Tito.

*   *   *

Space does not permit me to go into the pertinent and thoroughly misrepresented cases of Communist "anticommunism:" Milovan Djilas (*The New Class and Conversations with Stalin*), Imre Nagy, the Communist "martyr for freedom," Boris Pasternak, the great Communist champion of "humanism," and their ilk. Nor do we have space to go into the cases of United States participation in bringing Castro to power, or American aid to Communist Chedi Jagan, or Communist Wladyslaw Gomulka, or Communist Ben Bella. What must be emphasized is that the United States policy, supposed to defend the national interests of the United States and defeat the maneuvers of its enemies, has actively helped known and avowed Communists, in spite of their overwhelmingly documented work against our interests and in favor of World Communism.

And last, there is the fact that, as we have worked for our enemies, we have rejected our allies and worked against them.

The conviction, that if you want to get American help you must be against America, started as a cautious joke. But in the course of years it has become a matter of undisputable fact.

6

A Fresh Look at the Communist Bloc[*]

SENATOR J. W. FULBRIGHT

Senator Fulbright insists that the Communist bloc is not a monolithic unit unless we make it so by our policies. He foresees the possibility of gradually lessening tensions and believes that the United States should be constantly on the alert to exploit such possibilities. If the Fulbright thesis were adopted, what attitude should we take toward developing trade with East Europe? Toward disarmament proposals? Toward suggestions for cooperation in the exploration of space?

❋   ❋   ❋

The master myth of the cold war is that the Communist bloc is a monolith composed of governments which are not really governments at all, but organized conspiracies, divided among themselves perhaps in certain matters of tactics, but all equally resolute and implacable in their determination to destroy the free world.

I believe that the Communist world is indeed hostile to the free world in its general and long-term intentions, but that the existence of this animosity in principle is far less important for our foreign policy than the great variations in its intensity and character both in time and among the individual members of the Communist bloc. Only if we recognize these variations, ranging from China, which poses immediate threats to the free world, to Poland and Yugoslavia, which pose none, can we hope to act effectively upon the bloc and to turn its internal differences to our own advantage and to the advantage of those bloc countries which wish to maximize their independence. It is the responsibility of our national leaders, both in the executive branch and in Congress, to acknowledge and act upon these realities, even at the cost of saying things which will not win immediate widespread enthusiasm.

For a start, we can acknowledge the fact that the Soviet Union, though still a most formidable adversary, has ceased to be totally and implacably hostile to the West. It has shown a new willingness to enter mutually advantageous arrangements with the West and, thus far at least, to honor them. It has therefore become possible to divert some of our energies from the prosecution of the cold war to the relaxation of the cold war and to deal with the Soviet Union, for certain purposes, as a normal state with normal and traditional interests.

If we are to do these things effectively, we must distinguish between communism as an ideology and the power and policy of the Soviet state. It is not communism as a doctrine, or

* From J. W. Fulbright, *Old Myths and New Realities* (New York: Random House, Inc., 1964), pp. 8-14, 77-78. © Copyright 1964 by J. William Fulbright. Reprinted by permission of Random House, Inc.

communism as it is practiced *within* the Soviet Union or *within* any other country, that threatens us. How the Soviet Union organizes its internal life, the gods and doctrines that it worships, are matters for the Soviet Union to determine. It is not Communist dogma as espoused within Russia but Communist imperialism that threatens us and other peoples of the non-Communist world. Insofar as a great nation mobilizes its power and resources for aggressive purposes, that nation, regardless of ideology, makes itself our enemy. Insofar as a nation is content to practice its doctrines within its own frontiers, that nation—except under certain extreme circumstances—is one with which we have no proper quarrel. We must deal with the Soviet Union as a great power, quite apart from differences of ideology. To the extent that the Soviet leaders abandon the global ambitions of Marxist ideology, in fact if not in words, it becomes possible for us to engage in normal relations with them, relations which probably cannot be close or trusting for many years to come but which can be gradually freed of the terror and the tensions of the cold war.

In our relations with the Russians, and indeed in our relations with all nations, we would do well to remember, and to act upon, the words of Pope John in the great Encyclical *Pacem in Terris*: "It must be borne in mind," said Pope John, "that to proceed gradually is the law of life in all its expressions; therefore, in human institutions, too, it is not possible to renovate for the better except by working from within them, gradually . . . Violence has always achieved only destruction, not construction, the kindling of passions, not their pacification, the accumulation of hate and ruin, not the reconciliation of the contending parties. And it has reduced

men and parties to the difficult task of rebuilding, after sad experience, on the ruins of discord. . . ."

Important opportunities have been created for Western policy by the development of "polycentrism" in the Communist bloc. The Communist nations, as George Kennan has pointed out, are, like the Western nations, currently caught up in a crisis of indecision about their relations with countries outside their own ideological bloc. The choices open to the satellite states are limited but by no means insignificant. They can adhere slavishly to Soviet preferences or they can strike out on their own, within limits, to enter into mutually advantageous relations with the West.

Whether they do so, and to what extent, is to some degree within the power of the West to determine. If we persist in the view that all Communist regimes are equally hostile and equally threatening to the West, and that we can have no policy toward the "captive nations" except the eventual overthrow of their Communist regimes, then the West may enforce upon the Communist bloc a degree of unity which the Soviet Union has shown itself to be quite incapable of imposing—just as Stalin in the early postwar years frightened the West into a degree of unity that it almost certainly could not have attained by its own unaided efforts. If, on the other hand, we are willing to re-examine the view that all Communist regimes are alike in the threat which they pose for the West—a view which had a certain validity in Stalin's time—then we may be able to exert an important influence on the course of events within a divided Communist world.

We are to a great extent the victims, and the Soviets the beneficiaries, of our own ideological convictions and of the curious contradictions which they involve. We consider it a form of subverision of the free world, for example, when the Russians enter trade relations or conclude a consular convention or establish airline connections with a free country in Asia, Africa, or Latin America—and to a certain extent we are right. On the other hand, when it is proposed that we adopt the same strategy in reverse —by extending commercial credits to Poland or Yugoslavia, or by exchanging ambassadors with a Hungarian regime which has changed considerably in character since the revolution of 1956—then the same patriots who are so alarmed by Soviet activities in the free world charge our policymakers with "giving aid and comfort to the enemy," and with innumerable other categories of idiocy and immorality.

It is time that we resolved this contradiction and separated myth from reality. The myth is that every Communist state is an unmitigated evil and a relentless enemy of the free world; the reality is that some Communist regimes pose a threat to the free world while others pose little or none, and that if we will recognize these distinctions, we ourselves will be able to influence events in the Communist bloc in a way favorable to the security of the free world. "It could well be argued," writes George Kennan, ". . . that if the major Western powers had full freedom of movement in devising their own policies, it would be within their power to determine whether the Chinese view, or the Soviet view, or perhaps a view more liberal than either would ultimately prevail within the Communist camp."[1]

There are numerous areas in which we can seek to reduce the tensions of the cold war and to bring a degree of normalcy into our relations with the Soviet Union and other Communist countries—once we have resolved that it is safe and wise to do so. We have already taken important steps in this direction: the Antarctic and Austrian treaties and the nuclear test ban treaty, the broadening of East-West cultural and educational relations, and the expansion of trade.

On the basis of recent experience and present economic needs, there seems little likelihood of a spectacular increase in trade between Communist and Western countries, even if existing restrictions were to be relaxed. Free-world trade with Communist countries has been increasing at a steady but unspectacular rate, and it seems unlikely to be greatly accelerated because of the limited ability of the Communist countries to pay for increased imports. A modest increase in East-West trade may nonetheless serve as a modest instrument of East-West *détente*—provided that we are able to overcome the myth that trade with Communist countries is a compact with the Devil, and to recognize that, on the contrary, trade in nonstrategic goods can serve as an effective and honorable means of advancing both peace and human welfare.

✻　✻　✻

The cold war and all the other national rivalries of our time are not likely to evaporate in our lifetimes. The major question of our time is not how to end these conflicts but whether we can find some way to conduct them without resorting to weapons that will resolve them once and for all by wiping out the contestants. A generation ago we were speaking of "making the world safe for democracy." Having failed of this in two World Wars, we must now seek ways

---

[1] George Kennan, "Polycentrism and Western Policy," *Foreign Affairs,* January, 1964, p. 178.

of making the world reasonably safe for the continuing contest between those who favor democracy and those who oppose it. It is a modest aspiration, but it is a sane and realistic one for a generation which, having failed of grander things, must now look to its own survival.

Extreme nationalism and dogmatic ideology are luxuries that the human race can no longer afford. It must turn its energies now to the politics of survival. If we do so, we may find in time that we can do better than just survive. We may find that the simple human preference for life and peace has an inspirational force of its own, less intoxicating perhaps than the sacred abstractions of nation and ideology, but far more relevant to the requirements of human life and human happiness.

There are, to be sure, risks in such an approach. There is an element of trust in it, and we can be betrayed. But human life is fraught with risks, and the behavior of the sane man is not the avoidance of all possible danger but the weighing of greater against lesser risks and of risks against opportunities.

We have an opportunity at present to try to build stronger foundations for our national security than armaments alone can ever provide. That opportunity lies in a policy of encouraging the development of a habit of peaceful and civilized contacts between ourselves and the Communist bloc. I believe that this opportunity must be pursued, with reason and restraint, with due regard for the pitfalls involved and for the possibilty that our efforts may fail, but with no less regard for the promise of a safer and more civilized world. In the course of this pursuit, both we and our adversaries may find it possible one day to break through the barriers of nationalism and ideology and to approach each other in something of the spirit of Pope John's words to Khrushchev's son-in-law: "They tell me you are an atheist. But you will not refuse an old man's blessing for your children."

7

Creating an Atlantic Community *

JOHN F. KENNEDY

One concept that has captured the imagination of both Europeans and Americans in the post–war world has been that of an Atlantic Community, with the ocean serving as a bond, rather than as a dividing factor. In a military sense this movement created a North Atlantic Treaty Organization. Politically and economically it was less fully realized. On German soil, President Kennedy offered his eloquent arguments for such an arrangement.

Would such an arrangement be to the advantage of the United States? Why? Are we prepared to enter into a full partnership with West European nations? Even if tariffs come tumbling down? Even at the sacrifice of some of our sovereignty? Or do we expect these concessions to be made only by the Europeans? More basically, do we really share common foreign–policy goals with France, Great Britain, and West Germany?

❀   ❀   ❀

. . . Today there are no exclusively German problems or American problems. There are world problems—and our two countries and continents are inextracably bound together in the task of peace as well as war.

Partners for Peace

We are partners for peace, not in a narrow bilateral context, but in a framework of Atlantic partnership. The ocean divides us less than the Mediterranean divided Greece and Rome. Our constitution is old and yours is young—and our culture is young and yours is old—but in our commitment we can and must speak and act with one voice. Our roles are

distinct but complementary—and our goals are the same: Peace and freedom for all men, for all time, in a world of abundance, in a world of justice.

That is why our nations are working together to strengthen NATO, to expand trade, to assist the developing countries, to align our monetary policies and to build the Atlantic Community. I would not diminish the miracle of West Germany's economic achievements. But the true German miracle has been your rejection of the past for the future—your reconciliation with France, your participation in the building of Europe, your leading role in NATO, and your growing support for constructive undertakings throughout the world.

Your economic institutions, your constitutional guarantees, your confidence in civilian authority, are all harmonious with the ideals of older democracies. And they form a firm

* From John F. Kennedy, "A New Social Order," *Vital Speeches of the Day*, 29, No. 19 (July 15, 1963), 578-81. This address was originally delivered at Frankfurt, West Germany on June 25, 1963. Reprinted by permission of the publisher.

pillar of the democratic European community.

But Goethe tells us in his greatest poem that Faust lost the liberty of his soul when he said to the passing moment: "Stay, thou art so fair." And our liberty, too, is endangered if we pause for the passing moment, if we rest on our achievements, if we resist the pace of progress. For time and the world do not stand still. Change is the law of life. And those who look only to the past or the present are certain to miss the future.

The future of the West lies in Atlantic partnership—a system of cooperation, interdependence and harmony whose people can jointly meet their burdens and opportunities throughout the world. Some say this is only a dream, but I do not agree. A generation of achievement—the Marshall Plan, NATO, the Schuman Plan, and the Common Market—urges us up the path to greater unity.

There will be difficulties and delays, and doubts and discouragement. There will be differences of approach and opinion. But we have the will and the means to serve three related goals —the heritage of our countries, the unity of our continents and the interdependence of the Western alliance.

Faithful in Alliances

Some say that the United States will neither hold to these purposes nor abide by its pledges—that we will revert to a narrow nationalism. But such doubts fly in the face of history. For 18 years the United States has stood its watch for freedom all around the globe. The firmness of American will, and the effectiveness of American strength, have been shown in support of free men and free governments, in Asia, in Africa, in the Americas, and above all, here in Europe we have undertaken, and sustained in honor, relations of mutual trust and obligation with more than 40 allies. We are proud of this record, which more than answers doubts. But in addition, these proven commitments to the common freedom and safety are assured, in the future as in the past, by one great fundamental fact —that they are deeply rooted in America's own self-interest. Our commitment to Europe is indispensable—in our interest as well as yours.

It is not in our interest to try to dominate the European councils of decision. If that were our objective, we would prefer to see Europe divided and weak, enabling the United States to deal with each fragment individually. Instead we have and now look forward to a Europe united and strong—speaking with a common voice—acting with a common will— a world power capable of meeting world problems as a full and equal partner.

This is in the interest of us all. For war in Europe, as we learned twice in 40 years, destroys peace in America. A threat to the freedom of Europe is a threat to the freedom of America. That is why no administration in Washington can fail to respond to such a threat—not merely from good will but from necessity. And that is why we look forward to a united Europe in an Atlantic partnership— an entity of interdependent parts, sharing equally both burdens and decisions, and linked together in the task of defense as well as the arts of peace.

❄   ❄   ❄

Economic Unity

Second: Our partnership is not military alone. Economic unity is also imperative—not only among the nations of Europe, but across the wide Atlantic.

Indeed, economic cooperation is needed throughout the entire free world. By opening our markets to the developing countries of Africa, Asia and Latin America, by contributing our capital and skills, by stabilizing basic prices, we can help assure them of a favorable climate for freedom and growth. This is an Atlantic responsibility. For the Atlantic nations themselves helped to awaken these peoples. Our merchants and our traders ploughed up their soils—and their societies as well—in search of minerals and oil and rubber and coffee. Now we must help them gain full membership in the 20th century, closing the gap between the rich and the poor.

We must not return to the nineteen-thirties when we exported to each other our own stagnation. We must not return to the discredited view that trade favors some nations at the expense of others. Let no one think that the United States—with only a fraction of its economy dependent on trade and only a small part of that with Western Europe—is seeking trade expansion in order to dump its goods on this continent.

Trade expansion will help us all. The experience of the Common Market—like the experience of the German Zollverein—shows an increased rise in business activity and general prosperity resulting for all participants in such trade agreements, with no member profiting at the expense of another. As they say on my own Cape Cod, "A rising tide lifts all the boats." And a partnership, by definition, serves both partners, without domination or unfair advantage. Together we have been partners in adversity—let us also be partners in prosperity.

❖   ❖   ❖

Controls Needed

And third and finally, our partnership depends on common political purpose. Against the hazards of division and lassitude, no lesser force

will serve. History tells us that disunity and relaxation are the great internal dangers of an alliance. Thucydides reported that the Peloponnesians and their allies were mighty in battle but handicapped by their policy-making body—in which, he related "each presses its own end . . . which generally results in no action at all . . . they devote more time to the prosecution of their own purposes than to the consideration of the general welfare—each supposes that no harm will come of his own neglect, that it is the business of another to do this and that—and so, as each separately entertains the same illusion, the common cause imperceptibly decays."

Is this also to be the story of the grand alliance? Welded in a moment of imminent danger, will it disintegrate into complacency with each member pressing its own ends to the neglect of the common cause? This must not be the case. Our old dangers are not gone beyond return, and any division among us would bring them back in doubled strength.

❖   ❖   ❖

Europeans Must Agree

The great present task of construction is here on this continent where the effort for a unified free Europe is under way. It is not for Americans to prescribe to Europeans how this effort should be carried forward. Nor do I believe that there is any one right course or any single final pattern. It is Europeans who are bulding Europe.

Yet the reunion of Europe, as Europeans shape it—bringing a permanent end to the civil wars that have repeatedly wracked the world—will continue to have the determined support of the United States. For that reunion is a necessary step in strengthening the community of freedom. It would strengthen our alliance for defense. And it would be in our national interest as well as yours.

It is only a fully cohesive Europe that can protect us all against fragmentation of our alliance. Only such a Europe will permit full reciprocity of treatment across the ocean, in facing the Atlantic agenda. With only such a Europe can we have a full give-and-take between equals, and equal sharing of responsibilities, and an equal level of sacrifice. I repeat again—so that there may be no misunderstanding—the choice of paths to the unity of Europe is a choice which Europe must make. But as you continue this great effort, undeterred by either difficulty or delay, you should know that this new European greatness will be not an object of fear, but a source of strength, for the United States of America.

*   *   *

Free Choice for All

I preach no easy liberation and I make no empty promises, but my countrymen, since our country was founded, believe strongly in the proposition that all men shall be free and all free men shall have this right of choice.

As we look steadily eastward in the hope and purpose of new freedom, we must look—and evermore closely—to our trans-Atlantic ties. The Atlantic Community will not soon become a single overarching superstate. But practical steps toward stronger common purpose are well within our means. As we widen our common effort in defense, and our three-fold cooperation in economics, we shall

inevitably strengthen our political ties as well. Just as your current efforts for unity in Europe will produce a stronger voice in the dialogue between us, so in America our current battle for the liberty and prosperity of all our citizens can only deepen the meaning of our common historic purposes. In the far future there may be a great union for us all. But for the present, there is plenty for all to do in building new and enduring connections.

*   *   *

New Social Order Is Goal

To realize this vision, we must seek a world of peace—a world in which peoples dwell together in mutual respect and work together in mutual regard—a world in which peace is not a mere interlude between wars, but an incentive to the creative energies of humanity. We will not find such a peace today, or tomorrow. The obstacles to hope are large and menacing. Yet the goals of a peaceful world—today and tomorrow—must shape our decisions and inspire our purposes.

So we are all idealists. We are all visionaries. Let it not be said of this Atlantic generation that we left ideals and visions to the past, not purpose and determination to our adversaries. We have come too far, we have sacrificed too much, to disdain the future now. And we shall ever remember what Goethe told us—that the "highest wisdom, the best that mankind ever knew" was the realization that "he only earns his freedom and existence who daily conquers them anew."

8

The Crisis in the Western Alliance *

HANS J. MORGENTHAU

Western Europe has occupied a very special place in United States foreign policy. Great Britain and France were our allies in the two World Wars of this century. We spearheaded plans for the economic, political, and military unification of the continent after World War II. The present generation of Americans assumed without much questioning that United States interests and those of Western Europe coincided. American hegemony was often more or less implicit, although other Americans talked of an Atlantic Community or a cooperative partnership.

The following article challenges these assumptions and declares that European interests do not parallel those of the United States. How valid is this thesis? Is European intransigence a phenomenon that centers around Charles de Gaulle? Or is de Gaulle merely a symbol of a permanent estrangement? Can a different United States foreign policy preserve the Atlantic Community? Or is it dead beyond recall?

. . . For a century and a half, we accepted, and acted upon, this formulation of our relations with Europe which Washington's Farewell Address gave us. Our interventions in the two World Wars we considered at the time as temporary exceptions to the rule of non-involvement, justified by "extraordinary" vicissitudes, combinations, and collisions. But in the spring of 1947, we radically changed the conception and course of our foreign policy by identifying our interests with those of Europe in what we thought was virtual permanence through the Truman Doctrine, the Marshall Plan and the military containment of the Soviet Union.

Since then, Europeans have from time to time expressed their fear that we might again come to define our interests differently from theirs and

go back into isolation. It was for us to reassure them. Now Europe is turning George Washington's formulation against us and proclaiming the separateness of its interests from those of America. I have advisedly attributed this proclamation to "Europe" and not to Charles de Gaulle alone; for de Gaulle has but given trenchant and uncompromising expression to a mood and trend which is by no means limited to the French leader.

*   *   *

De Gaulle's policy may well be wrong in that it will either prove unsuccessful or, if it should succeed, detrimental to France. It may also run counter to the interests of the United States and must therefore be opposed by American policy. Yet whatever one's conclusions are, they ought to derive not from emotional reactions but from a rational under-

* Reprinted from *Commentary*, by permission; copyright © by the American Jewish Committee.

standing of what de Gaulle is after. Whatever his chances for success may be and in whatever ways his success or failure may affect the interests of France and the United States, de Gaulle's design is rational in itself and not devoid of audacity and even grandeur. . . .

De Gaulle's European policy derives from five basic propositions, which are not peculiar to France but are of general validity.

First, an alliance among nations unequal in power inevitably gives the most powerful nation a decisive voice in determining the policies of the alliance. . . .

Second, this dependence is tolerable for the weak only if there exists so complete an identity of interests between the weak and the strong that the policies pursued by the strong in their own interests also serve the interests of the weak. Such identity of interests is rare in peace and cannot even be taken for granted in war. It exists among the members of the Atlantic Alliance only on the most general plane: the Atlantic Alliance is united in its opposition to Communist aggression and subversion. But this interest is not policy in itself; it must be implemented by common policies. Such policies, to which all members of the Alliance are committed, do not at present exist.

❖   ❖   ❖

The third of the five propositions on which de Gaulle's European policy rests is that the availability of nuclear weapons to the United States and the Soviet Union has administered a death blow to the Atlantic Alliance, as it has to all alliances. It has made alliances obsolete. In the pre-nuclear age, a powerful nation could be expected to come to the aid of a weak ally provided its interests were sufficiently involved, risking at worst defeat in war, the loss of an army or of

territory. But no nation can be relied upon to forfeit its own existence for the sake of another.

. . . Since no nation can be expected to risk destruction for the sake of another nation, all nations must protect themselves as best they can. While France could not hope to match the deterrent of a major nuclear power quantitatively, she is capable of developing an invulnerable deterrent sufficient for her purposes. She could say to a major nuclear power: If you do this I shall cut off your leg. And the major nuclear power could reply: If you do that I shall kill you. But is it likely that an issue might arise between France and a major nuclear power for the sake of which the latter would be willing to risk losing a leg?

Fourth, what has been said of alliances also applies to federations of states. Strong and weak nations can federate effectively only on a hierarchial and not an equalitarian basis.

❖   ❖   ❖

De Gaulle sees himself choosing between a Europe dominated by the United States and a Europe dominated by the Franco-German combination. He sees Great Britain not only as the spearhead of American power but also as a non-European influence within Europe by virtue of its worldwide interests and commitments. Furthermore, the British presence in Europe would endanger the viability of the Franco-German combination; for the British political presence could offer Germany an alternative to the association with France and threaten France with isolation. In other words, it would be a threat to the predominance of France.

Lastly, de Gaulle realizes that Europe thus united under Franco-German auspices is but a fragment of the true Europe, the other half of which forms the Western part of the Soviet empire. To merge these two parts is the task of a united Western Europe and, more particularly, of France. The accomplishment of that task is of course predicated upon an accommodation with the Soviet Union. The main issue of such an accommodation is the stabilization of the territorial and military status quo in Central Europe.

* * *

It is de Gaulle's paradoxical good fortune that he can count upon the protection of America regardless of what he says and does. However much he may annoy American sensibilities and antagonize American interests, we cannot help but protect him, not for his sake but for ours. What was true in 1953 when John Foster Dulles threatened France with an "agonizing reappraisal" is true today. Regardless of what France does or does not do, we have a vital interest in preventing the addition of French and, through it, European power to that of the Soviet Union. In the awareness of that vital interest of the United States which makes France secure, de Gaulle can afford to attempt the realization of his grand design, the purpose of which is to be done with the need for American protection altogether. Hegel would have enjoyed seeing "the ruse of the idea" thus at work.

Regardless of whether de Gaulle succeeds or fails, the relations between the United States and Europe can never again be what they were before January 14, 1963. For de Gaulle has laid bare in simple and stark outline the ills which ailed the Atlantic Alliance for a decade and which governments on both sides of the Atlantic have been pleased to gloss over with fine phrases and manipulate with petty schemes. We may be able to continue this convenient yet self-defeating tradition for the

time being; but the sooner we face the facts, however startling and unpleasant they may be, and act upon them, the better will we be capable of molding them to our interests.

There are only two possible ways to resolve this issue. Either the United States retains its power of decision, in which case the present Atlantic Alliance must be transformed into a true federation capable of reducing the political interests peculiar to its members to a common denominator. Or the power of decision must be put into the hands of those individual allies who wish to exercise it, in which case the alliance will for all practical purposes be diᵃ solved. The former alternative requires for its achievement a series of constructive and delicate political settlements and arrangements, eliminating the present points of friction among the allies. The other alternative requires the return of the United States to isolation in a world which will be dominated by four power centers instead of two: the United States, the Soviet Union, Europe, and China. In other words, the alliance will either go forward or backward, but it cannot stand still. Nor is there a middle ground for reconciling the two alternatives.

* * *

Whether or not we find these policies to our taste or in our interest, we are indebted to de Gaulle for having posed the great issues of the day with simple and accurate clarity. De Gaulle has made clear what some of us have pointed to for a decade without anybody listening—that the political, military, and economic foundations upon which the Atlantic Alliance was constructed are in the process of erosion or have altogether ceased to exist and that hence the institutional superstructure of the Alliance has lost its empirical supports.

CHAPTER THIRTEEN

Government and the Economy:
Direction Without Domination?

In an earlier age Americans believed that politics and economics were distinct and separate activities. The business cycle moved through its various phases—prosperity, recession, depression, recovery—without attracting more than passing attention from political spokesmen. Business leaders created vast industrial empires without any government intervention. The impact of new machines on the labor force was largely ignored by governors and presidents.

Today, domestic economic issues automatically become political questions. The earlier sharp distinction separating government and the economy had been replaced by active government intervention in economic affairs.

OVERALL DIRECTION: CAN GOVERNMENT CURB THE BUSINESS CYCLE?

The United States experienced major economic crises during the administrations of Martin Van Buren, James Buchanan, U. S. Grant, and Grover Cleveland without government showing any great concern for falling prices, unemployment, and breadlines. When President Cleveland vetoed a bill that would have given federal funds for farm relief, he firmly declared that the people should support the government but that government should never support the people. This philosophy was discarded during the Great Depression of the 1930's. In the face of wholesale disaster a demand arose that government become a team captain who would organize the economy's players (business, labor, farmers, consumers) into a winning combination called prosperity. If depression or inflation threatens today, we assume that it is the responsibility of government to take action that will restore relative price stability. The big question today is no longer "should we" but "can we?" It is an article of faith among world Communists that a "boom-bust" cycle is part of the very nature of capitalism. Max Lerner, a famous American commentator on the current scene, has written that "It is on the test of stability that American capitalism is most vulnerable." Recently the government's "new economists" have grown increasingly certain that they can eliminate those frightening extremes that have marred our history. Although critics have predicted the eventual failure of their methods, these "new economists" have used money supply, interest rates, taxes, spending, and the public debt as tools in their drive for stability. Will their maneuvers be permanently successful? Will they require government regulation so vast as to threaten personal freedom? From which direction do we face the greatest threat? The unchecked business cycle? The "new economics"?

BIG BUSINESS AND GOVERNMENT: LOGICAL PARTNERS OR NATURAL ENEMIES?

The relationship between business and government is a matter of much concern to Americans. At one extreme are those who argue that the country should be governed by those who own it, that since businessmen have a great financial stake in the country they have the greatest concern that government policies do not thwart that interest—or more positively, that government must become an active agent to preserve national prosperity. In one form, at least, this policy is reduced to the simple formula, "What's good for United States Steel is good for the United States." Expressed in another way, a comparison between business and government operations is made, with the conclusion that "we need more business in government."

At the other extreme in this debate are those who view with alarm the role played by business leaders in political affairs. To buttress their argument these spokesmen advance evidence of political control through campaign contributions, the staffing of regulatory agencies, and the attempt of corporate leaders to speak for their stockholders and employees. At a more basic level, C. Wright Mills has described a ruling class in the United States composed of business, military, and political leaders, many of whom are subject to no democratic controls.

Questions of policy are debated within the foregoing framework. Do we need more business in government? Do we already have too much? Should rigid restriction be placed on business campaign contributions and other avenues of influence? Should unions be similarly restricted? Should business and labor groups be encouraged to compete for voter favor? Finally, how can we dispose of the concern (expresssed in the following pages by former President Eisenhower) that we face a constant danger from the dual alliance between business and the military establishment?

AMERICA FACES AUTOMATION: BOON OR BLIGHT?

Automation is a "good" or "bad" word, depending largely upon the experience of the reader. To many Americans it means that man has finally conquered his environment, that he will no longer be harnessed to heavy, dull, repetitive tasks. Instead, in a society of growing leisure he will be able to practice the arts and commune with his soul while a mounting tide of goods rises around him.

This rosy picture bears no resemblance to the bleak reality of West Virginia's desolate coal towns, filled with unemployed miners who have been replaced by machines. Nor does it parallel the soaring unemployment patterns in steel, automobile, and railroad towns, where automatic processes have displaced workers by the thousands.

What does automation really mean? Can the present period be compared to a highway detour, carrying the sign "the inconvenience is temporary—the improvement is permanent?" Or is automation a spreading danger? Does it contain self-adjusting forces that guarantee that "machines make jobs"? Perhaps, instead, problems should be disposed of in orderly fashion through negotiation by labor-management leaders. Or is the issue so great that only intervention by the national government can provide for the retraining, unemployment compensation, and adjustment of hours and wages that automation demands?

1

The "New Economists" Take Over*

NEIL W. CHAMBERLAIN

During the past 20 years a number of sophisticated theories and policies have been developed to stabilize the business cycle and stimulate economic growth. Put forward by the so-called "new economists," these policies require bold, decisive action on the part of the national government. Contemporary debate over government action is unintelligible without an understanding of the assumptions upon which such action is based.

In the article that follows the economic thinking that has governed our historical development is categorized in three periods. Several questions should be answered by the careful reader. Why did Keynesian economists reject the "housekeeping" concept of the budget? How did they propose to achieve a balanced budget? How do the "new economists" differ from the Keynesians in their attitude toward balanced budgets?

The effect of the 1965 income tax cut was not only to prolong a period of prosperity but also to consolidate a revolution in economic thought. The federal government had undertaken deficit financing in the past, but always in times of depression or war. This time it purposely pursued a budgetary deficit when the economy was still in the throes of a protracted peacetime expansion, when wise men of a previous generation would have urged a prudent surplus in order to reduce the national debt. The unbalanced budget, which had so recently been an object of revulsion, had taken on respectability. Government deficits had ceased to be a sin and had themselves become the mark of a shrewd Administration's prudence.

This upheaval in applied economic theory is one of the most significant social devolpments in modern times. The intellectual innovations which led to its adoption can take their place with the more spectacular discoveries in the physical sciences in terms of potential importance to man's welfare. This was not the case of a government stumbling onto a good thing and then converting a political accident into an economic principle. It came as a planned maneuver, based on new concepts which were partly fashioned by the cadre of young economists who came to Washington with the Kennedy Administration but who—as in most such cases—were building on the work of contemporaries and predecessors.

The history of this remarkable delopment can be traced most simply in three stages of thought concerning the government's budget and when it should be balanced. We commit only slight violence to the facts bv

* From Neil W. Chamberlain, "The Art of Unbalancing the Budget," *The Atlantic Monthly*, January, 1966, pp. 58-61. Copyright © 1966 by The Atlantic Monthly Company, Boston, Mass. 02116. Reprinted bv permission of the author and publisher.

treating these as three neat and successive intellectual epochs, as future historians will doubtless do anyway.

The first period lasted longest, from the earliest conception of a nation's governmental budget almost to World War II. During it, the federal budget was regarded as an instrument of governmental housekeeping, performing the same function as a family's budget. The government had certain functions to perform, which had been assigned to it by society: keeping order, carrying the mails, running the courts, providing a monetary system, regulating interstate and foreign commerce, manning the army and navy. A well-administered government would see to it that in carrying out these functions it lived within its means, a feat of good housekeeping comparable with that of the prudent household. Taxes were levied only to provide the revenue needed for the performance of the services which society required. If special circumstances—most commonly a war—obliged the government to borrow funds, this was to be viewed as an unfortunate but temporary expedient. The sooner the debt was extinguished, the better. To produce a surplus at the end of the fiscal year, which could be applied against the national indebtedness, won for a government a crown of glory.

*   *   *

It conceived the government's economic role in the same terms as it would any other economic unit, private or public: private business performed certain economic functions, such as providing goods; households performed other economic functions, such as providing labor services; and similarly, the federal government performed still other economic functions. The federal budget was the largest of all budgets, to be sure, even

though not by the same margin as today, but this was a difference in degree and not in kind.

Or was it? Was there something about the government's budget that distinguished it from that of the Jones family and of U.S. Steel? Was there some special function connected with it which gave it a purpose other than the economical provision of particular services? There was indeed, said a school of economists, whose minority voice failed to attract much notice until the late 1930s, when John Maynard Keynes became its spokesman. Their view gained ascendancy largely as a consequence of the Great Depression, which lingered on until finally dispelled by wartime activity, and memories of which provided the emotional undertow on which full employment policies rode to legislative approvals in post-war Western Europe and North America. The second stage of our budgetary history was thereby ushered in.

Managed Prosperity

This second-stage school of economic theorists looked on the budget as performing not just one function—proper federal housekeeping—but two. The second function was to preserve the economic health of the nation as a whole. It was the government's duty, said this group, to see that the nation remained prosperous, a duty no less important than preserving law and order and maintaining courts and other such time-honored governmental services. The nation's economic health was the business of the government because no other agent or institution could serve as doctor.

The doctor's implements were not only monetary policy—making money cheaper to use in depressions so that businesses and households would use more of it, hopefully returning the nation to prosperity; the instrument kit of the federal government as economic doctor included its budget as well. In times of depression, it could spend more than it took in, thereby directly putting people and plants to productive use. It did not have to wait for businesses and households to become optimistic enough to borrow money at lower rates of interest. It could put money in their pockets directly by cutting its tax take, or it could itself spend on a variety of projects, or it could increase the amount of money it transferred to people who could be counted on to spend it. All these ways would put the government budget in the red, but it would increase the nation's economic activity. It would put people and plants to work whose services would otherwise be irretrievably lost.

All very well, said more traditional economists, but how long could this go on? How many times could the medicine be repeated? If the government persisted in deficit spending, its debt would double, its credit would crumble, and it would find no buyers for its bonds. Fiscal responsibility could not be evaded. The balanced budget was not a luxury to be dispensed with under pressure but a necessity of a solvent government.

Cyclical Balancing

The economic freethinkers had an answer. It might be true that the government could not afford to go on piling up new debt on old every time there was a downturn of business activity. But it would not have to; the fear that government credit would sooner or later go under, in a persistently rising sea of debt, was unwarranted. The alarmists were ignoring the existence of the business cycle, with its alternating phases of boom and depression.

If the economy was depressed at times, experience showed that this was followed by periods of excessive —inflationary—activity. The government as doctor was no less needed in the one case than in the other, but the remedy for one was the opposite of the remedy for the other. In depressions it would spend more than it took in and use budget deficits to bring the economy back to normal. In inflations it would take in more than it spent, and use budget surpluses to restore economic normality. And the surpluses of the inflation end of the business cycle could be used to pay off the deficits of the depression phase of the cycle.

Was it necessary to balance the budget? Yes, but only over the period of a business cycle. Annual balancing was an error, since it ignored the cyclical rhythm of the nation's health. Outgo and income could be matched over an appropriate span of years, in which the minuses of some were wiped out by the pluses of others.

*   *   *

Planned Deficits

A more daring set of economists began to feel their way toward a different answer. The nation could not count on regular budgetary surpluses to wipe out regular deficits. There was no reason to expect that such cyclical balancing would ever occur. But if the budget were balanced in the good years, then one could afford to run deficits in those years when the economy slowed down. This would mean that the national debt would steadily rise over the years, but this need not cause alarm, since the nation's assets and income were also growing. Not annual budget balancing, not even cyclical balancing, but balancing only in the years of plenty was looked on as the appropriate policy.

*   *   *

This was the general line of reasoning behind the income tax cut of 1965 and the excise tax cuts projected for the next few years. By reducing taxes to a level which at full employment *would* produce only as much revenue as *would* be needed to cover expenditures, the government necessarily collects less *now*. It leaves more money in the business and household sectors; if they spend it, as they will in large proportion, this augments economic activity and brings us nearer the full-employment goal.

Tax-Cutting: New Fiscal Toy

It is this phenomenon that has given rise to the colorful description of the new fiscal policy as "spending our way to prosperity." In effect, we can buy more and be better off for doing so.

Skeptical politicians have wondered whether such a policy courts inflation. They are uneasy with a policy which appears to reward profligacy. An amusing instance of this attitude occurred during Senate hearings over the proposed income tax reduction. A New England lawmaker asked Walter Heller, then chairman of the President's Council of Economic Advisers, why so many people resisted the new fiscal philosophy if, in effect, it promised reward for self-indulgence. Heller said he supposed any public disapproval stemmed from a residual Puritanism—to which the New England senator, still dubious but not doleful, replied that he himself was more of a puritan than a Heller.

But any earlier doubts now seem largely to have been dispelled as a result of the success of the 1965 tax reduction, and an increasing number

of legislators appear to embrace the new approach with enthusiasm. What politician can for long resist the appeal of voting for tax reductions? Is there, then, danger that the new fiscal toy will be overused with inflationary consequences?

Any policy is of course subject to abuse, but as long as the size of budgetary deficits is geared to the full-employment surplus, there is a built-in monitor. In the final analysis, the new fiscal policy is based less on deficit budgeting than on budget balancing. When the potential GNP is reached, the government's outlay will be in line with its income, since that is the point at which the government's budget is *planned* to be in balance.

Balance the budget? Of course, but what budget? The answer which is now being given is the full-employment budget. At levels short of full employment this means balancing not an actual but a hypothetical budget, the budget as it would be if we were operating at potential GNP. This is not a matter of running in the red in a vague hope that this will do the economy some good, as the bloodletting of earlier days was expected to restore a patient's health. It is the incurring of deficits in an amount which is guided by calculations of potential GNP, which in turn is based on computations of the level of acceptable compromise between unemployment and price increases.

National Debt No Mortgage

. . . There is of course no basis for believing that economic "truth" about budget balancing has now, finally, been divulged. We can be sure that a fourth stage in our thinking lies somewhere over the horizon. We might even surmise that it has something to do with relative advantages of tax cuts versus government expenditures, a matter which so far has been more the subject of vocal inflection than cerebral reflection.

But of one other thing we can also be sure. Our present stage-three thinking represents a vast improvement over its predecessor stages. And whether it appears excessively simplistic to some or dubiously synthetic to others, it is a product of contemporary social science no different in its fundamental importance from current innovations in the physical sciences.

2

The Other Side of the "New Economics" *

MAURICE H. STANS

Although the "new economics," with its stress on government as the prime moving force, has won widespread acceptance, the verdict is not unanimous. Many critics and skeptics believe that political control of the business cycle is neither possible nor desirable. Some of their doubts are summarized by Maurice Stans, Director of the Budget under President Eisenhower. Among the questions suggested by Stans are the following: (1) Can the "new economics" prevent inflation? (It has a very spotty record here). (2) Can we safely use taxes, spending, and the national debt as regulatory tools while ignoring balanced budgets? (3) Do we run the danger of downgrading such old-fashioned American virtues as thrift, frugality, and self-reliance? (4) Is the "new economics" a will-o'-the-wisp that promises more than it can ever fulfill?

We are witnessing in Washington a daring attempt to devise new concepts for a solution of the persistent problem of the uneven distribution of the national wealth and output.

There is, in fact, under way in our seat of Government the biggest economic experiment the world has ever seen. It is important that each of us understand clearly what it is and what it seeks to achieve, and what risks are involved, for our personal fortunes and our national future are at stake on the outcome.

The national economic policy which is now so aggressively being tested is not designed as a temporary expedient to meet a momentary difficulty. It is an avowed way of life.

If it succeeds, it will be a major turning point in the the economics of government. Historians will record it as a complete reversal in direction for the science of political management.

If it fails, it will be an equally historic event that may forever shatter the strength of our free democratic processes.

These wide-scale economic experiments are the brain children of a

* Maurice H. Stans, "The Other Side of the 'New Economics,'" *U.S. News and World Report*, December 13, 1965, pp. 82, 84, 86. Copyright 1965 U.S. News & World Report, Inc. Reprinted by permission of the publisher.

present generation of liberal economists holding considerable influence in Government affairs. They do not comprise a compact group, and their ideas are not uniform, but in general they endorse and support these propositions of governmental economics:

1. That a Government can spend a nation into prosperity and assure full employment and resources—by a process of force-feeding the economy through planned deficits;
2. That a limited amount of inflation is good for the country—or, at least, does no harm;
3. That a tax cut, when a deficit exists, will stimulate the economy and thereby enhance total revenues—enough to achieve future surpluses;
4. That the national debt need never be reduced—and should, in fact, be increased as the national output grows.

Behind the principles is the confident belief that the future of a nation can be successfully assured through closely designed economic blueprints, enforced by a system of central control values that regulate the economic stream to accomplish desired social objectives.

In short, government should intervene more in economic planning and management. Only then can we gain a satisfactory annual rate of growth and a suitable level of living.

All this is usually described as the "new economics." To the advocates of these precepts, any thing else is an incantation from the forgotten past, an ancient cliché, a worn-out tradition. There are immediate questions that these propositions bring to mind:

Can a government successfully cast out the long-accepted tenet that, to be financially strong, it must live within its income?

Will persistent deficit spending really provide enough steam to iron out the wrinkles and gaps in employment of manpower and resources?

To what extent and for how long can annual deficits be suffered and national debt be accumulated without imposing severe inflation, with its consequent loss of values and of security, especially harsh for those on fixed incomes?

Can a small degree of inflation be encouraged without serious risk that it will get out of control?

As a part of all this, how safe is it for a government to offer its people the attractive carrot of recurring tax reductions when there is already an existing substantial gap between revenues and expenses?

If the "new economics" succeeds, it would without a doubt create a new era for the United States and, in fact, for the entire community of nations. Never again would a national government need to be inhibited in the scope of its services to the people by old-fashioned thinking. Central economic planning would become a major tool of progress, and a planned full economy for the United States would be a key weapon against the Soviet threat of domination. This is apparently what the liberal economists hope and believe.

It may be boldness even to question these policies when, after a few years, they already seem to be highly successful. But a few years of success do not insure their long-time survival in the face of the inevitable pressures of a democratic society, and it is over the long term that their ultimate value will be judged.

What Happened in Brazil

Take the case of Brazil as one examples:

Jose Pereira, down in Sao Paulo Brazil, doesn't know much about the theories of economics. Except for the complaints he hears from his fellow workmen in the glass factory about the stupidity of the politicians way off in Brasilia, he doesn't understand much about his Government's affairs. And he wouldn't recognize a fiscal policy at any distance.

But Jose knows some things about his own income and outgo. He knows that when his wife, Maria, goes to the market she needs three times as much money to fill her basket with groceries as she did two years ago. He knows that the medicines he needs when the doctor comes are nine times as expensive as they were five years ago. He knows that the huaraches that cost him 20 cruzeiros in 1953 have gone to 70 cruzeiros in 1955, to 200 cruzeiros in 1960, to 2,000 cruzeiros today.

Jose has had increases in his pay during all this time, but they never seem to catch up. What good is a 50 per cent increase in pay when living costs have gone up 60 per cent since the last one, less than a year ago? There is nothing left to save now, and the 3,000 cruzeiros he put away in the big bank for a nest egg 10 years ago are hardly worth going after. They will barely pay for one piano lesson now for little Marquita, and he and Maria had once had such hope that someday it would grow to buy a piano for her so her musical talents could be developed.

To Jose, his meager pay must be spent quickly before it loses its value. Saving is useless, and the future is dark and foreboding.

There are some things we could tell Jose that might make him understand his plight:

1. In the last 12 years, the cruzeiro has dropped from 18½ to the dollar to 1,850 to the dollar. It has lost 99 per cent of its buying power.
2. In the same period, the Government of Brazil has consistently operated with large deficits, financed with borrowed and printed money. The national debt is astronomical, and foreign obligations cannot be met even with large amounts of new aid.
3. Meanwhile, the cost of living has been spiraling. It increased 23 per cent in 1960—43 per cent in 1961—52 per cent in 1962—75 per cent in 1963—85 per cent in 1964—and is still going up, despite all efforts of a new reform Government.

Until the present administration, the successive Governments of Brazil were following exactly the same new economic philosophy that is being urged on the United States today. It started about 10 years ago when a President of Brazil called the traditional economics "fuddy-duddy" and set out to use deficits and inflation as a purposeful economic device. He promised 50 years of progress in five. But, in the words of one expert a few years ago: "He achieved 40 years of inflation in four. Today, the only thing behind the cruzeiro is the printing press. Fiscal irresponsibility is at the root of Brazil's present problems."

❋   ❋   ❋

Grounds for Skepticism

Certainly in these experiences, and many others around the globe there are grounds for skepticism about the optimistic and confident assurances of the liberal economists. The evidence is that they may well be overlooking or minimizing some imposing risks involved in their propositions. Perhaps among the long-term risks of the "new economics" in the United States are these:

1. The risk of failure—with a high penalty in accumulated debt, loss of value of our currency, disastrous inflation, and loss of our position of world leadership.
2. The risk of success—which might, paradoxically, bring about another epidemic of failures in weaker nations

tempted by the sweet smell of our achievement, but unable to keep their programs in bounds, and might also tempt us to demand too much of a good thing and thereby bring about our downfall.

3. The risk of degradation of the national purpose and spirit—which would be an inevitable accompaniment of a reversal of the deep-seated traditions of thrift, self-responsibility, freedom of choice, and driving ambition that built a great nation out of a mixture of insecure racial and ethnic strains.

4. The risk of loss of personal freedoms— a price which most likely would have to be paid for the all-powerful central government that long-range economic planning and controls would bring and high spending would create.

In the absence of proof that the new theories are workable, these risks need careful evaluation. As a matter of fact, it can be said, to a degree, we have already tested this new economic philosophy in this country. All through the 1930's our Government promised to balance the budget "over the cycle" and tried to reduce unemployment and "prime the pump" of the economy by running deliberate deficits—some as much as 50 per cent of the revenues.

The adoption of the economic ideas of compensatory fiscal policy, of deliberate spending to "prime the pump," of "a little inflation is good for us," were moves of desperation at the time, to induce a recovery from the depression of the 1930s. They failed. The cycle never came around, there were 13 consecutive deficits in 13 years, unemployment held at 10 per cent or more, and it took a world war to pull the economy out of the doldrums.

Risk: Depreciation of Our Money

The risk of failure, therefore, is the risk that, after a period of years, we find what we have really achieved is an ever-increasing debt, continued depreciation of our money, a flight of capital, loss of our gold, and loss of our national strength and international prestige.

Even deeper than its impact on today's living costs or tomorrow's debts and taxes is the potential danger of weakening the national ability to fight Communism. We may be playing right into their hands by extravagant fiscal policies that carry such overwhelming risks. How do we preserve the flexibility and reserve strength to meet emergencies if we constantly pursue a course of fiscal brinkmanship, of government by credit card?

The chances for successful use of the "new economics" depend on finding a delicate line of overspending that nevertheless does not tip the balance to disaster. No country has ever found that formula.

The proponents of the "new economics" deny the validity of the American traditions. They characterize our national beliefs in frugality, thrift and self-responsibility as archaic, primitive and Puritan. A balanced budget, they tell us, is an old cliché.

But, these roots are deep in American history. In establishing their Government, the American people adopted the principle of frugality and sought to avoid the accumulation of debt. This was not a casual policy. It was expressed as the national will by every President from Washington to Eisenhower. And it was effectively carried out for 155 years after independence. The early debt of the Revolution was paid in full in 1834. The new debts incurred in later wars were progressively reduced in peace time.

Despite the massive expenditures of World War I, the national debt by 1930 had been brought down to a mere 16 billion dollars. It is only since then that we have defaulted in our direction: Since 1930, we have paid our bills only six times and have added to the debt in the other 30 fiscal years.

We Were Taught to Be Thrifty

This tradition of thrift in government was paralleled in the personal lives of our people. We were taught to be thrifty, to be self-reliant, to provide for our future. The savings of individuals became the capital that built the vast industrial complex that carried us safely through our wars and brought us from a primitive rural economy to the world's most advanced. Until the recent few decades, we heard no economic "principles" in conflict with this kind of progress.

All of this we are now asked to abandon. All of this, we are told, is an illusion, a repetition of stale phrases, an inheritance of stereotype, a hoary tradition to be buried. There is an easier way and we have missed it all along.

The "new economics" dismisses all this as mythology. It asks the nation to give up its moral legacy from the past. In offering the primrose path, it may be risking the destruction of the American spirit that built American greatness.

Perhaps most serious of all, the liberal economists, right or wrong, may be risking the loss of our personal freedoms in advancing their new policies.

Of all the instruments which subvert personal freedoms, inflation is the worst. Millions of people today know this lesson. But almost as bad are the controls that will seemingly be necessary to hold us together if the "new economics" becomes the new order.

Where does the new economic planning stop? We know that it includes deliberate expenditures to stir up the economy, that it includes artificial interest rates, that it includes tax cuts regardless of deficits, that it includes a growing national debt, and that it includes some acceptable inflation.

We know also that, sooner or later, it necessarily involves Government influence or control over prices or wages, over conditions of work, over investment and investment returns, over business policies, over the flow of money and credit, and over economic education.

And we know that the control mechanisms themselves and the bureaucracies that grow to superintend the flow of spending add up to ever enlarging power over the lives and actions of the people.

Certainly not all Government growth or Government control is to be condemned.

The population explosion and an accelerating pace of existence require more agencies to protect rights and balance out opportuniites. National defense in a threatening world requires manpower and money. These are proper Government functions.

A Pleasant Irresponsibility

In summary, the new economic theories have the attractions of promising much, providing a pleasant euphoria of irresponsibility and postponing the reckoning to other generations. But the evidence of experience is unanimous in showing that they cannot be sure of success.

The case for the "new economics" has never been proved. It rests on a sandy foundation that has never in history supported a nation's long-term progress. It has failed under every test. It is failing right now in many other countries.

Yes, the liberal economists may be overlooking some things in advocating this course: the likely risks of failure and its disastrous consequences; the intoxicating pitfalls of temporary success; the deep-seated beliefs of the American people in fiscal integrity, both in government and in their personal affairs, and the loss of national character that will ensue if these beliefs are brainwashed; the danger that by pursuing their course they may build over us a dictatorship of economic planners and of central bureaucratic Government, destroy our freedoms, and in the end make us easy victims of Communism.

Is the "new economics" a blueprint for Utopia or a temporary mess of economic pottage?

Only history will tell, but the signs so far suggest that there are more reasons for skepticism than seem to be generally recognized.

3

Applying the New Economics *

PAUL A. SAMUELSON

Economic theory in the abstract cannot be checked against performance. But the new economists insist that theirs is a practical science that should be judged by its results in the market place. In the article that follows a leading practitioner of the new economics, Professor Paul A. Samuelson, evaluates the American economy for a single year. Certain insights with respect to modern economic theory are revealed almost as a by-product of this analysis. For instance, what does Samuelson regard as the key post in determining economic trends? What role does he suggest for economists?

How would he rank Eisenhower, Johnson, and Herbert Hoover? What "blunder" does he charge to Johnson? Why should taxes have been raised in 1966? Why does he oppose a tax increase for 1967? The concepts revealed by these questions are far more important than any specific answers.

The fiscal year, like the academic year, has two semesters. Now that we are moving into the second half, I find it natural to reach for pen to fill in the report card for the American economy.

The over-all grade is a high one—say B-plus.

* Paul A. Samuelson, "State of the Economy," Copyright *Newsweek*, January 23, 1967, p. 81. Reprinted by permission of the publisher.

On employment the performance is better than that: with unemployment down to 4 per cent of the labor force, a good solid A has been earned. An A-plus must be withheld because youth and Negro unemployment remain high enough to warn us that there remain elements of structural unemployment that still need to be faced by education and manpower-mobility programs.

Real growth also merits an A grade.

Who would have expected a rise of 4 per cent or more in the sixth year of an economic expansion?

Where price stability is concerned the record darkens. Only in the last months of 1966 have wholesale prices ceased to rise. The best mark I can mete out is C. Although this is better than the flunking grades so richly merited by the Brazilian kind of inflation—40 per cent per year and more —price behavior in 1966 has not been good enough.

The Score at the Top

Up until now, I have been grading happenings. You can no more praise or blame the gross national product than you can award gold stars to the wind for blowing sweetly or to an apple for falling to the earth quadratically. What about responsible wills —I mean, people?

Along with being Commander in Chief of the armed forces, the President is architect of our economic destiny. It is a favorite sport these days to criticize President Johnson for every error of commission and omission. If a batch of fudge goes bad, LBJ is often the scapegoat.

When I try to look objectively at what government has been doing in the economic sphere, comparing these actions with what ought to be done but also taking into account what policies are politically feasible, mine is not the hand to throw the first stone—or the tenth.

Moreover, when you judge people, you need some kind of a scale. What is the "statistical curve" against which you calibrate a person's performance? Anyone who followed Herbert Hoover might have looked pretty good. And General Eisenhower—particularly during his second term—managed to make both his predecessor and suc-

cessor look pretty good as economic statesmen.

For 1966 I have to award President Johnson a grade of B in economic leadership.

Decisions Past and Yet to Come

Since 1966 was definitely a year of demand-pull inflation (and recognizable as such fairly early in the year), the President's greatest blunder was in not asking for a tax rise early in the year.

When he tells us that not a single economic expert gathered together last March in the White House raised his hand in the affirmative when queried about the wisdom of a tax rise, we can only wonder how the invitation list had been compiled. If the Council of Economic Advisers did not advise the President to raise tax rates while the 1966 pot of dollar demand was overboiling, it is scarcely credible that they have advised him to do so in January 1967 when new soft spots are being reported daily.

Now that Dwight D. Eisenhower is out of office, we can dare voice the suspicions nursed during the 1958 recession—that the general was then acting as his own professional economist and, as the lawyers cannily say, had a fool for a client.

President Johnson may turn out to be lucky in having called for a 1967 surcharge of 6 per cent on corporation and personal income taxes. But in 1925 Winston Churchill, when he mistakenly put England back on the gold standard at an overvalued prewar parity, did not prove to be lucky. History remembers, and not all the power of the surviving Churchill family can serve to wash out half a line of it.

When President Truman requested higher taxes in 1948, the lethargy of Congress saved him from thereby making the end-of-year recession worse. Since President Johnson has suggested the new tax not go into

effect until July 1, that could happen again. Sometimes they also serve who only sit and drowse.

4

The Power of Big Business *

ROBERT L. HEILBRONER

The power of any major institution, such as the giant corporation, is hard to measure out. Some contemporary analysts view modern American big business with alarm, while others hail it as a benign force. Still others regard it as an aging Sampson, shorn of its earlier strength. Although the Sherman Anti-Trust Act was enacted over three-quarters of a century ago, on the surface, at least, the multi-million dollar corporation expands and thrives in the shadow of this fundamental law. Should Americans fear this expansion? Are political leaders dwarfed by the power of their corporate counterparts? Or has big government made the modern corporation a pale, housebroken imitation of its nineteenth-century counterpart?

The power of big business is an apparition that has haunted almost as many men as has the specter of Communism. Like the cartoon of the bearded Bolshevik with his bomb, the picture of the big businessman is familiar to all of us, with his top hat and frock coat, a dollar sign across his bulging vest, one foot trampling the scenery of America and the other crushing its workmen, the fingers of one gloved hand picking the pockets of the ordinary citizen while those of the other manipulate legislators and even Presidents.

It is a caricature, of course—but how much of a caricature? How much significance should we accord to the

fact that six hundred businesses produce goods worth half the entire gross national output, or that an average one of these supercorporations handles as much revenue in a year as an average state? How alarmed should we be that the national defense and offense of the United States has become the chief source of profit of some of its large corporations, and that the heads of these corporations enjoy easy access to the corridors of the White House and the Pentagon? What attention should we pay to the opinion of Professor A. A. Berle, one of the most informed and least hysterical students of big business power, who has said, "Some of these corporations can be thought of only in somewhat the way we have heretofore thought of nations"?

These are the kinds of awkward but all-important questions to which a

* Robert L. Heilbroner, "The Power of Big Business," *Atlantic Monthly*, September, 1965, pp. 89-93. Copyright © 1965 by The Atlantic Monthly Company. Reprinted by permission of William Morris Agency, Inc.

consideration of business power leads us. Perhaps we should realize at the outset that the questions cannot be answered altogether objectively—wish, suspicion, and apology crowd in irresistibly along with the facts. Nevertheless, they are questions with which we must try to come to grips if we are to understand our society. So let us begin by examining one aspect of the problem of business power where the facts are pretty clear. This is the question of what is happening to the sheer size of big business within the economy.

The answer may come as something of a surprise to those who are familiar with the trend of corporate amalgamation in the past. Thirty years ago, when Professors Berle and Means made the first brilliant study of the two hundred biggest nonfinancial corporations, they came up with the half-fanciful prognostication that if the observed rate of expansion of the big corporations relative to the smaller ones were maintained for another 360 years, all the nation's corporations would have disappeared into one mammoth concern, which would then have a life expectancy roughly equivalent to that of the Roman Empire. Long before that day, however—in fact, by 1950—Berle and Means warned, the two hundred largest corporations would already have absorbed 70 per cent of all corporate wealth.

Well, 1950 has come and gone, and it appears that these worst fears have not been realized. We do not have statistics exactly comparable with the Berle and Means estimates, but a study published by A. D. H. Kaplan of the Brookings Institution is close enough. It shows that the top one hundred industrial corporations in 1960 had amassed 31 percent of all industrial corporate assets, compared with 25 percent in 1929. This is evidence of continuing concentration, but at nothing like the rate envisaged in the Berle and Means projection.

Why? One main reason is simply that the great corporations, for all their enormous mass, are not totally invulnerable to attack, to erosion by technology, or to suicide by incompetent management.

A complementary reason for the standstill in the trend toward concentration lies in a change that has affected the big corporation from within rather than from without. This is the growing reluctance of the big companies to ram home the economic advantage that is theirs by running their competitors out of business. General Motors, for example, makes three times as much profit as the entire asset value of American Motors, but no one expects GM to "compete" by eliminating its rival from the field.

Do these standard explanations promise a continuance of the relative stability of big business size within the economy? We do not know. There is some evidence that the vulnerability of the topmost corporations is decreasing, lessening the chances that they will be displaced by other firms; between 1948 and 1960 only twenty-four of the top hundred had their places usurped, whereas between 1909 and 1919, forty-one leaders were displaced. Then, too, large areas of the economy—construction, for instance, or the service industries—are still characterized by small or medium-sized business, and it would be in line with past experience if largescale enterprise eventually "rationalized" these fields. Finally, the new technology of administration and control, automation, may provide the techniques and the impetus to further concentration.

Thus the relative quiescence of the "monopoly" problem today does not guarantee as much for tomorrow. It is at least possible that the economic pressures toward agglutination will again rise. In that case much will depend on the attitude of the top corporation officialdom and on the counter-pressures exerted by other groups in society.

The Men at the Top

Fifty or sixty years ago it would have been a much easier task to form an opinion about the attitudes of big businessmen, for the supercorporations were then still dominated to a considerable extent by the supermen who started them. Not alone the names but also the personalities of Rockefeller, Carnegie, Morgan, Harriman, Frick were familiar to every reader, albeit often in romanticized versions. Today it is not so simple to identify or to dissect the business elite. We are confronted with a largely faceless group known as "the management." How many well-informed people can name or describe in any way even one of the chief executive officers (except Henry Ford, Jr.) in the ten biggest industrial firms: GM, Standard Oil of New Jersey, Ford, General Electric, Socony, U.S. Steel, Chrysler, Texaco, Gulf, Western Electric? . . . it seems clear to me, comparing the big businessman of today with those of a few decades back, that the contemporary executive represents a generation of administration rather than of acquisition. This is not merely a matter of the statistics of concentration we have already examined. It refers as well to a style of business leadership in which "good public relations" have come to play an extraordinarily important role. Here perhaps is where the increased educational exposure, the lengthened training, the so-called "professionalization" of the executive, should be given its due.

One result of this new style, par-ticularly noticeable among the executives of the biggest firms, is a certain caution in utterance and action quite untypical of their predecessors a generation back. In the main, the approved managerial tactics are now those of long-run security rather than short-run risk, of staying out of trouble rather than of taking a chance, of bucking for the title of "business statesman" rather than "tycoon." Among the smaller firms, we still see something of the uninhibited drive of the past, but at the top, inhibition itself begins to appear as a managerial virtue.

Another characteristic of the business elite is its essentially reluctant relationship to political power. Noise, oratory, and table-thumping to the contrary notwithstanding, I think that what is noticeable about the great majority of big businessmen in America is a striking absence of real political involvement. What is visible instead is a profound unwillingness to get embroiled in anything that might take them away from their jobs, or that might not look good in the newspapers, or that might incur the displeasure of their main customers or their boards. There is in the big business world a great deal of political rhetoric but not much political commitment—what could be more significant than the fact that for all the endless business talk of freedom, not a single major corporate executive found the Alabama Freedom March important enough to warrant leaving his desk, although educators, government officials, housewives, trade unionists, students, and scientists felt the need to go to Selma, despite the nuisance, the call of other duties, or the danger to which it exposed them.

The New Elites

All this discussion of the structure of big business and the sociological attributes of big businessmen circles around our main subject—the power of big business—and yet fails to engage it squarely. What is big business power? What does it look like in ordinary life?

The oldest and purest exercise of business power has always been the market exploitation of the weak. We think of labor, the historic victim of the big corporation, working a twelve-hour day and a seven-day week (with a twenty-four-hour shift every two weeks) as late as 1919 in the dangerous mills of the United States Steel Corporation. We think of little business, undersold and outbought and forced to pay additional freight charges to the railroads, who then turned the money over to the Standard Oil combine. We think of the consumer, pictured by a commentator of the 1890s as "born to the profit of the Milk Trust and dead to the profit of the Coffin Trust."

To recall these instances from the past does more than give reality to one meaning of the words "business power." It also serves to give some historical perspective on the trend of that power. Surely the strength of labor vis-a-vis big business has been enormously enhanced since the days when labor unions were literally afraid of the big company. So, too, although less noticed, has the position of little business improved. We often forget that it was the political pressure of little business and not of the public that brought about the passage of most anti-big-business legislation, including the antitrust acts. But this animus of the past seems largely to have evaporated. Now and again there is some anti-big-corporation talk, as when the auto dealers rose up against General Motors or when small business complains that big companies get all the defense contracts. But the complaints, however true, quickly subside. From the peace

that prevails, it is hard not to conclude that little business no longer feels the brunt of big business power as it did in the past.

It is less easy to make an unambiguous determination in the case of the third historic target of business power in the marketplace, the consumer. Certainly he is more ardently wooed than in the public-be-damned days, but the wooing is sometimes accompanied by breach of promise; not too long ago, for instance, the Federal Trade Commission found that General Foods was charging more per unit of weight for its "economy-sized" packages than for its regular packages. Nor does leafing through Consumer Reports overwhelm one with a sense of corporate solicitude for the consumer. Still more important, perhaps, although the trusts have gone, there is no evidence that profit margins have declined over the past fifty years or so. General Motors, for example, makes almost as much in profits before taxes per car as it pays out for wages on that car.

But even if we leave the case of the consumer undecided, it seems fair enough to conclude that the power of big business to throw its weight around in the marketplace has been considerably restricted in the past three or four decades. Yet that does not fully satisfy our inquiry. For everyone knows that market exploitation, however bad, is not all of what we mean by "big business power." In fact, what usually comes to mind when we say the words is not so much these instances of market abuse, but larger and subtler kinds of influence —for instance, the use of the national government to create new domains of private profit such as the enormous land-grabs of the railroad era, or the insinuation of business goals into foreign policy such as the banana-republic diplomacy that once made the world safe for United Fruit, or the

374 The Power of Big Business

blind deference accorded to business views just because they were business views, as in the general adulation of the businessman during the 1920s.

It is difficult to assay the trend of this hugely varied exercise of power with much accuracy. Certainly, we cannot airily dismiss the influence of big business on the nation's affairs as being a thing of the past. Nonetheless, I would still hazard the opinion that its ability to manipulate public affairs or to have its way in the formation of national policy is declining.

I base this opinion not so much on the static size of big business within the economy or on the quieter bearing of its executives as on another development that strikes me as being of signal importance. This is the rise within our society of new elites, whose competence for government is rapidly becoming of greater importance for national survival or even well-being than that of business leaders. One such new elite consists of the military professionals. A second is composed of advisers from the fields of science, economics, sociology, and the academic world in general. A third includes the civil servants and the career administrators of public programs.

These new elites play increasingly central roles in the elaboration and exercise of government policies in the crucial areas that now confront us: education, civil rights, poverty, urban renewal, foreign aid, the scale of the military establishment, the determination of fiscal and monetary policy, and the conduct of foreign affairs. At the same time, it seems undeniable that the voice of big business in the delineation of these specific programs is much smaller than in comparable programs of the past.

Further, it seems to me that this swing of power toward the new elites is likely to become intensified. I expect to see fewer big businessmen in positions of power in Washington and more soldiers, scientists, educators, and government administrators; to see fewer big businessmen as trustees of universities and more of the new men of power there; to hear less about the sanctity of private investments abroad and more about international government-to-government programs; to find less attention paid to the aging rhetoric of laissez-faire and more to the academic language of neo-Keynesianism and input-output tables. To be sure, we still live in a civilization in which the accumulation of individual wealth is believed to be the most admirable objective of human life, and in such a civilization great centers of wealth must perforce be great centers of influence. Nonetheless, I think the exercise of business power in the direction of national affairs is on the wane and that the power of new nonbusiness groups is sharply on the rise.

Managed Capitalism

As for the new elites that now contest with businessmen for the control of the levers of the nation's working programs, they are certainly not antibig business. The new elites have no thoughts of nationalization, of extensive decommercialization, of far-reaching changes in the enjoyment of property incomes. At most, their programs imply a kind of managed capitalism in which the great corporations, largely maintained intact, would be coordinated within the national effort by some form of permissive planning. But it is in itself indicative of the total acquiescence in the ideology of business that even the formulation of such mild goals comes as something of a shock, and that most of the elites would plead that they have no goal other than a day-to-day "pragmatic" approach.

If this is true, what does it portend for the future? There are, it seems to me, important possibilities for social evolution still unexplored within the business system, and I would hope that in the hands of a new guard, uncommitted to the ideological fundamentalism of the old guard, a liberal capitalism might develop greater stablity, less poverty, more public concern. At the same time there is also a less pleasant possibility. The prospect of a business society no longer made uncomfortable by the presence of alternative social formu- lations presents the threat of a human community arrested at a still primitive level of striving and quieted by an intellectual asphyxiation and a moral dullness. But this brings us far beyond the bounds of permissible speculation. Perhaps at the moment we can say no more than that we seem to stand at the threshold of a new era of contained capitalism, in which the power of big business is more constrained— and yet less contested—than in the past. What may be the horizons and what the limitations of such a society we must now begin to find out.

5

Big Business, Militarism, and Democracy *

DWIGHT D. EISENHOWER

During the past decade the relationship between government and the economy has changed most drastically in the field of military expenditures. More than 10 per cent of the American gross national product is now spent each year for defense purposes. A single military contract can be worth five or six billion dollars. Cancellation of a contract can mean economic disaster for an entire area. A multimillion dollar award means boom times. With so much at stake it is not surprising that an uneasy business-military power axis has arisen. President Eisenhower voices his concern over this new facet of American life in the article that follows. Why does he believe that "The potential for the disastrous rise of misplaced power exists and will persist"? What is the basis for his contention that the independence of the universities is threatened?

My fellow Americans: Three days from now, after half a century in the service of our country, I shall lay down the responsibilities of office as, in traditional and solemn ceremony,

the authority of the Presidency is vested in my successor.

This evening I come to you with a message of leavetaking and farewell and to share a few final thoughts with you, my countrymen.

Like every other citizen, I wish the new President and all who will labor with him Godspeed. I pray that the

---

* Excerpts from the "Farewell to the Nation" speech delivered by President Dwight D. Eisenhower over radio and television on January 17, 1961.

coming years will be blessed with peace and prosperity for all.

II

We now stand ten years past the midpoint of a century that has witnessed four major wars among great nations. Three of these involved our own country. Despite these holocausts, America is today the strongest, the most influential, and most productive nation in the world. Understandably proud of this preeminence, we yet realize that America's leadership and prestige depend not merely upon our unmatched material progress, riches, and military strength but on how we use our power in the interests of world peace and human betterment.

III

Throughout America's adventure in free government our basic purposes have been to keep the peace, to foster progress in human achievement, and to enhance liberty, dignity, and integrity among people and among nations. To strive for less would be unworthy of a free and religious people. Any failure traceable to arrogance or our lack of comprehension or readiness to sacrifice would inflict upon us grievous hurt both at home and abroad.

Progress toward these noble goals is persistently threatened by the conflict now engulfing the world. It commands our whole attention, absorbs our very beings. We face a hostile ideology—global in scope, atheistic in character, ruthless in purpose, and insidious in method. Unhappily the danger it poses promises to be of indefinite duration. To meet it successfully there is called for not so much the emotional and transitory sacrifices of crisis but rather those which enable us to carry forward steadily, surely, and without complaint the burdens of a prolonged and complex struggle—with liberty the stake. Only thus shall we remain, despite every provocation, on our charted course toward permanent peace and human betterment.

Crises there will continue to be. In meeting them, whether foreign or domestic, great or small, there is a recurring temptation to feel that some spectacular and costly action could become the miraculous solution to all current difficulties. A huge increase in newer elements of our defense, development of unrealistic programs to cure every ill in agriculture, a dramatic expansion in basic and applied research—these and many other possibilities, each possibly promising in itself, may be suggested as the only way to the road we wish to travel.

But each proposal must be weighed in the light of a broader consideration: The need to maintain balance in and among national programs—balance between the private and the public economy, balance between cost and hoped-for advantage, balance between the clearly necessary and the comfortably desirable, balance between our essential requirements as a nation and the duties imposed by the nation upon the individual, balance between actions of the moment and the national welfare of the future. Good judgment seeks balance and progress; lack of it eventually finds imbalance and frustration.

The record of many decades stands as proof that our people and their government have, in the main, understood these truths and have responded to them well in the face of stress and threat. But threats, new in kind or degree, constantly arise. I mention two only.

IV

A vital element in keeping the peace is our military establishment.

Our arms must be mighty, ready for instant action, so that no potential aggressor may be tempted to risk his own destruction.

Our military organization today bears little relation to that known by any of my predecessors in peacetime, or indeed by the fighting men of World War II or Korea.

Until the latest of our world conflicts, the United States had no armaments industry. American makers of plowshares could, with time and as required, make swords as well. But now we can no longer risk emergency improvisation of national defense; we have been compelled to create a permanent armaments industry of vast proportions. Added to this, 3½ million men and women are directly engaged in the defense establishment. We annually spend on military security more than the net income of all United States corporations.

This conjunction of an immense military establishment and a large arms industry is new in the American experience. The total influence—economic, political, even spiritual—is felt in every city, every statehouse, every office of the federal government. We recognize the imperative need for this development. Yet we must not fail to comprehend its grave implications. Our toil, resources, and livelihood are all involved; so is the very structure of our society.

In the councils of government we must guard against the acquisition of unwarranted influence, whether sought or unsought, by the military-industrial complex. The potential for the disastrous rise of misplaced power exists and will persist.

We must never let the weight of this combination endanger our liberties or democratic processes. We should take nothing for granted. Only an alert and knowledgeable citizenry can compel the proper meshing of the huge industrial and military machinery of defense with our peaceful methods and goals so that security and liberty may prosper together.

Akin to and largely responsible for the sweeping changes in our industrial-military posture has been the technological revolution during recent decades. In this revolution research has become central; it also becomes more formalized, complex and costly. A steadily increasing share is conducted for, by, or at the direction of the federal government.

Today the solitary inventor, tinkering in his shop, has been overshadowed by task forces of scientists in laboratories and testing fields. In the same fashion the free university, historically the fountainhead of free ideas and scientific discovery, has experienced a revolution in the conduct of research. Partly because of the huge costs involved, a government contract becomes virtually a substitute for intellectual curiosity. For every old blackboard there are now hundreds of new electronic computers.

The prospect of domination of the nation's scholars by federal employment, project allocations, and the power of money is ever present and is gravely to be regarded.

Yet, in holding scientific research and discovery in respect, as we should, we must also be alert to the equal and opposite danger that public policy could itself become the captive of a scientific-technological elite.

It is the task of statemanship to mold, to balance, and to integrate these and other forces, new and old, within the principles of our democratic system—ever aiming toward the supreme goals of our free society.

6

Caught on the Horn of Plenty *

W. H. FERRY

Traditionally, every dilemma has at least two horns. But the horn of plenty is generally regarded as a cornucopia, rather than one facet of a dilemma. Mr. Ferry suggests that the American horn of plenty does have a price tag attached. On the one hand it promises abundance for all; on the other hand it promises mounting unemployment. To solve this paradox will require more than "massage and Band-Aids." Instead, it will require a reordering of American society, with government intervening more and more in the nation's industrial life. Why does Ferry believe that economic planning by government "is indispensible if the United States is going to make sense out of its future?" Why does he argue that "We shall have to find means, public or private, of paying people to do no work?"

Strangely enough, Americans are having a hard time getting used to the idea of abundance. Abundance is not only a relatively recent state of affairs. There is also an idea current that it may not last very long. The barriers to general comprehension of the possibilities and demands of abundance are numerous. There is, for example, tradition, and a mythology that seeks to confine the growing abundance of this country inside the old political and social enclosures. Happily there is also the beginning of a less dusty literature on the topic.

As consumers, Americans are joyously sopping up affluence, quarter after quarter sending private debt for consumer goods to record levels, and inventing new categories of services. But the lesson of abundance is even

* W. H. Ferry, "Caught on the Horn of Plenty," *Bulletin*, Center For The Study of Democratic Institutions (Santa Barbara, Calif., January 1962). Reprinted by permission of the publisher.

here ambiguous; for while there is enough to go around for all, not all are sharing. There is enough in our ever-swollen granaries so that no American need to go to bed hungry. Yet millions do, while millions of others are vaguely uneasy and feel guilty about so absurd a situation. The American farm is technology's most notorious victory. That the disaster of abundance on our farms has so far resisted solution is a portent of greater dilemmas in other areas.

For the country may soon be in the same fix with regard to consumer goods and services—more than enough for all, but without the political wit to know how to bring about a just distribution. We may, in fact, be in that situation at present. There is evidence that something like 30 per cent of our productive facilities are standing idle most of time. Much of our machinery is obsolete. Everyone knows that the steel industry spent about a year in the doldrums of 50 per cent of capacity production. Planned obsolescence, which is the design and sales strategy of many manufacturers, is latent abundance, just as the fields left unturned by wheat and barley and rice farmers are latent abundance. It is not only what is produced that counts up to a total of abundance, but what is capable of being produced.

Not the least of our troubles occurs over definitions. Abundance of this self-evident variety, for example, is not the opposite of the classical idea of scarcity. And what are resources? How do you tell when a resource is scarce? Or not scarce? Are people resources? Are people without jobs or skills resources? What is prosperity? This is a particularly hard definition. The recession is said to be past. Newcomers by the millions are thronging into the stock market. The gross national product is at a 3.4 rate. And around 5,000,000 people are out of jobs. Is this prosperity? What are today's definitions of work, leisure, play, affluence? Our vocabulary is tuned to yesterday's industrial revolution, not to today's scientific revolution. Abundance might, for instance, be defined as the capacity—here meaning resources, skill, capital, and potential and present production—the capacity to supply every citizen with a minimum decent life. We have the capacity, so this makes us an abundant society. Yet some 30,000,000 Americans are living below the poverty line.

This paper focuses on a disagreeable abundance—the ironic and growing abundance of unemployment. Radical technological change is producing a surplus of labor, and radical measures will be required to deal with it. Since no such radical measures have been, or seem likely to be, proposed by the federal government, technological unemployment may soon grow to the proportions of a crisis. For generations the dictum that Machines Make Jobs was demonstrably valid. Now the dictum is losing its force and generality. Machines are replacing workers. Some part of the 50,000 new jobs that have to be provided weekly to keep the American economy going are, to be sure, being supplied by new machines. But what the machine giveth at one place it taketh away at another: hence, structural unemployment.

The prospect is that through the 1960's the gross national product will continue to rise. Profit and dividend levels and stock market prices will continue upward. So will the total number of employed. But the likelihood is that the absolute and relative number of unemployed will also be growing, as will the number of distressed areas.

How will this state of affairs be described? There is no word or combination of words at present to define such economic sunshine-and-shadow. We are used to thinking of major economic phenomena moving in roughly parallel lines. But it might turn out that the number of unemployed in the United States is at the lowest point today—around 6.5 to 7 per cent—that it will reach again. Current attacks on technological unemployment have produced more disappointment than results. The labor force is growing at a rate of 1,250,000 annually, and technological progress permits the discharge of another 1,250,000 each year. The dimensions of the situation are becoming plain. . . .

The question is whether jobs can be manufactured fast enough to approach full employment, using the present definition of jobs and the means of providing them that are presently regarded as acceptable. The essential contention of this paper is that the answer is no. An apparently unavoidable condition of the Age of

Abundance is increasing structural unemployment and underemployment.

The novelty of this proposition is that the majority of victims of technological displacement will be *permanently* out of work. They will not just be "resting between engagements." They will not just be waiting for the next upturn, or for expansion of the industry or company in which they were working. They will no longer be the objects of unemployment insurance plans, for these plans are designed to fill the gap between jobs, not to provide a permanent dole.

The rapidly emerging fact is that every year from now on we shall be able, because of accelerating technology, to produce the goods and services needed by the nation with fewer and fewer of the available hands—say 90 per cent or less.

I use the phrase "90 per cent or less" advisedly although it does not comport with the 6.5 to 7 per cent unemployment figure mentioned earlier. It is a delicate way of bringing in the touchy issues of featherbedding and underemployment. Everyone knows what featherbedding means. Underemployment describes workers who continue to hold jobs after it has been established that the jobs can be done as well or better by machines or people who work only part-time. The underemployed, according to some authorities, total as high as 25 per cent of the labor force. The underemployed include also a million or more agricultural workers who stay on the farm because there is no work in industry for them, 5,000,000 women who would like jobs, and 2,000,000 part-time workers. Note must be taken also of double-job-holding—"moonlighting"—by hundreds of thousands of workers.

The unemployed and underemployed are no longer almost exclusively the unskilled, the recent immigrants, the colored, the groups at the end of the economic scale, who have customarily borne the heaviest weight of economic slides. White collar workers are joining this group as automation reaches the office. There is some reason for thinking that white collar workers will after a few years comprise most of the growing category of technologically displaced. Herbert Simon has observed that by 1985 machines can do away with all of middle management, "if Americans want it that way." Since middle management is considered the ultimate destination of much of middle-class America, Simon's words have an air of clammy prophecy about them.

Senator William Proxmire commented recently on the assertion that there is nothing really novel about the present situation:

"I call for a frank recognition, especially among our experts on economic policy, that we do not have the answers to the perplexing problem of unemployment in a rapidly-automating, work-force-growing free economy. A vigorous search for answers consistent with economic freedom is urgently needed."

Harvey Swados remarked some time ago in a brilliant essay that the question of work would be the biggest domestic political issue of the 1960's. Part of his argument was that accelerating technological displacement would harden into an established economic pattern; the country would sooner or later be driven to the knowledge that it is not dealing with a regrettable but transient phenomenon. And, Swados said, there is a serious question whether Americans can accommodate themselves either to the idea or to the use of abundant leisure. The revolutionary consequences of leisure in a nation committed to economic dynamism and to work, any kind of work, as a good in itself have found no radical echoes yet in public policy. The likelihood is that the country will stay for a while with the policies that the administration has chosen.

These will be accompanied by spread-the-work campaigns, by union demands for shorter hours, union-management agreements to retrain employees or to share the shock of automation (as West Coast shippers and the long-shoremen's union have done), early retirement schemes, and more public works programs by local and regional authorities. There is nothing wrong with stop-gaps of this nature. It is only wrong to think of them as solutions instead of palliatives.

Mention of the word "planning" rouses instant suspicion. When coupled with the word "national"—that is, national planning—it sends editorial writers headlong to their typewriters. Yet national planning is indispensable if the United States is going to make sense out of its future. Can anyone imagine an unplanned transition from war to peace production, or an unplanned highway program? For those willing to acknowledge that free enterprise is not a divine dispensation and capitalism not a dictate of natural law, the need is evident everywhere. Such is the acceleration of technical and social change that international planning may be expected within the next decade or so.

The essential elements of the program proposed here are: First, national planning authorized by Congress, and not national planning administered by a bureaucratic ogre to be appointed by the CIO, the NAM, or the ADA. . . . Second, a scheme based on what W. Arthur Lewis calls "planning by inducement," by which he means the use of politics and persuasion, in their various guises, to achieve a more reasonable utilization of resources and a better distribution of income. . . . Finally, recognition of

today's economic order for what it is, an enormously complicated piece of machinery which cannot be run by the instruction manuals of the eighteenth and nineteenth centuries. National hypocrisy has in few places as many facets as it has in the simplistic rhetoric of the opponents of planning. The most violent antiplanners are the same men who expertly plan the future of their corporations for ten to thirty years, and who rely on planners to keep their suburbs from infestation by junkyards and filling stations.

National planning will be recognition that the government bears the final responsibility for the quality and content and prosperity of the nation. This may perhaps be called modern mercantilism. Those who construe these proposals as some dark version of new and unholy economic doctrines are advised to refer to economic planning in sixteenth and seventeenth century England or, even better, to the economic history of the Eastern seaboard of this country in the eighteenth and early nineteenth centuries.

In an abundant society the problem is not an economic one of keeping the machine running regardless of what it puts out, but a political one of achieving the common good. And planning is one of its major means.

But whether or not we can figure out some such way of taking systematic advantage of the bewildering fact of abundance, we shall within a short while have to discard attitudes that grew up in the dog-eat-dog phase of capitalism and adopt others suitable to modern mercantilism. For example, we shall have to stop automatically regarding the unemployed as lazy, unlucky, indolent, and unworthy. We shall have to find means, public or private, of paying people to do no work.

This suggestion goes severely against the American grain, and it will have to be adopted slowly. The first steps have been taken. Unemployment insurance and supplementary unemployment benefit plans reached by company-union negotiations are examples. As these have come to be accepted as civic-industrial policy, so may plans for six-month work years, or retirement at 50 or 55 at full pay until pension schemes take hold. So may continuation of education well into adult years, at public expense. So may payment from the public treasury for nonproductive effort, such as writing novels, painting pictures, composing music, doing graduate work, and taking part in the expanding functions of government. Is a physicist more valuable to the community than a playright? Why? The responsibility of the individual to the general welfare runs far beyond the purely economic.

Abundance will enable a reversal of the old order of things. Modern mercantilism will remove the economic machine from the middle of the land-scape to one side, where, under planning by inducement, its ever more efficient automata will provide the goods and services required by the general welfare. Humanity, with its politics and pastimes and poetry and conversation, will then occupy the central place in the landscape. Management of machines for human ends, not management by them, is the true object of industrial civilization.

This is the promise of modern mercantilism, and if the time is not yet, it is yet a time worth striving for. Meanwhile, the chief necessity is to revive respect for law and government as the proper instruments of the general welfare. Without this respect the economic future of this country and that of other nations linked to it will be determined, and stultified, by the accidents of private ambition and the hope of private gain. With this respect the Age of Abundance can be made into the Age of the General Welfare, and the United States can become in fact the moral commonwealth it has always claimed to be.

7

Labor Unions Wrestle with Automation *

NEIL W. CHAMBERLAIN

What stance should labor unions take in the face of automation? Should they oppose it as threatening worker security? Should they welcome it as providing the promise of abundance? What responsibility do they have toward displaced workers? Should union leaders, like their management counterparts, accept the idea of fluid assets (the skills of their members) rather than trying to preserve the status quo?

The constancy of change in our society creates inevitable insecurity. There is less than one can hold on to, whether in the realm of personal beliefs or bodies of professional knowledge, or in the realm of corporate market position or individual job tenure. We must learn to deal with change if we wish to survive, or at least if we wish to survive well.

Strangely enough, although it is management which speaks most conservatively, it is management which has learned most effectively how to come to grips with change in its own sphere of activity, the world of business. To put it briefly, management no longer conceives of itself as running a furniture business or an automobile plant or a meat-packing establishment or a chemical works; it views itself as managing a bundle of assets which may take one form today and another tomorrow.

This change in outlook is partly a product of, and partly gave rise to, the systems of corporate planning and budgeting which are developments of the last few decades. The notion that management can set a target for itself, usually in the form of a rate of return on investment, and then plan and manipulate its operations in order to come as close as possible to that goal, is an idea of such recent vintage that it is still far from standard practice. But among the corporate leaders it is gospel, and the planning goes on with respect not only to the year's current operations but to the firm's five- to ten-year future.

The budget—that homely device matching out-go against income—has been converted into a highly sophisticated instrument for ensuring that plans do not remain dreams because they lack resources for their accomplishment. The budget is the mold in which plans are cast. It is an elaboration of the planned composition and level of the inflows and outflows of funds on the strength of which the company's goal can be achieved. This planning-cum-budgeting re-

* Neil W. Chamberlain, "What's Ahead For Labor?" *The Atlantic Monthly*, July, 1964, pp. 34-37. Copyright © 1964 by The Atlantic Monthly Company, Boston, Mass. 02116. Reprinted by permission of the author and publisher.

quires a time horizon which extends into a virtually indefinite future. A business firm assembles and nurtures assets which grow over the years, and the uses of which vary from year to year and decade to decade in response to changing tastes, population shifts, market structures, production processes, and inventions. The use of almost any company's assets is quite different now from what it was ten years ago and from what it will be ten years from now. A company may thus be viewed as a bundle of assets which are frozen in one form today and which it is management's job to metamorphose into a continuingly different form as time goes by. If it fails in this task, the bundle of assets which it is managing lose their value.

In effect, what happens is that management freezes (that is, invests) funds in certain forms for specific purposes. These frozen funds are becoming liquid all the time as inventories are liquidated, as credit is repaid, as depreciation reserves accumulate, as earnings are retained. And management must make decisions all the time as to whether the assets which have become liquid shall be frozen into the same forms again or into new forms.

Sometimes the decision is relatively routine. If inventories become depleted of a product for which sales are brisk, it takes no soul-searching to decide whether to replenish them. But at other times the problem is more difficult. When an old piece of machinery has put in its time and has to be relegated to a standby role or scrapped, should the company buy another like it? The chances are that it could not do so if it wanted to, since technological improvements will have taken place. But even if it could, rival machinery producers or the company's own engineers may have other ideas as to how the job of the old machine can be done better. What form shall the replacement take?

Complicate the problem further. Should the machine even be replaced? Perhaps technological change has so outdated the whole production process that it is preferable to scrap not just that piece of equipment but the whole process, substituting a more efficient one. To carry that off effectively, it might be wiser to build a whole new plant. But if the company is to build a new plant, it does not have to place it in the same location; it might be more efficient to move it closer to a shifting source of materials or a shifting outlet for sales.

The alternatives do not end there. If a firm is going to invest in a new plant and a new process, perhaps it should use these for a new product. How much longer will the product in question remain profitable before being outmoded by something else? Perhaps the company had better consider putting its resources into something with a longer potential life.

We could multiply the questions which management must answer as it determines over and over again the form in which assets now liquid (through the sale of goods and the return of once-invested capital, through loans, through new equity issues) shall be freshly frozen. The answers to these questions relate to different points in the firm's future. The decision to invest in rebuilding inventories is one that affects operations in the next few weeks. Equipment replacement may be a matter of months. Process substitution may take a year or two. New-product development, at least as long or longer. The location of a new plant takes at least three years, more likely five to ten. And all these things are going on simultaneously. The decisions relating to projected actions at various points in a firm's time stream must all find room in the company's plans and must be incorporated into its budget—given concreteness by having resources allocated to their phased accomplishment.

Much more could be said about new approaches to management, but perhaps this is enough to convey the sense of what may be reasonably termed the "asset revolution." Compare this relatively abstract view of a business firm as a bundle of assets whose form and function must be continuingly modified with the more romantic and increasingly obsolete view of a business firm as identified with some product, some brand name, some location, even some family.

But it is that romantic and increasingly obsolete outlook, in their own sphere of activity, which still characterizes the labor unions. The assets which they are managing are the skills of their members. The function of the unions is to preserve the value of those assets, and to secure for their members a favorable rate of return on them. But the approach which they adopt is old-world and out-of-date. They look on the skills of their members not as something whose value can be retained only by constant adaptation and transformation, but as representing a more or less fixed set of characteristics whose value can best be assured by trying to preserve work opportunities making use of those characteristics. They still look to work rules, which require so many workers or certain types of workers for given functions, or rules based on "past practices," or rules preserving job "rights" through such devices as seniority, as the principal means for shoring up the worth of their members' skills. When these fail, they turn to shorter hours as an instrument for spreading the available work.

This old, familiar craft-oriented approach denies change rather than adapts to it. It regards the assets of union members in the same way that an old family firm might have regarded its business assets—frozen in a particular form, designed to do a particular job, seeking markets as long as there are markets, and fatalistically failing if and when markets dry up.

The asset revolution has not yet touched the unions. When it does, as it must in time if they are to survive, they will be driven to adopt the same asset orientation that management has learned to live with and profit from. The lifetime careers of their members will be recognized as something for which short-run and long-run plans must be made. They will anticipate the obsolescence of skills—before obsolescence has destroyed the value of existing assets—by planning for a continuing metamorphosis of old skills into new. This can be done only by explicit attention to career development through programs designed to upgrade the general abilities and specific qualifications of their members. They will recognize that their members' welfare is not secured by attempting to hold on to present rights, growing out of past service, but by projecting a present position into some competence to be realized in the future.

The present improvisations which are intended to preserve the value of skills by hanging on to diminishing work opportunities will be recognized for the Canutelike efforts which they are. The desperate search for ways of retaining market outlets for job abilities which are less and less wanted and needed will give way to a more rewarding examination of ways in which on-the-job training can be coupled with off-the-job educational opportunities to give their members qualifications which are continuously in demand.

This type of career planning costs money and means that unions must sell their membership on the desirability of substituting for the now relatively meaningless money demands on managements the much more significant demand for the financing of training programs, over the nature of which the unions would negotiate and, if need be, strike. The drive for shorter hours would suddenly acquire new meaning when coupled with study and training for future advancement. Shorter hours employed in this fashion would not be just a costly way of spreading work but a self-financing means of increasing productivity.

How far the unions are from such a way of thinking is neatly demonstrated by the "revolutionary" concession of a three-month vacation which the Steelworkers won in last year's negotiations. In accordance with time-honored custom, the vacation bonus went to the employees with the longest service. The upper half of the labor force, in terms of seniority, were to enjoy the three months of leisure every five years. The new fringe benefit was trumpeted as creating additional work opportunities for younger men who would take their places.

If the Steelworkers had been thinking in terms of asset management, however, they would have sought released time for skill upgrading rather than for vacation. Recognizing that older employees who have lost the habits of study would be less likely than younger workers to benefit from a training program, they would have given the opportunity to those who would gain most from such exposure, regardless of seniority. They would have recognized that the additional work they were cadging for younger employees had little or no relevance to their long-run earning opportunities, and no significance in terms of providing security through an improvement of their "asset structure."

To be sure, political realities may force a union to modify a position which it would prefer to adopt. Union leadership cannot force a point of view on a reluctant membership. Senior employees, for example, may be in a position to exact some advantage for themselves without respect to the organization's preferred program. Nevertheless, good management would call for a clear distinction between what is desirable and what is expedient or necessary. Unless such a distinction can be made, there is no possibility of bending the latter in the direction of the former, or even of knowing in what direction the leadership should seek to lead.

At the present time unions have no evident sense of direction. They are looking for ways to meet the growing sense of job insecurity on the part of their memberships, but are experiencing an increasing sense of frustration at the lack of success of the relatively minor measures they have been able to provide. The exaggerated boasting over the importance of some contract term which they have won from management is betrayed by their shrill criticism of government and the intellectuals for failing to come up with programs which will provide genuine and long-run job security.

Admittedly, they cannot meet that problem alone. Admittedly, the government has a role to play which it has so far played rather badly. Admittedly, the intellectuals have been less inventive than society, including the unions, might reasonably expect. But the unions cannot put the entire burden on others. They are themselves woefully behind the times, running their affairs with approximately the same skill as a family concern might have been managed two or three generations ago.

Not until they catch up with the idea that change not only creates problems but also offers opportunities, which can be realized only by proper management of assets, will they and their members be able to face the future with some assurance. The skill of their members is not only something which can lose its value, but it is also something whose value can be increased, with proper management. The rate of return on the assets of their members—the qualifications which they bring to their jobs—can be improved by upgrading the quality of those assets more than by trying to extract a few additional pennies an hour for unchanged assets which technological change is rapidly obsolescing.

It takes programs and planning to move in that direction. It takes a radical reorientation in the thinking of leadership and membership alike. Undeniably it is easier to proceed along familiar patterns, shutting one's eyes to the inevitable outcome or placing the blame on others. But until genuine career planning for the future substitutes for makeshift efforts to hang on to present job opportunities, the unions will continue resolutely to face the past. Their time stream will continue to flow in the wrong direction.

It would be uncharitable and unhelpful to criticize labor for its failure to manage its members' assets with more insight and purpose without at the same time recognizing that in certain ways labor has a more difficult job than the managers of business assets. The new breed of corporation executive being spawned by our business schools has been taught to regard administration as its profession—administration in itself, not the administration of a steelworks or the administration of a power plant or the administration of a shoe factory, but the administration of anything. It is easy for a McNamara to make the transition from the Ford Motor Company to the Department of Defense because the Harvard Business School has taught him that this is simply part of a career line.

There is really no parallel career concept in the case of the average worker. When his job as tool-and-die maker or foundryman or miner disintegrates before a technological onslaught, it is hard for him to cease to regard himself as a diemaker and to learn to think of himself as, say, a computer programmer. There is no continuing career line, but rather a career break.

Some present jobs, it is true, may lead naturally into evolving future opportunities. For example, younger electricians have occasionally learned electronics and gone on to better jobs, sometimes with the assistance of their union, in one of the few instances of genuine asset management on the part of a union leadership. But by and large, old jobs do not metamorphose so neatly into new professions. New functions must be learned to replace those that are being outworn. Basic skills may be transferable or upgradable but do not offer the substance of a career line. There is an emotional wrench in abandoning what has come to be one's occupational way of life.

This tie to an occupation, the identification of one's *self* with a bundle of job characteristics, is part of the fabric of the economic society which is passing, and it will unquestionably complicate the asset management of a union official. Part of his problem is to induce in his members' minds the notion that in their lifetime they may have to develop new career lines, and sometimes change career courses, but that this possibility holds out promise and fulfillment as well as challenge and risk.

The new approach to a person's career must in time supplant the increasingly romantic notion that a person *is* a garage mechanic or a postman or a newspaper reporter. It will not be easy to fix the idea that occupationally a person never *is*, in any continuing sense, but is always *becoming*. Until that career concept is generally accepted, the union official who attempts to perform like an asset manager can expect bitterness and frustration. Nevertheless, he will have two influences working on his side. First, the pressure of circumstance, the prevalence of the *fact* of broken careers, will temper workers to the need to plan for such eventuality. And second, in time our school systems will incorporate the ethos of our changing economic society into classroom instruction. Workers will then mature conditioned to accept change as part of a career pattern, just as managers have been conditioned by the business schools to that expectation.

Unions face a more difficult problem than business managers do in another respect. It is easier to shift plants than people. Plants do not form communities, but people do, and they become attached to them, so that movement is referred to as "uprooting." This is perhaps a more tractable matter, however. Here the problem is basically government's, not the unions'. A full-employment economy which offers good jobs to all comers will reduce the fear of movement. It will be easier to pull stakes because mistakes can be corrected by pulling stakes again. And area redevelopment programs, of the sort with which we have lately begun to experiment, can be expected to assist in situations where whole communities fall under the shadow of a declining industry.

Let us recognize, then, that our

unions have a difficult job on their hands even when they have stopped playing Rip Van Winkle. But let them recognize that aid and comfort will be more readily forthcoming when they cease to rest their long-run policy on premises such as railroads *need* firemen on diesel engines, or preassembling parts constitutes a violation of some social commitment to continued hand assembly.

If the unions are to survive as active agents rather than as a resistance movement, it is up to them to take the initiative in the effective management of the assets of their members. In doing so, they may appropriately put pressure on government to come forward with facilitating measures, but it is the essence of their function to supply the direction and the leadership.

Management, too, has a stake in whether the unions decide to join the asset revolution. If the labor movement proves unable to adapt to the needs which the processes of change force on our industrial society, and widespread insecurity is the companion of progress, we can be sure that pressures on government for more radical solutions will not be wanting. Perhaps it is time that advanced managements—advanced at least in this respect, since they, too, have their own areas of backwardness—lend technical assistance to the underdeveloped union organizations. Joint exploration of the potentials and limitations of private planning for career advancement may be doubly rewarding. The future not only of unions but of private enterprise may be at stake.

CHAPTER FOURTEEN

The Politics of Poverty: Alleviation or Elimination?

In modern America government engages in a wide range of activities designed to protect the individual from economic disaster. Minimum wages, old age pensions, unemployment insurance, Medicare, aid for the physically and mentally handicapped, and public housing programs are all facets of a central issue—American poverty. The controversy over poverty centers around two basic questions:

1. Who is poor and why are they poor?
2. Should government concentrate its efforts on alleviating or eliminating poverty? The two questions are interrelated and the answers given to one determine the answers given to the other.

AMERICAN POVERTY: WHO AND WHY?

What causes poverty? Who are the poor? Why is poverty concentrated in certain areas (insular poverty)? Why is it concentrated in certain groups (case poverty)? Do the poor tend to reproduce themselves? If so, why? Is poverty the result of a lack of opportunity? Mental incapacity? Physical handicaps? Illness? Broken homes? Racial prejudice? Lack of education? Unproductive work?

Or are the causes more sophisticated, perhaps a combination of moral, physical, and mental decadence? Are the poor an inevitable by-product of our industrial society, a kind of national slag pile that is the hallmark of a productive nation? Or should they be viewed as a kind of silent reproach and rebuke to those millions of Americans who bask in the greatest affluence the world has ever known?

WHAT ROLE FOR GOVERNMENT: ALLEVIATION OR ELIMINATION?

Should poverty be regarded as evil and un-American, a virus in our economic bloodstream that we should be pursued and eliminated? Or should it be regarded somewhat complacently as an individual challenge, a necessary handicap that spurs men to action? Is the eradication of poverty an individual problem or is it more properly the concern of government?

If the elimination of poverty is accepted as a concern of government, other problems remain. Should our major effort be directed toward raising general productivity and living standards? If we raise the national standard of living, will the impoverished be benefitted automatically? Or does this group represent a peculiar, isolated segment of our people, whose life is outside the mainstream of the American economy? Perhaps the impoverished should be regarded as charity cases, and tax dollars should be diverted to them as a salve to the national conscience? Or is the welfare of these people a basic component of our national prosperity? By aiding the physically and mentally handicapped, the unemployed, and the aged, are we not actually taking out an economic insurance policy for the nation? In other words, are the charity aspects of the case secondary to our concern for general welfare and prosperity?

A final set of questions centers around the question "How"? Assuming that the reduction of poverty is accepted as a national goal, how can it be achieved? What role should be assigned to education? Medicine? Housing? What about a government-guaranteed annual wage? How should these various conditioning factors be blended? How can a static acceptance of poverty ("The poor ye have always with ye") be replaced by an aggressive, positive policy? In its early days the Johnson administration began a host of new programs (Job Corps, Operation Head Start, Vista, Appalachia Program, federal school aid) with a great deal of fanfare under the general banner of a "War on Poverty." Very soon President Johnson's critics were complaining that the War on Poverty, however noble in concept, was badly managed, too expensive, and lacking in results. So the debate over American poverty continues.

1

Penury amid Affluence *

JOHN K. GALBRAITH

Having denied that the automatic functioning of our economy will solve the problem, Galbraith suggests an over-all pattern of governmental action that will break the poverty cycle. How do slum clearance, health facilities, and education fit into this program? How can we prevent the self-perpetuating character of poverty? Why does Galbraith believe that we must spend the most for government services in poor areas? Why does he conclude that "in the contemporary United States [poverty] ... is a disgrace"?

An affluent society that is also both compassionate and rational would, no doubt, secure to all who needed it the minimum income essential for decency and comfort. The corrupting effect on the human spirit of a small amount of unearned revenue has unquestionably been exaggerated as, indeed, have the character-building values of hunger and privation. To secure to each family a minimum standard, as a normal function of the society, would help insure that the misfortunes of parents, deserved or otherwise, were not visited on their children. It would help insure that poverty was not self-perpetuating. Most of the reaction, which no doubt would be almost universally adverse, is based on obsolete attitudes. When poverty was a majority phenomenon, such action could not be afforded. A

poor society, as this essay has previously shown, had to enforce the rule that the person who did not work could not eat. And possibly it was justified in the added cruelty of applying the rule to those who could not work or whose efficiency was far below par. An affluent society has no similar excuse for such rigor. It can use the forthright remedy of providing for those in want. Nothing requires it to be compassionate. But it has no high philosophical justification for callousness.

Nonetheless any such forthright remedy for poverty is beyond reasonable hope. Also, as in the limiting case of the alcoholic or the mental incompetent, it involves difficulties. To spend income requires a minimum of character and intelligence even as to produce it. By far the best hope for the elimination, or in any case the minimization, of poverty lies in less direct but, conceivably, almost equally effective means.

The first and strategic step in an at-

* John K. Galbraith, *The Affluent Society* (Boston, Mass.: Houghton Mifflin Company, 1958), pp. 329-33. Reprinted by permission of the publisher.

tack on poverty is to see that it is no longer self-perpetuating. This means insuring that the investment in children from families presently afflicted be as little below normal as possible. If the children of poor families have first-rate schools and school attendance is properly enforced; if the children, though badly fed at home, are well nourished at school; if the community has sound health services, and the physical well-being of the children is vigilantly watched; if there is opportunity for advanced education for those who qualify regardless of means; and if, especially in the case of urban communities, law and order are well enforced and recreation is adequate—then there is a very good chance that the children of the very poor will come to maturity without grave disadvantage. In the case of insular poverty this remedy requires that the services of the community be assisted from outside. Poverty is self-perpetuating because the poorest communities are poorest in the services which would eliminate it. To eliminate poverty efficiently we should invest more than proportionately in the children of the poor community. It is there that high quality schools, strong health services, special provision for nutrition and recreation are most needed to compensate for the low investment which families are able to make in their own offspring.

The effect of education and related investment in individuals is to enable them either to contend more effectively with their environment, or to escape it and take up life elsewhere on more or less equal terms with others. The role of education as an antidote to the homing instinct which crowds people into the areas of inadequate opportunity and frustration is also clear. However, in the strategy of the attack on insular poverty a place remains for an attack on the frustrations of the environment itself.

This is particularly clear in the case of the slum. Slum clearance and expansion of low and middle income housing removes a comprehensive set of frustrations and greatly widens opportunity. There is a roughly parallel opportunity in the rural slum. By identifying a land use which is consistent with a satisfactory standard of living, and by assisting with the necessary reorganization of land and capital, public authority can help individuals to surmount frustrations to which they are now subject. The process promises to be expensive and also time-consuming. But the question is less one of feasibility than of will.

Nor is case poverty in the contemporary generation wholly intransigent. Much can be done to treat those characteristics which cause people to reject or be rejected by the modern industrial society. Educational deficiencies can be overcome. Mental deficiencies can be treated. Physical handicaps can be remedied. The limiting factor is not knowledge of what can be done. Overwhelmingly it is our failure to invest in people.

It will be clear that to a remarkable extent the requirements for the elimination of poverty are the same as for social balance. (Indeed a good deal of case poverty can be attributed to the failure to maintain social balance.) The myopic preoccupation with production and material investment has diverted our attention from the most urgent questions of how we are employing our resources and, in particular, from the greater need and opportunity for investing in persons.

Here is a paradox! When we begin to consider the needs of those who are now excluded from the economic system by accident, inadequacy, or misfortune—we find that the normal remedy is to make them or their children productive citizens. This means that they add to the total output of goods. We see once again that even by its *own terms* the present preoccupation with material as opposed to human investment is inefficient. The parallel with investment in the supply of trained and educated manpower discussed above will be apparent.

But increased output of goods is not the main point. Even to the most intellectually reluctant reader it will now be evident that enhanced productive efficiency is not the *motif* of this volume. The very fact that increased output offers itself as a by-product of the effort to eliminate poverty is one of the reasons. No one would be called upon to write at such length on a problem so easily solved as that of increasing production. The main point lies elsewhere. Poverty—

grim, degrading, and ineluctable—is not remarkable in India. For few the fate is otherwise. But in the United States the survival of poverty is remarkable. We ignore it because we share with all societies at all times the capacity for not seeing what we do not wish to see. Anciently this has enabled the nobleman to enjoy his dinner while remaining oblivious to the beggars around his door. In our own day it enables us to travel in comfort through south Chicago and the South. But while our failure to notice can be explained, it cannot be excused. "Poverty," Pitt exclaimed, "is no disgrace but it is damned annoying." In the contemporary United States it is not annoying but it is a disgrace.

2

Our Invisible Poor *

DWIGHT MACDONALD

Much of the contemporary literature on poverty in the United States starts with the bland assumption that it is a kind of anachronism that survives temporarily in the midst of general abundance. In the article that follows, Mr. Macdonald denies this pleasant assumption and portrays present and future American poverty as a tough, unyielding blight that encompasses one-fourth of the nation. Rather than being a temporary phenomenon, he believes that American poverty will require Herculean efforts to dislodge it. Why does the author conclude that "Forty or fifty million people are becoming increasingly invisible"? In a country where nobody starves, why does he write that our present system "reduces life for many of the poor to a long vestibule to death"?

In his significantly titled "The Affluent Society" (1958) Professor J.

* Dwight Macdonald, "Our Invisible Poor," *The New Yorker*, January 19, 1963, pp. 82, 84, 91, 92, 94, 96, 98, 128-32. As adapted by the Sidney Hillman Foundation. © 1963 by The New Yorker Magazine, Inc. Reprinted by permission of the publisher.

K. Galbraith states that poverty in this country is no longer "a massive affliction [but] more nearly an afterthought." Dr. Galbraith is a humane critic of the American capitalist system, and he is generously indignant about the continued existence of even this nonmassive and afterthoughtish poverty. But the interesting thing about his pronouncement, aside from the fact that it is inaccurate, is that it was generally accepted as obvious. For a long time now, almost everybody has assumed that, because of the New Deal's social legislation and —more important—the prosperity we have enjoyed since 1940, mass poverty no longer exists in this country.

Dr. Galbraith states that our poor have dwindled to two hard-core categories. One is the "insular poverty" of those who live in the rural South or in depressed areas like West Virginia. The other category is "case poverty," which he says is "commonly and properly related to [such] characteristics of the individuals so afflicted [as] mental deficiency, bad health, inability to adapt to the discipline of modern economic life, excessive procreation, alcohol, insufficient education." He reasons that such poverty must be due to individual defects, since "nearly everyone else has mastered his environment; this proves that it is not intractable." Without pressing the similarity of this concept to the "Social Darwinism" whose fallacies Dr. Galbraith easily disposes of elsewhere in his book, one may observe that most of these characteristics are as much the result of poverty as its cause.

Now Michael Harrington, an alumnus of the *Catholic Worker* and The Fund for the Republic who is at present a contributing editor of *Dissent* and the chief editor of the Socialist party bi-weekly, *New America*, has written *The Other America: Poverty in the United States*.[1] In the admirably short space of under two hundred pages, he outlines the problem, describes in imaginative detail what it means to be poor in this country to-

day, summarizes the findings of recent studies by economists and sociologists, and analyzes the reasons for the persistence of mass poverty in the midst of general prosperity.

In the last year we seem to have suddenly awakened, rubbing our eyes like Rip van Winkle, to the fact that mass poverty persists, and that it is one of our two gravest social problems. (The other is related: While only 11 per cent of our population is non-white, 25 per cent of our poor are.) What is "poverty"? It is a historically relative concept, first of all. "There are new definitions [in America] of what man can achieve, of what a human standard of life should be," Mr. Harrington writes. "Those who suffer levels of life well below those that are possible, even though they live better than medieval knights or Asian peasants, are poor.... Poverty should be defined in terms of those who are denied the minimal levels of health, housing, food, and education that our present stage of scientific knowledge specifies for life as it is now lived in the United States." His dividing line follows that proposed in recent studies by the United States Bureau of Labor Statistics: $4,000 a year for a family of four and $2,000 for an individual living alone. (All kinds of income are included, such as food grown and consumed on farms.) This is the cut-off line generally drawn today.

Mr. Harrington estimates that between 40 and 50 million Americans, or about a fourth of the population, are now living in poverty. Not just below the level of comfortable living, but real poverty, in the old-fashioned sense of the word—that they are hard put to it to get the mere necessities, beginning with enough to eat. This is difficult to believe in the United States of 1963, but one has to make the effort, and it is now being made.

[1] Michael Harrington, *The Other America: Poverty in the United States* (New York: The Macmillan Company, 1962).

The extent of our poverty has suddenly become visible. . . .

The Limits of Statistics

Statistics on poverty are even trickier than most. . . . It is not, therefore, surprising to find that there is some disagreement about just how many millions of Americans are poor. The point is that all recent studies [2] agree that American poverty is still a mass phenomenon.

The model postwar budgets drawn up in 1951 by the Bureau of Labor Statistics to "maintain a level of adequate living" give a concrete idea of what poverty means in this country— or would mean if poor families lived within their income and spent it wisely, which they don't. Dr. Kolko summarizes the kind of living these budgets provide:

Three members of the family see a movie once every three weeks, and one member sees a movie once every two weeks. There is no telephone in the house, but the family makes three pay calls a week. They buy one book a year and write one letter a week.

The father buys one heavy wool suit every two years and a light wool suit every three years; the wife, one suit every ten years or one skirt every five years. Every three or four years, depending on the distance and time involved, the family takes a vacation outside their own city. In 1950, the family spent a total of $80 to $90 on all types of home furnish-

[2] The studies, all of which are referred to by the author, include Dr. Gabriel Kolko, *Wealth and Power in America* (New York: Frederick A. Praeger, Inc., 1962); "Poverty and Deprivation in the U.S.," Conference on Economic Progress, April 1962, Washington, D.C., 1001 Conn. Ave., N.W.; Dr. James N. Morgan, et al., *Income and Welfare in the United States* (New York: McGraw-Hill Book Company, Inc., 1962); "Poverty and Deprivation" (pamphlet), Conference on Economic Progress, Leon H. Keyserling and others.

ings, electrical appliances, and laundry equipment. . . . The family eats cheaper cuts of meat several times a week, but has more expensive cuts on holidays. The entire family consumes a total of two five-cent ice cream cones, one five-cent candy bar, two bottles of soda, and one bottle of beer a week. The family owes no money, but has no savings except for a small insurance policy.

One other item is included in the B.L.S. "maintenance" budget: a new car every twelve to eighteen years.

This is an ideal picture, drawn up by social workers, of how a poor family *should* spend its money. But the poor are much less provident—installment debts take up a lot of their cash, and only a statistician could expect an actual live woman, however poor, to buy new clothes at intervals of five or or ten years. Also, one suspects that a lot more movies are seen and ice-cream cones and bottles of beer are consumed than in the Spartan ideal. But these necessary luxuries are had only at the cost of displacing other items—necessary, so to speak—in the B.L.S. budget.

The distinction between a family income of $3,500 ("poverty") and $4,500 ("deprivation") is not vivid to those who run things—the 31 per cent whose incomes are between $7,500 and $14,999 and the 7 per cent of the top-most top dogs, who get $15,000 or more. These two minorities, sizable enough to feel they *are* the nation, have been as unaware of the continued existence of mass poverty as this reviewer was until he read Mr. Harrington's book. They are businessmen, congressmen, judges, government officials, politicians, lawyers, doctors, engineers, scientists, editors, journalists, and administrators in colleges, churches, and foundations. Since their education, income, and social status are superior, they, if anybody, might be expected to accept responsibility for what the Constitution calls "the general welfare." They have not done so in the case of the poor. And they have a good excuse. It is becoming harder and harder simply to *see* the one-fourth of our fellow-citizens who live below the poverty line.

The poor are increasingly slipping out of the very experience and consciousness of the nation [Mr. Harrington writes]. If the middle class never did like ugliness and poverty, it was at least aware of them. "Across the tracks" was not a very long way to go. . . . Now the American city has been transformed. The poor still inhabit the miserable housing in the central area, but they are increasingly isolated from contact with, or sight of, anybody else. . . . Living out in the suburbs, it is easy to assume that ours is, indeed, an affluent society. . . .

Clothes make the poor invisible too: America has the best-dressed poverty the world has ever known. . . . It is much easier in the United States to be decently dressed than it is to be decently housed, fed, or doctored. . . .

Many of the poor are the wrong age to be seen. A good number of them are sixty-five years of age or better; an even larger number are under eighteen. . . .

And finally, the poor are politically invisible. . . . They are without lobbies of their own; they put forward no legislative program. As a group, they are atomized. They have no face; they have no voice. . . . Only the social agencies have a really direct involvement with the other America, and they are without any great political power. . . .

Forty to fifty million people are becoming increasingly invisible.

These invisible people fall mostly into the following categories, some of them overlapping: poor farmers, who operate 40 per cent of the farms and get 7 per cent of the farm cash income; migratory farm workers; unskilled, unorganized workers in offices, hotels, restaurants, hospitals, laundries, and other service jobs; in-

habitants of areas where poverty is either endemic ("peculiar to a people or district"), as in the rural South, or epidemic ("prevalent among a community at a special time and produced by some special causes"), as in West Virginia, where the special cause was the closing of coal mines and steel plants; Negroes and Puerto Ricans, who are a fourth of the total poor; the alcoholic derelicts in the big city skid rows; the hillbillies from Kentucky, Tennessee, and Oklahoma who have migrated to Midwestern cities in search of better jobs. And finally, almost half our "senior citizens."

Perpetuating Poverty

It seems likely that mass poverty will continue in this country for a long time. The more it is reduced, the harder it is to keep on reducing it. The poor, having dwindled from two-thirds of the population in 1936 to one-quarter today, no longer are a significant political force, as is shown by the Senate's rejection of Medicare and by the Democrats' dropping it as an issue in the elections last year. Also, as poverty decreases, those left behind tend more and more to be the ones who have for so long accepted poverty as their destiny that they need outside help to climb out of it. This new minority mass poverty, so much more isolated and hopeless than the old majority poverty, shows signs of becoming chronic. "The permanence of low incomes is inferred from a variety of findings," write the authors of the Morgan survey. "In many poor families the head has never earned enough to cover the family's present needs."

For most families, however, the problem of chronic poverty is serious. One such family is headed by a thirty-two-year-old man who is employed as a dishwasher. Though he works steadily and more than full time, he earned over

$2,000 in 1959. His wife earned $300 more, but their combined incomes are not enough to support themselves and their three children. Although the head of the family is only thirty-two, he feels that he has no chance of advancement partly because he finished only seven grades of school. . . . The possibility of such families leaving the ranks of the poor is not high.

Children born into poor families today have less chance of "improving themselves" than the children of the pre-1940 poor. Rags to riches is now more likely to be rags to rags. "Indeed," the Morgan book concludes, "it appears that a number of the heads of poor families have moved into less skilled jobs than their fathers had." Over a third of the children of the poor, according to the survey, don't go beyond the eighth grade and "will probably perpetuate the poverty of their parents." There are a great many of these children. In an important study of poverty, made for a congressional committee in 1959, Dr. Robert J. Lampman estimated that 11 million of the poor were under 18. "A considerable number of younger persons are starting life in a condition of 'inherited poverty,' " he observed. To which Mr. Harrington adds, "The character of poverty has changed, and it has become more deadly for the young. It is no longer associated with immigrant groups with high aspirations; it is now identified with those whose social existence makes it more and more difficult to break out into the larger society." Even when children from poor families show intellectual promise, there is nothing in the values of their friends or families to encourage them to make use of it. Of the top 16 per cent of high-school students—those scoring 120 and over in I.Q. tests—only half go on to college. The explanation for this amazing—and alarming—situation is as much cultural as economic. The children of

the poor now tend to lack what the sociologists call "motivation." At least one foundation is working on the problem of why so many bright children from poor families don't ever try to go beyond high school. . . .

The federal government is the only purposeful force—I assume wars are not purposeful—that can reduce the numbers of the poor and make their lives more bearable. The effect of government policy on poverty has two quite distinct aspects. One is the indirect effect of the stimulation of the economy by federal spending. Such stimulation—though by war-time demands rather than government policy —has in the past produced a prosperity that did cut down American poverty by almost two-thirds. But I am inclined to agree with Dr. Galbraith that it would not have a comparable effect on present day poverty:

It is assumed that with increasing output poverty must disappear [he writes]. Increased output eliminated the general poverty of all who worked. Accordingly it must, sooner or later, eliminate the special poverty that still remains. . . . Yet just as the arithmetic of modern politics makes it tempting to overlook the very poor, so the supposition that increasing output will remedy their case has made it easy to do so too.

He underestimates the massiveness of American poverty, but he is right when he says there is now a hard core of the specially disadvantaged—because of age, race, environment, physical or mental defects, etc.—that would not be significantly reduced by general prosperity. (Although I think the majority of our present poor *would* benefit, if only by a reduction in the present high rate of unemployment.)

To do something about this hard core, a second line of government policy would be required; namely, direct intervention to help the poor. We have had this since the New Deal, but it has always been grudging and miserly, and we have never accepted the principle that every citizen should be provided, at state expense, with a reasonable minimum standard of living regardless of any other considerations. It should not depend on earnings, as does social security, which continues the inequalities and inequities and so tends to keep the poor forever poor. Nor should it exclude millions of our poorest citizens because they lack the political pressure to force their way into the welfare state. The governmental obligation to provide, out of taxes, such a minimum living standard for all who need it should be taken as much for granted as free public schools have always been in our history.

"Nobody Starves"

It may be objected that the economy cannot bear the cost, and certainly costs must be calculated. But the point is not the calculation but the principle. Statistics—and especially statistical forecasts—can be pushed one way or the other. Who can determine in advance to what extent the extra expense of giving our 40,000,000 poor enough income to rise above the poverty line would be offset by the lift to the economy from their increased purchasing power? We really don't know. Nor did we know what the budgetary effects would be when we established the principle of free public education. The rationale then was that all citizens should have an equal chance of competing for a better status. The rationale now is different: that every citizen has a right to become or remain part of our society because if this right is denied, as it is in the case of at least one-fourth of our citizens, it impoverishes us all. Since 1932, "the government"—local,

state, and federal—has recognized a responsibility to provide its citizens with a subsistence living. Apples will never again be sold on the street by jobless accountants, it seems safe to predict, nor will any serious political leader ever again suggest that share-the-work and local charity can solve the problem of unemployment. "Nobody starves" in this country any more, but, like every social statistic, this is a tricky business. Nobody starves, but who can measure the starvation, not to be calculated by daily intake of proteins and calories, that reduces life for many of our poor to a long vestibule to death? Nobody starves, but every fourth citizen rubs along on a standard of living that is below what Mr. Harrington defines as "the minimal levels of health, housing, food, and education that our present stage of scientific knowledge specifies as necessary for life as it is now lived in the United States." Nobody starves, but a fourth of us are excluded from the common social existence. Not to be able to afford a movie or a glass of beer is a kind of starvation—if everybody else can.

The problem is obvious: the persistence of mass poverty in a prosperous country. The solution is also obvious: to provide, out of taxes, the kind of subsidies that have always been given to the public schools (not to mention the police and fire departments and the post office)—subsidies that would raise incomes above the poverty level, so that every citizen could feel he is indeed such. "*Civis Romanus sum!*" cried St. Paul when he was threatened with flogging—and he was not flogged. Until our poor can be proud to say "*Civis Americanus sum!*" until the act of justice that would make this possible has been performed by the three-quarters of Americans who are not poor—until then the shame of the Other America will continue.

3

*Poverty on the Land**

JOHN STANLEY

Rural America is a study in economic contracts and extremes—from shiny Cadillacs and sleek cattle to corn bread, grits, and subsistence farming. The following description is an accurate portrait of impoverished rural America—the 30 per cent of farmers who produce only 3 per cent of agricultural sales. For this group such issues as parity payments and the soil bank are remote. Unless they have part-time jobs, these people are almost completely outside our present money economy. Why does Stanley conclude that the rural poor "have a culture so different from the bulk of their middle-class compatriots that "foreigner" is not a completely illegitimate term to use on them?"

The shower of snow mutes the ragged outlines of a farm that embarrasses the hopeful, willing country in New York and Kentucky and Maine and the rest of the states. The snow is both a promise of suffering and its alleviation; at least there will be water now after the long summer that has dried up the shallow spring up the hill; but with snow will come the cold wind that cuts its way through the thin boards. The family will huddle around the kitchen range, and the children will whine and the parents will scold—it will be a situation that is beyond homework and no one will want to go to the wintry cold bedrooms. Everyone will be longing for rest; there will be the dry fatigue that always comes from a constant diet of thin food, unsatisfying clothes and a steadily deteriorating situation. Every decade millions leave this

sort of thing and move into town. They are as worn out as the land they leave behind them. They realize that they are not receiving their share of what this country has to offer. They feel like an out-group, they're not as smooth and shiny as everyone else, and everything else, is getting to be. It takes cash to get into the national rhythm and shape, and the place to do this is in town. So, at a certain point in the complex pattern of endurance and desire, and urged by the sharp pricking of abrupt personal dissatisfaction, the farmer decides to go and share the things the city can provide, even though this may, will, mean the loss of an increasingly dubious "independence," fresh air and the shredded remnants of an inherited tradition.

❋   ❋   ❋

Picture this: a frame house of skimpy proportions, two stories high with a shaky, narrow porch along one

* John Stanley, "Poverty on the Land," *The Commonweal*, November 18, 1955, pp. 161-63. Reprinted by permission of the publisher.

side, built of second-hand lumber and covered with tar shingles pressed to look like yellow brick. It's on a dirt road pocked with ruts and stones—dust in August, a slough in March and a mad toboggan-slide in December; two cars cannot pass. It's more than a mile to the nearest paved road, and three miles more to the nearest general store and post office and school. The view is magnificent: a thousand feet below and miles away is a winding river lined with rich black farms where the land is as carefully utilized as it is in France. In the distance there are lavender hills, and in the winter moonlight, blue snow and black trees. Inside the kitchen door hangs the only light bulb in the whole house. Last year there was electricity for the first time in the area but there was only enough credit to wire the one room. You go to the "bathroom" and up to bed by candlelight, which makes for an atmosphere not of romance but of melancholy, and the mother of small children is ever on the alert for disaster. There is neither radio nor telephone. In the summertime the cooking is done on a kerosene stove that smokes and stinks if it is not carefully tended and expertly used; in the winter there is a kitchen range. If cash and credit are relatively adequate there is the luxury of coal, usually bought by the hundred-weight, which is more expensive than by the ton. And when things get really difficult the derelict barn gives a few more boards, and these are sawed up by hand.

The poor, both rural and urban, are forced to live constantly in extravagant debt: they must buy cheap shoes that wear out quickly, cheap foods that do not keep the body in top form, cheap tools that break and are inefficient, second-hand, broken down, wasteful cars that bad roads soon tear up completely. The result is exhaus-

tion that permits no rest, no growth, and little joy at the bright vistas in the fertile valleys below. There is only weary dragging on from day to day, almost a guilt-sense of failure at such poverty in the midst of the nation's storied progress recorded in much expensive color in the shiny magazines each week.

Here there is no fieldstone pumphouse with cedar shingles snugly housing a plump tank of cold and sweet artesian water; there is only the shallow spring that drools the water through for half the year; when the trickle stops, water must be fetched in buckets down the road, starting in the summertime when all the fields in the valley below are being worked by men who cannot spend their time carting water in a bucket; they're out producing. Here the fields are full of wild flowers, with only patches cultivated for the sake of quaint, small fruit that makes one say, "Well, it's not worth it, cheaper to buy it in town."

At one time this land was cleared of trees and made to yield some fruit, support some families. Up the road there is still the heaped-up wreckage of a one-room schoolhouse that served a score of families until sometime between 1918 and 1939. Now the trees are growing back, along with untidy brambles and black-eyed Susans, thistles and grape vines that run wild. Little foxes scoot across the road, and the dog barks on the leash. The children stand in the mud near the postbox in their thin clothes waiting for the school bus moving carefully in the November weather. They do not come home again until it is almost dark.

There is no hot water in the house except for what can be heated on the stove in a bucket so, except in warm weather, there are mostly sponge baths in the kitchen. There is an outhouse, frigid in winter and alive with flies and stench and foraging rats in the summer, a sweatbox under the slow-moving sun. In winter the house is a cave of draughts because everything is fitted poorly.

Discouragement and fatigue and loss of vision line the face of rural poverty. It is difficult to see beyond the muddy dooryard in the grey morning, and the mood lasts all day. No one comes and no one goes. A longing sets in for a little escape from the water-stained walls and unmended furniture, the cracked saucer and the wrinkled housedress. The supreme objective becomes the capture of a moment of spice, covered with spangles and filled with bubbles; a jukebox, a movie, a glass of lemon and lime or a comic book for the children, a permanent wave—which are wasteful as the thrifty and virtuous know. And there is always alcohol.

It is quite something to pass through a West Virginia town that looks like a movie set for a Wild West film circa 1903. There are only timber houses and covered wooden sidewalks, and a big raw sign that yells *whiskey*. There seems to be a lot of fierce-looking dark-eyed young men squatting on their haunches in the open in the middle of a weekday morning. Their eyes seem to follow strangers, and they roll cigarettes and seem silent. The report is that they don't do much of anything, many of them; they hunt and fish and from time to time cut down a tree and sell it; they make their own liquor and sell some of it. They are the men one wrote letters for in the army. They have a culture so different from the bulk of their middle-class compatriots that "foreigner" is not a completely illegitimate term to use on them.

Rural poverty is lived in isolation, in the imprisonment of broken fences and unpruned fruit trees that bear small, hard, wormy fruit. Rural poverty is as various as the terrain of the country. It is the lot, in God's mysterious justice, of millions of human beings, including the "single-men-in-barracks" types, the dark-skinned pickers in the "factories-in-the-fields," and the blue-eyed "crackers," some of whom have their huts dug into the sides of the red hills planted with stunted corn, and whose principal passion is a transference of all their resentment and frustration to a hatred of the Negro—a fellow prisoner. The rural poor are weighted down with chains of poor health and lassitude and ignorance. Their final humiliation is their removal—in one light it looks like a deliverance—from their wasted properties, rented or mortgaged, to the great institution of the industrial slum or housing project. Thomas Jefferson died a long time ago.

4

Government Can't Cure Poverty *

BARRY GOLDWATER

In his campaign speeches of 1964 the Republican presidential candidate, Barry Goldwater, examined and rejected the philosophical underpinnings of the War on Poverty championed by President Johnson. Although Goldwater lost the presidential race, his ideas reflect the thinking of millions of Americans. If the Goldwater arguments are accepted, what answers would be given to the following questions? In what manner has American prosperity been created? Are any Americans truly poor? If so, how many? What does society owe to the impoverished individual? What provisions should be made for the able-bodied unemployed? In our long history how have most Americans conquered poverty?

This nation has a choice to make. It is a choice on which history, not just election-year rhetoric, will hinge and turn. If that choice can be bought by promises, by pie-in-the-sky, by smiles at business meetings, then the future of the American enterprise system is bleak indeed. The choice is not one of detail or trimmings, but of basic direction.

The present Administration, like its Democratic predecessors, says the bureaucracy in Washington can solve all problems, end poverty, and create prosperity.

The Republican alternative is men and women working and investing in thousands of industries, freed from bureaucratic interference, building the wealth that best fights poverty. The Republican alternative says men and women in their own homes, communities, and states can best solve

* Barry Goldwater, *Where I Stand* (New York: McGraw-Hill Book Company, Inc., 1964), pp. 109-110, 112-16. Copyright © 1964 by Barry Goldwater. Reprinted by permission of the publisher.

their own problems and need pass along to the Federal government only those problems, national or international in nature, which clearly call for a single answer.

Diversity, of which we hear so much but see so little in the actions of the present Administration, can best be achieved by choosing the best tools of diversity—the initiative and creativity of individual Americans. Certainly no evidence indicates that this is in any way, shape, or form the choice of the present Administration—no matter what their claims to the contrary . . .

. . . Many of the new programs with which we are to be faced are said to be part of a "war on poverty." And who can be against that? America, for most of its years, has waged a war on poverty. And wherever it has waged that war, in factories, in laboratories, in shops, over counters, and under the enterprise system, it has won that war. It has won it, *is* winning it, more surely than any nation on earth.

And I say that this war on poverty can *only* be won that way. I say that when we *work* our way to wealth, we win that war. I say that when government tries to *spend* its way to wealth, we lose that war. Santa Claus dreams, or rolled-up sleeves! We have to make a choice.

Not so many years ago one of the Democratic Party's principal trouble-shouters, John Galbraith, wrote a book, *The Affluent Society*, to prove that consumers were wallowing in luxury while government was being starved. The individual, he said, should be taxed more heavily to support government in a style to which he wanted it accustomed. He found that there were basically only two types of private poverty left in the United States: insular poverty in areas whose economic base had been eroded; and case poverty-families or individuals who, because of personal deficiencies, are unable to earn an income which permits a contemporary American standard of living. . . .

The first question, of course, is how many Americans are poor? Franklin Roosevelt said that a third of the nation was impoverished and you still see the same figure cited, although the Administration's current official figure is one-fifth. Also, a few years ago, some called a family poor if its income was below $1,500. Now it is $3,000. Others say that any family is poor if it can't afford what the Department of Labor computes to be the standard of living of the average urban worker. In a country as wealthy as ours, it is implied, everyone should somehow be *above* our average! An interesting statistical exercise.

The fact is, of course, that these income levels are regarded as true wealth in the rest of the world. Workers in many other countries cannot earn as much as our welfare clients receive. As our production and in-

come levels have moved up over a hundred years, our concepts of what is poor have moved up also—we hope they always will, as indeed they always *should*. But, of course, you never can fully catch up; statistically there will always be a "lowest" one-third or one-fifth.

The truth is that the income of our lowest one-fifth of households, as expressed in dollars of constant purchasing power, has risen more than 100 per cent over the past quarter-century. This upward trend has been consistent. It will continue, so long as we are people of enterprise, of energy, of risk-taking. It will grind to a halt if we become a people of relief-check stagnation and government regimentation.

Our overall economic growth already has slowed. Under the governmental policies of the Big Government Party in power for most of the past three decades, we have reduced rewards for good work and also reduced the penalities for laziness or waste. We have been draining the fuel that fires the engines of progress. We have been quenching the fire and then wondering why the engines didn't run faster.

If somebody set out deliberately to slow down economic growth he could not do better than to reduce the incentives for enterprise and abolish the consequences of inertia. And that is what the New Deal started in the 1930s. It is what the Fair Deal continued in the 1940s. It is what the Fast Deal is now proposing to do in the 1960s.

I strongly believe that all people are entitled to an opportunity—let me stress that—*to an opportunity*, to get an education and to earn a living in keeping with the value of their work. I also believe that those in trouble through no fault of their own must be helped by society. I believe that those in trouble *through* their own fault should always have an opportunity to work themselves out of it. But I do not believe that the mere fact of having little money entitles everybody, regardless of circumstances, to be *permanently* maintained by the taxpayers at an average or comfortable standard of living.

This, it seems to me, raises the question of an essential safeguard we should place on public welfare programs—those who are physically able to work should be put to work to earn their benefits at a specified rate per hour. There are community projects aplenty that could be powered this way, performing jobs otherwise not done, and completing them without gaudy new Federal programs.

We have talked of many aspects of this overall problem. But we are talking, basically, about only two principles: enterprise *versus* regimentation; a society fluid in its opportunity *versus* a society hardened into a government mould.

Specifically, in a society where the vast majority of people live on a standard that is envied by all other nations, it must be appropriate to inquire whether the attitude or the action of the small group not participating in the general prosperity has anything to do with the situation. The

aim of such an investigation should not be to condemn anybody but to help, and to help effectively. We must know what *is* wrong, and not assume that big government alone has the answers.

I would seek a greater role for the Federal government in removing restrictions rather than imposing new ones—at every level of the economy. I stand on the side of individual responsibility and individual choice and creativity. I stand against the gray sameness of growing government, against the conformity of collectivism —regardless of excuses.

There is no such thing as a free lunch. Not even Santa Claus can whip one up. Most of our parents came to this land with little or nothing but honest energy and honest ideals. Most came from poverty and to poverty. But they built a great nation. They worked hard at it. They extended helping hands where needed and deserved. They were the greatest builders of history. And we, their descendants, still have that energy, still have that heart.

We have only to make the choice: will we use the energy and revitalize the heart, or will we abandon both for false securities? In this choice we will either build tomorrow or write our epitaph.

5

The War on Poverty *

LYNDON B. JOHNSON

In the past the relationship of the national government to poverty has often been a fragmented, uncoordinated series of programs, programs which had little in common. An attempt to pull together all old and new programs was made by President Johnson, who began an "all-out" "War on Poverty," coordinated by the Office of Economic Opportunity. What are the assumptions of the President regarding causes of poverty? At what groups were his proposals aimed? Why did he believe the time was ripe for such a "War." How did he justify it in constitutional and economic terms?

We are citizens of the richest and most fortunate nation in the history of the world.

One hundred and eighty years ago we were a small country struggling for survival on the margin of a hostile land.

Today we have established a civilization of freemen which spans an entire continent.

With the growth of our country has come opportunity for our people—opportunity to educate our children, to use our energies in productive work, to increase our leisure—opportunity for almost every American to hope that through work and talent he could create a better life for himself and his family.

The path forward has not been an easy one.

But we have never lost sight of our goal: an America in which every citizen shares all the opportunities of his society, in which every man has a chance to advance his welfare to the limit of his capacities.

We have come a long way toward this goal.

We still have a long way to go.

The distance which remains is the measure of the great unfinished work of our society.

To finish that work I have called for a national war on poverty. Our objective: total victory.

There are millions of Americans—one-fifth of our people—who have not shared in the abundance which has been granted to most of us, and on whom the gates of opportunity have been closed.

What does this poverty mean to those who endure it?

It means a daily struggle to secure the necessities for even a meager existence. It means that the abundance, the comforts, the opportunities they see all around them are beyond their grasp.

Worst of all, it means hopelessness for the young.

The young man or woman who grows up without a decent education,

* *Congressional Record*, 1964, House Document No. 243, March 16, 1964, pp. 5287-89.

in a broken home, in a hostile and squalid environment, in ill health or in the face of racial injustice—that young man or woman is often trapped in a life of poverty.

He does not have the skills demanded by a complex society. He does not know how to acquire those skills. He faces a mounting sense of despair which drains initiative and ambition and energy.

Our tax cut will create millions of new jobs—new exits from poverty.

But we must also strike down all the barriers which keep many from using those exits.

The war on poverty is not a struggle simply to support people, to make them dependent on the generosity of others.

It is a struggle to give people a chance.

It is an effort to allow them to develop and use their capacities, as we have been allowed to develop and use ours, so that they can share, as others share, in the promise of this Nation.

We do this, first of all, because it is right that we should.

From the establishment of public education and land-grant colleges through agricultural extension and encouragement to industry, we have pursued the goal of a nation with full and increasing opportunities for all its citizens.

The war on poverty is a further step in that pursuit.

We do it also because helping some will increase the prosperity of all.

Our fight against poverty will be an investment in the most valuable of our resources—the skills and strength of our people.

And in the future, as in the past, this investment will return its cost manifold to our entire economy.

If we can raise the annual earnings of 10 million among the poor by only $1,000, we will have added $14 billion a year to our national output. In addition, we can make important reductions in public assistance payments which now cost us $4 billion a year, and in the large costs of fighting crime and delinquency, disease and hunger.

This is only part of the story.

Our history has proved that each time we broaden the base of abundance, giving more people the chance to produce and consume, we create new industry, higher production, increased earnings, and better income for all.

Giving new opportunity to those who have little will enrich the lives of all the rest.

Because it is right, because it is wise, and because, for the first time in our history, it is possible to conquer poverty, I submit, for the consideration of the Congress and the country, the Economic Opportunity Act of 1964.

The act does not merely expand on programs or improve what is already being done.

It charts a new course.

It strikes at the causes, not just the consequences of poverty.

It can be a milestone in our 180-year search for a better life for our people.

This act provides five basic opportunities.

It will give almost half a million underprivileged young Americans the opportunity to develop skills, continue education, and find useful work.

It will give every American community the opportunity to develop a comprehensive plan to fight its own poverty—and help them to carry out their plans.

It will give dedicated Americans the opportunity to enlist as volunteers in the war against poverty.

It will give many workers and farmers the opportunity to break through particular barriers which bar their escape from poverty.

It will give the entire Nation the opportunity for a concerted attack on poverty through the establishment, under my direction, of the Office of Economic Opportunity, a national headquarters for the war against poverty.

This is how we propose to create these opportunities.

First. We will give high priority to helping young Americans who lack skills, who have not completed their education, or who cannot complete it because they are too poor.

The years of high school and college age are the most critical stage of a young person's life. If they are not helped then, many will be condemned to a life of poverty which they, in turn, will pass on to their children.

I therefore recommend the creation of a Job Corps, a work-training program, and a work-study program.

A new National Job Corps will build toward an enlistment of 100,000 young men. They will be drawn from those whose background, health, and education make them least fit for useful work.

Those who volunteer will enter more than 100 camps and centers around the country.

Half of these young men will work, in the first year, on special conservation projects to give them education, useful work experience, and to enrich the natural resources of the country.

Half of these young men will receive, in the first year, a blend of training, basic education, and work experience in job training centers.

These are not simply camps for the underprivileged. They are new educational institutions, comparable in innovation to the land-grant colleges. Those who enter them will emerge better qualified to play a productive role in American society.

A new national work-training program operated by the Department of Labor will provide work and training for 200,000 American men and women between the ages of 16 and 21. This will be developed through State and local governments and nonprofit agencies.

Hundreds of thousands of young Americans badly need the experience, the income, and the sense of purpose which useful full- or part-time work can bring. For them such work may mean the difference between finishing school or dropping out. Vital community activities from hospitals and playgrounds to libraries and settlement houses are suffering because there are not enough people to staff them.

We are simply bringing these needs together.

A new national work-study program operated by the Department of Health, Education, and Welfare will provide Federal funds for part-time jobs for 140,000 young Americans who do not go to college because they cannot afford it.

There is no more senseless waste than the waste of the brainpower and skill of those who are kept from college by economic circumstances. Under this program they will, in a great American tradition, be able to work their way through school.

They and the country will be richer for it.

Second. Through a new community-action program we intend to strike at poverty at its source—in the streets of our cities and on the farms of our countryside among the very young and the impoverished old.

This program asks men and women throughout the country to prepare longrange plans for the attack on poverty in their own local communties.

These are not plans prepared in

Washington and imposed upon hundreds of different situations.

They are based on the fact that local citizens best understand their own problems, and know best how to deal with these problems.

These plans will be local plans striking at the many unfilled needs which underlie poverty in each community, not just one or two. Their components and emphasis will differ as needs differ.

These plans will be local plans calling upon all the resources available to the community—Federal and State, local and private, human and material.

And when these plans are approved by the Office of Economic Opportunity, the Federal Government will finance up to 90 percent of the additional cost for the first 2 years.

The most enduring strength of our Nation is the huge reservoir of talent, initiative, and leadership which exists at every level of our society.

Through the community action program we call upon this, our greatest strength, to overcome our greatest weakness.

Third. I ask for the authority to recruit and train skilled volunteers for the war against poverty.

Thousands of Americans have volunteered to serve the needs of other lands. Thousands more want the chance to serve the needs of their own land. They should have that chance.

Among older people who have retired, as well as among the young, among women as well as men, there are many Americans who are ready to enlist in our war against poverty.

They have skills and dedication. They are badly needed.

If the State requests them, if the community needs and will use them, we will recruit and train them and give them the chance to serve.

Fourth. We intend to create new opportunities for certain hard-hit groups to break out of the pattern of poverty.

Through a new program of loans and guarantees we can provide incentives to those who will employ the unemployed.

Through programs of work and retraining for unemployed fathers and mothers we can help them support their families in dignity while preparing themselves for new work.

Through funds to purchase needed land, organize cooperatives, and create new and adequate family farms we can help those whose life on the land has been a struggle without hope.

Fifth. I do not intend that the war against poverty become a series of uncoordinated and unrelated efforts —that it perish for lack of leadership and direction.

Therefore this bill creates, in the Executive Office of the President, a new Office of Economic Opportunity. Its Director will be my personal chief of staff for the war against poverty. I intend to appoint Sargent Shriver to this post.

He will be directly responsible for these new programs. He will work with and through existing agencies of the Government.

This program—the Economic Opportunity Act—is the foundation of our war against poverty. But it does not stand alone.

For the past three years this Government has advanced a number of new proposals which strike at important areas of need and distress.

I ask the Congress to extend those which are already in action, and to establish those which have already been proposed.

There are programs to help badly distressed areas such as the Area Redevelopment Act, and the legislation now being prepared to help Appalachia.

There are programs to help those without training find a place in today's complex society—such as the Manpower Development Training Act and the Vocational Education Act for youth.

There are programs to protect those who are specially vulnerable to the ravages of poverty—hospital insurance for the elderly, protection for migrant farm-workers, a food stamp program for the needy, coverage for millions not now protected by a minimum wage, new and expanded unemployment benefits for men out of work, a housing and community development bill for those seeking decent homes.

Finally there are programs which help the entire country, such as aid to education which, by raising the quality of schooling available to every American child, will give a new chance for knowledge to the children of the poor.

I ask immediate action on all these programs.

What you are being asked to consider is not a simple or an easy program. But poverty is not a simple or an easy enemy.

It cannot be driven from the land by a single attack on a single front. Were this so we would have conquered poverty long ago.

Nor can it be conquered by government alone.

For decades American labor and American business, private institutions, and private individuals have been engaged in strengthening our economy and offering new opportunity to those in need.

We need their help, their support, and their full participation.

Through this program we offer new incentives and new opportunities for cooperation, so that all the energy of our Nation, not merely the efforts of Government, can be brought to bear on our common enemy.

Today, for the first time in our history, we have the power to strike away the barriers to full participation in our society. Having the power, we have the duty.

The Congress is charged by the Constitution to "provide . . . for the general welfare of the United States." Our present abundance is a measure of its success in fulfilling that duty. Now Congress is being asked to extend that welfare to all our people.

The President of the United States is President of all the people in every section of the country. But this office also holds a special responsibility to the distressed and disinherited, the hungry and the hopeless of this abundant Nation.

It is in pursuit of that special responsibility that I submit this message to you today.

The new program I propose is within our means. Its costs of $970 million is 1 per cent of our national budget—and every dollar I am requesting for this program is already included in the budget I sent to Congress in January.

But we cannot measure its importance by its cost.

For it charts an entirely new course of hope for our people.

We are fully aware that this program will not eliminate all the poverty in America in a few months or a few years. Poverty is deeply rooted and its causes are many.

But this program will show the way to new opportunities for millions of our fellow citizens.

It will provide a lever with which we can begin to open the door to our prosperity for those who have been kept outside.

It will also give us the chance to test our weapons, to try our energy and ideas and imagination for the many battles yet to come. As conditions change, and as experience illuminates our difficulties, we will be prepared to modify our strategy.

And this program is much more than a beginning.

Rather it is a commitment. It is a total commitment by this President and this Congress, and this Nation, to pursue victory over the most ancient of mankind's enemies.

On many historic occasions the President has requested from Congress the authority to move against forces which were endangering the well-being of our country.

This is such an occasion.

On similar occasions in the past we often been called upon to wage war against foreign enemies which threatened our freedom. Today we are asked to declare war on a domestic enemy which threatens the strength of our Nation and the welfare of our people.

If we now move forward against this enemy—if we can bring to the challenges of peace the same determination and strength which has brought us victory in war—then this day and this Congress will have won a secure and honorable place in the history of the Nation, and the enduring gratitude of generations of Americans yet to come.

CHAPTER FIFTEEN

The Crisis in Urban Government: Will Cities Remain Habitable?

Long-range population trends in the United States indicate a steady shift away from the original rural majority. While total population of the United States has risen by one-third since 1950, farm population has declined by over one-half. Ours is increasingly an urban civilization. At the present time, no major geographical division of the United States has a rural majority and only 12 states (Vermont, North Dakota, South Dakota, Virginia, West Virginia, North Carolina, South Carolina, Kentucky, Mississippi, Arkansas, Idaho, Alaska) are thus classified. In contrast, New Jersey, Rhode Island, and California are nearly 90 per cent urban and the 225 largest standard metropolitan areas (central cities and their suburbs) hold well over half of all Americans. Furthermore, we must assume that most of our population increase in the next 50 years (variously estimated between 122 and 275 million) will be absorbed by these same areas. Inevitably, therefore, most domestic American problems are urban problems.

DOES A CRISIS EXIST?

How serious are the problems that confront American cities? Is the total situation properly described as a crisis, a term that in its medical sense implies a choice between recovery and death? Or are the present problems, however difficult, only the growing pains of a new world? In recent years the prophets of disaster have spoken without many challengers. It is commonly said that American cities are becoming uninhabitable. The catalogue of particulars is long and grim. What is more, according to the critics, in every particular the situation becomes worse every year. Implicit in this analysis is a suggestion that American cities may die, unable to cope with their increasingly complex problems.

Other observers are more optimistic. Although they recognize the present plight of most metropolitan areas, they believe that the very pressure of events will generate solutions. In effect, they believe that once the crisis is widely recognized, it will receive the scientific, financial, and political attention it deserves. Also, say the optimists, American cities in their present state have much to recommend them. Most migration to them has been voluntary; the older rural America was not the Arcadia pictured by some urban critics.

WHAT ARE THE MAJOR PROBLEMS?

The major problems of American cities are rather easily identified, although satisfactory solutions are apt to require massive scientific and financial efforts and a complete reshuffling of the present governmental structure.

Consider, for a moment, the shifting population patterns within metropolitan areas. Nearly every central city has lost population during the past 20 years to its satellite suburbs. Meanwhile the racial-ethnic composition of the remaining residents has changed radically. As older immigrant groups have headed for the suburbs they have been replaced by the modern "underdogs" of contemporary America—Southern Negroes, Puerto Ricans, Mexican Americans. Many core cities are well on their way toward becoming super-ghettos, filled with impoverished slum dwellers. An old result of this process, of course, is a shrinking tax base as financial needs increase. Another byproduct appears to be a rising threat to personal safety—"crime in the streets."

Meanwhile, a large percentage of suburban residents daily enter and leave the central city—most of them by private automobile. The number of such vehicles has nearly tripled in the past 20 years, with no end to the growth rate in sight. Within the core cities they jam expressways as quickly as they are built and create gigantic parking problems. As a byproduct they also contribute to air pollution.

Pollution of water and air are a direct result of our booming economy. Most water pollution is caused by industrial wastes; air pollution comes from our factories, power plants, and automobiles. Both types of pollution are now a universal metropolitan problem. Clean water is in short supply; clean air is being replaced by smog.

Inevitably, the problems outlined above become political problems, but our present political structure is ill-suited to deal with such issues. Most metropolitan areas are fragmented into dozens of political units. The Pittsburgh metropolitan area, for instance, has nearly 200 political subdivisions, each largely independent of the others. The relationship between cities, states, and the national government is also being subjected to reappraisal in the face of these issues. The older cry of "states rights vs. central control" appears somewhat shopworn in this context. What governmental unit can best deal with pollution and transportation problems? How do we check slums? Perhaps there are clear-cut answers. Is a solution to be found in some new kind of cooperative effort? Cooperative federalism between central cities and suburbs? Cooperative federalism between cities, states, and the national government?

What Is the City's Future?

For most of us the future of American cities is closely bound up with our own future. Faced with a multitude of immediate problems, it is easy to conclude that the pessimists are right—that the outlook for American cities is a bleak one indeed. As an antidote to this depressing conclusion we present a rather optimistic description of American urban life in the year 2000. Although life in the twenty-first century will not be without problems, according to the author we will have surmounted many dilemmas.

1

The American City in Travail *

PETER F. DRUCKER

Two facts concerning American metropolitan areas are almost immediately apparent: (1) they are growing at a fantastic rate, as they absorb rural immigrants and as their own birth rate soars; (2) this growth is creating a host of problems that overwhelm our antiquated city governments. Regarding the trend of population growth there appears to be no turning back. Regarding the escalation of problems and the need for governmental reorganization to cope with them there appears to be little disagreement among those who face the issues. The chief issue, then, appears to be one of political education. What are the problems of metropolitan America? How can they be solved? Who will give direction? Who will foot the bill? How can we design governments that match the scope of the problems?

That our big cities are hell-bent on committing suicide is hardly news.

* Peter F. Drucker, "American Directions: A Forecast." Copyright © 1965 by Peter F. Drucker. Originally appeared in *Harper's Magazine* and reprinted by permission of Harper & Row, Publishers. From the forthcoming book *American Directions* by Peter F. Drucker.

They are rapidly becoming unlivable. Attempts to assuage the disease seem to aggravate it. New freeways create more traffic jams and more air pollution; urban renewal dispossesses the poor or moves them from the jungle of the slum into the desert of the housing development; zoning for "racial balance" ends up by creating another Black Belt or Bronzeville.

A real solution, if one can be found, will have to be primarily aesthetic (or if you prefer the word, moral). At stake is the environment of modern man, rather than administration. We need a city that enriches and ennobles rather than degrades the individual, and not one that most efficiently fits him into well-planned public services. But long before we can hope to come to grips with the city as a human environment we will have to come to grips with the city as a government.

And the need is desperate. Within a few years three-quarters of the American people will live in a fairly small number of metropolitan areas, fewer than 200. Nearly two-fifths of the population will live in or close by the three monster supercities—one spreading from Boston to Norfolk, another from Milwaukee to Detroit (if not to Cleveland), and a third from San Francisco to San Diego. We will have to be able to supply people in the metropolis with water, sewers, and clean air. We will have to provide decent housing and schools for them, plus easy mobility for people, things, and ideas—which is the very reason for the existence of a city.

And for all this we shall need governmental institutions that will, of necessity, cut across or replace a whole host of local governments in existence today.

The Government We Lack

The metropolis is the decisive community today. But it does not exist as a government at all. Instead our system is built on the old preindustrial units of town, county, and state. No attack on the problems of the metropolis is possible without attacking at the same time these most deeply entrenched political bodies of our tradition and laws.

The tax issue alone will make sure of that. Within the next five years, local government expenses will double —from fifty billions to one hundred billions, very largely for education. But most of the big cities have already drained their tax reservoirs. We might tackle the financial problem of the big city by bringing the suburbs into the metropolitan tax system; by using the taxing powers of the states to finance the cities; or through large-scale grants from the federal government. My guess is that we will use all three methods. And each of them is sure to touch off a major political fight.

Similarly the "war on poverty" will raise the issue of metropolitan government. For the hard core of present-day poverty consists of city people who dwell outside our affluent, high-education society. Compared to them, the unemployed coal miners in the hollows of West Virginia or the submarginal farmers of Appalachia are a mopping-up operation.

The battle over the city's place in American government has already been joined. The Supreme Court decision last spring on reapportionment decreed that state legislatures must give equal representation to all voters regardless of their residence. It was fully as revolutionary as was that other Supreme Court decision, ten years ago, that decreed racial integration for the public schools. And like the school decision, reapportionment clearly was just the first skirmish in what will be a long and bitter fight. Lieutenant Governor Malcom Wilson of New York was not exaggerating when he warned (in a speech to the County Officers Association of New York last September 22) that reapportionment eventually might lead to the end of counties as units of government. Connecticut has already abolished them. And when New Jersey celebrated its Tercentenary in 1964, quite a few of its inhabitants must have wondered whether their state now serves any real purpose—with a population divided between residents of Metropolitan New York and residents of Metropolitan Philadelphia, separated rather than held together by Princeton Junction.

Of course, the issue will be fought out on specifics. It will be fought out as an issue of power balances within the nation, over tax sources and their division, and over the by-passing of states and counties by a federal government which increas-

ingly works directly in cooperation with the cities.

Mass transportation in and out of our big cities is, for instance, likely to be entrusted to a new federal agency before very long.* In our largest cities (New York, Philadelphia, and Chicago) it requires planning beyond the boundaries of one state, and money beyond the capacity of any local government.

But such specifics are only symptoms of a great constitutional crisis of our poltical institutions and structure.

* Mr. Drucker's forecast has been confirmed. A new cabinet-level Department of Transportation was created by Congress in 1966.

2

A Second Look at the Urban Crisis *

IRVING KRISTOL

Today there is general agreement that ours is an urban society. Also, it is generally agreed that this urban society is faced with problems that bid fair to be insoluble. At this point there is value in reviewing all of the evidence for some ray of hope. Are we being urbanized in an inexorable fashion? Or do the population statistics actually show something else? Will the urban ghetto spread without check? Are traffic conditions growing steadily worse? Are slums spreading? And, if we managed to survive these challenges are we doomed to polluted water, smog, and crime in the streets? Mr. Kristol challenges the assumptions that most Americans accept without much thought or reflection.

Do we, in fact, have an urban crisis? Most people by now are con-

* Irving Kristol, "Not A Bad Crisis To Live In," *The New York Times Magazine*, Jan. 22, VI, 23. As condensed in the *St. Louis Post-Dispatch*, February 8, 1967. © 1967 by The New York Times Company. Reprinted by permission of the author and publisher.

ditioned to believe so. But would we believe any of the following propositions?

1. Since 1920, the percentage of the American population living in cities of over 250,000 has remained just about stationary. We have not become a nation of big cities—only 10 per cent of Americans live in cities

of over 1,000,000, not significantly more than in 1910. And only 29 per cent today live in cities of over 100,000. We have become to a greater extent than before, a nation of suburban and exurban towns and villages and of "cities" with less than 50,000 population.

2. Since World War II, there has been a steady decline in the proportion of substandard urban housing units. In 1960, according to the Census Bureau, less than 3 per cent of dwelling units in cities of 50,000 or more were substandard.

3. Since World War II, it has been estimated the proportion of our urban population living below the poverty line has been approximately halved.

4. Only 22 per cent of the American people—according to Gallup—want to live in cities, even small ones, whereas fully half prefer towns or rural areas. Put another way: There are many more people interested in leaving our larger cities than in inhabiting them.

5. The overwhelming majority of Negroes and Puerto Ricans on New York's Upper West Side, when polled, report that they like living in the area, and that their squalid housing represents a clear improvement over their previous living conditions.

6. In Philadelphia (population 2,000,000), 70 per cent of the homes are owner-occupied. That particular urban "behavioral sink" contains three trees per inhabitant.

7. While it is true that traffic in a half-dozen or so of our largest cities is worse today than it was in 1940, such evidence as we have suggests strongly that it is no worse than in 1900, or perhaps even 1850. (There were fewer people and vehicles then, of course; but there were also fewer thoroughfares and traffic was slower-moving.) In any case, most "city dwellers" live outside our big cities and have no intolerable traffic problem.

8. By any objective, statistical index, our slum areas today appear positively benign in comparison with the teeming, filthy slums of yesteryear. They are certainly less densely populated than they used to be.

If anything is certain about the direction in which American society is moving, it is this: more and more people are going to be living in suburbs. (More and more are going to be working there, too: perhaps 70 per cent do so already. Even now, it is probable that the total suburban population is greater than the total central city population of the nation.

And I should say that it is equally certain that the new suburbs of today are not going to permit themselves to be swallowed up by their nearest big city. Why should they? It used to be the case that the big city had vital services to offer its outlying townships—sewage, road-building, electricity. This is no longer so.

It seems safe to say that, for most Americans today, the central city serves as a point of entry—a vast staging ground—for the suburbs they will end up in. To these Americans, the "urban problem" consists of saving enough money to get out of the city. All sorts of people regard this as deplorable. But that's the way it is.

It is indisputable that our central cities have some very serious problems—problems which everyone is aware of, though confusedly.

The first problem, of course, is money. City income, though increasing, just cannot keep up with the increase in city expenditures.

Then, there is "the revolution of rising expectations" among the urban poor. These people will not be satisfied with a very slow, modest improvement of their conditions, but insist that the improvement be substantial and swift. The only real way out of this dilemma is economic growth which would create jobs.

To create the jobs that are needed, one would have to entice businesses to establish themselves in the central city. But, for historical reasons, trade unions are extremely powerful in the central city, and their high wage rates and restrictive practices are not inviting to new business.

Moreover, the political administrations of most of our large cities are "liberal" in complexion, and it is very difficult for them to do anything that might be construed as giving "Handouts" to business men. Smaller towns, either in the suburbs or beyond, are not so handicapped; and that's where the business men go.

The greatest single disaster in the history of American big city government, during these past decades, has been the decline of the "machine" and of the political boss. Yes, the machine and the boss were more often than not corrupt. Unfortunately, our new breed of incorruptible and progressive mayors is deficient in one not unimportant respect; they seem unable to govern.

The old-time boss could use his power to "get things done." He could, for instance, expel several thousand squatters from an underdeveloped area of the city in order to create Central Park, as we know it. Can anyone imagine John Lindsay expelling—or even relocating—several thousand people from a rural section of Staten Island in order to create a park? The real-estate developers, the merchants, the construction unions, and CORE would rise up in wrath and indignation. It wouldn't be done.

But our urban poor will doubtless survive the economic mismanagement of our cities. They will make it on their own—to the suburbs: what is now a trickle of Negroes and Puerto Ricans will become a stream and then a flood.

By the time some of the fancier new programs for "rehabilitating" the "local community" begin to have an appreciable effect, many of the people who constitute this "community" will have been largely dispersed and the area itself will be—who can say what it will be then? At that point, we shall be living in a very different world, and coping with some very different "urban crisis."

3

The Commuting Motorist: Urban Enemy Number One *

C. W. GRIFFIN, JR.

Each year our major cities expend millions of dollars in a losing battle to solve the transportation crisis created by suburban motorists. Each year the traffic jams grow longer. Each year the metropolitan areas become more thickly populated with automobiles and people.

This pattern is familiar to all Americans. Our instinctive solution is to do more of what we have traditionally done—more parking lots, more expressways, more bridges, tunnels, and skyways. The author of the following article is a professional engineer and city planner. After describing the American transportation crisis, he makes specific recommendations for reform. In capsule form he would wage war against the motorist who uses downtown streets and divert tax dollars from highway building to mass transit.

Having examined the evidence, the reader may have unanswered questions. Are desirability and feasibility always matched in a society governed on the principle "one man, one vote"? In other words, will voters who are also motorists agree that the commuting motorists be regarded as "a public nuisance"? How can the present image of mass transit be made more appealing? Still more basic, how can our metropolitan areas, with their dozens of independent political units, develop a unified transportation policy?

Sam Jepson is an intrepid knight of the highway who lives in northern New Jersey and works in Manhattan. At half past seven on a typical weekday morning, he lights a cigar, pulls out of his driveway in Lake Hontapocus, and starts the thirty-mile trek to New York.

After a short spell of easy driving, Sam is in stop-and-go traffic as cars, trucks, and buses converge on the main highway. Now he draws upon his long experience as a commuting motorist. Negotiating each bottleneck is a test of skill, brains, and daring. Tense and eager at every impending

showdown, he questions and admonishes his unresponding enemies aloud while cunningly gauging their speed and intentions—and above all, their determination. Occasionally, Sam discreetly chickens out when an undaunted rival stubbornly holds his lane as the highways merge. A sudden swerve of the Lake Hontapocus bus nearly forces Sam into the guard rail. He jams on the brakes, mutters un-Christian sentiments about the bus driver, but, hardened by years of such irritations, quickly regains his grim composure.

Approaching the Lincoln Tunnel, traffic slows to the speed of chilled molasses. Sam's tactics now become more aggressive—and so do his adversaries'. At this crawling pace, you can usually count on the other fel-

* C. W. Griffin, Jr., "Car Snobs, Commuters, and Chaos." Copyright © 1962, by Harper's Magazine, Inc. Reprinted from the July, 1962 issue of Harper's Magazine by permission of the author.

low's brakes if you cut in front of him.

As traffic oozes through the tunnel, Sam dourly puffs his cigar, inhales the exhaust fumes perfuming the tunnel, and mumbles about "too damned many cars on the roads." Finally—an hour and twenty-minutes after his departure—he pulls into his midtown Manhattan garage, slightly jaded and cheered by the thought that driving home will be worse than driving in.

Even in summer, on those horrible Monday mornings and Friday evenings when his trip may take two hours or more, Sam's faith remains unshaken. Never will he yield the sacred right of the commuting American to jam streets and highways; never will he submit to the ignominy of riding the train or bus.

Sam Jepson is a life member of the brotherhood of commuting motorists who cause so much of our transportation mess. Their cars crawling in and out of our cities are as costly as they are inefficient. Even the most rabid automaniac knows that rapid transit is a far faster and cheaper way to move masses of people into densely built downtown areas. (A single rapid-transit track can carry as many people as sixteen to twenty freeway lanes occupying ten times as much land.) But the automobile manufacturers, the automobile clubs, and the bridge and tunnel authorities whose revenues swell with traffic congestion defend motorized commuting as a basic American Freedom. "Freedom of Automobility," a slogan of the National Highway Users Conference, is the citizen's inalienable right to drive his car wherever and whenever he damned well pleases. . . .

Big Wheels on Wheels

. . . The national bias favoring highway transportation is supported by a durable myth—long cultivated by automobile manufacturers—that highway users pay for their facilities. This premise is false, especially in the big cities. A Chicago study in the midfifties revealed an average annual city subsidy of $84.54 for each motor vehicle using the city streets; a similar study in Milwaukee showed an annual average subsidy of $90. Bureau of Public Roads statistics indicate that in 1960 the nation spent about $1.5 billion more for building, maintaining, and policing streets and highways than was received by federal, state, and local governments from highway users.

Commuting motorists also receive other less direct subsidies. Real-estate-tax assessment policies in most states reward owners for using valuable land for parking lots. According to the general manager of the Chicago Transit Authority, the city loses an estimated $6.3 million in tax receipts a year because some thirty-five acres of privately owned land in the Loop are devoted to parking automobiles and are hence assessed far below the potential value. Expressways are even more parasitical devourers of land than parking lots. The vast acreages they carve out of cities are removed from the tax rolls to become a permanent financial liability. In short, the city's property owners subsidize the street and highway users.

Because of the bias favoring automobile travel, federal highway spending is not balanced by any comparable program for mass transit. Since Washington finances 90 per cent of the cost of urban freeways under the interstate program, the highway solution to surface-transportation problems is almost irresistible, for a city must bear the full burden of financing a mass-transit system. Thus a rapid-transit network that costs only one fifth as much as a federally aided expressway system would actually cost the local government twice as much. . . .

People vs. Automobiles

. . . One of the most radical proposals to date calls for permanent weekday banning of private automobiles from Manhattan, except in the downtown financial district and the midtown shopping and theatre district. The architect-writer team of Percival and Paul Goodman proposes a basic pattern of traffic arteries forming grid squares roughly 400 yards on a side. This would mean closing to general traffic about four out of five crosstown streets and alternate avenues. With its 25 per cent gain in usable space, each block could add recreation areas and trees. The closed streets would become pedestrian walks, as well as roads for service vehicles. An occasional tennis court, ice-skating rink, or softball diamond might bloom in the largest traffic-free intersections. Buses and small electric taxis could shuttle people around at speeds far greater than today's congestion permits. . . .

Less utopian but more likely is a car-banning scheme designed for downtown Fort Worth by architect-planner Victor Gruen, who has long been a champion of the pedestrian. Although his plan has been stymied for the past six years by lack of funds, it is still very much alive. Gruen proposes converting the present downtown core—about one square mile—into a pedestrian island. Electrically powered shuttle cars would transport the lame, the lazy, and the package-laden, and tunnels would admit trucks and taxis. Six huge garages along the belt roadway encircling the core would project into the island, as would bus loops, so that the longest walk would be about two hundred yards. . . .

On the other side of the continent, the undistinguished core of Los Angeles' smog-polluted, traffic-harassed metropolis is well on its way to becoming a vast complex of intersections bordered by parking garages and a few buildings standing as nostalgic reminders that once upon a time the downtown had a purpose. Less dismal but similar prospects menace just about every metropolitan area in the U.S.

The Right Track

Many measures, well this side of utopia, can help counter the threat. An obvious first step is to institute rush-hour tolls on all congested highways, bridges, and tunnels in and around a city. Adjusted to limit traffic to manageable volume, these tolls would not only put the charge where it belongs, they would also make the motorist aware of expenses other than operating costs. They might even convert him to mass transit. . . . Repeal of the 10 per cent federal transportation tax on interstate rail and bus fares, which tends to encourage automobile commuting.
. . . Amendment of federal highway legislation to include financing of rapid-transit track construction on the rights-of-way of urban expressways. . . .

Along with policies discouraging automobile commuting, cities would, of course, have to expand and improve public transportation. Reserving street or freeway lanes for rush-hour buses speeds commuters' trips in several cities—notably Chicago, Baltimore, and Nashville. Express buses are four times as efficient as cars; in bumper-to-bumper traffic, probably fifteen times as efficient. Park-ride service between strategically located parking lots and downtown cores, with buses speeding along a reserved lane while cars fight with trucks for the remaining lanes, should win friends for public transportation. The stale arguments against public transportation disintegrate in the light of a few facts. Contrary to anti-transit propaganda, many commuters who don't use the antiquated mass-transit facilities generally available today will patronize a modern system. Within three years, Philadelphia's subsidized rail program, with its improved schedules and faster trains, has increased patronage of commuter railroads by 44 per cent—and at a bare fraction of the public cost of building freeways for the added riders. In the San Francisco area, according to consulting engineers Parsons, Brinkerhoff, Quade & Douglas, 77 per cent of the commuters patronize mass transit if it's as quick as car travel. And 2,600 commuting drivers in three major cities questioned by *Fortune* magazine in the mid-'fifties overwhelmingly favored mass transit if it could match their driving time. For a saving of ten minutes or more a day, five out of six said they would desert their cars. . . .

The propagandists urging ever-increasing hordes of automobiles in the cities have neither economics nor civilized values on their side. They understand little of the need for dense, pedestrian-oriented development to preserve the cities as thriving centers of commerce and culture, and they care even less.

Like the freedom to pollute air and water, the unrestricted right to jam city and suburban highways can't be tolerated as we crowd ever more densely around our great urban centers. We must stop treating the commuting motorist as an aristocrat whose whims must not only be indulged, but subsidized. We should treat the commuting motorist as a public nuisance. He hogs a disproportionate share of public space; he robs pedestrians and bus riders of time, lost in the traffic jams he creates; he endangers public health as his idling engine pollutes the air with poisonous exhausts. As Lewis Mumford counseled the American Institute of Architects:

"Forget the damned motor cars; design the cities for friends and lovers."

4

America, the Dirty *

CLARE BOOTHE LUCE

In one sense, at least, American problems of polluted air and water are a direct result of our size, wealth, and affluence. In 1945 we had slightly over 30 million motor vehicles; today we have nearly 100 million, each one discharging over six pounds of contaminants daily. In 1940 we had to provide water and sewage facilities for 130 million people; today we must provide for over 70 million more. Several years ago John Kenneth Galbraith suggested the paradox of our time: "The greater the wealth the thicker will be the dirt."

Obviously, this result is not predestined. But without determined effort it is apt to prevail. How can we check and reverse the process? What is technically possible? Who will pay the bill? What responsibility does government have? Which government?

Recently, a British author called the United States "the biggest slum on earth," and he added, "The mess that is man-made America is a disgrace of such proportions that only a concerted national effort can hope to return America to the community of civilized nations." President Johnson seems bent on making that effort—or, rather, on challenging his countrymen to make the effort.

His conservation program is now in the legislative mills of Congress—which, like the mills of the gods, grind exceedingly slow and fine. It is to be hoped, for the sake of all Americans, that they will grind out the legislation the President has called for more rapidly than our engines and machines are grinding out the fine matter that has brought a new and terrible word into our language—*smog*. Smog is the polluted

air that hangs like a pall over many of our cities—the most expensive pall any nation has bought for what may prove to be the funeral of the Great Society.

According to Howard R. Lewis, author of a grim but fascinating book called *With Every Breath You Take*, about 60 per cent of our people live in areas government experts classify as air-polluted. These people breathe poison every minute of their lives.

By the daily dumping of litter and refuse, man has systematically poisoned and defiled his major rivers and lakes—until, government authorities say, all our major river systems are polluted. But man can live for several days without water. He can live, at most, two minutes without air. Each of us breathes about 35 pounds of air a day. The inevitable consequence of regularly breathing noxious or toxic air is some degree of ill health, if not death.

Science Digest reports that, in 1962,

* Clare Boothe Luce, "America, the Dirty," *McCall's*, July, 1965, p. 28. Reprinted by permission of the author.

United States physicians encountered 1,600,000 cases of illness in which air pollution figured. Among the ailments linked with smog are catarrh, tuberculosis, pneumonia, emphysema, dyspnea, headache, chest constriction, choking, nausea, sore throat, common colds. All respiratory and heart ailments are worsened by polluted air.

In 1952, when a heavy smog settled over London, 4,000 more deaths occurred than the weekly average. And for three months after the smog crisis, there were 8,000 deaths in excess of the normal death rate. Experts insist that such a disaster—given proper weather conditions—can strike almost any great city in America. The vulnerability of Los Angeles is proverbial. But even Phoenix, Arizona, once celebrated for the "pure air of the wide open spaces," is rapidly becoming one of the smog-affected communities.

Dirty air also attacks man's engines, shelters, and possessions. It dissolves clothing, corrodes metal, disintegrates stone, rots wood, erases paint, and kills plant and animal life. America's annual bill for its ravages is estimated as about 14 billion dollars.

The worst offender in urban areas is, paradoxically, also the source of much of our material progress and prosperity—the automobile. Exhaust fumes account for about 50 per cent of all air contamination. Everyone knows that death can quickly result from breathing the exhaust fumes from a running motor in a closed garage. These same fumes enter the air of cities, and when they do so in sufficient quantities, with every poisoned breath we take, we die a little.

Household heating systems and incinerators, city dumps and refuse-disposal plants, industrial smoke stacks, engines and machines of all kinds, airplanes spraying insecticides are constantly creating smokes, gases,

and clouds full of chemical poisons, which impregnate those minuscule solid particles we call dust, dirt, soot, and grime.

Nature itself is a villain. Dust and sandstorms, forest fires, earthquakes, landslides, volcanic eruptions, windborne pollens are some of the ways nature pollutes the air. But if nature in the raw is seldom mild, in air pollution she is, on the whole, a very lamb compared with man. He has, in this century and country, developed a monstrous capacity for crippling or killing himself and deliberately dirtying the one thing he cannot live without—reasonably clean air.

The causes of air pollution are so complex, the menace is so widespread and is increasing so rapidly, that controlling it is a formidable undertaking. The federal government began to tackle the problem with the Clean Air Act of 1963, and the President's conservation program proposes amendments to the act that will make it more efficient. Even the most confirmed states-righter must accept a large degree of federal responsibility for combatting pollution. What, for example, can one state do about the contaminated air that blows across its border from the industrial smokestacks of a neighboring state? Nevertheless, if the problem is to be met, the people themselves must agitate for more energetic state and city action.

It is some comfort to know that many technical solutions for pollution —especially in the case of the automobile—have been found. At long last, the automobile industry is building cars for the sore eyed, and Los Angeles car buyers will be able to greatly cut down exhaust fumes by better combustion of fuel. But why shouldn't we all? The majority of industries can, if state or federal law insists on it, install wash-and-filter systems that will greatly reduce the tons of poisonous matter they spew into the air.

A paradox at which nature sadly mocks is that detergents—man's invention to do away with the dirt his adored engines produce—are increasingly polluting our water systems and rivers. (If you are a city dweller and want to know how much waste detergent you drink, half fill a bottle with tap water, and shake it. If the water clouds and foams, it contains some of the detergent waste from your own sinks, tubs, and washing machines, and your city's water-filter-ing system is beginning to be over-burdened.

The task of beautifying America and cleansing it of pollution, which is the task of winning the race between wisdom and waste, in order to preserve the common estate, is the greatest challenge our nation faces—except for preventing that act of complete uglification, despoliation, and pollution called nuclear war. This challenge must be met, or the cream of the cosmic jest may be that America will bring about its own destruction with the fallout from peaceful and prosperous skies.

5

Towards a Super-Ghetto *

JOSEPH ALSOP

Among the mounting problems of American cities are those involving a racial imbalance that is increasing at break-neck speed. Throughout American history the city has been the melting pot, where diverse nationalities, races, and cultures were amalgamated into something uniquely American. That traditional pattern is now being replaced by a society that is structured around a metropolitan area divided along racial-economic lines. The central city is well on its way toward becoming a vast Negro, Puerto Rican, or Mexican ghetto, surrounded by middle– or upper-class white suburbs. This sharp division along racial lines has already taken place in many cities. Unless it is reversed or modified it will surely be an added barrier to political integration of our metropolitan areas. Certain questions are obvious. Can the existing ghetto patterns be altered to encourage "open housing"? Will Americans accept the creation of giant ghettos at the very heart of their vaunted civilization: New York's Manhattan, the Chicago Loop, Boston's Hub? Are certain government policies encouraging the rise of these ghettos? If so, can they be reversed?

The Census Bureau has been doing some further work on population trends in the United States. The results point to the same old demographic nightmare of the American future—an urbanized nation with affluent white suburbs encircling rot-ting, mainly Negro core-cities. On the

* Joseph Alsop, "Towards a Super-Ghetto," *St. Louis Post Dispatch*, December 22, 1966, p. 30. Reprinted by permission of the author.

surface, the results may not appear quite as hair-raising as they really are, for one must know how to read the figures. Briefly, between 1960 and 1965, America's cities suffered a net decline of 270,000 in their total white population. The Negro population of the cities meanwhile grew by 2,000,-000. And while the suburbs gained 9,252,000 whites, they admitted only 400,000 additional Negroes.

But these are over-all figures, covering all the growing cities of this country, including the larger cities that have not as yet become targets of intensive Negro immigration, and, above all, including the numerous smaller cities whence the white emigration to suburbs has not yet become a headlong flight.

Even so, an immense suburban immigration is concealed in the over-all totals. For the white population of the cities, instead of declining slightly, ought to have grown by 4,500,000 in the period in question. Thus nearly 5,000,000 people in the increased population of the suburbs are in fact refugees from the center-cities, the rest being former country dwellers and results of normal population growth.

One or two studies of individual cities have also been done by the Census Bureau. They were made for special reasons, and thus did not cover any of the more extreme and interesting cases, such as Baltimore or St. Louis.

One of the cities studied by the bureau was Cleveland. Its total population is now a bit above 800,000, which is a 65,000 decline from the former peak. Behind that decline, there is a loss of white population of 91,000, and a gain of Negro Clevelanders of 26,000. Overall, therefore, Cleveland is now 34.5 per cent Negro.

Buffalo is another city where the basic trend is not far advanced. With just above 480,000 population, it is still only 17.4 per cent Negro. But since 1960, Buffalo, too, has lost 13.5 per cent of its white population, and has increased its Negro population by 14.4 per cent.

For the most advanced cases—the cities that show us where we are really heading—over-all figures are lacking, alas. But in Washington, D.C., the Negroes in the elementary school population have again moved up a notch, from just under 90 per cent to 92.8 per cent. In Baltimore, too, the Negro percentage of elementary school children has gone from 64.3 to 65.4, and in St. Louis, there has been a rise from 63.5 per cent to 64.5 per cent. The school figures obviously predict the ghetto of the future.

Behind this process that is transforming our center-cities into huge Negro ghettos, there are of course two sub-processes. One is the white immigration to the suburbs, above mentioned. The other is the Negro emigration from the South.

Most of the gain in Negro population in the center cities represented this immense flight from the South. In the period since 1960, more than 2,000,000 Negroes moved from South to North, and the South's share of the total Negro population dropped from more than 60 per cent to about 53.4 per cent. Furthermore, this emigration is continuing.

The pressures that cause it are even being subsidized by the Federal Government. In Mississippi, for instance, soil bank payments are widely used by white farmers to retire part of their land from cultivation, and to mechanize the rest of their farming operation. As a result, by the best estimate available, at least 30,000 former sharecroppers and tenant farmers, all Negroes of course, are being driven each year to leave Mississippi for the Northern cities.

In one sense, perhaps, this trend is

a good thing. While the Negro problem remained predominantly a rural problem, America's unequal treatment of its Negro citizens was merely a national dishonor. It was not a danger. Now that the Negro problem is rapidly becoming a predominantly urban problem, however, it is becoming acutely dangerous to the whole fabric of American society. And so we may be forced to face the need to do something about it.

Let no one think, either, that white Americans can escape the Negro problem by the simple act of fleeing to the affluent suburbs. It is an urgent, a desperately urgent problem for every single American. And there is only one solution—to muster the resources even if these be counted in tens of billions, that are needed to give our Negro citizens the jobs, the quality education, and the career opportunities they require.

6

Urban America in the Year 2000 *

MITCHELL GORDON

In modern America the gap between science fiction and cold, sober reality has constantly narrowed. The article that follows originally appeared in a newspaper dedicated to the interests of the business community. The editors noted that their reporters had "talked to experts in many fields to get the best-informed opinions on probable developments between now and the year 2000."

If this is indeed the shape of the future, with what problems will government be compelled to wrestle during the next quarter century? Is centralized direction of urban growth a necessity or should it be regarded as a threat? What justification can be offered for "New Towns," "corridors," and malls? How and by whom can transportation problems be solved? What changes can we anticipate in the structure of major cities? Why do some experts believe that the racial ghetto will have disappeared by the year 2000?

If you don't like urban life, start running.

Houses and concrete and businesses and schools will spill over more of the country-side in coming decades. In the central sections of cities buildings will soar higher and the atmosphere will grow still more impersonal. The

noise level will climb as new types of short-haul intercity aircraft capable of operating from tiny downtown landing strips begin adding their jet roar to the present din.

But the citified society of the future may not be quite as grim as some pessimists would have you believe. Though urban "sprawl" is expected to continue, most planners are confident their campaigns for land-use projects that leave green spaces for

* Mitchell Gordon, "Urban America in the Year 2000," *Wall Street Journal*, January 30, 1967, pp. 1, 16. Reprinted by permission of the publisher.

recreation will start to pay off soon. Transit experts predict that dramatic progress in their field will ease commuting for poeple who work in the central city but live in new suburbs 100 miles or more distant; "air-cushion" vehicles that shoot through tubes at speeds up to 600 miles an hour or more are one of the proposed new modes of commuter transportation.

In the core areas of cities, slums will largely disappear, though some aging, ill-planned suburban subdivisions will take on a slum-like aspect. The crime rate will drop in cities, partly because television and other surveillance devices will improve police efficiency. Racial tensions also will decline sharply, in the view of some sociologists.

Another urban problem, downtown congestion, will be alleviated by turning many crowded streets into pedestrian malls and by barring private cars from some areas. Restrictions on the use of autos—or at least on those powered by internal-combustion engines—may also help combat air pollution. And some researchers go so far as to predict that a number of urban communities will solve the pollution problem completely by enveloping themselves in vast air-conditioned plastic canopies where residents will breathe filtered air—and bask in an ideal climate year round.

Planners balk at setting precise timetables for many of the changes they foresee in urban areas between now and the year 2000. True, marvels like domed cities or jet-speed commuting face enough technological and other problems so their advent probably can be safely assigned to the closing years of the century, if then.

Politics and Progress

But in some fields, such as pollution and land-use planning, the pace of change hinges to a considerable extent on the ability of local and regional administrative units to co-operate. Otherwise, confused, overlapping jurisdictions will frustrate efforts to carry out rational solutions to the problems of growing urban areas. With a few exceptions, urban planners note, past attempts to achieve metropolitan and regional cooperation have met dogged resistance, and the experts can't predict when problems will become serious enough to break down such opposition.

The role of the Federal Government is another imponderable in the future of cities. Rightly or wrongly, cities look to Washington for massive help in attacking slums and crime and in improving mass transit. So the rate of progress in these fields will depend to a high degree on the money and impetus from Washington—which, in turn, may depend on how preoccupied the U.S. remains with overseas problems, such as Vietnam.

Nevertheless, certain urban trends are clear. The most unmistakable one is that more and more people will live in urban areas.

At present some 70 per cent—or 139 million—of the total U.S. population of 198 million are classed as city dwellers under Census Bureau standards. By 2000 a minimum of 83 per cent—or 281 million—of a total population of 338 million are expected to be living in urban areas. Some analysts regard the 83 per cent projection as far too low, contending the proportion of city residents will top 90 per cent by the end of the century.

Experts agree that almost all these new urban dwellers will settle in the suburbs, at least through the next couple of decades or so. Typically, Robert C. Wood, Under Secretary of the Department of Housing and

Urban Development, says that what he terms the "spread city of the 1940s-60s era" will remain "the dominant form for some time to come."

Urban and suburban sprawl will produce immense metropolitan areas—"megalopolises"—in some parts of the U.S. By 2000, some experts say, unbroken stretches of urban civilization will run from just above Boston to below Washington, D.C., some 450 miles; from Chicago to Detroit, over 250 miles; from Cleveland to Buffalo; and from Santa Barbara (100 miles north of Los Angeles) to the Mexican border.

Many authorities think that central cities, most of which have lost population in recent decades, eventually will have a new surge of growth. The suburbs will continue to grow, too, but, says William L. C. Wheaton, a professor of planning at the University of California, "by the 1990's cities will be exciting enough to be drawing people back in, causing many with homes in the country to take up apartments in the city as well."

Squatters in Calcutta

Metropolitan areas abroad as well as those in the U.S. are expected to grow rapidly, and in some poorer parts of the world in Asia, the Mideast and Africa the expanding throngs of urban dwellers may pose almost insuperable problems. It is difficult to envision how the Indian city of Calcutta, for example, will be able to cope with the population of 30 million —five times the present total—that is forecast for it by 2000; already 600,-000 residents of Calcutta are said to be homeless squatters.

But in the U.S. urban planners hope they can shape growth so tomorrow's vast metropolises will be manageable by governments and hospitable to residents.

❋   ❋   ❋

At present planning agencies can generally do little more than recommend the directions in which metropolitan areas should grow, but even with this limited function they are beginning to make headway. Consider the efforts of the Maryland-National Capital Park Planning Commission, which consists of representatives of two Maryland counties, Montgomery and Prince Georges, that are suburbs of Washington.

The commission's assignment is to guide the municipalities in the counties so that their housing, business and recreational development will fit into an overall scheme. The commission says that so far the municipalities have largely adhered to its plan, now three years old.

A Sense of Identity

This plan calls for development to be channeled along six "corridors" radiating 40 to 50 miles out from Washington. Each corridor contains four or five cities, some new, some well established. Parkways or strips of greenery will prevent cities in the same corridor from blending into each other, while the wedges of open space between the corridors will provide close-in recreational areas for all. The plan creates the dense lines of development needed for low-cost mass transit, planners note. It also preserves physically separate towns, which sociologists say creates a sense of identity that stimulates civic pride and makes for safer, more attractive communities.

❋   ❋   ❋

The "New Town" movement offers another approach to the problem of urban sprawl. It envisions the creation in open countryside of new communities that would have their own employment opportunities, stores and recreational facilities, so residents would not have to travel long distances daily.

❋　　❋　　❋

The expectation that governments will encourage the construction of New Towns is based on the assumption that the need for some sort of planning to insure ordered urban growth eventually will be recognized by almost everyone. As Edward J. Logue, boss of Boston's redevelopment agency, puts it: "By the year 2000 some kind of green belt or open space policy will be effectively in force as the discovery is more generally made that sprawl just doesn't make sense."

But not all forecasters are this optimistic. Daniel Bell, a Columbia University professor of sociology and chairman of the Commission on the Year 2000, which was established in 1965 by the American Academy of Arts and Sciences to examine a variety of future problems, fears many large metropolitan areas won't take the ambitious planning measures needed to make their growth rational. Consequently, he expects smaller cities, particularly well-situated ones in the 50,000 to 100,000 category, to grow fastest in the future, simply because they will be more livable and therefore more attractive to job-generating industries.

Programs for rebuilding the old central cities of metropolitan areas could well prove easier to carry out than plans to guide suburban growth. One reason is that in core-area planning only one local government is involved, eliminating the need to reconcile the views of several jurisdictions.

Strong political pressures also are likely to speed the renaissance of metropolitan cores. Says Edward C. Banfield, professor of government at Harvard: "There's too much political power in our central cities for the Federal Government to let the cities go under and too much power in central business districts for central cities to let their downtowns go under."

As a result of such factors, authorities expect most city centers to undergo drastic transformations in the years ahead. Some aspects of these transformations will have their detractors. A number of critics complain, for example, that rebuilding programs break up close-knit neighborhoods. But the majority of urban planners obviously think the benefits far outweigh the drawbacks.

Rebutting the criticism of the disruption of old neighborhoods, they note that many of these are Negro ghettos. Dispersion of the residents into formerly all-white neighborhoods, while it may produce frictions initially, could contribute significantly to improved race relations in the long run. "By 2000 we'll be wondering what all the shouting was about," says sociologist Daniel P. Moynihan, newly appointed director of the Joint Center for Urban Studies at Massachusetts Institute of Technology and Harvard.

Some of the decaying structures due for destruction will be replaced by vertical cities within the city. These immense complexes may achieve heights of 200 or more stories, compared with 102 for the Empire State Building. They will contain apartments for tens of thousands of families, along with offices, shops, and recreational areas. In theory, residents would hardly ever have to step outside.

A Forerunner in Los Angeles

Century City in Los Angeles is considered a forerunner of the city-within-a-city of the future. Located on a former movie lot, it now boasts two major office buildings, a hotel, two luxury apartment towers and a shopping center. Century City will accommodate some 12,000 residents and provide 20,000 jobs by the time all segments are completed in the late 1970's.

The creation of pedestrian malls to make downtown areas more pleasant aroused wide interest several years ago, and a handful of cities tried them out. Some merchants objected, however; they feared loss of business if customers couldn't draw up at the front door in their cars. Some cities, including Toledo and Springfield, Ore., laid out malls, then had second thoughts and turned the streets to auto traffic again.

But now the mall concept is reviving as city planners convince the critics that malls can unclog downtown streets and make them more attractive places to shop and work. Los Angeles, Detroit, Houston, Minneapolis, Cincinnati, Elizabeth, N.J., and Philadelphia are either planning pedestrian malls or already building them.

Philadelphia will have a particularly extensive and elaborate pedestrian mall. Scheduled for completion in 1975, it will run for 10 blocks in the heart of the city. Edmund Norwood Bacon, Philadelphia's top city planner, says the mall will have benches, fountains, sculpture and plantings. Within 10 years, the city also hopes to install a moving belt or "carveyor" —individual seats on a belt—to carry people along at least part of the mall, according to Mr. Bacon. Transit lines and delivery vehicles will travel on a level beneath the mall—an idea a number of other cities may copy by simply building malls over existing streets.

Domed Communities

Still another feature of the Philadelphia mall—a glass roof to protect pedestrians from the elements—foreshadows the much more ambitious efforts to build domed communities.

Eugene B. Konecci, a staff member of a Presidential space advisory panel whose studies of habitations for men in the hostile environment of space are closely related to research on domed communities on Earth, is one of several authorities who expect such communities to begin appearing by the year 2000.

❊   ❊   ❊

Greatly improved mass transit will be essential to link tomorrow's central cities and the ever more distant fringes of metropolitan areas, urban planners stress. Though many jobs will move to the suburbs along with families, armies of commuters will still pour into the metropolitan cores daily. As these trips become longer and expressway traffic becomes more congested, swift new transit will be the only recourse.

How quickly transit needs are met is particularly dependent on developments in the political field. In major metropolitan areas transit lines must cross municipal, county and even state lines, making cooperation among several governmental units vital. The trials faced by the San Francisco area in its efforts to build a new $1 billion-plus rapid transit system illustrate some of the problems; routes have had to be redrawn time after time in keeping with the demands of the communities the system will serve.

Help From Washington

Though San Francisco is managing with little help from Washington, experts think many metropolitan areas will be unable to create new transit systems without Federal funds.

Some methods for improving transit—such as the reservation of expressway lanes for the exclusive use of buses—are relatively simple. But in most places the provision of adequate transit service will be an enormously expensive undertaking, and local governments and private firms are likely to lack the resources to tackle it.

Already Washington is taking on some responsibilities in transit. Under a 1964 law the Government can offer communities loans or grants to improve mass transit, plus aid for transit research. The Federally supported project to run 110-mile-per-hour trains between New York and Washington starting next fall is part of a broad program of Federal research into high-speed ground transportation that could eventually pay off in better mass transit systems.

Transit specialists are exploring many ideas. New or expanded subway systems will serve at least as short-term solutions to transit problems in some cities. Monorail is still considered a good possibility for single-leg transit service, such as the new monorail line linking Tokyo's airport and downtown. But difficulties with switching may rule out monorail for complex systems.

Far swifter than subway train or monorail, however, would be the 600-mile-an-hour air-cushion vehicles now under development. Laboratory models of such vehicles have been built at the University of Manchester in Britain and at MIT. Garrett Corp., a Los Angeles subsidiary of Signal Oil Co. that makes components for space vehicles and electric power

systems, last year received a Federal contract to study the feasibility of the concept.

Electromagnetic energy from a power source embedded in a concrete roadbed would pull the wheelless vehicles along. When at rest or slowing down they would settle onto the roadbed, but at other times they would travel inches above the surface. They would blast jets of air against the walls of the tube enclosing the system in order to keep centered over the roadbed and on course. The tube would muffle noise from the vehicles that might otherwise disturb areas along the right-of-way.

The high-speed air-cushion vehicles, which researchers think are 20 to 30 years off, could supplement air transport on heavily intercity routes. But they would also be suitable for the long-distance commutes of the future.

A West Coast executive could live on a hilltop overlooking the Pacific Ocean at Carmel, Calif., for example, and commute the 300 miles to Los Angeles with ease. He might board his reserved-seat air-cushion coach at Carmel at 8:15 a.m. It would lift off the roadbed, whirl around an acceleration loop and plunge into the main tube running from Seattle to San Diego. Little more than half an hour later the car would peel off into the deceleration loop in downtown Los Angeles. By 9 A.M. the executive would be at this desk.

CHAPTER SIXTEEN

American Civilization:
Government's Quest for a Great Society

The United States is frequently described as a materialistic nation. Certainly there is much evidence of our preoccupation with the production and consumption of material goods. In fact, when Americans compare their country with others they often cite comparative national statistics on the number of telephones, automobiles, bath tubs, TV sets, and electric razors. Both American conservatives and liberals have been caught up in this thought pattern, and the full platform of American liberalism for many years seems to have concentrated on higher living standards (more goods) for the underprivileged.

Perhaps every civilization eventually achieves what it believes to be important. At any rate Americans seem to be on the edge of achieving a surfeit of goods for most U. S. citizens. It is no longer only the wild-eyed dreamer who believes that we can provide abundance for all. Our engineers and factory managers have the blue prints at hand.

This development promises to provoke a great deal of soul searching during the next decade. In its simplest form the new problem can be phrased thus: Is material abundance enough? Can any society be numbered among the great simply because its citizens are all steam heated in winter, air conditioned in summer, and have full bellies from the cradle to the grave? Are material goods enough, or are they only the threshold to a Great Society? Furthermore, is the quest for a great society a proper function of the government, or is it best left to the individual or informal groups?

A GREAT SOCIETY: CAN POLITICAL LEADERS POINT THE WAY?

In this section you are asked to examine two conflicting interpretations of the role of government in providing a "good life" for modern man. One analysis finds that modern man is alienated from his world, that under both capitalism and communism men are becoming well-fed, well-clad automatons headed towards ever-increasing insanity. The solution proposed is the reorganization of the modern world into small groups and de-emphasis of the large nation-state.

The other analysis visualizes the nation-state as playing a major role in evolution towards a Great Society. First the remnants of poverty will be mopped up. Then government will open new doors that lead toward beauty, knowledge, and rewarding leisure.

In one version, government itself is part of the problem. In the other, government becomes the chief instrument for achieving the good life.

BEYOND ECONOMICS: WHAT GOALS FOR AMERICANS?

If economic goals are no longer to be the chief stock in trade of aspiring politicians, what will replace the older "pork chop" liberalism. Rather than attempt any definitive answer we have tried to provide a wide range of goals and problems that may result from the new leisure and abundance.

Prominent on any list is education, which Americans view as a liberating force. But the new dimensions of American life will require a new kind of education at a time when the whole educational process is in flux. A sexual revolution is also in process, which will inevitably revamp our basic social patterns. Increased leisure will also destroy older patterns of behavior and values. Finally, the intricate relationship between the political process and American culture is involved. Can we expect rival political candidates of the future to argue the relative value of representational versus non-representational art? Will "programmed learning" become a national issue? Will highway beautification become a platform plank? What stand will the Republican party take on the sexually emancipated woman?

1

Towards a Sane Society *

ERIC FROMM

The German-born psychoanalyst, Eric Fromm, has been commenting on the contemporary world for more than a quarter of a century. In the selection that follows he presents a penetrating critique of modern industrial society and offers his proposals for reform. Why, according to Fromm, does increased economic well-being fail to satisfy modern man? What do Capitalism and Communism have in common with respect to goals and organization? Other than atomic war, what great danger does modern man face? Why is he alienated? What is Fromm's solution? How does it differ from proposals by President Johnson?

... [I]n the middle of the twentieth century, a drastic change is occurring, a change as great as ever occurred in the past. The new techniques replace the use of the physical energy of animals and men by that of steam, oil and electricity; they create means of communication which transform the earth into the size of one continent, and the human race into one society where the fate of one group is the fate of all; they create marvels of devices which permit the best of art, literature and music to be brought to every member of society; they create productive forces which will permit everybody to have a dignified material existence, and reduces work to such dimensions that it will fill only a fraction of man's day.

Yet today, when man seems to have reached the beginning of a new, richer, happier human era, his existence and that of the generations to follow is more threatened than ever. How is this possible?

Man had won his freedom from clerical and secular authorities, he stood alone with his reason and his conscience as his only judges, but he was afraid of the newly won freedom; he had achieved "freedom from"— without yet having achieved "freedom to"—to be himself, to be productive, to be fully awake. Thus he tried to escape from freedom. His very achievement, the mastery over nature, opened up the avenues for his escape.

In building the new industrial machine, man became so absorbed in the new task that it became the paramount goal of his life. His energies, which once were devoted to the search for God and salvation, were now directed toward the domination of nature and ever-increasing material comfort. He ceased to use production as a means for a better life, but hypostatized it instead to an end in itself, an end to which life was subordi-

* Eric Fromm, *The Sane Society* (Fawcett Publications, Inc., 1965), pp. 308-15. Copyright © 1955 by Eric Fromm. Reprinted by permission of Holt, Rinehart and Winston, Inc.

nated. In the process of an ever-increasing division of labor, ever-increasing mechanization of work, and an ever-increasing size of social agglomerations, man himself became a part of the machine, rather than its master. He experienced himself as a commodity, as an investment; his aim became to be a success, that is, to sell himself as profitably as possible on the market. His value as a person lies in his salability, not in his human qualities of love, reason, or in his artistic capacities. Happiness becomes identical with consumption of newer and better commodities, the drinking in of music, screen plays, fun, sex, liquor and cigarettes. Not having a sense of self except the one which comformity with the majority can give, he is insecure, anxious, depending on approval. He is alienated from himself, worships the product of his own hands, the leaders of his own making, as if they were above him, rather than made by him. He is in a sense back where he was before the great human evolution began in the second millennium B.C.

He is incapable to love and to use his reason, to make decisions, in fact incapable to appreciate life and thus ready and even willing to destroy everything. The world is again fragmentalized, has lost its unity; he is again worshiping diversified things, with the only exception that now they are man-made, rather than part of nature.

The new era started with the idea of individual initiative. Indeed, the discoverers of new worlds and sea lanes in the sixteenth and seventeenth centuries, the pioneers of science, and the founders of new philosophies, the statesmen and philosophers of the great English, French and American revolutions, and eventually, the industrial pioneers, and even the robber barons showed marvelous individual initiative. But with the bureaucratization and managerialization of Capitalism, it is exactly the individual initiative that is disappearing. Bureaucracy has little initiative, that is its nature; nor have automatons. The cry for individual initiative as an argument for Capitalism is at best a nostalgic yearning, and at worst a deceitful slogan used against those plans for reform which are based on the idea of truly human individual initiative. Modern society has started out with the vision of creating a culture which would fulfill man's needs; it has as its ideal the harmony between the individual and social needs, the end of the conflict between human nature and the social order. One believed one would arrive at this goal in two ways; by the increased productive technique which permitted feeding everybody satisfactorily, and by a rational, objective picture of man and of his real needs. Putting it differently, the aim of the efforts of modern man was to create a sane society. More specifically, this meant a society whose members have developed their reason to that point of objectivity which permits them to see themselves, others, nature, in their true reality, and not distorted by infantile omniscience or paranoid hate. It meant a society, whose members have developed to a point of independence where they know the difference between good and evil, where they make their own choices, where they have convictions rather than opinions, faith rather than superstitions or nebulous hopes. It meant a society whose members have developed the capacity to love their children, their neighbors, all men, themselves, all of nature; who can feel one with all, yet retain their sense of individuality and integrity; who transcend nature by creating, not by destroying.

So far, we have failed. We have not

bridged the gap between a minority which realized these goals and tried to live according to them, and the majority whose mentality is far back, in the Stone Age, in totemism, in idol worship, in feudalism. Will the majority be converted to sanity—or will it use the greatest discoveries of human reason for its own purposes of unreason and insanity? Will we be able to create a vision of the good, sane life, which will stir the life forces of those afraid of marching forward? This time, mankind is at one crossroad where the wrong step could be the last step.

In the middle of the twentieth century, two great social colossi have developed which, being afraid of each other, seek security in ever-increasing military rearmament. The United States and her allies are wealthier; their standard of living is higher, their interest in comfort and pleasure is greater than that of their rivals, the Soviet Union and her satellites, and China. Both rivals claim that their system promises final salvation for man, guarantees the paradise of the future. Both claim that the opponent represents the exact opposite to himself, and that his system must be eradicated—in the short or long run— if mankind is to be saved. Both rivals speak in terms of nineteenth-century ideals. The West in the name of the ideas of the French Revolution, of liberty, reason, individualism. The East in the name of the socialist ideas of solidarity, equality. They both succeed in capturing the imagination and the fanatical allegiance of hundreds of millions of people.

There is today a decisive difference between the two systems. In the Western world there is freedom to express ideas critical of the existing system. In the Soviet world criticism and expression of different ideas are suppressed by brutal force. Hence,

the Western world carries within itself the possibility for peaceful progressive transformation, while in the Soviet world such possibilities are almost non-existent; in the Western world the life of the individual is free from the terror of imprisonment, torture or death, which confront any member of the Soviet society who has not become a well-functioning automaton. Indeed, life in the Western world has been, and is even now sometimes as rich and joyous as it has ever been anywhere in human history; life in the Soviet system can never be joyous, as indeed it can never be where the executioner watches behind the door.

But without ignoring the tremendous differences between free Capitalism and authoritarian Communism today, it is shortsighted not to see the similarities, especially as they will develop in the future. Both systems are based on industrialization, their goal is ever-increasing economic efficiency and wealth. They are societies run by a managerial class, and by professional politicians. They both are thoroughly materialistic in their outlook, regardless of Christian ideology in the West and secular messianism in the East. They organize man in a centralized system, in large factories, political mass parties. Everybody is a cog in the machine, and has to function smoothly. In the West, this is achieved by a method of psychological conditioning, mass suggestion, monetary rewards. In the East by all this, plus the use of terror. It is to be assumed that the more the Soviet system develops economically, the less severely will it have to exploit the majority of the population, hence the more can terror be replaced by methods of psychological manipulation. The West develops rapidly in the direction of Huxley's *Brave New World*, the East *is* today Orwell's

"1984." But both systems tend to converge.

What, then, are the prospects for the future? The first, and perhaps most likely possibility, is that of atomic war. The most likely outcome of such a war is the destruction of industrial civilization, and the regression of the world to a primitive agrarian level. Or, if the destruction should not prove to be as thorough as many specialists in the field believe, the result will be the necessity for the victor to organize and dominate the whole world. This could only happen in a centralized state based on force—and it would make little difference whether Moscow or Washington were the seat of government. But, unfortunately, even the avoidance of war alone does not promise a bright future. In the development of both Capitalism and Communism as we can visualize them in the next fifty or a hundred years, the process of automatization and alienation will proceed. Both systems are developing into managerial societies, their inhabitants well fed, well clad, having their wishes satisfied, and not having wishes which cannot be satisfied; automatons, who follow without force, who are guided without leaders, who make machines which act like men and produce men who act like machines; men, whose reason deteriorates while their intelligence rises, thus creating the dangerous situation of equipping man with the greatest material power without the wisdom to use it.

This alienation and automatization leads to an ever-increasing insanity. Life has no meaning, there is no joy, no faith, no reality. Everybody is "happy"—except that he does not feel, does not reason, does not love.

In the nineteenth century the problem was that *God is dead;* in the twentieth century the problem is that *man is dead.* In the nineteenth century inhumanity meant cruelty; in the twentieth century it means schizoid self-alienation. The danger of the past was that men became slaves. The danger of the future is that men may become robots. True enough, robots do not rebel. But given man's nature, robots cannot live and remain sane, they become "Golems," they will destroy their world and themselves because they cannot stand any longer the boredom of a meaningless life.

Our dangers are war and robotism. What is the alternative? To get out of the rut in which we are moving, and to take the next step in the birth and self-realization of humanity. The first condition is the abolishment of the war threat hanging over all of us now and paralyzing faith and initiative. We must take the responsibility for the life of all men, and develop on an international scale what all great countries have developed internally, a relative sharing of wealth and a new and more just division of economic resources. This must lead eventually to forms of international economic co-operation and planning, to forms of world government and to complete disarmament. We must retain the industrial method. But we must decentralize work and state so as to give it *human proportions*, and permit centralization only to an optimal point which is necessary because of the requirements of industry. In the economic sphere we need co-management of all who work in an enterprise, to permit their active and responsible participation. The new forms for such participation can be found. In the political sphere, return to the town meetings, by creating thousands of small face-to-face groups, which are well informed, which discuss, and whose decisions are integrated in a new "lower house." A cultural renaissance must combine work education for the young, adult education and a new system of popular art and secular ritual throughout the whole nation.

Our only alternative to the danger of robotism is humanistic communitarianism. The problem is not primarily the legal problem of property ownership, nor that of sharing *profits;* it is that of sharing *work,* sharing *experience.* Changes in ownership must be made to the extent to which they are necessary to create a community of work, and to prevent the profit motive from directing production into socially harmful directions. Income must be equalized to the extent of giving everybody the material basis for a dignified life, and thus preventing the economic differences from creating a fundamentally different experience of life for various social classes. Man must be restored to his supreme place in society, never being a means, never a thing to be used by others or by himself. Man's use by man must end, and economy must become the servant for the development of man. Capital must serve labor, things must serve life. Instead of the exploitative and hoarding orientation, dominant in the nineteenth century, and the receptive and marketing orientation dominant today, the *productive orientation* must be the end which all social arrangements serve.

*   *   *

Man today is confronted with the most fundamental choice; not that between Capitalism or Communism, but that between *robotism* (of both the capitalist and the communist variety), or Humanistic Communitarian Socialism. Most facts seem to indicate that he is choosing robotism, and that means, in the long run, insanity and destruction. But all these facts are not strong enough to destroy faith in man's reason, good will and sanity. As long as we can think of other alternatives, we are not lost; as long as we can consult together and plan together, we can hope. But, indeed, the shadows are lengthening; the voices of insanity are becoming louder. We are in reach of achieving a state of humanity which corresponds to the vision of our great teachers; yet we are in danger of the destruction of all civilization, or of robotization. A small tribe was told thousands of years ago: "I put before you life and death, blessing and curse—and you chose life." This is our choice too.

2

Towards a Great Society *

LYNDON B. JOHNSON

In the closing days of the presidential campaign of 1964, Lyndon Johnson attempted to define goals for America beyond economic necessities. Speaking in Madison Square Garden, he stressed the "quality of the lives that our people lead." This vision of a Great Society emphasized education, beauty, and creative leisure, rather than the older objectives of food, clothing, and shelter. This shift in emphasis was widely heralded as a new departure in American life—a pledge that government would become an instrument for achieving the "good life" beyond economic ends.

Should such a pledge be regarded as simply a vote-getting device? If this use of government is justified, how effective can it be in achieving a "Great Society"? On the other hand, can Americans ever "open the doors of learning, fruitful labor and rewarding leisure" without using government as an instrument of the national purpose?

We are going to work to enlarge the freedom of the American people, and we have the capacity to do that on a scale that's greater than ever before in the history of man.

First Objective

Our first task is to complete the work of the last 30 years, so we will work to give every citizen an equal chance to hold a job, to vote, to educate his children, to enjoy all the blessings of liberty, whatever his color, his religion or his race. Will you stand with me on that?

We will work to elminate the conditions which chain men to hopeless poverty and, in this way, to eliminate poverty in America.

Just 100 years ago Abraham Lincoln abolished slavery. Tonight the Democratic party pledges itself to abolish poverty in this land.

We will work to protect the old, and feed the hungry and care for the helpless.

Will you stand with me on that?

But this is just the beginning. We are rich and we are powerful, but that is not enough. We must turn our wealth and our power to a larger purpose.

Even the greatest of past civilizations existed on the exploitation of the many. This nation, this people, this generation, has man's first opportunity to create the Great Society.

It can be a society of success without squalor, beauty without barrenness, works of genius without the wretchedness of poverty. We can open the doors of learning, of fruitful labor and rewarding leisure—not just to the privileged few, but we can open them to everyone.

These goals cannot be measured by the size of our bank balance. They can only be measured in the quality of the lives that our people lead.

Millions of Americans have achieved prosperity, and they have found prosperity alone is just not enough. They need a chance to seek knowledge and to touch beauty—to rejoice in achievement and in the closeness of family and community, and this is not an easy goal.

It means insuring the beauty of our fields and our streams and the air that we breathe.

It means the education of the highest quality for every child in the land.

It means making sure that machines liberate men instead of replacing them.

It means reshaping and rebuilding our cities to make them safe, and make them a decent place to live.

Yes, it means all of these things and more—much more.

Answers Sought

I have already assembled more than a dozen groups, the best minds of America, the greatest talent that I could find, to help get the answers to these problems that I've talked to you about tonight.

For the first time in man's weary journey on this planet, an entire people has greatness almost within its grasp.

This is the goal within our sight. This is your goal.

This is America's goal.

This is the goal to which I pledge that I will try to lead all of you.

I have taken a long journey from a tenant farm in West Texas to this platform in Madison Square Garden.

I have seen the barren fields of my youth bloom with harvest.

I have seen despairing men made whole with enriching toil. I have seen my America grow and change, and I have seen it become a leader among the nations in the world.

In our early days some thought that the Mississippi would be our final boundary. The far-seeing Thomas Jefferson sent his explorers across the continent—and the American tide rolled after them. We, too, stand at the margin of decision.

Meeting the Future

Ahead is the prospect of a shining nation of towering promise. Behind is a threatening tide of change and growth, of expanding population and exploding science. And there is only one way to go.

The only way to preserve the values of the past is to meet the future.

The path to progress stretches in front of us, not back along the way we came.

And with the help of that Almighty God who has guided us whenever we have been true to Him, that is the way that we are going.

3

American Civilization: Beyond Economics *

PETER F. DRUCKER

The author suggests that old political loyalties are giving way in America to new alignments—that the economic questions that forged the New Deal, Fair Deal, and New Frontier are disappearing. The burning issues of the future, he suggests, will be concerned with the quality of American life. If Drucker's analysis is correct, what impact will this have on American politics? What will the "quality" issues be? Education? The fine arts? A war on the ugliness of the landscape? If not these issues, what others?

. . . The United States almost certainly is entering into a period of political turbulence unlike anything we have known for at least a generation. In the decades just ahead, our domestic politics will be dominated by unfamiliar issues—not only new, but different in kind from the things we have been arguing about since 1932. They will be concerned, not primarily with economic matters, but with basic values—moral, aesthetic, and philosophical. Moreover, the center of our political stage is now being taken over by a new power group: a professional, technical, and managerial middle class—very young, affluent, used to great job security, and highly educated. It will soon displace the old power centers—labor, the farm bloc, Big Business in the old-fashioned sense of that term. Around this new power center tomorrow's majority and tomorrow's consensus about the new issues will have to be built.

But the process will be accomplished only after eye-gouging struggles and bitter disagreement over the way to tackle our new set of national problems. For traditional power groups never give up their dominion gracefully; nor is it easy for any of us to turn our eyes away from the old, familiar issues which have preoccupied us for so long. Witness how the Goldwater people, during the last campaign, were obsessed almost exclusively with their yearning to repeal history.

The old questions—mostly economic—of course will not go away. Debate over the role and limitations of the unions surely will be with us for a good long time. So will our worry about intractable poverty in the midst of affluence . . . about the impact of automation . . . about tax policy, conservation, and many another ancient staple.

But the focus of domestic politics is likely to shift to two new areas: *the metropolis and the school.*

The major new issue of the last few years has been the Negro's integration into American society. It became a political issue precisely because economics alone could not solve the race problem. A good many civil-rights problems, of course, look as if they were primarily economic—access of the Negro to membership in craft unions, for instance. But at bottom we all know that it is our hearts, and not just our pocketbooks, that we are asked to open.

The central problem of the metropolis is not an economic one. It is concerned with political structure, indeed our political constitution. In the coming debate over the schools, educational policy and purpose will clearly be the focal points. In both cases, the ultimate issue is the quality of life in America. . . .

*   *   *

The Schools Move into Politics

Education has been our chief "growth industry" in the last twenty years. If the economists considered schooling part of the national product (as they should), our economic growth rate would have looked pretty good all through the postwar period.

But an even greater expansion is just ahead. It will catapult the American school into national politics. The colleges during the next few years—as by now everybody must have heard—will be hit by the wave of youngsters born during the "baby boom" following World War II (and unlike most booms this one was not followed by a bust, and there is no reduction in the numbers of young people in sight). Five to eight years from now, around 50 per cent more students should be in American colleges than are there today. The greatest growth will be in an entirely new and largely untried institution, the two-year "community college," which, unlike any earlier college in American history, is usually run by the same local school board that administers the public schools. Meanwhile, the private college, at least as far as undergraduate education goes, will become quantitatively an almost negligible factor.

Before we can digest the abrupt jump in college enrollment, the next wave will hit the elementary schools—the children being born now to the "baby boom" generation of the 1950s. This will increase public-school enrollment, grade by grade, by another 40 to 50 per cent until, around 1980 or so, this wave finally washes over the colleges once more.

The first consequence will be a drastic increase in the costs of education. And to make this increase even more drastic, salaries will certainly go up again, since the supply of qualified teachers cannot possibly keep up with this sudden jump in demand. It is hard to see how we can avoid large-scale federal support for education on all levels. In the poorer areas in particular, the schools already cost more than the local population can afford. It is sheer hypocrisy to pretend that federal support of education is possible without some considerable measure of national control. Will we support, for instance, schools that practice racial segregation? Or schools with curricula and standards below a national minimum, or with a short school year?

At the same time a technological revolution will hit American education. "Programmed learning" is the first major technological change in teaching and learning since the printed book—and likely to have equal impact.

The teacher shortage alone will hurry programmed learning, no matter how sturdily the teaching profession resists. However, only skills and knowledge can be transmitted through a program. Everything else—character, values, behavior, and above all the use of imagination and the discovery of the new and exciting—requires a teacher. Programmed instruction, therefore, predictably will unleash a debate over the function and methods of the American school such as we have not seen for a long time. Opponents will argue that it undermines the basic educational values and underfeeds the growing child. On the other side will be the fanatics who see in programmed instruction a panacea—which it surely will not be —and the doctrinaires who want to eliminate as "unscientific" whatever in the school curriculum cannot be programmed.

Altogether our society will be school-centered. At least one third of the American people will be in school a few years hence. (Only one fourth is there now.) Preschool children, ready for nursery school or kindergarten, will make up another tenth of the population. Teachers are already the largest single occupational group in the country. Total school expenditures, a few years from now, will exceed our present defense budget by a substantial amount. (Today they already run around thirty billions a year.) At the same time, the structure of American education, its purposes, values, content, and direction will all become hot issues.

Education is about to take over from the Welfare State as a basic commitment of the American people. One might call this new phenomenon the Knowledge State. Education is bound to become a focus of political life and political conflicts. So far, however, we have not even begun to think through national policies on education, let alone a national commitment to educational values and purposes. All we

have so far—and it is a great deal— is a national commitment to education in quantity, and for everyone.

The Young Take Over

President Johnson may be tempted to maintain a little longer the cozy illusion of an "Era of Good Feeling." But it can't last—partly because the new issues already are exploding, partly because a new power center is about to emerge on the American scene. Whatever the President may want, the educated young people who make up the professional, technical, and managerial middle classes will force on us new political alignments.

In 1960, when Kennedy was elected, the average American was about thirty-three years old. By 1968 the mid-age will have dropped to twenty-five or lower. This age drop—eight years within the span of eight years —is the biggest ever recorded in American history. It must also be one of the biggest any country ever went through. The reason is, of course, that because of the lean birth years of the 'thirties, relatively few Americans are now reaching middle age; while those born in the bumper years right after the war are now coming to maturity. (The over-sixty-five group, which has grown so rapidly in these past decades, will definitely become a static proportion of the population after 1970.) For the next fifteen years, then, the most rapidly expanding age group will be young adults reaching voting age. By 1970 ours will be the youngest country in the Free World. And the center of political gravity will soon lie with a generation that will know the New Deal and even World War II only out of history books, and as events that happened mostly before it was born.

In "psychological age" we will be even younger, and the jump between generations will be greater still. One out of every three Americans alive in the early 1970s is likely to be in school—a bigger percentage than in any other country. In their outlook on life and politics, students are "young," even if they are in graduate school and twenty-five years old, for they still consider themselves outside of the labor force.

More important than the age shift itself is the shift in expectations, from the New Deal and World War II generations to that now coming of age. Fully one half of the young men now reaching adulthood have education beyond high school. Consequently, most of them join the professional, technical, and managerial class expecting high opportunities for themselves and even greater for their children. By contrast, work as a machine operator or as a salesgirl was the normal expectation for the last large wave of young people to become voters—the generation that reached adulthood in the late 'twenties and the 'thirties; in education they had gone no further, by and large, than a year or two in high school.

The initiative in American politics has already shifted to this new group. Boys still in college or just out of it discovered Barry Goldwater ("invented him" might be a more appropriate term), made him their hero, and furnished the fanatical following which bludgeoned a reluctant Republican party into accepting him as its candidate. It was the educated young Negro who overthrew his old "moderate" leadership and forced the pace of civil rights. Both the Civil Rights Act and the forcing of school integration even in rural Mississippi are due largely to the explosive response of white youths in college and high school to the cry for racial justice. And the one innovation in American political institutions since President Truman has been the college students' very own Peace Corps.

The educated and affluent managerial, professional, and technical people are of course only one half—perhaps a little more—of the young adults. In the other half is a small but highly visible group: the "problems" (largely members of the minority groups in big cities) who become school dropouts, narcotics addicts, and unemployables. The more affluent our society becomes, the greater will be our concern with them—especially as we are unlikely to find a cure fast.

The Politics of Youth

But political and social power will not be where the "problems" are. It will lie increasingly with the successful, well-adjusted young people who are the beneficiaries of this high-pressure and high-education society of ours. Their buying will largely shape the economy. Economic policies will inevitably be tailored to their needs and aspirations. They are the community leaders of tomorrow. Above all they will have the voting power. They are not only the largest but the only homogeneous group among the new voters—and different from any earlier group. They already dominate the suburbs, which increasingly hold the decisive vote in the big states. Before long, no party and no major candidate will be able to win unless they carry at least a large minority of the affluent, young, educated middle class. And no national consensus will be possible which does not in large numbers reflect their beliefs, attitudes, and values. *Here is the center around which the New Majority will have to be built, and which will determine the direction and the character of American politics for the next generation.*

Yet this group, so far, is politically faceless. It has not aligned itself. Indeed, it does not fit into the present structure of American politics. To ask, say, whether these educated young people are "conservatives" or "liberals" makes practically no sense.

By the traditional yardsticks of American politics, they would appear to be highly conservative. They are the first "haves" in a long time to become a major new power center. Their incomes are well above average. Their jobs are as secure as jobs can be—or at least look to them secure enough—and their opportunities are great. They do not identify themselves with the traditional liberal groups. They are certainly not pro-labor. A proposal to do away with restrictive practices of the labor unions—for instance, by bringing labor under the antitrust laws—would probably be supported by most of them. If they identify themselves at all, in terms of economic interests or social position, it is with management. Even the young teachers are likely to think and speak of themselves as professional people.

Yet they also do not answer the traditional definition of the conservative in American politics. They are hired hands. Most of them have never met a payroll and do not expect ever to have to meet one. They surely have little in common with the small businessman. And even among the young engineers or market researchers in the big companies, who clearly identify themselves with management —indeed, even among the young owner-managers and entrepreneurs who form the membership of the Young Presidents Organization—John F. Kennedy, despite his much-publicized "hostility to business," would (according to all reports) have polled a larger vote than did Lyndon Johnson, whose "understanding of busi-

ness" had potent appeal to so many of the older big-business executives. A good many of the issues which traditionally marked the boundary line between "conservative" and "liberal" can hardly be explained to them.

I found this out last fall when I spent an evening with an extremely bright group of graduate students and young instructors at a large Midwestern university. Senator Goldwater had just proposed turning over the Tennessee Valley Authority to private enterprise. The proposal seemed quite reasonable to most of the young men, few of whom, otherwise, had much use for Goldwater. After all, they argued, why should the government do a better job than private enterprise as manager of power stations and fertilizer plants? "To plan and to build a TVA required government of course; but in running it is government likely to contribute much?" What puzzled them, however, was the reason for making an issue out of this. "Why not call in competent economists and management engineers and have them find out what would be most efficient?" Most of the men were political scientists or economists and had heard—if only vaguely—of yesterday's great private-versus-public-power controversy. But, in their own words, it seemed to them as irrelevant and as quaint as the debate over free silver.

A few years ago it was fashionable to explain this detachment from the burning issues of yesterday as "apathy." But the events of the last few years—the Goldwater movement, for instance, or the civil-rights explosion —have clearly shown that the educated young people of the new power center are passionate in their politics to the point of violence.

The true explanation may well be that these young people will not define themselves politically in the terms

in which American political alignments have been couched for seventy
years—since Mark Hanna created the
modern Republican party after 1896
—that is, in terms of economic issues
and interests. Feeling secure in their
jobs, they are free from the driving
fear of yesterday's "have-nots." Being
employees, they lack any grim determination to defend property rights.
But they care deeply for education—
for themselves and their children—
and for their community. They are
passionate about those matters that
directly touch them, and have a direct
impact on their security, opportunities, and place in society. They will,
therefore, be highly susceptible to
such new issues as metropolitan structure and educational purpose.

Economics Becomes a Bore

For the last seventy years at least,
economic issues have defined the
political position of an individual or
of a group in the American spectrum.
Non-economic issues were largely
treated as adjuncts; the position of a
man on economic issues determined,
by and large, where he stood on all
others. Where a non-economic issue
could not be folded into an economic
framework—for example, a good many
foreign-policy issues—we tried, on the
whole with success, to treat it as
"bipartisan."

But for the new power center, these
non-economic issues may well become
the core of political belief and action.
Consequently, the attempt to build a
new majority around this center—that
is, the attempt to find a community
of interests and viewpoints between
the new group and the older national
groups, such as labor and agriculture
—must center on non-economic issues.
It must focus on the quality of life,
rather than on the division of the
economic product.

Whenever a decisive new power
center has appeared in our history—
the New West of the 1820s, the skilled
worker around 1890, or the machine
operator in mass-production industry
between 1910 and 1930—the political
map of the country was overturned
as if by an earthquake. Such changes
are always dangerous. The general
confusion over issues and alignments
opens the door wide to the demagogue and the rabble-rouser. But such
an earthquake change also makes possible the creative leadership of an
Andrew Jackson, a Teddy Roosevelt,
or a Franklin Roosevelt. Each of these
managed to forge a new majority in
which the needs of the new power
center of his time became the foundation for effective national policy and
constructive political achievements.

Lyndon Johnson's Dilemma

Lyndon Johnson made his way to
the top as a superb tactician of the
American political process, with a rare
instinct for the timing needed to make
effective an already formulated idea,
and to push forward an already accepted policy. He has been commander rather than strategist. Now he
must demonstrate—if he has it—a different kind of talent: the art of political innovation, of leadership in formulating new issues and in designing
new policies.

In years of political service, Lyndon
Johnson (who first went to Washington as a Congressional assistant just
before Hoover left the White House)
is the most senior leader of the Free
World. Yet his Presidency will see a
generation-jump which will shift the
center of political gravity to an age-
group so young that it can barely
remember World War II, let alone
the Depression.

Johnson is the one original New
Dealer still prominent in American

political life, yet his success as President will largely depend on his attracting and inspiring a host of middle-class young people who have traditionally been somewhat right of center, and who barely understand the New Deal issues, emotions, and experiences. In this tension between what he has been and what he will have to be lies Lyndon Johnson's dilemma.

There is only one precedent in American history for the 1964 election, only one parallel to this President's situation. That is the 1896 election and the position of the victorious Republicans afterwards. There may be a powerful lesson for today in this parallel. In both elections the spotlight of the campaign was not on the winner—McKinley aroused as little popular enthusiasm as did Lyndon Johnson. The loser was the focal point.

There are striking similarities between Barry Goldwater and William Jennings Bryan, their respective campaigns and their defeats. Both men aimed at a coalition of the disaffected. Both embodied, in their righteous confusion, the frustration and bafflement of a great many Americans at the speed and ruthlessness with which change had plowed under all the landmarks of their accustomed world. Both, while publicly disavowing bigotry, exploited it. Both represented fundamentalism—that is, the refusal to think—as a considered political philosophy. Both hinged their strategy on the rural South and its revolt. Both thereby alienated large numbers of the one group they absolutely needed to win: the new power center. In 1896 this was the skilled industrial workers—foundrymen, printers, crane

operators in the steel mills; in 1964 it is the young technical, professional, and managerial middle class.

But the winners, too, found themselves in very similar positions. In choosing Lyndon Johnson as in choosing McKinley, the American people voted *against* irresponsibility, unreason, dissension, and bigotry. They did not vote *for* a man and even less *for* issues, programs, and policies. In both elections the victor was the last of his line. As Mr. Johnson is the last New Dealer, so McKinley was the last Civil War veteran to attain political prominence. Like Mr. Johnson today, McKinley in 1896 found himself in a new and alien world—with a new power center, and with no fresh issues to take the place of the old slogans of Reconstruction.

The Opportunity

The comparison with 1896 also suggests that such an election creates a tremendous opportunity. It is a great emotional trauma, which tears people off their old political moorings and sets them adrift—ready to be caught by new currents. It forces people who normally react to politics in terms of simple clichés—the great majority for whom politics is only of peripheral importance—to reexamine their stand. Altogether the year from President Kennedy's assassination to President Johnson's election was a year of shock, of self-questioning, of self-doubt such as must leave lasting effects. And it demonstrated that there is no going back to yesterday, even for the most nostalgic. As a result there is wide awareness of the need for something new, and receptivity to it.

4

Leisure Time: The Age of Fulfillment *

RALPH LAZARUS

Leisure has normally been equated with evil by Americans. Our tradition has stressed the virtues of work; we have told our children that the Devil makes work for idle hands to do. But today's shorter work week, longer and longer periods of adolescence and preliminary education, plus extended periods of retirement have made leisure a fact of life for millions of Americans.

How can we capitalize on our good fortune? Should the schools train students for both on-the-job and leisure time activity? Should government play a positive role? Is leisure in growing amounts a basic component of the good society?

❋   ❋   ❋

I shall begin with a proposition. Let us suppose, as many well-informed people believe, that the most important product of what is now being called the Second Industrial Revolution will turn out to be time—oceans of it. You may call it leisure time, idle time, unwanted time or free time, depending on your personal outlook on life. In any case, it is a commodity we are not presently prepared to consume in the bounteous quantities in which it is going to be presented to us by the new factory and office systems that are now being dreamed up in our automation laboratories.

❋   ❋   ❋

Public speculation about future disposable time has, as you know, taken all sorts of forms. Those who base their predictions on the past point to the historical trend of productivity—

the raw material which we convert into shorter hours or higher living standards. They do not expect the pace of productivity to increase too much, except in fits and starts, and they believe that we will continue, as we have in recent years, to prefer to exchange its fruits for more material goods and services rather than for shorter working hours, days or years. In other words, in their view, the American people will continue to prefer being rich to being idle. The unpredictable factors that they believe might upset this forecast are an abrupt end to the cold war or our continued failure to solve what is now called hard-core unemployment. Either could lead to the political solution of shortening the work week by law.

There are others who state with varying degrees of emotion that those who depend on the past as a reliable guide in the age of automation have their heads buried in the sand. They point out that just as mechanization replaced man's muscles with the machine, automation is gradually re-

* Ralph Lazarus, "The Age of Fulfillment," *Vital Speeches of the Day,* March 1, 1964, pp. 301-4. Reprinted by permission of the publisher.

placing his senses of sight and touch. Perhaps the best way to visualize the result of this is through the words that an excutive in an automated plant used to describe a machinist's new job. "All he has to do," the executive said, "is press the button to start the machine and then monitor it. All he has to know is what his machine looks like so he can find it when he comes to work."

❊   ❊   ❊

What will be the future impact of automation on work? No one knows, but a few imaginative people are guessing. John Diebold, one of the young prophets in this new field, wrote an article recently for *McCall's* to which an excited editor attached this headline: "When Will Your Husband Be Obsolete?" In it Diebold predicted that within the next generation the work of 60 million Americans is "practically certain to be obsolete."

If we work with known facts, we need to make only a few fairly conservative assumptions, in my opinion, to reach the conclusion that our economy is going to provide us with substantial blocks of spare time in the next 15 or 20 years. Between 1900 and 1940 technological advances allowed us to reduce the work week by one-third, or from 60 down to 40 hours, while more than tripling real per capita income. Though we have slowed the pace of turning productivity gains into greater leisure since 1940, it seems to me we shall soon have to quicken it again because of the pressure from scientific research and development—commonly called R & D—which has been preparing quite a package of goodies to unload on us in the near future. The government alone has multiplied its commitments for R & D spending more than five times since 1955 and last

year it obligated $15 billion, or 15 cents out of every tax dollar, for this purpose.

❊   ❊   ❊

These discoveries will produce countless new products and new jobs, but their impact on working time is sure to be considerable. If we were able to cut working time by one-third during the first 40 years of this century, it should now take us fewer decades to repeat the performance. One-third of a working life is more than 15 years. It therefore seems to me that a reasonable hypothesis on which to proceed is that by, let us say, 1985, we should have accumulated at least a decade of disposable time per person.

Let us skip over the intervening years now and take a look at life in 1985. I suggest this, not to belittle the enormous human and social problems that will confront us between now and then, as the speed of technological change steps up, but because I want to focus your attention on the goal ahead—the society of fulfillment that I believe is within the grasp of our children. If we think now, we can create that society so that they can live in it later. If we know what our goal is, we can wend our way far more successfully through the maze of problems that lie between us and it.

The first thing to think about is our attitudes toward non-work, for by 1985 automation may have forced our nation to turn leisure from a luxury into a virtue. We are automatically repelled by such an idea. It runs directly counter to the work ethic, which was rooted in our culture as far back as the third chapter of Genesis, when the Lord threw Adam out of the Garden of Eden. He condemned man to eternal labor in these memorable words, "In the sweat of thy face shalt thou eat bread."

Work has been integrated into man's moral code since the beginning. Social organization had its inception as a device to get the working and fighting done effectively. Only when these tasks were organized with real efficiency could more than 10 to 15 per cent of any society live at much above the starvation level. This has been true up until the last five minutes of history.

This country was built on the Puritan belief that honest toil was the foundation of character, the cement of society and the uphill road to progress. Idleness was a sin. With such a heritage, only the exceptional American feels comfortable with the philosophy of the pensioned steel worker who said he hopes never to die because he thinks it is such a fine joke to be paid for doing nothing.

As a result, we treat free time today as a conditional joy. We permit ourselves to relax only as a reward for hard work or as the recreation needed to put us back into shape for the job. The aimless, delightful play of children gives way in adult life to a serious dedication to golf, the game that is so good for business.

Because of these attitudes, the prospect of having additional time off in blocks large enough to add up to a disposable decade is greeted with a reaction that is far closer to fright than to eagerness. To our guilt about idleness is added a fear akin to that of unemployment. Unemployment no longer brings starvation, but it does threaten that a life built around work could be robbed of meaning. It is an awesome prospect that the new leisure might force us to search for the meaning of life within ourselves. For this is a truly under-developed territory, one whose resources society has hardly encouraged us to explore.

Those of you who think historically may feel that I have been painting a rather distorted picture. You may think that to treat leisure as a plague is like treating love as a communicable disease. To be liberated from the prison of work has been a consuming desire of man ever since he learned to write down his dreams. "The wisdom of the scribe cometh by opportunity of leisure," says Ecclesiasticus, "and he that hath little business shall become wise."

Leisure was a passion to the Greeks, as we all know. It was the duty of the state to provide it. It was neither work nor play but the opportunity to enjoy the fruits of the mind, to enlarge vision and understanding, to cultivate individualism and perfect the art of government. Without the political theory, sculpture, architecture, drama, philosophy and history that flowed out of this sunburst of leisure, modern man would be measurably poorer. And with the Athenians' ideas of science and freedom we might still be living under an absolute monarch and just beginning to invent the steam engine.

*   *   *

If the skeptics feel inclined to point out that Greek leisure was built on the labor of slaves, it can be rejoined that we now have the opportunity of building it on the labor of machines, which even now provide every man, woman and child in the U.S. with the power equivalent of more than 70 slaves apiece. Even this was foreseen by the Athenians. Listen carefully to Aristotle as he dreamed about automation out loud: "If every tool when summoned, or even of its own accord, could do the work that befits it . . . if the weaver's shuttle were to weave itself, then there would be no need either of workers by masters or of slaves by lords."

Perhaps the leisure of Greek life seems to us to be slightly un-American. If so, let us skip forward two millenia in time, hopping warily over the Puritans, and land in Philadelphia right in the midst of our own Periclean Age, the era of Jefferson. We find that glorious product of colonial leisure in the second-floor parlor of a house at Seventh and Market Streets writing the words: "We hold these truths to be self-evident, that all men are created equal, that they are endowed by their Creator with certain inalienable rights, that among these are life, liberty and the pursuit of happiness."

"The pursuit of happiness" was not just the whimsical phrase of one man, it went through all the re-drafts of the Declaration without change. It was central to Jefferson's complex philosophy. John Adams did not consider it even a novel political theory. "Upon this point all speculative politicians will agree," he wrote, "that the happiness of society is the end of government, as all divine and moral philosophers will agree that the happiness of the individual is the end of man."

Most of our contemporaries are extremely uncomfortable with this concept, which was based on faith in man, faith that his pursuit of self-fulfillment would not end up in just a pursuit of self-indulgence. Jefferson's faith got lost somewhere in the nineteenth century. What emerged out of the night of Victorian materialism was Josh Billings' definition of happiness: "Most of the happiness in this world konsists in possessing what others kant git."

* * *

We have to be thinking of a decade of disposable time, according to my guess, by 1985 or a decade and a half within 30 years. This is a third of a working lifetime.

We do not know, of course, how this free time will be divided up among our occupations. The presumption is that common labor will be hit first and that free time will move upwards and sideways through the skills on an unpredictable and erratic basis. The cynics say that those who have the lowest capacity for using free time constructively will get the most and that people like the members of this audience will actually have to work longer hours, since the demand for highly educated talents will far exceed the supply. But those who are bemused by the decision-making potential of the computer feel that some areas of middle management may face this problem, too. In any case, whether automation turns out to be an opportunity or a disaster, we must make sure that its effects are distributed equitably.

We do not know, either, in what kind of packages we will prefer to wrap this time. We may continue to use the old devices of shorter workdays and workweeks, holidays, vacations, later school years and earlier retirement. But none of these, for one reason or another, seems adequate to the task of bailing us out of the ocean of free time with which we will be inundated.

We must, therefore, free our imaginations enough to devise new forms for time away from regular jobs. The one that opens the most attractive horizons seems to be the sabbatical year. This, strangely enough, is an American invention, devised some 70 years ago but available as yet only to professors. Its purpose is to give them every seventh year off for study, travel and renewal.

If we adopted the sabbatical year for the rest of the population, what, you may ask, would they do with it?

The answer is that they would do with it what they wanted; I do not believe we should delegate their opportunities to the anxious planning of the social engineers.

Some of them would try to loaf, play or indulge their passing fancies. But few of them would make a success out of hedonism. Their neighbors and their children—particularly those children who are now studying harder than their parents ever did —will make it hard for them. But mainly they will make it hard for themselves. Much of the meaning of modern life has been built around work and man seems to fear emptiness more than he does sudden annihilation.

*   *   *

Let us concentrate then on breaking through the cast iron bonds of millenia of habits, philosophy and history that are holding back our imagination. For the task ahead is literally unprecedented; we shall have to invent the future. Perhaps a few ideas at this point would be helpful.

We might try to chase the meaninglessness out of modern life and search for a new purpose for man. Even after we dethrone work, we shall still have a few things left, such as love, beauty, truth, the endless frontiers of science and the Sermon on the Mount.

I suspect, though, that most of us find a new purpose in life most easily through what we do. And once we shift our sights as a people, we will find plenty to do. All around us there are mountains of unfinished business to tackle. If, in an automated society, we shall be able to pay men to loaf, why can't we pay them to finish unfinished business? And I am not thinking of a mammoth WPA. Certainly the government will play a role in this

future, but I hope private citizens and institutions will find enough daring and initiative to keep that role a minor one. But let us not forget that the government can be creative, too. Without expressing myself on any of its controversial details, it is clear that the concept of TVA still lifts the spirit and brightens the image of America throughout the world.

How much time and energy would it take to beautify our central cities and produce an atmosphere for living that would bring back the vast middle class? And what about our slums? The other day in New York I listened to a radio interview with a Puerto Rican who was describing the rooms in Harlem in which his family had been living, including the rats, the holes in the ceiling and the pipes that had been leaking steadily for five years. The general attitude on the program was that you can't fight City Hall. Can you imagine what would happen to City Hall if 10,000 sabbatical man-years were turned loose against it?

How much time and energy would it take to transmit the knowledge and technical skills that would enable the under-developed countries to abolish poverty, disease and ignorance so that they can secure for themselves their own versions of the better life? How much will it take to bring the neglected hordes of our own people up to the scale of health, wealth and education that we call the American way of life?

How many man-years of patient skill will we need to reverse the tide of school drop-outs for those who are capable of absorbing further education? What would happen if we decided to stockpile parks, forests and other recreational facilities ahead of the time when they will be gone forever?

There is no end to unfinished business. Our education can be expanded in quality, quantity and variety way beyond the hopes of our most visionary pedagogues. That we should do this is, in fact, the sternest commandment of the coming era of automation. The speed of change and the growing complexity of both knowledge and the world will force us to extend formal education throughout life in order to keep up with the demands of new and old occupations, starting with science, technology, medicine and foreign affairs. And, far more difficult than that, will be the reorientation of education in the earlier years from its primary emphasis on preparation for life to preparation for living. This is a revolution that will take a few decades to work our way through.

The character of the living process has hardly been touched in recent years. We have done a relatively good job of insuring domestic tranquility in the state within the meaning of the

Constitution. But how much domestic tranquility do we have in the family? How much serenity do we have in our lives? And how important is this to the future of the state?

I agree with David Riesman that there can be a surfeit of things but that the market for intangibles and the people who produce them is truly insatiable. . . .

And so I come back to Jefferson's concept of the pursuit of happiness. It was a central concept of the American Revolution, whose real meaning was not freedom from something but freedom for something. It was centered on man, not on the state. It was freedom for man to fulfill his ancient promise. This he has done, at least in part, by building a paradise of plenty. Let us now pick up the gauntlet where Jefferson dropped it in 1776 and use this plenty as the opportunity to fulfill the rest of the promise. Let us now start to build a home fit for the human spirit.

5

Technology and Education *

LEWIS PAUL TODD

The impetus towards quantitative measurement and statistical prediction is being extended to nearly every aspect of American life. Frequently this trend carries with it an assumption that everything can be reduced to such terms—that because the vocabulary of quality is imprecise, it does not actually exist. This attitude is now evident in American education, which is turning to the computer, teaching machine, and programmed learning. Can man retain his central position in the new educational patterns? Will he give way to a school system in which the process itself becomes the end? Are humaneness and the human qualities it implies to be victims of the new education?

Our present system of higher education, focused almost exclusively on the unlimited mass production of scientific truths, is utterly incapable of dealing with the most pressing problem of our age: namely, that of coping with the larger system of automation of which it is a part.

The indictment is Lewis Mumford's. He leveled it three years ago in an address delivered before the National Conference on Higher Education. In the address, "The Automation of Knowledge: Are We Becoming Robots?" Mumford sharply—and at times bitterly—attacked man's obsessive preoccupation with science and technology, and urged his audience, composed in large part of college and university administrators, to dedicate their institutions to the creation of "fully dimensioned human beings."

Mumford's warning, though pointed directly at higher education, was—and

is—just as relevant to education at the elementary and secondary levels. No, it is even more relevant, for if in the early years of schooling we sacrifice the human qualities of life on the altar of specialization and efficiency, the damage will be irreparable.

Plus and Minus

In order to understand what is happening to us, one must stand back, as Mumford does, and look at the problem from the large perspective of history.

Through the ages men have dreamed of human flight, instantaneous communication, and total control over the environment. They have dreamed of an economy of abundance in which "the shuttle would weave by itself, the lyre would play by itself, and loaves of bread would spring out of the oven untouched by human hand."

In our time all of these dreams, and achievements beyond the wildest imagining of earlier days, have been

---

* Lewis Paul Todd, *Civic Leader,* February 13, 1967, pp. 1-2. Reprinted by permission of the publisher.

realized. Powers the ancients attributed only to the gods of earth and sea and sky are today commonplace to even the poorest among men. In this respect, we are the most fortunate of all humans who have ever lived.

We owe our good fortune to those among us who over the past four centuries have developed modern science and technology. "But," Mumford reminds us, "as often happens when fairy stories come true, we are at last beginning to discover that there was a concealed catch in the original promise." The catch? We have become the captives of the system itself, thralls of the science and technology that have produced the riches, the material goods, we now enjoy.

The weakness, the fatal flaw, is inherent in the system itself. From the beginnings of modern science in the sixteenth and seventeenth centuries, "we find," as Mumford puts it, "that the very words *human, history, value, purpose* and *end* were excluded as extraneous and undesirable for any method of quantitative measurement and statistical prediction." In brief, as machines have become an increasingly integral part of life, we have become more and more dehumanized.

Men or Machines?

Mumford's quarrel is not with science and technology as such. He is as mindful as anyone else of the immense benefits they have conferred upon mankind and of the literally unlimited promise they hold for the future. He quarrels only with the notion—one unhappily all too widely entertained—that automation is so beneficial that the process should be extended into every field of activity, including of course education.

"If," he comments,

the human organism had developed on that principle, the reflexes and the autonomic nervous system would have absorbed all the functions of the brain, and man would have been left without a thought in his head. Organic systems are infinitely more complex than automatic systems; and what makes them so is the margin of choice, the freedom to commit and correct errors, to explore unfrequented paths, to incorporate unpredictable accidents with self-defined purposes, to anticipate the unexpected and to plan the impossible—all traits that no efficient automatic system can countenence.

The danger of attempting to automate everything is that man and the machine will exchange roles. Man, forced to adjust to the new conditions imposed by the system he has created, may one day discover that it is the system, not its creator, who is calling the tune.

An obvious case in point (Mumford calls it a "classic demonstration of destructive automation") is the automobile. In its earlier days the privately owned motor car provided an invaluable supplement to public transportation. Today we are dependent upon the auto. In many areas of the country there is no other means of transportation. Moreover, the nation's economy requires a healthy automotive industry. Cars *must* keep rolling off the automated assembly lines, which means people *must* buy them, or the economic system will be in real trouble. Meanwhile, our cities are choked with traffic, our countryside desecrated, and the death toll on our highways mounts higher every year.

Somewhere along the line we could have anticipated these (and other) problems. "We didn't because the machine itself fascinated us, and we ignored the human factor, the quality of life. As a result, the machine took over and is now imposing its own

456   *Technology and Education*

conditions. There is a lesson here for all of us, educators included.

The Trap

Modern science and technology have enabled mankind to accumulate prodigious quantities of knowledge. One measure of the mounting flood is the increase in scientific journals. Starting with a single journal in 1665, the number grew to one hundred by 1800, one thousand by 1850, ten thousand by 1900, and we are now on our way toward the hundred thousand figure. In a single subject, chemical engineering, five thousand journals deal with petroleum research alone! "Here," Mumford points out,

we face the great paradox of automation, put once and for all in Goethe's fable of the Sorcerer's Apprentice. Our civilization has cleverly found a magic formula for putting the academic brooms and pails of water to work by themselves, in ever-increasing quantities, at an ever-increasing speed. But we have lost the great Magician's formula for halting this process when it ceases to serve a direct human purpose, and as a result we are already, like the apprentice, beginning to drown in the flood.

In a desperate effort to cope with this tidal wave of knowledge we have created hundreds of journals devoted to abstracts and digests, and we are now building computerized retrieval centers where on command information from a vast variety of sources is placed at the scholar's disposal. And in a further desperate effort, the specialist is becoming increasingly specialized, devoting his life to an ever smaller part of the whole. But to what end? We have trapped ourselves in a process that feeds upon itself.

"In my reading," Mumford observes,

the mischief we now confront began when the scientific leaders of western thought dismissed as unworthy of their attention that immense fund of accumulated human experience which was embodied in language, religion, art, literature, morals, folklore, and in the annals of human history as a whole. Without that foundation, it is impossible to create fully dimensioned human beings. . . . By attempting to eliminate the human factor, by reducing all experience to supposedly ultimate atomic components describable in terms of mass and motion, science discarded mankind's cumulative knowledge of history and biography and paid attention only to discrete passing events. The typical vice of this ideology, accordingly, is to overvalue the contemporary, the dynamic, and the novel and to neglect stability, continuity, and the time-seasoned values of both collective history and individual human experience. The scientific intelligence, however magnified by its capacity to handle abstractions, is only a partial expression of the fully dimensioned personality, not a substitute for it.

The Challenge

[A recent report] reminded us of Mumford's apprehension about the direction of contemporary education was devoted to the new technology—classroom television, language laboratories equipped with multiple-station recording machines, mechanical teaching machines, and (newest of all) the computer. These and other devices promise to revolutionize education, even as science and technology have already revolutionized other aspects of life.

But, as experience should have taught us, the promise must be qualified. The crucial question, "to what end?" must first be answered. We know that the new technology will enable us to speed up learning and make education more efficient. Whether, given our current inclination to consider science and technology as ends rather than means, we can make education more meaningful in terms of the development of "fully dimensioned human beings" is an entirely different question.

We agree with Lewis Mumford's assessment of the basic problems of education today. "Shall we," he asks, restore man to his central position as the actor and director in a historical drama; or shall we banish him into the wings, first as a mere agent of an automatic control system, but eventually as a desperately bored super-numerary with no more active responsibility than a union stagehand in a modern drama that doesn't use scenery? Unless we tackle this question swiftly, we shall soon find that the last word in automation is automatic Man.

Date D

DATE DUE
